Unreal Engine 5 for Beginners

A step-by-step guide to building your first playable third-person game

Zhenyu George Li
Charles Shih-I Yeh
Michael Oakes

<packt>

Unreal Engine 5 for Beginners

Portfolio Director: Rohit Rajkumar
Relationship Lead: Nivedita Pandey
Program Manager: Sandip Tadge
Content Engineer: Shreya Sarkar
Technical Editor: Tejas Mhasvekar
Indexer: Pratik Shirodkar
Proofreader: Shreya Sarkar
Production Designer: Salma Patel
Growth Lead: Chayan Majumdar

First published: August 2026

Production reference: 1280826

Published by Packt Publishing Ltd.
Grosvenor House
11 St Paul's Square
Birmingham
B3 1RB, UK.

ISBN 978-1-80610-591-5
`www.packtpub.com`

To my wife Alison, whose patience, understanding, and steadfast support gave me the time and space to dedicate countless hours to writing this book. I could not have done this without you.

I would also like to express my sincere gratitude to my co-authors, Charles and Mike, for their collaboration and contributions throughout this project. I am also thankful to the entire editorial team at Packt and the technical reviewers for their hard work, thoughtful feedback, and dedication throughout the development of this book. Their expertise and guidance have been invaluable in shaping this work.

– Zhenyu George Li

To my wife and son, whose patience, understanding, and unwavering support gave me the extra time and encouragement needed to write this book. I could not have completed it without you. It means so much to me.

I would also like to express my sincere gratitude to my editor and technical reviewers, Eric Rico, Eduardo J. Reyes, and Sulbha Jadhav, for their insightful guidance, thoughtful feedback, and contributions throughout the development of this book.

– Charles Shih-I Yeh

To my wife Camie, whose patience and support gave me the time and motivation to lock myself away for hours on end to work on this book. In memory of my wonderful mother Sally, who I miss terribly and who always encouraged and helped me with everything I did. And a huge thanks to my loving sister Janet, who has always been there to support and encourage when I've needed it over the years.

I would also thank my fellow authors George and Charles, the Packt editorial team, and the technical reviewers. Particularly Shreya Sarkar, Eduardo J. Reyes, Sulbha Jadhav, and my good friend Eric Rico for their invaluable guidance, thoughtful feedback, and contributions throughout the development of this book.

– Michael Oakes

Contributors

About the authors

Zhenyu George Li is a passionate video game developer with over 20 years of experience in the field. As a seasoned software engineer, George has contributed significantly to the development of numerous games throughout his career. He currently serves as a senior development consultant at Unity.

George's fascination with video games sparked during his college studies, igniting a passion that would shape his professional journey. During the early stages of his game development endeavors, George immersed himself in technologies such as Visual Basic, C/C++, DirectX, OpenGL, and Windows GUI. These foundational experiences laid the groundwork for his subsequent success in the industry.

Throughout his career, George has made substantial contributions to various commercial games. Notable titles in his portfolio include *Halo Infinity*, *Magic Arena*, *Stela*, *Dead Rising 2*, and *The Bigs 2*. His involvement in these projects has allowed him to gain extensive knowledge and practical experience in a wide range of domains, including programming, game engines, gameplay and AI, graphics, animation, multiplayer, game physics, frontend, and multiplatform. In practical application, George used both the Unreal and Unity engines in the development of real game projects.

In addition to his achievements as a game developer, George has also honed his teaching abilities during his eight years of college-level instruction. He has shared his knowledge and expertise with aspiring developers, serving as a lecturer at the Vancouver Film School, College of Interactive Arts, and Hefei Union University. During his teaching at VFS, George instructed students in the intricacies of Unreal Engine.

Charles Shih-I Yeh studied computer science at the University of Southern California and began his career in games in the early 2000s. He has built proprietary engines, developed DCC tools to optimize pipelines, and designed gameplay mechanics, multiplayer systems, and tournament services for MMORPGs. Dedicated to education, Charles has lectured on game programming at several universities. He is the author of two game design books and the official Mandarin translator of several well-known programming titles, including *Game Programming Gems IV*.

Michael Oakes (BSc, PGDip, MSc) is an XR Specialist with Volvo in Gothenburg, Sweden who previously worked in game development at Unity for 6 years. He has over a decade in games and 30 years in IT, and holds a Master's degree in Computer Science with Games and Graphics Development from the University of Hull.

Michael's expertise includes XR/VR/AR Design and Development, Shader Programming, AI, Software Engineering & Management, and Multiplayer Systems.

Michael has also contributed as a technical consultant to books such as *Unity Learn ML-Agents*, Practical AI on the Google Cloud Platform, *Unreal Engine 5 Game Development with C++ Scripting*, and *Data Structures and Algorithms for Game Programming in C++*.

About the reviewers

Eric Rico is a Senior Software Developer on the Unity Studio Productions team, where he works alongside studios from indie to AAA on optimization, porting, and co-development to help them ship their games. Before joining Unity, he led development on enterprise AR/VR applications across XR, PC, and WebGL. He is also an independent developer, working as 3D artist and programmer on the VR title *Break Stuff VR*, released on PlayStation VR2 and Meta Quest.

I would like to thank my wife, Erica, for her patience during the evenings spent reviewing chapters, and the authors and editorial team at Packt for the opportunity to contribute to this book.

Eduardo J. Reyes is a Technical Artist and University Professor based in Barcelona. He specializes in shaders, procedural modeling, and pipeline tools. His experience encompasses instructing as an Unreal Authorized Instructor at companies like Scopely and universities like La Salle-URL in Barcelona, producing and developing games for Prime Video, and managing teams at B-Water Studios as a Production Coordinator.

I would like to thank the editorial team for the opportunity to review this book, and my fiancée and friends for their continued support throughout the process.

Sulbha Jadhav is an educator, technology professional, and Unreal Engine specialist with experience in immersive technologies, XR, HMI, simulation, digital twins, 3D visualization, and interactive applications. She holds a Master's degree in Information Technology and is an Unreal Engine Authorized Instructor. She has also contributed as a technical reviewer for *Architectural Visualization in Unreal Engine 5* and *Procedural Content Generation with Unreal Engine 5*. Her work focuses on emerging technologies, practical learning, and real-world applications.

I would like to thank the authors and editorial team for the opportunity to contribute to the book and for the collaborative review process. I also gratefully acknowledge my daughter for her patience, understanding, and support throughout the review.

Table of Contents

Chapter 2: Building Your First Game World in the Level Editor 25

Chapter 5: Handling Player Input 185

Preface

Game development is a unique and fascinating field where creativity meets technical expertise. For beginners, making games is an exciting learning journey, but taking that first step can be daunting. It requires a broad range of knowledge and skills, such as programming, art creation, AI technology, networking, input handling, and more. This steep learning curve often feels like a barrier in taking the first steps.

Game engines were originally developed by game studios as internal toolsets to accelerate production, streamline workflows, and reduce costs. Over time, these powerful tools became accessible to the public. With the integrated toolset of a modern game engine, the difficulty of starting game development has significantly lowered, allowing beginners to explore this complex and rewarding field with greater confidence than ever before.

What exactly is a game engine? Think of it as a collection of software tools bundled together to help developers build games more efficiently. Instead of writing code for graphics, sound, input, and physics every time they start a new project, developers can rely on a game engine to handle these common tasks. This allows them to focus on what makes their game unique, such as its story, characters, and gameplay mechanics.

The concept of game engines emerged naturally as game development grew more complex. In the early days, each game was built from the ground up with its own code for almost everything. As studios produced multiple titles, they began reusing code from previous projects to save time. Eventually, these reusable code libraries evolved into what we now call game engines.

Companies like id Software popularized this approach in the 1990s with games like *Doom* and *Quake*, whose technology was later licensed to other developers. Over time, game engines became standalone products available to anyone, not just large studios. Today, **Unreal Engine** stands as one of the most powerful and accessible engines in this long evolution.

This book, *Unreal Engine 5 for Beginners*, is designed to help readers who have no previous game development experience or technical skills to start developing a basic playable game. Whether you are ambitious to pursue a career in the game industry or simply want to build a personal hobby creating games without an engineering background, this book should be your first choice.

Unlike advanced books that focus purely on programming or theoretical design, this guide walks you through the entire development process step by step, explaining each concept as it becomes relevant. You do not need to write a single line of C++ code – Blueprint Visual Scripting will be your primary tool.

Who this book is for

This book is written for absolute beginners who have no prior game development experience. If you have never written a line of code, opened a game engine, or created any digital art, you are exactly the reader this book aims to help. You should, however, have basic computer skills and be familiar with common video game controls, mechanics, and objectives.

This book is also suitable for traditional software developers or IT professionals who want to explore game development as a new creative outlet. If you already understand programming concepts, you will appreciate the logic behind Blueprint scripting, but you can still learn how Unreal Engine structures gameplay without touching C++.

Artists and designers who want to see their creations come to life inside an interactive game world will also find this book valuable. The visual scripting system allows you to build gameplay logic without writing traditional code, making it possible to focus on the visual and experiential aspects of game creation.

Finally, this book is for hobbyists and aspiring indie developers who want to build a complete, playable game from start to finish. Rather than jumping between disconnected tutorials, you will follow a single project from initial setup to final gameplay. By the end, you will have a finished third-person action game and the confidence to begin your own projects.

Irrespective of your background, if you are willing to learn step by step and follow along with the exercises, this book will guide you through the journey of making your first game with Unreal Engine 5.

Learn what you need, when you need it

This book is structured around two parallel tracks: *learning the development environment* and *building an actual game*.

On the environment side, you will learn how to set up Unreal Engine, navigate its user interface, import content, manage level assets, and use essential tools like **Modeling Mode** and Blueprint scripting. On the game development side, you will apply these skills to create a complete third-person action game named *Pangaea*. You will design a castle level, place enemies, set up mission objectives, program gate logic, and connect a heads-up display (HUD), all within a single, coherent project.

The learning strategy of this book is simple: *learn what you need, when you need it*. Unlike an engine manual or an exhaustive reference guide, this book does not attempt to explain every UI detail or every tool in Unreal Engine. Instead, it introduces only the knowledge and tools required to complete the current task at hand.

For example, when the time comes to create an intro cutscene, the book guides you through creating a **Level Sequencer**, adding a camera track to the timeline, animating the camera path, and placing the sequence into your game level. It does not cover every feature of the **Sequencer** or every possible camera effect. The remaining details are left for you to explore later at your own pace through your own channels.

The benefit of this learn-to-use model is clear: you avoid unnecessary noise and focus only on what is immediately useful. At the same time, the reward of seeing a completed task, such as a working cutscene or a functional game level, motivates you to continue learning and tackle the next goal.

To keep this book readable and approachable for beginners, certain solutions have been simplified. For example, the Blueprint logic, character setup, and level design presented in these chapters prioritize getting the game to work clearly and reliably rather than pursuing the most optimized or production-ready solutions.

This means you may encounter Blueprint graphs that are *intentionally* kept linear and easy to follow, even if they could be condensed into fewer nodes. The character movement and combat systems are configured with straightforward settings so you can see immediate results, even though a commercial game requires more refined tuning.

Similarly, the level design uses simple shapes and modular pieces to illustrate concepts quickly, rather than demanding custom art assets or complex geometry. The goal is to reduce friction and keep you moving forward.

Once you have completed the book and built a working game, you will have a solid foundation to revisit these systems and explore more advanced techniques, such as optimizing Blueprint logic, enhancing character responsiveness, or designing more efficient level workflows, on your own.

What this book covers

This book provides a beginner-friendly guide to creating a complete playable game using **Unreal Engine 5**, focusing on practical skills rather than exhaustive technical reference. It begins by guiding you through the installation of the **Epic Games Launcher** and the Unreal Engine editor, then walks you through setting up your first game project using built-in templates.

You will explore essential tools such as the **Level Editor** for building game worlds, the **Blueprint Visual Scripting** system for creating gameplay logic without writing code, and the **UMG UI** designer for crafting menus and heads-up displays (HUDs).

The book delves into character creation, covering asset import, animation setup, and camera configuration, followed by AI development for enemy characters using navigation, perception, and Behavior Trees.

Later chapters cover gameplay mechanics design, mission and objective systems, cinematic cut-scene creation with the **Sequencer**, and finally packaging your game for release.

Each chapter combines clear instructions with hands-on steps, providing practical experience in building an efficient, playable, and polished game from start to finish.

Below is a list of chapters with brief descriptions to give you a quick overview of the book's structure and the key topics covered.

Chapter 1, Installing Unreal Engine and Creating Your First Game Project, introduces Unreal Engine and guides you through setting up your development environment. You will install the **Epic Games Launcher**, use it to manage different engine versions, and create your first game project using built-in templates, such as a first-person or third-person shooter. The chapter also covers the essential parts of a new Unreal project and basic project settings, building a strong foundation for your game development journey.

Chapter 2, Building Your First Game World in the Level Editor, helps you begin working with the Unreal Engine editor to design and build game levels. You will explore the editor's user interface, learn its layout and key panels, and use the Level Editor to manipulate actors, work with volumes, adjust lighting, and navigate the core components of a game scene. The chapter also introduces fundamental level design concepts and shows how to apply them using basic geometry tools.

Chapter 3, Learning the Basics of Blueprints, dives into the fundamentals of Unreal Engine's Blueprint system: the powerful visual scripting tool that enables game logic development without writing code. You will explore different types of Blueprints and learn how to use logic structures, such as sequences, branches, and loops, to control game behavior. Through hands-on examples, you will handle key events and practice creating interactive Blueprints that bring your game ideas to life.

Chapter 4, Creating a Player Character, teaches you how to create and configure a fully functional player character. You will begin by importing key assets such as 3D models, textures, skeletons, animations, and sound effects into your Unreal project. Step by step, you will create a Character Blueprint, configure the third-person gameplay camera, connect animations using an Animation Blueprint and Blend Space, and even attach weapons to your character.

Chapter 5, Handling Player Input, shows you how to create interactive and responsive gameplay by configuring Unreal Engine's input system. You will learn about hardware input and input mapping, use the **Enhanced Input** system to define player actions and bind them to game controls, and apply input handling techniques to control player behavior and trigger in-game events.

Chapter 6, Creating an AI Character, introduces you to creating non-player characters (NPCs) that can navigate, sense, and respond to their environment using Unreal Engine's AI tools. You will design an enemy character, enable intelligent movement through AI navigation components, implement environmental perception for hearing and vision, and build decision-making logic using Behavior Trees.

Chapter 7, Game UI with Unreal Motion Graphics, explores Unreal Engine's powerful UI creation system, **UMG**, to design responsive and visually engaging game interfaces. You will learn to create essential UI elements, such as main menus, in-game HUDs, and pause menus using widgets and Blueprints, as well as integrate UI elements directly into the 3D world.

Chapter 8, Designing and Implementing Gameplay Mechanics, focuses on the practical implementation of gameplay systems. You will learn how to design clear player objectives, manage gameplay progression, control game flow through scripted interactions, place and spawn actors, set up reliable collision detection, and enable interactions between in-game elements.

Chapter 9, Creating Cinematics and Cut-Scenes, teaches you how to use Unreal Engine's **Sequencer** to produce cinematic cut-scenes, scripted events, and dynamic camera movements that enhance storytelling. You will create a game introduction cut-scene with character movement and animation, configure camera transitions, and integrate your cinematic sequences seamlessly into gameplay.

Chapter 10, Polishing and Packaging Your Game, brings your game project to completion by addressing any unfinished elements and applying final polish. You will refine the level and gameplay experience, add audio and visual effects, and package your game as a standalone version ready for release.

To get the most out of this book

To successfully follow along with this book and complete the *Pangaea* game project, you should have the following basic knowledge and experience:

- **Operating system knowledge**: You should have operational knowledge of your computer's operating system, such as Microsoft Windows. This includes basic tasks like navigating folders, installing software, managing files, and understanding where downloaded files are stored on your system.

- **GitHub basics**: You should know how to clone and pull project files from a GitHub repository. The complete demo project for this book is available online, and being able to download the latest version will help you compare your work with the finished project if you get stuck. If you are not familiar with GitHub, you can also download the project as a ZIP file from the repository webpage (see the *Get the code/resource bundle* section for access instructions).
- **Basic gaming experience**: You should have basic knowledge and experience playing video games. Understanding common game conventions, such as moving a character with a keyboard and mouse, navigating menus, and recognizing what a health bar represents, will help you focus on learning the development side rather than struggling with basic gameplay concepts.

No prior game development experience, programming knowledge, or art skills are required. This book starts from the very beginning and guides you through each step. If you meet the three basic requirements above, you are ready to begin.

Hardware and software requirements

Before installing Unreal Engine, make sure your computer meets the minimum requirements to run the engine smoothly. While **Unreal Engine 5** is a professional tool, it can still run on modest hardware for learning purposes.

Minimum hardware requirements

These specifications are suitable for learning and running the sample project:

Software/Hardware covered in the book	Requirements/Specifications
Operating system	Windows 10 (64-bit) or Windows 11
Graphics driver	DirectX 12-compatible graphics driver. Make sure your GPU drivers are updated to the latest version from NVIDIA, AMD, or Intel.
CPU	Quad-core Intel or AMD processor, 2.5 GHz or faster
GPU	DirectX 11- or DirectX 12-compatible graphics card (for example, NVIDIA GTX 1060 or AMD Radeon RX 580 equivalent)
RAM	16 GB of system memory
Storage	50 GB of free disk space for the engine and project files

Recommended hardware for a better experience

To have fast response from the engine operations and get results within an acceptable waiting time and performance, it is recommended to upgrade your system to the following specifications:

Software/Hardware covered in the book	Requirements/Specifications
CPU	6-core or 8-core Intel Core i7/i9 or AMD Ryzen 7/9
GPU	NVIDIA RTX 2070 or higher (or AMD equivalent)
RAM	32 GB of system memory
Storage	100 GB or more of free space on an NVMe SSD

Here are a few additional notes worth considering:

- **Laptop users**: While Unreal Engine can run on laptops, performance will depend on your hardware. Make sure your laptop uses its dedicated GPU rather than integrated graphics when running the engine.
- **Internet connection**: A stable internet connection is required to download the **Epic Games Launcher**, install Unreal Engine, and access the demo project files from GitHub.
- **Non-Windows users**: If you run the samples on systems other than Windows, such as macOS, the appearance may differ from the screenshots captured on Windows in this book.

Note that the authors acknowledge the use of cutting-edge AI, such as ChatGPT, with the sole aim of enhancing the language and clarity within the book, thereby ensuring a smooth reading experience for readers. It's important to note that the content itself has been crafted by the authors and edited by a professional publishing team. Packt does not accept AI-generated content that replaces expert authorship.

Download the example code/resource files

This book includes a complete downloadable code/resource bundle containing all the example projects and files used throughout the chapters. We recommend downloading the bundle so you can follow along smoothly and experiment with the examples.

Use the bundle as a practical starting point. Modify it, extend it, and apply what you learn by creating your own variations as you progress through the chapters.

Get the code/resource bundle

If you bought the book directly from Packt:

1. Go to `packtpub.com`.
2. Click your profile picture and select **Your Orders**.
3. Find this book and click **Download Code**.

If you bought this book from Amazon or any other channel partner:

1. Go to `packtpub.com/unlock` or scan the following QR code:
2. Search for this book.
3. Sign up or log in to your free Packt account.
4. Upload your proof of purchase and download the code/resource bundle locally.

Usage note: You're free to use and modify this code/resource for personal learning and non-commercial projects. All the demo projects and the complete game project for this book are available in the GitHub repository. This is a useful resource if you get stuck on a specific step or want to compare your work with a finished, working version.

The repository is organized by chapters. Each chapter has its own branch containing the demo project as it should appear at the end of that chapter. This allows you to jump directly to a specific chapter without needing to complete all the previous work.

- **Chapter branches**: Navigate to a specific chapter branch (for example, `Chapter04`, `Chapter08`) to see the demo project exactly as it is presented in that chapter.
- **Development branch**: The full, final, completed *Pangaea* game project is located under the development branch. This includes all the features, polished assets, and final gameplay logic from every chapter.

Once downloaded, you can open the `.uproject` file in Unreal Engine to explore the project. The repository will help you learn by seeing a professional implementation of the exact concepts you are building.

Note

Using the project files

The project files for each chapter are organized into separate **Git branches**. Select the appropriate `ChapterXX-Start` branch to follow along with a chapter, or the `ChapterXX` branch to view the completed project. If you clone the repository, you can switch between these branches locally. If you download the files as a ZIP from GitHub, make sure you select the required branch before downloading, as the ZIP contains only the currently selected branch.

Download the color images

Some screenshots contain detailed Unreal Engine interface elements that may be easier to inspect in the included color PDF edition, which supports zooming. Your purchase includes a color, DRM-free PDF copy of this book, ideal for viewing color images, screenshots, and diagrams. Refer to the *Free benefits with your book section* at the end of the *Preface* to unlock your PDF copy.

Conventions used

There are several text conventions used throughout this book.

`CodeInText`: Indicates code words in text, database table names, folder names, filenames, file extensions, pathnames, dummy URLs, user input, and X (formerly Twitter) handles. For example: "Set the values to (`0.0, 0.05, 0.2`), which indicates a dark blue color."

A block of code is set as follows:

```
Receive Execute AI:
    → Get Blackboard value InitLocation
    → Find a random reachable point near InitLocation
    → Move the AI pawn to that point
    → Finish Execute
```

Bold: Indicates a new term, an important word, or words that you see on the screen. For instance, words in menus or dialog boxes appear in the text like this. For example: "The following example gives an overview of a **For Loop** Sequence Blueprint that creates a variable (**Index**) with a starting value of **0** (**First Index**), and a **Last Index** variable of **19**."

Any command-line input or output is written as follows:

```
r.setres 1280x720w
```

> **Note**
>
> Warnings or important notes appear like this.

> **Tip**
>
> Tips and tricks appear like this.

Acknowledgments

This book would not have been possible without the valuable contributions of many individuals.

Keven Lai, a senior technical artist, provided the Hero character, the 3D player model, along with the animations and weapon models used in the *Pangaea* game.

Grace Li, an artist and university student, contributed the concept art for the *Pangaea* game featured in this book.

Sincere gratitude is also extended to the technical reviewers and the entire team at Packt Publishing for their guidance, feedback, and support throughout the writing process.

Get in touch

Feedback from our readers is always welcome.

General feedback: If you have questions about any aspect of this book or have any general feedback, please email us at `customercare@packt.com` and mention the book's title in the subject of your message.

Errata: Although we have taken every care to ensure the accuracy of our content, mistakes do happen. If you have found a mistake in this book, we would be grateful if you reported this to us. Please visit `http://www.packt.com/submit-errata`, click **Submit Errata**, and fill in the form.

Piracy: If you come across any illegal copies of our works in any form on the internet, we would be grateful if you would provide us with the location address or website name. Please contact us at `copyright@packt.com` with a link to the material.

If you are interested in becoming an author: If there is a topic that you have expertise in and you are interested in either writing or contributing to a book, please visit `http://authors.packt.com/`.

Subscribe to Game Dev Assembly Newsletter!

We are excited to introduce **Game Dev Assembly**, our brand-new newsletter dedicated to everything game development. Whether you're a programmer, designer, artist, animator, or studio lead, you'll get exclusive insights, industry trends, and expert tips to help you build better games and grow your skills. Sign up today and become part of a growing community of creators, innovators, and game changers.

Scan the QR code to join instantly!

https://packt.link/gamedev-newsletter

Free benefits with your book

This book includes free benefits designed to support your learning and help you apply what you learn effectively. Activate them now for instant access (see the *How to unlock* section for instructions).

Here's a quick overview of what you can instantly unlock with your purchase:

How to unlock

Scan the QR code (or go to `packtpub.com/unlock`). Search for this book by name, confirm the edition, and then follow the steps on the page.

UNLOCK NOW

Note: Have your invoice handy. Purchases made directly from the Packt website don't require an invoice.

Share your thoughts

Once you've read *Unreal Engine 5 for Beginners*, we'd love to hear your thoughts! Scan the QR code below to go straight to the Amazon review page for this book and share your feedback.

https://packt.link/r/1806105918

Your review is important to us and the tech community and will help us make sure we're delivering excellent quality content.

Part 1

Your First Steps in Unreal Engine 5

Part 1 introduces you to Unreal Engine 5 and builds the foundation you need to start creating games. You will set up Unreal Engine, create your first project, and become familiar with the Level Editor and its essential tools. You will then begin building game worlds by working with actors, lighting, volumes, and basic level design techniques. From there, you will explore Blueprints, Unreal Engine's visual scripting system, and use fundamental logic structures to add interactivity and gameplay behavior without writing code.

By the end of this part, you will have the foundational skills to build game worlds and add basic gameplay logic in Unreal Engine.

This part of the book includes the following chapters:

1

Installing Unreal Engine and Creating Your First Game Project

Unreal Engine (UE), developed by Epic Games, is one of the most powerful and widely used game engines in the world. It has powered numerous acclaimed titles such as *Fortnite*, *Gears of War*, *Street Fighter V*, and the recent blockbuster *Black Myth: Wukong* – a visually stunning action RPG built with Unreal Engine 5. These examples demonstrate the engine's ability to deliver cinematic quality, immersive worlds, and high-performance gameplay across genres.

Despite its professional-grade capabilities, Unreal Engine remains remarkably beginner-friendly. With a wealth of tutorials and learning resources available online, newcomers can start creating games quickly and confidently. One of its most notable features, the **Blueprint Visual Scripting** system, enables developers, including those without programming experience such as designers and artists, to construct gameplay logic through an intuitive, node-based interface. The *Unreal Engine 5 for Beginners* book not only introduces essential tools and practical blueprinting techniques but also guides you through building a complete game project where you'll apply what you learn step by step in an authentic development workflow.

This chapter serves as your first step into the world of Unreal Engine game development. You'll begin by setting up your development environment, downloading and installing the Unreal Engine through the **Epic Games Launcher**. You'll then learn how to use the launcher to manage different engine versions and create your first game project using a built-in template: a third-person project. Once your project is created, you'll explore the Unreal Editor interface, understand its main panels and tools, and gain hands-on experience with basic knowledge and operations using the editor.

This chapter covers the following topics:

- Introducing Unreal Engine
- Downloading and installing the Epic Games Launcher
- Exploring the Epic Games Launcher interface
- Installing and managing game engine versions
- Creating your first game project
- Learning the essential parts of the new project

By the end of this chapter, you will have a fully functioning Unreal project and a clear understanding of the essential tools needed to begin your game development journey.

> Note
>
> **Download the code/resource bundle and the PDF version of this book**
>
> Your purchase includes a DRM-free PDF copy of this book, the code/ressource bundle, and a range of exclusive benefits. To unlock everything, follow the *Free benefits with your book* section in the *Preface.*

Technical requirements

Before starting this book, you should have basic computer operation skills and a general understanding of how video games work. This includes familiarity with common game controls (such as movement, camera, and interaction), awareness of basic game mechanics (like health, scoring, or objectives), and an understanding of typical game goals that define a player's experience. Having this foundational knowledge will help you better relate the Unreal Engine tools and Blueprints introduced in this book to real gameplay scenarios and design concepts.

To follow along with the demos and build the sample game projects in this book, you will need to install **Unreal Engine 5.6.1** or a later version on your computer. The examples and features discussed throughout the chapters are based on this version to ensure compatibility and consistent results. Please make sure your system meets Unreal Engine's hardware requirements before installation.

Your computer should meet the following system requirements for the development environment:

Minimum requirements

- **Operating System**: Windows 10 64-bit
- **CPU**: Quad-core Intel or AMD processor, 2.5 GHz
- **Memory (RAM)**: 16 GB
- **Graphics Card**: DirectX 12–compatible GPU (e.g., NVIDIA GTX 1060 or AMD RX 580)
- **Storage**: 100 GB of free disk space
- An internet connection

Recommended requirements

- **Operating System**: Windows 11 64-bit
- **CPU**: Octa-core Intel i7/i9 or AMD Ryzen 7/9
- **Memory (RAM)**: 32 GB
- **Graphics Card**: NVIDIA RTX 3070 / AMD RX 6800
- **Storage**: 200 GB of free disk space

If you are using **macOS** or **Linux**, or would like to learn more detailed information, please refer to the official Unreal Engine system requirements at: `https://docs.unrealengine.com/5.0/en-US/hardware-and-software-specifications-for-unreal-engine/`.

> **Note**
>
> Please note that the requirements listed here are intended as practical guidelines for following the tutorials and may differ from the official recommendations.

Using GitHub

To access the sample game projects and required assets for this book, you will need access to **GitHub**. All demo source code, supporting files, and downloadable content are hosted in the book's official repository.

You can download the example project and code files for this book by following the instructions in the *Download the example code/resource files* section in the *Preface* of this book.

This chapter's code/resource files are included in the downloadable code/resource bundle.

Please ensure you have a GitHub account and basic familiarity with downloading or cloning repositories, as this will allow you to retrieve the materials easily and follow along with the hands-on examples throughout the chapters.

Note

GitHub

GitHub is a cloud-based version control system that helps developers track changes to their code over time. A GitHub repository serves as a project storage space, containing all project files along with the complete history of every change made to them. The basic operations covered in this book include `clone`, which downloads an exact copy of the entire repository, including all files, branches, and history, to your local computer, and `pull`, which syncs the latest updates from the remote repository on GitHub to your local machine. Additionally, branches allow you to maintain isolated lines of development, enabling experimentation and feature work without affecting the main codebase.

Sample projects for each chapter are organized into repository branches. Typically, a chapter includes two branches: `Chapter#_Start` and `Chapter#`. The `Start` branch provides a pre-configured project to begin the lesson, while the `Chapter#` branch contains the finished demo.

For instance, when working through *Chapter 2*, you should check out the `Chapter02_Start` branch to begin building the game content; you can then switch to the `Chapter02` branch to view the final, completed version. The sample project for this chapter is available for download from the following branch in the GitHub repository:

- `Chapter01` **branch:** Contains the initially created *Pangaea* third-person game project.

Introducing Unreal Engine

Unreal Engine is a powerful real-time 3D creation tool developed by Epic Games. First released in 1998 alongside the first-person shooter Unreal, the engine quickly gained popularity for its advanced graphics and flexibility.

Over the years, Unreal has evolved through several major versions, from Unreal Engine 1, which introduced real-time 3D rendering, to Unreal Engine 5, which brings cutting-edge technologies such as Nanite for virtualized geometry and Lumen for dynamic global illumination. These innovations have established Unreal Engine as one of the most widely used platforms in the world, not only for video games but also for film, architecture, and interactive visualization.

Unreal Engine provides a comprehensive suite of tools that cover nearly every aspect of game creation. Its core components include:

- **Unreal Editor**: The main workspace for building and editing game worlds.

- **Blueprint Visual Scripting**: A node-based system that allows developers to create game logic visually without writing code.
- **Material and Animation Editors**: Tools for designing realistic surfaces, characters, and motion.
- **Physics, AI, and Audio systems**: Built-in modules that enable realistic behavior, intelligent movement, and immersive sound design.
- **Sequencer and Cinematics tools**: A system for creating cut-scenes, camera animations, and storytelling sequences.

The **Epic Games Launcher** plays a central role in managing Unreal Engine. It serves as the main hub for users to install, update, and launch different engine versions, as well as for creating and organizing projects. The launcher also connects users to the **Fab** (Unreal's marketplace, `https://www.unrealengine.com/marketplace/en-US/`), which offers free and paid assets, such as 3D models, materials, Blueprints, and plugins, to help you accelerate the game development process.

Before you can begin creating your own projects, you'll need to download and install the **Epic Games Launcher**. The next section will guide you through this process step by step, ensuring your development environment is ready for Unreal Engine.

Downloading and installing the Epic Games Launcher

Before you can begin developing your first Unreal Engine project, you need to install the **Epic Games Launcher**, the central application used to manage Unreal Engine versions, projects, and marketplace assets. The launcher acts as your entry point into the Unreal ecosystem, providing access to all the tools and content you'll need throughout this book.

> **Note**
>
> Please note that the steps described below are based on the current layout of the official Unreal Engine website and may change in future updates made by Epic Games.

Follow these steps to download and install the launcher:

1. Visit the official Unreal Engine website at `https://www.unrealengine.com/` and click the **Download** button in the top-right corner.
2. Click the **Download Launcher** button to download the installer (for example, **EpicInstaller-18.10.0.msi** on Windows), as shown in *Figure 1.1*:

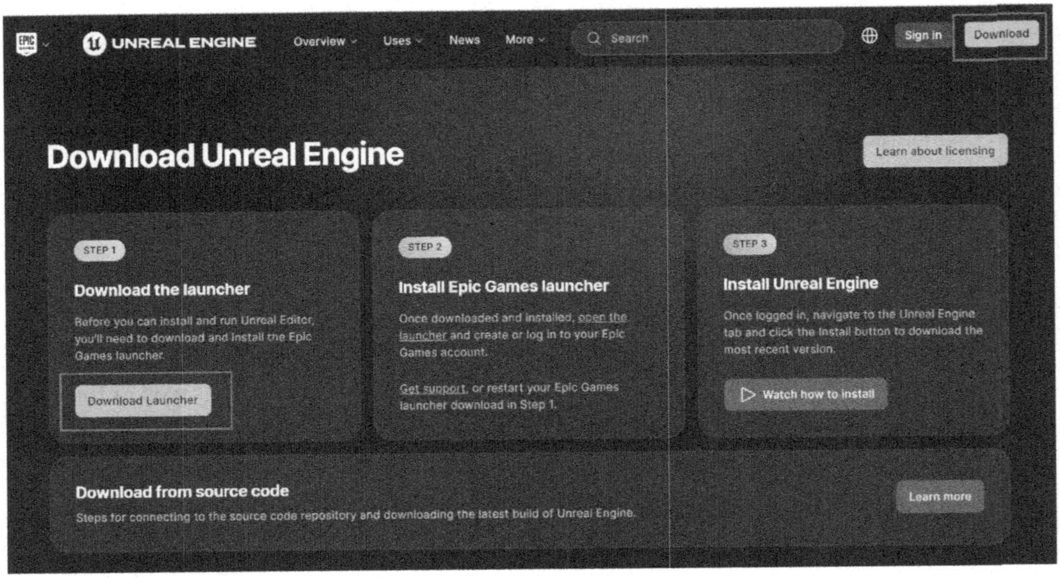

Figure 1.1 - Download the Epic Games Launcher

3. After the installer file finishes downloading, double-click it to launch the installation wizard.
4. Follow the on-screen instructions to complete the setup.

Once the installation is complete, you should see the **Epic Games Launcher** icon added to your desktop, as shown in *Figure 1.2*:

Figure 1.2 - Desktop shortcut icon for Epic Games Launcher

Double-click this icon to start the launcher. At the first launch, you'll be prompted to sign in with your Epic Games account. If you don't already have an Epic Games account, you'll need to sign up first, then sign in using your account credentials. For detailed instructions on creating a new account, visit the official documentation site **at Install Unreal Engine | Unreal Engine 5.7 Documentation | Epic Developer Community**.

With the Epic Games Launcher successfully installed, let's take a closer look at its user interface to understand the main sections and how each one helps you manage your engine versions, projects, and assets.

Exploring the Epic Games Launcher interface

After installing the **Epic Games Launcher**, the next step is to start the application and become familiar with its interface. When you launch the program for the first time, you'll be asked to sign in with your Epic Games account or create one if you're a new user. Once logged in, the launcher opens to its main dashboard, which provides access to everything related to Epic's ecosystem: Unreal Engine versions, projects, purchased assets, marketplace assets, and settings.

Open the Epic Games Launcher (e.g., by clicking the icon on the desktop), and you will see the launcher's main user interface. It is organized into several key sections accessible from the left-hand sidebar, as shown in *Figure 1.3*. Understanding these tabs will help you navigate efficiently and locate the tools you need for your development workflow.

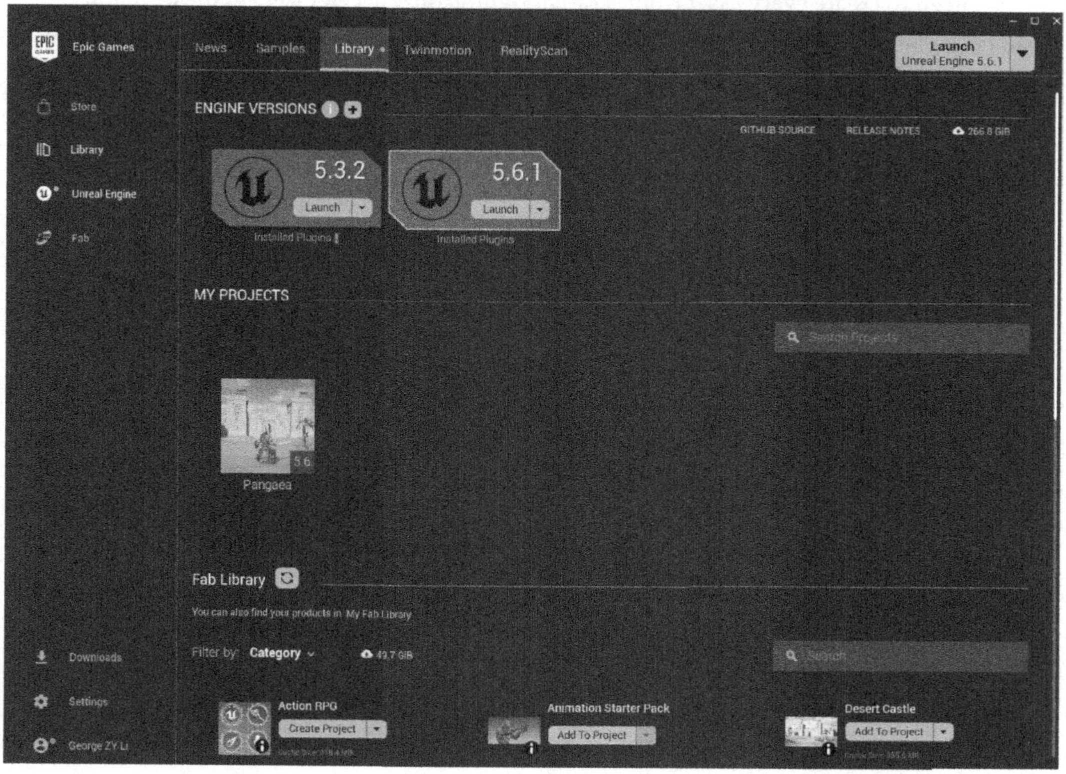

Figure 1.3 - Using the Epic Games Launcher

Let's look at the purpose of each main section:

- **Store**: The **Store** section is where Epic distributes games and applications, like Steam. Here, you can browse and purchase both free and paid games, as well as claim Epic's regular free game offers. While this area is primarily for players, developers can also use it to explore how games are marketed, discover new titles built with Unreal Engine, and gain inspiration from published projects.
- **Library**: This section is used to manage purchased and installed games.
- **Unreal Engine**: This is the core area for developers. Within this section, you can download and install Unreal Engine, launch the editor, and create new projects, making it the central hub for starting and managing your development work.
- **Fab**: As mentioned previously, this is the digital marketplace for discovering, downloading, and purchasing assets that can be directly used in your projects. Fab hosts a vast library of 3D models, materials, sounds, animations, and environment packs created by professionals and community contributors. Fab helps to reduce the need to create every asset from scratch, significantly accelerating game development.

Now that you're familiar with the main layout of the **Epic Games Launcher**, it's time to focus on the part most relevant to game developers: the **Unreal Engine** tab. This section serves as your central hub for accessing engine versions, learning materials, and creative tools.

Exploring the Unreal Engine tab

Once the Epic Games Launcher is opened, click the **Unreal Engine** section from the left sidebar to access all tools and resources related to Unreal Engine. Along the top of this section, you'll see several horizontal menu items that organize key development resources and options (see *Figure 1.3*):

- **News**: Displays the latest announcements, updates, and feature highlights from Epic Games, helping you stay informed about new engine releases, tutorials, and community events.
- **Samples**: Provides access to a variety of example projects and learning templates that demonstrate Unreal Engine's features and best practices.
- **Library**: Lists all installed and available Unreal Engine versions, as well as your own projects, allowing you to create, launch, update, or manage them from one place.

- **Twinmotion**: Offers a specialized real-time visualization tool built on Unreal Engine, designed for architecture, engineering, and design professionals to create high-quality images, videos, and scenes quickly.
- **RealityScan**: Integrates Epic's photogrammetry tool that transforms real-world photos into 3D models.

With the launcher interface explored, the next step is to install the Unreal Engine version you'll use for your project.

Installing and managing game engine versions

Before creating your first project, you need to install the proper version of Unreal Engine.

> **Note**
>
> This book uses **Unreal Engine 5.6.1** as the reference version because it offers a strong balance between stability and modern features. At the time of writing, version 5.6.1 is relatively new and close to the latest release, ensuring access to the most up-to-date tools and improvements.
>
> However, newer versions can sometimes introduce experimental features or interface adjustments that may affect compatibility with the examples in this book. By standardizing on version 5.6.1 or later, we provide a stable, reliable learning environment while still leveraging the advanced capabilities of Unreal Engine 5.

If you haven't yet installed the required Unreal Engine version, such as 5.6.1, follow these three steps to add it:

1. Click the + button to create a new engine slot.
2. In the newly added slot, open the drop-down menu on the right and select the version you want to install.
3. Click the **Install** button to begin downloading and installing the selected engine version.

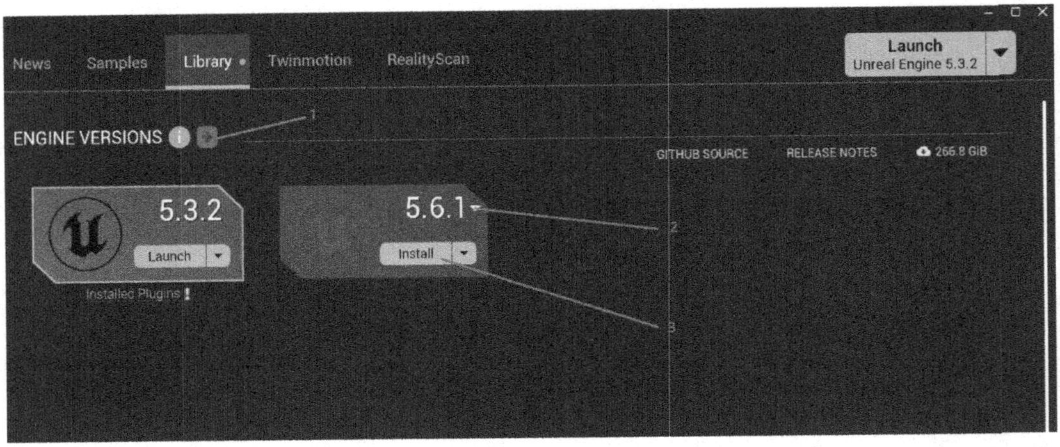

Figure 1.4 - Managing multiple Unreal Engine versions: (1) Adding a new engine version thumbnail; (2) Opening the options menu for this engine version; (3) Installing the engine

The installation process may take some time, depending on your internet speed and the available disk space on your system.

With the engine installed, let's take a closer look at how the **Library** panel helps you manage engine versions, projects, and downloaded assets.

Managing game engine versions, projects, and downloaded assets

On the **Library** panel under the **Unreal Engine** section, you'll find three key areas that organize your development resources (see *Figure 1.4*):

- **Engine Versions**: Displays all Unreal Engine versions currently installed on your computer. You can click the + button (Install a new version of the Unreal Engine) to add a new version of the engine or use the drop-down options on the right of an existing engine version to launch, update, or remove it, as shown in *Figure 1.5*.

Figure 1.5 - Using the drop-down options on an installed engine version

- **My Projects**: Lists all the Unreal projects you created through the launcher. From here, you can open a project directly in the editor and view its file location. For example, the **Pangaea** project is shown as a sample user project in *Figure 1.3*.
- **Fab Library**: Displays all asset packages you've purchased or downloaded from the Fab marketplace.

Figure 1.3 illustrates an example Library view containing two installed engine versions (**5.3.2** and **5.6.1**), one custom project (**Pangaea**), and three downloaded asset packages (**Action RPG**, **Animation Starter Pack**, and **Desert Castle**).

With the needed version of Unreal Engine now installed and ready to use, let's move on to the most exciting step: creating your first game project and stepping into the world of Unreal.

Creating your first game project

To create a new game project, you must launch the Unreal Engine. Click the **Launch** button on the selected engine version slot, **5.6.1** for example, in the **Epic Games Launcher**. The launcher will minimize to the system tray, and the Unreal Project Browser window will appear. This browser serves as the starting point for all your Unreal Engine projects. From here, you can choose a template, define project settings, and create or open existing projects.

The Project Browser is divided into several panels that guide you through the setup process, as shown in *Figure 1.6*:

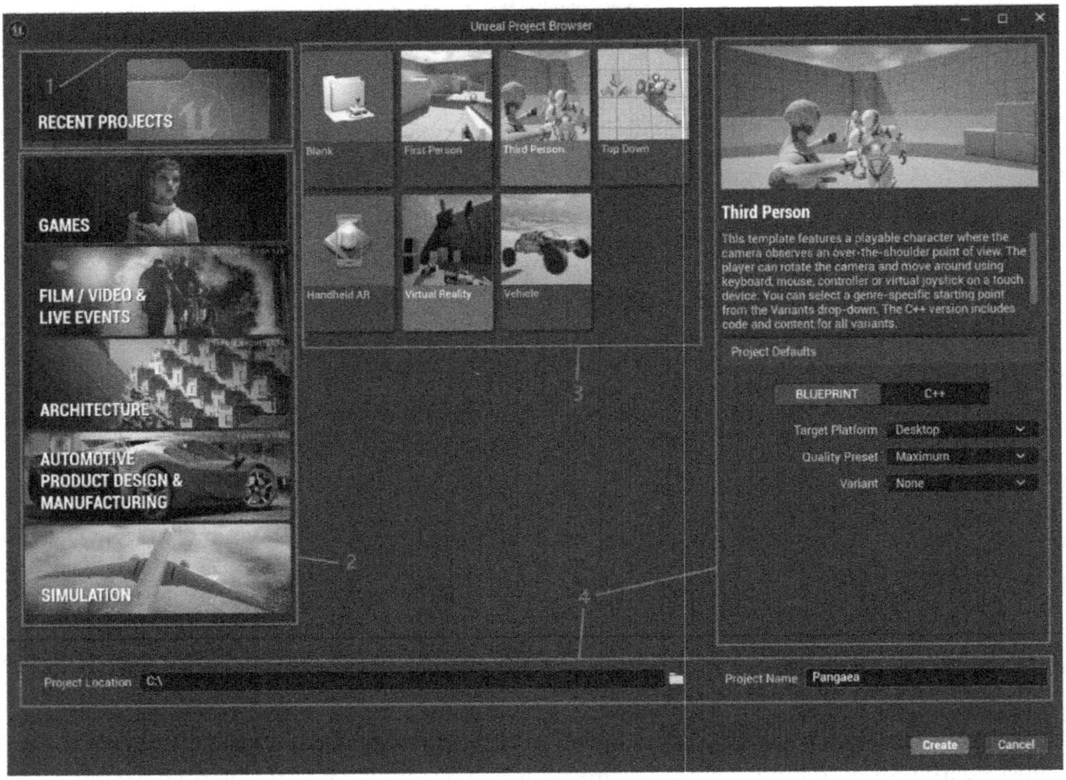

Figure 1.6 - Creating a new project in Unreal Project Browser

Let's explore these sections in greater depth:

1. **RECENT PROJECTS**: Displays a list of recently opened or created projects for quick access.
2. **New Project Categories**: Lets you select from several categories, such as **Games**, **Film/Video**, **Architecture**, or **Other**, with each category offering a set of templates tailored to different types of projects and creative goals.
3. **Project Templates**: Under each category, you'll find several predefined templates. For example, the **Games** category includes templates such as **Blank**, **First Person**, **Third Person**, **Top Down**, and more. Each template provides basic gameplay elements and configurations to help you get started quickly.
4. **Project Settings Panel**: Located on the right side, this area lets you specify project options such as **Blueprint** or **C++**, **Target Platform** (**Desktop** or **Mobile**), and **Quality Preset**. You can also define the **Project Location** and the **Project Name** here.

In this book, our goal is to guide you through building a third-person game called **Pangaea**. To meet the project requirements, you will create the game using Blueprints only (not C++), targeting desktop platforms with maximum graphics quality. Based on these requirements, start by selecting the **Games** category, then choose the **Third Person** template with **Blueprints** as the scripting method. This template includes a ready-to-use character, camera setup, and environment, making it an ideal starting point for learning core editor tools and gameplay mechanics.

Next, name your project `Pangaea` and specify the folder where it should be saved. For example, choosing `C:\Pangaea` as the target directory will create the project at `C:\Pangaea\Pangaea\Pangaea.uproject`. Once all settings are configured, click **Create** to generate the project. Unreal Engine will prepare the necessary files and then open the Unreal Editor, loading the default level of your new project for the first time, as shown in *Figure 1.7*:

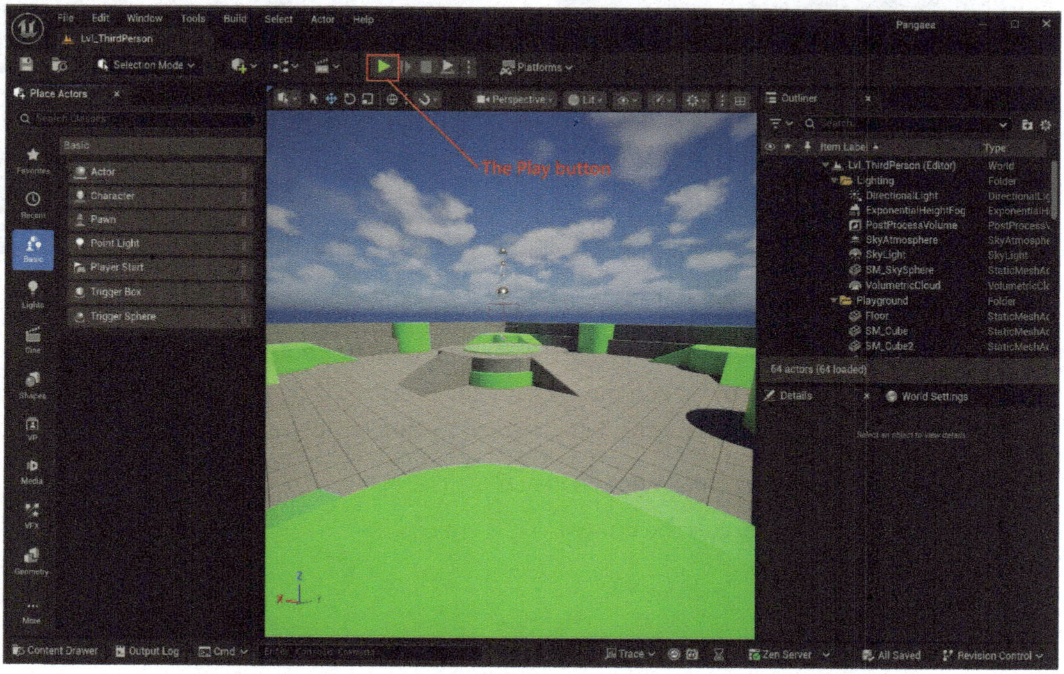

Figure 1.7 - Clicking the Play button to launch the game in Unreal Editor

Once your project has been created and opened in the Unreal Editor, you can click the **Play** button (see *Figure 1.7*) to run the game directly inside the editor.

Figure 1.8 shows the game in play, with the player character spawned directly in front of the camera in a third-person view:

Figure 1.8 - Running the third-person game inside the editor

Once the game starts, click anywhere inside the gameplay window to set focus on the view. The mouse cursor is hidden by default during gameplay, but you can press *Shift* + *F1* to make it visible again. The basic controls for the default **Third Person** template are as follows:

- *W/A/S/D* or *arrow keys*: Move the character
- *Mouse movement*: Rotates the camera
- *Spacebar*: Jump
- *Esc*: Exit Play mode

Congratulations! You've just created your first playable third-person game. Even though Unreal Engine handled most of the initial setup for you, it's completely normal to feel like you've only scratched the surface of game creation. From this point forward, you'll begin taking control and shaping the game yourself. This book will guide you step by step through that process.

To begin with, the next section introduces the essential parts of your new project, helping you understand how your game is structured and where key assets and systems are located.

Learning the essential parts of the new project

After playing your new project for the first time, you might start wondering how everything works behind the scenes and asking questions such as:

- Where does the character come from?
- How is the character defined?
- Can you replace it with your own custom character?
- Is it possible to build your own level, change game controls, or customize the gameplay entirely?

These are excellent questions, showing that you're thinking like a game developer and eager to dive deeper. We are now on the same page and ready to move forward. These questions will be answered naturally as you progress through the project and build each step along the way.

In this section, we'll first explore the core settings of your project and begin uncovering how Unreal Engine organizes the essential components of a game.

Project settings

The **Project Settings** window is where Unreal Engine gathers all the fundamental options that shape your game, giving you a single place to adjust how the project behaves, what features it uses, and how different systems are configured.

To open the **Project Settings** window, go to the editor's main menu and select **Edit | Project Settings...** on the pop-up menu:

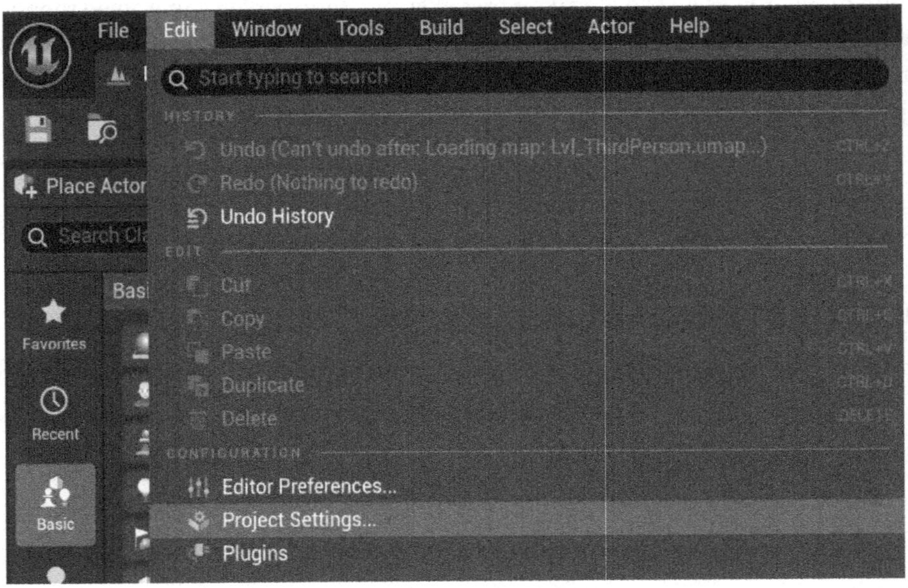

Figure 1.9 - Open the Project Settings window in Unreal Editor

When the **Project Settings** window opens, you'll see a two-panel layout designed to help you quickly find and adjust the settings you need.

On the *left side*, a long list of categories is organized into groups such as **Project**, **Game**, **Engine**, **Editor**, **Platforms**, and **Plugins**, each containing specific options that affect different parts of your game. When you select a category, the *right side* displays all related settings, arranged as editable fields, checkboxes, or dropdown menus, as shown in *Figure 1.10*. This layout allows you to browse through high-level categories on the left and fine-tune the detailed options on the right, making it easier to understand and configure how your project behaves.

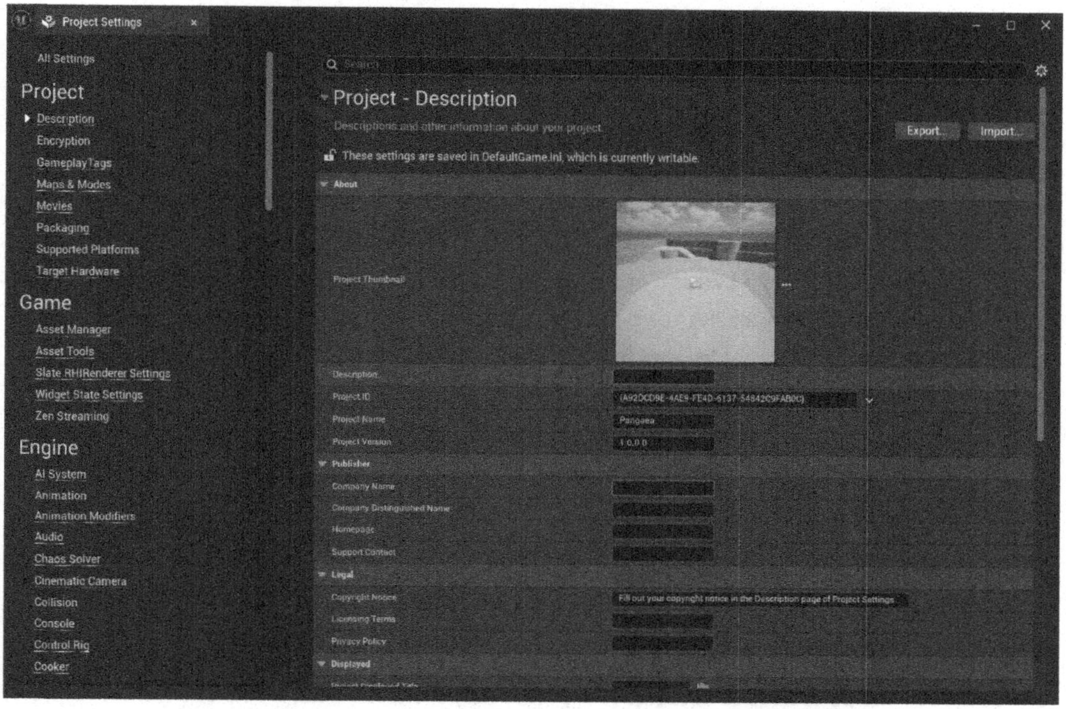

Figure 1.10 - The Project Settings window: Project - Description

The **Project Settings** window contains a large number of options, many of which are beyond the scope of this book and not required for our current goals. Whenever you need more detail, you can always refer to the official documentation: `https://dev.epicgames.com/documentation/en-us/unreal-engine/unreal-engine-5-6-documentation?application_version=5.6`.

For now, we will focus only on a few key settings, specifically those found in the **Description** and **Maps & Modes** sections under the **Project** category.

Project – Description

The **Project – Description** settings provide general information about your project, such as its name, version, and other metadata that help identify the game during development and distribution. These settings don't affect gameplay directly, but they define how your project is represented inside the editor and in packaged builds.

We'll look at the following key settings in this section (see *Figure 1.10*):

- **Thumbnail**: Lets you assign an image that represents your project in the Unreal Project Browser, making it easier to spot among multiple projects. If you don't provide a custom image, Unreal Engine will automatically generate one by capturing a snapshot of your game.
- **Project ID**: A unique identifier automatically generated by Unreal Engine to distinguish your project from others. This value is used internally by the engine and usually does not need to be changed.
- **Project Name**: Defines the official name of your game as used by Unreal Engine. For this project, you can enter `Pangaea` to match the game you are building in this book.

Project – Maps & Modes

The **Project – Maps & Modes** settings (see *Figure 1.11*) control which levels and gameplay rules your project uses by default. This is where you specify the starting map when the game launches, the editor startup map for development, and the overall game mode that defines core behaviors such as the default player character, controller, Heads-Up Display (HUD), and game rules.

> **Note**
>
> You'll see several class-based settings in this section – terms like *Pawn, Game State,* and *Player Controller*. Don't worry if these sound unfamiliar right now. You won't need to change most of them for your first projects. Think of this section as a map: you're just learning where things live so you can find them later when you need them.

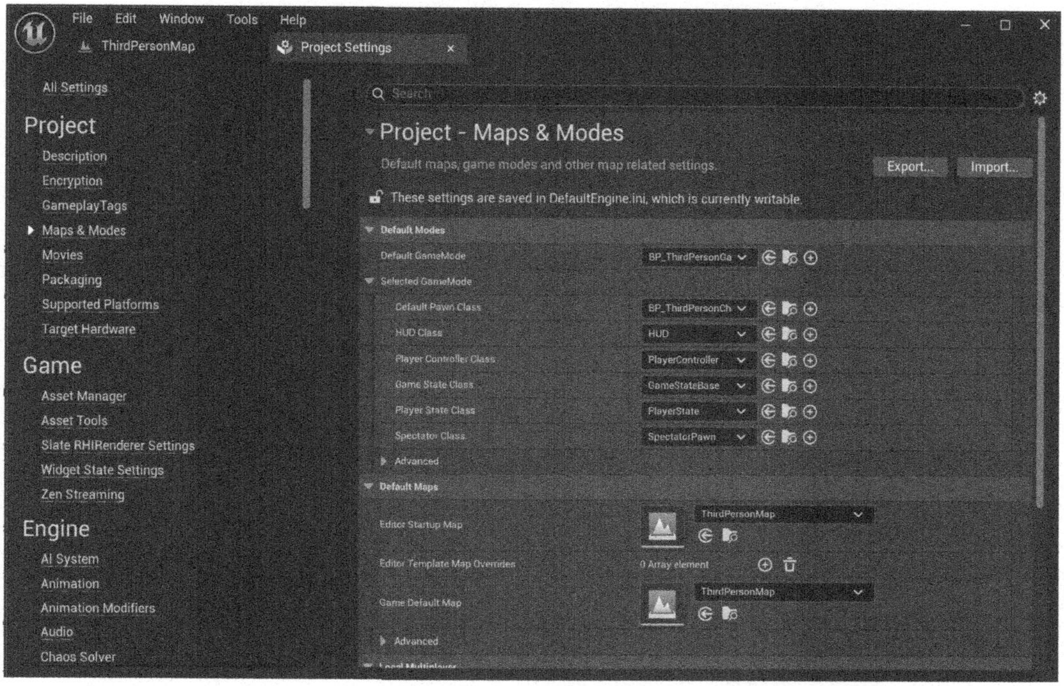

Figure 1.11 - The Project Settings window: Project - Maps & Modes

We'll briefly introduce the following settings in this section:

- **Default Game Mode**: Defines the overall gameplay rules for your project. Under the **Selected GameMode** section, you'll find settings for which character, controller, and HUD classes the game uses. Changing these establishes your game's core behavior.
- **Default Pawn Class**: Specifies the character or object the player controls when the game starts. For a **Third Person** template, this is the third-person character Blueprint.
- **Player Controller Class**: Determines how the player receives and processes input. This class translates keyboard, mouse, or gamepad actions into gameplay actions in the world.
- **Editor Startup Map**: Sets which level loads automatically when you open the Unreal Editor. This is useful for choosing the map you work on most often during development.
- **Game Default Map**: Specifies the level that loads first when you play or package the game. This becomes the starting point for your players.

- **Game State Class**: Manages information shared across the entire game, such as match status, remaining time, or team scores. It is mainly used for games that need to track global gameplay data.
- **Game Instance Class**: A persistent class that stays active while the game is running, even when changing levels. It is ideal for storing data that must carry over between maps, such as player settings or loaded save information.

Together, the **Project – Description** and **Maps & Modes** settings form the foundation of how your game is identified, organized, and launched within Unreal Engine. Although many of these fields may seem simple at first glance, they play an important role in shaping the structure and behavior of your project.

As we continue building the Pangaea game, you will revisit these settings, along with the **Input** and **Packaging** configurations, in later chapters, where we will adjust each of them in practical, hands-on steps to support the features and gameplay systems you develop. This early overview ensures you understand where these options are located and why they matter as your project grows.

With the essential project settings covered, the next step is to explore the project's directory structure to see where Unreal stores your game content and configuration files.

Project directories

When a new Unreal Engine project is created, the engine automatically generates a collection of subfolders inside the project's root directory, as shown in *Figure 1.12*:

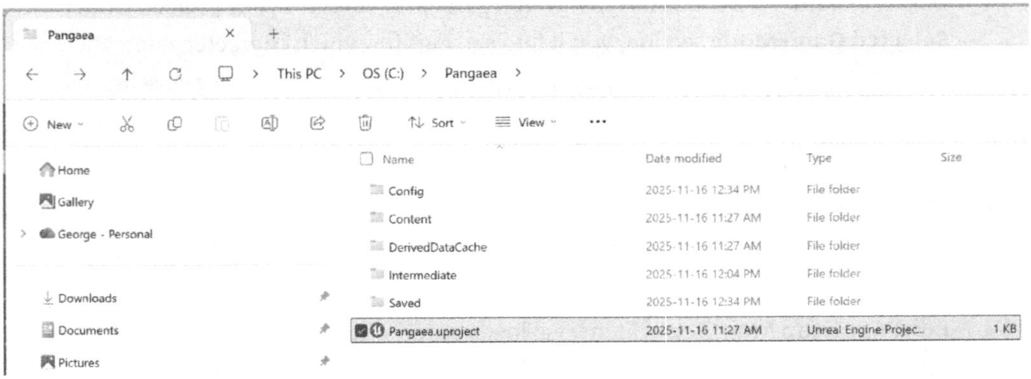

Figure 1.12 - Subfolders in the project's root directory

Each of these subfolders serves a specific purpose. Let's take a quick tour of the subfolders so you know where Unreal stores the different types of files that make up your project:

- `Config`: This folder contains configuration files (`.ini` files) that define many of your project's settings, such as input bindings, engine behavior, editor preferences, and gameplay rules. These files are stored in plain text and are updated automatically when you change settings inside the editor.

- `Content`: The `Content` folder is the heart of your project. It stores all game assets, including Blueprints, levels, materials, textures, sound files, and imported models. Everything you create or import through the **Content Browser** (explained in *Chapter 2*) in Unreal appears here.
- `DerivedDataCache`: This folder stores optimized versions of assets that are generated automatically. Cached files help Unreal Engine improve loading times and performance.
- `Intermediate`: Unreal stores temporary files in this folder.
- `Saved`: The `Saved` folder contains logs, backups, autosaves, crash reports, and packaged builds. It's useful for troubleshooting issues, recovering work from autosaves, or accessing output files after packaging your project.

When copying your entire project to another location, you can safely omit the `DerivedDataCache` and `Intermediate` folders, as Unreal Engine will automatically recreate them the next time you open the project in the editor.

With your development environment now properly set up and your very first Unreal Engine game created from scratch, you've taken the most important first step in your journey.

Summary

In this chapter, you set up the foundation for your Unreal Engine development journey. You installed the **Epic Games Launcher**, explored its interface, and learned how to access key resources such as engine versions, sample projects, and marketplace assets.

You also learned how to install and manage multiple versions of Unreal Engine, create your first third-person project, and run it inside the editor. From there, we introduced the essential settings that define your project, such as **Project – Description**, **Project – Maps & Modes**, and examined the important folders that make up a project's directory structure.

By understanding where your game's core components live and how Unreal organizes them, you now have a solid starting point for moving deeper into development.

In the next chapter, we will explore the Unreal Editor interface and learn how to use its tools to create and modify a game level.

2

Building Your First Game World in the Level Editor

This chapter introduces the core concepts and tools you need to begin building **Levels** in Unreal Engine. You start by learning how objects are positioned using Unreal's **World** and **Local coordinate systems**, giving you a clear understanding of how location, rotation, and scale are calculated in 3D space. You then explore the **Level Editor** and its main interface panels, including the **Viewport**, **Outliner**, **Details** panel, and **Content Browser**, along with the basic controls for navigating the scene.

You also learn how to manipulate objects using the **Translate**, **Rotate**, and **Scale** tools, as well as how snapping features help you position and transform Actors with accuracy. The chapter then explains the role of blockout geometry in early game prototyping.

You will then follow step-by-step instructions to prototype a simple Level, adding geometry, lighting, sky elements, and a character to bring the scene together. Finally, you are given a Level outline and description and get to build out a Castle prototype Level on your own.

This chapter demonstrates the prototyping phase of development, where you will build out a prototype Bridge Level. You will then follow that process for the development of our *Pangaea* game and create a Castle prototype Level with blockout geometry that forms a temporary representation of the Castle within the game.

In this chapter, we'll cover the following topics:

- Understanding coordinate systems
- Introducing the Level Editor
- Exploring Viewport controls

- Level prototyping and design
- Building out a Castle Level prototype

By the end of this chapter, you will understand how objects are positioned and manipulated within Unreal Engine and be comfortable navigating the Level Editor and its core tools. You will also gain hands-on experience creating and modifying geometry, setting up lighting and environments, and applying these skills to build a complete prototype Level.

Technical requirements

The sample project for this chapter is available for download from the following GitHub repository and branch:

- `Chapter02-Start` branch: The game project to begin learning in this chapter.
- `Chapter02` branch: The completed game project for this chapter, featuring the **Bridge Prototype** and **Castle Prototype** Levels, which can be found in the **Content Browser** under **Content** | **LevelPrototyping** | **Levels**.

You can download the example project and code files for this book by following the instructions in the *Download the example code/resource files* section in the *Preface* of this book.

This chapter's code/resource files are included in the downloadable code/resource bundle.

Understanding coordinate systems

Unreal utilizes two distinct methods to accurately track the placement and movement of objects within a 3D space. These are the **World Space coordinate system** and the **Local Space coordinate system**. Let's explore these in more detail in the subsequent sections.

World Space coordinate system

When working in Unreal Engine, everything in the 3D world is positioned using three numbers called **coordinates**. These numbers tell the engine where something is inside the world—just like giving directions on a map.

To understand this, imagine a big 3D grid. Every point inside the grid can be found using three coordinates:

- *X* **(axis)**: Forward or Backward
- *Y* **(axis)**: Left or Right
- *Z* **(axis)**: Up or Down

Together, these *X*, *Y*, and *Z* axes make up Unreal's **World Space coordinate system** (or **World Space**), which tells Unreal Engine *exactly* where an object is placed in the world. *Figure 2.1* illustrates this concept as follows:

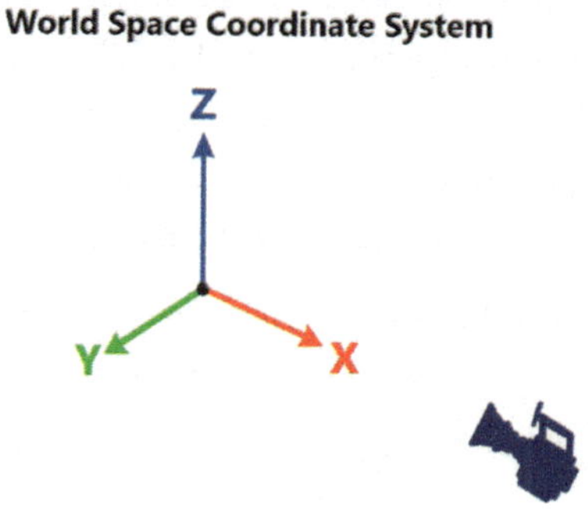

Figure 2.1 - World coordinate system

The World Space coordinate system acts like a giant invisible map that covers the whole level. Some key facts to note here are:

- The very center of the world is **(0, 0, 0)**, which is called the **world origin**.
- Every object's position is measured from this point.
- If an object has world coordinates **(100, 3, 5)**, it means:
- In an Unreal level, the default unit of measurement is 1 unit which equals to 1 centimeter. So, the object is 100 cm forward (*+X*) from the center, 3 cm right from the center, and 5 cm up from the center.
- If an object has world coordinates **(-100, -3, -5),** it means:
- It is 100 cm backward (*-X*) from the center, 3 cm left (*-Y*) from the center and 5 cm down (*-Z*) from the center.

Having explained the use of the World coordinate system, you will now go on to learn about the Local Space coordinate system in the next section.

> Note
>
> **Understanding Pivot Points and Hierarchy**
>
> Before manipulating objects using **Local Space** coordinates, it is essential to understand the concept of an object's *pivot point*. The **pivot point** represents the **local origin** (the absolute (0,0,0) coordinate point) within an object's own Local Space, serving as the definitive anchor for all its transformations. Every vertex, polygon, and component that makes up that 3D asset calculates its position relative to this local

origin. When you translate, rotate, or scale an Actor in the Viewport, Unreal Engine executes that calculation directly from this point.

This local coordinate system becomes even more dynamic when you introduce the Parenting of objects, which establishes a hierarchical relationship between Actors. When you attach a child Actor to a parent Actor, the child abandons its relationship with World Space and begins calculating its position, rotation, and scale relative to the parent's local origin. If the parent Actor moves or rotates, the child moves and rotates with it automatically, maintaining its exact local offset from the parent's pivot point.

This hierarchy allows you to build complex, multi-part objects, such as wheels attached to a car chassis, while keeping individual placement logic perfectly localized.

Local Space coordinate system

Like World Space, **Local Space** is also positioned using a three-number coordinate system that tells the engine where something is inside the world. However, rather than being relative to the *world origin*, **Local Space Coordinates** are relative to the **local origin**.

The local origin (0, 0, 0) is either the object's own pivot point (if it is an unparented root-level object) or its immediate parent's pivot point (if it is a parented object). Simply put, each object also has its own mini coordinate system attached to it.

To understand how Local Space works, first look at these core principles:

- The local coordinates for an unparented (root level) object are identical to its world coordinates.
- When the parent object moves, rotates, or scales, the child object moves with it, maintaining its local offset from its parent's pivot point.
- The world transform for a child object can be calculated by adding its local transform to the parent's world transform.

Now let's look at a simple example to see how this works in practice.

If a parent object has world coordinates **(0, 1, 1)**, and a child object attached to it has a local position of **(2, 2, 3)**, this means the child object would be 2 cm forward, 2 cm right, and 3 cm up from the parent object.

To calculate the child object's world position, add the child object's local position **(2, 2, 3)** to the parent's world position **(0, 1, 1)**. This gives a world position of **(2, 3, 4)**.

If the parent object is moved to **(0, 2, 2)**, it means:

- The child object's local position does not change and remains at **(2, 2, 3)**.
- The child object's world position does change and will now be **(2, 4, 4)** - **(2, 2, 3)**, added to the parent world position **(0, 2, 2)**.

We will now give you an example of how to visualize the difference between the World Space coordinate system and the Local Space coordinate system.

Visualizing the difference between the World Space coordinate system and the Local Space coordinate system

This parent-child hierarchy makes it easy for objects to have parts that move together like a nose on a face, bones on a character, or a door on a car.

Imagine you have a toy car sitting on the floor. **World space** (shown in *Figure 2.2*) is like the room the car is in. It is the big map that everything in the game shares. If we say:

- The car is at **(100, 100, 0)** on the big map.
- World space tells us where the car is in the whole world.

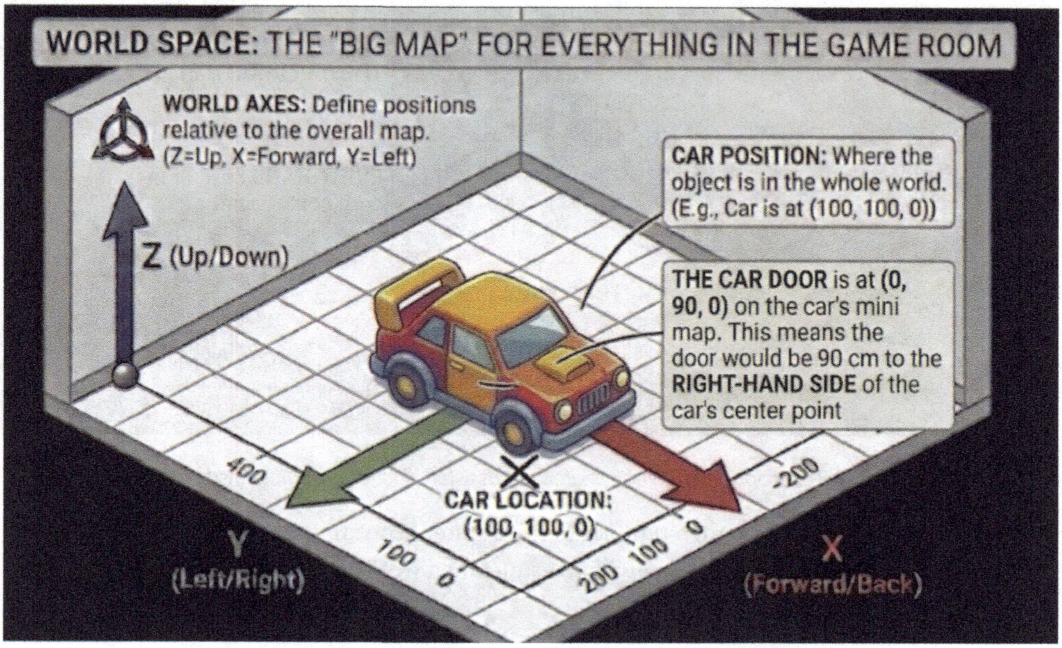

Figure 2.2 - World Space coordinate system (AI-assisted illustration, edited by the author)

Local space (shown in *Figure 2.3*) is like a mini map stuck to the car itself. This mini map moves and rotates with the car. If we say:

- The car door is at **(0, 90, 0)** on the car's mini map. This means the door would be 90 cm to the right-hand side of the car's center point.
- Local space is where the car door is on the car.
- If you rotate the door around the hinge in the door's local space, it swings and opens the door around the hinge pivot no matter where the car is.
- When the car moves or turns, the door's world position also moves because the whole car is moving, but the door's local position stays the same because on the car's mini map, it is still 90 cm to the right-hand side of the car's center point.

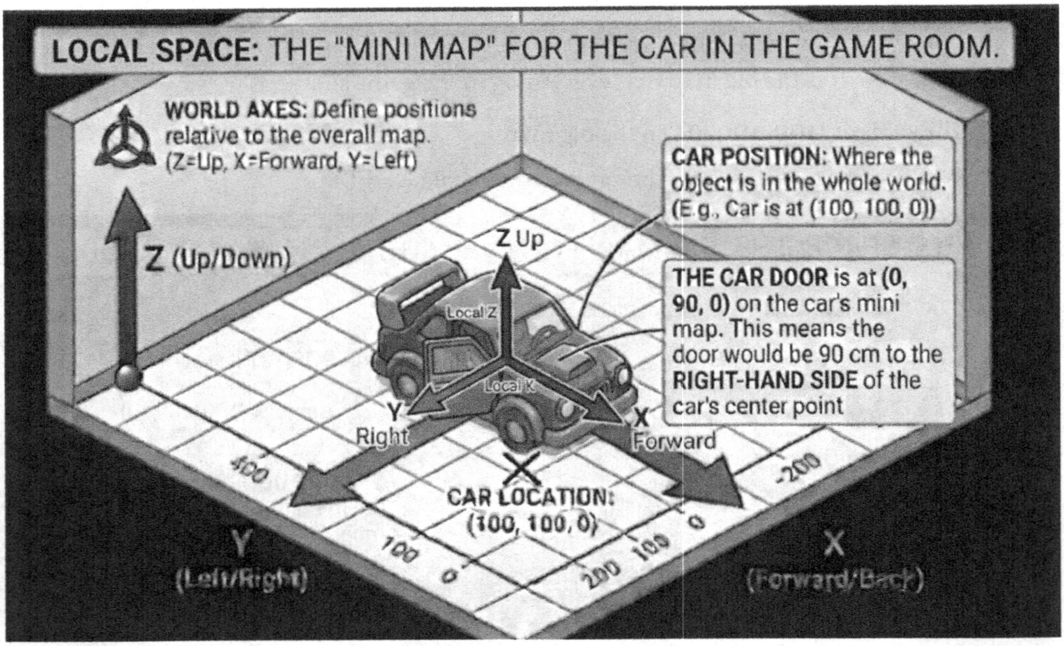

Figure 2.3 - Local Space coordinate system (AI-assisted illustration, edited by the author)

Now that you have a visual understanding of the different coordinate systems, we will give an overview of the Level Editor that you will be using when working with the Unreal Editor.

> **Tip**
>
> If you would like detailed information about the **coordinate system**, the Unreal Engine system documentation delves deeper into the subject and can be found here: `https://dev.epicgames.com/documentation/unreal-engine/coordinate-system-and-spaces-in-unreal-engine?application_version=5.6`.

Introducing the Level Editor

With an understanding of the Unreal coordinate systems, we will now examine the main window of the Unreal Engine: the **Level Editor**.

The **Level Editor** includes a collection of tools for manipulating both the World and Local coordinates of objects in the Level, configuring core gameplay logic, and crafting level environments. It is made up of several panels for different functions (as highlighted in *Figure 2.4*), which we'll explore in the subsequent sections.

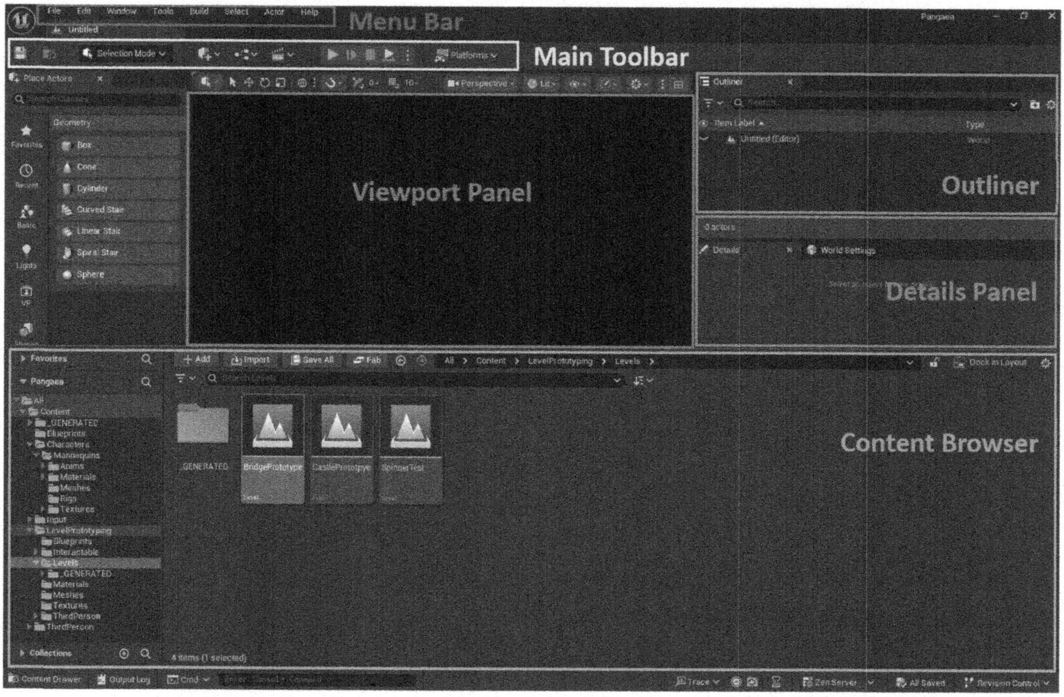

Figure 2.4 - Level Editor Overview

Main Menu Bar

The **Main Menu Bar** provides access to all major editor functions through its submenus, as shown in *Figure 2.5*:

Figure 2.5 - Unreal Engine Main Menu Bar

Let's understand the function of these submenus:

- **File** includes options for opening and saving projects and levels.
- **Edit** contains **Project** and **Editor Settings**, **Plugins**, and standard operations such as **Undo/Redo**, **Cut**, **Copy**, **Paste**, **Delete**, and **Duplicate**.
- **Window** allows you to open additional panels and customize the editor layout.
- **Tools** offers utilities for organizing assets, updating Blueprints, merging or converting Actors, and using automation or debugging features. The subjects of Blueprints and Actors will be covered later in the book.
- **Build** provides commands for building the current project, or specific level elements, including lighting, geometry, and shaders.
- **Select** helps you filter and highlight objects by type, class, relationship, or state—useful for managing large levels.
- The **Actor** menu includes actions for managing Actors placed in a Level, such as attaching, grouping, converting, or modifying them.
- The **Help** menu links to documentation, tutorials, support resources, and learning materials.

> Note
>
> **Actors in Unreal Engine**
>
> An **Actor** in Unreal Engine is any object that can be placed in a Level, such as a character, light, camera, or piece of geometry, that has a position, rotation, and scale within the game world. An Actor's movement is determined by its *origin (pivot) point*, which is assigned when the asset is imported.

We will not be using the Main Menu Bar very much at this stage of the game development process for our *Pangaea* game, but we will be using functions of the **Main Toolbar**, which we will now describe.

Main Toolbar

The **Main Toolbar** sits beneath the main menu and provides quick access to the **Level Editor**'s commonly used tools, as shown in *Figure 2.6*:

Figure 2.6 - Unreal Engine Main Toolbar

This includes the following tools:

- **Save** button to save the current Level.
- **Open Level Select** button to navigate to and select the current Level in the **Content Browser**.
- **Selection Mode** to switch the editor to different modes and change the context and behavior of what is being edited:
    - **Selection**: Used to select, move, rotate, and scale Actors and objects within the Level.
    - **Landscape**: Tools for creating and sculpting terrain, including shaping mountains, valleys, and painting landscape materials.
    - **Foliage**: Allows you to quickly paint and scatter vegetation such as grass, bushes, and trees across surfaces in a level.
    - **Mesh Painting**: Enables painting directly onto meshes to modify vertex colors or blend materials on the surface.
    - **Modeling**: Provides built-in modeling tools for creating, editing, and modifying 3D geometry directly inside Unreal Engine.
    - **Fracture**: Used to break meshes into destructible pieces for physics-based destruction using Chaos Fracture tools.
    - **Brush Editing**: Allows editing of BSP (Binary Space Partition) brushes used for quickly blocking out and shaping level geometry.
    - **Animation**: Opens tools for working with **Control Rig** and animation editing directly within the Level Editor.
- **Level Sequence** options to create a new Level Sequence or select an existing one.
- **Quick Add** button provides a list of objects and actors the user can create and add to the Level, and a dropdown list of Blueprints available for creation or editing.
- **Play Mode Controls**, which include **Play**, **Stop**, **Advance a Single Frame**, etc.
- **Platforms** provides options for configuring and deploying to different platforms.

Viewport panel

The **Viewport panel** is the main visual interface into the game, allowing you to see the game, move around the current Level, and interact with the game world. *Figure 2.7* shows the Castle Level Prototype, which you will build later in this chapter, as viewed from the Unreal **Viewport** panel:

Figure 2.7 - Unreal Engine Viewport panel

The Viewport panel can display a Level in either **Orthographic** or **Perspective Camera** view and has several view modes, including the following:

- **Lit**: Displays the scene exactly as it would appear in-game, with full lighting, materials, textures, shadows, and post-processing effects applied.
- **Unlit**: Shows the scene without lighting or shadow calculations, displaying only the base colors of materials, which is useful for inspecting textures and color values.
- **Wireframe**: Renders all geometry as wireframe lines, allowing you to see the underlying polygon structure and topology of meshes in the Level.
- **Lighting Only**: Displays only the lighting information affecting the scene while ignoring material textures and colors, making it easier to evaluate light placement, shadows, and overall lighting quality.

- **Reflections**: Visualizes how reflective surfaces capture their environment by highlighting reflection data from reflection captures, screen space reflections, or other reflection methods.
- **Path Tracing**: Uses Unreal Engine's physically accurate path tracing renderer to produce highly realistic lighting, reflections, and global illumination, often used for high-quality previews or cinematic rendering.

Clicking the **Play** button on the Main Toolbar transitions the Viewport panel into **Play Mode** – the interactive mode that allows you to *play* your Level as if you were running the standalone game, but without leaving the editor.

Outliner

The **Outliner** displays a selectable hierarchical tree of objects in the current Level with editable names. Objects can be organized using container folders, and multiple object selection allows for property changes to be made to multiple objects simultaneously.

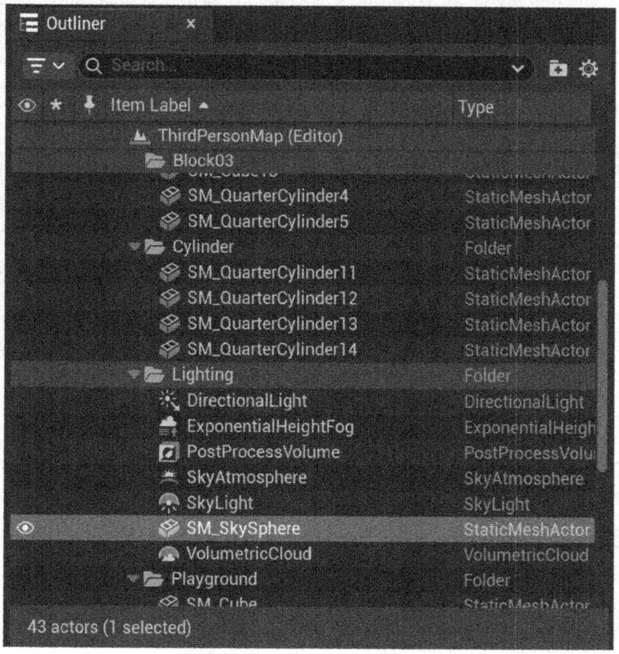

Figure 2.8 - Unreal Engine Outliner panel

Selecting an object in the **Outliner** panel causes its properties to display in the **Details** panel, which we'll explore next.

Details panel

The **Details panel** (see *Figure 2.9*) can usually be found on the right-hand side of the Level Editor, underneath the **Outliner** panel, and displays all the settings and properties for the object currently selected in either the Viewport panel or the **Outliner**.

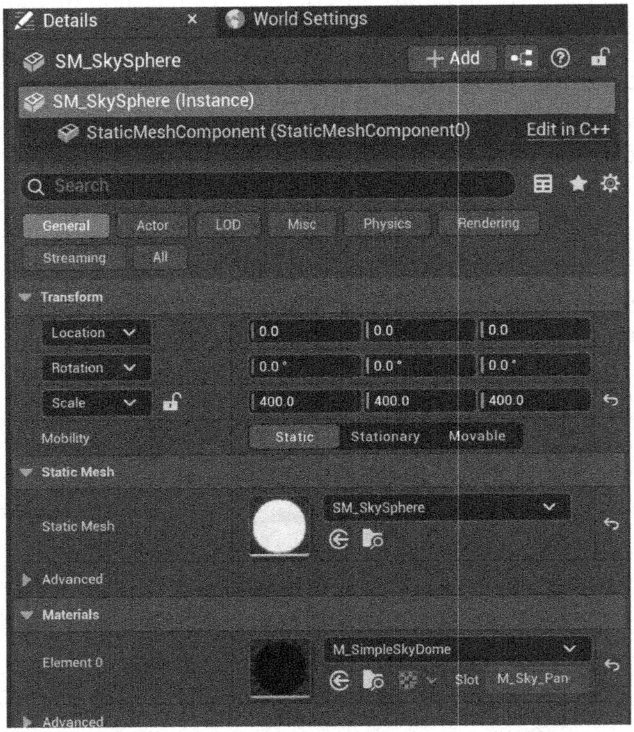

Figure 2.9 - Unreal Engine Details panel

The **Details** panel allows you to search for and edit properties in the currently selected object. Common properties include the name of the object and three sets of coordinate values as we previously described, with one each for **Location**, **Rotation**, and **Scale** of the object in the Level.

Content Browser

The **Content Browser** panel is usually minimized when first opening Unreal Engine but can be expanded by clicking on the **Content Browser** header title at the very bottom left of the Level Editor. It is a central area for managing a project and its assets – essentially a file explorer where you can view and organize all the items that your project is composed of. You can organize assets into folders, rename, copy, move, delete assets, search for assets, import and export assets, and perform other asset-management tasks.

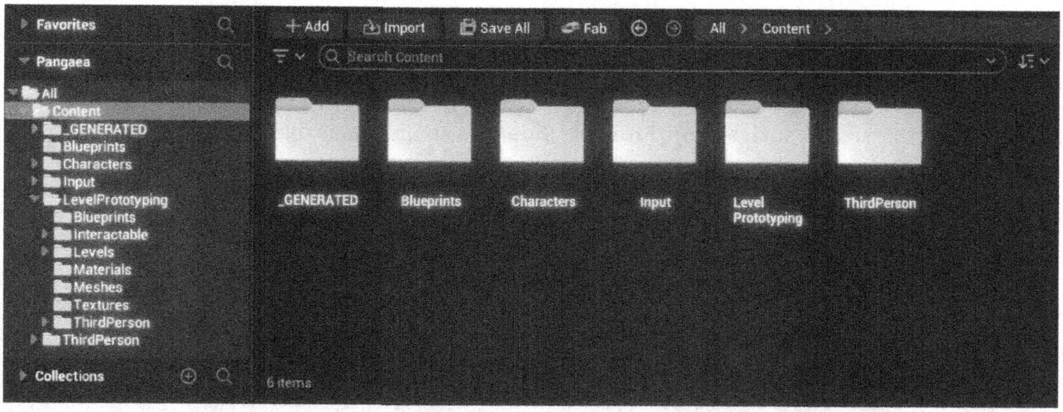

Figure 2.10 - Unreal Engine Content Browser panel

Having had an overview of the Level Editor interface, you will now learn the controls used to navigate the Viewport panel.

> **Tip**
>
> If you would like to learn more detailed information about the **Level Editor** to supplement your understanding, refer to the official Unreal Engine system documentation at: `https://dev.epicgames.com/documentation/en-us/unreal-engine/level-editor-in-unreal-engine?application_version=5.6`.

Exploring Viewport controls

When creating a Level, most of your time will be spent working within the Viewport panel, as this is your main visual view of the Level you are putting together. It is important to learn how to navigate in the Viewport and understand how to manipulate objects in the Level. So, we will provide a short primer on how to do that in this section.

> **Note**
>
> **Orthographic versus Perspective**
>
> When working in the Unreal Engine Viewport, you can view your Level through two fundamentally different viewing modes: *Perspective* or *Orthographic*. **Perspective View** is the default 3D camera mode that mimics how human eyes and real-world cameras perceive the world. Objects appear smaller the further away they are from the camera, creating a natural sense of depth, distance, and 3D scale that is perfect for testing lighting, playing your game, and navigating your world.

> The **Orthographic View** mode flattens your 3D world into a 2D Viewport, completely removing perspective distortion and depth perception. Objects remain the same size regardless of their distance from the camera, allowing you to view your Level from perfect, flat angles, such as **Top**, **Front**, or **Side**. It is an indispensable tool for beginners when precise object alignment is required.

Viewport Viewing Modes

Perspective and **Orthographic** (**1** and **2** in *Figure 2.11*, respectively) view modes are both available in the Viewport panel:

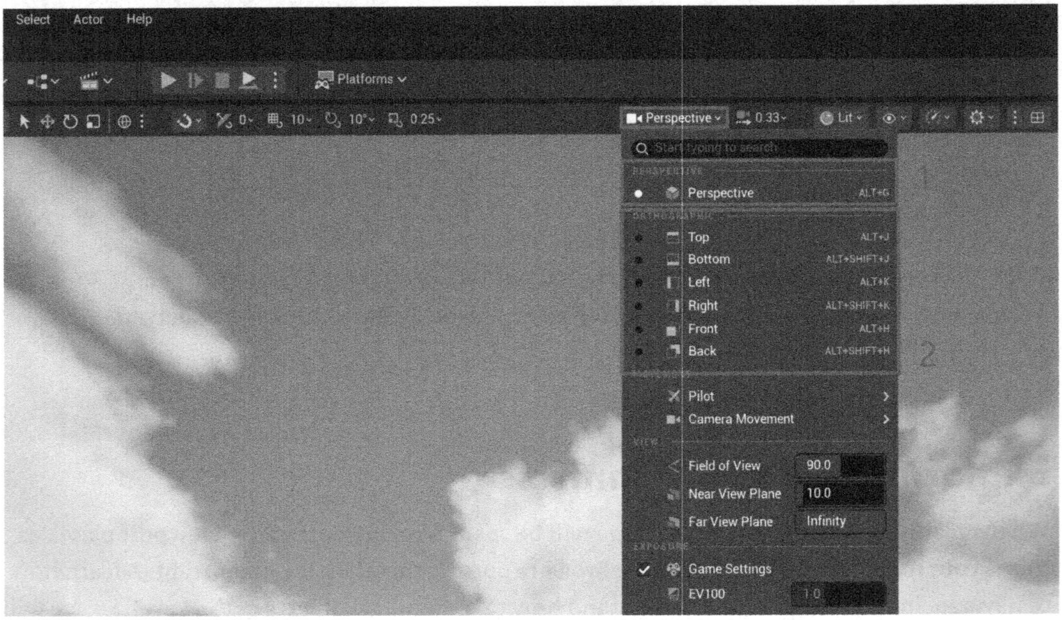

Figure 2.11 - Camera options dropdown showing available Perspective and Orthographic modes

For **Orthographic** mode, there are six sub-modes: **Top**, **Bottom**, **Left**, **Right**, **Front**, and **Back**, which are self-explanatory in that they give an orthographic view of the Level from that side. These view modes can be changed from the **Camera Options** dropdown in the Viewport toolbar, as highlighted in *Figure 2.11*.

We will mainly be working in **Perspective** view mode during the exercises in this book, and so that will be our focus here.

To adjust the camera view of the Viewport in **Perspective** viewing mode, you can use the following options:

- *Left-Click and Drag*: Move the Camera Forward/Back, Rotate the Camera Left/Right
- *Right-Click and Drag*: Rotate the Camera
- *Any Mouse Click and W*: Move the Camera Forward
- *Any Mouse Click and S*: Move the Camera Backward
- *Any Mouse Click and A*: Move the Camera Left
- *Any Mouse Click and D*: Move the Camera Right
- *Any Mouse Click and Q*: Move the Camera Down
- *Any Mouse Click and E*: Move the Camera Up

While navigating the Viewport allows you to move the camera around the Level and explore the environment, building a scene also requires you to position and adjust the objects within it. Once you are comfortable moving around the Viewport, the next step is learning how to manipulate the Actors (explained in the next section) that make up your Level. Unreal Engine provides a set of *transformation tools* that allow you to move, rotate, and scale objects directly in the Viewport. These tools form the core workflow for placing and arranging assets when designing a level.

Manipulating objects with transformation tools

The main **transformation tools** that you will use to build out your scene are the **Move** (or **Translate**), **Rotate**, and **Scale** tools. These tools allow you to visually manipulate objects in the Viewport, indirectly changing their associated **Location**, **Rotation**, and **Scale** values under the **Transform** section of the **Details** panel.

The advantage of using these tools rather than manually setting the values in the **Details** panel is that they allow you to physically move objects visually in the Viewport to position the objects where you require.

These tools can be selected from the **Viewport** toolbar and are highlighted **(1)** in *Figure 2.12*.

Figure 2.12 - Viewport toolbar with the transformation (1) and selection (2) tools

They can also be selected using the following shortcut keys when the Viewport panel is selected:

- *W*: Use the **Translate** tool
- *E*: Use the **Rotate** tool
- *R*: Use the **Scale** tool

Tip

Be sure to click the target object inside the Viewport panel first before using the shortcut keys; otherwise, the shortcuts will not register.

To exit any of these transformation tools and return to object selection mode in the Viewport panel, you can either click on the **Select Object** button (**2** in *Figure 2.12*) below or use the *Q* shortcut key. You can also use the *F* shortcut key to have the Viewport camera focus on the object currently selected.

Note

Object Snapping

Unreal Engine's transformation tools have a **Snapping** feature that allows you to manipulate objects in fixed, predictable increments rather than smooth, arbitrary values. This functionality lets you translate (move), rotate, and scale objects in precise, predetermined steps, making exact alignments significantly easier to achieve.

This is particularly useful when building levels with modular assets where objects, such as walls, floors, and props, need to align neatly with each other to avoid gaps or overlaps. Ultimately, utilizing transform snapping helps maintain consistent spacing, proportions, and scale across your scenes, which drastically improves both visual consistency and overall development efficiency.

Translate tool

The **Translate tool** lets you move an Actor to a new position within the Viewport's 3D space and is one of the most frequently used transformation tools in Unreal.

To use the **Translate** tool, select the Actor in the Viewport or **Outliner**, then activate the tool using the **Translate** icon in the Viewport toolbar (**1** in *Figure 2.13* below) or the *W* key. A **Gizmo** with *three colored* arrows will appear (**2** in *Figure 2.13* below), allowing you to drag an Actor along a single axis. Additionally, the colored squares at the axis intersections let you move it along two axes at once.

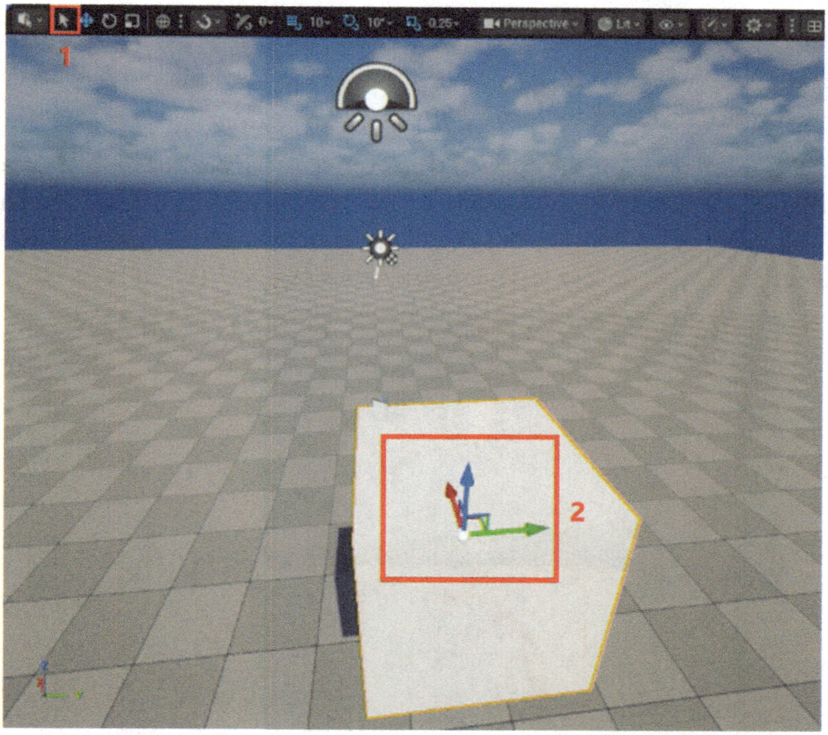

Figure 2.13 - Translate tool

The Gizmo follows Unreal's standard color coding for the axes – *red* for *X*, *green* for *Y*, and *blue* for *Z* – which is consistent across the editor. These same colors also appear in the **Details** panel beside the **Location**, **Rotation**, and **Scale** fields, helping you quickly identify which axis you are adjusting.

You can toggle Translation snapping on or off using the **translation-snap** icon in the Viewport toolbar (see *Figure 2.14*), and adjust the snap distance (e.g., `1`, `5`, `10`, or `50` units) from the same control.

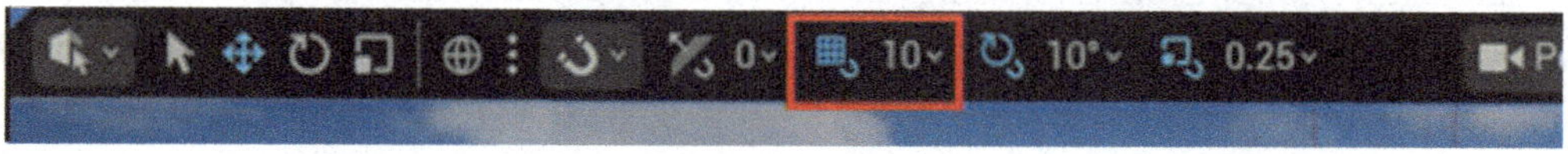

Figure 2.14 - Translate Snapping

When enabled, the Actor moves in these set increments as you drag the Translate Gizmo, ensuring consistent and accurate positioning throughout your Level.

Rotate tool

The **Rotate tool** lets you rotate an Actor around its pivot point within the Viewport's 3D space and is another core transformation tool in Unreal.

To use it, select the Actor in the Viewport or **Outliner**, then activate the tool using the **Rotate** icon (**1** in *Figure 2.15*) or the *E* key. A Rotation Gizmo with three colored circular bands will appear (**2**), allowing you to drag any ring to rotate the Actor around its corresponding axis. Rotation around the *X*, *Y*, and *Z* axes is referred to as *roll* (*X*), *pitch* (*Y*), and *yaw* (*Z*), respectively.

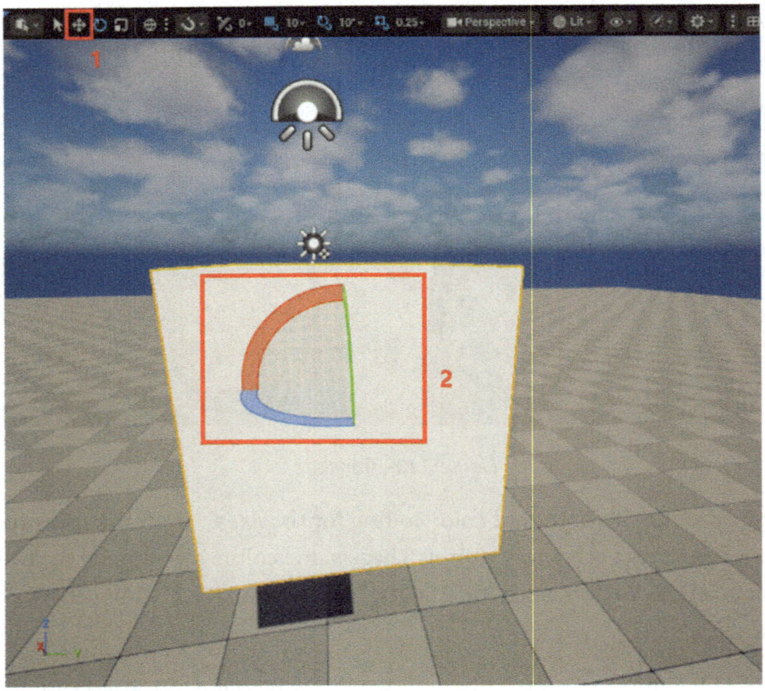

Figure 2.15 - Rotate tool

You can toggle snapping on or off using the **rotation-snap** icon in the Viewport toolbar (see *Figure 2.16*), and adjust the rotation angle increment value (e.g., `5°`, `10°`, `15°`, or `45°`) from the same control.

Figure 2.16 - Rotation Snapping Icon

When enabled, the Actor rotates in these set increments as you drag the Rotation Gizmo, ensuring you keep rotations accurate and consistent within your Level.

Scale tool

The **Scale tool** lets you adjust an Actor's size from its pivot point within the Viewport's 3D space.

To use it, select the Actor in the Viewport or **Outliner**, then activate the tool using the **Scale** icon (**1** in *Figure 2.17*) or the *R* key. A Scaling Gizmo with three colored handles and three colored squares will appear (**2**), allowing you to drag a handle to scale along a single axis or drag a square to scale along two axes. Dragging the *white* cube at the center scales the Actor uniformly across all axes.

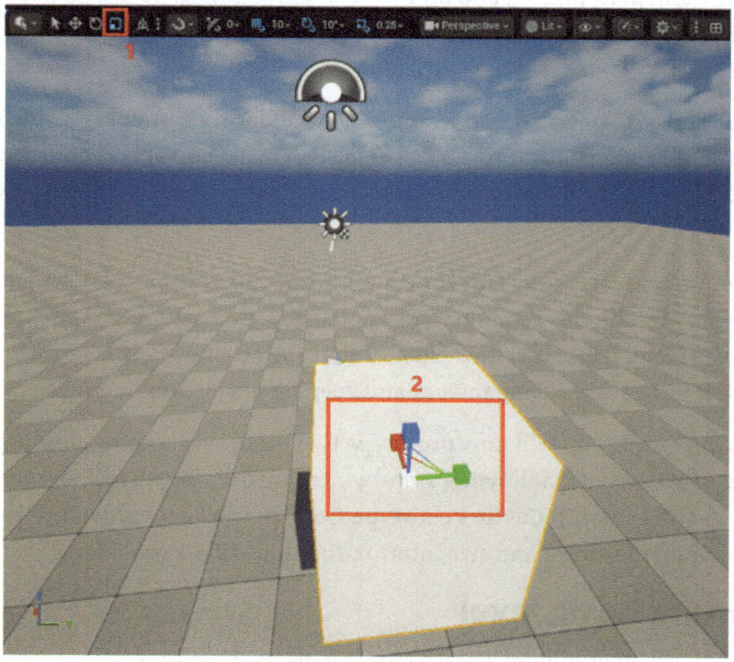

Figure 2.17 - Scale tool

Scaling can be applied non-uniformly (different values per axis) or uniformly (the same value on all axes), depending on which handle or control you drag.

You can toggle snapping on or off using the **scale-snap** icon in the Viewport toolbar (see *Figure 2.18*), and adjust the scale increment value (e.g., `0.1`, `0.25`, `0.5`, or `1.0`) from the same control.

Figure 2.18 - Scale Ratio Snapping Icon

When enabled, the Actor scales in these set increments as you drag the Scale Gizmo, ensuring you achieve precise and uniform scaling of objects within your level.

Now that you have learned how to use the transformation tools in Unreal, you will learn about Level Prototyping and use these skills to create prototype Levels for the *Pangaea* game.

Level prototyping and design

During early game development, teams often prototype levels using simple placeholder geometry (sometimes called **blockout** or **greybox meshes**). This approach allows designers to focus on testing gameplay, pacing, and layout before investing time in detailed art assets. Using simple shapes makes it easier to experiment, iterate quickly, and identify design issues early in development.

Blockout geometry also plays an important role in validating **gameplay scale**. By testing the level with placeholder shapes, designers can ensure that spaces such as doorways, corridors, platforms, and traversal paths feel correctly sized for the player character and gameplay mechanics.

Once the gameplay and level flow are refined and approved, technical artists and environment artists replace the placeholder geometry with polished, optimized assets that match the final visual style of the game. This workflow ensures that the artistic effort is spent on content that is already proven to work, reducing rework and keeping development efficient.

Following this approach, you will now prototype two basic Levels using simple geometry. First, you will create a **Bridge Level** following step-by-step instructions. Then, based on what you have learned, you will create a **Castle Prototype Level** in the next section for the *Pangaea* game, using geometry location and size information that will be provided.

Prototyping a basic level

Now that you have been familiarized with the Unreal Level Editor, you will get hands-on and prototype a simple Level using geometry. You will create a bridge, add sky, add placeholder statue geometry, and add placeholder water geometry.

Creating a new empty level

The following steps will guide you through creating a new empty Level in Unreal Engine 5:

1. Open the `Pangaea` project in `Chapter02-Start`.
2. In the **Content Browser**, navigate to **All** | **Content** | **LevelPrototyping** folder.
3. Click on the **Add** button and select **New Folder**.

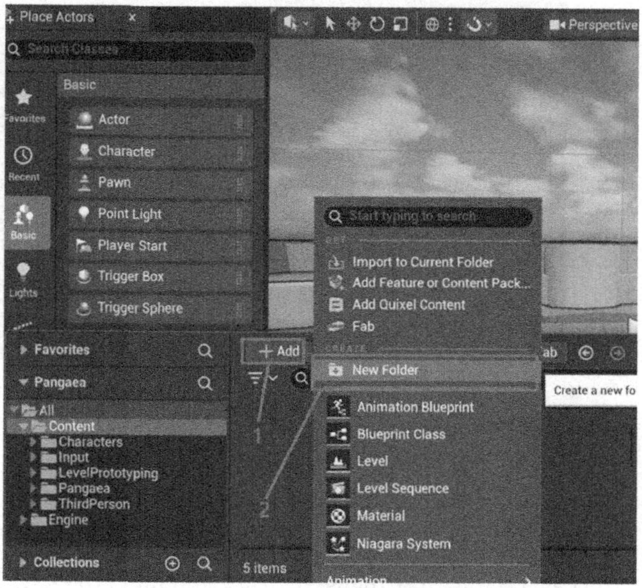

Figure 2.19 - Create a New Levels Folder

4. Name the new folder `Levels` and press *Enter*.
5. Create a New Level by selecting **File** | **New Level** in the Main Menu.
6. Select the **Empty Level** icon.
7. Press the **Create** button to create and open your new Level, which will be empty and black.

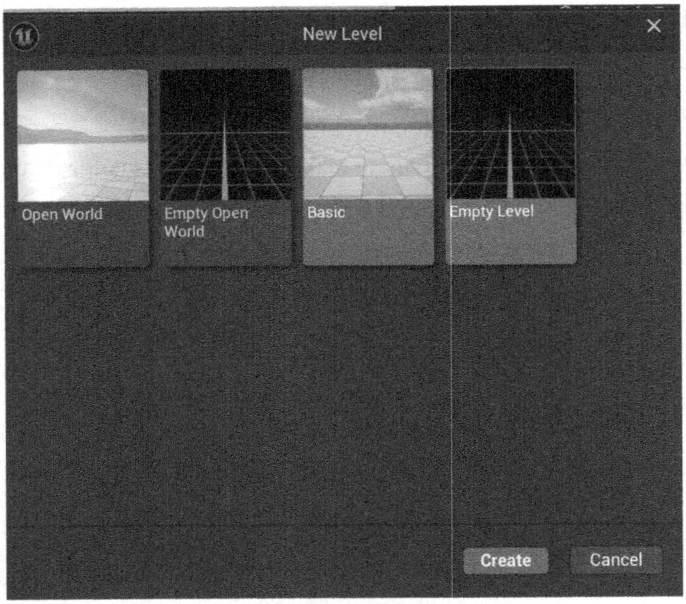

Figure 2.20 - Create a New Level

8. In the Main Menu, select **File** | **Save Current Level As...**
9. Navigate to the **All** | **Content** | **LevelPrototyping** | **Levels** folder that you created in *step 2*.
10. Change the Level Name to `BridgePrototype` and press the **Save** button to save the new Level, as shown in *Figure 2.21*.

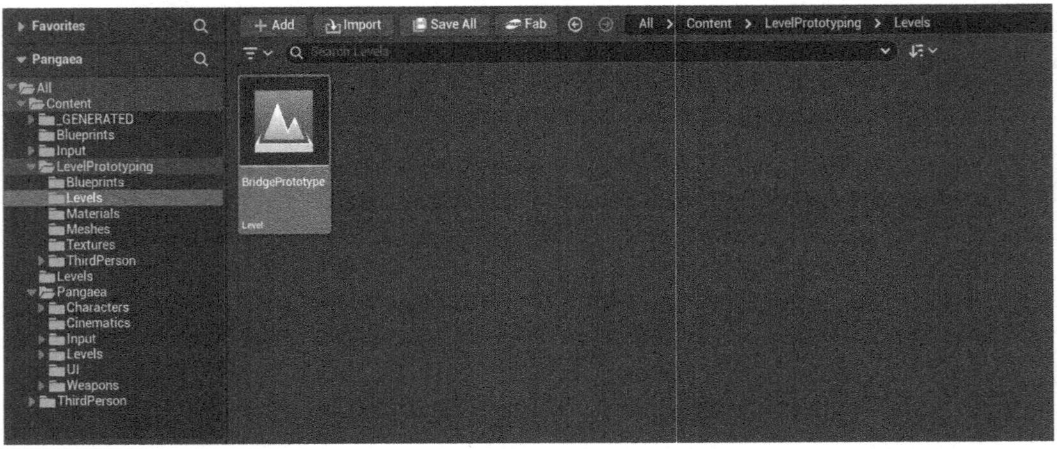

Figure 2.21 - BridgePrototype Level Saved in the Levels Folder

Now that the empty Level has been created and saved, the next step is to begin constructing an environment. You will do this by adding and editing geometry to form the basic structure of a bridge.

Creating the Bridge geometry

In this section, we will create a Bridge by editing Geometry in the Level:

1. In the Main Toolbar, change the **Context Mode** dropdown of the Level Editor to **Modeling Mode** (see *Figure 2.22*).
   Modeling Mode provides tools for creating and editing geometry directly inside Unreal Engine, allowing you to generate basic shapes and modify meshes without using an external 3D modeling application. This makes it ideal for quickly prototyping level geometry such as the bridge we will build in this section.

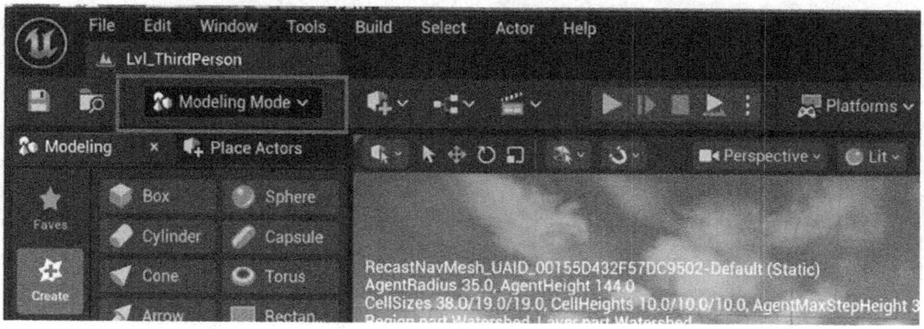

Figure 2.22 - Change Level Editor Context to Modeling Mode

2. Click the **Create** button on the left-hand side of the Modeling Toolbar.
3. Select **Box** in the Modeling Toolbar (**2** in *Figure 2.23*) and move the created Box object into position in the Viewport panel using your mouse, then left-click to select the desired position.
4. In the **Create Box** window that appears, click the **Accept** button.
5. In the **Details** panel, underneath the **Transform** section, you will find 3 sets of coordinates for **Location**, **Rotation**, and **Scale**. Edit the boxes for the location coordinates (**2** in *Figure 2.23*) to `0.0`, `0.0`, and `20.0`, and then edit the boxes for the scale coordinates (**3** in *Figure 2.23*) to `1.0`, `1.0`, and `0.2`.

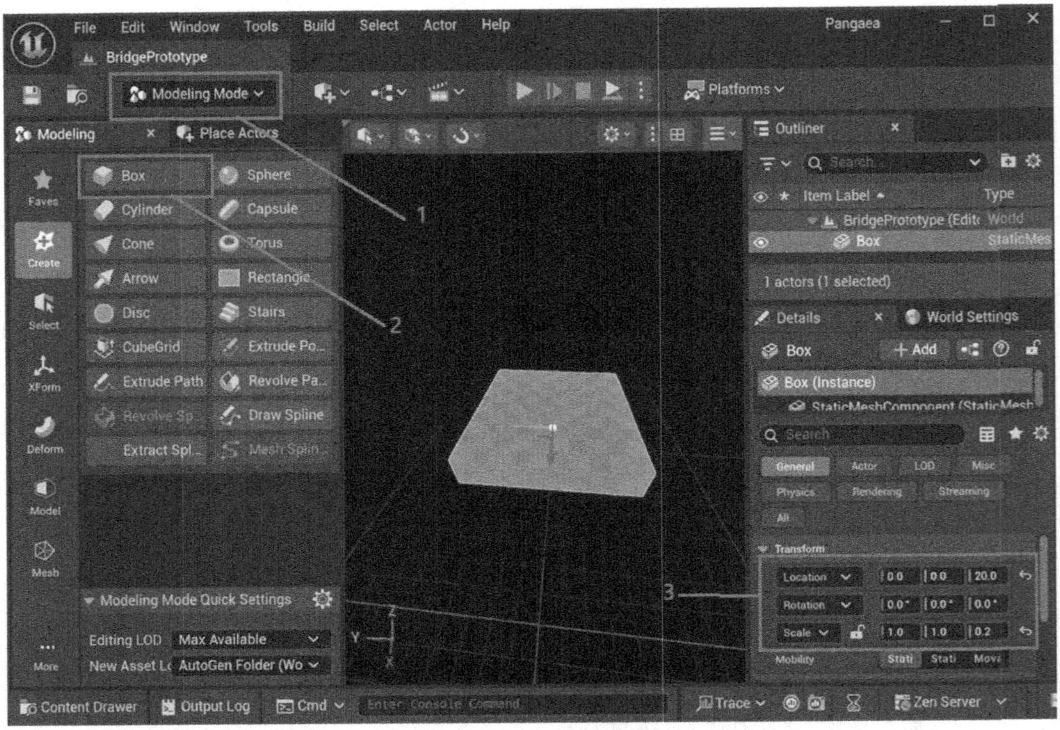

Figure 2.23 - Add a Box to the Level

6. Select the newly created box and press *Ctrl* + *D* to create a duplicate of the box.
7. In the **Outliner**, select the newly created box and edit its location coordinates to hold the values of (`0.0`, `-100.0`, and `20.0`) as shown in *Figure 2.24*.

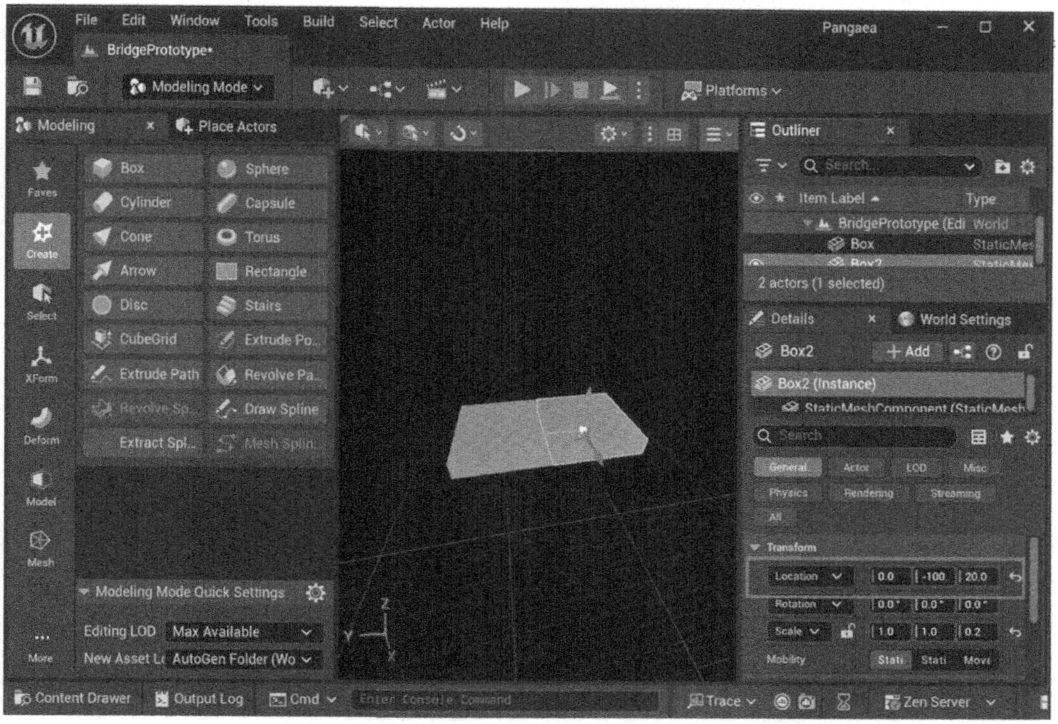

Figure 2.24 - Duplicate and place a second box

8. Repeat this process to create three more duplicate boxes and position these boxes as follows:
    - Set the first box's **Location** coordinates to (`0`, `-200`, `20.0`)
    - Set the second box's **Location** coordinates to (`0`, `-300`, `20.0`)
    - Set the third box's **Location** coordinates to (`0`, `-400`, `20.0`)
9. Hold *Ctrl* and select each of the newly created boxes, then click the **Mesh** button (**3** in *Figure 2.25*) on the left-hand side of the Modeling Toolbar and select **Union** (**4** in *Figure 2.25*) in the right-hand window of the Modeling Toolbar and press the **Accept** button at the bottom of the window. This will Union (or combine) the five boxes into one single mesh named **Merge**. Rename it to `Bridge`.

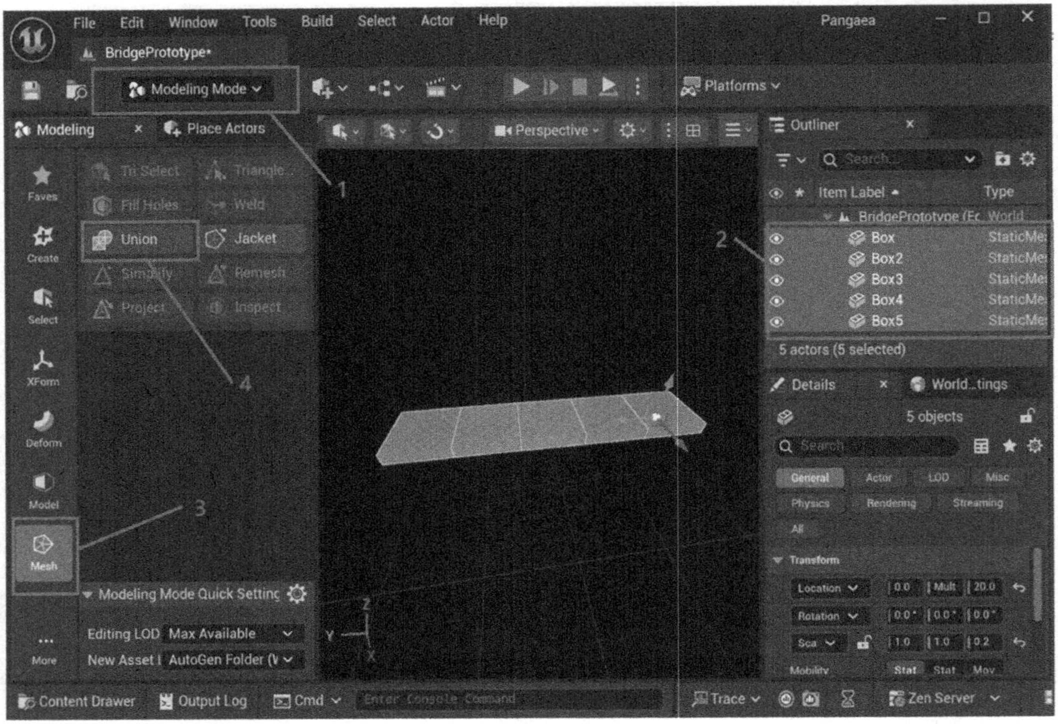

Figure 2.25 - Use Union to combine the 5 Box meshes into a single Box mesh

10. In the **Outliner** window, select the newly combined Box (that is the Bridge) and edit its location coordinates to hold the values of `0.0`, `-200.0`, and `10.0`.

11. Click the **Model** button (**1** in *Figure 2.26*) on the left-hand side of the Modeling Toolbar and select **PolyGroup Edit** (**2** in *Figure 2.26*) to enter the **PolyGroup Edit** mode.

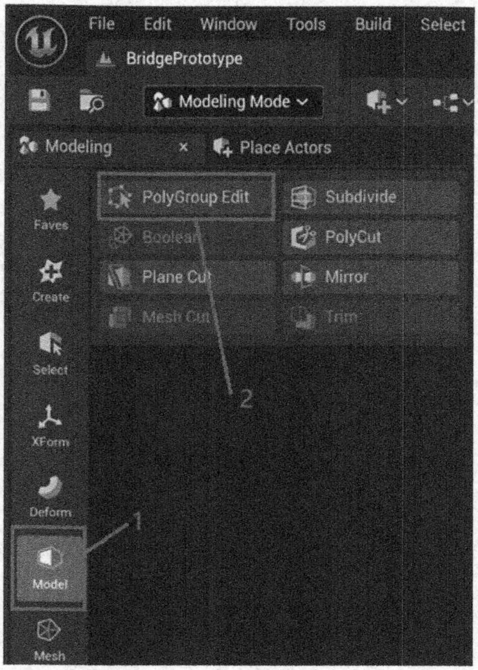

Figure 2.26 - Selecting PolyGroup Edit on the combined single Box mesh

12. In **PolyGroup Edit** mode, change the **Selection Filter**, found near the bottom of the **PolyGroup Edit panel**, to only select **Vertices** by clicking the points icon (**1** in *Figure 2.27*).
13. Now press *Shift* and select the 4 central corner points (Vertices) of the top face of the Box (highlighted as *yellow* dots in *Figure 2.27*) and drag these up to a height of around 1 unit (**2** in *Figure 2.27*).

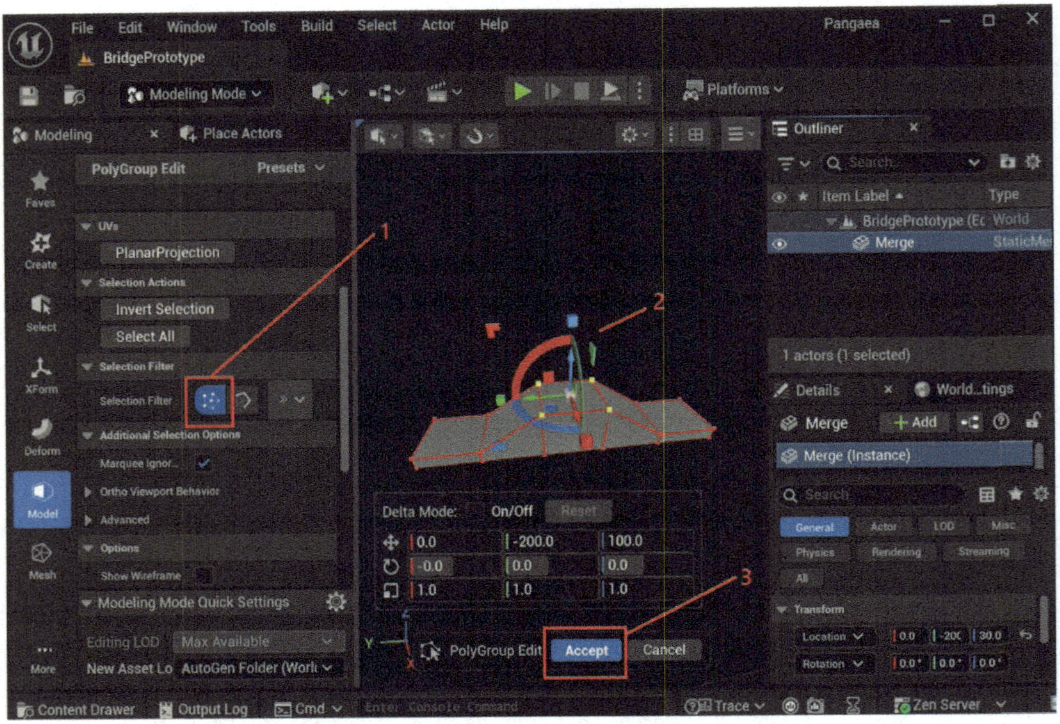

Figure 2.27 - Pull the four centre vertices of the Box up one unit

14. Click on the **Accept** button (**3** in *Figure 2.27*) to confirm the extrusion of the central vertices of the Box. This gives us our base Bridge geometry.
15. Click the **Create** button on the left-hand side of the Modeling Toolbar (**1** in *Figure 2.28*).
16. Select **Cylinder** in the Modeling Toolbar and move the created Cylinder (**2** in *Figure 2.28*) object into the Viewport panel using the mouse.
17. Position it in front of the Bridge Geometry (created in the earlier steps), then left-click to select the desired position.
18. In the **Create Cylinder** pop-up, click the **Accept** button (**4** in *Figure 2.28*).

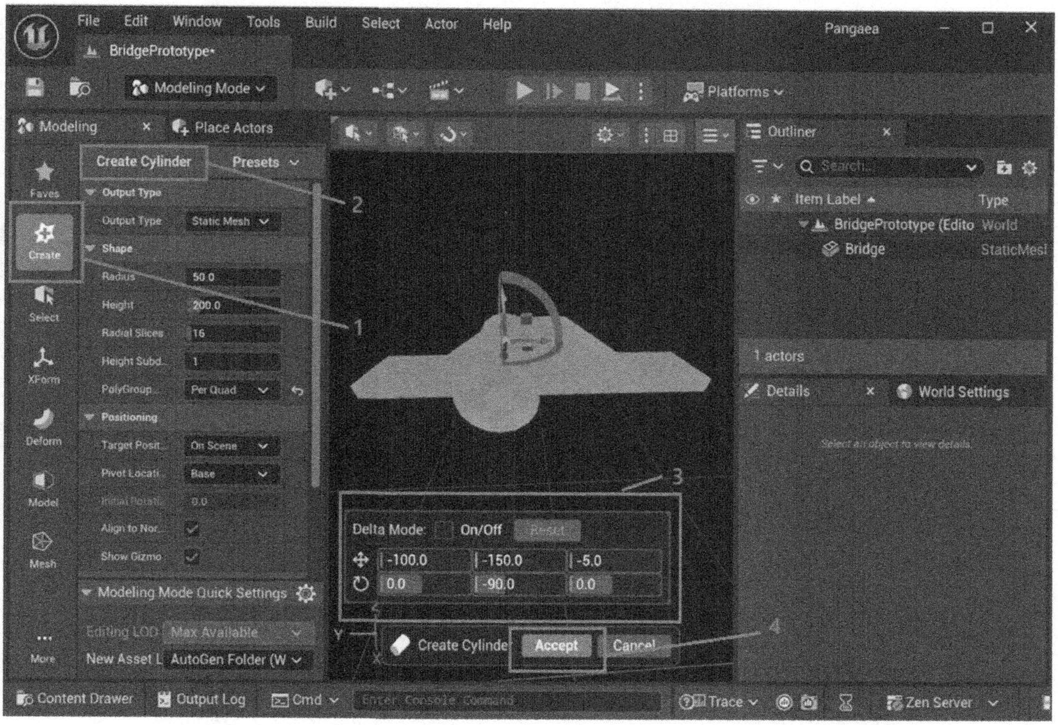

Figure 2.28 - Creating and positioning the Cylinder

19. In the **Details** panel for the Cylinder, under the **Transform** section, set the following properties to position it as shown in *Figure 2.29*:
    - Set the **Location** coordinates to (`-100`, `-150`, `-5.0`)
    - Set the **Rotation** coordinates to (`0`, `-90`, `0`)
    - Set the **Scale** coordinates to (`0.5`, `0.5`, `1.0`)

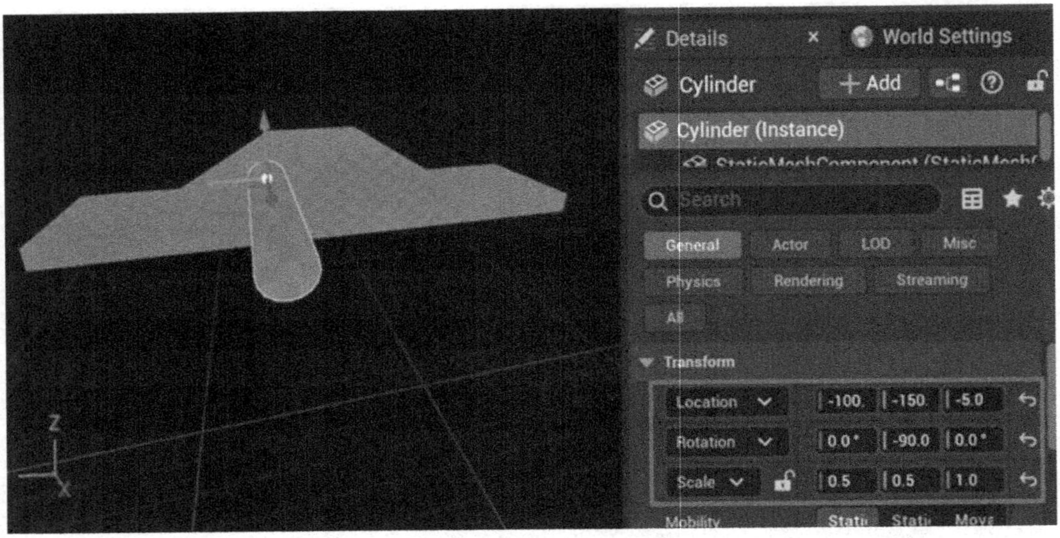

Figure 2.29 - Positioning and scaling the Cylinder

20. Holding down the *Shift* key, first click on the Bridge Geometry to select it, then click on the **Cylinder** to select that as well (still holding down the *Shift* key; see **1** in *Figure 2.30*):
21. If it is not already selected, click the **Model** button (**2** in *Figure 2.30*) on the left-hand side of the Modeling Toolbar.
22. Select **Boolean** (**3** in *Figure 2.30*) in the right-hand window of the Modeling Toolbar *(note that Boolean operations are explained in the next section)*. This will configure a Boolean Operation between Object A (the first selected object, which was Bridge Geometry) and Object B (the second selected object, which was the Cylinder).

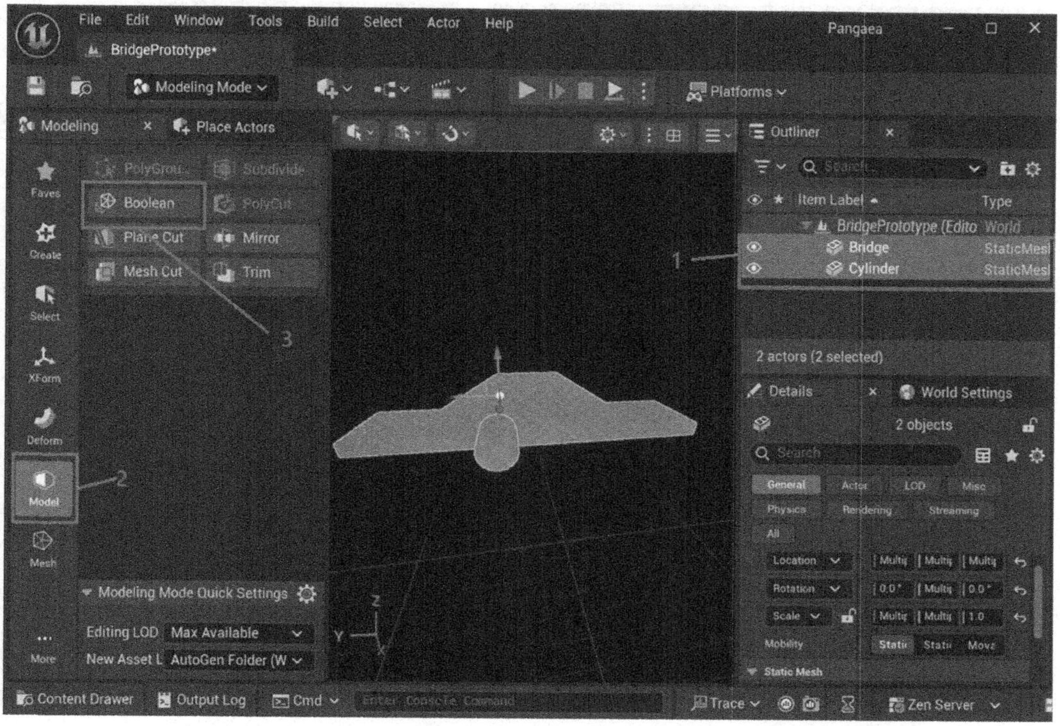

Figure 2.30 - Configure a Boolean Operation with the Bridge and Cylinder

23. In the **Boolean Operation** dropdown, make sure to choose the setting **Difference A-B**. This will subtract the geometry of Object B from the geometry of Object A and give us a tunnel under the left-hand side of the Bridge (see *Figure 2.31*).
24. In the **Mesh Boolean** pop-up, click the **Accept** button.

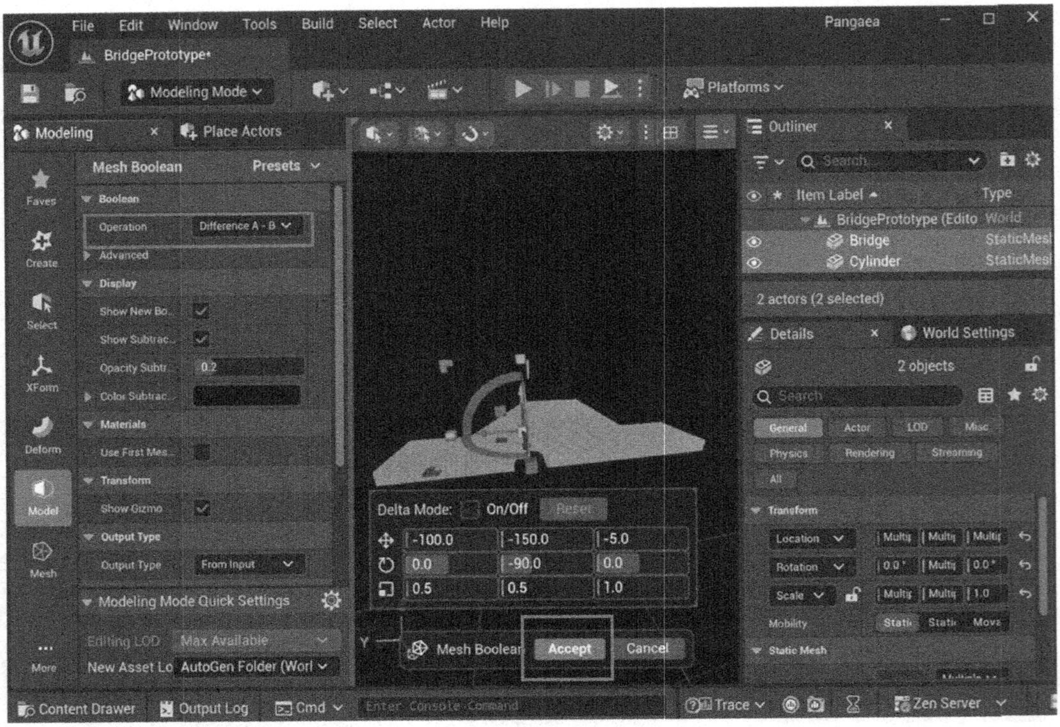

Figure 2.31 - Tunnel resulting from a Boolean operation on the Bridge and Cylinder

To reinforce your understanding of the previous Boolean steps, the next section will give a short explanation of Boolean Operations.

Understanding Boolean operations

The type of Boolean Operation that is carried out between Object A and Object B is dictated by the Boolean Operation chosen in the dropdown setting (highlighted in *red* in *Figure 2.31*). The following settings options are possible:

- **Difference A - B**: Subtract the geometry of Object B from that of Object A
- **Difference B - A**: Subtract the geometry of Object A from that of Object B
- **Intersection**: Subtract the geometry of Object A and Object B that do not intersect with each other
- **Union**: Combine the geometry of Object A and Object B

Now repeat *steps 15 to 24* (inclusive) to create a tunnel under the right-hand side of the bridge, add a Directional Light (covered in the next section), and set its **Rotation** to (`145, -30, -15`).

You should see a bridge with two tunnels as shown in *Figure 2.32*:

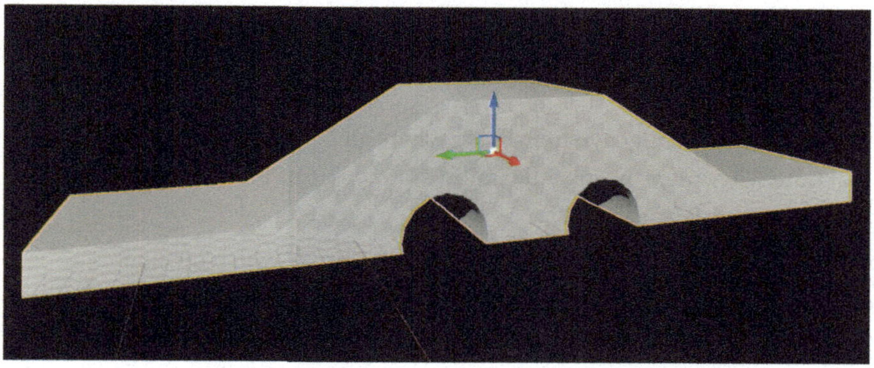

Figure 2.32 - Bridge Geometry with Two Tunnels

The process should be identical to the previous steps, other than the settings for the Cylinder, which are given below.

In the **Details** panel for the Cylinder, set the following properties underneath the **Transform** section:

- Set the **Location** coordinates to (`100, -250, 15.0`)
- Set the **Rotation** coordinates to (`0, 90, 0`)
- Set the **Scale** coordinates to (`0.5, 0.5, 1.5`)

With the Bridge Geometry created, we will now provide an overview of available lighting options that can be added to the Level.

Adding lighting to the level

Unreal Engine provides several lighting types that can be used individually or combined. But it's important to remember that adding many lights in Unreal Engine can be performance-expensive, particularly with certain types of light mobility and settings like dynamic shadows.

Unreal Engine supports three main light mobility types, each designed for different performance and gameplay needs:

- **Static Lights**: The most performance-efficient lights. Their lighting and shadows are precomputed and baked into lightmaps, meaning they cannot change during gameplay. They are best used for stable environments and general ambient lighting.

- **Stationary Lights**: Provide a balance between quality and performance. They use baked lighting for static objects but allow certain properties, such as color and intensity, to change during gameplay while still casting dynamic shadows from movable objects.
- **Movable Lights**: Fully dynamic lights where all lighting and shadows are calculated in real time. They offer the most flexibility for moving or interactive light sources but have the highest performance cost.

There are several different types of lights available in Unreal, which include:

- **Directional Light**: Simulates light from an infinitely distant source, like the sun or moon, casting parallel rays across the Level. It's used to simulate outdoor environments and day-night cycles.
- **Point Light**: Light is emitted in all directions emanating from a single point, similar to a light bulb. A good choice for small, localized light sources.
- **Spot Light**: Light is projected in a cone shape like a flashlight or a stage spotlight, with dynamic properties for position, direction, and angle of spread. A great choice when you need to illuminate a specific, localized area with a focused, controllable beam of light.
- **Rect Light**: Soft, diffused light is emitted from a flat, rectangular area. Ideal for simulating light from sources like windows or large screens.
- **Sky Light**: Ambient lighting information is captured from the sky to provide overall, soft global illumination and realistic ambient shadows. It is often paired with cube maps or HDRI images, which provide a simulation for the sky.

You will now add a **Directional Light** into the Level. This will simulate light from the sun and is appropriate because this level is set outdoors. Follow these steps:

1. Add a **Directional Light** to the Level by clicking on the **Quick Add** button in the Main Toolbar, then navigating to **Lights | Directional Light** (see *Figure 2.33*).

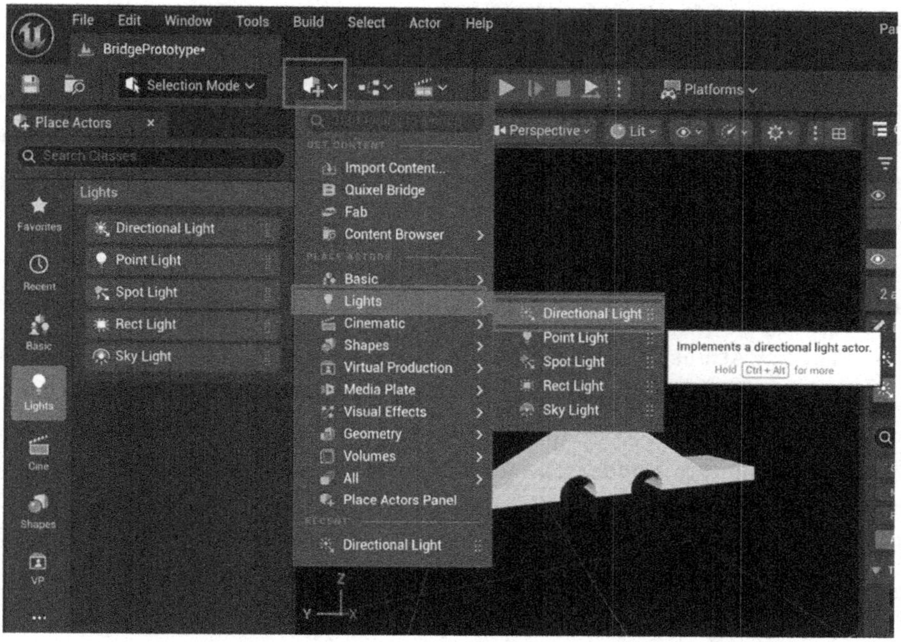

Figure 2.33 - Add a Directional Light to the Level

2. Underneath the **Transform** section, change the **Rotation** coordinate values to adjust the lighting until you are happy with how it looks. In the example provided, the **Rotation** is set to (`0, 116, 0`).

   Remember that you adjust the **Rotation**, not the **Location**, to change the effect of Directional lights. A **Directional Light** simulates an infinitely distant light source like the sun, so consequently, all the light rays hitting your Level are considered perfectly parallel. So, changing the location of the light source will not produce a noticeable effect. The angle of the light determines how it will illuminate the scene, so rotating the Directional Light is the best way to change the direction of these parallel rays and alter how objects are lit and where shadows will fall.

Now that there is a **Directional Light** added to the Level, we will add a Sky Environment to give it a more realistic feel.

Adding a realistic sky environment

Unreal Engine provides an **Environment Light Mixer** tool for quickly creating and adjusting core components for outdoor lighting and the sky environment, such as Directional Light, Skylight, Sky Atmosphere, And Exponential Height Fog. It is a central interface allowing you to control these elements without having to go and find each of them in the Level and adjust them in the **Details** panel.

To better understand how these systems work together, let's briefly look at the main components used to build the sky and ambient lighting in a Level.

- The **Sky Atmosphere component** is a rendering system that creates realistic skies by physically simulating light interaction with a planetary atmosphere. It can be customized to create a variety of effects, from Earth-like skies with day-night cycles to exotic alien atmospheres, by adjusting settings for light scattering, color, and other atmospheric properties. It depends on a Directional Light and a Sky Light to function properly and can be integrated with other systems like volumetric clouds and height fog to create complete environments.
- The **Sky Light component** captures ambient light from the environment and applies it to the Level to create realistic, bounced lighting. It is used to illuminate areas that are not directly hit by Directional Light, such as the underside of objects. It can be set up to capture either the real-time atmosphere or a pre-made cube map, like an HDRI.
- The **Volumetric Cloud component** is a physically based rendering system that can be used to create realistic real-time clouds by ray-marching a 3D volume texture. Cloud appearance can be controlled by modifying parameters in the cloud material, such as density, coverage, and noise. It supports dynamic movement, time-of-day cycles, cloud casting and receiving shadows, and integrates with the Sky Atmosphere and Sky Light systems. Play around with some of the cloud properties to see what effects you generate with your clouds.
- The **Exponential Height Fog component** is a global system that creates a height-based fog effect which is denser at lower altitudes and thins out at higher altitudes. It allows for a two-color configuration, provides a smooth transition between foggy areas and clear areas, with properties available to adjust the fog density, color, height offset, and height falloff. There is an option to enable Volumetric Fog for more physically based light scattering, allowing light shafts and other complex atmospheric effects. Experiment with some of these fog properties to see what sort of effects you can generate with your fog.

In the following steps, you will use the **Environment Light Mixer** to create a realistic Sky Environment within your Level using the default settings for these Unreal Engine environmental features:

1. Open the window for the **Environment Light Mixer** tool by navigating to **Window | Env. Light Mixer**.

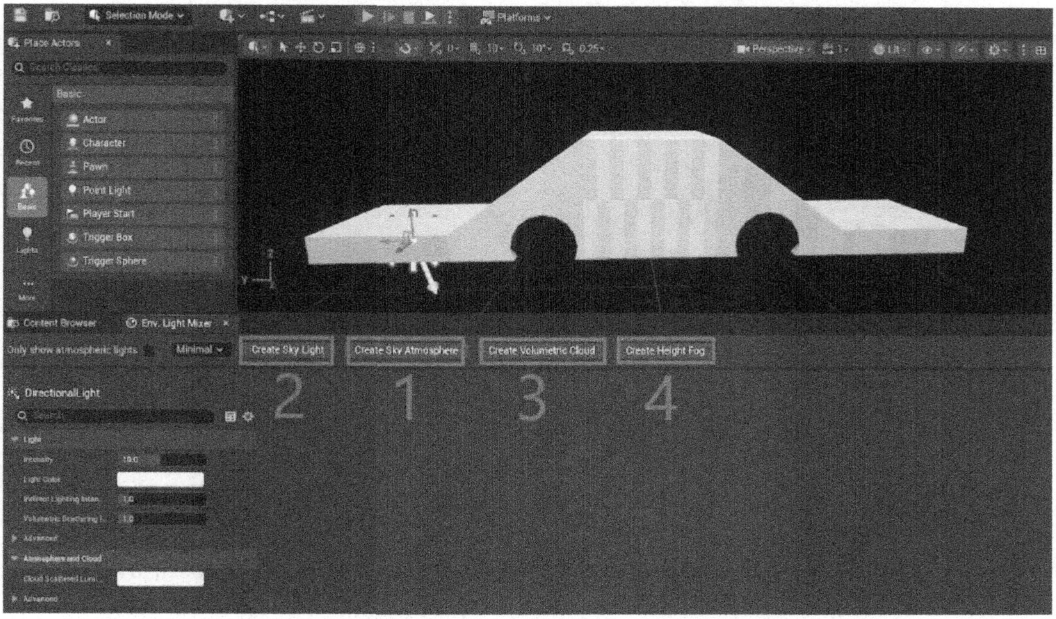

Figure 2.34 - Open the Environment Light Mixer

2. Click on the **Create Sky Atmosphere** (**1** in *Figure 2.34*) and **Create Sky Light** (**2**) buttons to create the **Sky Atmosphere** and **Sky Light**.
3. **Click** on the **Create Volumetric Cloud** button (**3**) to add **Volumetric Clouds** to the Level.
4. Click on the **Create Height Fog** button (**4**) to add **Exponential Height Fog** to the Level.

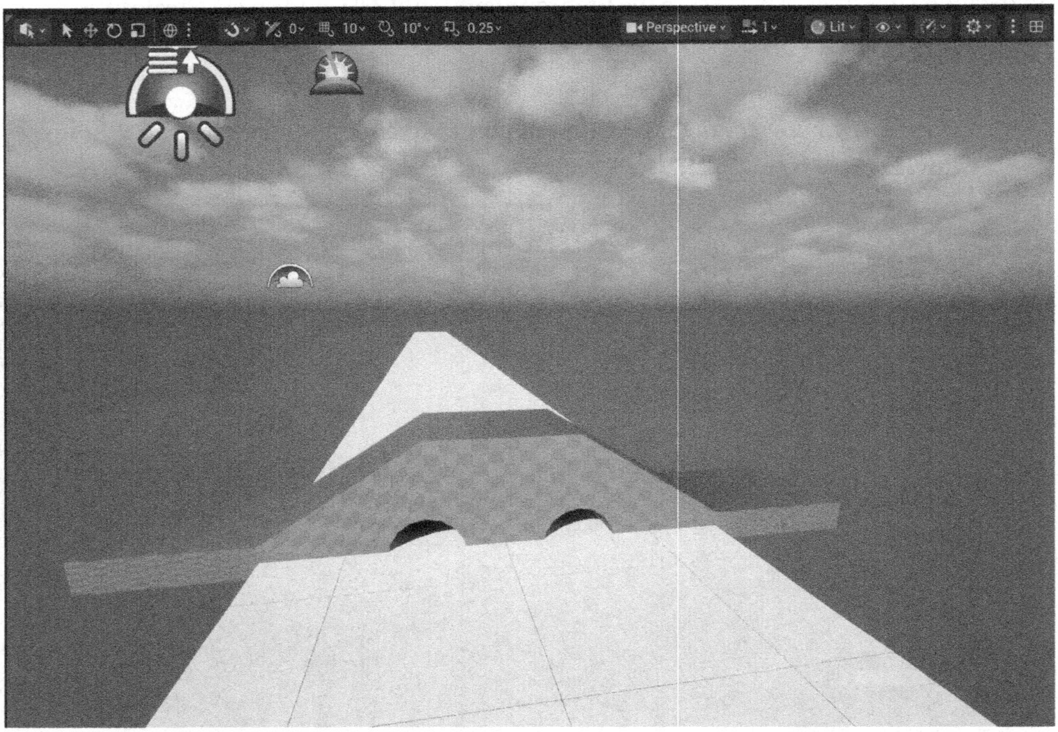

Figure 2.35 - Sky Atmosphere, Sky Light, Volumetric Clouds and Height Fog added to the Level

There is now a realistic Sky Environment in the Level, with a Sky Light, Sky Atmosphere, Volumetric Clouds, and Exponential Height Fog, as shown in *Figure 2.35*. In the next section, we will add a default Unreal Engine character into the Level.

Tip

If you would like to learn more detailed information about the **Environment Light Mixer** to supplement your understanding, refer to the official Unreal Engine system documentation at: `https://dev.epicgames.com/documentation/unreal-engine/environmental-light-with-fog-clouds-sky-and-atmosphere-in-unreal-engine?application_version=5.6`.

Adding the default UE5 character

Unreal Engine offers two standard character mannequins. A female character named `Quinn` and a legacy male mannequin named `Mannequin`. Both these characters' skeletal meshes share the same Epic skeleton structure that is the foundational design used for characters in Unreal, helping to ensure consistency when reusing animations between Unreal and third-party character assets.

The following steps will add a character to the level:

1. In the **Content Browser**, navigate to the **All** | **Content** | **Characters** | **Mannequins** | **Meshes** folder and click and drag the `SKM_Quinn_Simple` asset (shown in *Figure 2.36*) into the Level Viewport to place an instance of the Quinn mannequin.

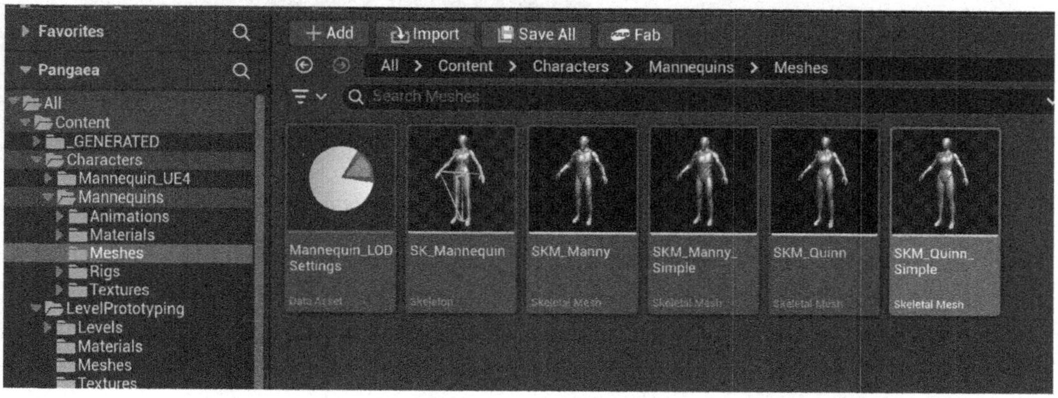

Figure 2.36 - SKM_Quinn_Simple asset path shown in the Content Browser

2. Select the `SKM_Quinn_Simple` character in the **Outliner** panel and scale down the size of the asset. Set the **Scale** to (`0.3`, `0.3`, `0.3`), the **Location** to (`20`, `-20`, `20`), and the **Rotation** to (`0`, `0`, `-180`).

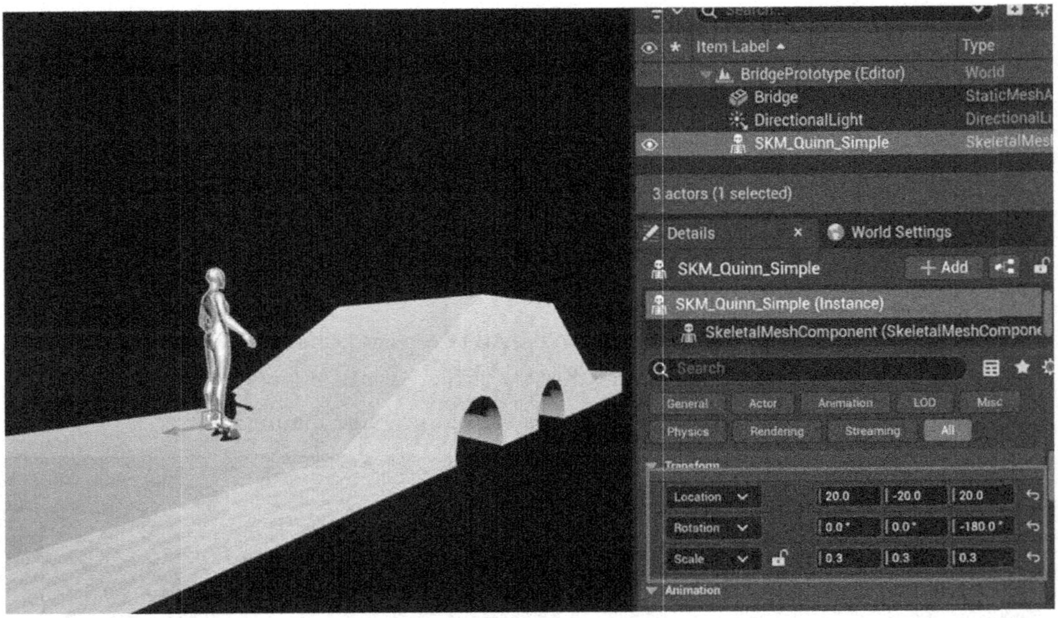

Figure 2.37 - UE5 Character Mannequin positioned in the scene

Note that this step is for prototyping only, not for adding a playable character. Pressing **Play** on this Bridge Level will spawn an oversized player character, which is not intended for this prototype. The technique for properly adding a playable character to a Level is covered later in *Chapter 4*.

Now that there is a character added to the Level, we will look to add a little more decoration by adding placeholder geometry to represent the placement of a statue.

Adding statue placeholder geometry

Even with the bridge and the character added, the Level is still a little sparse. So, we will make it a little more interesting and give you some further practice creating geometry by adding a statue placeholder through the following steps:

1. Click the **Create** button in the Main Toolbar and select **Shapes | Cylinder** from the pop-up menu to add a Cylinder to the Level.

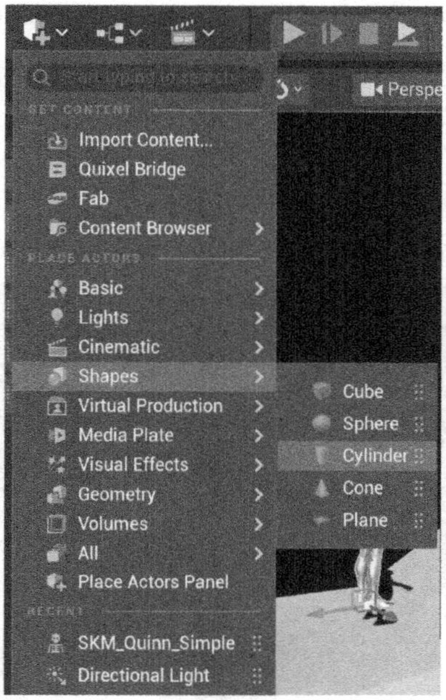

Figure 2.38 - Add a Cylinder and Sphere to the Level

2. Select the **Cylinder** asset in the **Outliner** panel and set the **Location** coordinates to (`0, -200, 90`) using either the **Move** tool or by setting the location in the **Details** panel.
3. With the **Cylinder** still selected, set its **Scale** coordinates to (`0.1, 0.1, 0.5`) using either the **Scale** tool or by setting the **Scale** in the **Details** panel. The bottom of the placed **Cylinder** should be flush against the surface of the bridge. There may be some leeway adjustment needed here depending on how high you dragged up the bridge height, so adjust the **Z** value of the **Cylinder** accordingly.
4. Click the **Create** button in the Main Toolbar and select **Shapes | Sphere** from the pop-up menu to add a **Sphere** to the Level (see *Figure 2.38*).
5. Select the **Sphere** asset in the **Outliner** and set the **Location** coordinates to (`0, -200, 120`) using either the **Move** tool or by setting the **Location** in the **Details** panel.

6. With the **Sphere** still selected, set its **Scale** coordinates to (`0.2,0.2,0.2`) using either the **Scale** tool or by setting the **Scale** in the **Details** panel. The bottom of the **Sphere** should be touching the top surface of the **Cylinder**. There may be some leeway adjustment needed here depending on how high you dragged up the bridge height, so adjust the **Z** value of the **Sphere** accordingly.

You now have statue placeholder geometry placed on the bridge in the scene:

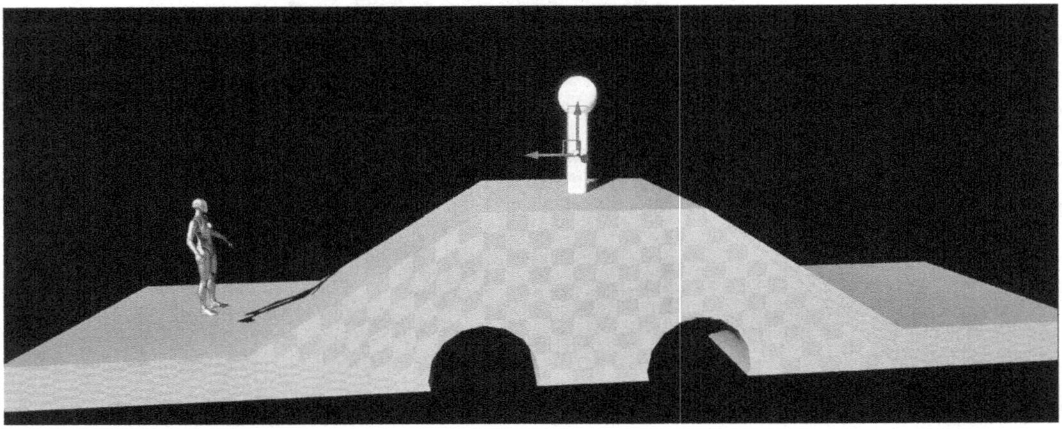

Figure 2.39 - Cylinder and Sphere Geometry Statue Placeholder Added to the Level

Now that the statue placeholder has been added to the Level, we will add a simple plane shape that will form a placeholder for water in the Level, which runs under the Bridge.

Adding a simple plane

The following steps will add Plane geometry to the Level to create a water placeholder:

1. Click the **Create** button in the Main Toolbar and select **Shapes | Plane** from the pop-up menu to add a Plane to the Level.

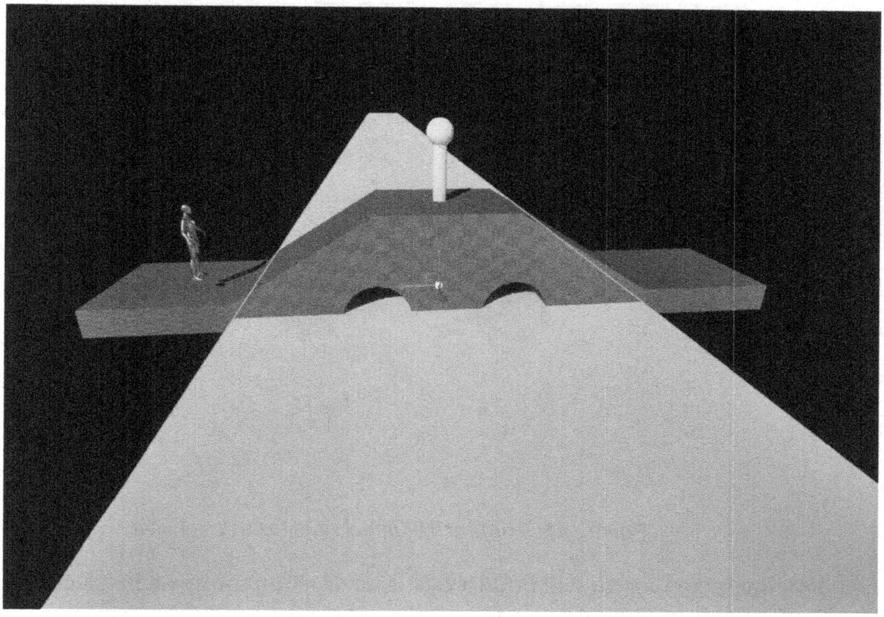

Figure 2.40 - A plane water placeholder added to the Level

2. Select the **Plane** asset in the **Outliner** panel and set the **Location** coordinates to (`0`, `-200`, `1`) using either the **Move** tool or by setting the **Location** in the **Details** panel.
3. With the **Plane** still selected, set its **Scale** coordinates to (`100`, `3`, `1`) using either the **Scale** tool or by setting the **Scale** in the **Details** panel.

Having added the Plane water placeholder and completed the Bridge prototype Level with step-by-step instructions, you will now move on to build out a new Castle prototype Level on your own using a layout image and scale and location details for the placeholder geometry.

Building out a Castle Level prototype

The following exercise is designed to help you apply the Level Editor and transformation skills you have learned in the previous sections to build out a prototype Castle Level on your own. *Figure 2.41* shows the image of what the Castle Level should look like once you have finished prototyping:

Figure 2.41 - Image of the Unreal Level to be Prototyped

In the following sections, you will build a Castle Level using the given instructions and your understanding of the Level Editor and transformation tools.

Before moving on to the next steps to create the Castle prototype itself, first create a new Level to work in called `CastlePrototype` under the **All | Content | LevelPrototyping | Levels** folder. If required, refer to the *Prototyping a basic level* section for a refresher of the process. The steps in the following sections should be completed inside the `CastlePrototype` Level.

Directional light, floor, and outer walls

1. Add a Directional Light.
2. Create a Floor placeholder by adding a Cube at position `(0, 0, -50)` with a scale of `(40, 40, 0.1)`.
3. Create Castle placeholder geometry and scale and place it as follows, to build the Castle prototype, as shown in *Figure 2.42*:
    - A Cube at position `(-1950, 0, 172)` with a scale of `(1, 40, 4.5)`
    - A Cube at position `(1950, 0, 172)` with a scale of `(1, 40, 4.5)`
    - A Cube at position `(0, 1950, 172)` with a scale of `(40, 1, 4.5)`
    - A Cube at position `(0, -1950, 172)` with a scale of `(40, 1, 4.5)`
    - A Cube at position `(-1850, 0, 50)` with a scale of `(1, 38, 2)`
    - A Cube at position `(1850, 0, 50)` with a scale of `(1, 38, 2)`

- A Cube at position (`0, -1850, 50`) with a scale of (`36, 1, 2`)
- A Cube at position (`0, 1850, 50`) with a scale of (`36, 1, 2`)

Figure 2.42 - Castle prototype with Directional Light, Floor and Outer Walls added

Half-cylinder towers

1. Enter **Modeling Mode**, and from the **Create** menu add a temporary Box with a **Width** of `500`, a **Depth** of `500`, and a **Height** of `600` at position (`0, -250, 600`).
2. Add one Cylinder with a **Radius** of `250` and a **Height** of `400` and move it to position (`0, 0, 600`).
3. Use the **Boolean** tool, in **Modeling Mode**, to subtract the temporary Box from the Cylinder to essentially crop it across the diameter, to create a Half-Cylinder.
4. Return to **Selection Mode** and duplicate the Half-Cylinder a further three times, so you have four Half-Cylinders.
5. Delete the temporary Box from the Level.
6. Place the four Half-Cylinders at the following locations, to mimic the center building and ramps (see *Figure 2.43*):
   - 1 Half-Cylinder at position (`0, 1775, 160`), rotated to have its flat side flush against the wall

- 1 Half-Cylinder at position (`0, -1775, 160`), rotated to have its flat side flush against the wall
- 1 Half-Cylinder at position (`1775, 0, 160`), rotated to have its flat side flush against the wall
- 1 Half-Cylinder at position (`-1775, 0, 160`), rotated to have its flat side flush against the wall

Figure 2.43 - Castle prototype with the Half-Cylinder Towers added

Center building and ramps

1. Add a Cube with a scale of (`10, 10, 2`) at position (`0, 0, 50`).
2. Enter **Modeling Mode** and, from the **Create** menu, add four Boxes, each with a **Width** of `300`, a **Depth** of `300`, and a **Height** of `200`.
3. Return to **Selection Mode** and position the Boxes at the following locations: (`0, 650, -50`), (`0, -650, -50`), (`650, 0, -50`), and (`-650, 0, -50`).

4. Enter **Modeling Mode** and, for each box, use vertex selection and drag them down to make them slope to the ground away from the center cube to mimic the center building and ramps.

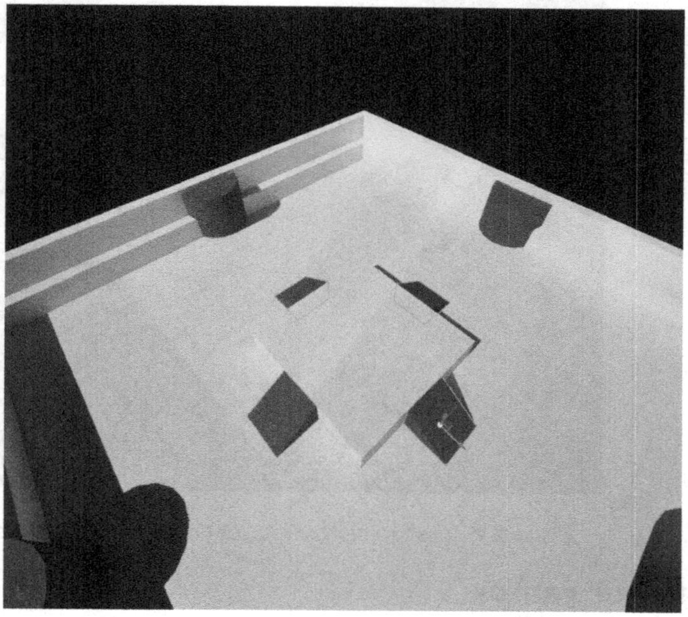

Figure 2.44 - Castle prototype with the Center Building and Ramps added

Corner tower buildings

1. Add four Cubes, each with a scale of (`6, 6, 2`).
2. Position them at the following four locations: (`1500, 1500, 50`), (`-1500, 1500, 50`), (`-1500, -1500, 50`), and (`1500, -1500, 50`) to create the corner tower buildings.

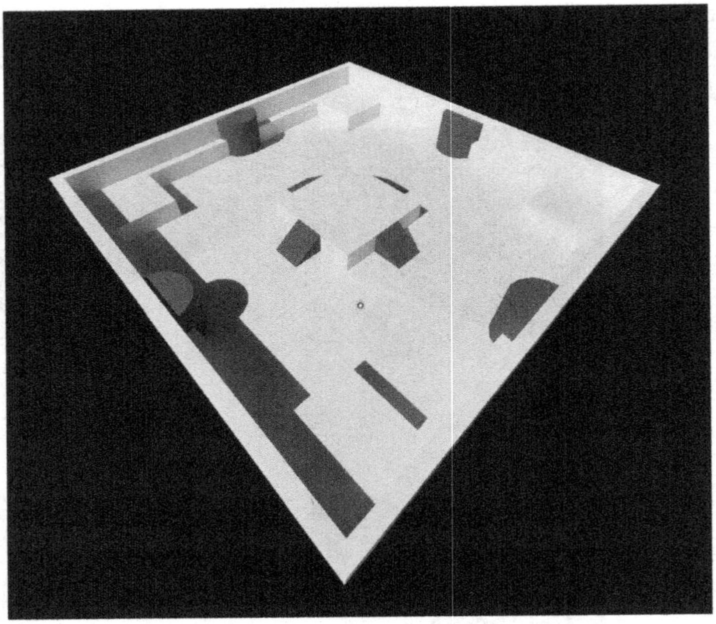

Figure 2.45 - Castle prototype with the Corner Tower Buildings added

Corner tower ramps

1. Enter **Modeling Mode** and, from the **Create** menu, add eight Boxes, each with a **Width** of `300`, a **Depth** of `300`, and a **Height** of `200`.
2. Return to **Selection Mode** and position them at the following locations: `(1700, 1050, -50)`, `(-1700, 1050, -50)`, `(1700, -1050, -50)`, `(-1700, -1050, -50)`, `(-1050, -1700, -50)`, `(1050, -1700, -50)`, `(-1050, 1700, -50)` and `(1050, 1700, -50)`.
3. Enter **Modeling Mode** and, for each of the boxes, use vertex selection and the **Extrude** tool to make them slope to the ground away from the corner cubes to which they are adjacent, rotating where necessary to mimic the corner cubes with ramps.

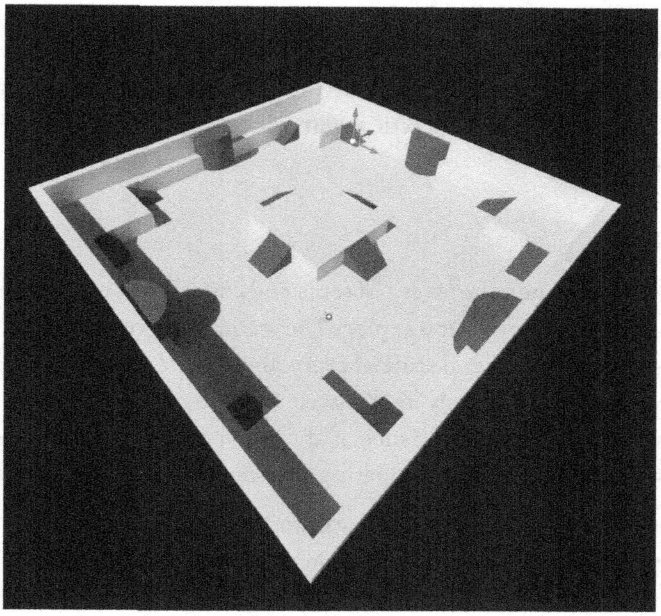

Figure 2.46 - Castle prototype with the Corner Ramps added

Realistic sky environment

To create a realistic sky environment, add the Sky Atmosphere, Sky Light, Volumetric Clouds, and Exponential Height Fog components to the game level. Now, you should have a fully built-out prototype Castle Level.

Figure 2.47 - Completed Castle prototype Level

You should now understand how to build a Level prototype through the creation and manipulation of Geometry and setting up a realistic environment. This will prepare you to delve deeper into the techniques required to build a game in Unreal Engine 5, which will be introduced in this book through practical game development examples in the creation of the Pangaea game.

Summary

In this chapter, you learned the essential tools and concepts needed to begin constructing game worlds in Unreal Engine. You explored how Unreal's World and Local coordinate systems define the position, rotation, and scale of every object in your scene, giving you a clear foundation for working accurately in 3D space. From there, you were introduced to the Level Editor and its core interface panels, such as the Viewport, **Outliner**, **Details** panel, and **Content Browser**, and practiced navigating the scene using Perspective camera controls.

You also worked with the **Translate**, **Rotate**, and **Scale** tools, along with Unreal's snapping features, to precisely place and manipulate Actors in your Level. Building on those skills, you learned the importance of blockout geometry for early level prototyping and followed step-by-step instructions to create a simple bridge prototype using **Modeling Mode**, Boolean operations, and basic shapes. You then enhanced your scene by adding lighting, sky elements, atmosphere, clouds, and fog using tools like the **Environment Light Mixer**, giving the Level a realistic outdoor environment. You then added the Quinn mannequin for scale/reference purposes, along with placeholder geometry for statue and water elements.

Finally, you concluded the chapter by creating your own Castle Level prototype. By understanding how to navigate the editor, manipulate objects, and compose a simple playable space, you now have a strong foundation for building more advanced game worlds in Unreal Engine.

In the next chapter, *Learning the Basics of Blueprints*, you will gain an understanding of the Unreal Blueprint System and how to use textures and Materials in Unreal Engine.

3

Learning the Basics of Blueprints

Unreal Engine's **Blueprint Visual Scripting system** is one of its most defining and beginner-friendly features. While many professional engines require complex programming knowledge before you can make anything interactive, Unreal allows you to build game behavior visually – by connecting nodes together in a clear, logical flow.

This powerful system is used by indie developers, students, designers, and major AAA studios alike, enabling teams of all skill levels to prototype ideas quickly, refine mechanics, and build complete gameplay systems without writing a single line of C++. Learning the basics of Blueprints is essential because it allows you to start building gameplay logic visually without prior coding experience while developing a strong foundation for creating interactive experiences.

This chapter serves as your hands-on introduction to Blueprint scripting. You will learn how Blueprints fit into the Unreal Gameplay Framework, how to navigate the **Blueprint Editor**, and how to read and build Blueprint graphs. Starting with simple examples, such as sequential logic, conditional branching, and looping, you will gradually build understanding of how game logic flows.

This chapter covers the following topics:

- Understanding Blueprints
- Working with Blueprints
- Understanding Blueprint graphs
- Learning the Blueprint flow control structures
- Creating materials with Blueprints

By the end of this chapter, you'll be able to create your own custom Blueprints, understand how nodes interact, and apply your new knowledge to constructing your first material-based visuals.

> **Note**
>
> **Download the code/resource bundle and the PDF version of this book**
>
> Your purchase includes a DRM-free PDF copy of this book, the code/resource bundle, and a range of exclusive benefits. To unlock everything, follow the *Free benefits with your book* section in the *Preface*.

Technical requirements

The sample project for this chapter is available for download from the book's GitHub repository and branch:

- `Chapter03-Start` **branch**: The game project to begin learning this chapter.
- `Chapter03` **branch**: The completed game project for this chapter, featuring the `BridgePrototype` level with the sample Blueprints, which can be found in the **Content Browser** under **Content** | **LevelPrototyping** | **Levels**.

You can download the example project and code files for this book by following the instructions in the *Download the example code/resource files* section in the *Preface* of this book.

This chapter's code/resource files are included in the downloadable code/resource bundle.

Understanding Blueprints

Blueprint is Unreal Engine's powerful visual scripting system, and it sits at the very core of how developers create gameplay behavior without needing to write traditional code. Instead of typing commands, Blueprint lets you build logic by connecting visual blocks – called **nodes** – which represent actions, decisions, and events. It works on the same ideas found in traditional programming but presents them in a format that is more visual, more intuitive, and easier to experiment with.

Because Blueprints function like object-oriented classes, they allow developers and non-programmers alike to define objects, customize behavior, and extend the engine's functionality without needing to write C++ code. Blueprints are part of the engine, used by professional game studios at every scale.

A **Blueprint Class**, often simply called a "Blueprint," is an asset stored in your project that acts as a template for creating objects in your game. These Blueprints are built entirely inside

Unreal Editor, letting designers and artists add gameplay logic through visual tools instead of code. In the next section we give a high-level overview of how Blueprints work.

Understanding how Blueprints work

At the core of the Blueprint system are *nodes* and *graphs*. A **graph** is a workspace or canvas where you place nodes, connect them together, and shape the logic of your game. Each node represents something specific: an action, an event, a function call, a calculation, or even a decision. By arranging and linking nodes, you create the flow of behavior. Learning to follow the wires and understand the order in which nodes fire is a key skill when reading or creating Blueprints.

Blueprints operate using an **event-driven approach**. This means the game reacts when something happens – an input from the player, an overlap between two objects, the start of a level, the tick of a timer, and so on. Events are often where your graphs begin, acting like entry points that tell your logic *when* to run. Because games are inherently interactive, this system makes it easy to build responsive behaviors without worrying about constantly checking for changes.

While some nodes are simply instructions ("move this," "play a sound," "spawn an actor"), others are more like tools that help you shape logic. You can use nodes that make decisions (branches), process values (math or comparison operators), trigger functions, or communicate between different parts of your game. By combining these pieces, you can create anything from simple interactions, like opening a door, to advanced systems, such as health management, inventory logic, or AI behavior.

Together, these concepts form the foundation of how Blueprints work. They give you a visual way to design logic, react to events, and build complete gameplay systems using nodes that fit together like puzzle pieces.

Later in this chapter, you'll explore the **Blueprint Editor**, see how these systems work together, and build your first Unreal Engine Blueprint. But first, we'll cover a few more foundational topics, starting with the key benefits of using Blueprints.

Why use Blueprints?

Some of the key advantages of using Blueprints include:

- **Rapid prototyping**: You can build and test ideas instantly without waiting for code to compile, which accelerates experimentation and iteration.
- **Beginner-friendly and visual**: Because logic is represented through clear, connected visual steps rather than lines of code, Blueprints allow people with no programming background (such as artists, designers, beginners) to create functional gameplay systems.

- **Cross-team collaboration**: They create a shared language across disciplines: level designers, artists, technical artists, and programmers all work in the same visual environment, making it easier to communicate ideas and adjust gameplay together.
- **Scalable for advanced use**: Powerful enough for advanced developers to build complex mechanics, making it a flexible tool for the entire development team.
- **Real-time updates**: Since changes to Blueprint logic update in real time inside the editor, developers can fine-tune behavior on the fly and immediately see the results.
- **Integration with C++**: For advanced projects, Blueprints integrate seamlessly with C++, allowing teams to combine fast visual scripting with the power and efficiency of native code.

Together, these strengths make Blueprints one of the most flexible and approachable tools in Unreal Engine's ecosystem, and they can be used for implementing behaviors such as:

- Player movement
- Interactions (doors, pickups, switches)
- UI logic (health bars, menus)
- AI behavior (patrolling, chasing)
- Animations
- Level scripting
- Gameplay rules

With a good understanding of the benefits of using Blueprints in Unreal Engine, we will now examine the different types of Blueprints provided by Unreal Engine.

Types of Blueprints

Unreal Engine provides several specialized **Blueprint asset types**, each designed to help you organize your gameplay logic, data, and interactions in clean and efficient ways. While all Blueprints use the same visual scripting system, they serve different purposes depending on whether you're building reusable gameplay objects, controlling events in a level, managing shared communication, or storing small bits of logic. Understanding these Blueprint types early on helps you structure your project more clearly and avoids unnecessary duplication of work as your game grows.

Level Blueprint

A **Level Blueprint** is tied to a specific level and exists only within that level or map. It's perfect for handling logic that affects the level environment as a whole, such as triggering doors when a player enters a certain area, running cinematics, controlling timed sequences, or responding to events from objects placed directly in the level. Because a Level Blueprint is unique to each level, its logic is not reusable, so you should only use it for behavior that belongs exclusively to that map.

Blueprint Class

A **Blueprint Class** is the most commonly used Blueprint type and is the backbone of most gameplay systems. Unlike a Level Blueprint, a Blueprint Class is reusable across your entire project. It can contain components, variables, functions, event graphs, and custom logic. This makes it ideal for creating gameplay Actors such as Characters, interactable objects, enemies, projectiles, UI widgets, and much more. Technically, every Blueprint Class is a "child" of an existing C++ class in Unreal, meaning it inherits built-in engine features while allowing you to add your own visual scripting on top. For most of your gameplay objects, this is the Blueprint type you'll use the most.

Data-Only Blueprint

A **Data-Only Blueprint** is a simplified Blueprint Class that starts with no scripting of its own. Instead, it inherits all behavior from its parent class (either another Blueprint or a C++ class). This makes it ideal for creating variations of existing objects without rewriting or copying logic. For example, you might have a base enemy Blueprint with all the AI behavior for that enemy, and then create `Enemy_Basic`, `Enemy_Normal`, and `Enemy_Elite` as Data-Only Blueprints that simply change health values, colors, or default settings. This keeps your project clean and avoids having multiple Blueprints with duplicated scripts.

Blueprint Interface

A **Blueprint Interface** is a special asset that contains function names but no actual implementation. Think of it as a promise, or a contract, that any Blueprint using the interface will include working versions of those functions. This makes communication between different Blueprints clean and consistent. Interfaces are perfect for universal behaviors like `Interact()`, `TakeDamage()`, `Activate()`, or `ToggleState()`, where many different objects might need to respond in their own unique way. By using an interface, you ensure every object shares the same function name even if the internal logic differs, which improves organization and consistency and reduces errors.

Blueprint Macro Library

A **Blueprint Macro Library** is used to store small chunks of logic that you want to reuse across multiple Blueprints. Macros can create custom flow-control nodes or wrap up repeated logic patterns into single, tidy blocks. For example, you could use a macro for clamping movement values or checking if an Actor is valid before running code. Once created, macros from a library can be placed into any Blueprint in your project, reducing repetition and keeping your graphs cleaner and easier to read.

You've now seen the fundamental ideas behind the Blueprint system. In the next part of this chapter, we'll take those concepts further by working directly in the **Blueprint Editor** to create your first Blueprints.

Working with Blueprints

We will begin by introducing some of the core Blueprint classes and the roles they play within a game, then explore the **Blueprint Editor** and the essential tools you will use when creating behavior. From there, you will learn how to navigate Blueprint graphs, understand nodes, create variables, and build simple logic sequences. By the end of this section, you will have the foundational skills needed to start building your own Blueprints.

Understanding Unreal Engine's Gameplay Framework

Before you begin creating your own Blueprints, it's important to understand how Unreal Engine organizes the different parts of a game. Unreal uses a structured **Gameplay Framework** to define how players, characters, world objects, rules, and on-screen UI all work together. You don't need to learn every detail of this framework right now, but having a basic mental model will make it much easier to choose the correct type of Blueprint and understand how your game's systems communicate. Blueprints are built on top of this framework, so knowing these building blocks helps you create cleaner, more organized gameplay logic.

Core concept: roles and responsibilities

In Unreal Engine, *no single object* handles everything. Instead, the engine divides responsibilities across different Blueprint classes – some focus on controlling the player, some manage the game's rules, some exist in the world, and others display information on the screen. When you start creating Blueprint classes, you'll be choosing which of these roles your Blueprint belongs to. Understanding these roles early on helps you avoid confusion and build your game in a more organized way.

Understanding inheritance in Unreal Engine

Before we look at the individual gameplay classes, it helps to understand a foundational idea that Unreal uses throughout its system: **inheritance**. Inheritance means that one type of object automatically receives the features and capabilities of another type it is based on.

A simple analogy: vehicles and shared features

Imagine the way vehicles share features, as shown in *Figure 3.1*:

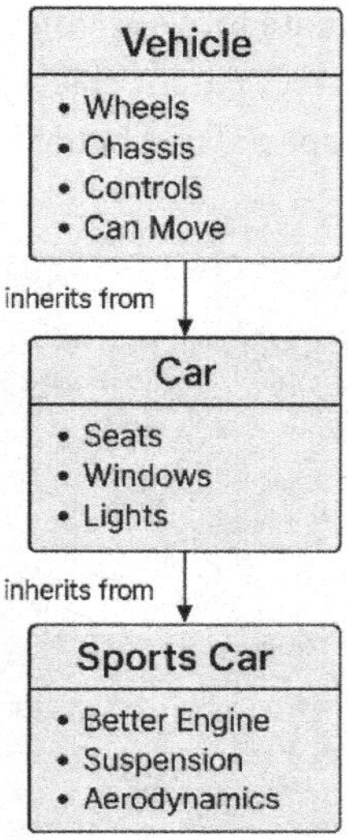

Figure 3.1 - Vehicle – Car – Sports Car Inheritance

Let's understand *Figure 3.1*:

- A **Vehicle** has **Wheels**, a **Chassis**, **Controls**, and the ability to **Move**.
- A **Car** is built on top of the **Vehicle** design and adds **Seats**, **Windows**, and **Lights**.
- A **Sports Car** is built on the **Car** template and adds a **Better Engine**, **Suspension**, and **Aerodynamics**.

Hence, each new design *inherits* everything from the one before it and adds more specialized features.

Unreal Engine works in the same way:

- General gameplay classes provide the *basic features.*
- More specialized classes *inherit those features and add new abilities.*
- Your Blueprint starts with everything its parent class already knows how to do.

Therefore, choosing the right parent class is like choosing the right vehicle design: you begin with the features that make sense for the job.

Exploring common parent Blueprint classes

Every time you create a new Blueprint in Unreal Engine, you are asked to select a parent class, which serves as the foundational template for your object. This choice is critical because of object inheritance: by choosing the correct parent class, your new Blueprint instantly inherits pre-built functionality, variables, and specialized behaviors designed for specific roles in your game.

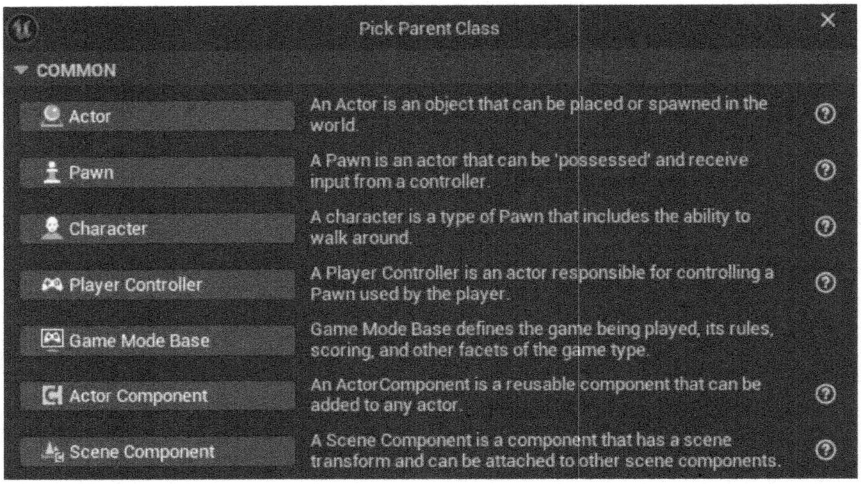

Figure 3.2 - Pick Parent Class dialog

The following sections explore some of these Blueprint parent classes in more detail to help you build a solid understanding of their intended purpose. It is essential to understand the primary architecture of these parent classes (ranging from simple inanimate props to complex, player-controlled characters and game-managing systems) so that you always write your visual scripting logic with the correct foundation.

Actor: the foundation of all gameplay objects

At the base of most gameplay objects is the *Actor*. An **Actor** is any object that can exist in a level. Props, doors, lights, moving platforms, pickups, triggers, and many visual effects all begin as Actors. Actors can contain components and run logic inside Blueprints, but they do not inherently support input, player control, or specific movement systems. Many of the more specialized Gameplay Framework classes you will meet next are built on top of Actors through inheritance.

Pawn and Character: controllable objects

A **Pawn** is a type of Actor that can be *controlled*. This control may come from the player or from AI. Pawns are ideal for anything that can be "possessed," such as vehicles, drones, cameras, or robots. Pawns don't include automatic movement; they gain movement behavior when you add a movement component such as a **FloatingPawnMovement**, or through custom Blueprint logic.

A **Character** is a more specialized type of Pawn. Characters inherit everything a Pawn can do but add built-in movement features such as walking, jumping, falling, and interacting with animations. Characters are most often used for humanoid players and creatures, and they are often the starting point for beginner player-controlled Blueprints.

Player Controller: the brain behind behavior

Unreal separates thinking from doing. A **PlayerController** or **AIController** acts as the *brain*, interpreting player input or AI instructions and telling a Pawn or Character what to do. This design allows players to switch between characters, possess vehicles, control cameras, or hand control over to AI without rewriting movement logic.

Controllers do not exist physically in the world; they exist to make decisions and drive behavior. When you create Blueprints that handle input or high-level actions, they will often belong to a Controller.

Game Mode Base: rules and shared information

A **GameMode** defines the overarching rules for your game or level. It decides which Pawn the player should control, which Controller to use, what HUD appears, and how the game should begin. You can think of it as the starting Blueprint for your level's logic.

In addition to the core classes introduced in this section, Unreal Engine provides a rich set of other foundational classes that play important roles in structuring and managing a game. Classes like `GameState`, `GameInstance`, `PlayerState`, HUD, and others are commonly used to handle global game data, match-level information, persistent state across levels, and player-specific data. To keep the learning process focused and approachable, these classes will be introduced progressively in later chapters at the point where they are needed in practical development scenarios, allowing you to understand not only what each class does, but also why and when it should be used.

How this all connects to Blueprints

Every Blueprint you create belongs to one of these classes. Whether you are building a door, a playable character, a scoring system, or an inventory UI, each Blueprint fits somewhere within the gameplay framework. Understanding these roles ensures that your logic ends up in the right place. For example:

- Movement → `Pawn` or `Character`
- Input and decisions → `Controller`
- Game rules → `GameMode`
- Shared data → `GameState`
- Player-specific data → `PlayerState`
- UI → `Widgets`
- Reusable behavior → `Actor Components`
- Visual structure → `Scene Components`

Thanks to inheritance, choosing the right parent class gives your Blueprint the features it needs – just as starting with the right vehicle design gives you the engine, wheels, and systems required for the job. This keeps your project clean, reduces duplicated work, and makes your Blueprints easier to manage as your game grows.

With the core Blueprint classes introduced, we can now move from concepts to practice. In the next section, we will explore the **Blueprint Editor** user interface, focusing on its main panels and tools so you can efficiently navigate and build Blueprint logic in the chapters ahead.

Exploring the Blueprint Editor

The **Blueprint Editor** is where you define the behavior of gameplay objects, configure their components, and script interactive logic using Unreal Engine's visual scripting system.

Just like the Level Editor, it is composed of several key panels, each with a dedicated purpose and workflow, as shown in *Figure 3.3*:

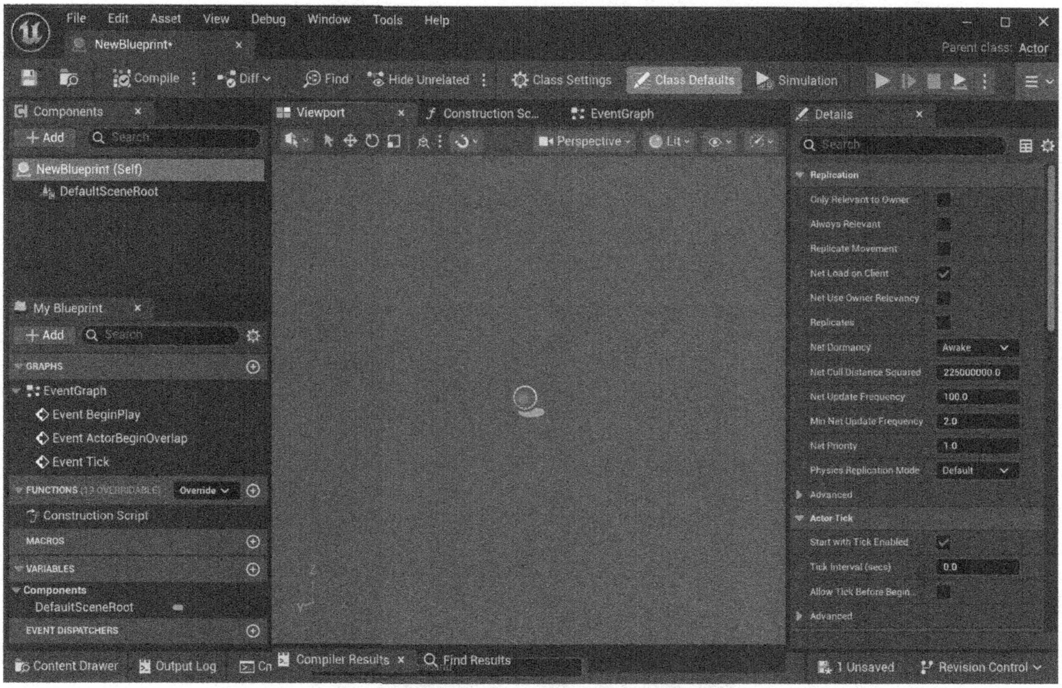

Figure 3.3 - Overview of the Blueprint Editor

The Blueprint Editor opens automatically when you create or double-click a Blueprint asset in the **Content Browser**. Although the exact layout can differ slightly depending on Blueprint type (such as Actor, Pawn, or Widget), all Blueprint Editors share the same core structure described in the sections that follow.

Main Toolbar

The Blueprint Editor's **Main Toolbar** runs across the top of the window and provides access to common operations for working with a Blueprint.

It includes buttons for saving the Blueprint, compiling changes, toggling simulation options, debugging tools, class settings, class defaults, and options for switching between different editing modes, as shown in *Figure 3.4*.

Figure 3.4 - Blueprint Editor Main Toolbar

Compiling is particularly important in Blueprints: it checks for errors and applies any logic changes, so they are ready to use in the level. You'll learn more about it in the *Compiling your Blueprint* section.

Components panel

Located on the left side of the **Blueprint Editor**, the **Components panel** displays the hierarchy of components that make up the Blueprint.

This panel is where you add, remove, rename, and organize components, such as static meshes, lights, collision shapes, cameras, audio sources, and more. The topmost item acts as the **root component**, which defines the transform (location, rotation, and scale) for the entire Blueprint. This is shown in *Figure 3.5* as follows:

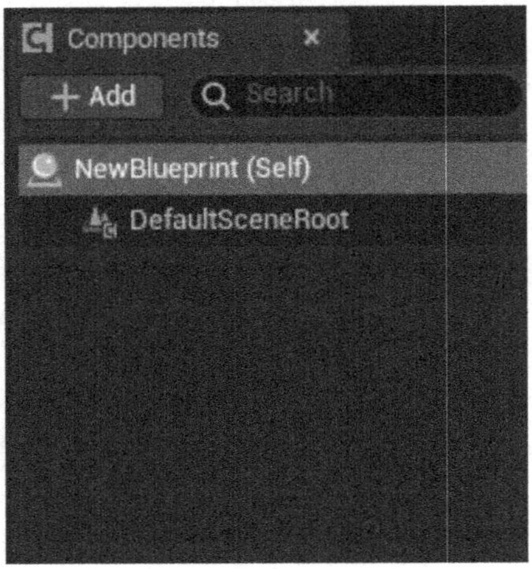

Figure 3.5 - Blueprint Editor Components panel

Selecting a component here determines what appears in the Viewport panel and what options are displayed in the **Details** panel.

Viewport panel

The **Viewport panel** is shown in *Figure 3.6* and provides a 3D preview of the currently selected Blueprint. Within this panel, you can arrange components, adjust transforms, and visually design the layout of the Blueprint's structure. Tools for moving, rotating, and scaling work the same way they do in the Level Editor Viewport.

This preview helps you confirm the appearance, orientation, and positioning of all components before using the Blueprint in a level.

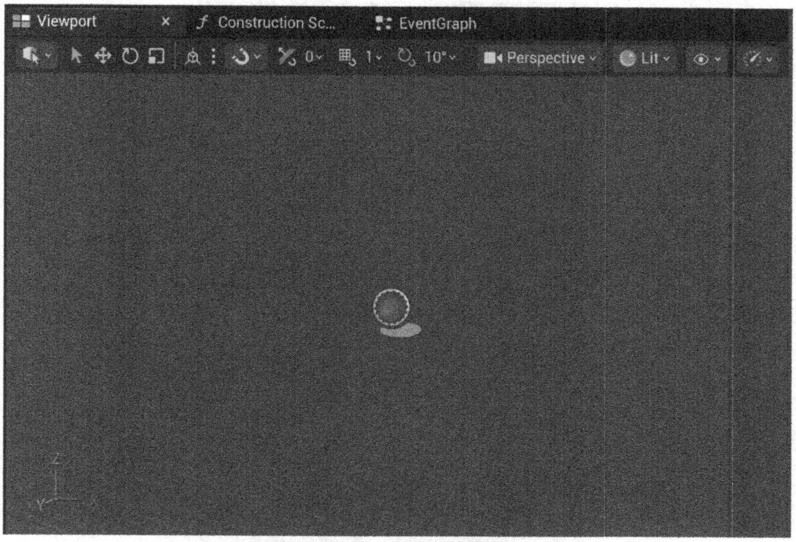

Figure 3.6 - Blueprint Editor Viewport panel

Common uses of the Blueprint Viewport include:

- Positioning meshes relative to the root
- Adjusting light placement or collision shapes
- Making sure pivot points are correctly aligned
- Checking visibility and scale relationships

My Blueprint panel

The **My Blueprint panel**, typically found to the left of the **Event Graph**, acts as the organizational hub of a Blueprint's logic elements. This panel shows all variables, functions, macros, event dispatchers, graphs, and any other script-related elements defined within the Blueprint. This is shown in *Figure 3.7* as follows:

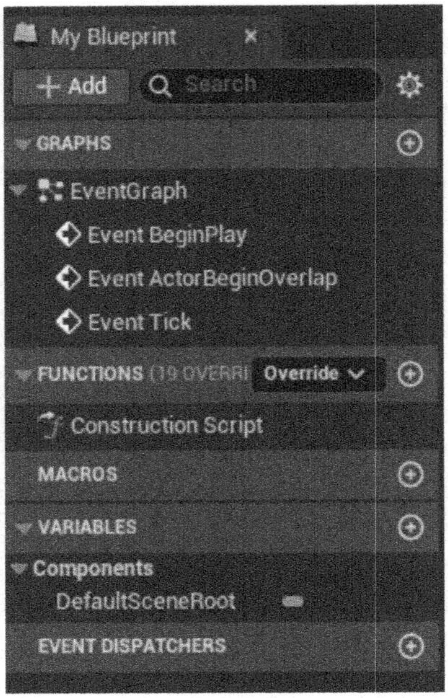

Figure 3.7 - Blueprint Editor My Blueprint panel

The panel allows you to create new variables (such as health, speed, timers), create functions, and manage all data or behaviors used in your scripts.

Whenever you introduce new logic, you will often begin here, adding a variable or function before wiring it into the Event Graph.

Event Graph

The **Event Graph** is the primary workspace for scripting behavior. This is where nodes are placed and connected to define how the Blueprint responds to events and executes gameplay logic. A typical Event Graph includes starting nodes, such as **Event BeginPlay**, **Event Tick**, or **Event ActorBeginOverlap**, which act as triggers for your logic. This is shown in *Figure 3.8* as follows:

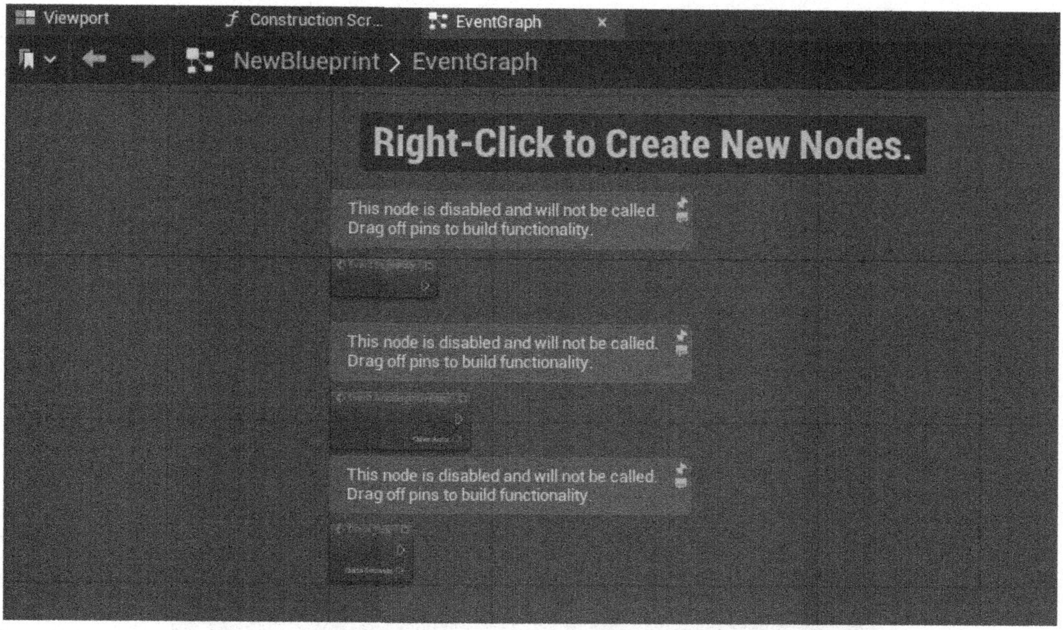

Figure 3.8 - Blueprint Editor Event Graph panel

Here, you can:

- Call functions
- Modify variables
- Create branches and loops.
- Use timelines and delays.
- Execute gameplay sequences.

The Event Graph uses **execution wires** (*white lines*) to show the order in which actions occur, and **data wires** (*colored lines*) to carry information between nodes. By combining these elements, designers can construct complex behaviors without writing traditional code.

Details panel

The **Details panel**, shown in *Figure 3.9*, sits on the right-hand side of the **Blueprint Editor**. This panel exposes editable properties including transforms, rendering settings, collisions, physics behaviors, default variable values, and Blueprint-specific settings.

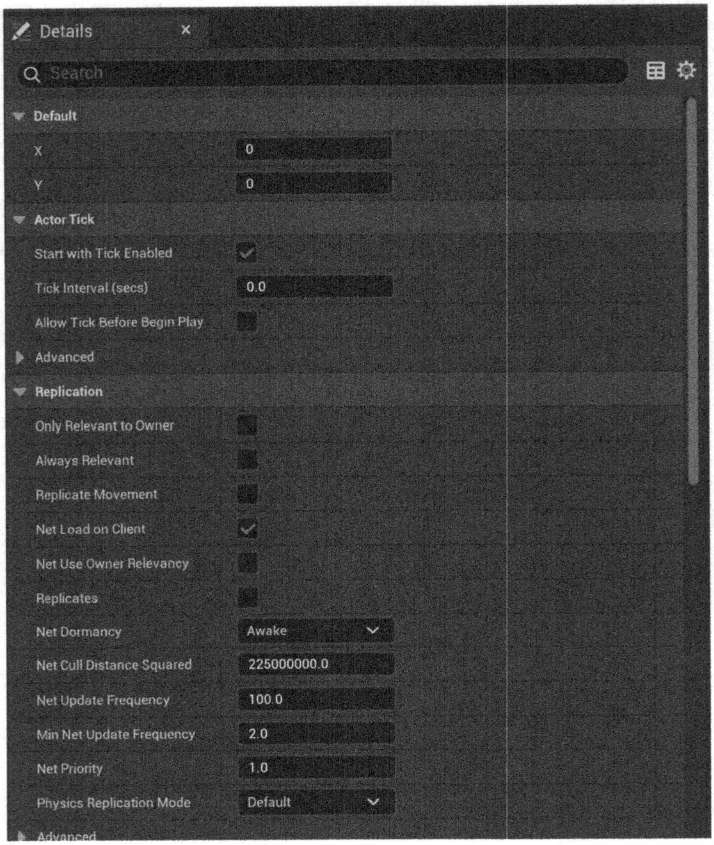

Figure 3.9 - The Details panel

Its displayed content changes depending on the item currently selected:

- Selecting a *component* shows its mesh, mobility, lighting, and physics options.
- Selecting a *variable* shows its type, default value, and metadata.
- Selecting a *node* shows configuration settings unique to that node's functionality.

Beginners will quickly find that the **Details** panel is crucial for refining both the structure and behavior of a Blueprint.

Blueprint tabs and modes

Depending on the type of Blueprint, additional tabs may be available at the top of the window, such as:

- **Construction Script**: Used for setup tasks that run both when the Blueprint is placed in the level and whenever its properties are modified in the editor. Avoid expensive operations in the Construction Script as it runs frequently during editing. This tab holds logic that affects component setup before gameplay begins.

Figure 3.10 - Blueprint Editor Construction Script Tab

- **AnimGraph**: Used for Animation Blueprints to evaluate and blend skeletal poses in real time. This tab holds nodes that determine how a character transitions between animations like walking, running, and jumping based on gameplay variables.
- **Designer Mode**: Used for Widget Blueprints to provide a visual drag-and-drop canvas for layout creation. This window allows you to position, style, and anchor user interface elements such as buttons, text, and images before writing their functional logic.

These tabs allow you to work across multiple aspects of the Blueprint's functionality without leaving the editor.

The **Blueprint Editor** brings together component authoring, scripting, and debugging into a unified workspace. By understanding how the main panels work together – the **Components** panel for structure, the **Viewport** panel for visual arrangement, the **My Blueprint** panel for logical organization, the **Event Graph** panel for scripting, and the **Details** panel for fine-tuning – you will be equipped to build interactive gameplay elements entirely through visual scripting.

With an understanding of the main panels in the **Blueprint Editor**, you will now examine how to navigate the Blueprint workspace in the next section.

Navigating the Blueprint Workspace

Your next step in learning Blueprints is to understand how to move around this workspace and recognize where the core scripting elements are stored. This will make you comfortable exploring a Blueprint before you move on to the next section and begin learning how the logic inside it actually works.

Finding events, variables, and functions in the Blueprint Editor

All logic-related elements inside a Blueprint are organized in the **My Blueprint** panel, which acts as the central directory for anything connected to your script. Events appear in the **Event Graph**, and you can always return to this graph by selecting its tab at the top of the editor.

You will mainly work with the following Blueprint elements:

- **Variables** are listed in the **VARIABLES** section within the **My Blueprint** panel. Selecting one reveals its details, such as type and default value, in the **Details** panel.
- **Functions** are stored under the **FUNCTIONS** category and can be opened, edited, or created directly from the **My Blueprint** panel.

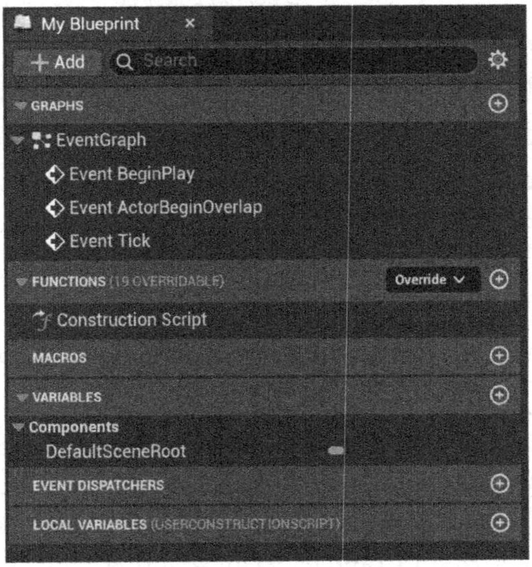

Figure 3.11 - My Blueprint panel showing Events, Variables, and Functions

This organization allows you to quickly find the elements you will later use when building gameplay behaviors.

Moving around the Event Graph

The **Event Graph** is the canvas where you will later place nodes and connect your logic. The following controls are used to navigate this space.

- *Right-mouse drag* lets you pan around the graph
- *Mouse wheel* zooms in and out
- Selecting any node allows you to move it by *dragging*

These controls make it easy to stay oriented even when graphs become large.

Adding and selecting nodes

Although the next section will explain the different types of nodes and how they work, it's helpful to know how to place one:

1. *Right-click* anywhere in the **Event Graph**.
2. Begin typing the name of the node you want.
3. Select it from the **Search** list.

This is shown in *Figure 3.12* as follows:

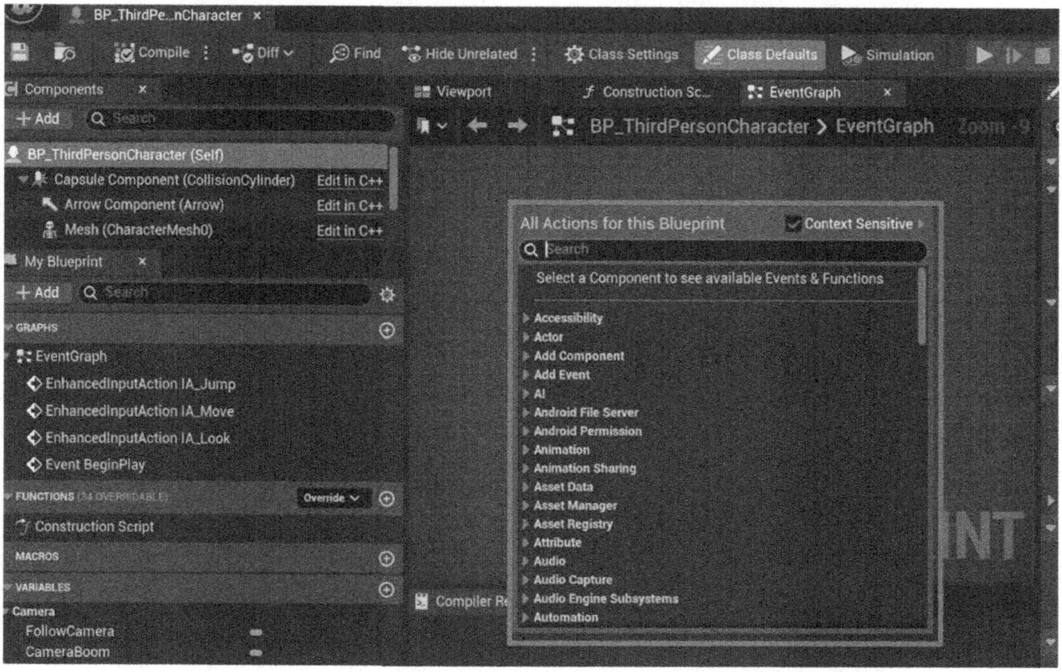

Figure 3.12 - Node Creation Menu highlighted in the Event Graph

You can reposition nodes by dragging them or delete them using the *Delete* key.

Compiling your Blueprint

The **Blueprint Editor** includes a **Compile** button in the Main Toolbar, which you will use frequently. **Compiling** applies any changes you've made, whether structural or logical, and checks your Blueprint for issues. A **status** icon beside the button displays whether the Blueprint is error-free.

Figure 3.13 - Compile button highlighted in the Blueprint Editor Main Toolbar

Even before learning the logic system, compiling is good practice whenever you make adjustments to components, variables, or the graph layout.

You should now be comfortable navigating the Blueprint workspace: finding events, variables, and functions; moving around the **Event Graph**; placing nodes; and switching between the main editing tabs.

In the next section, you will learn what these elements do and how they work together to create gameplay behavior.

Understanding Blueprint graphs

This section explains the core building blocks of Blueprint graphs: events, variables, nodes, and the visual connections that control how **execution flows** between them.

Blueprints allow you to script gameplay using visual nodes instead of written code. Each node performs a specific action, provides information, or responds to something happening in the game. By connecting these nodes together, you can define how your Blueprint reacts and what it does.

Events: what triggers your logic?

Events are the starting points for Blueprint behavior. They respond to specific moments during gameplay and automatically fire when their condition is met. Some events are built into every Actor-based Blueprint, while others appear only when certain components or features are present.

Common events include:

- **Event BeginPlay**: Fires once when the game starts or when the Blueprint first enters the game. Useful for setting up logic and tasks.

- **Event Tick**: Runs every frame, often used for continuous behavior such as movement or checking conditions. Running complex logic every frame is expensive, so use **Event Tick** sparingly.
- **Event ActorBeginOverlap**: Triggers when another object enters this Blueprint's collision area.

Events always appear on the left side of a graph and have a *white* execution output pin. The next section explains what happens after the event fires and how the Blueprint logic flows.

Understanding Blueprint Nodes

Blueprint nodes form the individual building blocks of a Blueprint graph, with each node performing a single action, such as:

- Reading a variable
- Making a comparison
- Waiting for a delay
- Moving a component

Understanding the basic node types in Unreal will help you recognize at a glance what a script is doing.

- **Event nodes**: Start the execution of your Blueprint. They have no execution input, only outputs.
- **Action nodes**: Perform operations or tasks, such as moving an Actor, printing text, playing a sound, or changing a variable.
- **Function nodes**: Run logic stored inside a function. They often take inputs, perform a calculation, and return outputs.
- **Pure nodes**: Return information without requiring execution flow. For example, getting an object's location or reading a variable's value. Pure nodes may evaluate multiple times if connected to multiple nodes, so avoid using them for expensive operations.
- **Flow control nodes**: Control the directional flow that your Blueprint logic takes. Examples include sequence, branches, and loops; these are explained in more detail in the *Learning the Blueprint flow control structures* section later in the chapter.

Each node type plays a different role, and by combining nodes you can build complex behaviors or logic from simple steps. We will gradually introduce nodes when using them to create Blueprints for the *Pangaea* game in later chapters.

In the next section, we will examine variables, which allow your Blueprints to store information.

Variables: storing and using information

Variables are containers that hold information that your Blueprint needs to keep track of. They allow your Blueprint to remember information, react to changes, and make decisions. For example, a variable might store:

- Whether an object is active
- How long a timed delay should last
- How many times something has been triggered

A variable can represent almost anything (numbers, text, true/false toggle states, object references to other actors, colors, vectors, etc.), and each variable has a *type*, such as:

- **Boolean** True/False.
- **Integer** or **Float**: An **integer** is a whole number without any decimals (e.g. 5 or -12). A **float** is a number that includes a fractional decimal point (e.g. 5.75 or -0.1).
- **Vector**: 3D position or direction.
- **Object** Reference: Link to another Actor.
- **String**: Text.

Variables can be both read from and written to during gameplay, allowing their values to change as needed. This makes them useful for calculations and tracking cumulative totals. For example:

- A health variable decreases when damage is taken.
- A Boolean (true/false) variable like `IsOpen` may control whether a door can be interacted with.
- A vector might store the starting point of a moving platform or another actor.

When a variable's value changes, it can be used to alter behavior or drive logic elsewhere in the Blueprint, especially through branches and loops (discussed in more detail in the *Learning the Blueprint flow control structures* section later in the chapter).

Variables are created in the **My Blueprint** panel, and once created, they can be used within a Blueprint graph as `Get` or `Set` nodes:

- `Get` **Variable**: Reads the value currently held by the variable
- `Set` **Variable**: Changes the value of the variable

We will introduce more variable types as we use them to create Blueprints for the *Pangaea* game in the following section and later chapters, but for now it is important to understand that variables represent the data your Blueprint uses to make decisions and control behavior.

Having learned the event-driven execution model and the Blueprint graph nodes, we can now examine how logic flows *after* an event is triggered.

Learning the Blueprint flow control structures

In Unreal Engine, **Blueprint flow control structures** are specialized nodes that regulate the execution order of your visual script. By default, a Blueprint executes sequentially along a path from left to right. Flow control nodes act as the traffic cops of this system: they introduce decision-making to the flow and can split, loop, delay, or halt that execution stream based on specific gameplay data or conditions.

Without flow control, your code would simply run in a straight line; with it, you can create dynamic, reactive game logic.

The following section introduces you to the Blueprint Sequence structure and two of the most common and important flow control structures every beginner should learn: branches and loops.

Sequence structure

Blueprints operate on a strict sequential execution flow, like a series of instructions followed step-by-step. The flow always begins with an event node (such as **Event BeginPlay** or a custom input event), which acts as the starting trigger. **Event BeginPlay** is one of the system's built-in events, and built-in events are usually triggered by engine events.

From the event node, execution travels along *white* execution wires that connect output pins to input pins. These wires determine the order of operations, ensuring that one action completes before the next begins. While *white wires* control *when* an action happens, *colored data wires* (like *cyan* for integers or *pink* for strings) control *what* data is used by that action.

The following example gives an overview of a Sequence Blueprint that creates two variables (**x** and **y**), adds them together, and then prints them to the screen, triggered when the game starts.

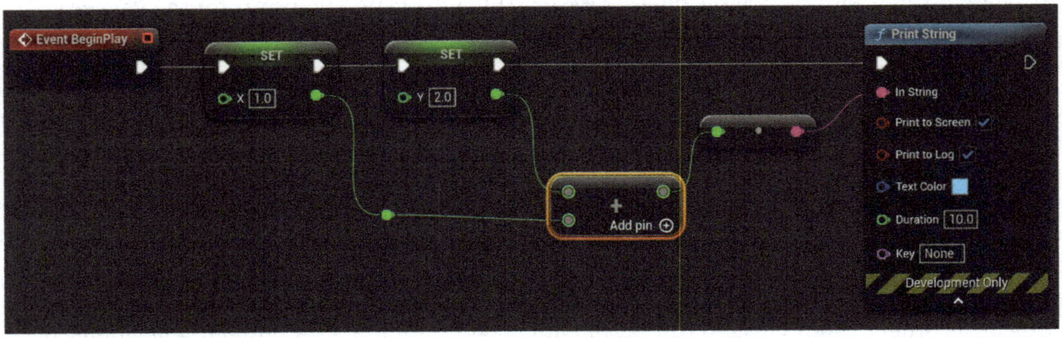

Figure 3.14 - Sequential Blueprint Graph

The entire process shown in *Figure 3.14* is a continuous chain, where the *white* execution wires guarantee the order of operations and the *colored* data wires reliably transport information between nodes.

Using the following step-by-step guide, you will build your first Blueprint and create the **variable addition sequence** described above using an Actor Blueprint:

1. In the **Content Drawer**, right-click and choose **New Folder** to create a new folder under `/Content`. Rename the new folder to `Blueprints`.
2. In the new `/Blueprints` folder, right-click and choose **Blueprint Class**. Select **Actor** as the parent class and name the new Blueprint item to be `BP_SequentialFlow`. Double-click to open the **Blueprint Editor**.
3. In the **My Blueprint** panel (left side), navigate to the **VARIABLES** section and click the **+ (plus)** icon to create a new variable. Then, rename the variable `X` and change its type to **Integer**.

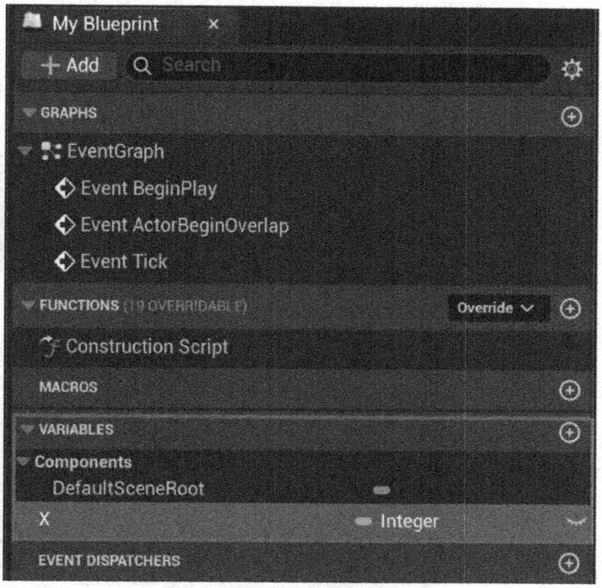

Figure 3.15 - Add X variable

4. Repeat *step 3* process to create the second **Integer** variable named Y.
5. In the **My Blueprint** panel, under **GRAPHS**, double-click **EventGraph** to open the Event Graph and locate the **Event BeginPlay** node. This is the starting point of your execution flow.
6. Now, we'll set the X variable:
    1. In the graph window, right-click to open the **All Actions for this Blueprint** window.

> **Note**
>
> The **Context Sensitive** checkbox controls filtering in the action menu. When checked, only actions relevant to the current context are shown. When you cannot find the action you are looking for, try unchecking this option to disable the filter and display all available actions. Be cautious when using nodes found with **Context Sensitive** disabled, as they may not be compatible with your current pin types, and this could cause compilation errors if connected incorrectly.

2. Type `SetX` to search and scroll down to the **Variables | Default** tab on the **All Possible Actions** window. If **Set X** does not appear in the search results, click **Compile** in the toolbar first, as variables only become available in the graph after compilation.

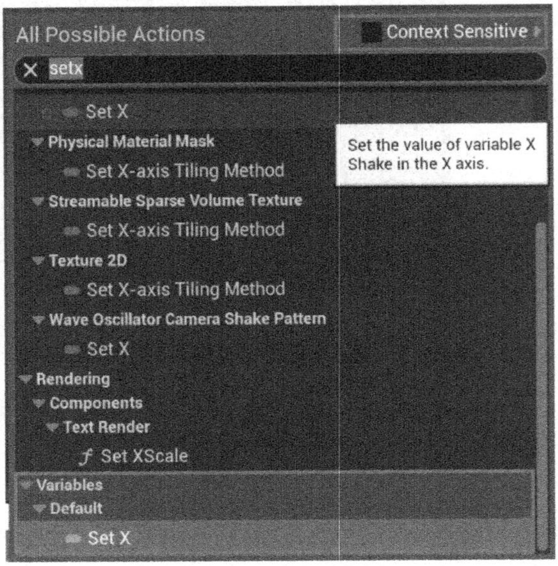

Figure 3.16 - Search for the Set X node in the node search window

3. A faster and more direct way to add the **Set X** node is to drag the variable directly into the graph window. When you release the left mouse button, select **Set X** from the pop-up menu.

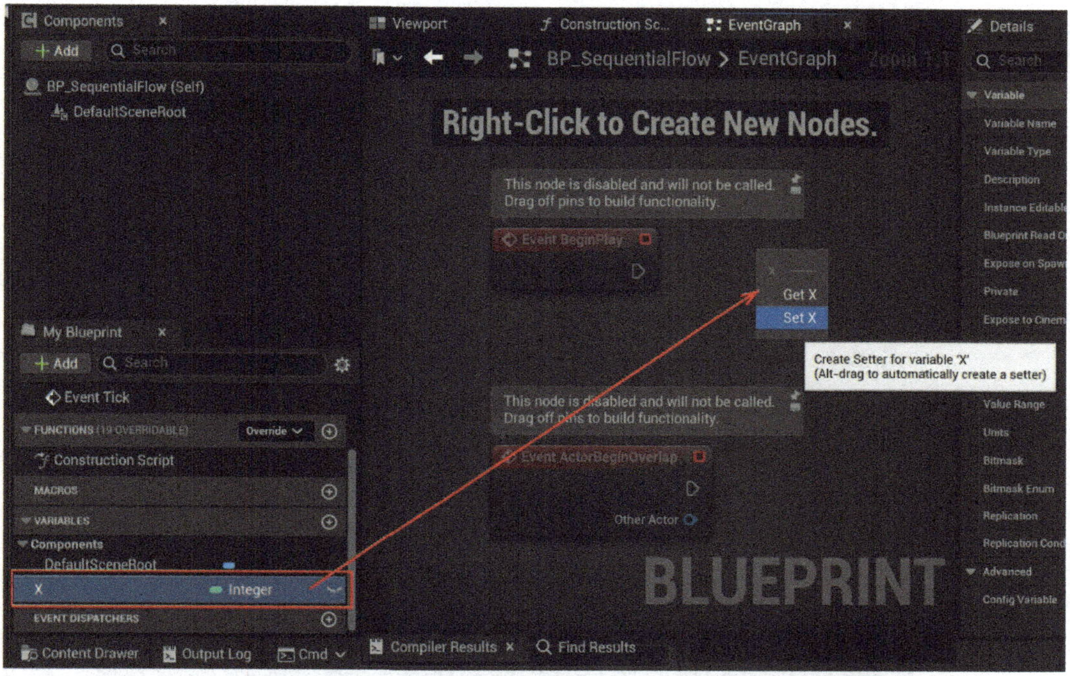

Figure 3.17 - Create the setter for variable X

4. For the **Set** node for **X**, enter a 1 into the Integer input pin to set its value.
5. Connect the *white* output execution pin of the **Event BeginPlay** node to the input execution pin of the **Set X** node.

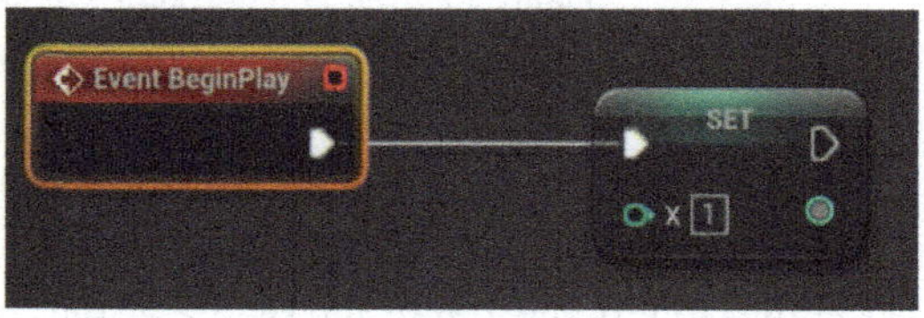

Figure 3.18 - Connecting the Event BeginPlay node to the Set X node

> **Note**
>
> Hold *Alt* and *left-click* a connection line to delete it and disconnect the two nodes.

7. To set the Y variable, repeat *step 6* to add the **Set Y** node and set the **Y** value to 2.

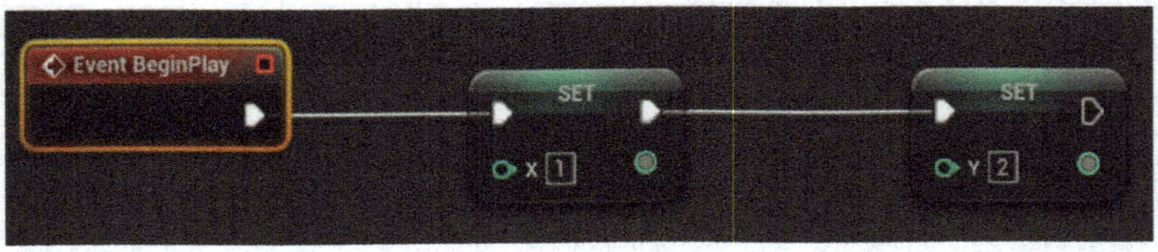

Figure 3.19 - Adding and connecting the Set Y node to the execution flow

8. Next, to add the X and Y variable values, follow these steps:
    1. Drag the *green* data pin (Integer output) from **Set X** and drop it in the graph window.
    2. Search for `Add`, scroll down to **Operators**, and select **Add**. This will create an **Add** node and connect it to the **Set X** node with a *cyan* wire.
    3. Drag the data pin (Integer output) from **Set Y** and connect it to the remaining input pin on the **Add** node.

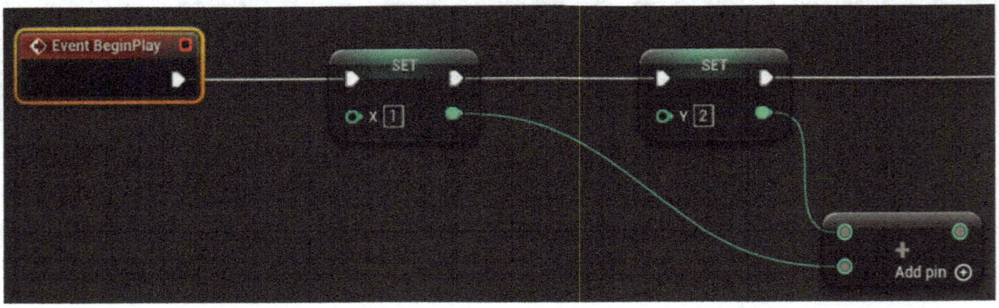

Figure 3.20 - Adding and connecting the Add node

> **Note**
>
> Double-clicking a connection line adds a **Reroute** node. By moving this node, you can adjust the shape of the connection curve, improve the overall layout of the graph, and reduce visual clutter caused by tangled wires.

9. Now, follow these steps to print out the result:
    1. Drag the white execution pin from the output of the **Set Y** node and drop it in the graph window.
    2. Search for `Print String` and select it. This will create a **Print String** node and connect it to the **Set Y** node with a *white* wire.

3. Drag the output green data pin (the result of the addition) from the **Add** node and connect it to the *pink* **InString** input pin on the **Print String** node.
4. This will automatically create a new conversion node, which converts the integer value result from the **Add** node into a string value, connected to the **Add** node with a *cyan* wire. It will also create a wire connecting the output pin of the **Conversion** node to the pink **InString** input pin on the **Print String** node.

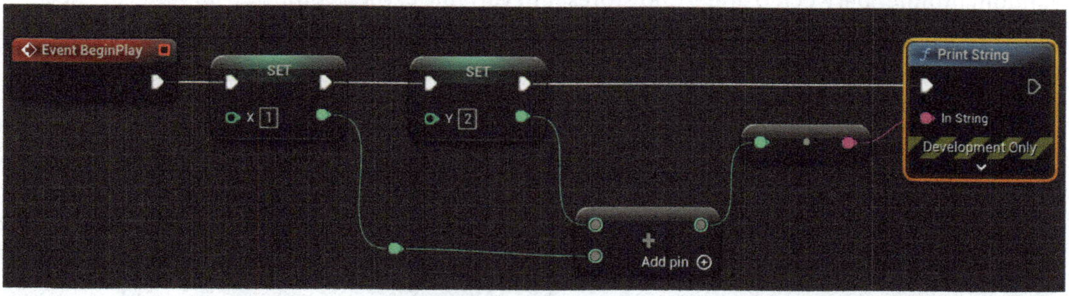

Figure 3.21 - Printing the result of X+Y

10. We'll finalize and test the Blueprint:
    1. In the Main Toolbar of the Blueprint Editor, first click the **Compile** button to validate the nodes and wires, then click the **Save** button to save the updated Blueprint.
    2. Close the **Blueprint Editor** and return to your Level Editor. Locate your new Blueprint (`BP_SequentialFlow`) in the **Content Drawer**.
    3. Click and drag the `BP_SequentialFlow` actor from the **Content Drawer** directly into the 3D Viewport panel of your level. Once placed, it will be visible in the **World Outliner** panel.
    4. Press the green **Play** button (usually at the top center of the Main Toolbar). The game will start, and since the **Event BeginPlay** node is triggered immediately, the entire sequential flow will execute.
    5. You should see the number **3.0** (the result of 1 + 2) briefly displayed in the top-left corner of your Viewport panel in blue, confirming that the step-by-step logic successfully ran in order.

Now that you have learned how to create a Blueprint in the editor, you will move on to two other fundamental control structures: Branch and Loop. Using the same workflow, you will practice building example Blueprints on your own and observe how these structures influence the flow of gameplay logic.

Branch structure

We now introduce the **Branch node**, which uses a Boolean (`True`/`False`) condition to split the white execution flow down one of two paths. This is essential for all conditional logic in Blueprints.

The following example gives an overview of a Branching Sequence Blueprint that generates a random number between 0 and 9 and stores it in variable a, then compares its value to check whether it is equal to 0. If the result evaluates to true, it prints a message to the screen stating that **a==0**; otherwise, it prints a message to the screen stating that **a is greater than 0**. The Blueprint for this entire process is shown below:

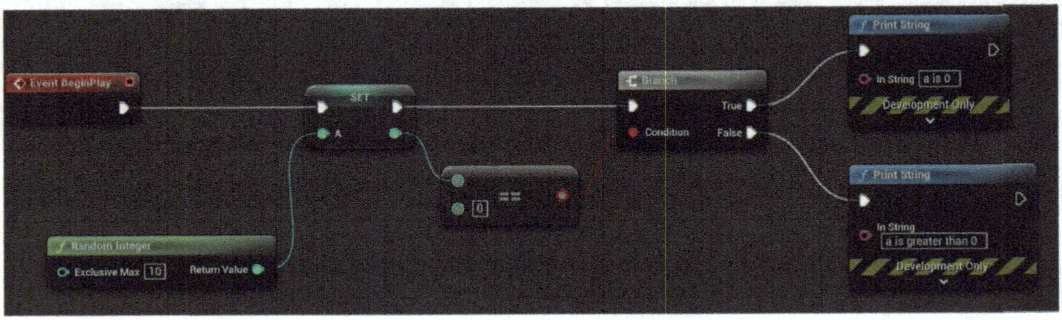

Figure 3.22 - Branching Blueprint Graph

You can test the Blueprint logic described above by building the Blueprint and launching a game to test it. If the logic successfully runs in order, then you should see either the message that **a is 0**, or the message **a is greater than 0** (depending on the random value generated by the **Random Integer** node in the Blueprint) briefly displayed in the top-left corner of your Viewport panel in *blue*.

With a good understanding of the concept of how branching works, we will now introduce you to the concept of Loop logic and how repeating logic can be implemented using `While` and `For` Loops.

Loop structure

Loops are crucial for automating repetitive tasks in Blueprints and changing the execution flow from a simple straight line. They allow a segment of execution logic to repeat multiple times before resuming the main white execution flow.

The two most common loop structures used in Blueprints are:

- The **While Loop** is a conditional loop: it executes repeatedly as long as a specific Boolean condition remains True.
- The **For Loop** is a count-controlled loop that executes a fixed number of times, making it ideal for iterating over a known range of values or a collection of elements.

To better understand how looping logic works in practice, let's create a simple `While` Loop Blueprint example next.

Creating the While Loop Blueprint

The **While Loop** can be implemented through either a standard **Branch** node, which loops back on itself, or with a dedicated **Do While** node for clarity. We'll use a **While Loop** node in the following example. Unlike sequential nodes, which only execute once, the loop node's *white* execution wire splits, allowing the loop body to execute its own sequential steps multiple times, only releasing the flow to continue with the rest of the graph once the Boolean condition becomes false.

The following example gives an overview of a **While Loop** Sequence Blueprint that creates a variable (**x**) with a value of `20`. It then performs a condition check to see if the value of **x** is greater than **0**. If the condition check is true, it executes the loop, which reduces the value of **x** by **1**. It then creates a message string containing **"x="** appended to the new value of **x** and prints this message string to the screen. The execution then returns to the start of the loop to check the condition again, repeating these loop steps until the condition check is false and **x** has a value of **0**.

When the condition check is false, it exits the loop and prints a message to the screen stating that **x is now 0**. The Blueprint for this entire process is shown below:

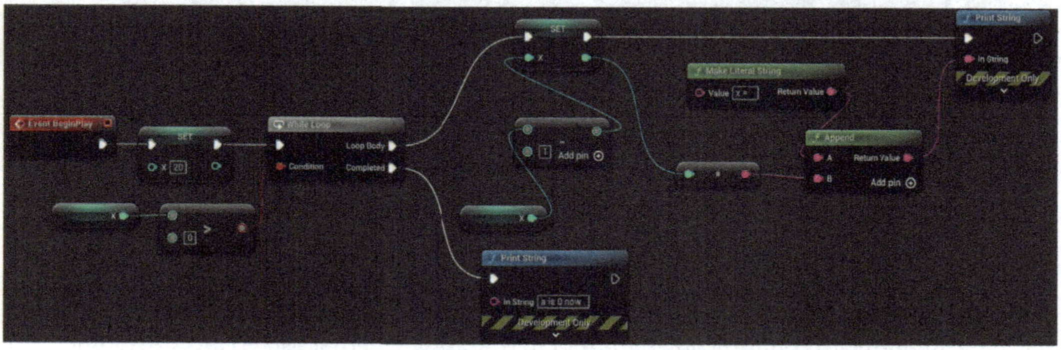

Figure 3.23 - While Loop Blueprint Graph

If you were to build the above Blueprint and launch a game to test it, you would see the message **x = repeated 20 times** on the screen (with each appended to a value ranging from 19 down to 0) on the left-hand side of the Viewport panel, and the message **x is now 0** at the top of these messages. This would confirm that the **While Loop** logic successfully ran as expected.

Creating the For Loop Blueprint

The **For Loop** allows a section of logic to repeat multiple times before resuming the main white execution flow (for example, running a piece of logic 10 times). The loop node's *white* execution wire splits, allowing the loop body to execute its own sequential steps multiple times based on a specified starting and ending index, only releasing the flow to continue with the rest of the graph once the final index is reached.

The following example gives an overview of a **For Loop** Sequence Blueprint that creates a variable (**Index**) with a starting value of **0** (**First Index**), and a **Last Index** variable of **19**. It then performs a condition check to see if the value of the **Index** is less than or equal to **19** (**Last Index**). If this evaluates to true, it executes the loop, which uses a branch to check whether the value of **Index** is even (using the **%** modulo operator). If it is, it appends the message string **"is an Even number"** to the current value of **Index** and prints this message string to the screen. Otherwise, it appends the message string **"is an Odd number"** to the current value of **Index** and prints that message string to the screen instead.

The loop then returns to the start of the **For Loop** again, where the value **Index** is increased by 1 before checking the condition again – repeating these loop steps until the condition check is false and **Index** has a value of `20`, when it exits the loop and prints **"Finished!"** to the screen.

The Blueprint for this entire process is shown in *Figure 3.24*:

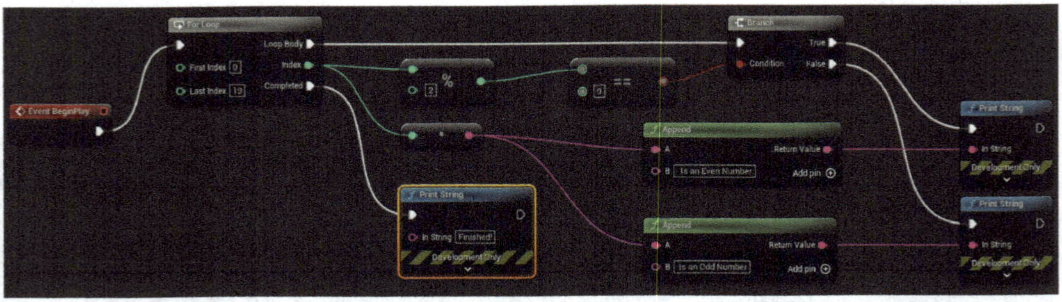

Figure 3.24 - For Loop Blueprint Graph

If you were to build the above Blueprint and launch a game to test it, you would see 20 messages on the left-hand side of the screen, with **Finished!** displayed on the top line, and each line underneath counting down from **19** to **0**, stating whether each is an even or odd number. This would confirm that the **For Loop** logic successfully ran as expected.

With the fundamental Blueprint flow control structures in place, you now have the tools to define how gameplay logic executes, branches, and repeats over time. In the next section, we will shift focus from controlling logic to creating visual results by introducing the basics of Materials.

Creating materials with Blueprints

While gameplay Blueprints define behavior, **Materials** and their **Material Graphs** (usually called **Materials** and **Material Graphs**) define appearance. Materials in Unreal Engine determine how objects *look* in the world: how they appear when lit, how they react to light, what colors they display, and what textures or patterns they show.

A **Material** in Unreal is created and edited using the **Material Editor**, which works similarly to the **Blueprint Editor** but focuses entirely on visual properties. Instead of scripting logic with events and functions, you build materials using a node graph that connects colors, textures, math operations, and special shading instructions.

Even though materials can become extremely advanced, the core ideas begin with three fundamental concepts:

- **Color**: This includes Red, Green, and Blue (RGB) channels
- **Texture map (normal, roughness)**: It is an image used to define how a surface looks
- **Color maps**: These are image textures that specifically control color

The following sections give an overview of these key concepts.

Understanding color representation

Colors in Unreal are represented using 3 color channels, or **RGB channels**. *RGB* stands for *red*, *green*, and *blue*, where each color channel contributes intensity of that color. Each of these channels carries a value between **0.0** and **1.0**, and by combining different intensities for each channel, you can create almost any color imaginable.

Table 3.1 illustrates this with some example **RGB** color channel settings:

Red	Green	Blue	Result
1	0	0	Pure red
0	0	1	Pure blue
0	1	0	Pure green
1	0	1	Magenta
1	1	0	Yellow

Red	Green	Blue	Result
0	1	1	Cyan
1	1	1	White
0	0	0	Black

Table 3.1 - RGB Color Values

Unreal also supports **RGBA colors**, which represent colors using a fourth channel, called the **Alpha** Channel. This additional channel is used to represent how transparent or solid the color appears (the **opacity**), and again carries a value between **0.0** and **1.0**, with 0 being fully transparent, 1 being fully opaque, and values in between being semi-transparent (like glass or smoke).

Knowing the Material Output pins

Every Material Graph includes a **Material Output** node, which defines the final appearance and rendering behavior of the material. This node serves as the endpoint of the graph, collecting all computed values and passing them to the renderer. The available input pins on the Material Output node correspond to the properties defined by Unreal Engine's *Physically Based Material system.*

Physically Based Rendering (PBR) materials use real-world lighting principles to describe surfaces using physical properties, such as Base Color, Normal, Roughness, Metallic, and Emissive, allowing Unreal Engine to produce realistic and predictable visuals in immersive game environments.

Each material input pin can accept either a constant color value or a texture map, which is simply an image file. A color value is useful for defining uniform surface properties, such as a solid base color, while texture maps allow adding visual detail by sampling color or data from an image. Let's learn and understand some frequently used texture maps:

- **Color map**, also known as a **base color texture**, defines the visible color information of a material's surface. It is an image that contains the painted details of an object, such as patterns, gradients, and surface variations. In Material Graph, the Color Map should be connected to the **Base Color** input of the **Material Output** node.
- **Normal map** is a special type of texture that adds surface detail without increasing the model's geometry. A normal map encodes surface direction data, which tells the lighting system how light should interact with the surface at each pixel. This allows a flat surface to appear with bumps, grooves, or ripples which dynamically respond to

lights. In the Material Graph, a normal map should be connected to the **Normal** input of the **Material Output** node.

- **Roughness map** controls how smooth or rough a surface appears and how light is scattered across it. Roughness maps are usually grayscale images, where darker areas represent smoother surfaces with sharp reflections (for example, mirror reflection) and lighter areas represent rougher surfaces with softer, more diffused reflections. In the Material Graph, the roughness map should be connected to the **Roughness** input to control the material's reflective quality.
- **Metallic map** defines whether areas of a surface behave like metal or non-metal. It is also typically a grayscale texture, where black values represent non-metal surfaces such as wood or plastic, and white values represent metallic surfaces like steel or aluminum. When connected to the **Metallic** input, this map determines how the material reflects light and interacts with its environment.
- **Emissive map** defines areas of a surface that emit light, making them glow regardless of the scene's lighting conditions. Emissive maps use brighter colors to indicate stronger emission, and darker areas emit little or no light. Emissive maps are commonly used for elements such as screens, LEDs, neon signs, or magical effects. In the Material Graph, the emissive map should be connected to the **Emissive Color** input.

Creating materials for the BridgePrototype Level

The bridge in the `BridgePrototype` Level is currently a very plain object constructed of default Unreal Geometry with no color or texturing, and it does not look very realistic. In the following sections, you will have the opportunity to get hands-on and create some materials to provide a more realistic look for the `BridgePrototype` Level.

Importing needed textures

To create the materials needed for the bridge and the river, we need to import the three texture maps: `Brick_Stone_Diffuse.PNG`, `Brick_Stone_Normal.PNG`, and `Water_Normal.PNG`.

In the **Content Drawer**, navigate to the **All** |**Content** | **LevelPrototyping** |**Textures** folder, right-click and choose **Import to Current Folder** from the pop-up menu. In the **Import** dialog, go to the **Pangaea_Assets** | **Textures** folder and import the needed texture maps from there.

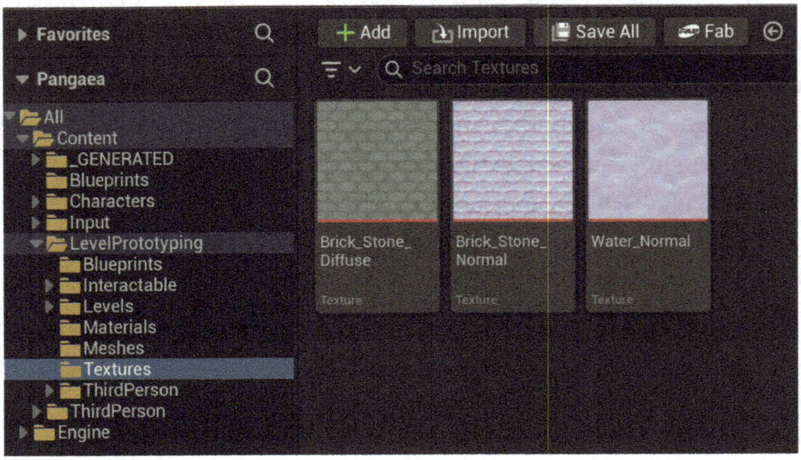

Figure 3.25 - Texture Maps in the Textures folder after importation

Now that the required texture maps have been imported, let's create the custom brick material for the bridge.

Creating the Bricks Material for the bridge

You will now create a new custom Material on your own to add a brick look to the Bridge in the `BridgePrototype` Level you created in *Chapter 2*. You should be able to accomplish adding a bridge texture similar to the one shown in *Figure 3.26* through what you have learned so far and through the instructions that follow.

Figure 3.26 - The BridgePrototype Level Using the Bricks Material

Let's get started:

1. Create a new Material in the **All** | **Content** | **LevelPrototyping** | **Materials** folder and name it `M_Bricks`.
2. Locate the `Brick_Stone_Diffuse` and `Brick_Stone_Normal` textures in the **All** | **Content** | **LevelPrototyping** | **Textures** folder and drag them into the **M_Bricks** graph as **Texture Sample** nodes.
3. In the Material Graph, connect the `Brick_Stone_Diffuse` **Texture Sample** node to the **Base Color** pin of the **M_Bricks** output node.
4. In the `Material Graph`, connect the `Brick_Stone_Normal` **Texture Sample** node to the **Normal** pin of the **M_Bricks** output node.

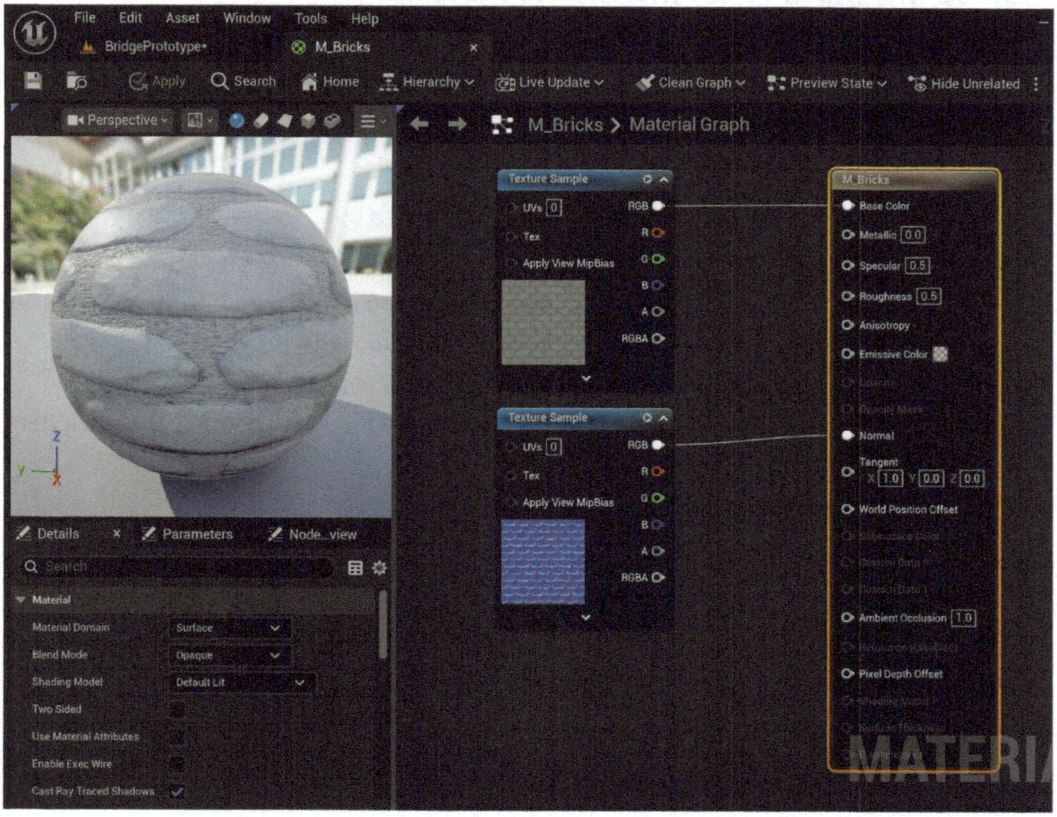

Figure 3.27 - The M_Bricks Material

5. Leave the rest of the pins' default values and click the **Save** button in the Material Editor toolbar to save the new material.
6. To apply the `M_Bricks` Material to the bridge, drag the material and drop it onto the bridge object.

You have now created your first `M_Bricks` Material using the step-by-step instructions above. It is noticeable, however, that after applying the `M_Bricks` Material to the bridge, each mesh face of the bridge doesn't have correct tiling sizes, and this is due to messy or inaccurate UV values. In the next section, we will explain what UV values are and how this issue can be solved using the **UV transformation** tool to adjust the offset, scale, and rotation of the texture for each surface.

Correcting the UVs on the Bricks Material

Think of UVs as the *instruction manual* that tells Unreal Engine exactly how to wrap a 2D image (like a texture) around a 3D object. **UV mapping** is the process of flattening a 3D object into 2D "islands" so a flat image can be painted onto it perfectly.

Imagine you have a 3D model of a brick, and you want to put a Brick Texture on it:

- The *3D model* is the box.
- The *Texture* is the wrapping paper.
- The *UVs* are the fold lines and tape marks that tell you which part of the paper goes on the top, bottom, and sides so the bricks don't look crooked or stretched.

In a 3D world, we already use *X*, *Y*, and *Z* to talk about moving left/right, up/down, and forward/backward. To avoid people getting confused, mathematicians chose to use the letters *U* and *V* for the 2D space of a texture:

- **U** is the horizontal axis (left to right)
- **V** is the vertical axis (top to bottom)

Most UV maps live in a coordinate system that goes from 0 to 1. So, a coordinate of (0.5, 0.5) is exactly the center of your image. Be aware that in Unreal Engine, *V=0* starts at the top of the texture, so the value of *V* increases downward.

When you're inside Unreal's Material Graph, you'll see a node called **Texture Coordinate**:

- This node represents the UV map.
- A **Multiply** node can be used to *tile* or repeat the texture multiple times across a surface, with the **Multiply** value of the node used to specify how many times the

texture is to be repeated. It should be noted that this is only if you leave the **Tiling Method** set to its default setting of **Wrap**.

- If your UVs are messy (a process called **bad unwrapping**), your texture will look like it's melting or glitching out on your 3D model.

This glitching is clearly visible on the material for the bridge model in our level, highlighted in *Figure 3.28*. You will now correct the look of the `M_Bricks` Material in the scene, so that it is sized and oriented uniformly across the bridge, by making corrections to the UVs related to the faces of the bridge mesh. The steps to achieve this are as follows:

1. Navigate to the **All** | **Content** | **LevelPrototyping** | **Levels** folder, open the `BridgePrototype` Level, and select the `SM_Bridge` Actor in the **Outliner**.
2. In the menu toolbar, change the **Context Mode** dropdown of the Level Editor to **Modeling Mode**.
3. Click the **UVs** button (**1** in *Figure 3.28*) on the left-hand side of the **Modeling** toolbar, select **UV Unwrap** (**2** in *Figure 3.28*), and press the *Enter* button on your keyboard to **Accept**. This will recompute the incorrect UV map for the bridge mesh.

Figure 3.28 - Unwrap the incorrect UVs for the bridge model

4. The recomputed UVs are more accurate; however, the brick texture material appears oversized and is not uniformly oriented across the bridge.

Figure 3.29 - Unwrapped Brick Material UVs oversized and incorrectly oriented

5. To correct this, you need to adjust the scale and rotation of the UV Islands for each of the corresponding faces on the bridge mesh. With the `SM_Bridge` Actor still selected, click the **UVs** button (**1** in *Figure 3.30*) and then select **Transform UVs** (**2** in *Figure 3. 30*):

Figure 3.30 - UV Transform Mode with UV islands outlined in red

6. The editor is now in **UV Transform** mode, with the UV Islands for each of the corresponding faces on the bridge being outlined in *red* (see *Figure 3.30*). To correct the scaling and orientation of a UV Island, click on the respective UV Island outlined in *red* on the `SM_Bridge` mesh in the Viewport panel (the UV Island will highlight in *green* when your cursor hovers over it) to select it.
7. With the UV Island selected, a **Details** panel will appear near the bottom of the Viewport panel. The **Scale** and **Rotation** properties (**3** in *Figure 3.31*) for the UV Island are made available to edit, and these should be adjusted manually until an accurate-looking scaling and orientation of the UV Island is achieved.

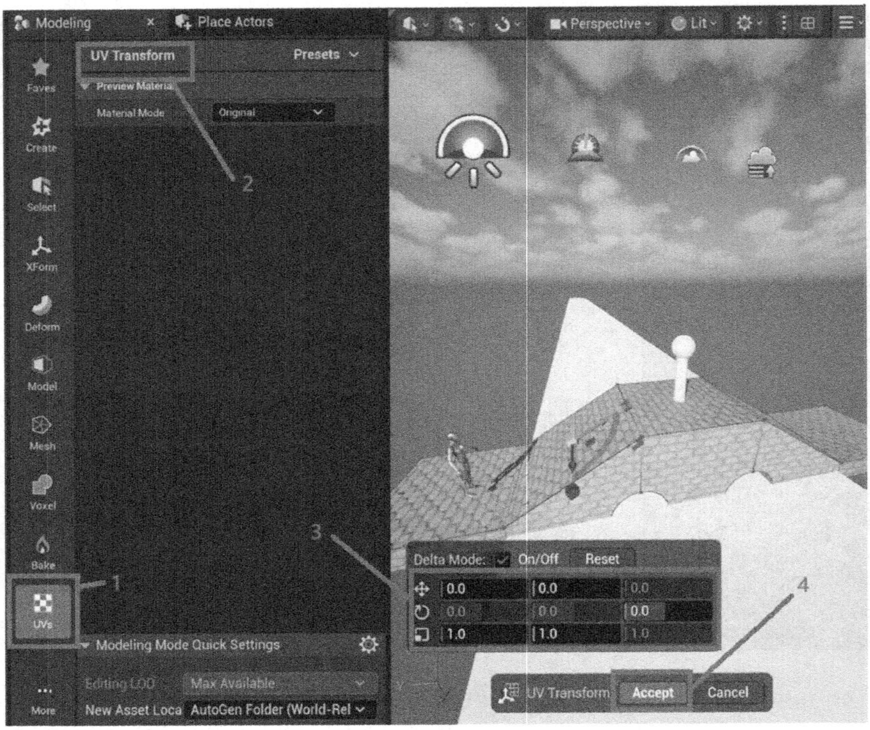

Figure 3.31 - Details panel with Rotation and Scaling properties available to edit

8. Repeat this process for all the remaining UV Islands on the `SM_Bridge` mesh until you are satisfied that the scaling and orientation of the Material on the bridge faces looks uniform and accurate.
9. Finally, press the *Enter* button to **Accept** (4 in *Figure 3.31*) the adjustments you have made to the **Transforms (Rotation and Scaling)** of the UV Islands. You can view the corrected bridge in the final scene image displayed in *Figure 3.33*.

Creating the M_Water Material for the river

Using the following step-by-step guide, you will create a Material to represent water and add it to the `BridgePrototype` Level. Following these steps will create a Material with a final node structure as depicted in *Figure 3.32*.

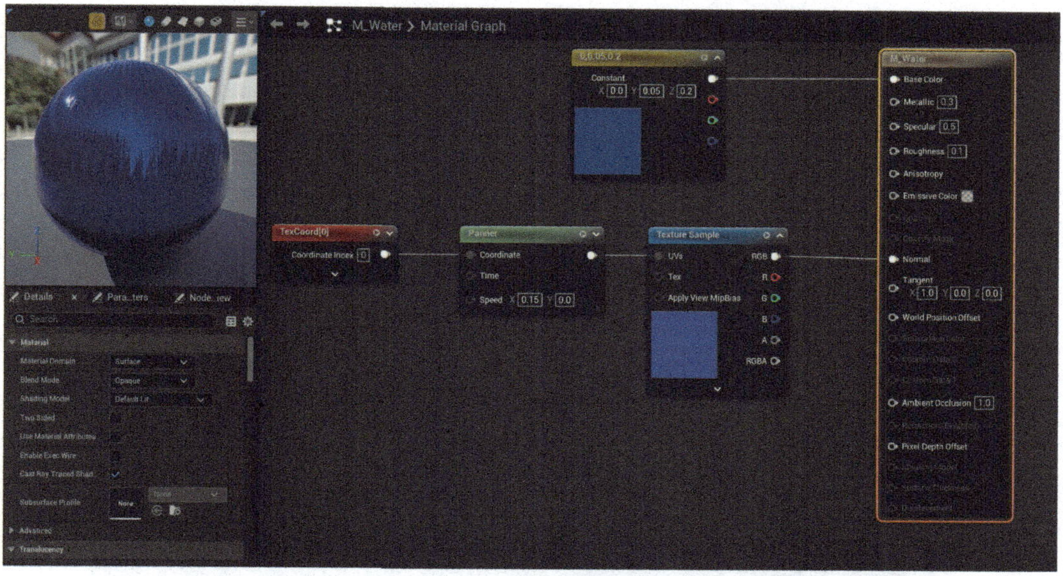

Figure 3.32 - The M_Water Material

1. Create a new `M_Water` Material in the **All** | **Content** | **LevelPrototyping** | **Materials** folder, double-clicking to open it in the Material Editor.
2. In the Material Graph, create a new **Const3Vector** node and connect it to the **Base Color** pin of the **M_Water** node. Set the values to (`0.0, 0.05, 0.2`), which indicates a dark blue color.
3. In the Material Graph, create the **Texture Sample** node from the `Water_Normal` texture located in the **All** | **Content** | **LevelPrototyping** | **Textures**.
4. To make the river water flow, add two nodes, **TexCoord** (**Texture Coordinate**) and **Panner**, in the Material Graph. Connect the **TexCoord**, **Panner**, and **Texture Sample** nodes, as shown in *Figure 3.32*.
5. Set `100` for the **UTiling** field for the **TexCoord** node. This value specifies 100 repetitions along the horizontal direction of the river.
6. Set the **Panner** node's **Speed** value to `(0.15, 0)`. It controls the tiled texture to move along the X direction over time.
7. Set the **Roughness** value to `0.1`, so that the water plane is smooth enough to have a reflection effect.
8. Apply the `M_Water` Material to the water plane. You should now obtain the same result displayed in *Figure 3.33*.

Figure 3.33 shows the final scene with both the complete Bridge Material and the Water Material:

Figure 3.33 - Final BridgePrototype Level with corrected bridge UVs and the M_Water Material applied

This chapter provided you with an understanding of the Blueprint Graphs. We will gradually introduce more nodes and functionality in future chapters when using them to create Blueprints.

Summary

In this chapter, you built a solid foundation for understanding and working with Unreal Engine's Blueprint Visual Scripting system. You explored the Gameplay Framework and learned how core classes, such as Actors, Pawns, Characters, Controllers, and Components, fit together to shape the structure of a game.

You then examined the **Blueprint Editor** in detail, gaining familiarity with essential panels such as the **Components** panel, **My Blueprint** panel, **Event Graph**, and **Details** panel. Building on this, you learned how Blueprint graphs operate by working with Events, Variables, Functions, Execution Flow, and a variety of node types. Through step-by-step, hands-on examples, you walked through creating Blueprints that used sequential logic, branching, a **While Loop**, and a **For Loop** to process data and control flow visually.

You were then introduced to Materials, learning how colors, texture maps, color maps, and normal maps contribute to realistic surface appearance. By following guided exercises, you built practical water and brickwork materials and applied them to objects in a level and corrected bad unwrapping on the bridge model's UVs.

With these skills, you now understand both how to construct gameplay behavior through Blueprints and how to define visual appearance using Material Graphs. You are well prepared to continue deeper into Blueprint scripting and begin combining these systems to create more interactive and visually engaging game elements.

In the next chapter, we explore creating a Player Character for the game.

Part 2

Creating Characters and Interactions for Your Game

Part 2 brings your game world to life with playable characters, enemies, controls, and user interfaces. You will create and animate a player character, attach a weapon, and use the **Enhanced Input** system to turn keyboard and mouse input into movement, camera control, and attacks. You will then build an AI-controlled enemy that can navigate the level, perceive the player, and make decisions using AI Controllers, Behavior Trees, and Blackboards. You will also use **Unreal Motion Graphics (UMG)** to create a main menu and an in-game HUD, connecting the interface to your game systems.

With these systems in place, you will be able to connect characters, controls, AI, and UI to create an interactive gameplay experience.

This part of the book includes the following chapters:

- *Chapter 4, Creating a Player Character*
- *Chapter 5, Handling Player Input*
- *Chapter 6, Creating an AI Character*
- *Chapter 7, Game UI with Unreal Motion Graphics*

4

Creating a Player Character

In this chapter, you will create the player character for the *Pangaea* project. A playable character in Unreal Engine is not just a 3D model. It is a collection of connected assets and systems: a Skeletal Mesh for the character's body, materials and textures for its appearance, animation clips for movement, a Character Blueprint for gameplay behavior, an Animation Blueprint for animation logic, and sockets for attaching equipment such as weapons.

We will build this character step by step. First, you will prepare and import the `Hero` model and textures. Then, you will fix the material so the character displays correctly. After that, you will import animation clips, create a Character Blueprint, set up an Animation Blueprint, blend movement animations with a Blend Space, and finally attach a sword to the Hero's hand. The full workflow for this chapter is as follows:

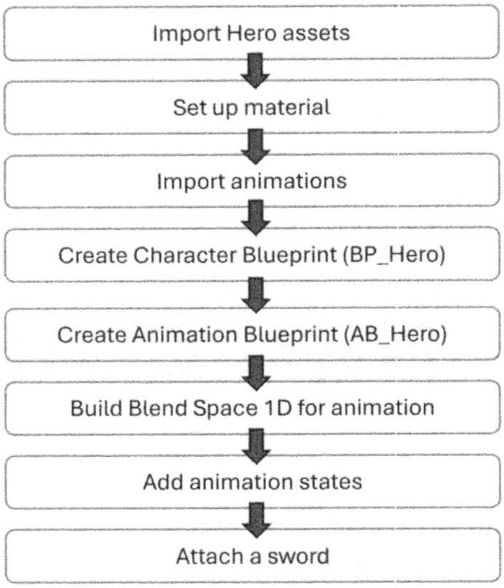

Figure 4.1 - The workflow for creating a player character

This chapter covers the workflow described in *Figure 4.1* with the following major sections:

- Preparing your assets before import
- Importing assets into your game project
- Creating the Character Blueprint
- Setting up the Animation Blueprint
- Attaching the weapon to the character

By the end of this chapter, the `Hero` character will appear correctly, play animations through an Animation Blueprint, and carry a sword attached to the correct hand socket. The character will not yet be fully controlled by player input – that connection will be added in the next chapter when we set up input and movement.

Technical requirements

The sample project for this chapter is available for download from the book's GitHub repository and branch:

- `Chapter04-Start` **branch**: The game project to begin learning in this chapter.

- `Chapter04` **branch**: The completed game project for this chapter.
- The source assets can be found under the `Pangaea_Assets` folder. This folder contains 3D models, character animations, and textures that can be imported into the *Pangaea* project for the player's Hero character and the sword.

You can download the example project and code files for this book by following the instructions in the *Download the example code/resource files* section in the *Preface* of this book.

This chapter's code/resource files are included in the downloadable code/resource bundle.

This chapter assumes you are using the Unreal Engine version specified in the book's introduction. If you are using a newer version of Unreal Engine, some button names or panel layouts may look slightly different, but the overall workflow remains the same.

Preparing your assets before import

Importing assets is the process of bringing external files, such as 3D models (with Static Mesh data or Skeletal Animation data), textures, audio, or data, into your game project so the engine can recognize, process, and reference them at runtime or in the editor.

Common asset categories include 3D models (FBX, OBJ, GLTF), textures (PNG, JPG, TGA, EXR), animations (FBX, BVH), audio (WAV, OGG, MP3), UI assets (2D sprites, icons, fonts), and other data assets (CSV, JSON, XML).

Naming your assets properly

A typical Unreal Engine project contains hundreds, or even thousands, of assets. As your project grows, maintaining a consistent naming convention becomes essential. A good naming convention allows you to identify an asset's type and purpose by looking at its name before opening it.

In practice, this usually means adding a standardized prefix to the beginning of each asset name. For example, a `Static Mesh` may begin with `SM_`, a Blueprint may begin with `BP_`, and a `Material` may begin with `M_`. These prefixes make assets easier to search, filter, and organize in the **Content Drawer**, especially when multiple characters, weapons, environments, and UI assets are added to the same project.

In this chapter, we will follow the naming convention shown in *Table 4.1* to name imported assets. You do not need to memorize every prefix immediately, but try to notice how each asset name tells you what kind of asset it is. Assets created or downloaded from other sources may not use this naming convention. Don't worry, we will rename the imported assets accordingly.

Prefix	Asset Type	Example Asset
`SM_`	Static Mesh	`SM_Rock`, a static rock mesh
`SK_`	Skeletal Mesh	`SK_Player`, the Skeletal Mesh of the main player character
`A_`	Animation	`A_Attack`, an attack animation
`T_`	Texture	`T_FloorTile`, a texture used for floor tiling
`M_`	Material (Master)	`M_Wheel`, a material (shader) for a car wheel in a racing game
`BP_`	Blueprint	`BP_Player`, a Blueprint controlling the player's movement
`AB_`	Animation Blueprint	`AB_Hero`, the Animation Blueprint that controls Hero animations
`BS_`	Blend Space	`BS_1D_Hero`, the Blend Space used for locomotion blending

Table 4.1 - Common Unreal Engine asset prefixes used in this chapter

Here are some other useful tips for preparing assets:

- **Avoid extremely long path names**: Windows has a limitation on the path string length
- **Avoid spaces in the path**: Instead of `My Game/Content`, use `MyGame/Content`
- **Add category segments for larger projects**: For bigger projects with many assets, add a category segment after the asset type prefix. *Table 4.2* illustrates this as follows:

Category	Example Asset Name
Character, or Char	`SK_Character_Player`, a Skeletal Mesh for the player character
Environment, or Env	`SM_Environment_Cliff`, a cliff mesh used as background environment in the game level

Table 4.2 - Optional category segments for larger asset collections

Let's look at the example in *Figure 4.2*. We can easily identify which FBX file contains the Hero character's model or animation, which one is for the color (albedo) texture, and which one is for the normal map:

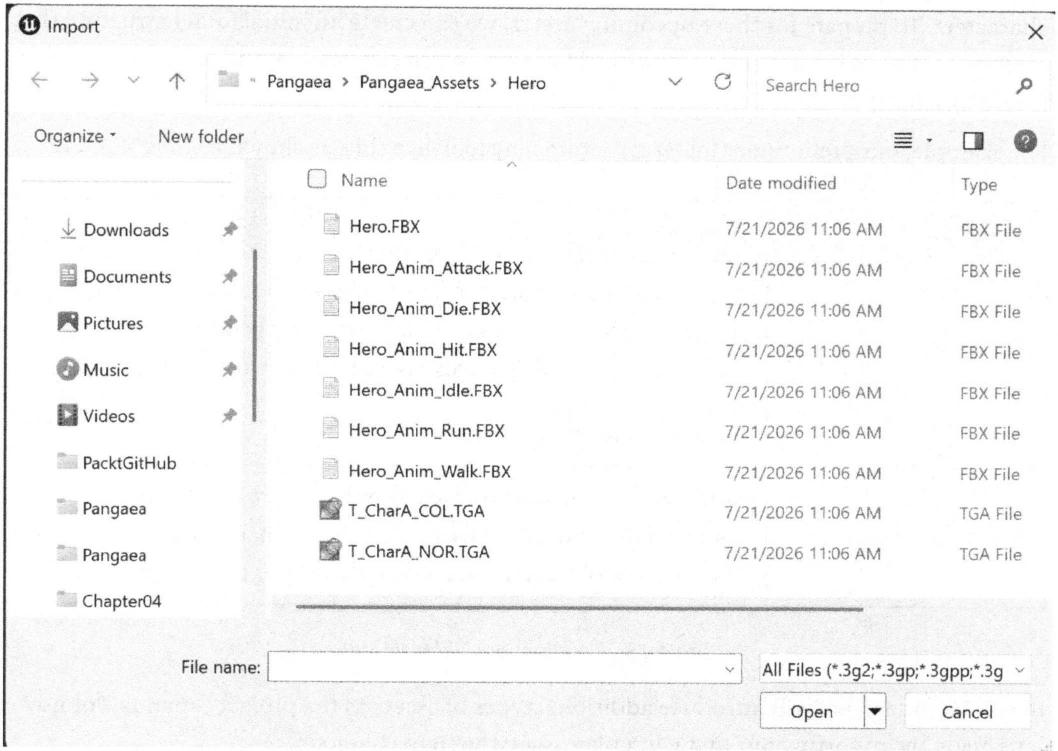

Figure 4.2 - Hero assets with proper studio naming convention

Adopting a standardized naming convention improves organization, reduces confusion, and makes collaboration much easier, especially in team environments. In the next section, we will start adding them to the game.

Importing assets into your game project

Before importing any assets, it is important to plan how you will organize your project's folder structure. A clean and logical **folder hierarchy** keeps your project manageable as it grows and prevents assets from becoming scattered or difficult to locate.

In Unreal Engine, all project assets are stored inside the **Content** folder. Rather than placing assets directly at the root level, it is considered best practice to group them under a project-specific folder.

Since our demo game is titled *Pangaea*, we will create a main folder named `Pangaea` inside the **Content** folder. All game-related assets will be organized under this directory.

In this chapter and the next few chapters, we will begin adding both player and enemy characters. To prepare for these upcoming assets, we can create an initial folder structure that anticipates future growth. Planning ahead helps maintain consistency and reduces the need for restructuring later.

For example, our preliminary folder structure may look like this, as shown in *Table 4.3*:

Location	Purpose
`Pangaea/Characters`	We will put game characters like the player hero character, enemy soldier, and boss characters in this folder. It's good practice to also create separate subfolders for assets of each character. For instance: `Pangaea/Characters/Hero`
`Pangaea/Weapons`	Since each weapon can be used by either a hero or an enemy character, we manage all weapons here. Again, it's also good practice to create subfolders for each weapon, like `Pangaea/Weapons/Sword`

Table 4.3 - A preliminary folder structure

In later chapters, we will introduce additional types of assets as the project expands. For now, let's begin by importing our first gameplay asset: the Hero character.

The `Hero` asset package includes the character's 3D model, textures, and animations shown in *Figure 4.2*. The main character model is provided as an FBX file that contains both the mesh and its rigging (skeleton) data. The skeleton defines the bone hierarchy that drives character animation. You can find all of these source asset files in the `Pangaea_Assets` folder.

We also provide several pre-made animation clips for this character. Each animation is exported as a separate FBX file. Although these animation FBX files may still contain the same mesh data, what we primarily need from them is the animation data itself, which will later be linked to the shared skeleton inside Unreal Engine.

To keep our project organized, let's create two new folders:

Location	Purpose
`Pangaea/Characters/Hero/Model`	We will import the FBX model file into this folder. The accompanying texture files will also be imported into this folder.
`Pangaea/Characters/Hero/Animations`	We will import all FBX animation data files in this folder.

Table 4.4 - Creating folders for project organization

We will begin our importing task in the next section.

Importing the Hero model

There are two common ways to import assets into Unreal Engine:

- Using the context menu inside the destination folder
- Dragging and dropping source files directly into the destination folder

Both methods achieve the same result, so you may choose whichever workflow you prefer.

To begin, let's set up the folder structure for importing the Hero model:

1. Open the **Content Drawer** from the bottom-left corner of the Unreal Editor. In *Chapter 2*, you were introduced to the **Content Browser**, which is the main panel used to browse, create, import, and organize project assets. The **Content Drawer** provides quick access to the same asset system from the bottom-left of the editor. You can think of it as a collapsible **Content Browser** that opens when you need it and stays out of the way when you return to Viewport. When the **Content Drawer** opens, it displays your project's `Content` folder by default.
2. Inside the `Content` folder, right-click and select **New Folder**, then name it `Pangaea`. As discussed earlier, it is good practice to organize your assets under a project-specific folder. All game-related assets for this project will be imported into the `Pangaea` folder to keep them properly organized from the start, as shown in *Figure 4.3*.

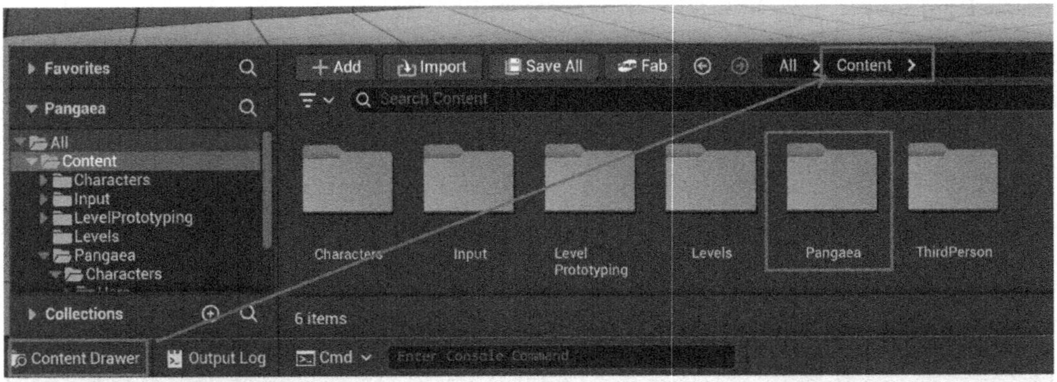

Figure 4.3 - Creating the folders to import your game assets

> **Note**
>
> If you prefer to keep the asset browser open permanently, click **Dock in Layout** in the top-right corner of the **Content Drawer**. This turns it into a docked **Content Browser** panel. Both workflows access the same project assets, so you can use whichever layout you prefer.

3. Now, create and navigate to the following folder: `Pangaea/Characters/Hero/Model`; this is our destination folder.
4. Inside the `Model` folder, right-click to open the context menu and select **Import to Current Folder**.
5. In the file browser window that appears, navigate to: `Pangaea_Assets/Hero` (see *Figure 4.2*).
6. In the file browser window, select `Hero.FBX` and click **Open**. Unreal Engine will display the **Import Content** dialog as shown in *Figure 4.4*. This dialog contains many settings for importing FBX files. For this first character model, we do not need to change the default import settings. The default settings are enough for Unreal Engine to import the `Hero` as a Skeletal Mesh and create the related Skeleton.

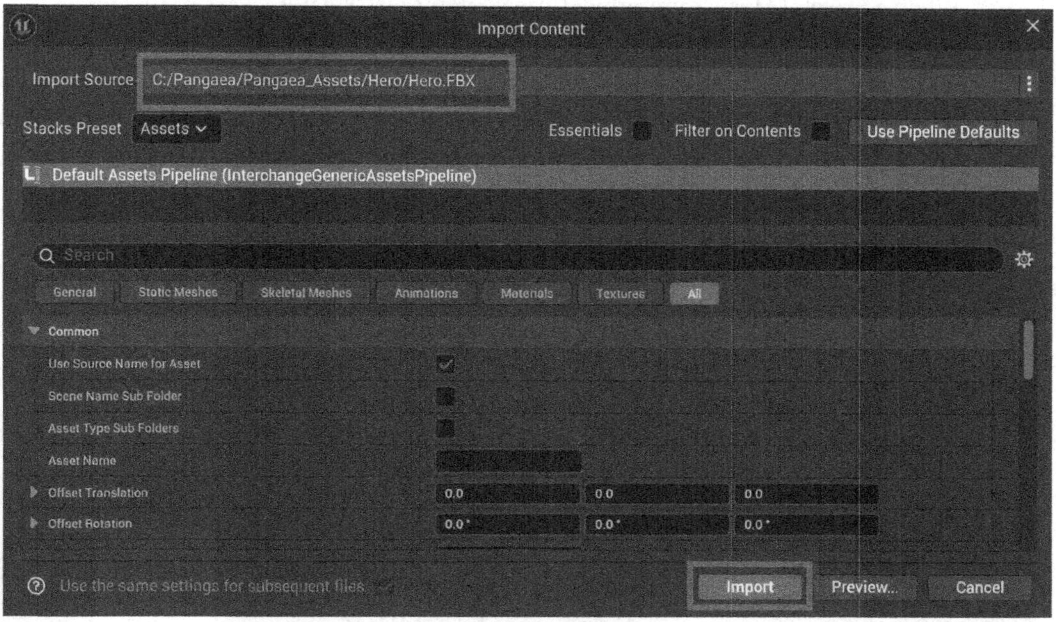

Figure 4.4 - Using default import settings for Hero.FBX

7. Click **Import** to begin the import process. Depending on the complexity and file size of the model, the import process may take several seconds. During this time, Unreal Engine reads the mesh and skeletal rigging data from the FBX file and creates the corresponding Unreal assets in the current folder. Now that the `Hero` model has been successfully imported, you can inspect it in the **Content Drawer** of Unreal Engine, as shown in *Figure 4.5*:

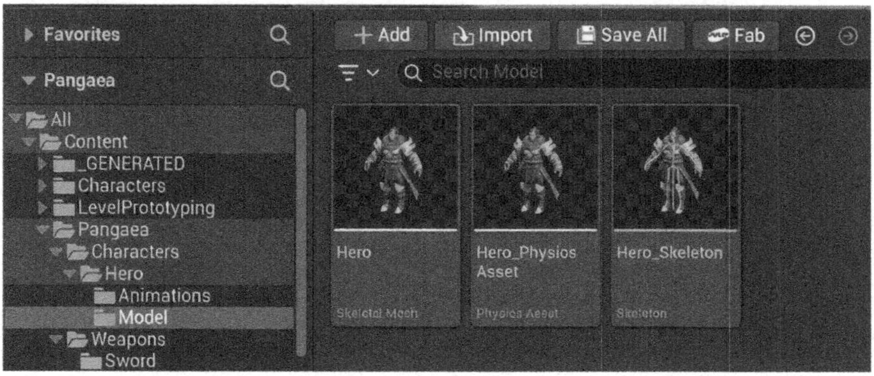

Figure 4.5 - The newly imported Hero mesh and skeleton

8. When a Skeletal Mesh is imported, Unreal Engine also creates a *Physics Asset* for it automatically. A **Physics Asset** contains simplified collision shapes attached to the skeleton's bones. These shapes are used for features such as hit detection, ragdoll physics, and physical animation. If a Physics Asset was not created during import, as in our case in *Figure 4.5*, you can create one manually by right-clicking `Hero` in **Content Drawer**, selecting the menu **Create | Physics Asset | Create and Assign** as shown in *Figure 4.6*:

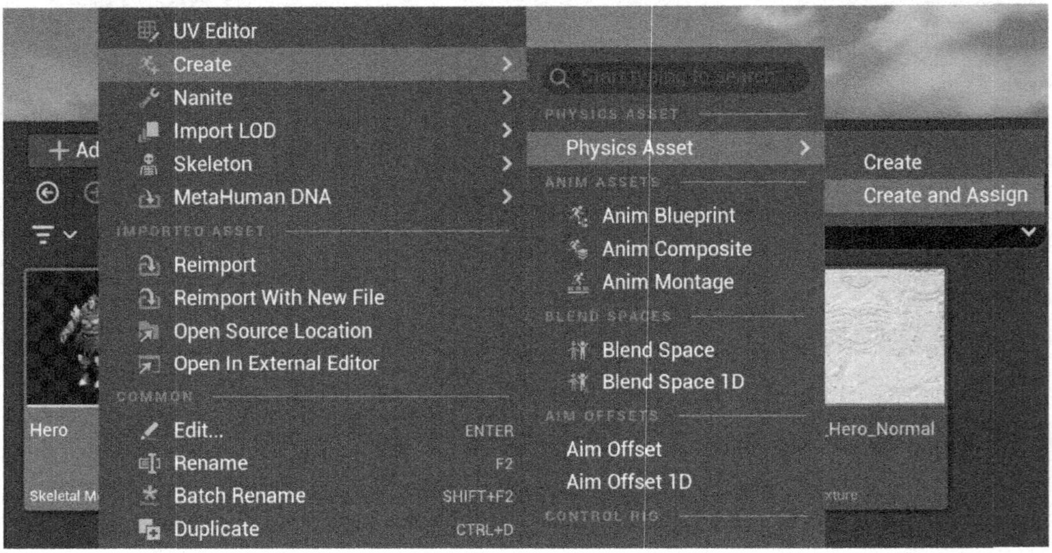

Figure 4.6 - Creating and assigning a Physics Asset to our Hero

9. Unreal Engine lets us tweak settings before creating a Physics Asset for our Hero. Make sure the **Primitive Type** is set to **Capsule** as shown in *Figure 4.7*. **Capsule** is a commonly used shape for humanoid characters. We can leave the rest of the settings as default and click **Create Asset** to generate a Physics Asset for Hero. A new `Hero_PhysicsAsset` will be created in the same `Model` folder.

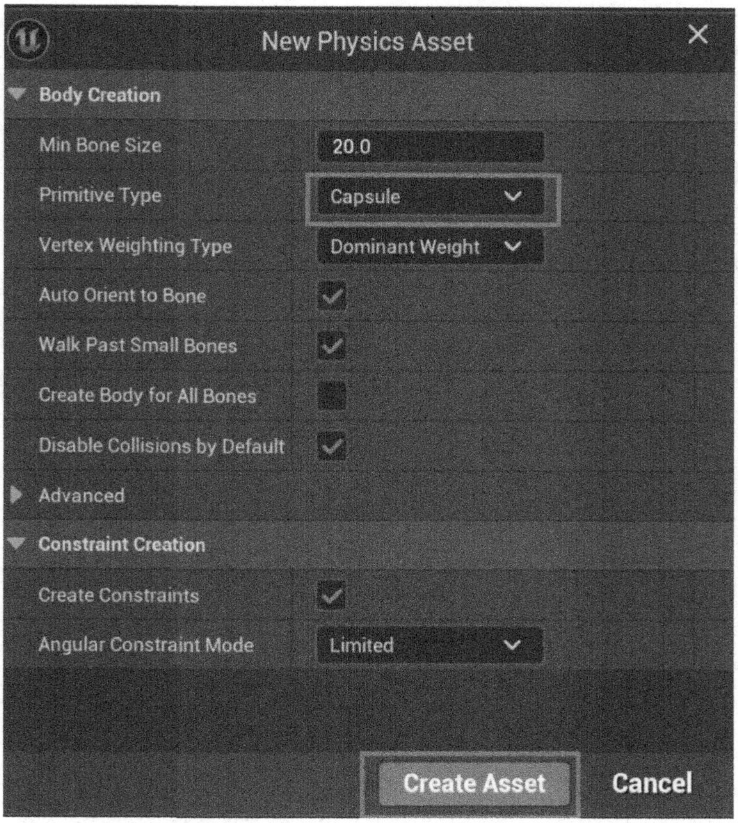

Figure 4.7 - Making sure the Primitive Type is set to Capsule before creating the asset

10. Unreal Engine may automatically open the Physics Asset Editor to let you inspect the detailed settings in the `Hero_PhysicsAsset`. It gives you a visual presentation of how a complex humanoid character can be covered by a few simplified shapes (see *Figure 4.8*) to accelerate the computing of physical interaction with other characters and environment objects. We do not need any further setup on the Physics Asset for now; let's close this Physics Asset Editor window and turn our focus back to `Hero` in the **Content Drawer**.

Figure 4.8 - A Physics Asset contains simplified geometry shapes for physical interactions

11. Double-click `Hero` to open the asset in the **Skeletal Mesh Editor**. It allows you to preview the character model, inspect its skeleton, review assigned materials, and check other mesh-related settings. You may also see settings related to **Level of Detail** (usually shortened to **LOD**). It is an optimization technique where a model can use simpler versions of itself when it is farther away from the camera. This helps improve performance because distant objects do not need to be rendered with the same amount of detail as objects close to the player. In this chapter, we will not modify the `Hero` character's LOD settings. For now, we only need to confirm that the Skeletal Mesh imported correctly and that the `Hero` model can be previewed inside Unreal Engine.
12. Inside the **Skeletal Mesh Editor**, you can rotate, zoom, and inspect the character to ensure the model has been imported correctly.

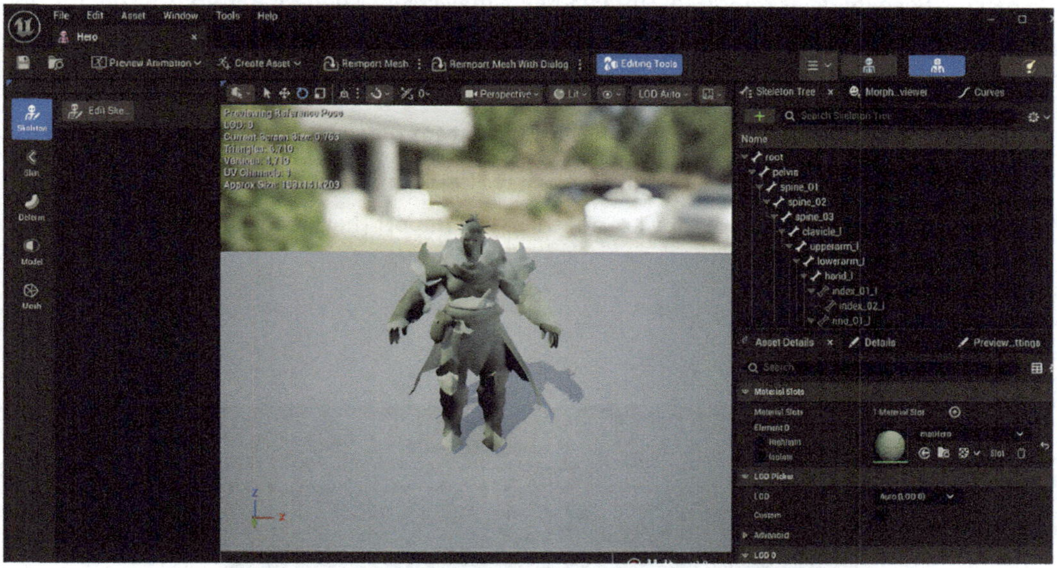

Figure 4.9 - Observing the Hero model that does not display correct texture settings

However, you might notice that the imported Hero model does not display its texture correctly, as shown in *Figure 4.9*. When importing an FBX file, materials like texture maps are not always automatically assigned. Let's fix this in the next section.

Setting up materials

After importing the `Hero` model, the next step is to review and fix the material assigned to the Skeletal Mesh.

As discussed in *Chapter 3*, a material controls how a surface appears in Unreal Engine. It defines properties such as base color, roughness, metallic value, and how the surface reacts to light. The Hero model uses two important texture maps:

- `T_Hero_Albedo`: The base color texture, which provides the visible color details of the character.
- `T_Hero_Normal`: The normal map, which changes how light reacts to the surface and makes details such as armor grooves, cloth folds, and surface dents appear more three-dimensional without adding extra geometry.

When the Hero model is imported, Unreal Engine may create a default material automatically. However, the imported material may not always use the correct texture maps. In this section, we will update the Hero material so the character displays correctly. Follow these steps:

1. In the **Content Drawer**, open this folder: `Content/Pangaea/Characters/Hero/Model`.
2. Make sure the two Hero texture assets have been imported into the `Model` folder as shown in *Figure 4.10*. If they are not there yet, import them from the `Pangaea_Assets/Hero` source folder:
   - `T_Hero_Albedo`
   - `T_Hero_Normal`

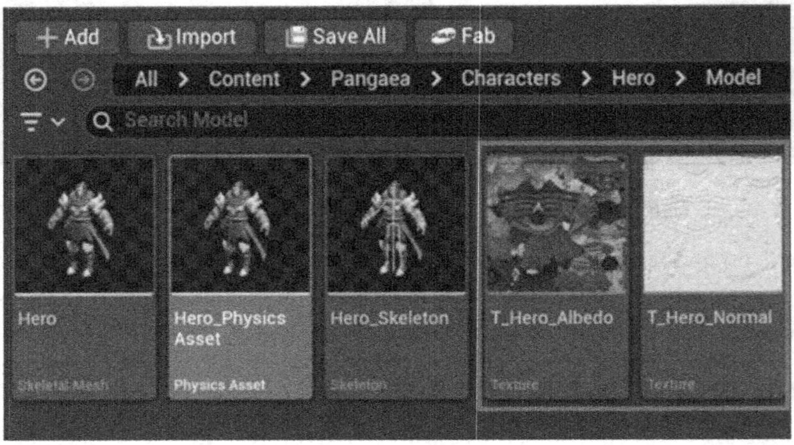

Figure 4.10 - Importing textures for Hero

3. Locate the `Hero` material created during the FBX import. Rename it to `M_Hero` if it does not already use that name. Double-click `M_Hero` to open it in the **Material Editor**. The **Material Editor** is where you build or modify a material by connecting texture, color, math, and parameter nodes to the final Material output node. For this chapter, we only need to connect the Hero's base color texture and normal map.
4. If the material already contains default texture nodes that are not using the `Hero` textures, select those unused texture nodes and delete them.
5. Drag `T_Hero_Albedo` and `T_Hero_Normal` textures from the **Content Drawer** into the **Material Editor** graph.
6. Connect the **RGB output pin** of `T_Hero_Albedo` to the **Base Color** input of the Material output node (see *Figure 4.11*).

7. Connect the **RGB output pin** of `T_Hero_Normal` to the **Normal** input of the Material output node (see *Figure 4.11*). Be careful not to connect the normal map to **Base Color**. The albedo texture provides the visible color of the character, while the normal map provides lighting direction information for surface detail.
8. Click Save in the **Material Editor** toolbar.

Figure 4.11 - Dragging both texture maps into the Material Editor

If everything has been set up properly, the Hero model will now appear with its intended visual details and surface shading like *Figure 4.12*.

Figure 4.12 - Hero model with correct material settings

One more task remains: rename the imported and generated assets for the Hero to match our naming convention. The change will be adding an `SK_` prefix to the asset names, including changing `Hero` to `SK_Hero`; `Hero_PhysicsAsset` to `SK_Hero_PhysicsAsset`; and `Hero_Skeleton` to `SK_Hero_Skeleton`.

At this point, our Hero model appears visually correct. However, it is still a static character and cannot move or perform any actions. To bring the character to life, we need to import and configure animation assets. In the next section, you will learn how to import pre-made animation clips and prepare them for use with the Hero's skeleton.

Importing animation data

In a video game, a character model does not move on its own. Movement is driven by **animation data**. Traditionally, animations are hand-crafted by artists using 3D software or recorded through motion capture and then cleaned up and refined.

Our Hero model includes several hand-made animation clips created by a human artist (see *Preface* for details), and they are ready for you to use.

To organize these assets properly, open the **Content Drawer** and create a new folder named `Animations` under `Content/Pangaea/Characters/Hero`.

Just like how you import the `Hero` model, let's select all animation FBX files at once and import them all into the newly created folder as shown in *Figure 4.13*:

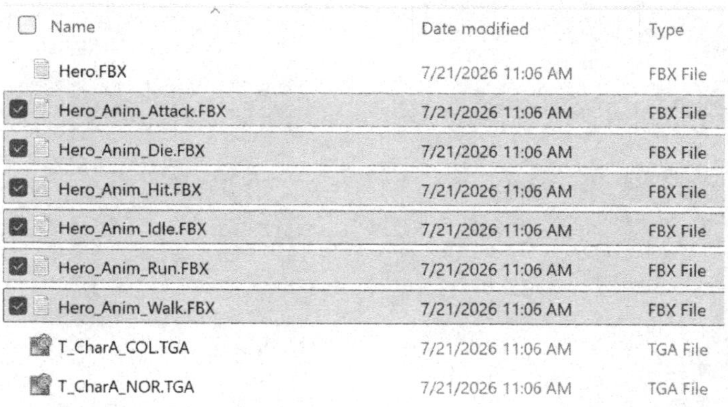

Figure 4.13 - Importing all animations at once

You can now import multiple pre-made animation files at once if they are created for the same skeleton. When you select multiple FBX animation files, Unreal Engine will display the same **FBX Import Options** dialog.

However, this time we must adjust the settings to ensure that only animation data is imported.

Scroll down to the **Common Skeletal Mesh and Animation** section. There are two very important settings you need to configure:

- **Import animation only**: Enable the **Import Only Animation** option (disable mesh import) as shown in *Figure 4.14*. Depending on the 3D software and export settings used, an animation FBX file may still contain mesh or skeleton data. We are not interested in importing duplicate Hero meshes or creating new skeletons – we only want data stored in the animation tracks.
- **Select the correct Hero skeleton**: The most important step when importing animations is selecting the correct Skeleton. In a real project, you may have many characters, each with its own skeleton. Every animation must be associated with the appropriate skeleton to function correctly. Use the **Skeleton** dropdown menu and select the Hero skeleton asset that was created earlier when you imported the Hero model (see *Figure 4.14*). This ensures that all imported animations are linked to the same skeleton and can be reused consistently.

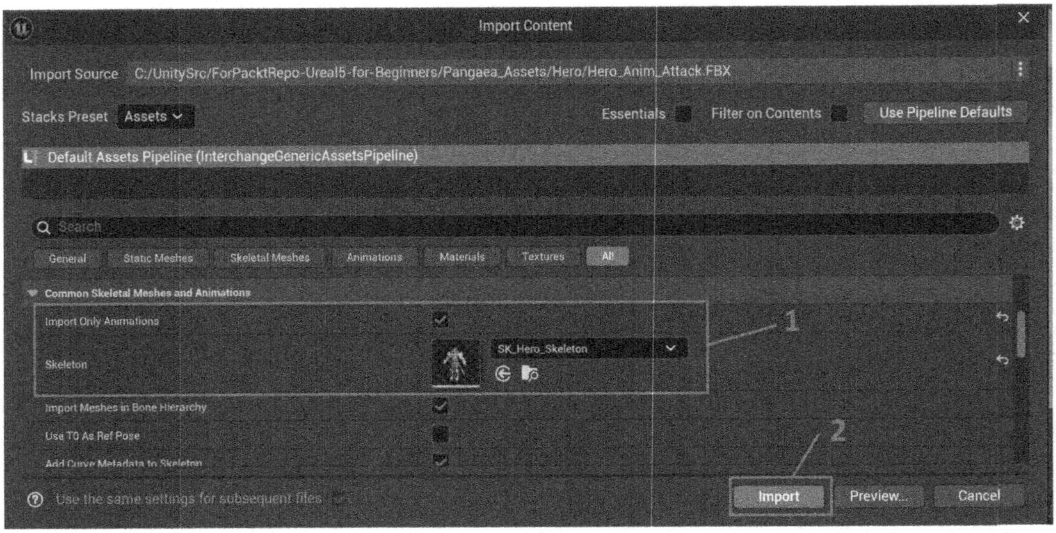

Figure 4.14 - Selecting SK_Hero_Skeleton when importing animation

- Click the **Import** button to start the importing process. You will see all animations ready, as shown in *Figure 4.15*:

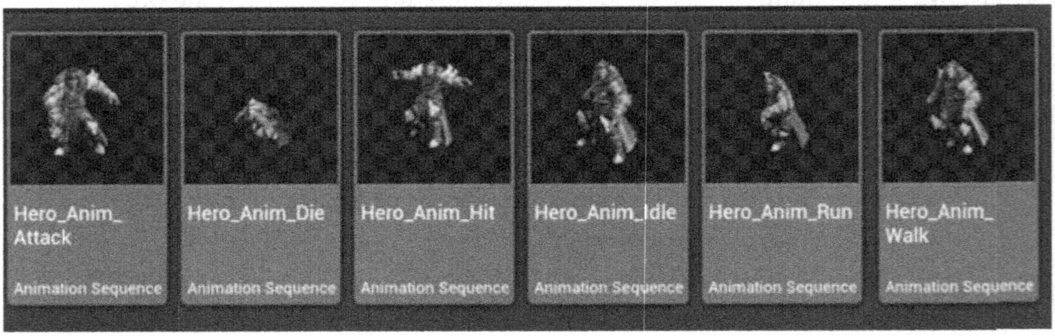

Figure 4.15 - Confirming all animations are imported

Note

When importing the provided Hero model and animation FBX files, Unreal Engine may display warnings such as **No smoothing group information was found for this mesh** or **Imported skeletal mesh has some invalid bind poses**. These warnings do not prevent the provided assets from being imported and used in this project. If the Hero mesh and animations display and play correctly after import, you can safely continue with the chapter.

Before we continue working on animations, it's also good to use consistent studio naming convention. Let's rename all these animations with an asset type prefix, as shown in *Table 4.5*:

Original animation asset name	Studio naming convention asset name
`Hero_Anim_Attack`	`A_Hero_Attack`
`Hero_Anim_Die`	`A_Hero_Die`
`Hero_Anim_Hit`	`A_Hero_Hit`
`Hero_Anim_Idle`	`A_Hero_Idle`
`Hero_Anim_Run`	`A_Hero_Run`
`Hero_Anim_Walk`	`A_Hero_Walk`

Table 4.5 - Renaming assets to meet studio naming conventions

Locate the Hero Skeletal Mesh asset in the **Content Drawer** and double-click it. This opens the asset in the Skeletal Mesh Editor.

The **Skeletal Mesh Editor** is a specialized editor used to inspect and configure Skeletal Mesh assets. A **Skeletal Mesh** is a mesh that can be animated by a skeleton, making it suitable for characters, creatures, and other objects that require bone-based movement. Inside this editor, you can preview the character model, inspect the skeleton, check assigned materials, preview animations, and review mesh-related settings.

For now, we will use the Skeletal Mesh Editor only to confirm that the `Hero` model imported correctly. You can rotate, pan, and zoom the Viewport to inspect the character from different angles. If the mesh, skeleton, and generated supporting assets were imported correctly, the Hero should appear in the preview window.

Figure 4.16 - Previewing imported animation in Skeletal Mesh Editor

Inside the **Skeletal Mesh Editor**, locate the **Preview Animation** option near the upper-left corner of the editor window (**2** in *Figure 4.16*). Click the dropdown menu to display a list of all animations that have been successfully imported and linked to the Hero's skeleton.

From this list, select any animation to preview it directly on the `Hero` model (**3** in *Figure 4.16*). This allows you to verify that the animation data has been correctly associated with the skeleton and that the character animates as expected.

If the import settings were configured correctly, the selected animation should play smoothly without distortion, incorrect scaling, or unexpected bone movements.

Now we have successfully set up an animated character. In the next section, we will need to create a Blueprint to manage and set up the Hero character.

Creating the Character Blueprint

You have already learned the fundamentals of **Blueprints** in Unreal Engine and how they function as visual scripting tools in *Chapter 3*. Now it is time to create a Blueprint for our `Hero`.

A **Character Blueprint** is a Blueprint based on Unreal's Character class in Unreal Engine used to create playable or AI-driven characters. This class is designed for characters that can move through a level, whether they are controlled by a player or by AI. It already includes several useful components, such as:

- **Capsule Component**: The main collision shape used by the character.
- **Mesh Component**: The visual Skeletal Mesh displayed inside the character.
- **Character Movement Component**: The built-in movement system used for walking, falling, jumping, and other character movement behavior.

Because these systems are already included, the `Character` class gives us a better starting point than a plain `Actor` Blueprint. Follow these steps to create the `Hero` Character Blueprint:

1. Navigate to the `Content/Pangaea/Characters/Hero` folder in the **Content Drawer**.
2. Right-click inside the folder and select **Blueprint Class** | **Character** as the parent class (see *Figure 4.17*):

Figure 4.17 - Creating the Hero's Blueprint from the parent class Character

3. In the **Pick Parent Class** window, select **Character** as the parent class.
4. Name the new Blueprint `BP_Hero`.

The **Character** class provides a solid foundation for building our playable Hero character. When the `BP_Hero` Blueprint opens, you will see the default components inherited from the **Character** class. The **Capsule Component** is the root collision component, and the **Mesh** component is where we will assign the Hero character's Skeletal Mesh. Let's continue with the detailed settings.

Setting up the collision capsule

Now, we need to configure the character's collision setup to ensure it interacts correctly with the game world.

We'll begin by double-clicking `BP_Hero` to open the Hero's Blueprint. By default, a newly created **Character Blueprint** includes a **Capsule Component**. This capsule defines the character's collision boundary and allows it to interact properly with the game world.

The capsule shown in *Figure 4.18* serves as the character's collision shape and will not be visible during gameplay. It represents the default size typically used for humanoid characters.

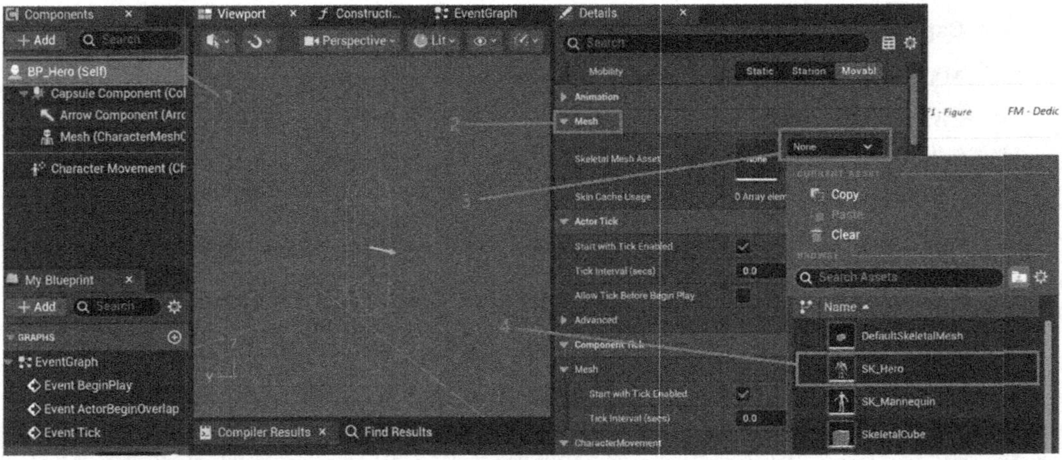

Figure 4.18 - The default capsule for collision detection

There is a *light blue* arrow inside the Blueprint Viewport. This arrow indicates the character's *forward-facing direction*, which aligns with Unreal Engine's default *X*-axis orientation.

Understanding the capsule and forward direction is important, as both directly affect movement, collision detection, and animation alignment.

Now we need to assign the `Hero` Skeletal Mesh to the `BP_Hero` Blueprint:

1. In the **Components** panel, select the **Mesh** component.
2. In the **Details** panel, find the **Skeletal Mesh** property.
3. From the **Skeletal Mesh** dropdown, select `SK_Hero` as shown in *Figure 4.19*:

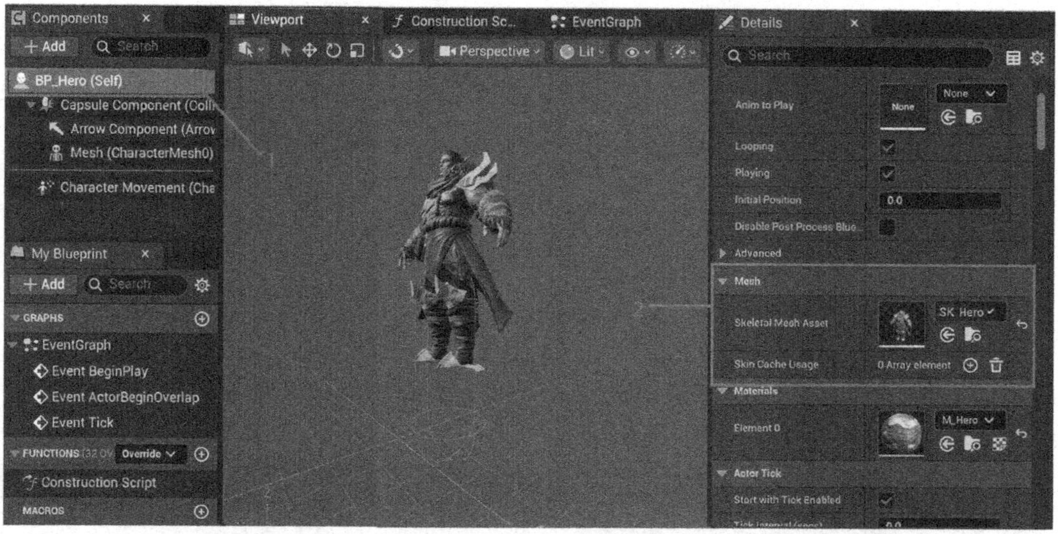

Figure 4.19 - Selecting the Mesh component and assigning SK_Hero as its Skeletal Mesh

After assigning the Skeletal Mesh, the `Hero` character model may not appear in the correct position or orientation inside the capsule. This happens because the source model's coordinate system and Unreal Engine's character setup do not always match perfectly. We will fix this by adjusting the transform values of the Mesh component.

You may also notice the mesh appears rotated incorrectly, positioned slightly above the ground, and if you are using your own model, it is scaled differently than expected.

This situation is common when importing character assets from external 3D software. The **Capsule Component** defines the character's collision boundary and root alignment, so the mesh must be correctly positioned inside it.

Depending on your design needs, there are two possible approaches:

- Adjust the Hero's Skeletal Mesh (rotation, position, and scale) to fit the default **Capsule Component**.
- Modify the **Capsule Component** dimensions to better match the Hero character's proportions.

In most cases, adjusting the mesh is the simpler and more controlled solution. So, we will go with the first approach to adjusting the mesh to fit perfectly with the capsule.

With the **Mesh** component still selected, update the **Transform** values in the **Details** panel. Follow the same order shown in the **Details** panel:

- **Location**: Set the *Z* value to move the mesh downward so the Hero's feet align with the bottom of the capsule. Suggested starting value: *Z* = `-90`. You can adjust the value as you see fit.
- **Rotation**: Rotate the mesh so the Hero faces the correct forward direction. Suggested starting value: *Z* = `-90`.
- **Scale**: Leave the **Scale** values at their default setting unless your imported model appears too large or too small. The default value is *X* = **1.0**, *Y* = **1.0**, *Z* = **1.0**. In this project, the Hero mesh only needs its **Location** and **Rotation** adjusted. The **Scale** values can remain at **1.0, 1.0, 1.0**.

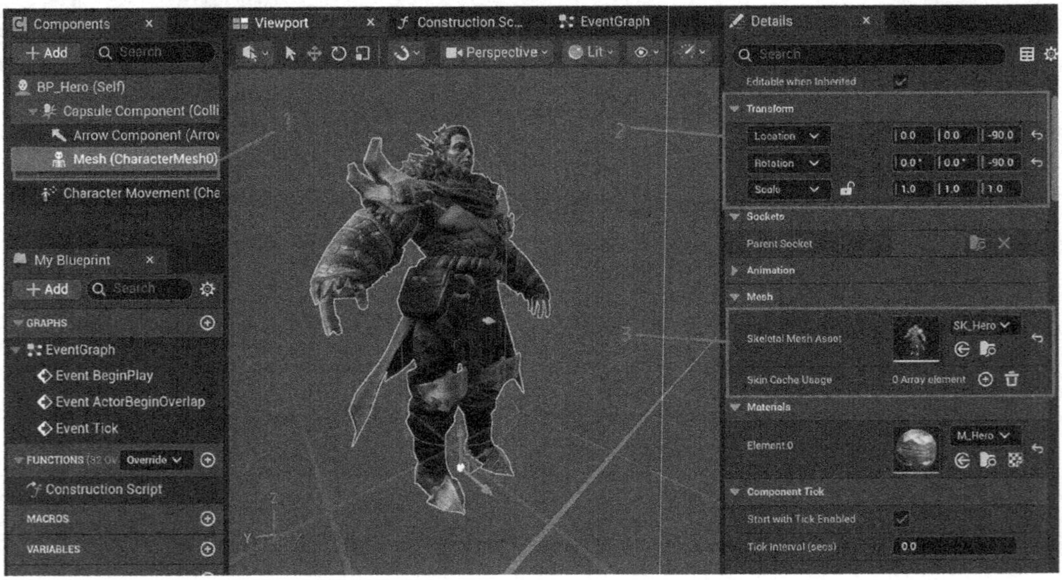

Figure 4.20 - Aligning the Skeletal Mesh with the Capsule Component

After applying these changes, the Hero model should sit correctly inside the **Capsule Component** with proper orientation and proportion (see *Figure 4.20*). Proper alignment at this stage is essential, as it directly affects collision detection, movement behavior, and animation accuracy later in development.

Click the **Save** icon on the top-left toolbar to save your changes. Now we have a basic Blueprint for the Hero character. The next step is to deal with the animation settings.

Setting up the Animation Blueprint

Importing assets and configuring the **Character Blueprint** are relatively straightforward steps. Now, we need to define how the character's animations behave during gameplay. This is accomplished by creating an Animation Blueprint.

An **Animation Blueprint** controls how animation clips are selected, blended, and transitioned based on gameplay conditions such as movement speed, jumping, or attacking.

To create one, follow these steps:

1. Navigate to the `Content/Pangaea/Characters/Hero` folder, then right-click and select: **Animation | Animation Blueprint**.
   Unreal Engine will ask you to choose which Skeleton this Animation Blueprint should be associated with. Select **SK_Hero_Skeleton** (see *Figure 4.21*). This was created earlier when importing the `Hero` model.

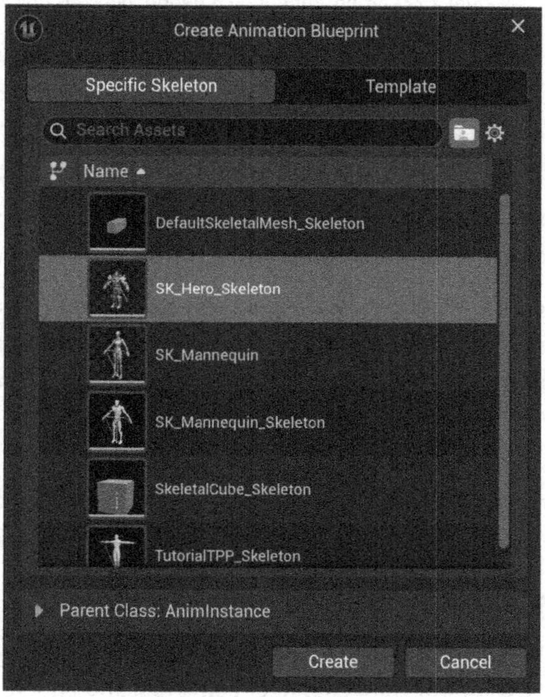

Figure 4.21 - Selecting skeleton for newly created Animation Blueprint

2. Name the new Animation Blueprint `AB_Hero`. After creation, double-click `AB_Hero` to open the **Animation Blueprint Editor**, where we will begin defining the character's animation logic:

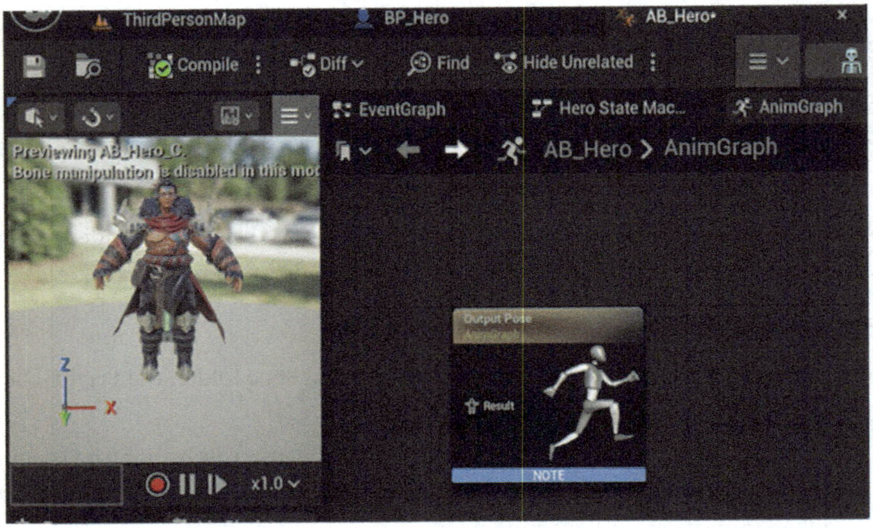

Figure 4.22 - Empty Animation Blueprint only has an Output Pose node

You will notice that it only has one node in *Figure 4.22*, **Output Pose**. The **Output Pose node** represents the final animation result applied to the character's skeleton. In other words, whatever animation data flows into the **Output Pose** becomes the character's visible movement in the game.

However, the **Output Pose** node alone does not determine which animation should play. We need to connect another node that defines how the final pose is generated.

As you might expect, this requires a node that evaluates conditions and determines which animation – or combination of animations – should produce the final result. In Unreal Engine, this is typically done using nodes such as **State Machine**, **Blend Space**, or direct animation playback nodes. We'll understand **State Machine** and **Blend Space** better in the subsequent sections.

However, before we start creating nodes, it helps to understand the animation logic we are going to build.

Planning the animation state behavior

Before continuing to modify the State Machine in `AB_Hero`, it is good practice to plan the overall animation flow for our Hero character using pen and paper.

For example, we might define the following high-level animation states:

- Locomotion (*Idle/Walk/Run Forward* and *Backward*) – all animations relate to movement

- Attack
- Hit reaction

Then we consider important questions, such as:

- Can the character attack while moving?
- Should an attack interrupt running immediately?
- Can the character be hit while attacking?
- After being hit, should the character return to Locomotion automatically (for example, keep running)?

Planning these relationships first helps us design a clean and maintainable *State Machine* before we start creating nodes in Unreal Engine.

A **State Machine** is a way to organize animation logic by separating character behavior into different *states*. Each **state** represents what the character is currently doing, such as standing, walking, running, attacking, being hit, or dying. In our Hero animation setup, *Locomotion* is one state and *Attack* is another state.

The lines between states are called *transitions*. A **transition** defines when the Animation Blueprint is allowed to move from one state to another. For example, the `Hero` can transition from Locomotion to Attack when the player presses the **Attack** button. After the attack animation finishes, the `Hero` can transition from Attack back to Locomotion.

Each transition has a rule or condition. The transition only happens when that condition is true. This structure keeps the animation logic clear: states describe what animation behavior is active, while transitions describe when the character is allowed to change behavior.

The simplest way to plan this is to map out the relationships between these animations, even on plain paper:

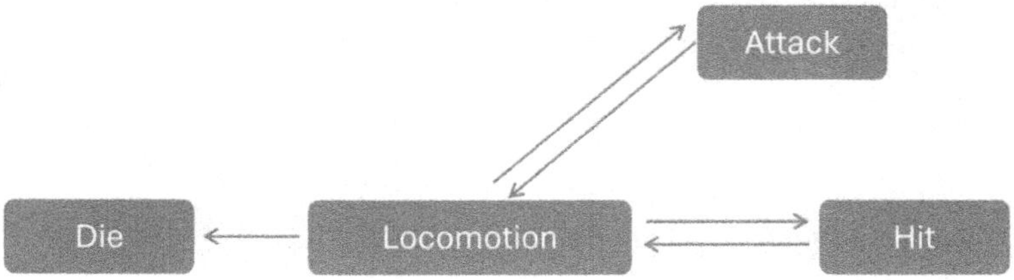

Figure 4.23 - Planning animation states and transitions first

Figure 4.23 demonstrates the animation plan before we build it. Each animation behavior is represented as a state, shown as a *green* block in the diagram. The directional lines between states represent possible transitions from one animation state to another.

For example, imagine a sequence where the Hero is hit, gets pushed back one step, and then launches a punch attack to retaliate. This sequence may trigger several state transitions: first from the Hit state back to Locomotion as the Hero recovers, and then from Locomotion to Attack when the punch begins.

These transitions depend on your game design. For example, you may choose to add a direct transition from Hit to Die if the Hero's health reaches zero. Each transition can have its own condition, and the transition only happens when that condition is met.

In the next step, we will add the appropriate node to control and generate the final animation pose for our `Hero` character.

Adding an Animation State Machine

If a character only remains idle in the game world, the animation setup would be very simple. We could directly connect an **Idle** animation node to the **Output Pose**, and the character would stay in that state indefinitely.

However, our Hero character needs to perform multiple actions, such as idling, walking, running, and so on. To manage these different animation states and switch between them smoothly, we need a more advanced system.

The solution is to use a **State Machine** node. Before diving into technical details, you can think of a **State Machine** as a smart graph that defines rules for determining which animation should be played at any given time. It allows us to organize animations into states and define transitions between them based on gameplay conditions.

To add one, follow these steps:

1. Open the **Animation Blueprint Editor**.
2. Inside the **AnimGraph**, right-click in the graph area. Search for `State Machine`, as shown in *Figure 4.24*, then add the node to the graph:

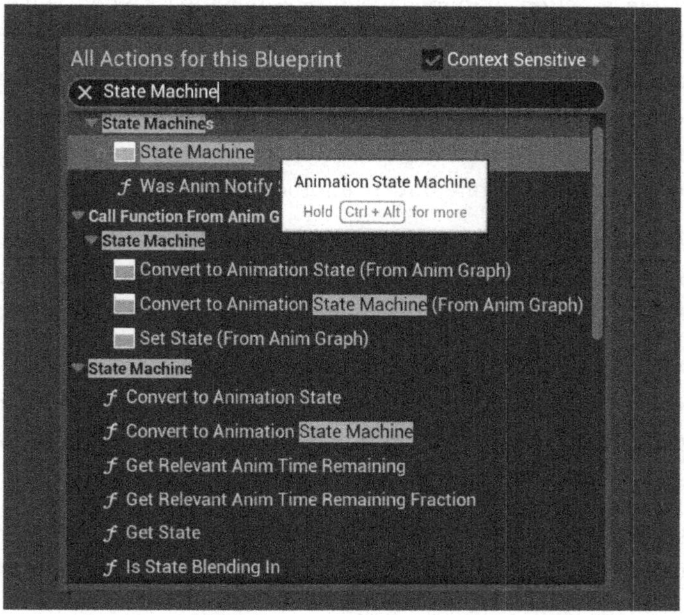

Figure 4.24 - Adding a State Machine node into the Animation Blueprint

3. The last step is to connect the output animation pin of the **State Machine** node to the **Output Pose** node (see *Figure 4.25*).

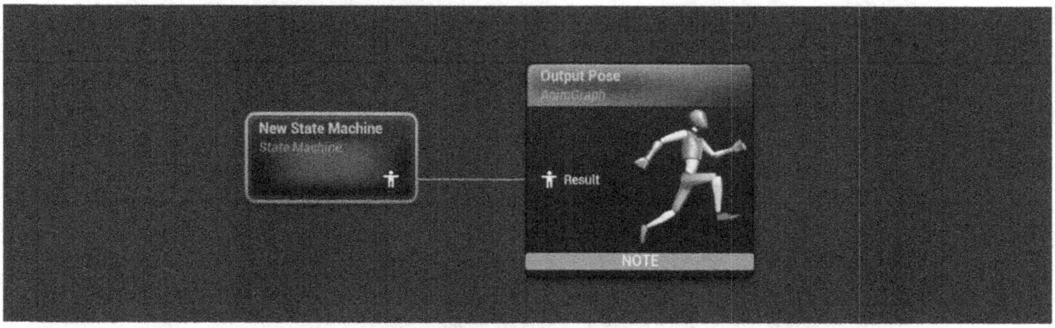

Figure 4.25 - Connecting State Machine node to Output Pose node

Now we can enter the **State Machine** and begin defining the animation states and transitions for our Hero character. Let's look at the steps to achieve this:

1. Double-click to open the newly created **State Machine** node. If we click the **Compile** button to build the Blueprint, it will display a warning that there is no state inside it. The **Compile button** checks the Blueprint graph, updates its generated data, and makes newly created variables or graph changes available to the rest of the Blueprint. If

a variable, function, or graph change does not appear where you expect it to, compiling the Blueprint is often the first thing to try.

A **State Machine** node contains a collection of animation states and uses a graph-based structure to define how those states relate to one another. Each state represents a specific animation (or animation blend), and transitions determine when and how the character moves from one state to another.

Inside the opened **State Machine** node, you will see a single **Entry** node, as shown in *Figure 4.26*. This node represents the starting point of the **State Machine**. At the moment, it does not connect to anything because no states have been created yet.

We will use this **State Machine** to organize and control the Hero's animations. Before proceeding, make sure you have renamed the animation assets to match our naming convention, as described earlier (see *Table 4.5*). Following the convention, we renamed all assets with the `Hero_Anim_` prefix to `A_Hero_` (see *Figure 4.26*).

2. Let's open the **Content Drawer** and navigate to the Hero's animation folder, locate the `A_Hero_Idle` animation asset, then drag it directly into the **New State Machine** graph, as shown in *Figure 4.26*:

Figure 4.26 - Adding an idle animation into the State Machine

This action creates a new state that plays the Idle animation.

3. Now we can connect the **Entry** node to this animation node, as shown in *Figure 4.27*. This means "apply the Hero's idle animation from the start."

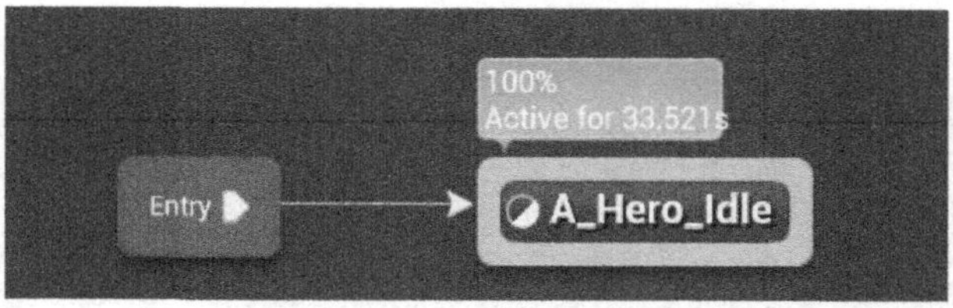

Figure 4.27 - Connecting Entry of State Machine to A_Hero_Idle

4. Now click on **AnimGraph**, go back to the **Animation Blueprint**, and compile again. The warning message is now gone. Rename the State Machine node to **Hero State Machine**, connect it to the **Output Pose** node, and the preview of the Hero character becomes the idle animation pose (see *Figure 4.28*). This means the output of **Hero State Machine** is the idle animation.

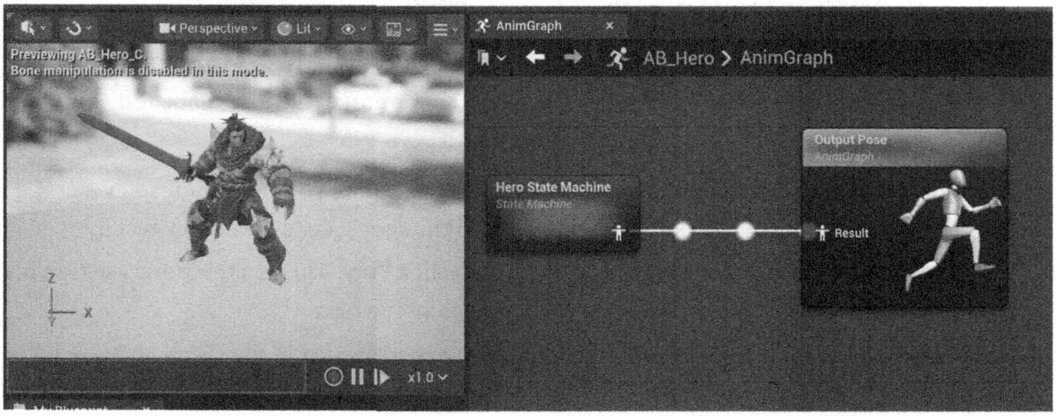

Figure 4.28 - Connecting State Machine to the Output Pose

The setup detailed in these steps represents the most basic and minimal form of an animation State Machine. At this point, the character will simply play the Idle animation by default.

Next, we need to tell our **Character Blueprint** to use this **Animation Blueprint**. Follow these steps:

1. Open `BP_Hero` again.
2. Select the **Mesh** (**CharacterMesh0**) component, then look at the **Details** panel on the right side.

3. Scroll down to the **Animation** section. Set the **Animation Mode** to **Use Animation Blueprint**, as shown in *Figure 4.29*.
4. Then, in the **Anim Class** dropdown menu, select the newly created `AB_Hero`. After you select the `AB_Hero`, it will be shown as **AB_Hero_C**.

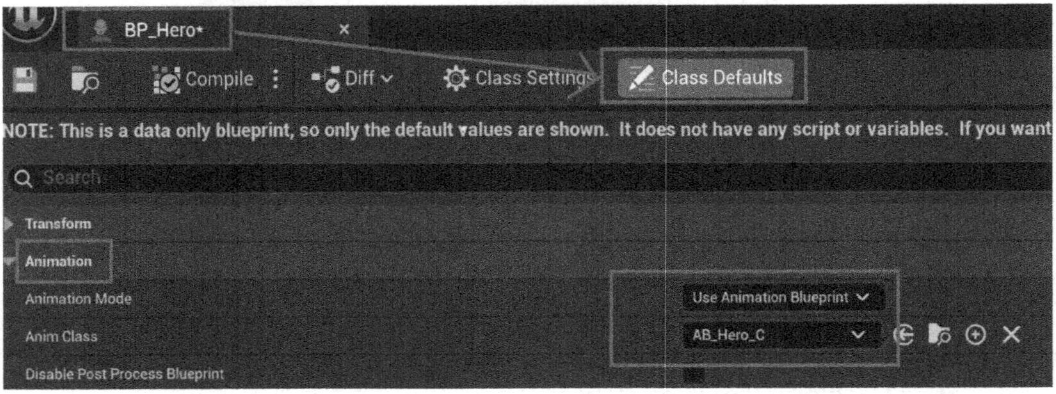

Figure 4.29 - Assigning Hero's Animation Blueprint to Hero's Character Blueprint

Once assigned, the `BP_Hero` Blueprint is now linked to the Hero's **Animation Blueprint**. During gameplay, the character's animation behavior will be fully controlled by the logic defined inside **AB_Hero**.

5. For now, save all changes and perform a quick test. Open your current test level and drag `BP_Hero` from the **Content Drawer** into the scene. Let's do a quick test by positioning the character on the ground, then click **Play**. This is a temporary action for quick testing; we will remove it after we complete the test.

If everything has been configured correctly, the Hero should appear in the scene and remain in the idle state continuously, as shown in *Figure 4.30*, since that is currently the only state defined in the Animation Blueprint.

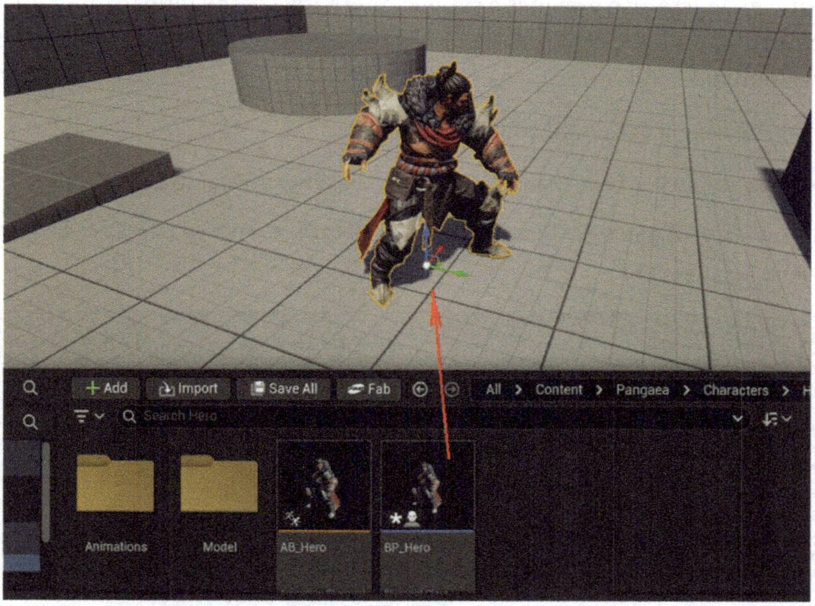

Figure 4.30 - Dragging your Hero's Blueprint into the test level

When previewing `A_Hero_Idle`, you may notice that the animation plays once and then stops. This does not mean the animation was imported incorrectly. The animation preview is only used to confirm that the clip is connected to the Hero skeleton and can play on the model. Later, when we use this animation inside the Hero's locomotion setup, we will make sure the idle animation loops so the character continues standing naturally during gameplay.

Once we confirm that the Character Blueprint and Animation Blueprint are properly connected, remove this testing character by selecting it and pressing the *Delete* key to remove it from the existing scene. In the next step, we will expand the State Machine to support additional movement animations, such as walking and running.

Making a new animation from an existing one

Now we want our character to move freely throughout the level. We already have forward movement animations: `A_Hero_Walk` and `A_Hero_Run`. These animations will be used when the player moves the character forward.

But what about moving backward?

One approach is to have an artist create dedicated backward walking and running animations in a 3D modeling tool, then import those animations into Unreal Engine. This method is ideal if you want subtle differences in body posture, weight distribution, or different upper-body motion when moving backward.

However, Unreal Engine also provides a simpler alternative. If the forward animation can be reused, we can create a backward version directly inside the **Content Browser** by duplicating the existing animation and reversing its playback.

Let's begin by creating a backward walking animation.

1. Navigate to the `Content/Pangaea/Characters/Hero/Animations` folder.
2. Right-click on `A_Hero_Walk` and select **Duplicate**, as shown in *Figure 4.31*, and name it `A_Hero_WalkBack`:

Figure 4.31 - Duplicating a new animation from the existing animation

3. Now open `A_Hero_WalkBack` in the **Animation Editor**, and locate the **Asset Details** panel. Find the **Rate Scale** property and change its value from `1.0` to `-1.0` (See *Figure 4.32*).

   By setting the **Rate Scale** to `-1.0`, the animation will play in reverse. You should immediately notice that the walking motion now plays backward, effectively creating a backward walking animation from the original forward animation.

This technique is useful when the forward and backward motions are symmetrical enough to reuse the same animation data. However, for more realistic character movement, especially in high-quality productions, dedicated backward animations created by an animator are usually preferred.

Figure 4.32 - Change Rate Scale value to create a backward-walking animation

Note that we also need to create an `A_Hero_RunBack` animation based on `A_Hero_Run`. Repeat the same process as detailed above: duplicate `A_Hero_Run`, rename it to `A_Hero_RunBack`, and set its **Rate Scale** to `-1.0` so it plays in reverse.

After completing this step, we now have five animation clips available:

- Idle (`A_Hero_Idle`)
- Walk Forward (`A_Hero_Walk`)
- Run Forward (`A_Hero_Run`)
- Walk Backward (`A_Hero_WalkBack`)
- Run Backward (`A_Hero_RunBack`)

These animations allow the character to transition between standing still, moving forward, and moving backward at different speeds.

In the next section, we will create a new animation setup that blends smoothly between these five animations. This will allow the character to transition naturally from idle to walking or running, in both forward and backward directions, using **Blend Space**.

Creating character movement using Blend Space

Now it is time to create a more advanced animation setup that allows the character to move smoothly forward and backward.

We will use the three original animations – idle, walk, and run – together with the newly created walk backward and run backward animations. Our goal is to blend these five animations smoothly to produce natural transitions between standing still, walking, and running in both directions.

To achieve this, we will create a new animation asset that blends between these five existing animations.

Since forward and backward movements occur along a single axis (one dimension), Unreal Engine provides a built-in solution called a **One-Dimensional Blend Space** (**Blend Space 1D**). Although Blend Space 1D is a legacy asset, it provides a simpler way for beginners to understand animation blending in a one-dimensional space. For this reason, we will use it as a learning tool to build foundational knowledge. The more advanced 2D blending capabilities of the newer Blend Space asset will be left for readers to explore on their own.

A **Blend Space 1D** allows animations to be blended smoothly based on a single input parameter. The value along this dimension is interpolated automatically, producing smooth transitions between animation samples.

In our case, this parameter will represent speed, and we will name it `Blend1D_Speed`. Five animations are blended with a single parameter (see *Figure 4.33*):

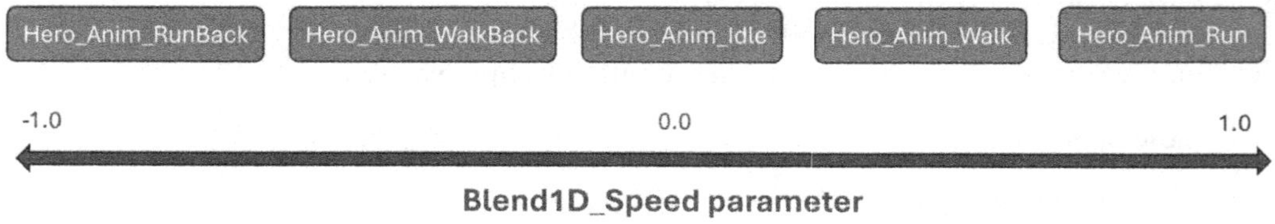

Figure 4.33 - Blending 5 animations with one parameter, Blend1D_Speed

In *Figure 4.33*, we configure the speed axis to range from **-1.0** to **1.0**, where:

- **0.0**: Character remains idle
- **1.0**: Character runs forward
- **Values between 0.0 and 1.0**: Character walks or transitions toward running forward
- **-1.0**: Character runs backward
- **Values between 0.0 and -1.0**: Character walks backward

By mapping movement speed to this range, Unreal Engine can automatically interpolate between Idle, Walk, and Run animations in both directions.

In the next step, we will create the Blend Space asset and place the five animations along this axis to complete the setup.

1. Once again, navigate to: `Pangaea/Characters/Hero/Animations`.
2. Right-click inside the folder to open the context menu. From the menu, navigate to **Animation | Legacy | Blend Space 1D** (see *Figure 4.34*):

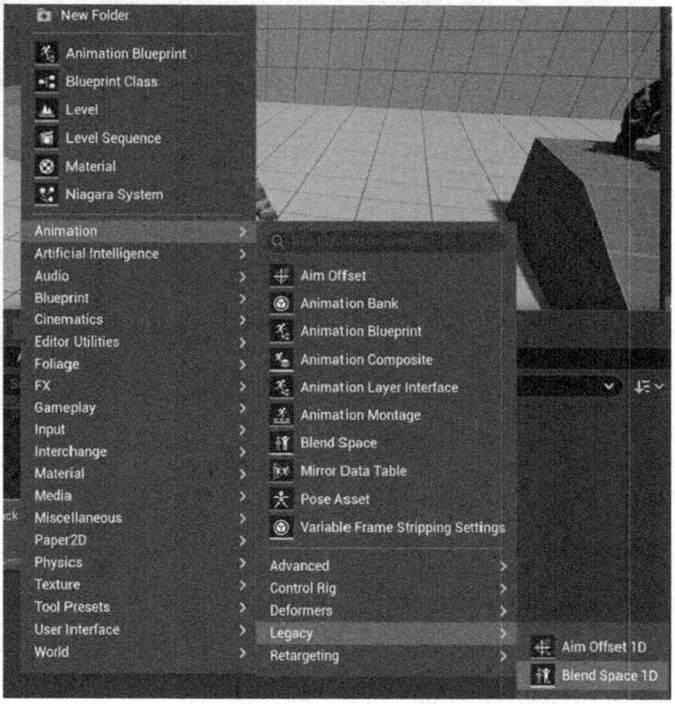

Figure 4.34 - Creating a Blend Space 1D animation

3. When prompted, select **SK_Hero_Skeleton** as the target skeleton for this Blend Space. This will create a new **Blend Space 1D** asset, which we will use to blend between the Hero's idle, walking, and running animations based on movement speed.

   Unreal Engine also provides a more generic **Blend Space (2D)** asset. However, since our movement only depends on a single parameter (forward/backward speed), we will use the simpler and more focused **Blend Space 1D**.

4. After selecting the skeleton, name the new asset as `BS_1D_Hero`.

To configure the Blend Space, follow these steps:

1. Open the **BS_1D_Hero** asset in the editor:
2. In the **Asset Details** panel, locate the **Horizontal Axis** settings under **Axis Settings**. Configure the following properties (shown in *Figure 4.35*):

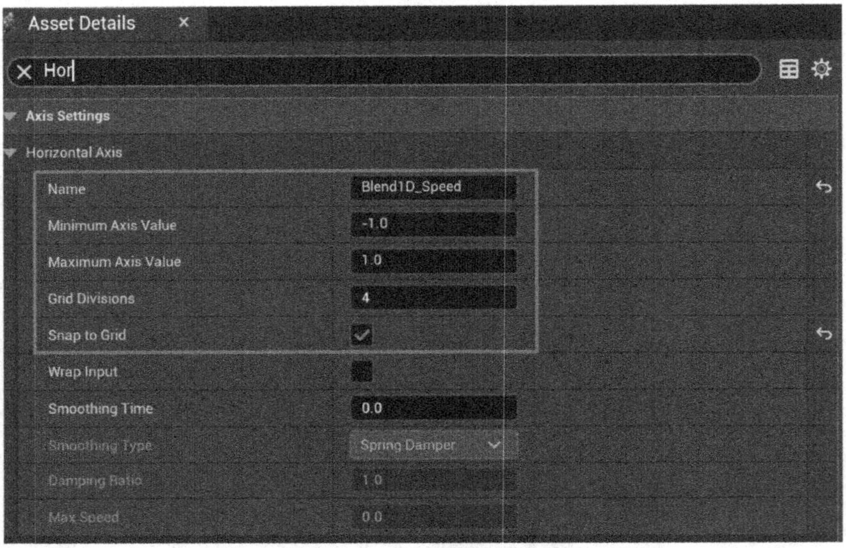

Figure 4.35 - Configuring Blend Space 1D

   - **Name:** `Blend1D_Speed`
   - **Minimum Axis Value:** `-1`
   - **Maximum Axis Value:** `1`
   - **Grid Divisions:** `4`
   - **Snap to Grid**: `Enabled`

   This defines the blending range for our speed parameter `Blend1D_Speed` that we defined previously in *Figure 4.33*.

With the axis configured, we are now ready to place the five animation samples along the Blend Space timeline to complete the blending setup. As discussed earlier, we will use five animations to smoothly blend the Hero's movement along the direction the character is facing. These animations will be positioned along the horizontal axis according to their corresponding speed values.

1. In the **Blend Space Editor**, locate the animation list in the lower-right panel. Drag the animation assets into the grid area beneath the preview Viewport.
   You may notice a small *green* **X** marker in the grid. This represents the current preview position of the **Blend1D_Speed** parameter.
2. Start by dragging `A_Hero_Idle` from the animation list and dropping it at the center position (value **0**) on the horizontal axis, as shown in *Figure 4.36*. This ensures that when the speed is zero, the character remains in the idle state.

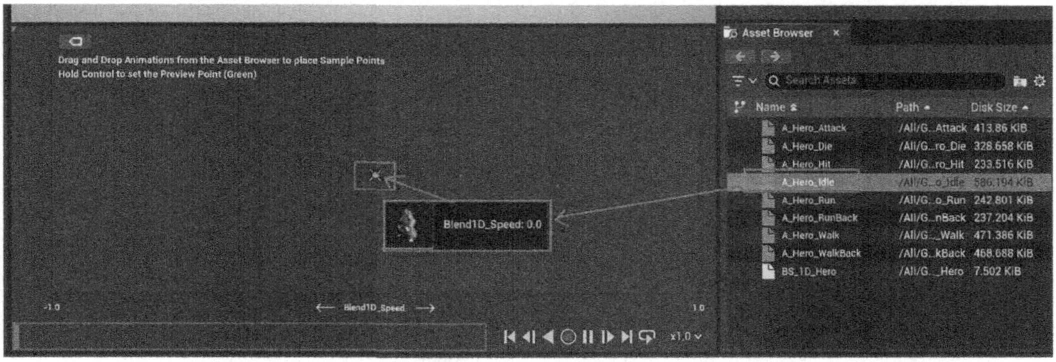

Figure 4.36 - Adding the first animation to the Blend Space Editor

3. Next, drag the forward movement animations to the positive side of the **Blend1D_Speed** axis, as shown in *Figure 4.37*:
   - Place `A_Hero_Walk` somewhere between **0** and **1** (for example, around **0.5**).
   - Place `A_Hero_Run` at **1.0**, representing maximum forward speed.

   Then, drag the backward movement animations to the negative side of the axis:
   - Place `A_Hero_WalkBack` between **0** and **-1** (for example, around **-0.5**).
   - Place `A_Hero_RunBack` at **-1.0**, representing maximum backward speed.

   After arranging the animations, your Blend Space layout should conceptually look like this:

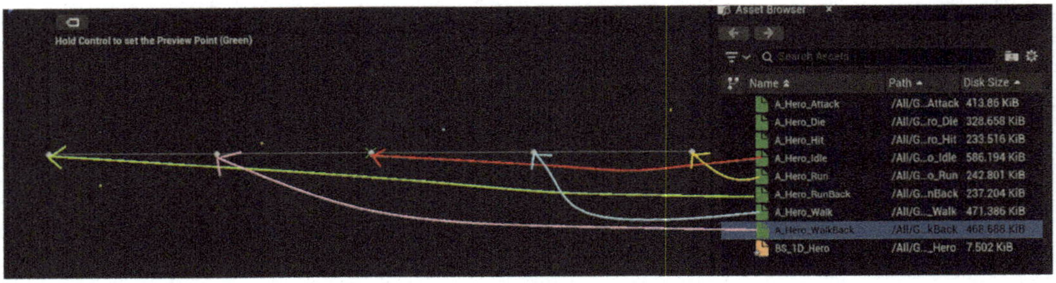

Figure 4.37 - Dragging all 5 animations along the Blend1D_Speed axis

4. Now click **Save** and close the **Blend Space Editor**.

At this point, we have created `BS_1D_Hero`, a new **Blend Space 1D** asset that smoothly blends between five animations: idle, walk/run forward, and walk/run backward. This asset is now ready to be used in our animation system.

In the next section, we will return to `AB_Hero` and learn how to drive this Blend Space from the **Animation Blueprint**, so the character's movement speed automatically controls the blended animation during gameplay.

Updating Animation Blueprint

Building on the Blend Space we just created, the next step is to return to `AB_Hero` and show how to control it from the **Animation Blueprint**. You will learn how to use the character's movement speed to automatically drive animation blending during gameplay.

In this section, we will update the Animation Blueprint to use Blend Space for controlling the character's movement animations. Follow these steps:

1. Return to our Hero's **Animation Blueprint**, `AB_Hero`, and reopen the **Hero State Machine** we created earlier.
   Previously, we added a simple `A_Hero_Idle` state as the default animation. Since we now have a Blend Space that handles idle, walking, and running in both directions, we no longer need that single idle state.

2. Let's first delete the existing `A_Hero_Idle` state. Next, right-click to create a new state and name it: `Locomotion`.

3. Connect the **Entry** node to this new **Locomotion** state. This ensures the character starts in the **Locomotion** state when gameplay begins.

4. Now, double-click the **Locomotion** state to open it. Inside, you will also see an **Output Animation Pose** node. At the moment, nothing is connected to it.

5. Look for **Asset Browser** (typically right next to the **Animation Preview Editor**), locate `BS_1D_Hero`, and drag it into the graph.
6. Then connect the output pin of `BS_1D_Hero` to the **Output Animation Pose** node (see *Figure 4.38*).

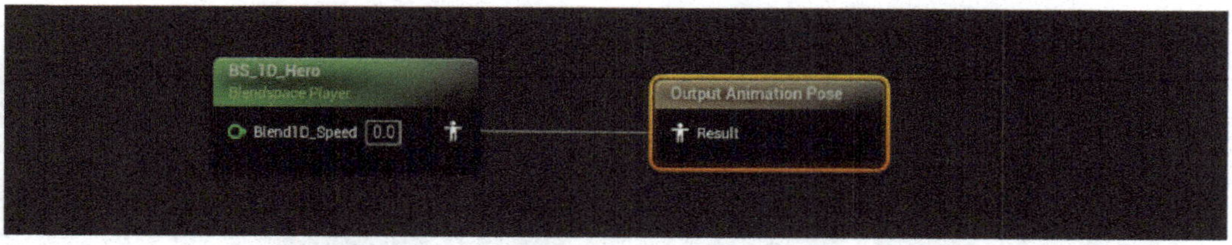

Figure 4.38 - Creating the BS_1D_Hero Blend Space for the Hero's locomotion animations

At this stage, the Blend Space is connected. But it still needs a speed parameter to drive the blending. In the next step, we will create and update a variable inside the Hero's **Animation Blueprint** to control the **Blend Space 1D** dynamically during gameplay.

And you can try to tweak the value of **Blend1D_Speed** between `-1` and `1` and observe how the Hero character blends/changes animations.

To drive the Blend Space dynamically, we need to create a variable that controls the animation speed. For this, we will create a variable inside the **Animation Blueprint**.

7. In the **Animation Blueprint Editor**, variables are created from the **My Blueprint** panel. In the default Unreal Editor layout, this panel is located on the left side of the editor, often near the bottom-left area. Under the **Variables** section, click the **+** button to add a new variable. Configure it with the following settings:
   - **Name**: **Speed**
   - **Type**: **Float**
8. Next, click the **closed eye** icon next to the variable name to make it **public** (which means Instance Editable, see *Figure 4.39*). This allows the variable to be accessed or modified by other Blueprints if necessary.

Figure 4.39 - Adding a new variable, Speed

9. After creating the variable, click **Compile** to apply the changes. This `Speed` variable will later be connected to the input parameter of **Blend Space 1D**, allowing the animation to respond dynamically to the character's movement speed during gameplay.

Now we can use this **Speed** variable to drive the **Blend Space 1D**.

10. Inside the **Locomotion** state graph, drag the **Speed** variable from the **Variables** panel into the graph. Choose **Get Speed** when prompted (see *Figure 4.40*).
11. Connect the **Speed** output pin to the **Blend1D_Speed** input on the **BS_1D_Hero** node.
12. Click **Compile** to apply the changes.

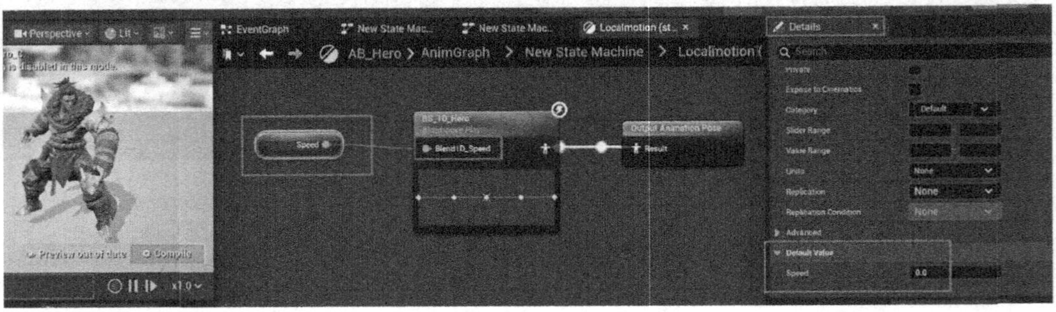

Figure 4.40 - Connecting Speed variable to BS_1D_Hero's Blend1D_Speed axis

13. Next, select the `Speed` variable in the **Variables** panel. In the **Details** panel, locate the **Default Value** section. The default value is currently set to `0`, which corresponds to the *Idle* animation.
14. You can temporarily change this value (for example, to `1`, `0.5`, or `-1`) to preview how the **Blend Space 1D** responds:
    - **0**: Idle
    - **Positive values**: Forward movement blending
    - **Negative values**: Backward movement blending

The **Speed** variable will control the Hero's locomotion Blend Space. When **Speed** is 0, the Hero will use the idle animation. As the value increases or decreases, the Blend Space will blend toward the walking or running animations.

In this chapter, we will use **Speed** to prepare and test the animation setup. In the next chapter, after we add player input and movement, we will update **Speed** from the Hero's actual movement, so the animation changes automatically during gameplay.

The default value allows you to preview the blended animation directly inside the **Animation Blueprint Editor**.

Adding animation states

At this point, the Hero character can move smoothly using the Locomotion Blend Space. However, movement is only part of a complete character animation system.

What about other actions, such as attacking or reacting to being hit? These events can occur at any time, whether the character is idle or running. Our animation system must be able to handle these dynamic situations.

As introduced earlier, a State Machine controls how animations transition between different states based on gameplay conditions. In this section, we will expand the current setup by adding more animation states and defining the conditions that control transitions between them.

In our **Animation Blueprint** (`AB_Hero`), we have already created a simple State Machine.

Based on our planning in *Figure 4.23*, let's think through how our animation transitions should behave:

- The player may trigger an **Attack** while the character is in the **Locomotion** state (idle, walking, or running).
- After the animation of the **Attack** finishes, the character should return to **Locomotion** automatically.
- The same logic applies to a **Hit** reaction animation.
- The character may also enter a death (**Die**) state, which typically should not transition back to other states.

We already have the **Locomotion** state in place. Now we need to add the remaining animation states to the existing State Machine inside `AB_Hero`. Follow these steps:

1. Open the **Hero State Machine** again.
2. From the **Asset Browser**, drag the `A_Hero_Attack`, `A_Hero_Hit`, and `A_Hero_Die` animation assets into the State Machine graph (see *Figure 4.41*). Each dragged animation will automatically create a new state node:
3. Click on the border of the Locomotion state. As the border becomes highlighted, drag the mouse to `A_Hero_Attack`. This will create a transition from the Locomotion state to the `A_Hero_Attack` state.

   You should see a **round-shaped two-way arrow** symbol on the side of the transition line. This defines the rule to activate the transition. We will assign the transition rule later; now we just create the transition and leave the rule unspecified.
4. Now you can add transitions based on our planning in *Figure 4.23*. The resulting animation states and transitions should be like the following *Figure 4.41*:

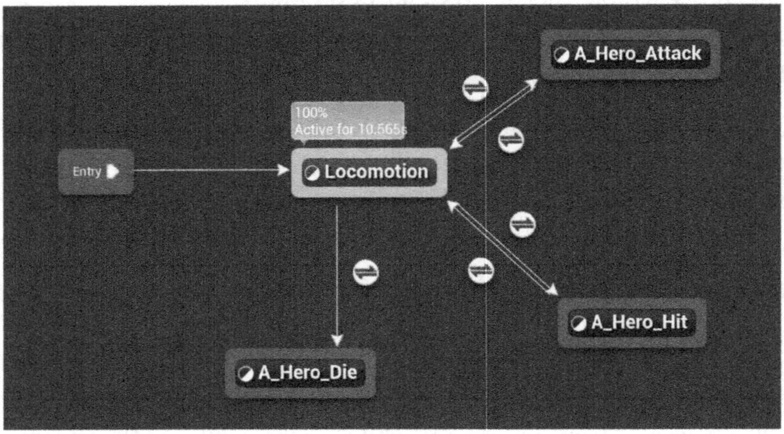

Figure 4.41 - Adding attack, hit, and die animations

Remember to compile after you finish setting all animations and transitions. You might see some warnings about there being no rule for transitions; that's fine for now.

After adding all the animation states, we need a way to determine which state should be activated during gameplay. To accomplish this, we can create a variable that stores the currently selected animation state. There are multiple ways to represent this:

- A **String variable** that stores the animation name (for example, `A_Hero_Attack`)
- An **Integer variable** that assigns a unique ID to each animation state

Using integers is generally more efficient and easier to manage in transition rules. For example, we could define a simple mapping like this:

Animation state	Unique integer ID
Locomotion (idle/walking/running)	0
`A_Hero_Attack` (attack)	1
`A_Hero_Hit` (hit reaction)	2
`A_Hero_Die` (dead)	3

Table 4.6 - Animation state IDs used by AB_Hero

In this case, we only need to use an integer variable to store the current animation state. Let's create a new integer variable `AnimState` in the same Blueprint on the left side panel (see *Figure 4.42*):

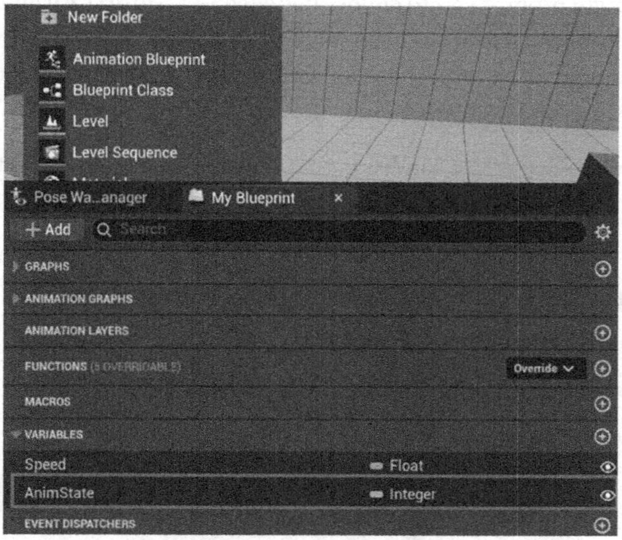

Figure 4.42 - Adding AnimState variable

Now that all animation states have been created, we can begin defining the transition conditions between them. Here is a step-by-step guide to achieve this:

1. Let's first configure the transition from **Locomotion** (for example, value 0) to `Attack` (value 1).
2. In the State Machine graph, double-click the **small circular** icon on the transition arrow between **Locomotion** and **Attack**. This will open the **Transition Rule** graph.
3. Inside the **Transition Rule** graph, drag the **AnimState** variable from the **Variables** panel into the graph and select **Get AnimState**, as shown in *Figure 4.43*:

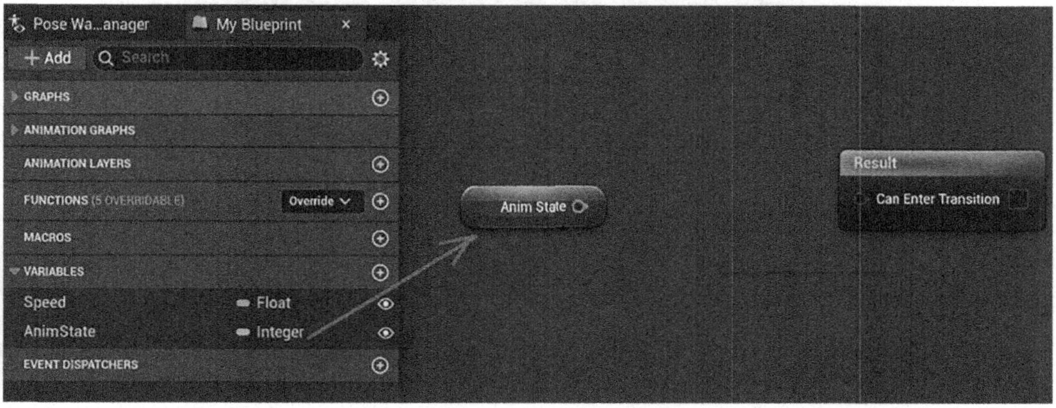

Figure 4.43 - Creating a Get AnimState node

Note that it will prompt you to choose between **Get AnimState** and **Set AnimState**. Since we only need to read the current value of **AnimState** to determine whether the transition should occur, we select **Get AnimState**. Using **Get** allows us to evaluate the variable without modifying it.

Now we need to define the condition that determines whether it is the correct moment to switch to `A_Hero_Attack`. Since we assigned the **Attack** state an ID value of `1`, we will check whether the value of **AnimState** is equal to 1.

4. Inside the **Transition Rule** graph, follow these steps (see *Figure 4.44*):
   1. Drag from the output pin of **Get AnimState**.
   2. In the search window, type == (which means *Equal To*).
   3. Select the **Equal** node.

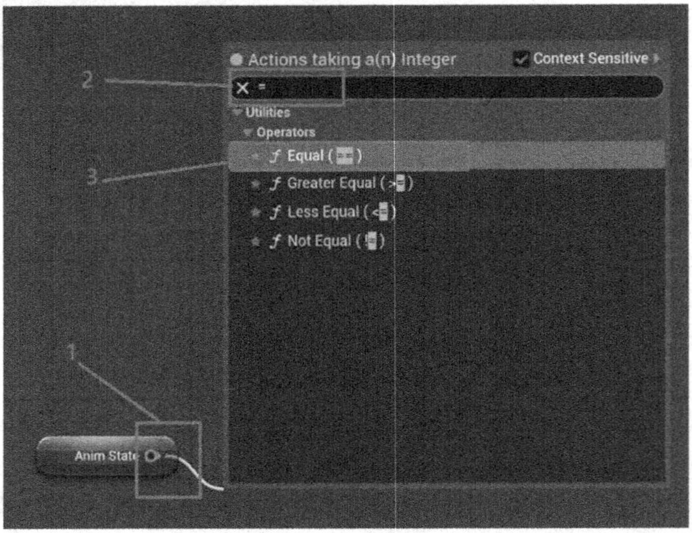

Figure 4.44 - Adding value comparison node

This will create a new value comparison node. Let's set the compared value to `1` (shown in *Figure 4.45*):

Figure 4.45 - Comparing whether AnimState is 1

5. Connect the output of the **Equal** node to the **Result** node. This means the transition from **Locomotion** → **Attack** will only occur when the value of **AnimState** is **1**.
6. After compiling, the State Machine will enter the Attack animation whenever the **AnimState** variable is set to 1.

Also, do you notice the warning sign on the result state in *Figure 4.45*? You need to hit the **Compile** button again, so the Blueprint can be up to date with your latest editing.

Now you can repeat the same process to define rules for the other transitions in the State Machine. As you work, you can click each transition's *rule* button to quickly review which logic has been applied and confirm that every arrow has a valid condition, as shown in *Figure 4.46*:

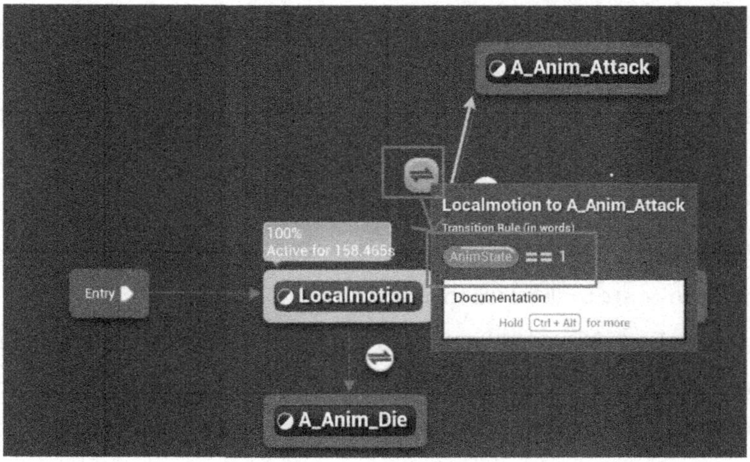

Figure 4.46 - Clicking the yellow icon to check each transition condition

The Hero also needs a transition from Attack back to Locomotion. Let's also add this transition. However, this transition does not happen automatically just because `A_Hero_Attack` reaches the end of the animation. A State Machine transition must have a rule that tells Unreal Engine when it is allowed to move from one state to another.

For now, we will leave the rule unspecified. Later, in *Chapter 5*, we will introduce how to use **Animation Notify** to trigger an event when the Attack animation reaches its end, so we can set the animation back to Locomotion.

Click **Compile**, then save your changes in the Hero's `AB_Hero`. At this point, we have completed the basic animation state structure for the Hero character. The State Machine now includes **Locomotion**, **Attack**, **Hit**, and **Die** states, along with the corresponding transition rules.

The animation logic is now almost structurally complete, but it is not yet driven by gameplay input. The next step is to learn how to assign values to the **AnimState** (and **Speed**) variables from the **Character Blueprint** or gameplay logic script.

> **Note**
>
> If a transition has no rule (or its **Result** is always `False`), the State Machine will never take that transition. So, it's worth double-checking each arrow before moving on.

Controlling Hero animations

We are now ready to work on the Hero character's behavior. This is done in the Hero's Blueprint `BP_Hero`.

Let's open this Blueprint. We want to be able to set the initial Hero animation state. This is basically done in the following steps:

1. Retrieving the animation instance from the mesh of the Hero character
2. Casting the animation instance to the Hero-specific Animation Blueprint, `AB_Hero`
3. Setting **AnimState** to the desired animation ID
4. Connecting the Animation Blueprint of the Hero character to **Event BeginPlay**

This is how we configure `BP_Hero` to set the Hero's initial animation state at startup. We will now explore each of these steps in more detail in the subsequent sections.

Retrieving the animation instance

In `BP_Hero`, go to the **Event Graph**. From the **Components** panel (upper-left side), drag the **Mesh (CharacterMesh0)** component into the graph. This creates a reference to the Hero's Skeletal Mesh, as shown in *Figure 4.47*:

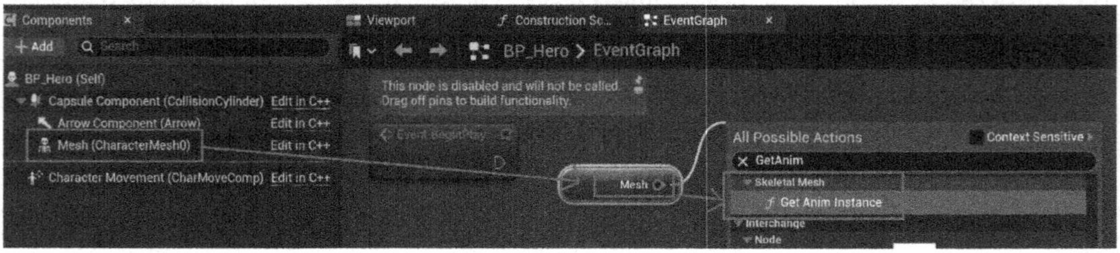

Figure 4.47 - Retrieving animation instance

From the **Mesh** reference node, drag out a connection and search for the `Get Anim Instance` node. This gives us access to the animation instance of the current Hero character.

Casting the Animation Blueprint to AB_Hero

Before BP_Hero can change variables inside AB_Hero, it first needs a reference to the Animation Blueprint instance currently running on the Hero's Mesh component.

The **Get Anim Instance** node returns the animation instance used by the Mesh component. However, this return value is generic. At this point, Blueprint only knows that it is an animation instance; it does not know that it is specifically our AB_Hero Animation Blueprint. Because of that, BP_Hero cannot directly access variables that only exist in AB_Hero, such as AnimState or Speed.

To access those Hero character-specific variables, we use **Cast To AB_Hero** (see *Figure 4.48*). **Casting** tells Blueprint, "Treat this animation instance as AB_Hero." Once the cast succeeds, we can use the **As AB_Hero** output pin to read or update variables inside the Hero's Animation Blueprint.

Follow these steps to get access to AB_Hero from BP_Hero:

1. Open BP_Hero.
2. In the **Components** panel, select the **Mesh** component, then drag it into the **Event Graph** to create a reference to it.
3. Drag from the **Mesh** reference and add a **Get Anim Instance** node.
4. Drag from the **Return Value** of **Get Anim Instance** and add a **Cast To AB_Hero** node.
5. From the **As AB_Hero** output pin, you can now access variables created inside AB_Hero, such as **AnimState** and **Speed**.

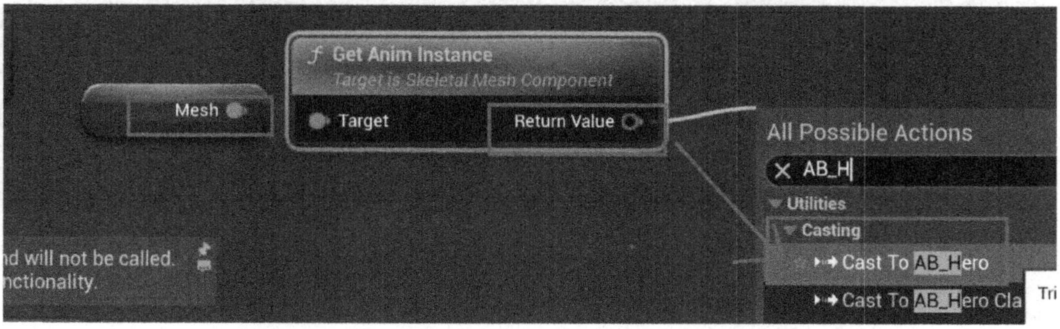

Figure 4.48 - Casting a generic animation instance to AB_Hero

This allows us to access the unique type of Hero's Animation Blueprint: AB_Hero. We will use this way to access unique variables in AB_Hero often in the following chapters.

Setting AnimState to the desired animation ID

With the AB_Hero reference available, drag from the **As AB_Hero** pin and add a **Set AnimState** node (see *Figure 4.49*). Now we can assign the value of **AnimState**; set the value to 0, the ID assigned to the **Locomotion** state:

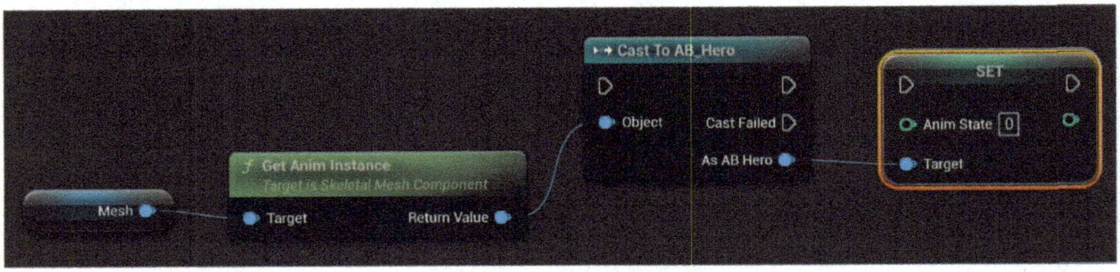

Figure 4.49 - Accessing AnimState variable

Now we can set the desired animation from the Blueprint of the Hero character. Let's do this in the next step.

Connecting the Animation Blueprint of the Hero character to Event BeginPlay

After completing the setup above, we now need to connect this logic to the **Event BeginPlay** event so that the Hero character starts in the Locomotion state when the game begins (see *Figure 4.50*).

Let's connect the **Event BeginPlay** event to the **Cast_To_AB_Hero** node:

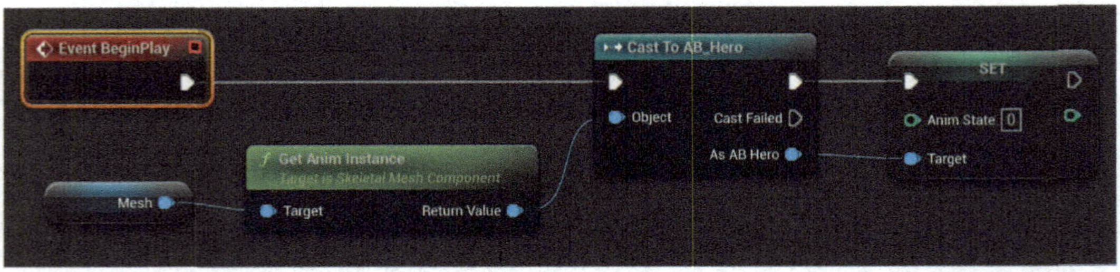

Figure 4.50 - Executing Cast_To_AB_Hero node from BeginPlay event

Save and compile this Blueprint. Now, we are ready to do some quick testing.

Let's drag BP_Hero directly into the game scene and hit the **Play** button. Now you can see our Hero character is loaded and set to the Locomotion state by default, as shown in *Figure 4.51*:

Figure 4.51 - Testing Hero character in play mode

At this stage, seeing only the idle animation is expected. The **Speed** variable still has its default value of **0.0**, and `BS_1D_Hero` uses that value to select `A_Hero_Idle`. We will connect **Speed** to real character movement in the next chapter.

We have a complete basic animation setup for our Hero character. Next, we will learn how to equip our Hero character with a weapon.

Attaching the weapon to the character

Once the `Hero` character (and other characters) is placed in the game scene, it is time to equip the character with items such as weapons, armor, or other accessories. In this section, we will demonstrate how to attach a sword to the Hero character.

Importing the Sword Model

First, we need to import the sword assets. A pre-made sword model is provided in the source assets folder: `Pangaea_Assets/Weapons/Sword/`.

1. Inside Unreal Engine, create a new folder: `Content/Pangaea/Weapons/Sword`.
2. Navigate to this folder and import `Sword.fbx`. When the **Import Content** dialog appears, select **Use Pipeline Defaults** (see *Figure 4.52*) before importing the sword mesh. This applies Unreal Engine's default Static Mesh import pipeline settings for the FBX file:

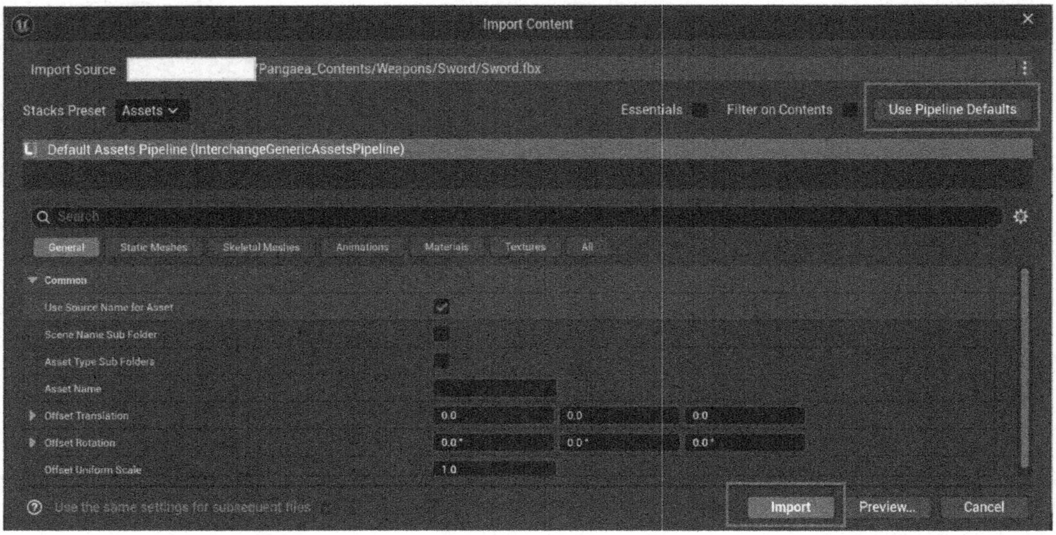

Figure 4.52 - Making sure to select Use Pipeline Defaults for Static Mesh import

3. After selecting **Use Pipeline Defaults**, click **Import**. Unreal Engine should import the sword as a Static Mesh asset in the current folder. Name the file `SM_Sword`.
4. The Sword FBX contains a material `BaphometSword_mat`; however, we can create our own new material in the `Sword` folder and name it `M_Sword`.
5. Also import the four textures provided with the Sword FBX file into the same `Pangaea_Assets/Weapons/Sword/` folder:

Sword texture	**Purpose**
`T_Sword_Albedo`	Diffuse (albedo) texture map
`T_Sword_Normal`	Normal texture map
`T_Sword_Metallic`	Metallic texture map
`T_Sword_Roughness`	Roughness texture map

Table 4.7 - Texture maps used by Sword asset

6. Open this material in the **Material Editor**. Assign the appropriate texture maps (for example, **Base** (Albedo), **Color**, **Normal**, **Metallic**, **Roughness**, etc., depending on the provided textures, as shown in *Figure 4.53*).

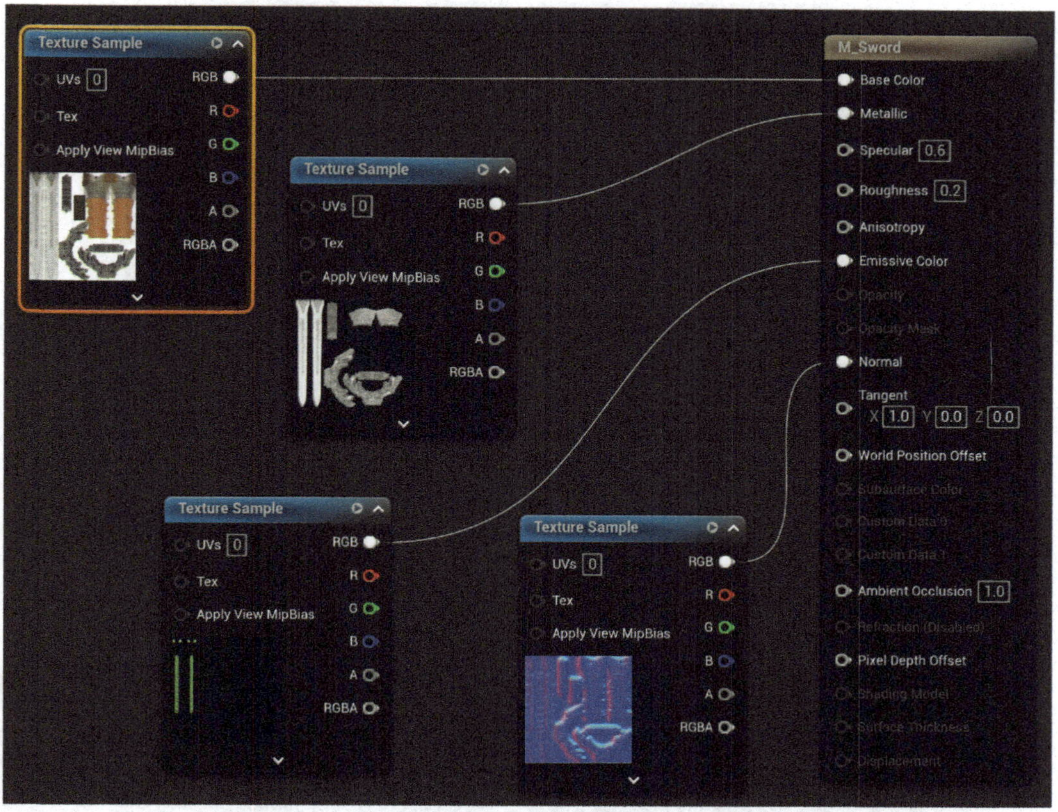

Figure 4.53 - Creating a material for the sword

7. After connecting the textures correctly, save the changes. Don't forget to open the `SM_Sword` model and assign the material we just created. It's the same process as how we assign the correct material to the `Hero` model; refer back to the material-assignment workflow in the *Setting up materials* section.

Now we need to create a Blueprint for the sword. Let's follow these steps:

1. In the **Content Drawer**, navigate to: `Content/Pangaea/Weapons/Sword`.
2. Right-click inside the folder and select **Blueprint Class**. Select **Actor** as the parent class, as shown in *Figure 4.54*:

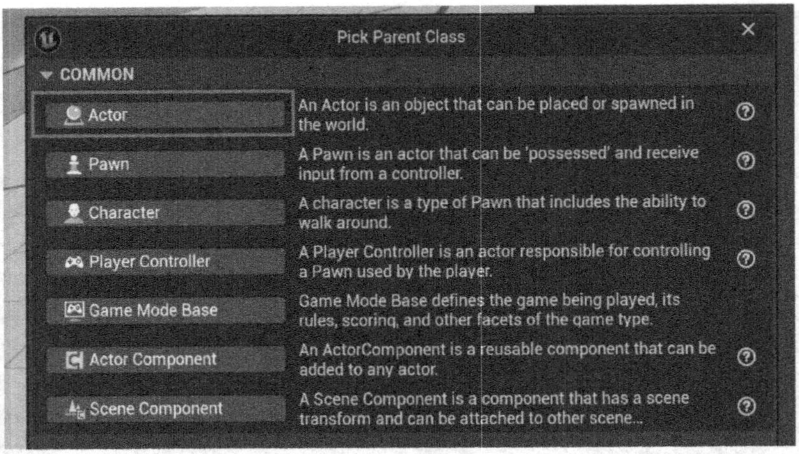

Figure 4.54 - Creating an Actor Blueprint for the sword

3. Name the new Blueprint: `BP_Sword`.
4. Double-click `BP_Sword` to open it in the Blueprint Editor.
5. In the **Components** panel, click **Add** and select **Static Mesh** (See *Figure 4.55*).

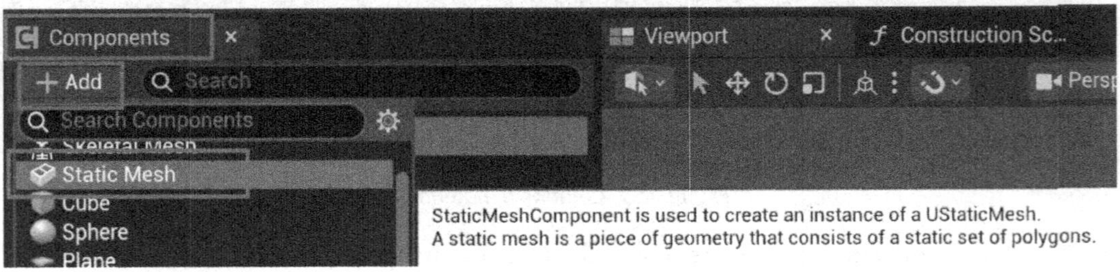

Figure 4.55 - Adding Static Mesh as a new component

6. Rename the new **Static Mesh Component** to: `SwordMesh`. This is the component that will display the sword mesh inside the Blueprint. In the following steps, **SwordMesh** refers to the **Static Mesh Component** inside `BP_Sword`, not the `SM_Sword` asset in the **Content Drawer**.
7. With the **SwordMesh** component selected, go to the **Details** panel. In the **Static Mesh** property, assign `SM_Sword`, as shown in *Figure 4.56*:

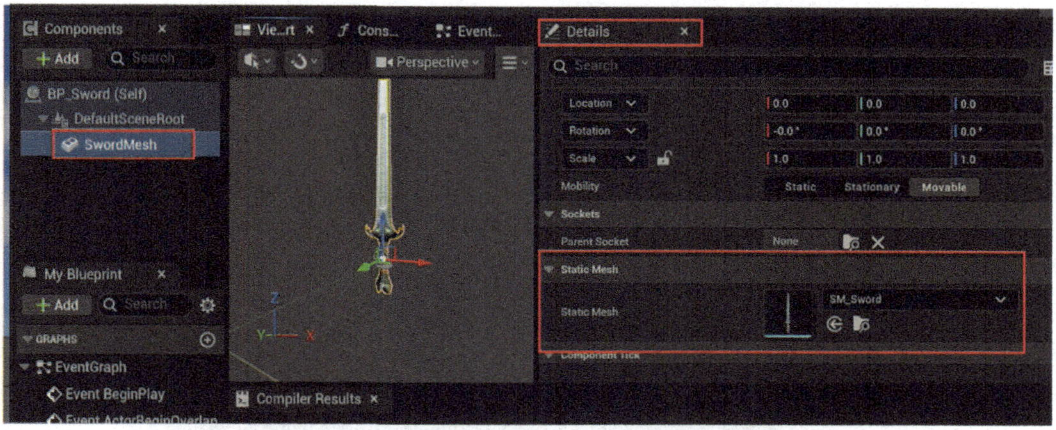

Figure 4.56 - Assigning sword mesh to the Static Mesh field of BP_Sword

We now have a Blueprint that controls the sword mesh. Compile and save `BP_Sword` for later use.

At this point, `BP_Sword` contains a component named `SwordMesh`, and that component displays the imported `SM_Sword` mesh. When we spawn `BP_Sword` later, Unreal Engine will spawn the Actor Blueprint, and the `SwordMesh` component will provide its visible sword model.

Next, we want to attach the sword to the Hero's hand during the startup of the game. Let's switch back to the Hero character's Blueprint, `BP_Hero`, and open it in the full **Blueprint Editor**:

1. In the **Event Graph**, locate **Event BeginPlay**.
2. Drag from the execution pin of **BeginPlay** and add the new node **Spawn Actor from Class** (see *Figure 4.57*):

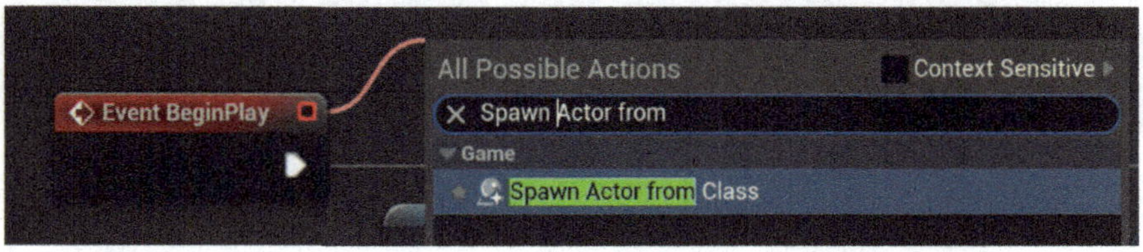

Figure 4.57 - Adding a Spawn Actor from Class node

3. Configure the **Spawn Actor from Class** node with the following settings (see *Figure 4. 58*):
    - **Class: BP_Sword**

- **Collision Handling Override: Always Spawn, Ignore Collision**
- **Transform Scale Method: Multiply Scale With Root Component Scale**

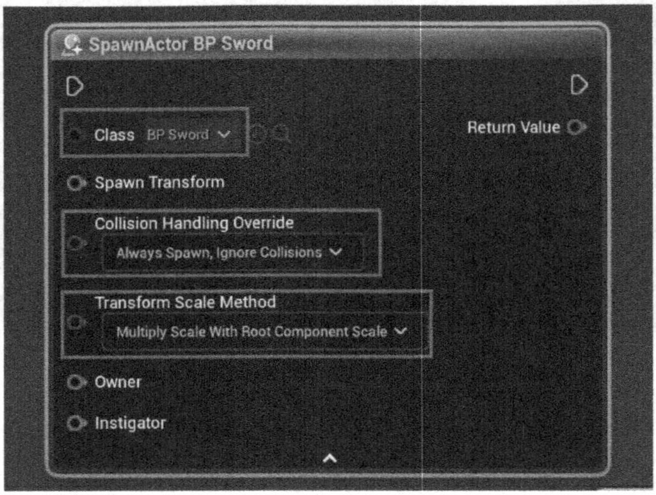

Figure 4.58 - Configuring Spawn Actor from Class with BP_Sword

Now we need to define the **Spawn Transform** for the sword:

1. Drag from the **Spawn Transform** pin on the **Spawn Actor from Class** node and search for: **Get Actor Transform** (see *Figure 4.59*):

Figure 4.59 - Setting up spawn transform

   Once the sword has been spawned, the next step is to attach it to the Hero's hand socket so it follows the character's animations correctly.

2. Drag from the **Exec** output pin of the **SpawnActor BP_Sword** node and search for: **Attach Actor to Component** (see *Figure 4.60*):

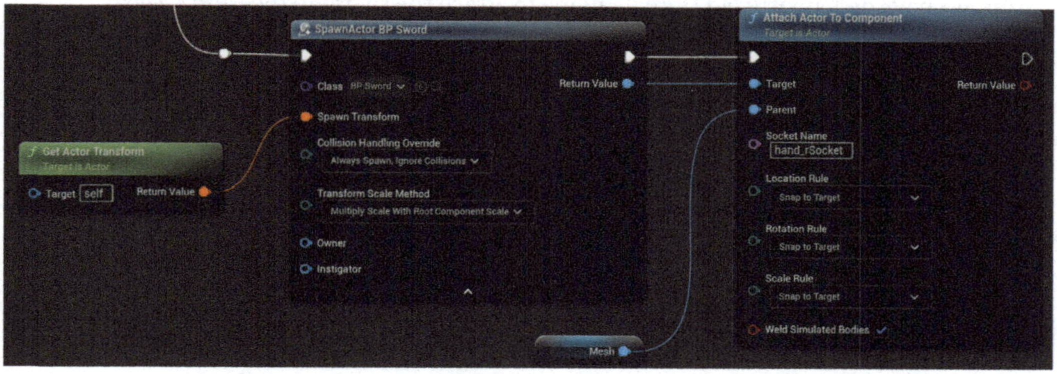

Figure 4.60 - Setting up Attach Actor To Component node

3. Now configure the **Attach Actor To Component** node as follows (see *Figure 4.60*):
   - **Target**: Connect the **Return Value** pin of the **SpawnActor BP Sword** node to the **Target** pin. This is the spawned sword instance.
   - **Parent**: Drag to the Hero's **Mesh (CharacterMesh0)** component.
   - **Socket Name**: Enter the name of the socket (`hand_rSocket`) for our `BP_Sword` to attach. We will create and configure this socket in the next section.
   - **Location, Rotation, Scale Rules:** Set to **Snap to Target**

Figure 4.61 shows the completed Blueprint connections/setup:

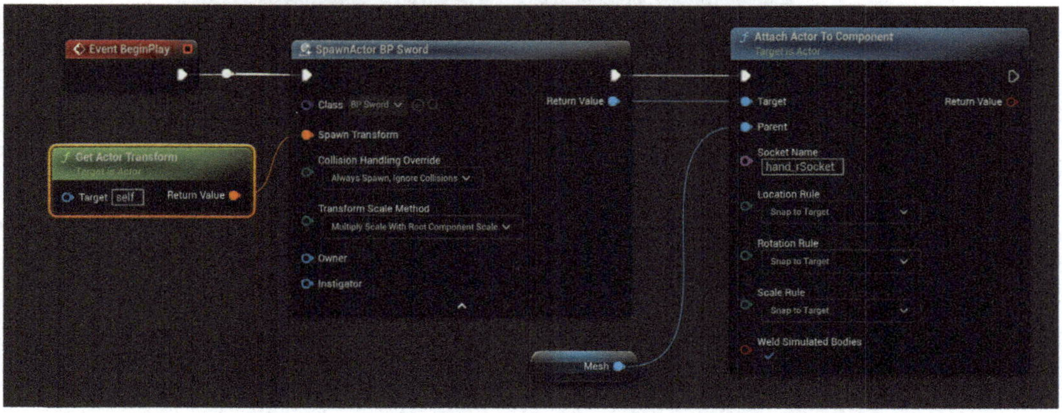

Figure 4.61 - Using Attach Actor to Component to attach SpawnActor BP Sword to Hero Mesh

We are not finished yet.

So far, we have only instructed Unreal Engine to attach the sword to the Hero's **Mesh** component. But we have not specified where on the mesh it should be attached. Should it attach to the left hand? The right hand? The torso?

To correctly attach a weapon to a character's hand, we must use a **Socket**.

A **Socket** is a special attachment point added to a bone in the skeleton. It acts as a connector that allows other Actors (such as weapons) to attach precisely to that bone and follow its animation.

Currently, our Hero skeleton does not include a predefined weapon socket, so we need to create one manually at the palm of the right hand.

1. Open `SK_Hero` asset in **Skeletal Mesh Editor**. In the **Skeleton Tree**, right-click the `hand_r` bone and add a socket on the right-hand palm mesh (see *Figure 4.62*):

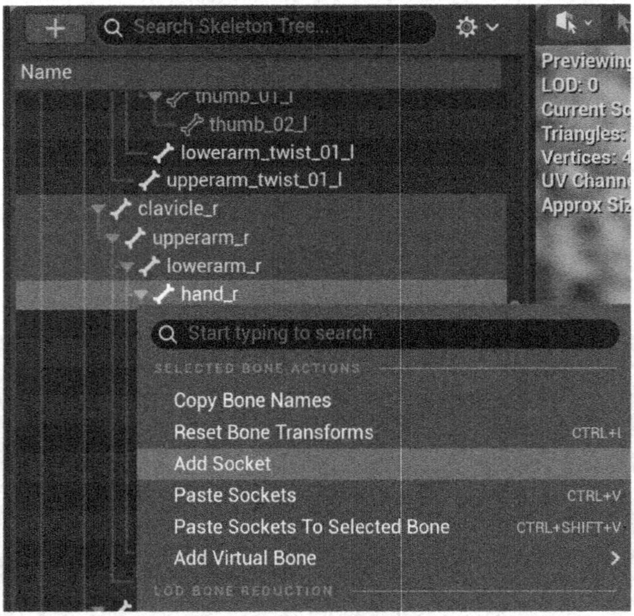

Figure 4.62 - Adding a socket to Hero's palm of right hand

When you add a socket to the `hand_r` bone, Unreal Engine may automatically name it `hand_rSocket`. We will use this exact socket name later when attaching `BP_Sword` to the `Hero`'s hand.

2. The position of the socket is aligned with the palm, but we need to preview if this is the right position. We can temporarily add a preview-only mesh of our sword (see *Figure 4. 63*):

Figure 4.63 - Adding preview-only mesh

The socket is now roughly aligned with the palm bone, but we should verify whether its position and rotation are correct.

A convenient way to test this is by adding a preview-only mesh to the socket. The steps to preview the sword on the socket are:

1. Select/right-click `hand_rSocket` in the **Skeleton Tree** (**1** in *Figure 4.63*).
2. Select **Add Preview Asset** from the context menu (2 in *Figure 4.63*).
3. Select `SM_Sword` from the asset picker (**3** in *Figure 4.63*).

   This will attach the sword as a preview mesh to the socket. The preview mesh is only visible inside the editor and does not affect gameplay. It is used purely for alignment and testing.

4. Now rotate, move, and adjust the socket transform (**Location** and **Rotation**) until the sword fits naturally in the Hero's hand.
5. Take your time to fine-tune (see *Figure 4.64*):
   - The blade direction (should face forward along the character's facing direction).
   - The grip alignment with the palm.
   - Any small positional offsets to prevent clipping through fingers.

6. Once satisfied, click **Save**.

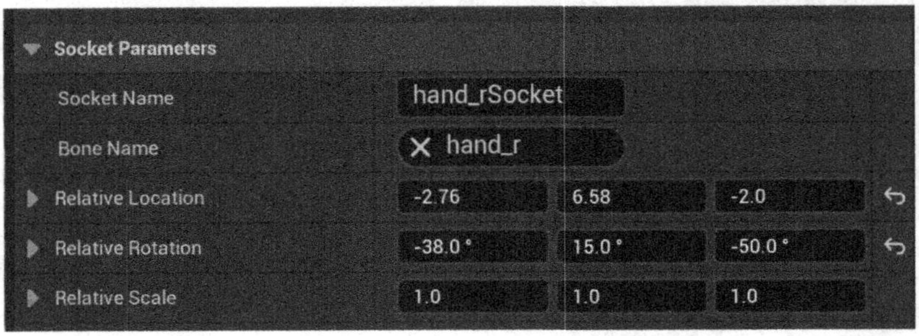

Figure 4.64 - Fine-tuning the socket location, rotation, and scale

Now bring back the `BP_Hero` Blueprint. In the **Attach Actor to Component** node, find the **Socket Name** field and enter `hand_rSocket` on the Hero's Mesh component.

> **Note**
>
> Make sure the spelling matches the socket name exactly; otherwise, the sword may attach to the mesh root or appear in the wrong location.

Also, make sure we set the **Location/Rotation/Scale** rules all to **Snap to Target**.

Before testing the result, let's quickly review the setup:

- `BP_Sword` contains a **Static Mesh Component** named `SwordMesh`
- `SwordMesh` uses the `SM_Sword` Static Mesh asset
- `SK_Hero` has a socket named `hand_rSocket` on the `hand_r` bone
- `BP_Hero` spawns `BP_Sword` from its **Event BeginPlay**
- The spawned `BP_Sword` actor is attached to the `Hero's Mesh` component
- The **Socket Name** field in the attach node is set to `hand_rSocket`

Now click **Play**. When the level starts, `BP_Hero` should spawn `BP_Sword` and attach it to the Hero's right-hand socket. If everything is connected correctly, the Hero should appear in the level holding the sword.

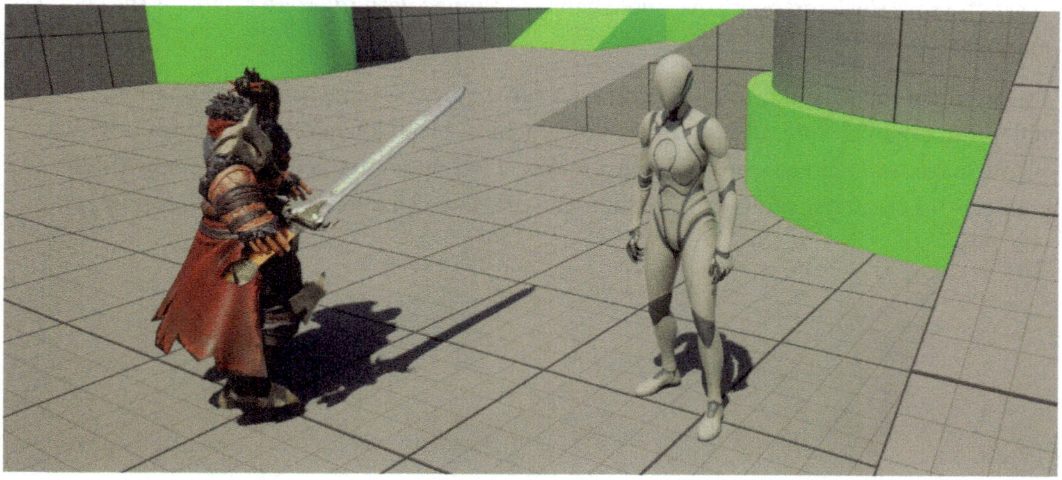

Figure 4.65 - Final testing shows Hero character with sword

Voilà! We have successfully spawned a sword attached to the Hero's right palm.

Summary

In this chapter, you built the Hero character from imported assets and connected several important Unreal Engine character systems together. You began by preparing and importing the Hero's Skeletal Mesh, textures, skeleton, Physics Asset, and animation clips. You then created and assigned materials so the Hero displayed correctly inside the engine.

After the assets were imported, you created `BP_Hero` as the playable Character Blueprint and assigned the Hero Skeletal Mesh to its Mesh component. You also created `AB_Hero`, the Animation Blueprint responsible for controlling the Hero's animation logic.

Inside the Animation Blueprint, you used a State Machine to organize animation behavior into states, such as Locomotion and Attack. A State Machine is useful because it gives animation logic a clear structure: each state represents what the character is doing, and each transition defines when the character is allowed to move from one state to another.

You also created `BS_1D_Hero`, a Blend Space used by the Locomotion state. A Blend Space solves the problem of switching smoothly between related movement animations. Instead of instantly changing from idle to walking or running, the Blend Space uses a value such as Speed to blend between those animations naturally.

Finally, you attached a sword to the Hero by creating a socket on the Hero's right-hand bone. A socket solves the problem of attaching gameplay objects to a moving skeleton. Because the socket follows the hand bone, the sword can stay aligned with the Hero's hand as the character animates.

By the end of this chapter, the Hero character can display correctly, use an Animation Blueprint, organize animations with a State Machine, blend locomotion animations with a Blend Space, and hold a sword through a socket attachment. In the next chapter, we will connect this character setup to player input so the Hero can move and respond to gameplay controls.

5

Handling Player Input

In this chapter, we will learn how to create interactive and responsive gameplay by configuring Unreal Engine's input system. The **input system** is responsible for receiving hardware input, such as keyboard keys, mouse movement, and gamepad buttons, then translating those signals into gameplay actions that the game can respond to. Instead of writing gameplay logic directly for each physical button, Unreal Engine allows us to define abstract input actions, such as moving, looking, or attacking, and map different devices to those actions.

We will begin by looking at how hardware input flows from the player's device into Unreal Engine. Then, we will use the **Enhanced Input system** to create **Input Action assets** and an **Input Mapping Context** for our Hero character. After that, we will connect those mappings to a Player Controller and route the input events into the character Blueprint so the player can move, rotate the camera, and trigger an attack.

The chapter also introduces Game Mode setup, which tells Unreal Engine which playable character and Player Controller should be used when the level starts. After working through this chapter, our *Pangaea* project will have a working player control setup that connects keyboard, mouse, and Blueprint gameplay logic into a playable character experience.

Player input is the bridge between the player and the game world. Up to this point, we have been preparing the character, assets, and basic project structure. Now we need to make the game respond to the player's commands. By learning how Unreal Engine receives input, maps it to gameplay actions, and routes it into Blueprints, you will understand the process used to turn a character from a placed asset into a playable Hero. This input foundation will also support later gameplay systems, such as attacking, interacting with objects, completing objectives, and responding to enemy AI.

Therefore, in this chapter, we'll cover the following topics:

- Understanding hardware input
- Setting up Input Actions and Input Mapping
- Working with the Enhanced Input system
- Handling and processing player input
- Configuring Input for your own game

By the end of this chapter, you will understand how Unreal Engine's input system manages player interaction. You will be able to create Input Action assets, map hardware controls to gameplay actions, add an Input Mapping Context to the local player, and handle input events inside Blueprints. You will also understand how Game Mode connects the level to the correct playable character and Player Controller.

Technical requirements

The sample project for this chapter is available for download from the book's GitHub repository and branch:

- `Chapter05-Start` **branch**: The game project to begin learning this chapter.
- `Chapter05` **branch**: The completed game project for this chapter. The Hero character is the player-controlled character.

This chapter assumes you have completed *Chapter 4* and followed the steps to create the *Pangaea* project and the Hero character. After opening the project, navigate to `Content/ThirdPerson/Maps/ThirdPersonMap` and open that level before beginning the exercises in this chapter. This will be the working level used throughout.

You can download the example project and code files for this book by following the instructions in the *Download the example code/resource files* section in the *Preface* of this book.

This chapter's code/resource files are included in the downloadable code/resource bundle.

Understanding hardware input

In a video game, **hardware input** refers to signals coming from devices such as keyboards, mice, game controllers, touch screens, or VR controllers. The game engine must detect these signals, interpret them, and convert them into meaningful gameplay. The typical input handling pipeline works as shown in *Figure 5.1*:

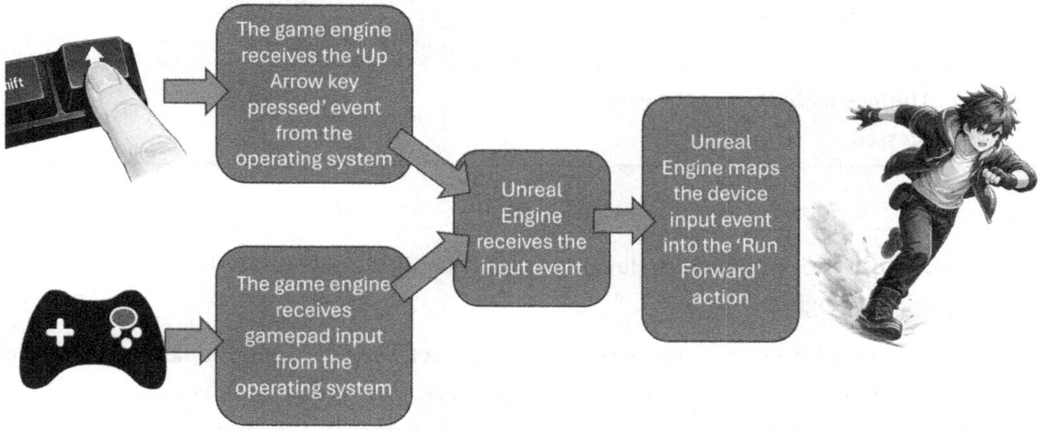

Figure 5.1 - Mapping different input device events into the same video game action (AI-assisted illustration, edited by the author)

Now, let's understand the preceding figure step by step:

- **Hardware device receives event(s)**: When a player presses a key, moves a joystick, or clicks a mouse/gamepad button, the hardware sends signals to the operating system.
- **The operating system processes the input event**: The OS converts the raw electrical signals into standardized input events, such as an *Up Arrow* key press or a forward-control button press on a gamepad.
- **Unreal Engine receives the input event**: The game engine polls or listens to these input events every frame. Many engines use an input system that collects the current input state from the OS.
- **Mapping input to gameplay actions:** Instead of responding directly to individual hardware buttons, modern games translate those inputs into abstract gameplay intentions, such as moving forward, jumping, or attacking. In Unreal Engine's Enhanced Input system, these intentions are represented by assets called Input Actions. We will create and configure these assets later in the chapter. For now, *Table 5.1* illustrates how different hardware inputs can represent the same general Run Forward action:

Input device event	**Action (defined by a developer like you)**
The *up arrow* key on the keyboard is pressed	Run forward

Input device event	Action (defined by a developer like you)
The *forward* button on the gamepad is pressed	Run forward

Table 5.1 - Mapping multiple hardware inputs to the same gameplay action

This abstraction allows developers to support multiple devices without rewriting gameplay logic.

- **The gameplay system reacts to the player's action**: After an input has been mapped to a gameplay action, the relevant gameplay system responds to it. For example, the character Blueprint can move the character when it receives a movement action, the camera system can rotate the view when it receives a look action, and the animation system can play an attack animation when it receives an attack action. This is the point where the player's physical input produces a visible result in the game.

In Unreal Engine, input handling is built around a flexible input mapping system that separates hardware input from gameplay behavior. In the rest of the chapter, we will walk through how to set up input actions, map them to controls, and connect them to gameplay.

Setting up Input Actions and Input Mapping

In UE5, input setup is usually handled through the Enhanced Input system. **Enhanced Input** is Unreal Engine's modern input framework for defining player controls in a flexible and reusable way. Instead of writing separate logic for each keyboard key, mouse button, or gamepad input, **Enhanced Input** lets us define gameplay actions first, then map different hardware input to those actions. This makes it easier to support multiple control schemes, remapping, and more complex input behavior later in the project.

Understanding how actions and mapping contexts work

The Enhanced Input system is built around two main concepts:

- **Input Action**, which represents a gameplay intent such as *jumping*, *moving*, or *looking*
- **Input Mapping Context**, which defines which hardware inputs, such as keyboard keys or gamepad sticks, are bound to those actions

In short, an Input Action defines *what* the player wants to do, while an Input Mapping Context defines *which hardware input* performs that action. For example, we can create a new input action `Action_Move` to represent the intent to move the character, while the mapping context connects that action to keys such as *W*, *A*, *S*, *D*, and the arrow keys.

Once these are created, the Input Mapping Context is added to the local player so Unreal Engine knows which controls are currently active. The Input Actions are then handled in the character or controller Blueprint, where they can call movement functions, rotate the camera, play attack animations, or trigger other gameplay responses.

Because **Enhanced Input** is UE5's standard input workflow, you should make sure the **Enhanced Input** plugin is enabled in the Unreal Editor's **All Plugins** (choose **Edit | Plugins** from the main menu to open the **Plugins** window) settings, as shown in *Figure 5.2*:

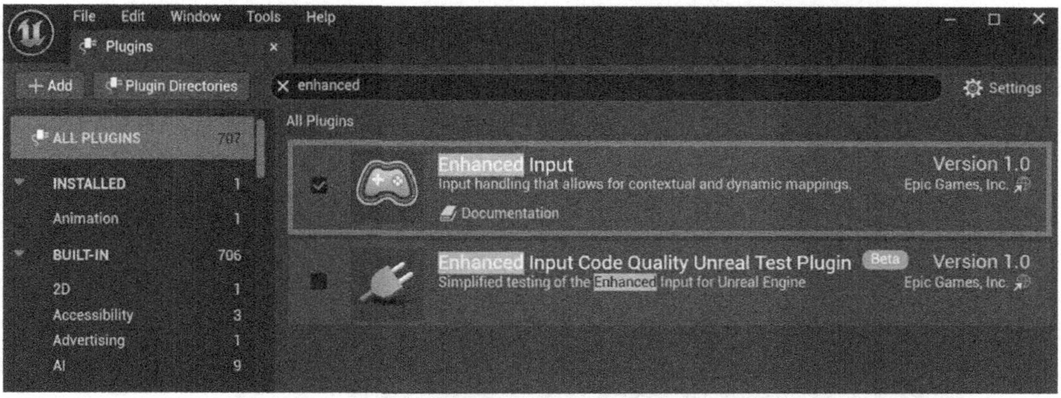

Figure 5.2 - Making sure the Enhanced Input plugin is enabled

We will start by creating the Input Action assets first, because these assets define the gameplay commands that the rest of the input setup will use.

Creating Input Action assets

As explained in the previous section, an Input Action represents a player's intent, such as jumping or crouching, and serves as the element that your gameplay code or Blueprint will bind to. We need to create an **Input Action asset** for each gameplay behavior we want to implement.

When creating an Input Action, make sure to set its **Value Type** based on the type of data it is expected to provide, as shown in *Table 5.2*:

Data type	**Explanation**
`Bool`	Used for simple pressed/released actions like jump, attack
`Axis1D`	Used for one-dimensional values like throttle or zoom

Data type	Explanation
Axis2D	Used for movement or camera look

Table 5.2 - Common Input Action Value Types

We want to create an individual Input Action asset for each gameplay behavior we want to support. Let's first create a folder structure to hold these input-related assets.

Navigate to `Content/Pangaea/` and create a child folder named `Input`. We will group all input-related settings and assets here. Now we can create the `Actions` subfolder under `Content/Pangaea/Input/` folder. We will store all Input Action assets here. Right-click to add a new **Input Action**, as shown in *Figure 5.3*:

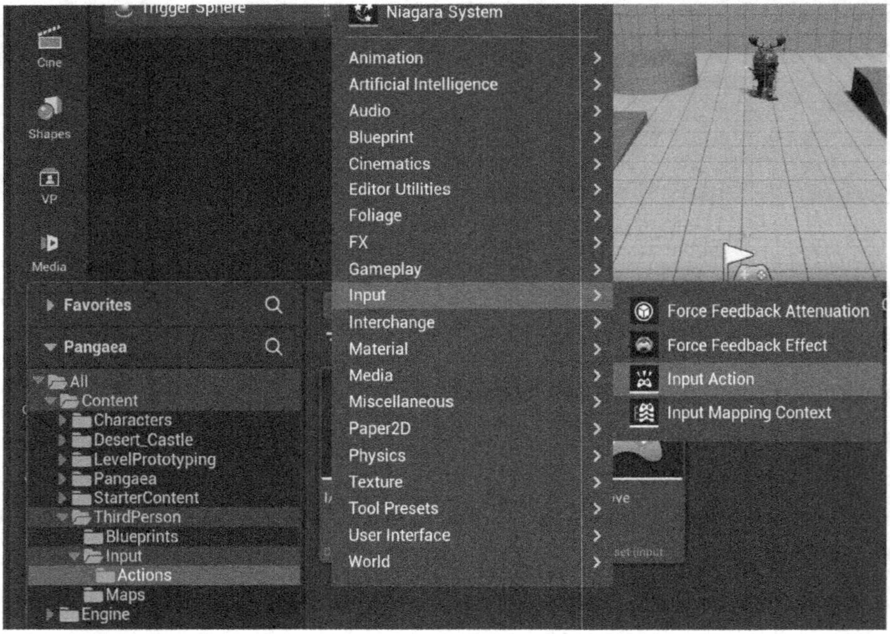

Figure 5.3 - Creating action from the Input submenu

The first action we will create is the character's movement action. Create a new **Input Action** named `Action_Move`. Then open the newly created asset and set its **Value Type** to **Axis2D**, as shown in *Figure 5.4*:

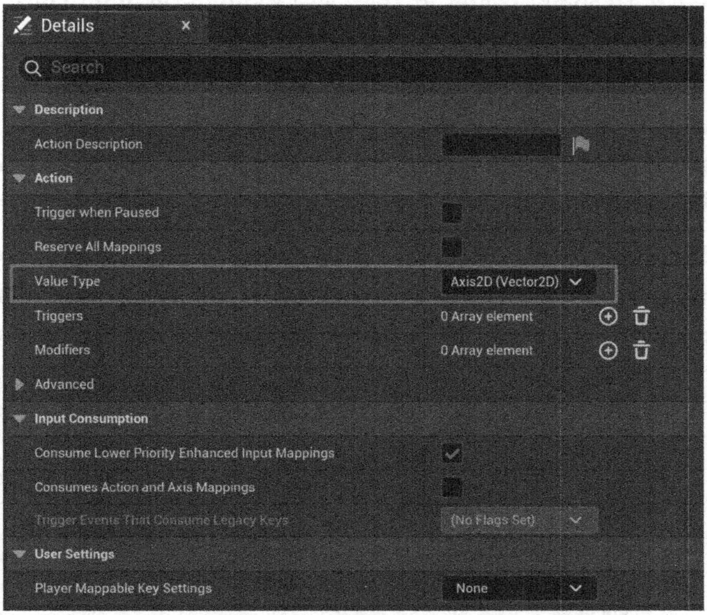

Figure 5.4 - Setting the Value Type of move action to Axis2D

Save your changes before closing the asset. Next, follow the same steps to create another Input Action named `Action_Hero_Look`, and set its **Value Type** to **Axis2D** as well.

The last action to create is `Action_Attack`. For this one, set the **Value Type** to **Bool**, which represents a true/false state. This is suitable for handling whether the attack input is currently active.

With these Input Action assets in place, we now have everything needed to create an Input Mapping Context and connect these actions.

Working with the Enhanced Input system

Creating Input Action assets alone is not enough. Now we need to create an Input Mapping Context. This asset contains the actual hardware bindings for your input setup.

The Enhanced Input system also supports *modifiers* and *triggers*. A **modifier** changes the input value before it reaches the gameplay logic. For example, it can reverse a value or move it from one axis to another. A **trigger** controls when an input action should fire, such as when a button is pressed, held, or released. Together, these features make Enhanced Input flexible enough to support more complex input behavior.

You must also add the mapping context to the player's **Enhanced Input Local Player Subsystem** later. Since mapping contexts can be added or removed at runtime, they determine which actions the player can currently use.

Now we will create the Input Mapping Context asset. This asset will hold all of the hardware bindings for our Hero character, including the attack button, movement keys, and camera look input. Follow these steps:

1. In the **Content Browser**, navigate to the `Content/Pangaea/Input folder`. Right-click in an empty area of the folder to open the context menu. Select **Input | Input Mapping Context**, as shown in *Figure 5.5*. Name the new asset `Pangaea_Input_Map`.

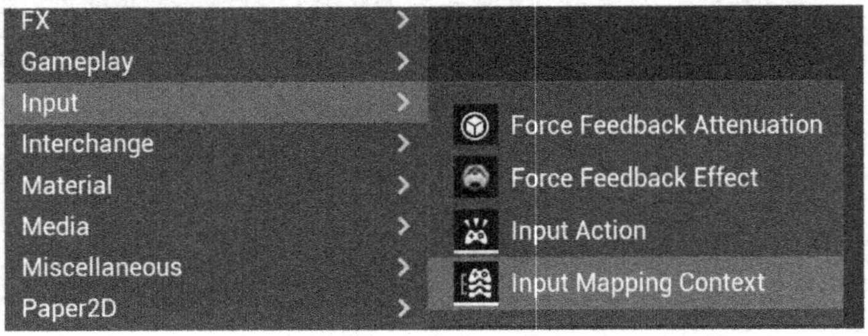

Figure 5.5 - Creating a new Input Mapping Context

2. Open `Pangaea_Input_Map`. In the **Details** panel, find the **Mappings** section. Click the **Add** button beside **Mappings** to create a new mapping entry. For each entry, use the **Input Action** dropdown to select one of the Input Action assets we created earlier, such as `Action_Attack`, `Action_Move`, or `Action_Hero_Look`, as shown in *Figure 5.6*:

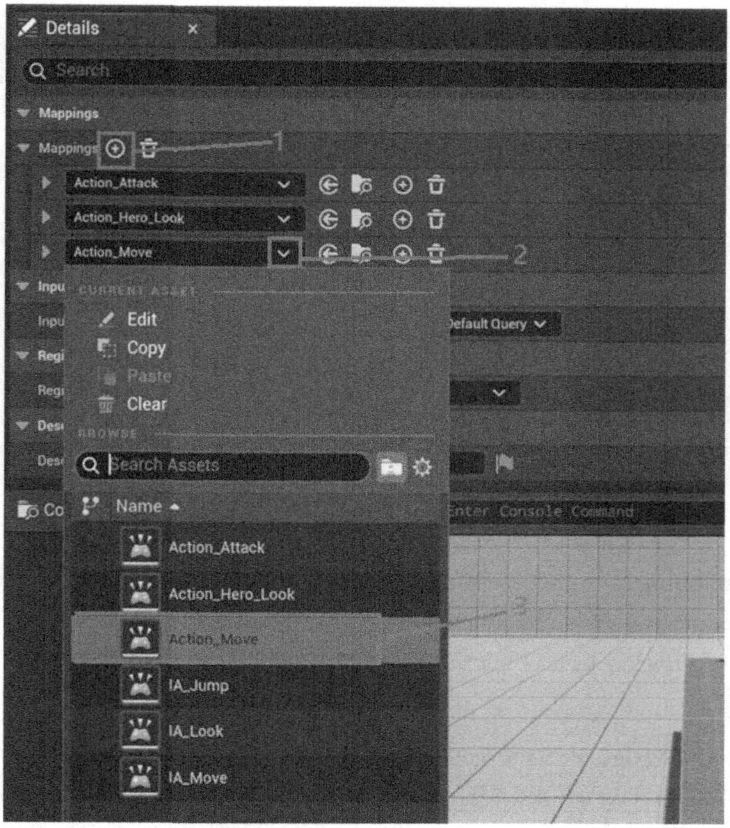

Figure 5.6 - Adding actions into the Mapping Context

3. Now we can assign actual mouse and keyboard input to these actions. Start with `Action_Attack` (**1** in *Figure 5.7*). In its mapping entry, set the input to **Left Mouse Button** (**2**), then expand the **Triggers** section (**3**) and add a trigger set to **Down** (**4**). This means the attack action will be triggered when the left mouse button is pressed down:

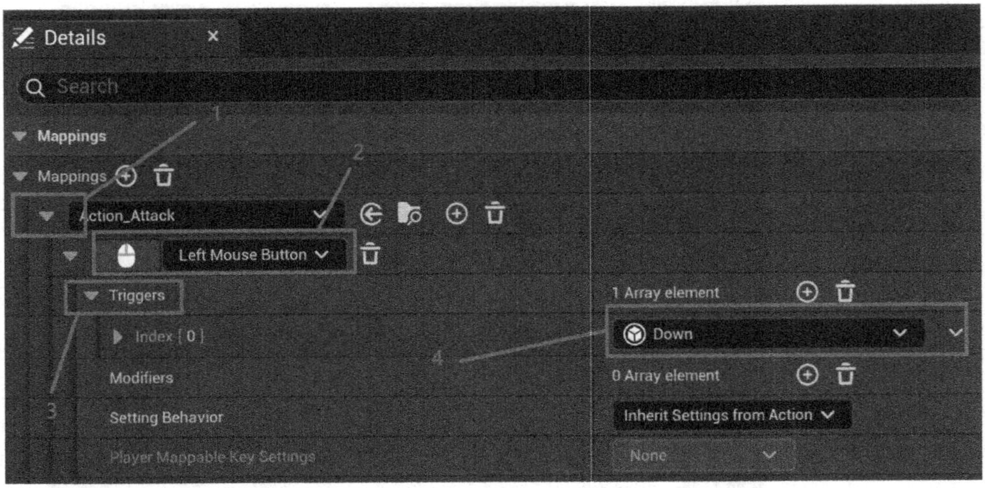

Figure 5.7 - Setting attack input with the left mouse button down

The next mapping to configure is `Action_Move`. Because `Action_Move` uses the **Axis2D** value type, it produces a two-dimensional input value. The *X* axis represents left and right movement, while the *Y* axis represents forward and backward movement.

> **Note**
>
> When setting up *WASD* movement with the Enhanced Input system, a common approach is to use one **Axis2D** Input Action instead of creating separate actions for each direction. This allows the movement Blueprint to read one movement vector and use it to move the character.

To support both *WASD* and arrow-key movement, we will create eight separate key mappings: *W*, *A*, *S*, *D*, *Up*, *Down*, *Left*, and *Right*, as shown in *Figure 5.8*. Each key contributes a directional value to the same `Action_Move` input.

The *D* key and the *Right Arrow* key should produce positive *X* movement. The *A* key and *Left Arrow* key should produce negative *X* movement, so these mappings use the Negate modifier. The **Negate modifier** reverses the input value. For example, a normal value of 1 becomes -1, which allows the same movement action to represent movement in the opposite direction.

The *W* key and *Up Arrow* key should produce positive *Y* movement. Since keyboard keys normally provide a single one-dimensional value, we use the **Swizzle Input Axis Values modifier** to move that value into the *Y* axis of the **Axis2D** input. The *S* key and the *Down Arrow* key also use Swizzle, but they additionally use Negate, so they produce negative *Y* movement.

Together, these modifiers convert individual key presses into directional values on a 2D movement axis. This allows the character movement logic to read one `Action_Move` value instead of checking each movement key separately.

Figure 5.8 - Creating all keyboard mappings

Before we configure each key, it is helpful to understand the purpose of these mappings. `Action_Move` uses an **Axis2D** value, so Unreal Engine expects movement input as a two-dimensional direction: *one axis for left and right movement, and another axis for forward and backward movement.*

However, each keyboard key only sends a simple pressed value. The following steps show how to convert those individual key presses into directional values on a 2D movement axis, so the same `Action_Move` input can correctly drive character movement in all four directions:

1. Start with the *W* key, which moves the character forward. Add a mapping for *W*, then add the **Swizzle Input Axis Values** modifier and set its order to **YXZ**, as shown in *Figure 5.9*. A keyboard key initially supplies its value on the *X* axis. The **YXZ order** swaps the *X* and *Y* values, moving the key's value to the *Y* axis used for forward and backward movement.
   A keyboard key produces a one-dimensional value on the *X* axis by default. However, `Action_Move` uses a two-dimensional value in which *X* represents left and right movement, while *Y* represents forward and backward movement. The **YXZ** swizzle order exchanges the *X* and *Y* components, placing the key's value on the *Y* axis. Therefore, pressing *W* produces ($X = 0, Y = 1$), which represents forward movement. The *Z* component is irrelevant for this two-dimensional input.

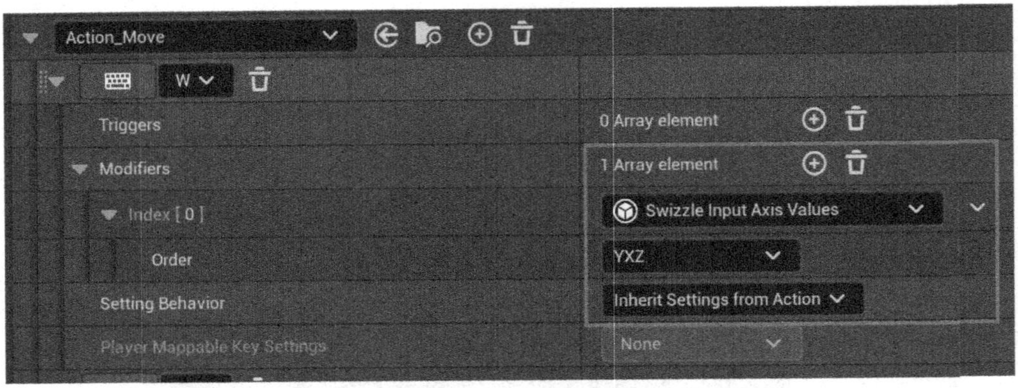

Figure 5.9 - Using Swizzle Input Axis Values to place the key value on the 2D movement axis

2. Next, set up the *S* key, which moves the character backward. Add the **Swizzle Input Axis Values** modifier and set its order to **YXZ**, then add the **Negate** modifier, as shown in *Figure 5.10*. Swizzle places the value on the *Y* axis, and **Negate** changes it to the opposite direction:

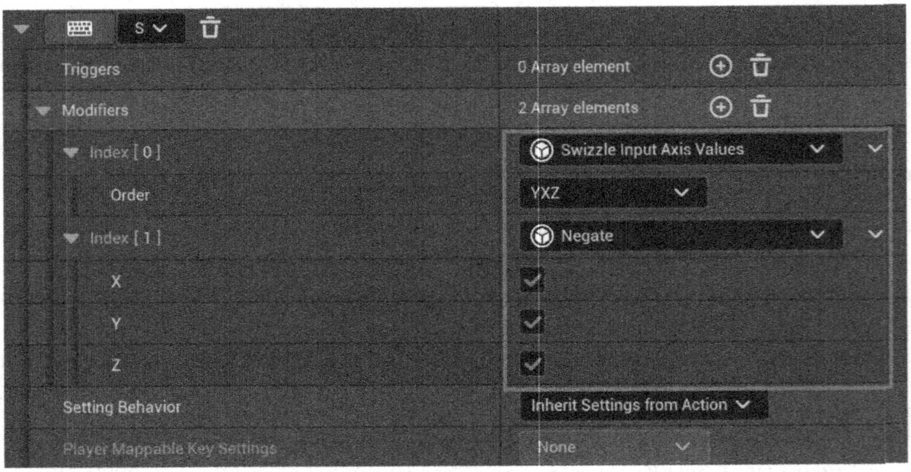

Figure 5.10 - Using two modifiers to move backward

3. Set up the *D* key and the *Right Arrow* key as positive *X* movement. These mappings do not need Swizzle because they already use the *X* axis.
4. Set up the *A* key and *Left Arrow* key as negative *X* movement by adding the **Negate** modifier to each mapping.
5. Set up the *Up Arrow* key the same way as the *W* key, using **Swizzle Input Axis Values**.

6. Set up the *Down Arrow* key the same way as *S* (in *step 2*), using both **Swizzle Input Axis Values** and **Negate**.
7. Finally, add a mapping for `Action_Hero_Look` and set its input to **Mouse XY 2D-Axis** and add a **Negate** modifier. This input already provides a two-dimensional value: mouse movement along the *X* axis controls horizontal looking, while movement along the *Y* axis controls vertical looking. No **Swizzle** modifier is required.

At this point, the input assets and hardware mappings are ready, but Unreal Engine still needs to know when this mapping context should be active. In the next section, we will create a Player Controller and add this mapping context to the local player when the level starts.

Handling and processing player input

In Unreal Engine, a **Player Controller** serves as the connection between the player and the `Pawn` or `Character` being controlled. It receives player input, manages player-specific systems, and passes gameplay commands to the controlled character. We use a separate **Player Controller Blueprint** instead of placing all input setup inside `BP_Hero` because the controller belongs to the player, while `BP_Hero` represents the character in the game world. Keeping these responsibilities separate allows the same controller to possess a different character later and prevents player-level input configuration, such as activating an Input Mapping Context, from becoming tightly coupled to one Character Blueprint.

The first step is to create a **Player Controller Blueprint** class for our Hero character. In this Blueprint, we will verify that it belongs to the local player and then activate the Input Mapping Context.

In this context, *local* means that the controller belongs to a player using the current device, rather than a remote player connected over the network.

Follow these steps to connect the input mappings to the **Player Controller**, so they can be used during gameplay:

1. In the **Content Browser**, navigate to the `Content/Pangaea` folder. Right-click in an empty area and select **Blueprint Class**. In the **Pick Parent Class** window, select **Player Controller**, as shown in *Figure 5.11*. Name the new Blueprint `BP_Hero_Controller`.

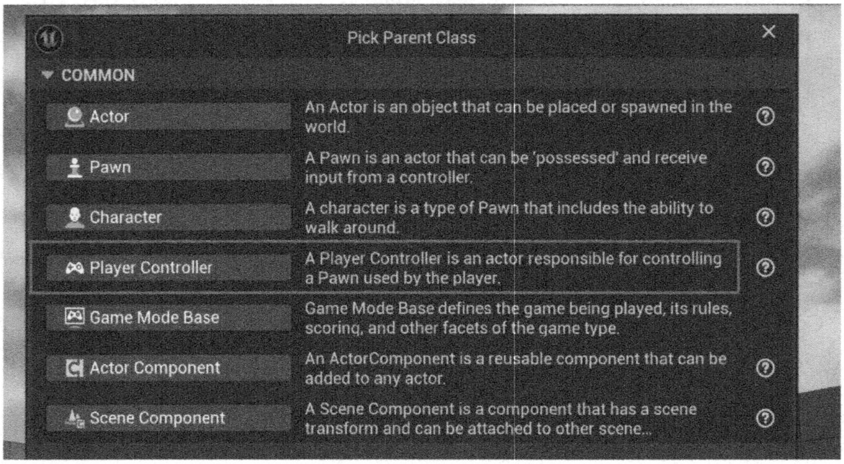

Figure 5.11 - You can select Player Controller class as the parent class

2. Let's open this newly created **Player Controller** and switch to the **EventGraph** tab (which was introduced in *Chapter 3*), as shown in *Figure 5.12*:

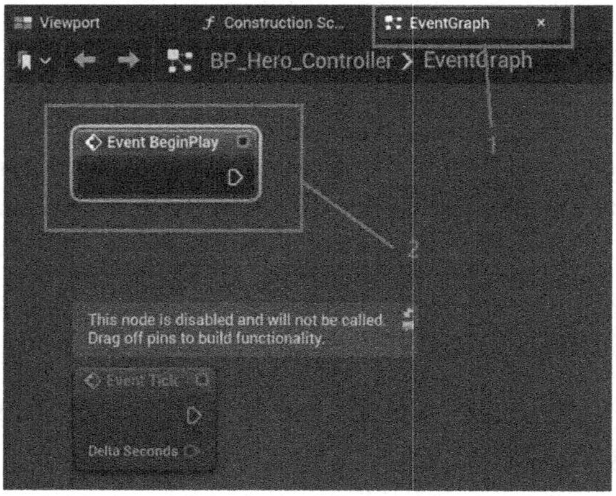

Figure 5.12 - The Event Graph of Player Controller class

3. Right-click in an empty area of the graph to add a **Get Player Controller** node. Drag from its **Return Value** pin to create a **Get Enhanced Input Local Player Subsystem** node, as shown in *Figure 5.13*.

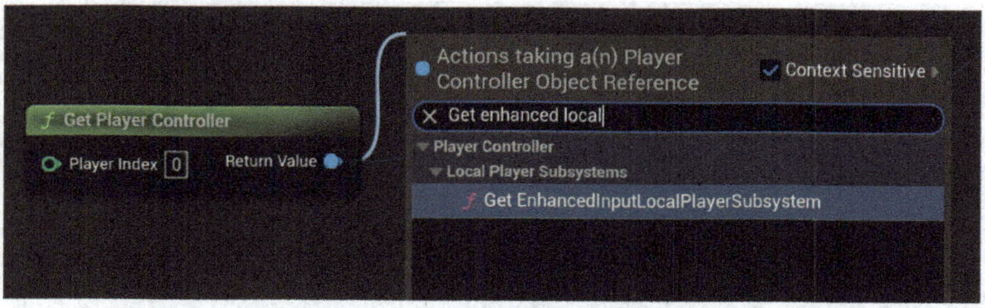

Figure 5.13 - Adding Get Player Controller and Get Enhanced Input Local Player Subsystem nodes

4. Drag from the **Return Value** pin of **Get Enhanced Input Local Player Subsystem** and add an **Add Mapping Context** node. This automatically connects the subsystem to the node's **Target** pin.

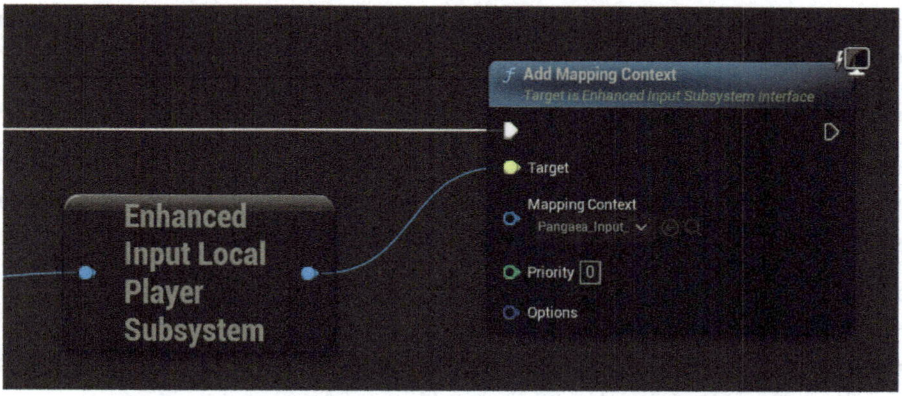

Figure 5.14 - Assigning the target to local input system by Get Enhanced Input Local Player Subsystem

5. Connect the **Event BeginPlay** execution pin to the execution input pin of **Add Mapping Context**.
6. On the **Add Mapping Context** node, set **Mapping Context** to `Pangaea_Input_Map`. Leave **Priority** at **0**, as shown in *Figure 5.15*, because this chapter uses only one mapping context. If multiple contexts are active later, a higher priority can be used to resolve conflicting mappings.
7. Compile and save.

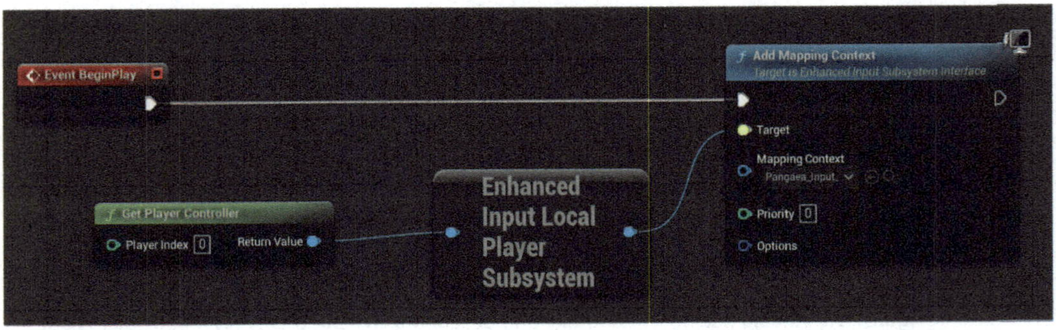

Figure 5.15 - The final BP_Hero_Controller Blueprint

When the level begins, `BP_Hero_Controller` first gets the `Player Controller` and feeds it to the **Enhanced Input Local Player Subsystem** and adds `Pangaea_Input_Map` with the **Add Mapping Context** node. This activates the keyboard and mouse bindings created earlier for the current player only.

Routing controls to a character's Blueprint

At this point, our `Pangaea_Input_Map` has been added to the local player through the Player Controller. This means Unreal Engine can now receive the input actions we created earlier, such as `Action_Attack`, `Action_Move`, and `Action_Hero_Look`.

However, adding the Input Mapping Context only makes the input actions available. We still need to decide what the character should do when those actions are triggered. For example, pressing the left mouse button should start an attack, pressing the movement keys should move the Hero, and moving the mouse should rotate the camera.

In the next section, we will do some additional work on `BP_Hero` and handle these input actions inside the character Blueprint.

Handling attack input

We will begin with the attack input because it is a simple button-style action. Earlier, we created `Action_Attack` as a `Bool` Input Action and mapped it to the left mouse button. Now we need to handle that action in `BP_Hero`.

Let's open `BP_Hero` and switch to the **Event Graph**. In the **Event Graph**, we'll right-click and search for the **Enhanced Input Action Event** for `Action_Attack`. Add this event to the graph, as shown in *Figure 5.16*. Leave it unconnected for now. We will return to this event after creating the `Attack` function.

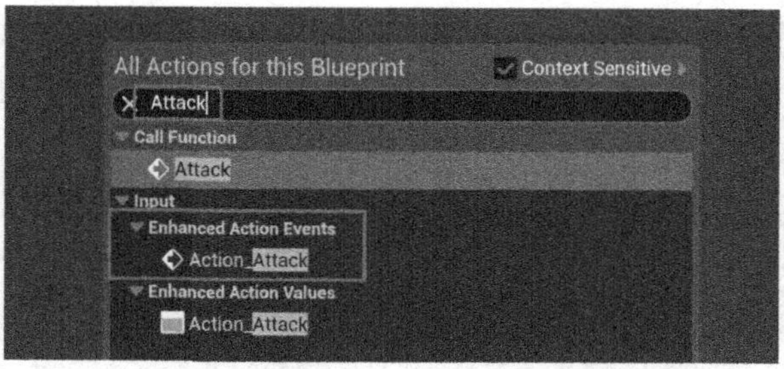

Figure 5.16 - Adding Action_Attack event to BP_Hero

When the attack input is triggered, we want the Hero to enter an attack animation state. To keep the Blueprint easier to read, we will create a reusable function named `Attack`, then call that function from the `Action_Attack` input event.

Using a function is helpful because it keeps the input Event Graph clean. Instead of placing all attack logic directly beside the input event, we can keep the attack behavior inside a named function. Later, if we need to add more attack checks, play sound effects, spawn hit effects, or trigger damage logic, we can extend the `Attack` function without making the input graph difficult to follow.

Writing functions in the Blueprint

Before writing the attack logic, we will create a helper function named `GetAnimInst`. This function retrieves the **runtime instance** of `AB_Hero` that is controlling the Hero's Skeletal Mesh. It does not return the Animation Blueprint asset itself; it returns the active instance whose variables can be read or changed during gameplay.

> **Note**
>
> A **Blueprint function** is a reusable block of nodes that performs a specific task, can accept input parameters and return output values, and executes only when explicitly called through an execution pin.

So, we'll create a new function in `BP_Hero` by clicking the + button on the **FUNCTIONS** section shown in *Figure 5.17*, and name it `GetAnimInst`.

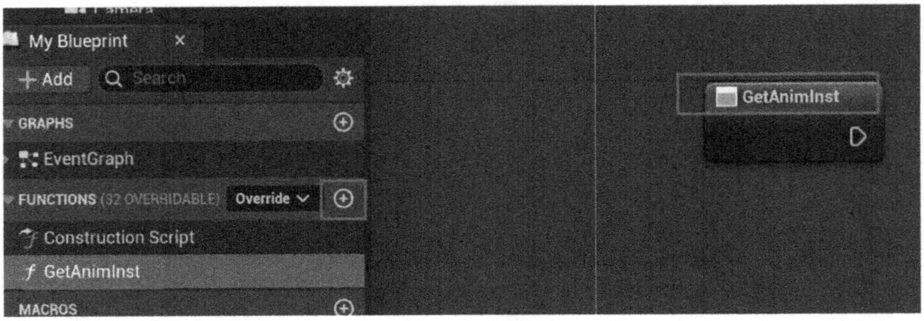

Figure 5.17 - Adding a function inside `BP_Hero`

Inside the new `GetAnimInst` function, follow these steps (see *Figure 5.18* for steps **1–7**):

1. In the **Components** panel, locate the inherited `Mesh` component. Drag it into the function graph and select **Get Mesh**.
2. Drag from the *blue* output pin of **Mesh**, search for **Get Anim Instance**, and add the node. This retrieves the Animation Blueprint instance currently controlling the Hero's Skeletal Mesh.
3. Drag from the **Return Value** pin of **Get Anim Instance** and search for **Cast To AB_Hero**. Add the cast node. The cast verifies that the retrieved animation instance uses the `AB_Hero` Animation Blueprint class and gives us access to its variables, including `AnimState`.
4. Connect the function entry node's *white* execution output pin to the execution input pin of **Cast To AB_Hero**.
5. Select the function's return node. In the **Details** panel, add an output parameter named **AnimInst** and set its type to `AB_Hero` **Object Reference**, set the `NewParam` name to be `AnimInst`, and set **Pure** to be `true`.

> **Note**
>
> In Unreal Engine, a **pure function** computes and returns a value without modifying any data or game state and does not require an execution pin to be called.

6. Connect the **As AB Hero** output pin of **Cast To AB_Hero** to the **Anim Inst** input pin on the **Return Node**.

7. Connect the successful execution output of **Cast To AB_Hero** to the execution input of the **Return Node**.
8. Compile and save `BP_Hero`.

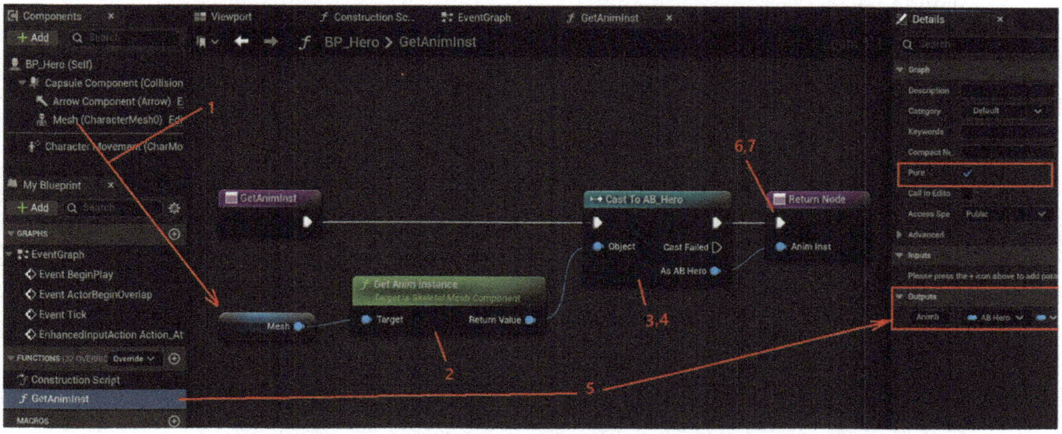

Figure 5.18 - Blueprint of GetAnimInst function

The function now returns a typed reference to the Hero's Animation Blueprint instance. Other functions in `BP_Hero` can call `GetAnimInst` and directly access variables defined in `AB_Hero` without repeating the same retrieval and casting nodes.

Writing the Attack function

Before we start to write the Attack function, let's recall how we set up animations for Hero in Chapter 4. The `AnimState` integer determines which animation state the Animation Blueprint activates:

AnimState	Animation
0	Locomotion
1	Attack
2	Hit

Table 5.3 - The AnimState values of Hero's animations

Create another function in `BP_Hero` and name it `Attack`, then follow these steps:

1. Drag the `GetAnimInst` function from the **My Blueprint** panel into the function graph and choose **Call GetAnimInst**.

2. Drag from the returned **Anim Inst** reference and add a **Get Anim State** node. This reads the current animation-state value from `AB_Hero`.
3. Drag from the **Anim State** output pin and add an **Equal (Integer)** node. Set the second value to `0`.
4. Add a **Branch** node. Connect the execution output of the function entry node to the **Branch**'s execution input.
5. Connect the Boolean result of the equality comparison to the **Branch**'s **Condition** pin.
6. Drag again from the **Anim Inst** reference and add a **Set Anim State** node.
7. Set the new **Anim State** value to `1`, which represents the attack state in the current Animation Blueprint.
8. Connect the **True** execution pin of the **Branch** to the execution input of **Set Anim State**. Leave the **False** pin unconnected.
9. Compile and save `BP_Hero`.

The complete `Attack` function is shown in *Figure 5.19*:

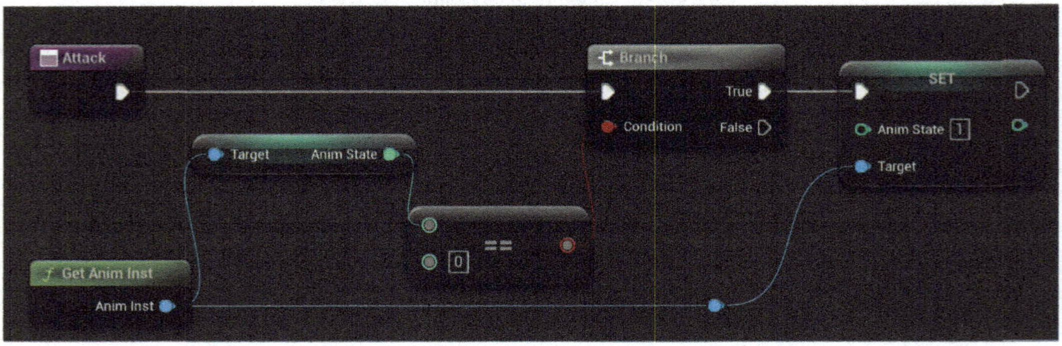

Figure 5.19 - Blueprint of the Attack function

The function starts an attack only when **Anim State** is **0**, which represents the normal locomotion state. If the Hero is already attacking or is in another animation state, the **Branch** follows the unconnected **False** path and no change is made. This prevents repeated input events from continually restarting the attack animation.

Now, connect the Action_Attack event to the Attack function by following these steps:

1. Return to the BP_Hero **Event Graph**, where you previously added the **EnhancedInputAction Action_Attack** event.
2. Drag the Attack function from the **My Blueprint** panel into the graph and choose **Call Attack**.
3. Connect the event's **Started** execution pin to the execution input of **Attack**. Using **Started** calls the function once when the left mouse button is initially pressed rather than repeatedly while it remains held.
4. Compile and save BP_Hero.

Creating an Animation Notify to finish the attack

Starting the attack is only half of the process. We also need to tell the Animation Blueprint when the attack animation has reached the point where the Hero can return to normal movement. Otherwise, AnimState will remain set to the attack state, and the Hero will never transition back to the normal idle, walk, or run state.

To solve this, we will add an **Animation Notify** to the attack animation. An **Animation Notify** is a marker placed on an animation sequence's timeline. When playback reaches that marker, Unreal Engine sends a corresponding event to the Animation Blueprint. We can handle that event to reset AnimState and allow the state machine to transition back to locomotion. Follow these steps:

1. In the **Content Browser**, locate A_Hero_Attack, then double-click it to open the attack animation in the **Animation Sequence Editor**. In the timeline at the bottom of the editor, move the playhead to approximately 80% of the animation, shortly before the attack finishes.
2. In the **Notify Tracks** panel below the animation timeline, locate **Notify Track 1**. Move the playhead to approximately frame 40, then right-click **Notify Track 1** and select **Add Notify | New Notify**, as shown in *Figure 5.20*. Name the new notify EndOfAttack1.

Figure 5.20 - Adding a new Animation Notify on animation track

The completed notify placement at approximately frame 40 is shown in *Figure 5.21*:

Figure 5.21 - Placing EndOfAttack1 at approximately frame 40

In this animation, frame 40 is approximately 80% of the way through the sequence. Placing the notify shortly before the final frame allows the Animation Blueprint to begin transitioning back to the locomotion state while the remaining portion of the attack animation blends out.

3. After creating and saving the `EndOfAttack1` notify, open `AB_Hero` and switch to its **Event Graph**. Right-click in an empty area of the graph, search for `AnimNotify_EndOfAttack1`, and add the corresponding `Animation Notify` event.
4. Next, drag the `AnimState` variable from the **My Blueprint** panel into the graph and choose **Set Anim State**. Connect the white execution output pin of **AnimNotify_EndOfAttack1** to the execution input pin of **Set Anim State**, then enter 0 as the new value.
5. Compile and save `AB_Hero`. The completed connection should look like *Figure 5.22*.

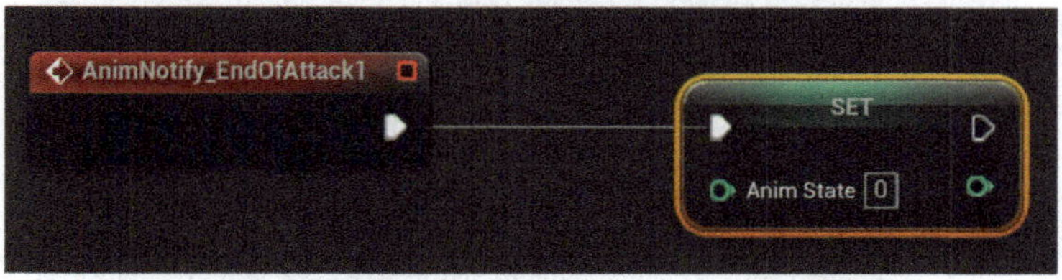

Figure 5.22 - Setting animation state back to 0 (idle/walk/run)

When the attack animation reaches the `EndOfAttack1` marker, Unreal Engine fires the `AnimNotify_EndOfAttack1` event in `AB_Hero`. The event sets `AnimState` to *0*, which represents the normal locomotion state. This satisfies the transition condition that allows the Animation Blueprint to blend from the attack animation back to idle, walking, or running.

The complete attack flow is now:

1. The player presses the left mouse button.
2. `Action_Attack` calls the `Attack` function.
3. The function changes `AnimState` from 0 to 1.
4. The Animation Blueprint transitions into the attack state.
5. The attack animation reaches `EndOfAttack1`.
6. `AnimNotify_EndOfAttack1` resets `AnimState` to 0.
7. The Animation Blueprint transitions back to locomotion.

Fixing the animation root motion defect

If you pay close attention to the Hero's attack animation, you may notice that the character moves forward during the attack and then snaps back to its original position when the animation returns to the first frame. This is a common issue caused by root motion in the animation. In most gameplay scenarios, we do not want the animation to control character movement, so we need to disable this behavior.

To do so, open the `A_Hero_Attack` animation asset. In the **Asset Details** panel, search for **Force Root Lock** and set it to True. This will prevent the animation from affecting the character's position.

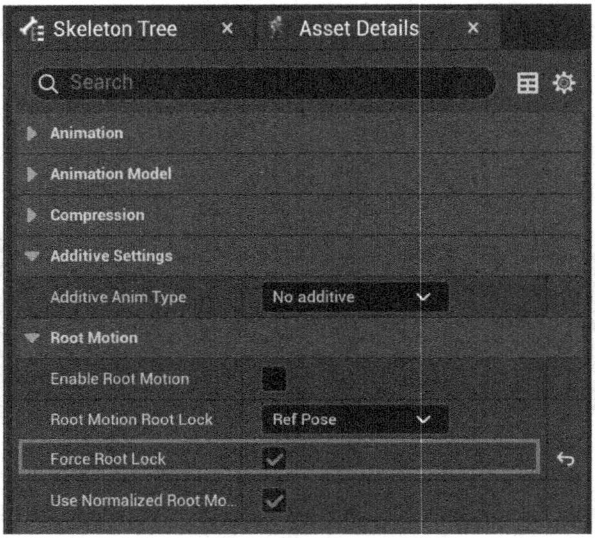

Figure 5.23 - Locking the Root Motion for the A_Hero_Attack animation

Handling movement input

Now that the attack input is connected and the attack animation can return to Locomotion, we can move on to player movement. Earlier, we created `Action_Move` as an **Axis2D Input Action** and configured the keyboard mappings to produce *X* and *Y* movement values. In this section, we will create a `MoveHero` function in `BP_Hero` and use those values to move or turn the character during gameplay.

Creating the MoveHero function

In `BP_Hero`, we'll create a new function named `MoveHero`. Select the function entry node and add two input parameters:

- **X Axis**, with the type `Float`
- **Y Axis**, with the type `Float`

These values will later come from the two components of the `Action_Move` Axis2D input.

Adding the movement state check

Figure 5.24 appears to contain a state check before movement is processed. The construction steps should therefore begin with that logic:

1. Add a **Branch** node and connect the **MoveHero** function entry node's execution output to the **Branch** execution input.
2. Drag the **GetAnimInst** function from the **My Blueprint** panel into the graph and choose **Call GetAnimInst**.
3. Drag from the **Anim Inst** output and add a **Get Anim State** node.
4. Drag from the **Anim State** output and add an **Equal (Integer)** node. Set the second value to `0`.
5. Connect the Boolean output of the **Equal (Integer)** node to the **Condition** pin of the **Branch** node, as shown in *Figure 5.24*.

Figure 5.24 - Checking the Hero's animation state before processing movement

Creating forward and backward movement

With the Locomotion-state check in place, we can now use the Hero's forward direction and the **Y axis** input value to implement forward and backward movement. Follow these steps (see *Figure 5.25*):

1. Drag from the **Branch** node's **True** execution pin and add an **Add Controller Yaw Input** node and continue dragging from the execution to add an **Add Movement Input** node. The **Branch** node ensures that movement is applied only when `AnimState` is 0, indicating that the Hero is in the Locomotion state.
2. Right-click in an empty area and add a **Get Actor Forward Vector** node.
3. Connect the **Return Value** of **Get Actor Forward Vector** to the **World Direction** pin of the **Add Movement Input** node.
4. Drag from **X Axis** of **MoveHero** to connect to the **Val** input pin of the **Add Controller Yaw Input** node.

5. Drag from **X Axis** of **MoveHero** to an empty area and add a new **ABS** (Absolute value of a target) node, then continue dragging from the output pin of the **ABS** node to add a new **Addition** node.
6. Drag from **Y Axis** of **MoveHero** to connect to the second input pin of the **Addition** node.
7. Finally, drag from the output pin of the **Addition** node to connect to the **Scale Value** input pin of the **Add Movement Input** node.
8. Don't forget to compile and save `BP_Hero`.

The completed setup should look like *Figure 5.25*:

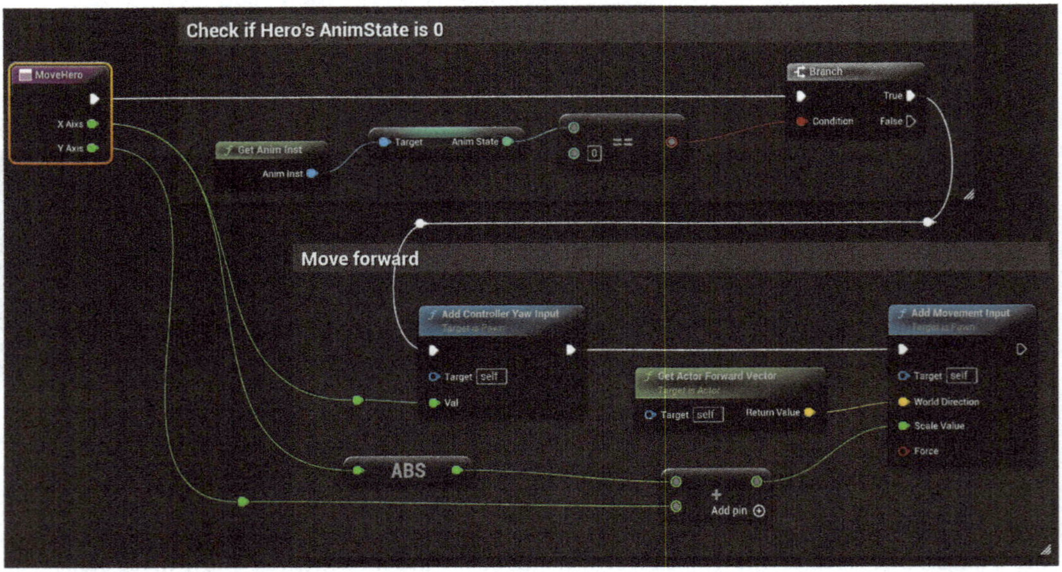

Figure 5.25 - The complete MoveHero function Blueprint

> **Note**
>
> To add a comment panel that groups a set of nodes, select the nodes and press *C* on the keyboard.

By using the **Axis2D** value from `Action_Move`, we can handle all movement keys through one input action instead of checking each key separately. This is the main benefit of the input mapping setup we created earlier.

This Blueprint logic allows movement only when **AnimState** is `0`, which represents the Hero's locomotion state. The **Branch** checks this state before allowing the movement logic to execute.

When the check succeeds, the Hero can move forward or backward using the **Y-axis** input, while the **X-axis** input moves and turns to the left or right.

After completing the `MoveHero` function, return to the `BP_Hero` **Event Graph** and follow these steps (see *Figure 5.26*):

1. Right-click in an empty area of the graph, search for `Action_Move`, and add the **EnhancedInputAction Action_Move** event.
2. Drag from the event's **Action Value** pin and add a **Break Vector 2D** node. This converts the input action value into a two-component vector.
3. Drag the `MoveHero` function from the **My Blueprint** panel into the **Event Graph** and choose **Call MoveHero**.
4. Connect the **Triggered** execution pin of **EnhancedInputAction Action_Move** to a Boolean **Branch** node.
5. Connect the **True** output pin of the **Branch** node to the execution input pin of **MoveHero**.
6. Connect the **X** output of **Break Vector 2D** to the **X Axis** input of **MoveHero**.
7. Connect the **Y** output of **Break Vector 2D** to the **Y Axis** input of **MoveHero**.
8. Compile and save `BP_Hero`.

The completed setup should look like *Figure 5.26*:

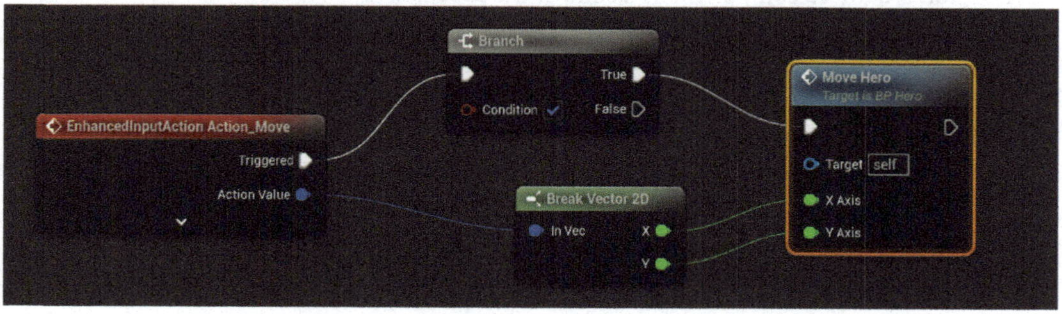

Figure 5.26 - Setting up event in BP_Hero for movement

While one or more movement keys are held, the **Triggered** output repeatedly calls **MoveHero** with the current two-dimensional input value. The function uses the *Y* component for forward and backward movement and the *X* component for left and right movement. When opposite directions are pressed together, their values can cancel each other out.

Creating a follow camera for the player character

Now we need to make sure the player can see and control the character comfortably during gameplay. A playable character usually needs a camera setup that follows the character from behind, keeps the player oriented in the game world, and responds smoothly as the character moves. Without this camera setup, the player may technically be controlling the character, but the gameplay experience will feel incomplete or difficult to navigate.

In UE5, a **Spring Arm** is typically used as an invisible camera boom for third-person characters. Instead of attaching the camera directly to the character, the Spring Arm holds the camera at a target distance behind the player. It can also help the camera avoid clipping into walls by shortening the arm when level geometry blocks the view, then extending it again when the path is clear. This makes it a standard component for building a third-person follow camera.

In our project, we will add a **Spring Arm** and **Camera** component to `BP_Hero`. The **Spring Arm** will control the camera's distance and collision behavior, while the **Camera** component will render the player's view.

1. In our `BP_Hero` Blueprint, switch to the **Viewport** tab so you can see the Hero.
2. Open the **Components** panel from the **Window** menu.
3. Under the character's root or the **Capsule** of `BP_Hero` hierarchy, add a **Spring Arm** component by clicking **Add**, as shown in *Figure 5.27*.
4. Add a **Camera** component as a child of the `SpringArm`.
5. Move the camera by adjusting the Spring Arm rather than manually placing the camera far behind the character.

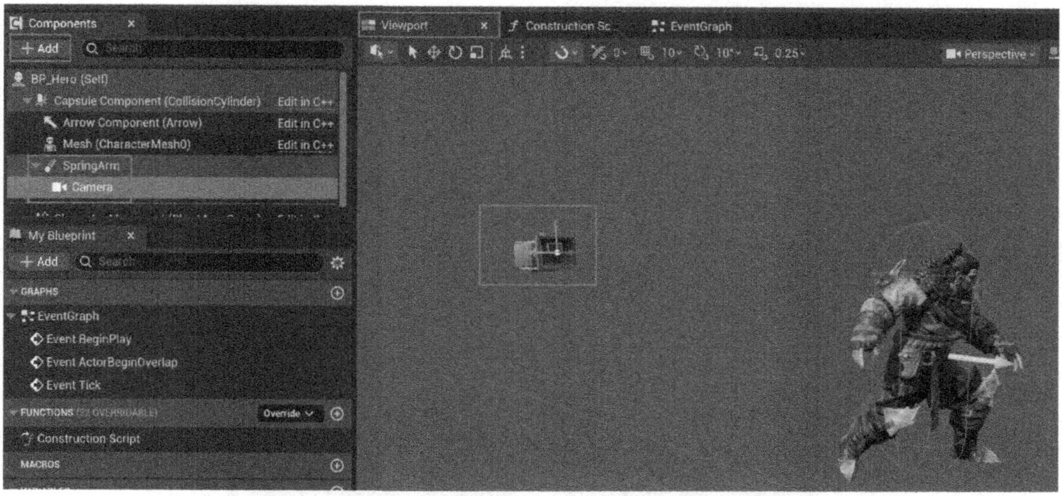

Figure 5.27 - Adding a Spring Arm and Camera component

Now we can start fine-tuning the `SpringArm` settings. For a basic follow camera, these are the main properties to tune. You can tweak these settings from the **Details** panel shown in *Figure 5.28*:

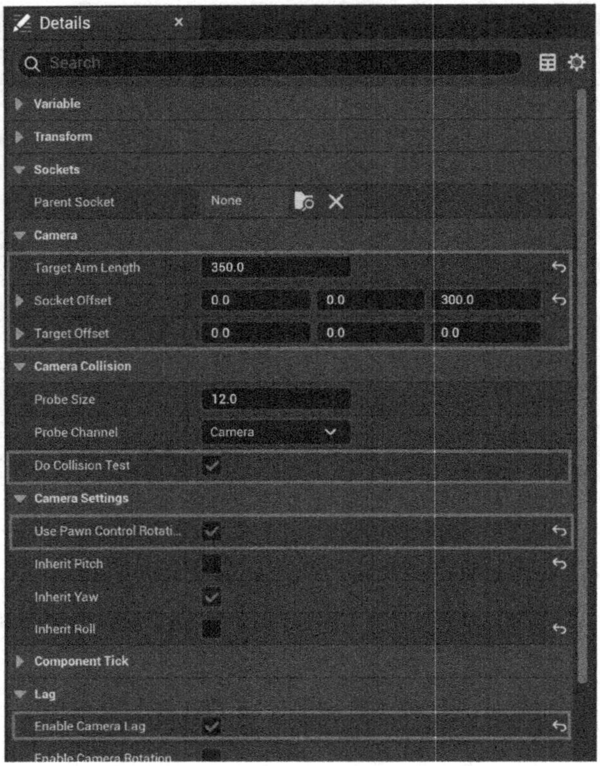

Figure 5.28 - Key Spring Arm settings

Let's explore the key settings for the `SpringArm` in more detail:

- **Target Arm Length**: Controls how far the camera stays from the player. A larger value places the camera farther back. You can start with `350` and adjust to your needs.
- **Socket Offse**t: Useful for shifting the camera slightly upward or sideways, such as over the character's shoulder. We can set it to (`0`, `0`, `300`) for a slight over-the-shoulder feel.
- **Use Pawn Control Rotation**: Lets the Spring Arm follow the controller's rotation, which is common for player-controlled cameras.
- Uncheck **Inherit Pitch** and **Inherit Roll**.
- **Do Collision Test**: Keeps the camera from clipping into walls by retracting the arm when something blocks it.
- Enable **Camera Lag** and **Camera Lag Speed**: Adds smoothing so the camera follows with a softer motion rather than snapping instantly. You can try to set the lag speed between `8` and `15`.

Next, select the **Camera** component from the **Components** panel to set the **Rotation** to (`0`, `-30`, `0`) in the **Details** panel:

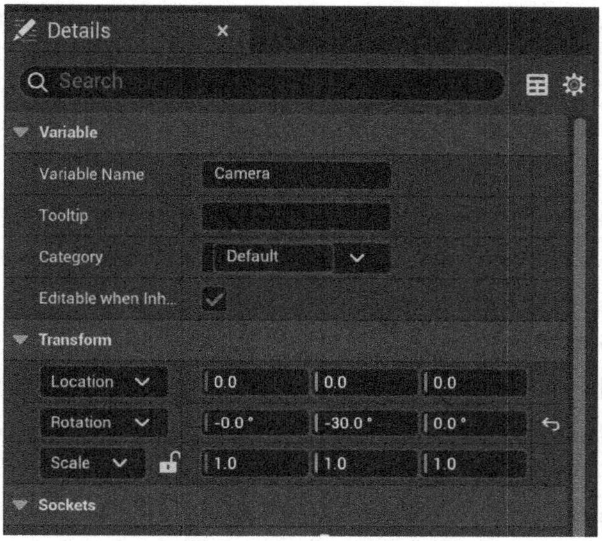

Figure 5.29 - Setting the Camera Rotation to (0, -30, 0)

In the **Components** panel, select `BP_Hero`. In the **Details** panel, search for `Use Controller Rotation Yaw`. Under the **Pawn** category, enable **Use Controller Rotation Yaw**.

You might wonder why we do not simply attach the **Camera** component directly to the Hero character. The reason is that a directly attached camera usually has less control over distance, collision, and smoothing. If the camera is attached directly to the character, you may run into the following problems:

- The camera can clip into walls.
- Movement can feel too rigid.
- Rotation changes can feel abrupt.

By using a Spring Arm, Unreal Engine can handle camera distance, obstruction, retraction, and smoothing for us.

Handling camera input

The final input action we need to handle is camera control. Earlier, we created `Action_Hero_Look` as a **Mouse XY 2D-Axis** Input Action. This action is used to read mouse movement so the player can rotate the view.

Creating the HeroLook function

In `BP_Hero`, create a new function named `HeroLook`. Select the function entry node, then add two input parameters named **X Axis** and **Y Axis** and set their type to **Float**.

Build the function using these steps (see *Figure 5.30*):

1. Add a **Make Rotator** node. This node converts the two mouse-axis values into a rotation that can be applied to the camera's **Spring Arm**.
2. Connect **X Axis** of **HeroLook** to the **Y (Pitch)** input of **Make Rotator**.
3. Connect **Y Axis** of **HeroLook** to the **Z (Yaw)** input of **Make Rotator**.
4. Drag the **SpringArm** component from the **Components** panel into the function graph and select **Get SpringArm**.
5. Drag from the **Spring Arm** node and add an **Add Relative Rotation** node.
6. Connect the output of **Make Rotator** to the **Delta Rotation** input of the **Add Relative Rotation** node.
7. Connect the execution output of the **HeroLook** function entry node to the execution input of **Add Relative Rotation**.

The Blueprint also includes a group of nodes that use the **Set Relative Rotation** node to clamp the up and down rotation angles of the Spring Arm. This prevents the camera from rotating too far over the character's head or below the feet. We will skip the detailed steps for this part and leave it for you to practice and experiment with on your own.

The completed `HeroLook` function uses the *X*-axis value to adjust the camera's pitch and the *Y*-axis value to adjust its yaw, as shown in *Figure 5.30*:

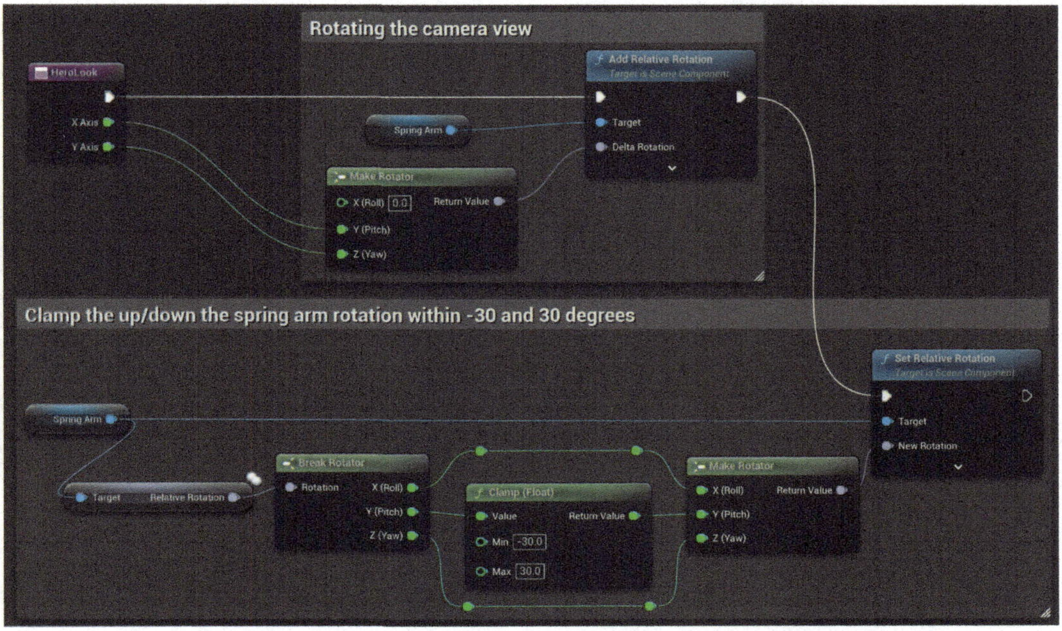

Figure 5.30 - Implementation of HeroLook function

This Blueprint handles camera rotation and limits the vertical viewing angle. The `HeroLook` input provides the *X* and *Y* axes, which are used to create a rotator that controls the Spring Arm's rotation. On the **Make Rotator** node, the **Y (Pitch)** input controls the up and down rotation of the camera, while the **Z (Yaw)** input controls the left and right rotation. To prevent the camera from rotating too far vertically, the **Spring Arm**'s relative rotation is clamped using a **Clamp** node, limiting the **Pitch** value between `-30` and `30` degrees. This ensures the camera stays within a comfortable viewing range.

Now is the time to connect the `HeroLook` function to the corresponding action.

Connecting Action_Hero_Look

Return to the `BP_Hero` **Event Graph** and complete the input connection (see *Figure 5.31*):

1. Right-click in an empty area and add the **EnhancedInputAction Action_Hero_Look** event.
2. Drag from its **Action Value** pin and add a **Break Vector 2D** node.
3. Drag the **HeroLook** function from the **My Blueprint** panel into the **Event Graph**.
4. Connect the event's **Triggered** execution pin to the execution input of **HeroLook**.

5. Connect the **X** and **Y** output of **Break Vector 2D** to the **X Axis** and **Y Axis** inputs of **HeroLook**.
6. Compile and save the Blueprint.

Figure 5.31 shows the completed `Action_Hero_Look` event process Blueprint:

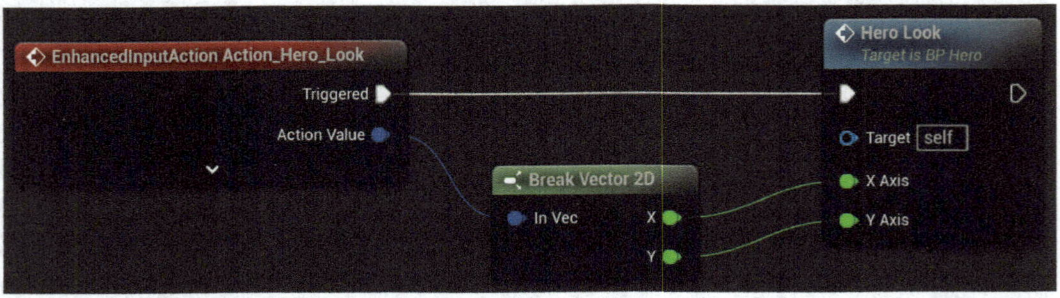

Figure 5.31 - Handling Action_Hero_Look event in BP_Hero

With this setup complete, the Character Blueprint now responds to all three main input actions:

- `Action_Attack` triggers the Hero's attack animation state.
- `Action_Move` moves the character forward, backward, left, and right.
- `Action_Hero_Look` rotates the camera using mouse movement.

We are all set now and need to complete the final step to sync the Hero's locomotion to its movement speed.

Syncing Character Animation with Movement Speed

To make the character's movement feel responsive and visually convincing, we need to synchronize its animations with its actual movement speed. This is achieved by hooking into the `BP_Hero` **Tick** event and passing a normalized forward movement speed – a value clamped between 0 and 1 – to the `AB_Hero` Animation Blueprint. This value is assigned to the `AnimSpeed` parameter, which drives a 1D blend space. Based on the current speed, the blend space automatically selects and plays the appropriate animation: *idle* when stationary, *walk* at moderate speeds, and *run* when moving at full speed. This creates a seamless visual transition between movement states and ensures the character's animation always matches what the player is doing on screen.

Use *Figure 5.32* as a reference and try creating this Blueprint logic on your own. The `Chapter05` branch (see the *Technical requirements* section; to access the GitHub repository, see the *Preface* for instructions) has full implementation of this in `BP_Hero`:

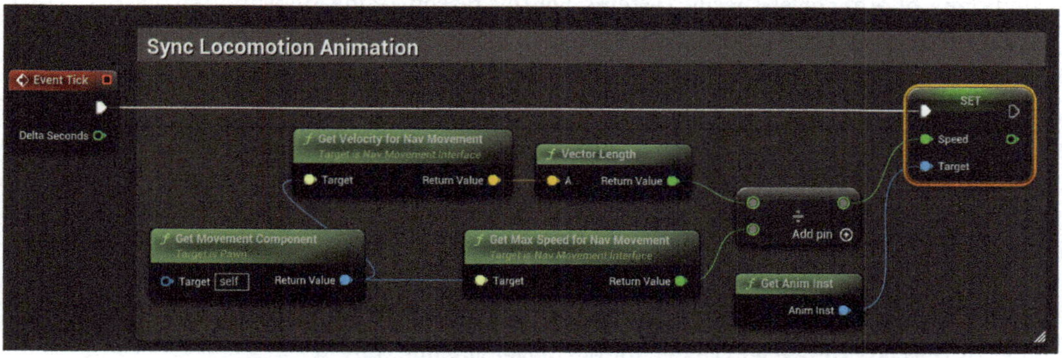

Figure 5.32 - Syncing the character's animation to its movement speed

The next step is to enable all the work we've done in our project by setting up the Game Mode, which brings the player input and level gameplay settings together.

Configuring input for your own game

Now that the input actions are mapped and handled inside `BP_Hero`, we need to make sure the level uses the correct character, controller, and camera setup when the game starts. In this final section, we will connect the input workflow to the playable level by configuring the follow camera, Game Mode, Default Pawn Class, and Player Controller Class.

Understanding the Game Mode in an input setup

Before players can move, interact, or complete objectives, the game needs a set of rules that define how the experience begins and how it is structured. In Unreal Engine, one of the main systems responsible for this is Game Mode.

Game Mode acts as a high-level controller for the current level or gameplay session. It defines the core rules of play and specifies which classes should be used for key gameplay elements, such as the default player character, Player Controller, game state, and HUD.

When a level begins, Unreal Engine checks the assigned Game Mode and uses it to establish the gameplay framework for that level. For example, it can define which Pawn the player controls at startup, what happens when a player joins, and which rules govern spawning, restarting, winning, or losing. This makes Game Mode a central part of building a playable game, as it helps organize the player's experience from the moment the level is loaded.

It is also important to note that Game Mode is not intended to contain all gameplay logic. Instead, it is used for *rules* and *setup behavior* that apply to the overall game session. In a simple single-player project, this may mean selecting the main playable character and defining how the game starts. In a larger game, it may also manage match flow, spawning rules, score conditions, or other level-specific systems. For this reason, Game Mode is often one of the first classes configured in a new project.

Your project may already include a default Game Mode, but for our game, *Pangaea*, we will create a new one of our own. Now that `BP_Hero` has the camera setup needed for player control, we can assign it as the playable character through our Game Mode.

Setting up the main character

We can assign the main playable character through the Game Mode's `Default Pawn Class`. Game Modes define the default classes used by the level, including the `Default Pawn Class`, which is the class Unreal will spawn for the player at game start.

There are two places we can assign Game Mode. One is the global Game Mode you can set in **Project Settings**. Another one is a level-specific Game Mode, which you can set for each individual level to override the global Game Mode. If a level does not have its own Game Mode assigned, it will apply the Game Mode set in **Project Settings**.

The basic idea behind the setup is:

- Your *Character Blueprint* is your playable character, such as `BP_Hero`.
- Your *Game Mode Blueprint* tells Unreal which pawn or character to spawn for the player.
- When the level starts, Unreal uses the Game Mode and spawns that class as the player's character.

Rather than modifying the template's **Game Mode** directly, we will duplicate it and create a Game Mode specifically for the `Pangaea` project. Follow these steps:

1. In the **Content Browser**, open the `Content/ThirdPerson/Blueprints` folder.
2. Locate `BP_ThirdPersonGameMode`, as shown in *Figure 5.33*.
3. Right-click `BP_ThirdPersonGameMode` and select **Duplicate**.
4. Rename the duplicated Blueprint `BP_PangaeaGameMode`.
5. Move `BP_PangaeaGameMode` to the `Content/Pangaea` folder.
6. Double-click `BP_PangaeaGameMode` to open it in the **Blueprint Editor**.
7. Click **Class Defaults** and locate the **Default Pawn Class** setting in the **Details** panel.
8. Set **Default Pawn Class** to `BP_Hero`, then compile and save the Blueprint.

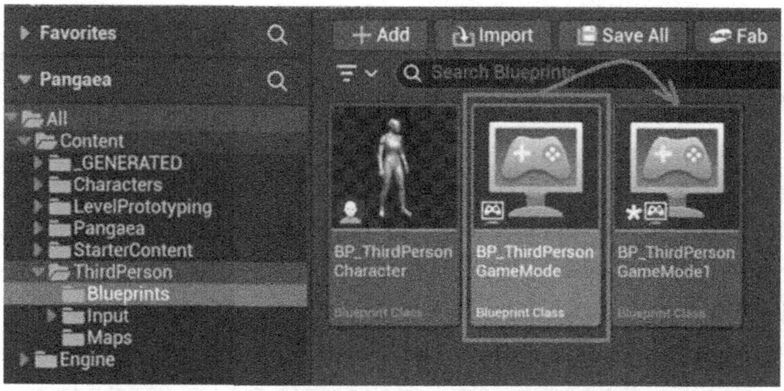

Figure 5.33 - Creating our GameMode class based on the existing BP_ThirdPersonGameMode class

The next step is to make your level use the Game Mode Blueprint. There are two common ways to do this:

- **Project-wide default**: The project-wide default Game Mode is the Game Mode used by the whole project unless a specific level overrides it. This method is useful when most levels in your game use the same player character, Player Controller, HUD, and general gameplay rules.

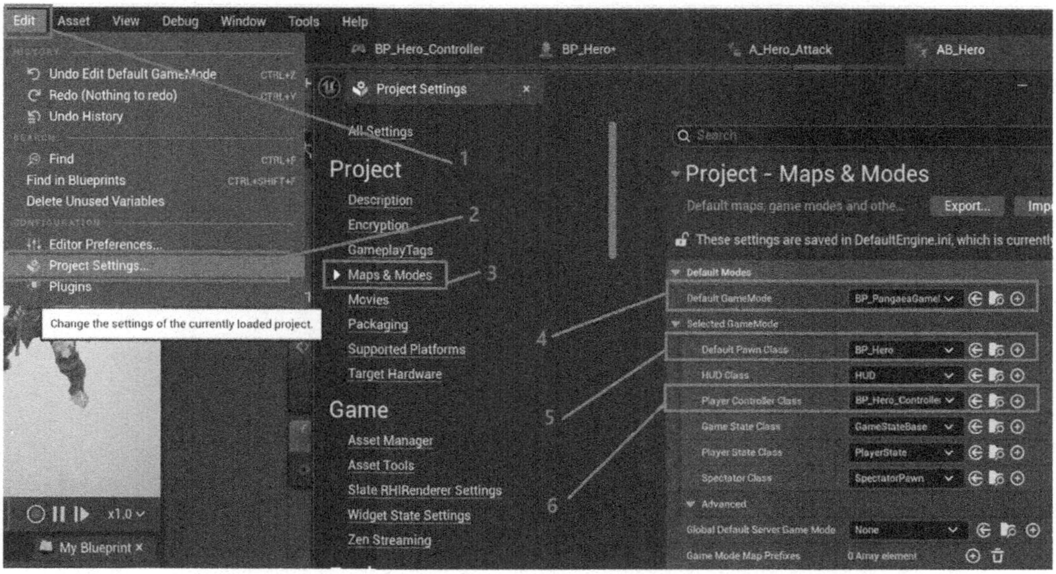

Figure 5.34 - Accessing the default Game Mode in the Project Settings dialog

By setting the default Game Mode in **Project Settings** | **Maps & Modes** as shown in *Figure 5.34*, you define the standard gameplay setup that Unreal Engine will apply whenever a level does not provide its own **Game Mode Override**.

- **Per-level override**: The per-level **Game Mode Override** lets a specific map use a different gameplay setup from the project-wide default. This is useful when a project contains multiple test maps, tutorial chapters, gameplay modes, or special levels that need their own playable character, Player Controller, HUD, or rules. When a level has a **Game Mode Override** assigned in **World Settings**, Unreal Engine uses that level-specific Game Mode instead of the default one from **Project Settings**.

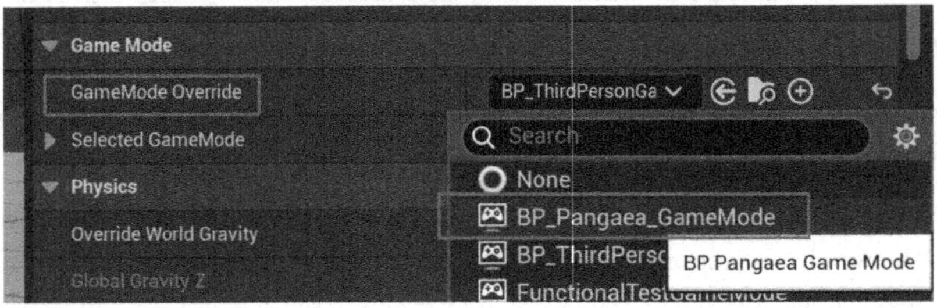

Figure 5.35 - Assigning our own Game Mode Blueprint for this level

As shown in *Figure 5.35*, we will use a level-specific Game Mode for this level. We chose per-level override here because this setup is only needed for the current test level. It lets this level use our custom `BP_PangaeaGameMode`, `BP_Hero`, and Player Controller without changing the default Game Mode for the entire project. This is useful when a project contains multiple maps or chapter demos, because each level can have its own gameplay setup while the global project settings remain unchanged.

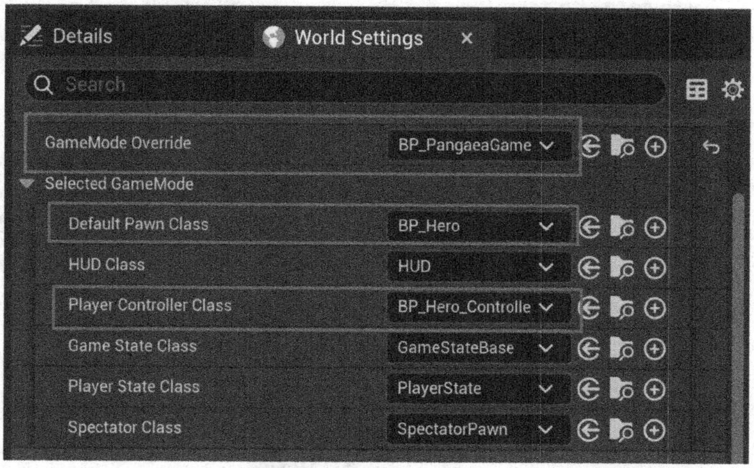

Figure 5.36 - Assigning the Hero Pawn and Player Controller classes

The per-level setting is done in the **World Settings** panel of our level, as shown in *Figure 5.36*:

1. From the Unreal Editor's main menu, select **Window | World Settings** to open the **World Settings** panel. In this panel, locate the **GameMode Override** setting and select `BP_PangaeaGameMode` from the dropdown list.
2. We set the **Default Pawn Class** to our Hero character class `BP_Hero` and set **Player Controller Class** to `BP_Hero_Controller`.

Now we are ready to run it inside Unreal Editor:

Figure 5.37 - Run the level for final testing

With the level-specific **Game Mode Override** assigned, this map now knows which gameplay setup to use when it starts. Unreal Engine will spawn `BP_Hero` as the playable character and use our custom Player Controller to connect the input mappings we created earlier.

This completes the high-level player setup for the level. Before we finish the chapter, let's review the complete input workflow so you can apply the same pattern to your own game projects:

- Add one Input Action per gameplay intent.
- Choose the correct value type: **Bool**, **Axis1D**, or **Axis2D**.
- Bind physical controls in an **Input Mapping Context**.
- Add the **Mapping Context** through the local **Player Controller**.
- Handle the input events in the **Character** or **Pawn** Blueprint.
- Use **Game Mode** to make sure the correct **Pawn** and **Player Controller** are used.

Summary

In this chapter, we explored how Unreal Engine's input system enables players to interact with gameplay in a responsive and meaningful way. We began by examining the foundations of hardware input, input mappings, and input actions, and then applied the **Enhanced Input** system to connect player controls directly to gameplay behavior. This provided a flexible and scalable framework for handling player interaction in a modern Unreal Engine project.

We also looked at how Unreal Engine's gameplay framework supports player control through the Player Controller, Character Blueprint, follow camera, and Game Mode setup. By using Blueprints, we created a gameplay flow that responds to player input and drives character behavior through input-driven logic. Together, these systems demonstrate how input handling becomes a key part of building complete and interactive gameplay scenarios.

Now, by the end of this chapter, you should be comfortable configuring input mappings, binding player input events, and applying input-driven logic to your own game projects. You should also have a stronger understanding of how Unreal Engine's gameplay framework connects the player, controller, character, and level setup into one playable experience.

Across *Chapters 4* and *5*, our focus has been on building and controlling the main playable character. In the next chapter, we will extend that foundation by exploring how to create and configure non-player characters (NPCs), allowing your game world to feel more dynamic, interactive, and alive.

6

Creating an AI Character

Now that we have a player character that can move around the game level, the world is starting to feel more interactive. However, a game world usually needs more than just the player. It also needs **non-player characters**, or **NPCs**, such as monster enemies, patrolling guards, or a guild receptionist who offers new quests.

Unlike the player character, NPCs are not directly controlled by the player. Their behavior is controlled by the game's AI system. In this chapter, we will learn how to create AI-controlled characters that can automatically move, sense the environment, make decisions, and respond to the player during gameplay. To build this kind of AI character, we need several Unreal Engine features working together, including Character Blueprints, AI Controllers, navigation, perception, animation, and Behavior Trees. The best way to learn how these systems connect is to build a complete enemy character step by step.

At this point in your learning journey, you already know how to create a player character and connect it to input. AI characters build on many of the same ideas, but their actions come from game logic instead of direct player input. Learning this distinction now will help you understand how Unreal Engine separates the character's body, controller, movement, animation, and decision-making systems.

This chapter uses **Warrok**, an enemy character, as a practical example so you can see how these systems work together in a real gameplay scenario. We have prepared the visual assets for Warrok. We will use these assets to create a fierce enemy NPC that can patrol the level, detect the player, chase the player, and attack when close enough.

In this chapter, we'll cover the following topics as we build the Warrok character step by step:

- Understanding AI character design in Unreal Engine
- Setting up the enemy NPC: Warrok
- Enabling AI navigation and movement

- Creating patrol behavior
- Implementing perception: hearing and vision
- Making decisions with Behavior Tree
- Developing an AI-controlled Enemy

By the end of this chapter, you will be able to create interactive NPCs that can navigate the level, perceive their surroundings, and make decisions in real time.

Technical requirements

The sample project for this chapter is available for download from the book's GitHub repository and branch:

- `Chapter06-Start` **branch**: The game project to begin learning this chapter.
- `Chapter06` **branch**: The completed game project for this chapter. The AI character `Warrok` is ready to fight against your Hero.

After opening the project, navigate to `Content/ThirdPerson/Lvl_ThirdPerson` and open that level before beginning the exercises in this chapter.

You can download the example project and code files for this book by following the instructions in the *Download the example code/resource files* section in the *Preface* of this book.

This chapter's code/resource files are included in the downloadable code/resource bundle.

Understanding AI character design in Unreal Engine

An **NPC** is any character or actor in the game world that is not directly controlled by the player. In a typical Role-Playing Game (RPG), this could be an enemy, a shopkeeper, a companion, a guard, or a creature wandering through the environment.

In our project, we will create an enemy NPC called `Warrok`, a fierce enemy guardian soldier. It will patrol the level, detect, chase, and attack the player character when close enough.

To make this possible, we first need to understand how Unreal Engine separates player-controlled logic from AI-controlled logic.

Figure 6.1 shows the type of enemy NPC we will create in this chapter. `Warrok` is not controlled by player input. Instead, we will use Unreal Engine's AI systems to make it patrol, detect the player, chase, and attack during gameplay.

Figure 6.1 - Creating an enemy non-player character

To better understand how `Warrok` will behave in the game world, let's first look at the difference between player-controlled characters and AI-controlled characters in Unreal Engine.

Player-controlled characters and AI-controlled characters

A **player-controlled character** receives input from the player. For example, when the player presses the *W* key, moves the left analog stick, or clicks the mouse, Unreal Engine receives that input and passes it to the player character or player controller. The character then responds by moving, rotating, jumping, attacking, or performing another action.

An **AI-controlled character** works differently. It does not wait for input. Instead, it uses pre-defined game logic to decide what to do. For example, an AI enemy may ask questions such as:

- Where should I patrol?
- Can I see the player?
- Is the player close enough to attack?
- Should I chase the player?
- Should I stop moving and play an attack animation?

These decisions are not made by the player. They are made by the AI behavior that we, as developers, define for the character. In Unreal Engine, both player-controlled and AI-controlled characters can use the same base `Character` class. They can both have a skeletal mesh, animations, collision, movement, health, and attack logic. The main difference is who controls the character: a player character is usually controlled by a `PlayerController`, but an AI character is usually controlled by an `AIController`. This separation is important because it allows us to create characters that share similar gameplay features but receive their instructions from different sources.

Role of AI Controller, Behavior Tree, and Blackboard

An AI Controller is the object responsible for controlling an AI character. You can think of it as the AI character's brain at runtime. Without an AI Controller, the enemy character can still exist at the level, but it will not have a proper decision-making system controlling it.

The AI Controller can perform tasks such as:

- Starting a **Behavior Tree**, which is a visual decision-making system used to organize AI behavior. It allows you to describe what AI should do under different conditions.
- Reading and writing the **Blackboard**, which is a shared data container (temporary memory storage specifically for AI) used by the AI Controller and Behavior Tree.
- Moving the character to a target location through Unreal Engine's navigation system.
- Reacting to perception events, which are used to give AI characters senses, such as sight and hearing. This allows an enemy to detect Actors in the world instead of always knowing exactly where they are.

Unreal Engine's AI system may seem like it has many separate parts, but each part has a clear responsibility. We can summarize these parts and the above explanation in *Figure 6.2* as follows:

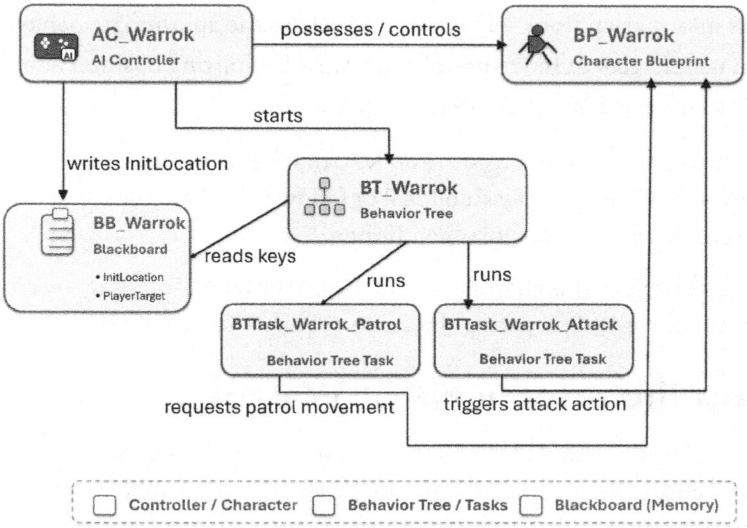

Figure 6.2 - Relationship between Warrok's AI Controller, Behavior Tree, Blackboard, Character Blueprint, and Behavior Tree tasks

Figure 6.2 summarizes how the main assets and systems used in this chapter work together:

- `BP_Warrok` is the Character Blueprint for the enemy body placed in the level. It contains the mesh, collision, movement, animation connection, health variables, and weapon attachment logic.
- `AC_Warrok` is the AI Controller Blueprint. It possesses `BP_Warrok`, starts the Behavior Tree, and updates AI-related information in the Blackboard.
- `BT_Warrok` is the Behavior Tree that decides which behavior Warrok should perform, such as patrolling, chasing, or attacking.
- `BB_Warrok` is the Blackboard that stores information shared by the AI Controller and Behavior Tree, including Warrok's starting location (`InitLocation`) and the detected player (`PlayerTarget`).
- `BTTask_Warrok_Patrol` and `BTTask_Warrok_Attack` are custom Behavior Tree tasks that perform specific actions, such as selecting a patrol destination or triggering an attack.
- The Nav Mesh defines where `Warrok` can move, while AI Perception allows Warrok to detect the player through sight and hearing.

When the game begins, AC_Warrok possesses BP_Warrok and starts BT_Warrok. The Behavior Tree then reads information from BB_Warrok and selects the appropriate behavior. For example, it can use InitLocation to patrol near Warrok's starting position or use PlayerTarget to chase and attack the detected player.

By combining these systems, we can create an NPC that behaves more like an active part of the game world. Warrok will not simply stand still or follow a fixed animation. It will move, sense, decide, and respond based on gameplay conditions.

In the following sections of this chapter, we will begin the hands-on setup by creating the Warrok enemy character and preparing the assets required for our AI-controlled NPC.

Setting up the enemy NPC: Warrok

Just as we built a player-controlled character in *Chapter 4*, the first step in building Warrok is to import its assets, create the required Blueprints, assign an AI Controller, and prepare the basic AI asset structure.

Importing the Warrok assets

Let's import the character model and its animation files first. To keep the project organized, we will place Warrok under the same character folder structure used by the rest of the Pangaea project.

In the **Content Browser**, create the following folder structure:

- Content/Pangaea/Characters/Warrok/
- Content/Pangaea/Characters/Warrok/Model/
- Content/Pangaea/Characters/Warrok/Animations/

You can find all required source files under the Pangaea_Assets/NPCs/Warrok folder, as shown in *Table 6.1*:

Source asset	Asset type	Project renamed target asset
Path: Pangaea_Assets/NPCs/Warrok		**Path:** Content/Pangaea/Characters/Warrok
Warrok.fbx	Model	Model/SK_Warrok
	Skeleton	Model/SK_Warrok_Skeleton
	Material	Model/M_Warrok
Warrok_Attack1.fbx	Animation	Animations/A_Warrok_Attack1
Warrok_Attack2.fbx		Animations/A_Warrok_Attack2
Warrok_Idle.fbx		Animations/A_Warrok_Idle
Warrok_Walk.fbx		Animations/A_Warrok_Walk
Warrok_Run.fbx		Animations/A_Warrok_Run
Warrok_Hit.fbx		Animations/A_Warrok_Hit
Warrok_Die.fbx		Animations/A_Warrok_Die

Table 6.1 - Folder structure of Warrok NPC

First, import Warrok.fbx into the Model subfolder. This file contains the Warrok skeletal mesh and skeleton, so rename the imported model and skeleton assets to SK_Warrok and SK_Warrok_Skeleton. After the import finishes, open the Skeletal Mesh and confirm that the Warrok model appears correctly in the **Skeletal Mesh Editor**.

Next, import the Warrok_*.fbx animation files into the Animations subfolder and rename the imported animation assets to A_Warrok_*. When importing each animation FBX file, make sure it uses the SK_Warrok_Skeleton skeleton.

> **Note**
>
> When importing the provided Warrok FBX files, Unreal Engine may display a **No smoothing group information was found** warning. You can safely ignore this warning for the supplied assets as long as `SK_Warrok` appears correctly shaded in the **Skeletal Mesh Editor**. It does not affect the skeleton or the imported animation clips. If you are exporting your own skeletal mesh from a 3D application, enable **Smoothing Groups** in the FBX export settings so Unreal Engine can preserve the intended surface shading. If the imported mesh shows visible shading problems, re-export it with smoothing groups or appropriate vertex normals instead of ignoring the warning.

The animation import should be set up as an animation-only import, because these files are meant to add animation clips to the selected skeleton rather than creating a new character mesh each time.

After importing the animations, open each animation asset and check whether the Skeletal Mesh, skeleton, and animations were imported correctly. You should be able to open the Skeletal Mesh and preview the Warrok model in the editor.

The automatically generated `Warrok_MAT` material is slightly more complex than the `Hero` material because it uses additional texture inputs, such as a specular map and a normal map. The *specular map* controls how shiny different parts of the surface appear, while the *normal map* adds small surface details without changing the actual model geometry.

Figure 6.3 shows the material node graph for reference, so you can understand how the imported texture maps are connected to the material. Since the `Warrok_MAT` is automatically generated when importing the model, *you don't need to build it from scratch*: just remember to rename the file to `M_Warrok` to match the naming convention.

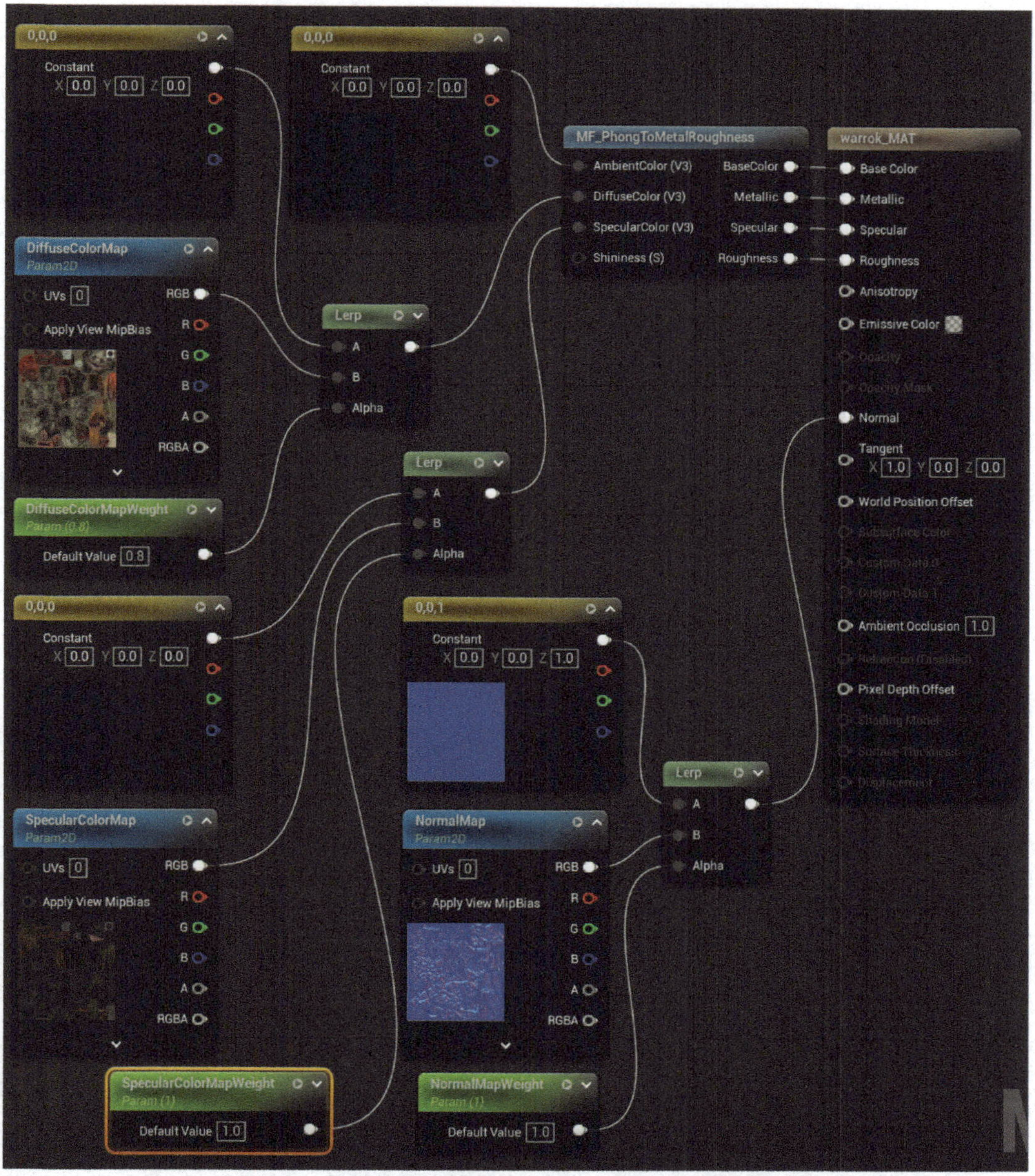

Figure 6.3 - Material settings of the Warrok model

At this stage, we are only preparing the assets. In the next section, we will create the Character and Animation Blueprints.

Creating BP_Warrok and AB_Warrok Blueprints

Now, we want to create the Blueprint that represents the Warrok character in the game world. This Blueprint will be based on Unreal Engine's Character class because Warrok needs character-style movement, collision, animation, and AI navigation support.

In the **Content Browser**, go to the folder `Content/Pangaea/Characters/Warrok/`. Right-click in the folder and select Blueprint Class. In the **Pick Parent Class** window, choose **Character**. Name the new Blueprint `BP_Warrok`.

After creating `BP_Warrok`, open it and set up the visible character mesh:

1. In the **Components** panel, select the **Mesh** component, and then in the **Details** panel, assign the **Skeletal Mesh** to `SK_Warrok`.
2. In the **Details** panel, assign `M_Warrok` to **Materials | Element 0**.
3. Adjust the **Mesh** component's **Location**, **Rotation**, and **Scale** values until the model stands correctly inside the capsule (see *Figure 6.4*). This also aligns the feet of Warrok to the bottom of the capsule.
4. To make Warrok's body mostly covered by the capsule, select the **Capsule component** in the **Components** panel and adjust the **Shape** parameters to provide a reasonable collision boundary for movement and gameplay (see *Figure 6.4*).

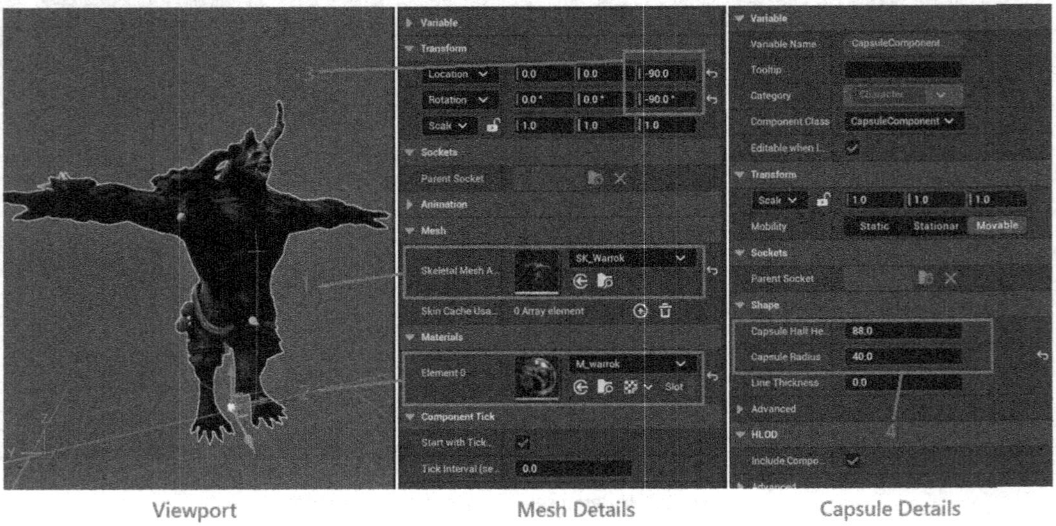

Figure 6.4 - Adjust collision capsule to fit the model

The BP_Warrok Blueprint will become the main enemy actor placed in the level. It is responsible for the visible character, collision, movement component, health variables, weapon attachment, and animation connection.

After creating BP_Warrok, we also need an Animation Blueprint for Warrok. The Character Blueprint controls the enemy actor in the level, while the Animation Blueprint controls which animation the skeletal mesh should play.

In the **Content Browser**, go to: Content/Pangaea/Characters/Warrok/Animations/. Right-click inside the folder and select **Animation | Animation Blueprint**. When Unreal Engine asks for the target skeleton, choose the SK_Warrok_Skeleton. Name the new Animation Blueprint AB_Warrok.

Next, assign AB_Warrok to BP_Warrok:

1. Open BP_Warrok.
2. Select the **Mesh** component in the **Components** panel.
3. In the **Details** panel, find the **Animation** section.
4. Set **Animation Mode** to **Use Animation Blueprint**.
5. Set **Anim Class** to AB_Warrok.
6. Compile and save BP_Warrok.

This connects Warrok's skeletal mesh to its Animation Blueprint. Later in this chapter, we will add animation variables such as Speed and AnimState inside AB_Warrok so the enemy can switch between idle, movement, hit, attack, and death animations.

The Warrok character also needs a weapon. We have prepared a hammer asset as the weapon used by Warrok. Just as we set up the sword for the Hero character, we need to import hammer assets from the Pangaea_Assets source folder and create a Hammer folder under the Content/Pangaea/Weapons folder. We learned how to import Hero's sword in *Chapter 4*; here we follow the same steps as in *Chapter 4* to import the hammer assets.

After successfully importing the model and hooking up the material, we need to create a BP_Hammer Blueprint to represent the weapon, as shown in *Figure 6.5*:

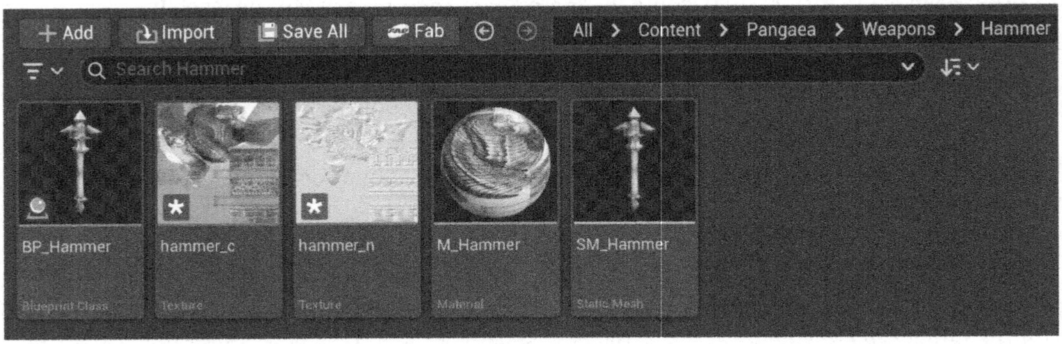

Figure 6.5 - Hammer assets

We want this hammer to be able to spawn and attach to Warrok during gameplay. We can repeat the same steps we have learned in *Chapter 4* of attaching the sword to the Hero character (shown in *Figure 6.6*). The important steps are to choose the correct socket, attach the weapon actor to the mesh component, and make sure the attachment transform places the weapon correctly in the character's hand.

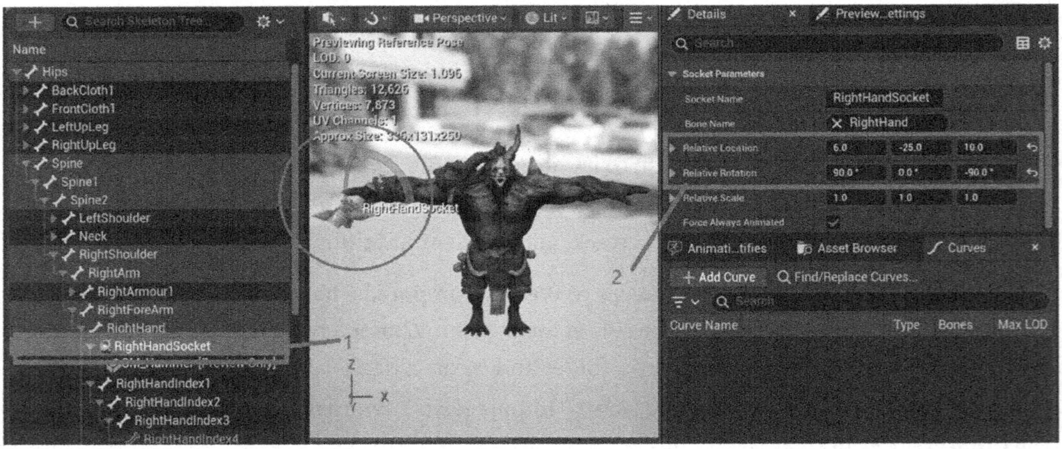

Figure 6.6 - Using a socket to attach the hammer

This setup gives the enemy a visible weapon before we create its attack behavior. Later, when the Behavior Tree triggers an attack task, Warrok will already have the hammer attached and ready to use.

In `BP_Warrok`, we need to spawn `BP_Hammer` and attach it to Warrok's hand when the game begins. This is the same runtime weapon attachment workflow we used for the Hero's sword in *Chapter 4*.

Figure 6.7 shows the Blueprint logic you need to recreate in `BP_Warrok`. The logic starts from **Event BeginPlay**. From there, use **Spawn Actor from Class** and set **Class** to `BP_Hammer`. The **Return Value** pin from **Spawn Actor from Class** is the hammer actor instance created at runtime.

Next, pass that **Return Value** into the **Target** pin of **Attach Actor To Component**. Set the **Parent** pin to Warrok's **Mesh** component and set the **Socket Name** to the weapon socket on Warrok's skeleton. This tells Unreal Engine to attach the spawned hammer actor to Warrok's right hand instead of leaving it at its spawn location in the level.

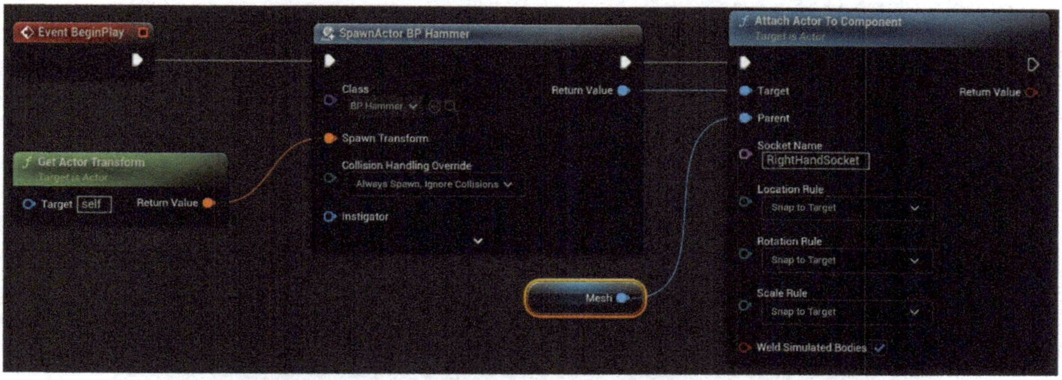

Figure 6.7 - Spawning and attaching the hammer to Warrok in BP_Warrok

The socket transform values shown here are adjusted specifically for the provided `Warrok` asset and hammer. If you use a different character mesh, skeleton, or weapon asset, these values may not produce the same alignment. Preview the weapon attachment and adjust the socket's **Location**, **Rotation**, and **Scale** until the hammer fits naturally in the character's hand.

Compile and save `BP_Warrok`, then press **Play**. Warrok should now hold the hammer in his hand. If the hammer appears but is incorrectly positioned or rotated, return to the **Skeleton Editor** and adjust the socket transform while previewing the attached weapon. If the hammer does not appear at all, confirm that **Spawn Actor from Class** uses `BP_Hammer`, that the spawned actor is connected to the **Target** pin of **Attach Actor To Component**, and that the correct socket name is entered.

Creating an AI folder

Before creating the AI assets, it is helpful to organize them in a dedicated folder. In the **Content Browser**, go to the Warrok character folder and create a new folder named `AI`:

`Content/Pangaea/Characters/Warrok/AI/`.

This folder will contain `Warrok`'s AI Controller, Behavior Tree, Blackboard, and custom Behavior Tree tasks.

First, create the AI Controller Blueprint:

1. Right-click inside the `Content/Pangaea/Characters/Warrok/AI/` folder.
2. Select **Blueprint Class**.
3. In the **Pick Parent Class** window, expand or search under **All Classes**, as shown in *Figure 6.8*.
4. Search for `AIController`.
5. Select **AIController** as the parent class.
6. Name the new Blueprint `AC_Warrok`.

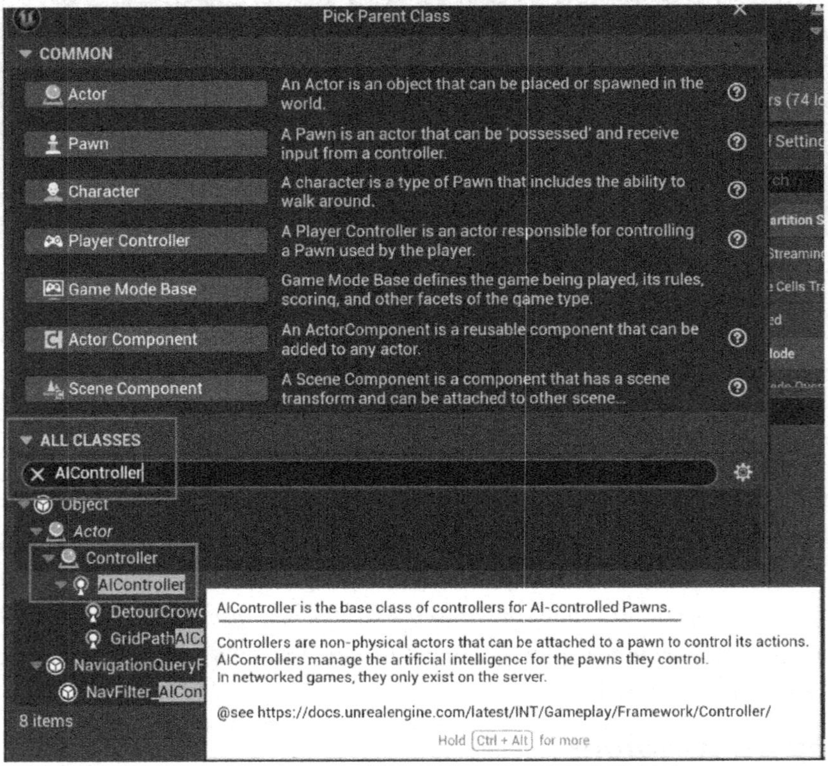

Figure 6.8 - Creating AI Controller – you need to select from "All Classes"

Note that the AC_ prefix means AI Controller. AC_Warrok will possess and control BP_Warrok during gameplay. Later, it will also start Warrok's Behavior Tree and write important values, such as Warrok's starting location, into the Blackboard.

This folder will contain the AI Controller, Behavior Tree, Blackboard, and custom Behavior Tree tasks used by Warrok. The core AI assets we will create for Warrok are listed in *Table 6.2*:

Asset	Type	Purpose
AC_Warrok	AI Controller Blueprint	Possesses BP_Warrok, starts BT_Warrok, and writes AI data into BB_Warrok
BT_Warrok	Behavior Tree	Defines Warrok's decision-making flow
BB_Warrok	Blackboard	Stores shared AI data such as patrol location and player target

Table 6.2 - The major assets needed to create a life-like enemy

In the next section, let's connect the AI controller and the enemy character's Blueprint.

Assigning the AI Controller to BP_Warrok

Creating an AI Controller is not enough by itself. We also need to tell Warrok's main Blueprint, BP_Warrok, to use that controller when the game starts. Follow these steps:

1. Open BP_Warrok and then open the **Details** panel.
2. Find the **Pawn** settings and locate the **AI Controller Class** property.
3. Set **AI Controller Class** to the Blueprint AC_Warrok.

This tells Unreal Engine that when Warrok is spawned or placed in the level, it should be controlled by AC_Warrok. You should also check the **Auto Possess AI** setting. For an enemy placed directly in the level, this is commonly set to **Placed in World** or **Spawned**, as shown in *Figure 6.9*:

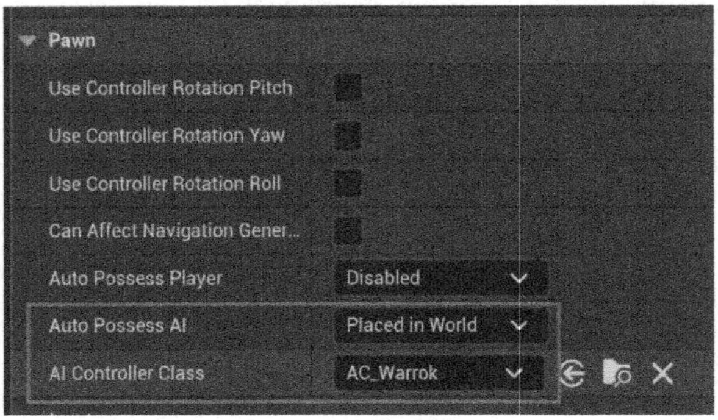

Figure 6.9 - AI Controller settings

This allows the AI Controller to automatically possess the Warrok, whether it was manually placed in the level or spawned during gameplay. The Warrok character now has a controller, but the controller still needs to start the Behavior Tree. We'll continue the setup in the next section.

Starting the Behavior Tree from the AI Controller

Let's create a new Behavior Tree by right-clicking under the `AI` folder and selecting **Behavior Tree** under the **Artificial Intelligence** sub-menu. Assign its name as `BT_Warrok`, as shown in *Figure 6.10*:

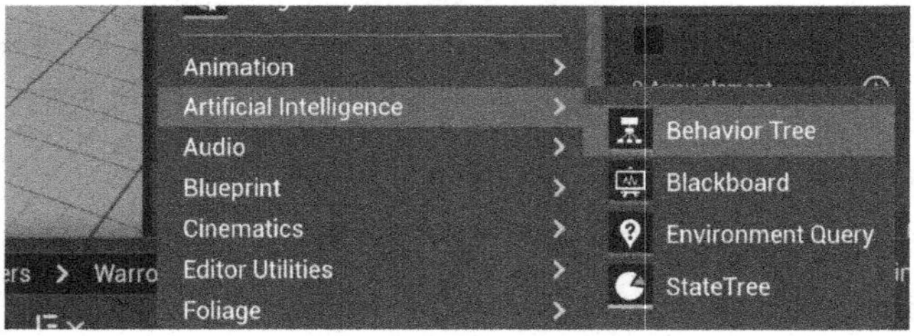

Figure 6.10 - Creating a new Behavior Tree

Now open `AC_Warrok`. This AI Controller will be responsible for starting `BT_Warrok` when it takes control of `Warrok`.

In `AC_Warrok`, switch to the **Event Graph** and create the logic shown in *Figure 6.11*:

1. Right-click in an empty area of the **Event Graph**.
2. Search for `Event On Possess` and add it to the graph.
3. Right-click again and search for `Run Behavior Tree`.
4. Add the **Run Behavior Tree** node.

5. Connect the execution output pin of **Event On Possess** to the execution input pin of **Run Behavior Tree**.
6. Leave the **Target** pin of **Run Behavior Tree** as self because `AC_Warrok` is the AI Controller that will run the Behavior Tree.
7. Set the **BTAsset** property of **Run Behavior Tree** to `BT_Warrok`.
8. Compile and save `AC_Warrok`.

Event On Possess runs when `AC_Warrok` successfully takes control of `BP_Warrok`. The **Run Behavior Tree** node then starts `BT_Warrok`, allowing Warrok's AI decision logic to begin.

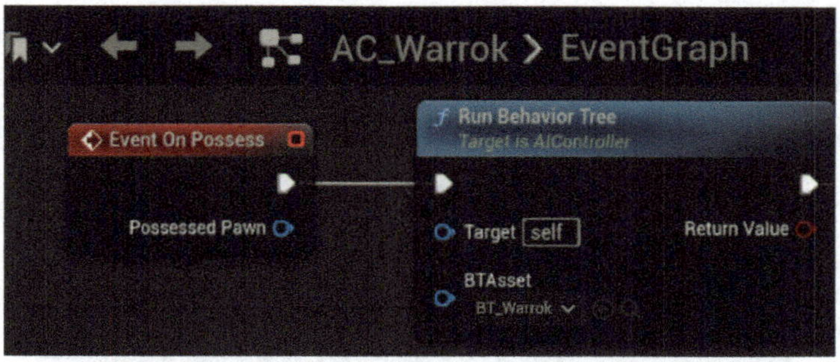

Figure 6.11 - Starting the Behavior Tree in AI Controller

After this setup, press **Play** and confirm that Warrok is using `AC_Warrok` as its controller. If the Behavior Tree does not appear to run later, return to this setup and check three common issues:

- `BP_Warrok` must have **AI Controller Class** set to `AC_Warrok`.
- **Auto Possess AI** must be set to **Placed in World or Spawned**.
- `AC_Warrok` must call **Run Behavior Tree** with `BT_Warrok` assigned as the **BTAsset**.

Once this is set up, `AC_Warrok` will start running `BT_Warrok` when the game begins. In the following sections, we will add more logic to this controller, such as setting Warrok's starting location in the Blackboard. For now, the important part is making sure the AI Controller can start the Behavior Tree successfully.

If we think of the Behavior Tree as the tool that helps the AI Controller decide what to do next, then the AI Controller also needs a place to store the information used by those decisions. For example, the AI may need to remember its starting location, the player it has detected, or the target it is currently chasing.

As described in the *Role of AI Controller, Behavior Tree, and Blackboard* section, in Unreal Engine, this shared data is stored in a Blackboard. In the next section, we will create a Blackboard for our AI character and use it to store the values needed by the Behavior Tree.

Creating a Blackboard as short-term memory for AI Actor

If we want the Warrok character to stay near a specific area and patrol around it, we need a way for Warrok to remember where it started. In this case, we will create a Blackboard to store its initial spawn location. Later, the Behavior Tree can read this location and use it as the center point for Warrok's patrol behavior. This allows the enemy to move around its assigned area instead of wandering randomly across the entire level.

Now let's create a Blackboard by right-clicking under the `AI` folder and selecting **Blackboard** under the **Artificial Intelligence** submenu. Set its name to `BB_Warrok`. Open `BT_Warrok` and assign its **Blackboard Asset** to `BB_Warrok` in the **Details** panel, as shown in *Figure 6.12*:

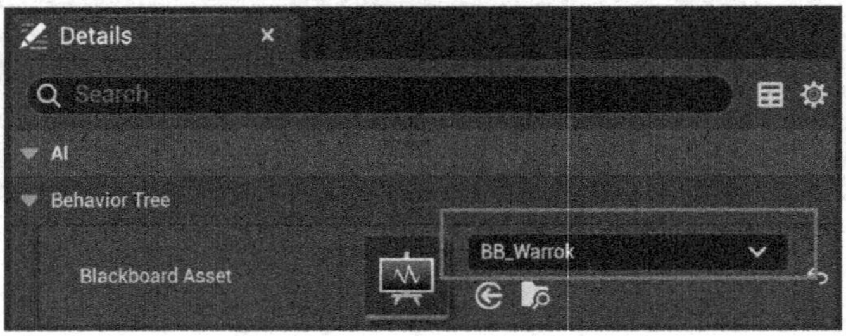

Figure 6.12 - Assigning Blackboard to Behavior Tree

After assigning the Blackboard, open `BB_Warrok`. You may already see a default key named **SelfActor**. This is normal. **SelfActor** represents the actor that owns or runs the Blackboard during gameplay, and Unreal Engine may create it automatically.

We will now add our own key. Add a new key with the **Vector** type and name it `InitLocation`, as shown in *Figure 6.13*:

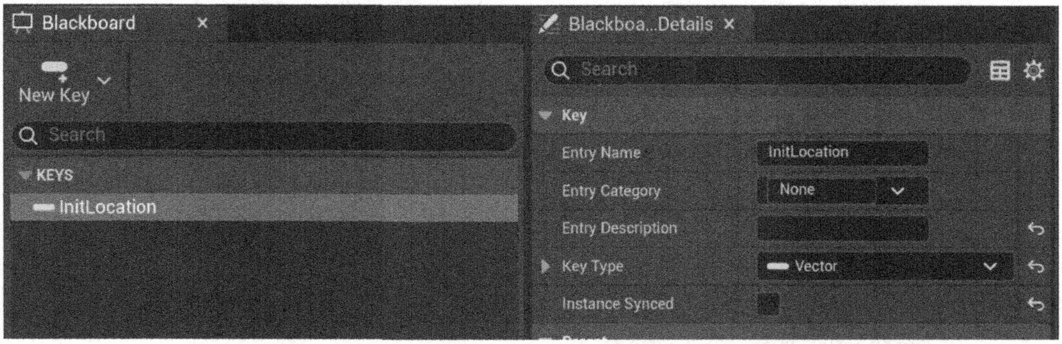

Figure 6.13 - Adding an InitLocation key

The **InitLocation** key will store the position where the Warrok begins. Later, the patrol task will use this value to choose patrol points around the starting area. This is useful because we usually do not want an enemy to wander anywhere in the entire level. By storing the starting location, we can make the enemy patrol around its own area.

At this point, our Warrok is not fully intelligent yet. It has a character body, an animation system, an AI Controller, a Behavior Tree, and a Blackboard, but the Behavior Tree does not yet contain useful behavior.

In the next section, we will set up AI navigation so Warrok can move through the level and begin patrolling around its starting location.

Enabling AI navigation and movement

Now we can start giving Warrok the ability to move through the level. Before an AI character can patrol, chase the player, or move toward an attack position, Unreal Engine needs to know which areas of the level are walkable. This is handled through Unreal Engine's **navigation system**.

The navigation system generates a special data structure called a **Nav Mesh**, short for **navigation mesh**. The Nav Mesh marks the surfaces where AI-controlled characters are allowed to move. Once a Nav Mesh exists in the level, AI movement nodes such as **Move To** can use it to calculate paths.

For example, if the player stands on the other side of a wall, the AI should not move in a straight line through the wall. Instead, it should find a valid route around the obstacle. The Nav Mesh helps Unreal Engine calculate this path.

In this section, we will set up the navigation area for Warrok and prepare the enemy for AI-controlled movement.

Setting up Nav Mesh

A Nav Mesh is generated from the level geometry. It identifies which surfaces can be walked on by AI characters. In most cases, flat floors, terrain, and ramps become valid navigation areas, while walls, steep slopes, and blocked objects are excluded.

For Warrok, the Nav Mesh will allow it to:

- Patrol around its starting location.
- Move toward a random patrol point.
- Chase the player after detection.
- Move close enough to enter attack range.

Without a valid Nav Mesh, Warrok may have a working AI Controller and Behavior Tree, but movement commands will not behave correctly. The character may stand still because Unreal Engine cannot find a valid navigation path.

To create this walkable area in our level, we need to place a Nav Mesh Bounds Volume.

Adding a Nav Mesh Bounds Volume

To generate a Nav Mesh, we need to add a **Nav Mesh Bounds Volume** to the level. This volume defines the area where Unreal Engine should calculate navigation data.

In the editor, open the level where Warrok will be placed. Then follow these steps:

1. Open the **Place Actors** panel. You can find this from the top **Window** menu.
2. Search for **Nav Mesh Bounds Volume** from the left side category panel, as shown in *Figure 6.14*.
3. Drag the **Nav Mesh Bounds Volume** into the level.
4. Move the **Nav Mesh Bounds Volume** so it covers the playable area where Warrok needs to move.
5. Scale the **Nav Mesh Bounds Volume** until it covers the full navigation area.

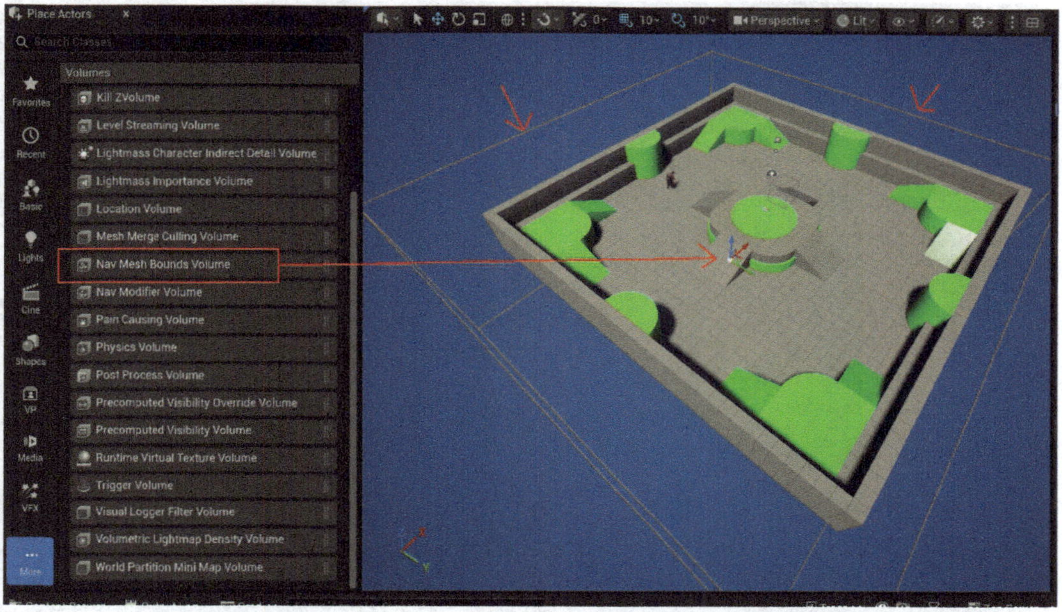

Figure 6.14 - Selecting Nav Mesh Bounds Volume to add into the level

Note

The Nav Mesh Bounds Volume does not need to cover the entire world. It only needs to cover the areas where AI movement should be possible. For example, if Warrok only patrols inside a small courtyard, the volume only needs to cover that courtyard and any nearby paths the enemy can use.

Visualizing the Nav Mesh

When we add a Nav Mesh Bounds Volume to the level, adjusted to cover the navigation area, we can visualize the generated Nav Mesh by pressing *P* in the Viewport, as shown in *Figure 6.15*:

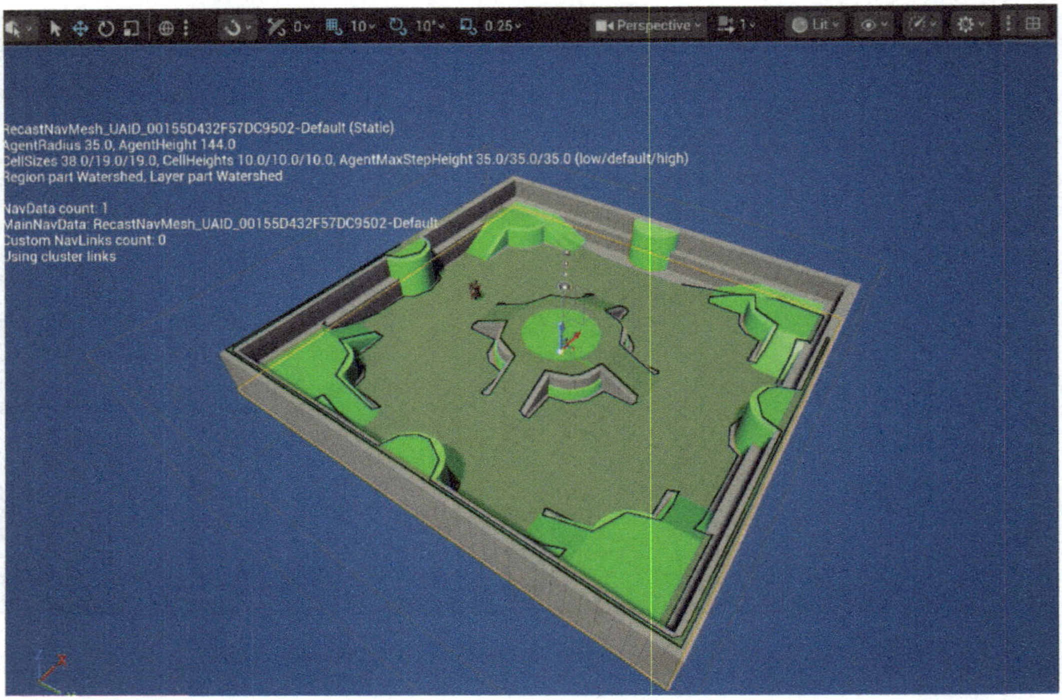

Figure 6.15 - Visualize the walkable area (overlaid with green shade) with Nav Mesh

You should see a *green* overlay on the floor or terrain inside the volume. This green overlay represents the walkable area.

The most common beginner mistake is placing the Nav Mesh Bounds Volume above or beside the playable area instead of covering it. Make sure the volume overlaps the ground where Warrok should walk.

Once the Nav Mesh is visible, place `BP_Warrok` inside the green area. The enemy should begin the game on a valid navigation surface. This is important because the AI movement works best when both the *starting location* and *target location* are on the Nav Mesh. If Warrok starts outside the generated navigation area, movement commands may fail.

You should also check that Warrok's capsule is not intersecting the floor or blocked by nearby objects. If the character starts inside collision geometry, it may not move correctly even if the Nav Mesh is valid.

Once Warrok is placed on a valid Nav Mesh area, we can start using Behavior Tree movement tasks to tell it where to go.

How AI movement works with the Behavior Tree

As discussed in the *Role of AI Controller, Behavior Tree, and Blackboard* section, AI movement is often controlled through a Behavior Tree. Instead of manually moving the character every frame, we can use Behavior Tree tasks to request specific AI actions.

A **Behavior Tree task** is a node that performs a particular operation, such as waiting, running custom logic, or moving toward a target. For AI movement, Unreal Engine provides a built-in task called **Move To**. We can browse and select these built-in tasks by right-clicking in empty space of the Behavior Tree to bring up the context menu:

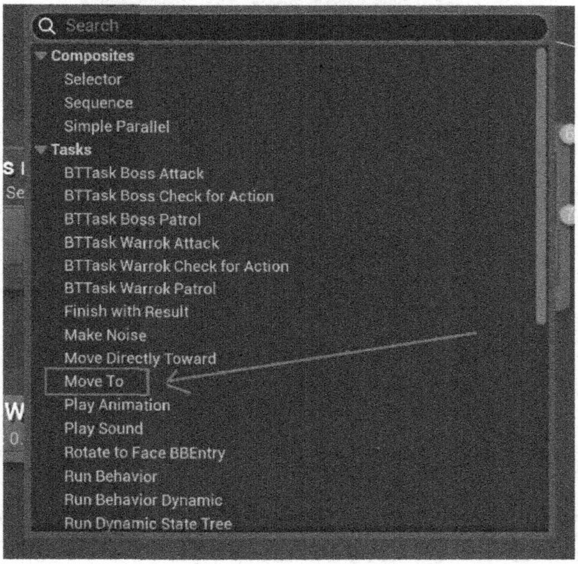

Figure 6.16 - Creating a new task from list of available built-in tasks

A **Move To** built-in task tells the AI to move toward a target location or actor. The target can be a position stored in the **Blackboard**, or it can be an Actor reference such as the player character.

Later in this chapter, we will use movement in two important ways: patrol and chase; both behaviors rely on the Nav Mesh. The Behavior Tree decides *where* Warrok should move, while the navigation system calculates *how* Warrok should get there.

This separation is useful because it keeps the AI logic clean. The Behavior Tree does not need to know every detail of the level. It only needs to request movement. The navigation system then handles pathfinding.

Preparing the Blackboard for movement

In the previous section, we created a Blackboard key named `InitLocation`. This key stores Warrok's starting position.

The patrol behavior will use this value as the center point for movement. Instead of wandering across the entire level, Warrok can choose patrol points near its original location.

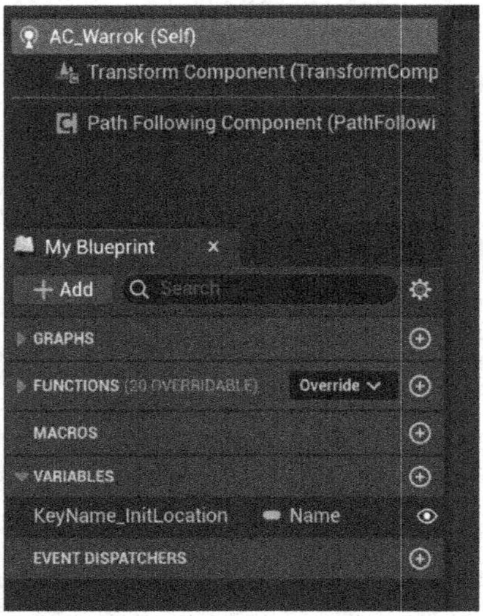

Figure 6.17 - Creating the KeyName_InitLocation variable in AC_Warrok

The `InitLocation` key will be set by `AC_Warrok` when the AI Controller possesses `BP_Warrok`. This lets `Warrok` remember where it started in the level.

Open `AC_Warrok` and create a new variable:

1. In the **My Blueprint** panel, click the + button beside **Variables**.
2. Name the variable `KeyName_InitLocation`, as shown in *Figure 6.18*.
3. Set its **Variable Type** to **Name**.
4. Compile the Blueprint.
5. Set the default value of **KeyName_InitLocation** to `InitLocation`.

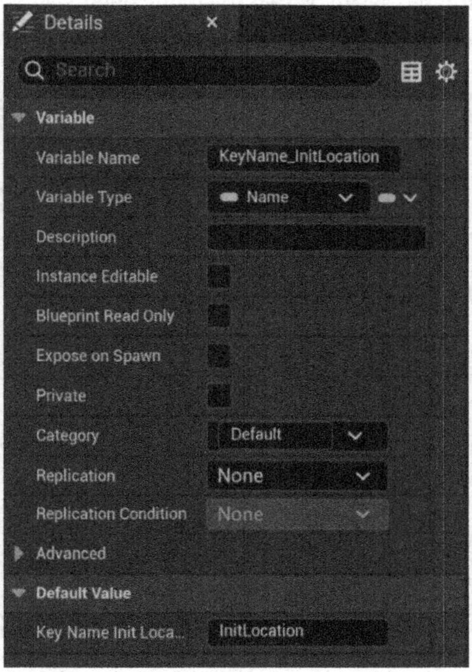

Figure 6.18 - Adding a new variable to store the key name

The variable name is `KeyName_InitLocation`, but the value stored inside it must match the Blackboard key name exactly: `InitLocation`. This avoids typing the key name directly into several Blueprint nodes.

Next, update the **Event Graph** in `AC_Warrok` so it writes `Warrok`'s starting position into the Blackboard when possession happens:

1. Use the existing **Event On Possess** node.
2. From the **Possessed Pawn** pin, add **Get Actor Location**.
3. Add **Get Blackboard** to access the Blackboard used by this AI Controller.
4. Add a **Set Value as Vector** node.
5. Connect the **Return Value** from **Get Blackboard** to the **Target** pin of **Set Value as Vector**.
6. Connect **KeyName_InitLocation** to the **Key Name** pin.
7. Connect the output value from **Get Actor Location** to the **Vector Value** pin.
8. Connect the execution flow so this logic runs when `Event On Possess` fires.

Figure 6.19 shows the completed setup. When the game begins, `AC_Warrok` gets the location of the possessed Warrok pawn and stores it in the Blackboard key named `InitLocation`:

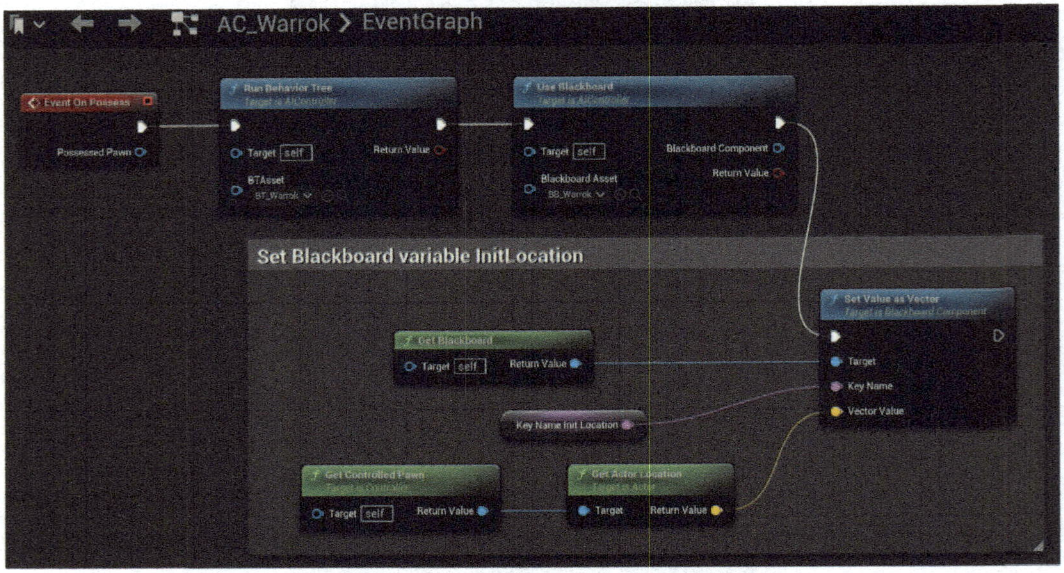

Figure 6.19 - Use Actor pawn's spawn location to set up Warrok's initial location

> **Tip**
>
> The `KeyName_InitLocation` variable stores the name of the Blackboard key we want to update. Using a variable instead of typing the key name directly in multiple places makes the setup easier to maintain. If the Blackboard key name changes later, we only need to update it in one place.

Once the value is stored in Blackboard, the patrol task can read it and choose a nearby navigation point. This gives the AI a simple memory of where it belongs. In the next section, we will build a patrol movement task for our Behavior Tree.

Creating patrol behavior

In the previous section, we enabled AI navigation by adding a Nav Mesh to the level and preparing Warrok for AI-controlled movement. Now we can use that navigation setup to create Warrok's first behavior: *patrolling around its starting location.*

Patrol behavior is one of the most common enemy AI patterns in games. Instead of standing still, an enemy can move around a small area, making the world feel more active. In our project,

Warrok will patrol near the position where it begins the game. Later, when Warrok detects the player, the Behavior Tree will switch from patrol behavior to chase behavior.

For now, we will focus only on the patrol behavior.

Understanding the patrol logic

Before building the Blueprint logic, it is helpful to understand what we want Warrok to do. When the game starts, Warrok should remember its initial position. This position will be stored in the Blackboard as a Vector value named `InitLocation`. The patrol task will then use this location as the center of the patrol area.

The basic logic of patrolling looks like this:

```
When the game starts:
    Save Warrok's starting position as InitLocation
During patrol behavior:
    Read InitLocation from the Blackboard
        Find a random reachable point near InitLocation
        Move Warrok to that point
        Wait briefly
        Repeat the process
```

The important part of this flow is that Warrok does not choose patrol points from the entire level. It first reads `InitLocation` from the Blackboard, then searches for a reachable point near that location. This keeps the enemy near its assigned guard area and prevents it from wandering too far away.

This gives Warrok a controlled patrol area. Instead of wandering across the entire level, it moves around its own starting position.

Creating patrol movement task

With the Nav Mesh and `InitLocation` key ready, we can create Warrok's first custom Behavior Tree task. This task will choose a random reachable patrol point near Warrok's starting location.

In the **Content Browser**, go to the `Content/Pangaea/Characters/Warrok/AI/` folder and create the patrol task Blueprint.

1. Right-click inside the `AI` folder.
2. Select **Blueprint Class**.
3. In the **Pick Parent Class** window, search for **BTTask_BlueprintBase**.

4. Select **BTTask_BlueprintBase** as the parent class.
5. Name the new Blueprint `BTTask_Warrok_Patrol`.
6. Open `BTTask_Warrok_Patrol`.

Inside `BTTask_Warrok_Patrol`, create a variable for the Blackboard key name:

1. In the **My Blueprint** panel, click the + button beside **Variables**.
2. Name the variable `KeyName_InitLocation`.
3. Set its variable type to **Name**.
4. Compile the Blueprint.
5. Set the default value of **KeyName_InitLocation** to `InitLocation`.
6. As before, the variable name is `KeyName_InitLocation`, but the value stored inside it must match the Blackboard key name exactly: `InitLocation`.

The minimum patrol logic flow runs as follows:

```
Receive Execute AI:
    → Get Blackboard value InitLocation
    → Find a random reachable point near InitLocation
    → Move the AI pawn to that point
    → Finish Execute
```

Here is the task Blueprint implementation shown in *Figure 6.20*:

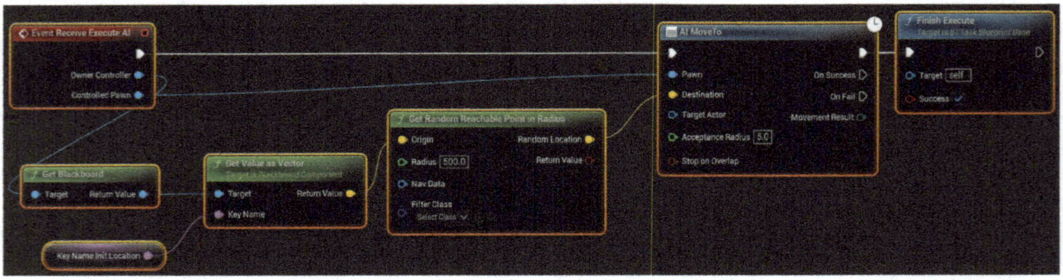

Figure 6.20 - The Blueprint of patrol behavior

Now we can build the task logic. When the Behavior Tree runs this task, Event Receive Execute AI will start the task. The task will read `InitLocation` from the Blackboard, ask the navigation system for a random reachable point near that location, move Warrok toward that point, and then finish the task so the Behavior Tree can continue.

Figure 6.20 implements the patrol logic with the following Blueprint nodes:

- **Event Receive Execute AI** starts the task when the Behavior Tree reaches `BTTask_Warrok_Patrol`.
- **Get Blackboard** gets the Blackboard component used by the AI Controller.
- **Get Value as Vector** reads the value stored in the `InitLocation` Blackboard key. This gives us the center point of Warrok's patrol area.
- **Get Random Reachable Point in Radius** asks the navigation system to find a random point near `InitLocation` that Warrok can actually reach on the Nav Mesh. In this chapter, we use a radius of 500 Unreal units.
- **AI MoveTo** sends the controlled Warrok pawn toward the random reachable point returned by the navigation query.
- **Finish Execute** tells the Behavior Tree that this task has finished. When the Behavior Tree loops back to this task later, Warrok can choose a new random patrol point.

As shown earlier in *Figure 6.17*, the startup logic in `AC_Warrok` stores the controlled pawn's current location in the Blackboard as `InitLocation`. This prevents the patrol task from choosing random locations from the whole level. Instead, it will choose points around this stored starting position.

> **Tip**
>
> The important part is that the patrol location must be reachable on the Nav Mesh. Unreal Engine provides navigation helper nodes, such as **Get Random Reachable Point in Radius**, that can find a random point within a navigable radius. This prevents the AI from choosing a target inside a wall or outside the playable area.

The patrol radius controls how far Warrok can move away from its starting location. For example, you can start with a value like `500`, which means Warrok will choose random patrol points within 500 Unreal units from its initial location. Because Unreal Engine uses centimeters by default, 500 units is approximately 5 meters.

Why use a random reachable point?

When creating patrol behavior, we should not simply choose a random point using raw *X* and *Y* values. That point might be inside a wall, outside the level, or in an area where the AI cannot walk.

Instead, we should choose a point that is reachable through the navigation system.

A reachable point means:

- The point is inside the Nav Mesh
- The AI can calculate a path to it
- The point is valid for movement

This makes the patrol behavior more reliable. Warrok will choose destinations that are actually usable by the AI navigation system.

Now that the patrol task can choose a valid destination, we can add it to `BT_Warrok` and let the Behavior Tree run it repeatedly.

Adding the patrol task to BT_Warrok

After creating `BTTask_Warrok_Patrol`, open `BT_Warrok`. For the first patrol version, let's create a simple Behavior Tree structure, as shown in *Figure 6.21*:

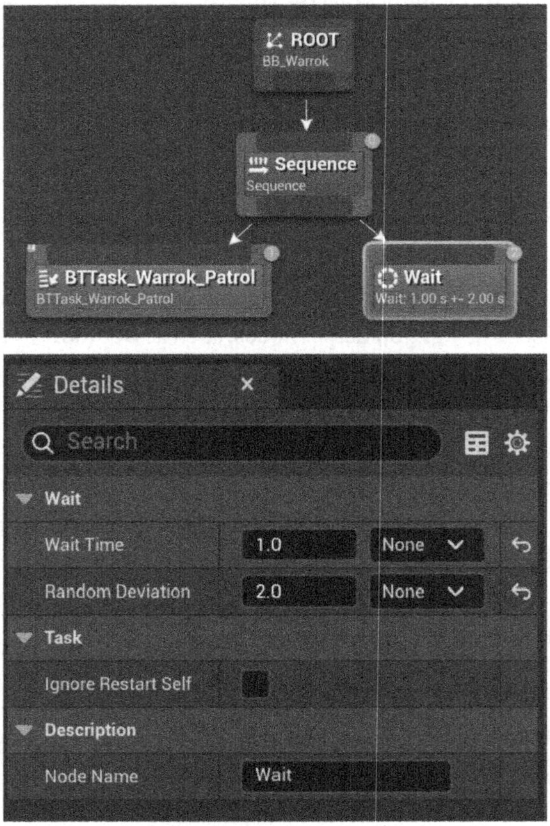

Figure 6.21 - Setting the simplest patrol behavior

In *Figure 6.21*, the BTTask_Warrok_Patrol node chooses a patrol point and starts the movement. The **Wait** node adds a short pause before the Behavior Tree runs the patrol task again. This pause prevents Warrok from immediately choosing a new destination every time it reaches a patrol point, which makes the patrol behavior look more natural. Without a wait, the enemy may immediately choose a new destination, which can make the patrol behavior look unnatural.

To configure the pause:

1. Select the **Wait** node in BT_Warrok.
2. In the **Details** panel, set **Wait Time** to 1.0.
3. Set **Random Deviation** to 2.0.

With these values, Warrok waits for a slightly varied amount of time before choosing the next patrol point. This small variation helps the patrol behavior feel less mechanical.

Before continuing, press **Play** and observe Warrok in the level. At this point, Warrok should move to a random point near its starting location, pause briefly, and then choose another nearby patrol point.

If Warrok does not move, check the following common issues:

- BP_Warrok must be placed on the *green* Nav Mesh area.
- BP_Warrok must have **AI Controller Class** set to AC_Warrok.
- **Auto Possess AI** must be set to **Placed in World** or **Spawned**.
- AC_Warrok must call **Run Behavior Tree** with BT_Warrok assigned.
- BT_Warrok must use BB_Warrok as its Blackboard Asset.
- BB_Warrok must contain the InitLocation key.
- AC_Warrok must write Warrok's starting location into InitLocation.
- BTTask_Warrok_Patrol must read InitLocation and use **Get Random Reachable Point** in **Radius** to find a valid patrol point.
- If the Behavior Tree is running but Warrok still does not move, press *P* in the Viewport and confirm that the Nav Mesh covers both Warrok's starting position and the patrol area.

In the next section, we will improve how Warrok looks while moving by connecting its locomotion animation and rotation settings to the AI movement system.

Improving Warrok locomotion and turning

At this point, Warrok can use the Nav Mesh to patrol around its initial location. However, AI movement is only one part of the result. If the character moves through the level but the animation does not match the movement, the enemy may appear to slide, rotate unnaturally, or move without proper body motion.

In this section, we will improve Warrok's movement presentation by connecting its locomotion animation to its movement speed and adjusting the character rotation settings. This will make Warrok look more natural while patrolling, chasing, and turning toward different destinations.

The goal is not only to make the AI move correctly, but also to make the movement visually believable.

Understanding locomotion for AI characters

Locomotion refers to the character's movement animation, such as *idle*, *walking*, *running*, and *turning*. For a player-controlled character, locomotion is usually driven by player input; for an AI-controlled character, the idea is similar. The difference is that the movement is not caused by player input. Instead, the AI Controller and Behavior Tree tell the character where to move. The **Character Movement** component then moves the character through the world.

Even though the source of movement is different, the Animation Blueprint can still read the character's velocity and use it to update the animation state.

The general flow looks like this:

1. Behavior Tree requests movement.
2. AI Controller moves Warrok through the Nav Mesh.
3. `BP_Warrok` updates its velocity.
4. `AB_Warrok` reads the velocity.
5. Animation changes from *idle* to *movement*.

This means we do not need a separate animation system just because Warrok is controlled by AI. We only need to make sure the Animation Blueprint reads the correct movement values. Let's work on this in the next section.

Syncing Warrok's movement with the Animation Blueprint

Let's improve the visual quality of Warrok's movement by synchronizing its movement speed with the Animation Blueprint, `AB_Warrok`. The Animation Blueprint needs to know whether Warrok is standing still or moving. A common way to do this is to calculate the character's speed from its velocity.

Open `AB_Warrok` and go to its **Event Graph**. Create a new **Float** variable named `Speed`. This variable will store Warrok's current movement speed.

Now let's build the following Blueprint logic:

1. Add or use **Event Blueprint Update Animation**.
2. Drag the `Speed` variable into the graph and choose **Set Speed**.
3. Connect the *white* execution output pin from **Event Blueprint Update Animation** to the *white* execution input pin of **Set Speed**.
4. Add **Try Get Pawn Owner**. This is a pure node, so it does not need an execution wire.
5. From the **Return Value** of **Try Get Pawn Owner**, add **Get Velocity**.
6. Connect the velocity value to **Vector Length**.
7. Set the result of **Vector Length** into the **Speed** variable.

With this setup, the Animation Blueprint updates `Speed` every animation update. The execution wire tells Unreal Engine when to set the variable, while the pure nodes provide the value that should be stored.

Here is the final Blueprint for synchronizing movement with the Animation Blueprint, as shown in *Figure 6.22*:

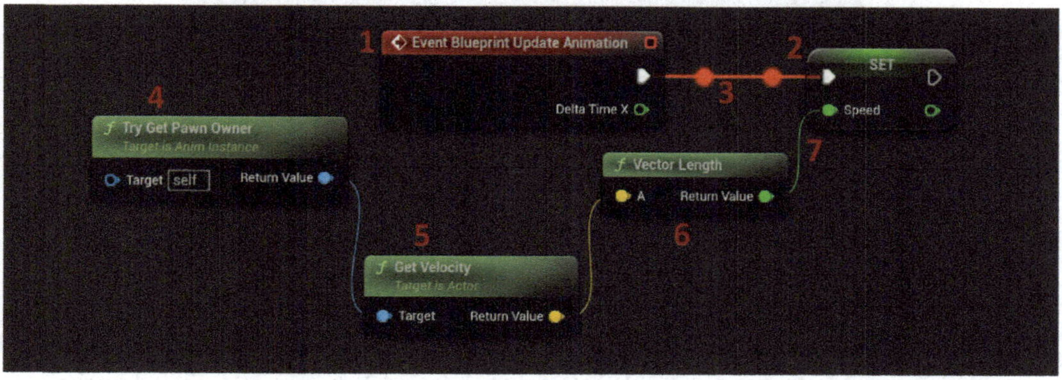

Figure 6.22 - The final Blueprint of synchronizing movement with animation

In *Figure 6.22*, the Animation Blueprint starts with **Event Blueprint Update Animation**. The **Try Get Pawn Owner** node gets the pawn that owns this Animation Blueprint. From that pawn, **Get Velocity** reads the character's current velocity, and **Vector Length** converts that velocity into a Float value. The result is stored in the `Speed` variable. The animation state machine can then use `Speed` to decide whether Warrok should play the idle animation or the movement animation.

To switch between different animations for Warrok, in the next section, we will build an animation state machine in **AnimGraph** as we did in *Chapter 4*.

Setting up Warrok's AnimGraph

Like the Hero character we built in *Chapter 4*, an AI-controlled character also needs to handle complex animation transitions. We have learned how to build an animation state machine for the Hero character in *Chapter 4*. The same process applies to AI-controlled characters.

1. Open the **AnimGraph** of `AB_Warrok` and create a **State Machine** named `Warrok State Machine`. Connect this **State Machine** to the final **Output Pose** node as shown in *Figure 6.23*.
2. Open `Warrok State Machine`, create a new animation state from the **Entry** node, and name it `Locomotion`. Later, we will create more animation states for attack, hit, and die. But we will focus on setting up the **Locomotion** animation state for now.

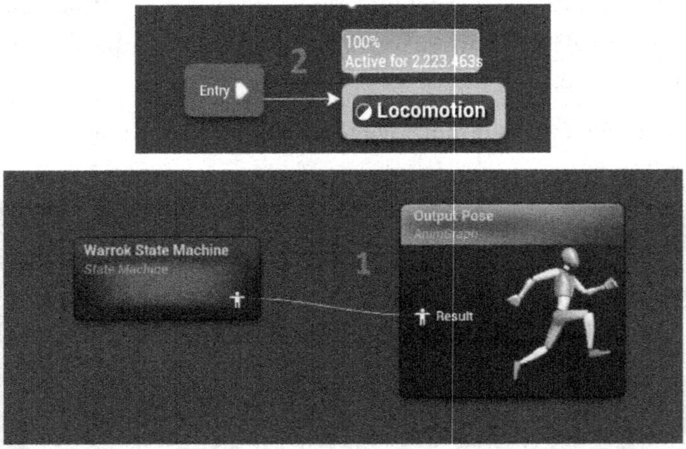

Figure 6.23 - Creating Warrok's animation state machine and first Locomotion state

In *Chapter 4*, we introduced how to use **BlendSpace_1D** to smoothly blend from idle, walk, and run animations with the `Speed` variable in Hero's Animation Blueprint. We will follow the same setup here: using the `Speed` variable in `AB_Warrok` to smoothly blend idle (`A_Warrok_Idle`), walk (`A_Warrok_Walk`), and run (`A_Warrok_Run`) with **BlendSpace_1D**.

However, here we don't repeat the steps you've learned in *Chapter 4* to create a **BlendSpace_1D** animation.

We will create a BS_1D_Warrok animation by using the value of the Speed variable to smoothly blend idle and move (walk/run) animations, as shown in *Figure 6.24*:

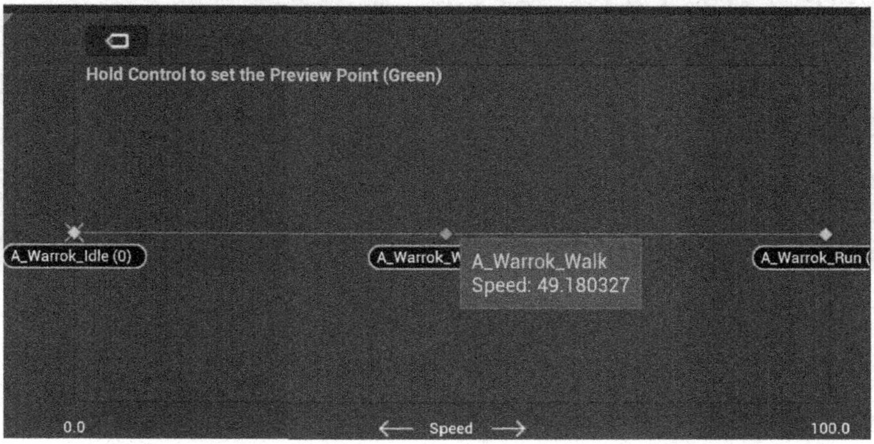

Figure 6.24 - Using BlendSpace_1D to blend from idle, walk and run animations

We choose the following settings:

- Warrok stays idle (A_Warrok_Idle) when Speed = 0.0
- Warrok walks (A_Warrok_Walk) when Speed = 50.0
- Warrok runs (A_Warrok_Run) when Speed = 100.0

Save the BS_1D_Warrok animation under Content/Pangaea/Characters/Warrok/Animations/ folder. We can set up the Locomotion state, as shown in *Figure 6.25*:

1. Open AB_Warrok, switch to **AnimGraph**, and open **Locomotion** state in Warrok State Machine.
2. Create a **BS_1D_Warrok Player** node, name it BS_1D_Warrok, and connect the output to **Output Animation Pose**.
3. Drag the Speed variable and connect it to the Speed input of the **BS_1D_Warrok** node.

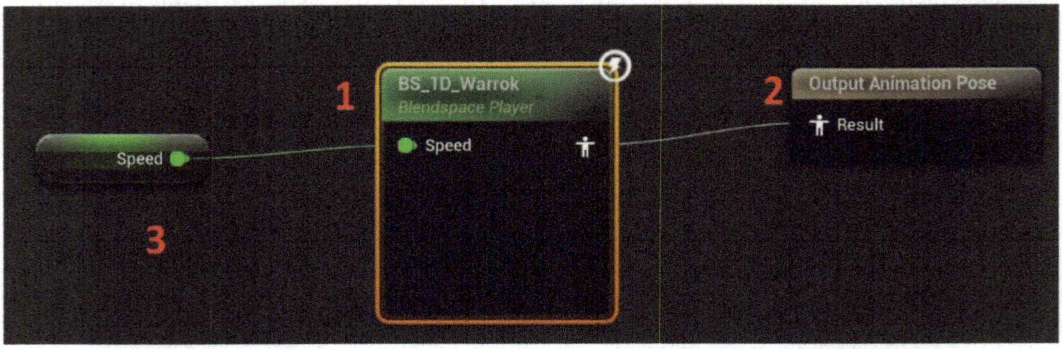

Figure 6.25 - Setup Locomotion animation state

After locomotion is working, the next improvement is turning.

Improving Warrok's turning behavior

AI characters often need to rotate while moving toward different patrol points. If rotation is not configured correctly, Warrok may snap to a new direction or move sideways while facing the wrong way. Since Warrok is controlled by AI movement, we do not need to manually rotate him toward every destination. Instead, we can let the **Character Movement** component rotate Warrok in the direction he is moving.

To improve this, open `BP_Warrok`, switch to the **Details** panel, and select the **Character Movement** component. Find the rotation settings and enable: **Use Controller Desired Rotation**. Then select the main `BP_Warrok` class defaults and disable: **Use Controller Rotation Yaw**. This is shown in *Figure 6.26*:

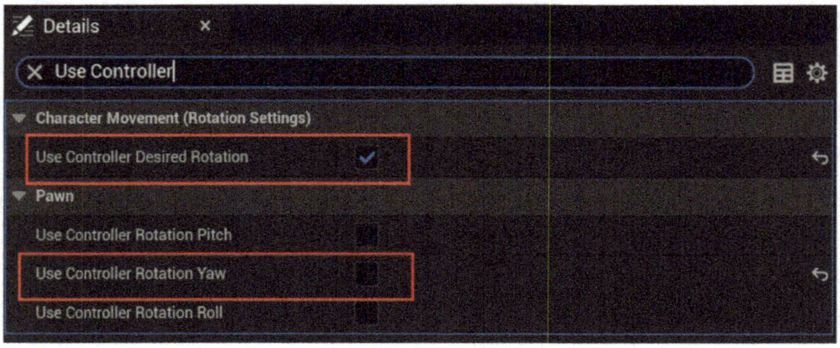

Figure 6.26 - Settings to work better with AI controller

These settings allow the character movement system to rotate Warrok toward the AI Controller's desired movement direction more smoothly.

The names of these settings can be confusing at first, so let's break them down:

- **Use Controller Desired Rotation**: It allows the **Character Movement** component to rotate the character toward the controller's desired direction. This works well with AI pathfinding because the AI Controller already knows where the character should move next. For Warrok, this combination helps make AI movement feel more natural.
  If Warrok turns too slowly or too quickly, you can adjust the rotation rate on the **Character Movement** component.
- **Use Controller Rotation** means the character directly uses the controller's yaw rotation. This can be useful for some player-controlled characters, especially when a character must always face the camera or aiming direction. However, for AI movement, this can sometimes create sharp or unnatural turning.
  For Warrok, we usually want the character to face the direction it is moving. That is why we disable **Use Controller Rotation Yaw**.

Search for the **Rotation Rate** section under the same **Details** panel. The yaw value controls how quickly the character can rotate left or right. For example: "**Rotation Rate Z** = `360`" means the character can rotate up to 360 degrees per second.

If Warrok feels too slow when turning toward a patrol point, increase the value. If Warrok snaps too quickly, lower the value. Warrok appears to be a heavier melee enemy, so a moderate value such as 360 can be a good starting point.

This gives us a stronger base for the next parts of the AI system.

At this point, Warrok can:

- Use the Nav Mesh for movement
- Remember its starting location
- Patrol around that starting location
- Update locomotion animation based on speed
- Turn more smoothly while moving

Press **Play** and observe Warrok while he patrols. He should now turn toward each patrol destination instead of sliding sideways or moving while facing the wrong direction. If Warrok still slides sideways, check that **Use Controller Rotation Yaw** is disabled and **Orient Rotation to Movement** is enabled on the **Character Movement** component.

In the next section, we will add AI Perception so Warrok can sense the player using sight and hearing. Once Warrok can detect the player, we can start switching from patrol behavior to chase behavior.

Implementing perception: hearing and vision

Warrok can now patrol around its starting location and move smoothly through the level. However, it still does not know anything about the player. It can move, but it cannot yet *sense* the world around it.

In this section, we will add AI Perception so Warrok can detect the player using sight and hearing. This will prepare the enemy for the next behavior change: switching from patrol mode into chase mode when the player is detected, as shown in *Figure 6.27*:

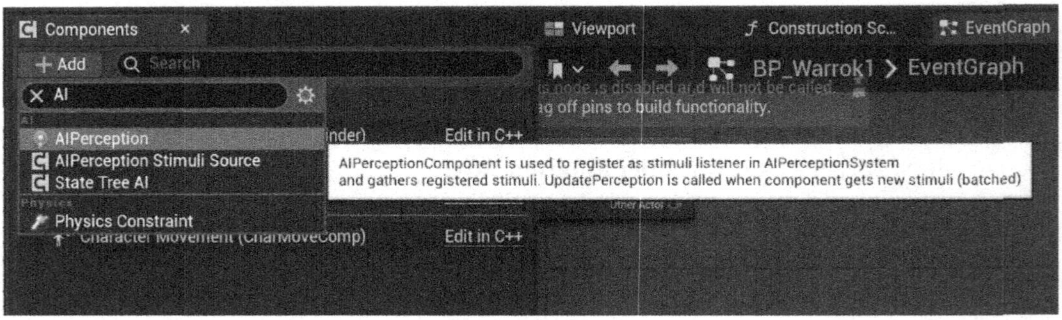

Figure 6.27 - Adding AI perception to BP_Warrok

AI Perception is Unreal Engine's system for giving AI-controlled characters senses. Instead of allowing the enemy to always know where the player is, perception lets the enemy react only when certain detection rules are met. For example, Warrok can see the player when the player enters its vision range or hear the player when a sound event happens nearby.

For our Warrok enemy, we will configure two senses:

- **Sight**: It will allow Warrok to detect the player within visible range and angle
- **Hearing**: It will allow Warrok to detect a sound-based event around it.

Working with AI Perception

AI Perception works through two main parts:

- **AI Perception Component** added to the AI character or controller so it can detect stimuli.
- **Perception Stimuli Source Component**: It is added to Actors that should be detectable.

In our case, Warrok is the AI actor that senses the world, so we will add an **AI Perception** Component to `BP_Warrok`.

The player character, `BP_Hero`, is the actor that Warrok needs to detect, so we will add a **Perception Stimuli Source** Component to `BP_Hero`.

This setup allows Warrok to receive perception events when the player enters or leaves its detection range.

Adding AI perception and senses to BP_Warrok

Follow these steps to add AI Perception to `BP_Warrok`:

1. Open `BP_Warrok` and add a new component in the **Components** panel: **AIPerception**, as shown in *Figure 6.28*:

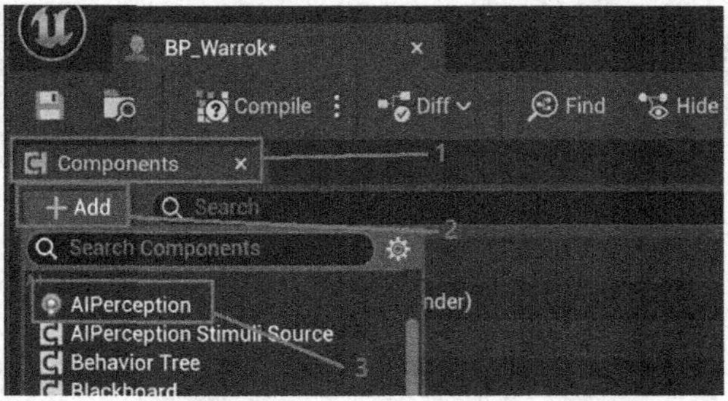

Figure 6.28 - Adding AI sight and hearing sense configuration

2. Name it something clear and meaningful, such as `AIPerception`.
3. Select the **AIPerception** Component and look at the **Details** panel. This is where we will configure the senses that Warrok can use. Use the + button to add new senses.
4. For our Warrok enemy character, we will add two types of senses. Let's add **AI Sight config** first, as shown in *Figure 6.29*.

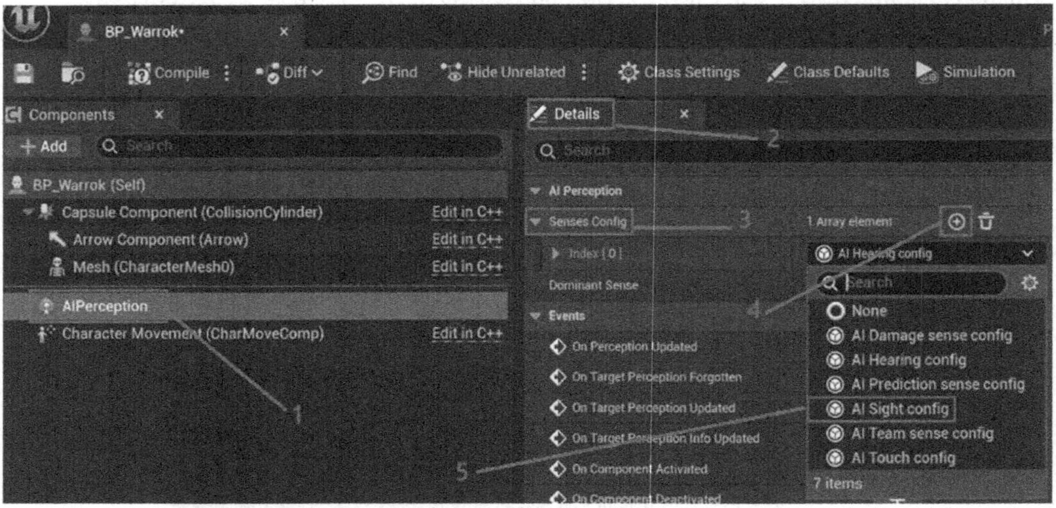

Figure 6.29 - Adding the first sense config

The sight sense will be used as the main detection method. It controls how far and how widely Warrok can see, as shown in *Figure 6.30*.

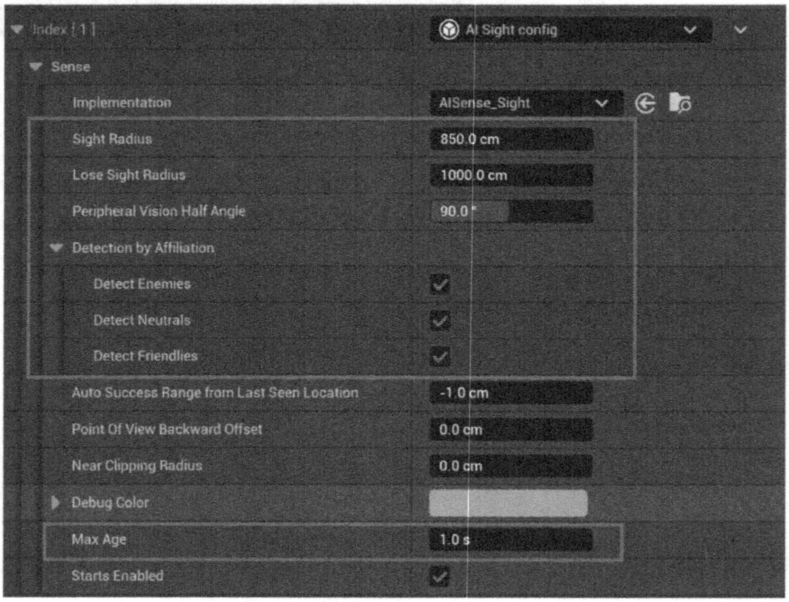

Figure 6.30 - Adding AI sight sense configuration

Some important settings you can adjust are:

- **Sight Radius**: How far Warrok can see other characters. With the usual setup, Warrok can see actors within 850 Unreal units and within its vision angle.
- **Lose Sight Radius**: How far a detected target can move away before Warrok loses sight of it. The lose sight radius is slightly larger, so Warrok does not immediately forget the player the moment the player steps slightly outside the sight radius.
- **Peripheral Vision Half Angle**: Half of the view angle. This controls how wide Warrok's vision is. A smaller value creates a narrow cone of vision, while a larger value makes Warrok more aware of actors to the side.
- **Detection by Affiliation**: This filter allows you to set if you only want to detect enemies (player's character), NPCs not for combat (Neutrals), or only friendlies (like the same team member). For our project, we just let Warrok see all the characters.
- **Max Age**: Controls how long the perception system keeps a stimulus after it is no longer sensed. For example, if **Max Age** is set to `1.0`, Warrok can remember the sight stimulus for about one second after the Hero leaves his field of view. After that, the stimulus expires. A small value makes the AI forget quickly, while a larger value lets the AI keep recent perception information for longer.

5. We also want to add another sense configuration: **AI Hearing Config**, as shown in *Figure 6.31*. Select the same **AIPerception** component in `BP_Warrok`. In the **Senses Config** array, press the + button again and choose **AI Hearing Config**:

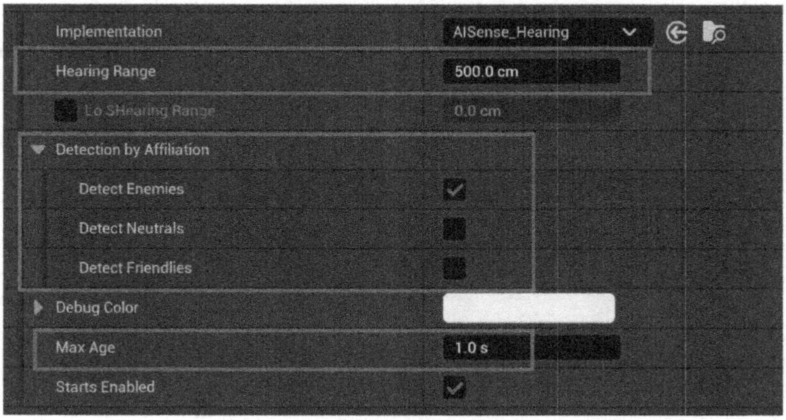

Figure 6.31 - Adding AI Hearing Config

The hearing sense will allow Warrok to respond to sound-related stimuli later. The setting is simpler; we'll tweak the **Hearing Range** value here. Warrok will not hear any sound greater than this distance. The sound is triggered via the following:

- The player runs nearby
- The player attacks
- The player triggers an object
- A projectile hits the environment
- Another actor makes noise

You should also check the **Detection by Affiliation** settings for the hearing sense, just as you did for sight. For this beginner setup, allow Warrok to detect the player through hearing so we can use the same perception system for both sight and sound-based detection later.

6. Set the **Dominant Sense** to: `AISense_Sight`. The last setting under **Sense Config** section of AI Perception's **Details** panel is **Dominant Sense** setting. This setting indicates the primary sense used when the AI system reports information about detected actors. Since Warrok is mainly a visual enemy, sight is a good default choice.

With sight and hearing configured, we can now choose which sense should be treated as the main source of perception information.

Adding a Perception Stimuli Source to BP_Hero

Warrok now has perception senses, but the player also needs to be registered as something the AI can detect:

1. Open `BP_Hero`, in the **Components** panel, add: **Perception Stimuli Source**.
2. Select the component and configure it to register the player as a source for: `AISense_Sight` and `AISense_Hearing`, as shown in *Figure 6.32*. It doesn't matter which sense (sight or hearing) you register first:

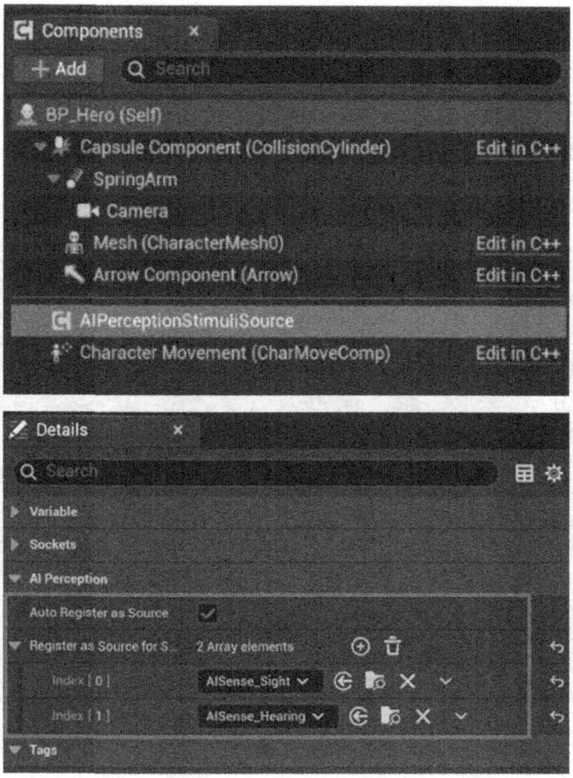

Figure 6.32 - Setting Perception Stimuli Source

The **Register as Source for Senses** list tells which senses can detect this actor. Each entry in the list is shown with an index, such as **Index [0]** or **Index [1]**. The index only represents the order of the array entries; it does not change how the senses behave.

Keep the **Register as Source for Senses** list on `BP_Hero` synchronized with the senses configured on `BP_Warrok`'s AI Perception component. The sense doesn't work if it's not registered as a source of senses.

What matters is that both `AISense_Sight` and `AISense_Hearing` are added to the list so Warrok can detect `BP_Hero` through both senses. This tells Unreal Engine that `BP_Hero` can be perceived through sight and hearing.

Now we have given Warrok the ability to see and hear the player through AI Perception. However, sensing the player is only the first step. The perception event must store the detected player in the Blackboard so that the Behavior Tree can decide how Warrok should react.

Tracking target player in the Blackboard

Since Warrok can now patrol and detect the player character, the next step is to store the detected player in the **Blackboard** before adding more reactive behaviors. This gives the Behavior Tree a shared reference to the detected actor (`BP_Hero`).

Let's add a new key in `BB_Warrok` and set the base class to be `BP_Hero`, as shown in *Figure 6.33*:

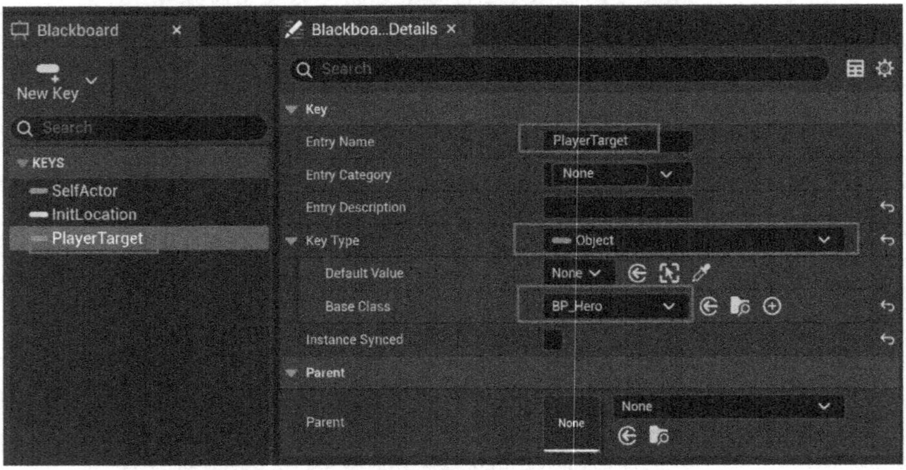

Figure 6.33 - Adding PlayerTarget key to the Blackboard

By saving the player character in the **PlayerTarget** key inside the **Blackboard**, any behavior branch can access the same target information. For example, the chase behavior can move toward **PlayerTarget**, while the attack behavior can use it to face and attack the player when Warrok is close enough.

Until now, our basic AI memory has contained two keys:

- **InitLocation** – a Vector value that stores Warrok's starting patrol location.
- **PlayerTarget** – an Object reference that stores the player character currently detected by Warrok.

These two keys will become one of the most important values in our AI system.

In the next section, we will connect Warrok's perception events to the Blackboard and Behavior Tree, allowing the enemy to change its behavior when it detects the player.

Making decisions with Behavior Tree

So far, we have only used Behavior Tree to execute a single patrol task. Now we will use its real strength: choosing different behavior branches based on conditions and priority. As the enemy becomes more complex, we need a clean way to organize its decisions. This is where a Behavior Tree becomes useful.

Our Warrok character can now patrol around its starting location and detect the player using AI Perception. The next step is to connect these systems so that perception can affect behavior.

For example, Warrok should not always perform the same patrolling action. It should patrol when the player has not been detected, chase when the player is found (via perception), and attack when the player is close enough. If Warrok is defeated, it should stop normal behavior completely. Managing all of these decisions directly inside `BP_Warrok` would quickly make the Blueprint difficult to read and maintain.

Behavior Tree allows us to break AI logic into smaller branches, where each branch represents a possible action or decision. Instead of writing one large block of logic, we can organize the enemy's behavior into clear sections, such as patrol, chase, attack, and death handling.

At this moment, Warrok's patrol logic and perception logic are separate. The patrol behavior moves Warrok around its initial location, while the perception system can detect the player.

To make the enemy feel reactive, we need to use the perception result to update the Blackboard. The Behavior Tree can then read the Blackboard and decide whether Warrok should continue patrolling or start chasing the player.

Updating PlayerTarget from AI Perception

Now a question: who is responsible for updating `PlayerTarget` data in the Blackboard when Warrok detects the player?

In a larger or production-ready AI system, the **AIPerception** component and its events are commonly handled by the AI Controller because the controller owns the character's decision-making logic and Blackboard access.

For this beginner project, however, we will handle the perception event in `BP_Warrok`, where the AI Perception component is already configured. This keeps the perception setup and its event handling together and makes the Blueprint flow easier to follow. The event will still access `AC_Warrok` to update the `PlayerTarget` value in the Blackboard.

Open `BP_Warrok` and select the **AIPerception** component. From the right-side **Details** panel, add a new **On Target Perception Info Updated** event by pressing the **+** (**plus**) button:

Figure 6.34 - Adding On Target Perception Info Updated to player perception

This event in *Figure 6.34* is triggered when Warrok receives updated perception information about an Actor. It can fire, for example, when the player enters Warrok's sight.

In this event graph, we need to check whether the detected actor is the player and whether the actor was successfully sensed. If both conditions are true, we set the `PlayerTarget` key.

The logic can be summarized like this:

```
On Target Perception Info Updated
     → Check if Actor is BP_Hero
     → Check if Sensed is true
     → Get Warrok's AI Controller
     → Get Blackboard
     → Set Value as Object
          Key Name = PlayerTarget
          Object Value = Detected Actor
```

This saves the player actor into the Blackboard. Once the Blackboard is updated, the Behavior Tree can react automatically. Follow the steps to build the Blueprint.

1. Select the **AIPerception** component in `BP_Warrok`.
2. In the **Details** panel, find the **Events** section and click **+** to add an **On Target Perception Info Updated** event, as shown in *Figure 6.35*. This will automatically create a new **OnTargetPerceptionInfoUpdated_Event** node in the **Event Graph**.
3. If you do not have your **Event Graph** currently visible inside the `BP_Warrok` window, you can manually switch to **Event Graph** from the **My Blueprint** tab. You should see a new **OnTargetPerceptionInfoUpdated_Event** node already created for you in the `BP_Warrok` Blueprint.

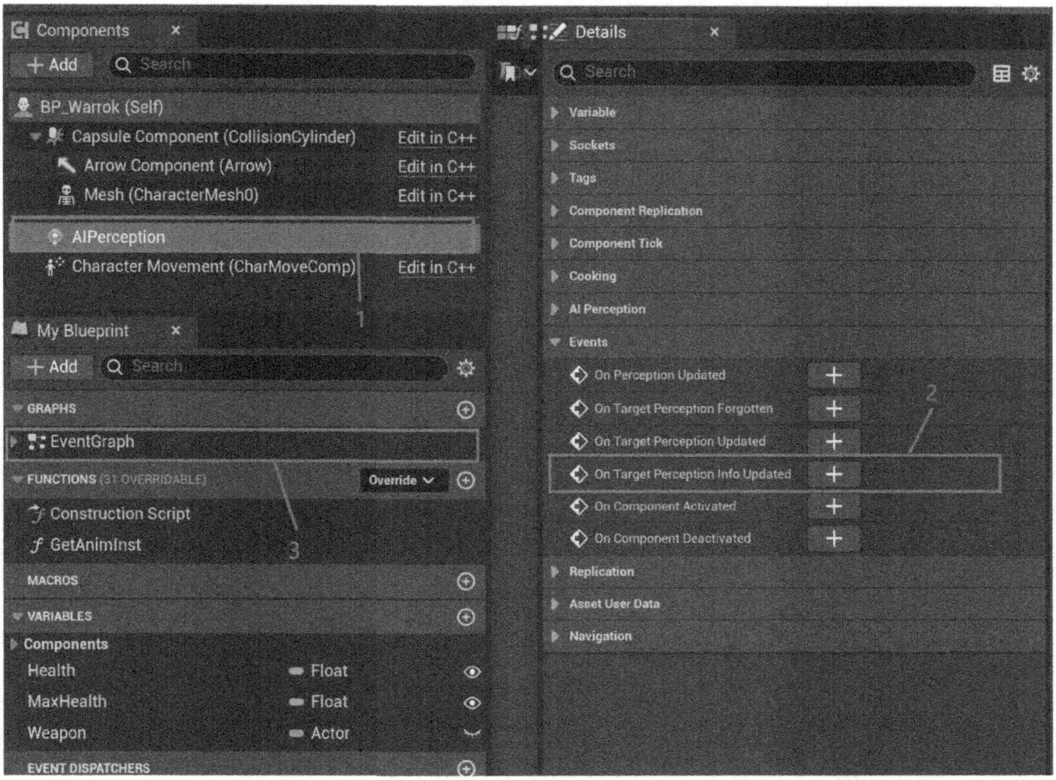

Figure 6.35 - Adding On Target Perception Info Updated event (Step 1–3)

4. From the **Update Info** output of the **OnTargetPerceptionInfoUpdated_Event** node, add a **Break Sensed Actor's Update Data** node.
5. Add a **Break AIStimulus** node and connect the **Stimulus** output of **Break Sensed Actor's Update Data** to its **AIStimulus** input.
6. Add a **Cast To BP_Hero** node and connect the execution output of the **OnTargetPerceptionInfoUpdated_Event** node to it.
7. Connect the **Target** output of **Break Sensed Actor's Update Data** to the **Object** input of **Cast To BP_Hero**, as shown in *Figure 6.36*.

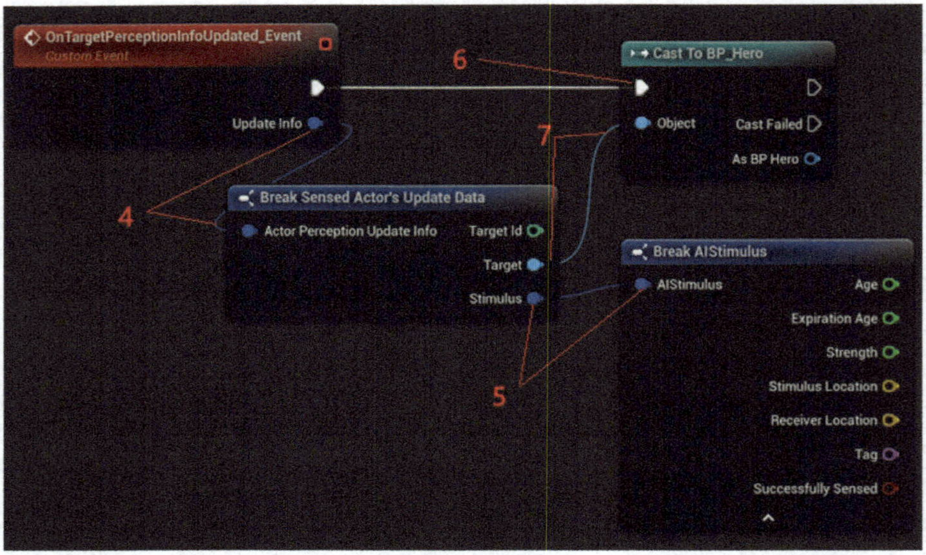

Figure 6.36 - Getting stimulus updates, steps 4–7

The **OnTargetPerceptionInfoUpdated_Event** provides the perception update data. **Break Sensed Actor's Update Data** separates this data into the sensed **Target** and **Stimulus**. The **Target** is cast to `BP_Hero`, while **Break AIStimulus** provides the **Successfully Sensed** value used to determine whether `PlayerTarget` should be set or cleared.

8. From the **Cast To BP_Hero** node, drag out an execution line and create a **Branch** node.
9. Connect the **Successfully Sensed** output of the **Break AIStimulus** node to the **Condition** input of the **Branch** node.
10. From the **True** output of the **Branch** node, add a **Set Value** as **Object** node.
11. Add a **Get AIController**, leaving its **Target** set to **self**.
12. Create a **Get Blackboard** node and connect the **Return Value** of the **Get AIController** to the **Target** input of the **Get Blackboard** node.
13. From the **Return Value** of **Get Blackboard**, create a **Clear Value** node. Connect the **Return Value** of **Get Blackboard** to the **Target** input of both **Set Value** as **Object** and **Clear Value**.
14. Add a **Make Literal Name** node and set its value to `PlayerTarget`. Then connect its **Return Value** output to the **Key Name** input of the **Set Value as Object** and **Clear Value** nodes.

15. Connect the **As BP Hero** output of **Cast To BP_Hero** to the **Object Value** pin of **Set Value as Object**. This stores the detected Hero in the Blackboard.
16. Connect the **Branch** node's **False** execution output to the **Clear Value** node. This clears the target when the Hero is no longer successfully sensed.

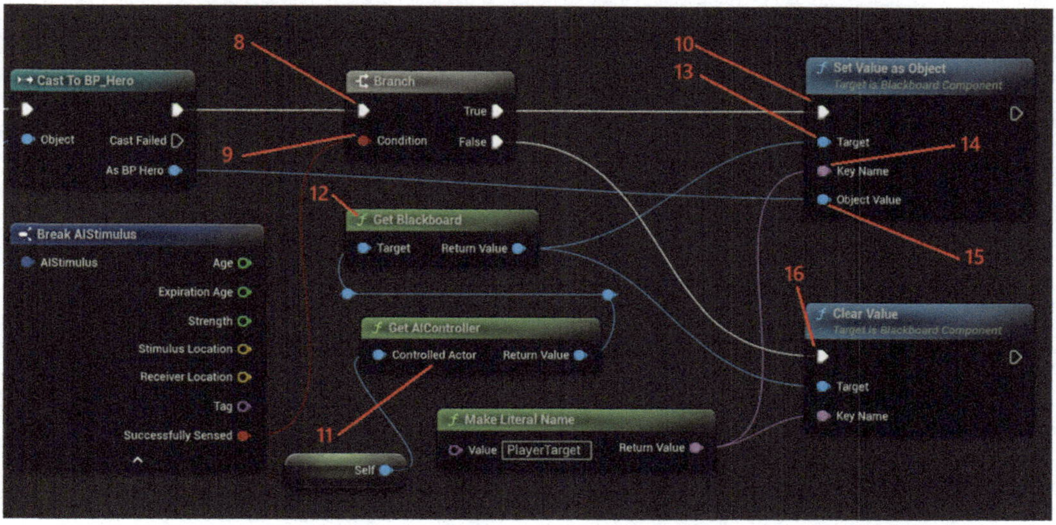

Figure 6.37 - Set or clear Blackboard PlayerTarget by checking if the sensed actor is Hero or not

Figures 6.36 and *6.37* show how the perception event updates the Blackboard. The **OnTargetPerceptionInfoUpdated_Event** node provides the perception update through its **Update Info** output. The **Break Sensed Actor's Update Data** node separates this information into the sensed **Target** and its associated **Stimulus**.

We connect the **Target** output to **Cast To BP_Hero** to verify that the sensed Actor is the player character rather than another detectable Actor in the level. The **Target** output is a generic Actor reference, so it does not guarantee that the detected Actor is the Hero. In a larger level, AI Perception might also detect other characters or Actors registered as perception stimuli.

If the cast succeeds and the stimulus reports that the Actor was successfully sensed, we get Warrok's AI Controller, access its Blackboard, and use the **Set Value as Object** node to store the detected player in the `PlayerTarget` key.

Once this value is stored, the Behavior Tree can use `PlayerTarget` for chase and attack behavior.

To avoid typing the same key name directly in multiple Blueprint nodes, you can create a `KeyName_PlayerTarget` variable for it, then use this variable when setting or getting the `PlayerTarget` object value on the Blackboard.

> **Note**
>
> Using key name variables is not required, but it makes the Blueprint easier to maintain. If you later rename the Blackboard key, you only need to update the variable's default value.

So far, we have given Warrok the basic ability to patrol the level and detect the player character. At this stage, however, Warrok still behaves more like a harmless bystander than a real enemy.

In the next section, we will make Warrok more threatening by adding aggressive combat behavior. We will allow it to chase the player, attack when close enough, and react appropriately during combat.

Understanding the Behavior Tree branch switch

Now that Warrok can patrol and detect the Hero, we can expand `BT_Warrok` so Warrok can choose between different behaviors. Each behavior is called a **branch** in the Behavior Tree.

Conceptually, Warrok will use three behavior branches:

- `Patrol`: Used when Warrok has no detected target.
- `Chase`: Used when Warrok has detected the Hero but is not close enough to attack.
- `Attack`: Used when the Hero is close enough.

A **Selector** chooses between these branches from left to right. The leftmost branch has the highest priority. For Warrok, we will eventually order the branches as `Patrol`, `Chase`, and then `Attack`.

Creating the patrol behavior branch

Now let's build this structure in the Behavior Tree. We'll open `BT_Warrok`, then in the Behavior Tree graph, we'll complete the following steps:

1. Double-click `BT_Warrok` to open it.
2. Make sure the **Root** node is visible.
3. Right-click under the **Root** node and add a **Selector**; name it `Warrok_Behavior`.
4. Connect the **Root** node to `Warrok_Behavior`.
5. Right-click under `Warrok_Behavior` and add a **Sequence**.
6. Rename this **Sequence** to `Patrol`.
7. Under the **Patrol** Sequence, add `BTTask_Warrok_Patrol`.
8. Under **Patrol**, add a **Wait** node.

Figure 6.38 shows the steps of creating the Behavior Tree. At this stage, the Behavior Tree still only performs patrol behavior. We are adding the **Selector** so the tree is ready for additional branches, such as Chase and Attack, in the next sections.

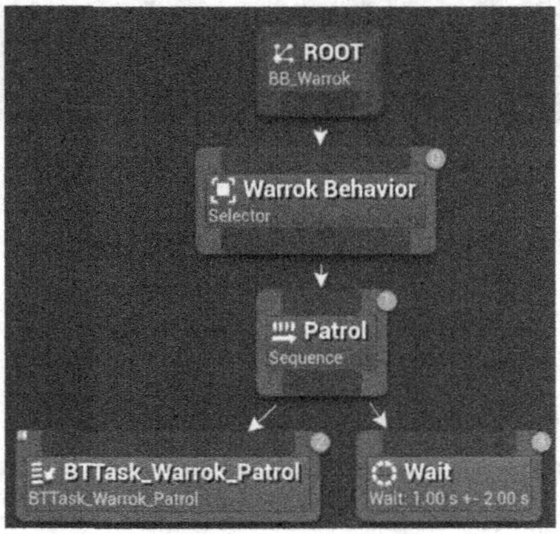

Figure 6.38 - Creating the Behavior Tree for Warrok

For the **Patrol** Sequence node, we want to add a **Blackboard Decorator** that checks whether the `PlayerTarget` key is not set. Right-click the **Patrol** Sequence node and select **Add Decorator | Blackboard** as shown in *Figure 6.39*:

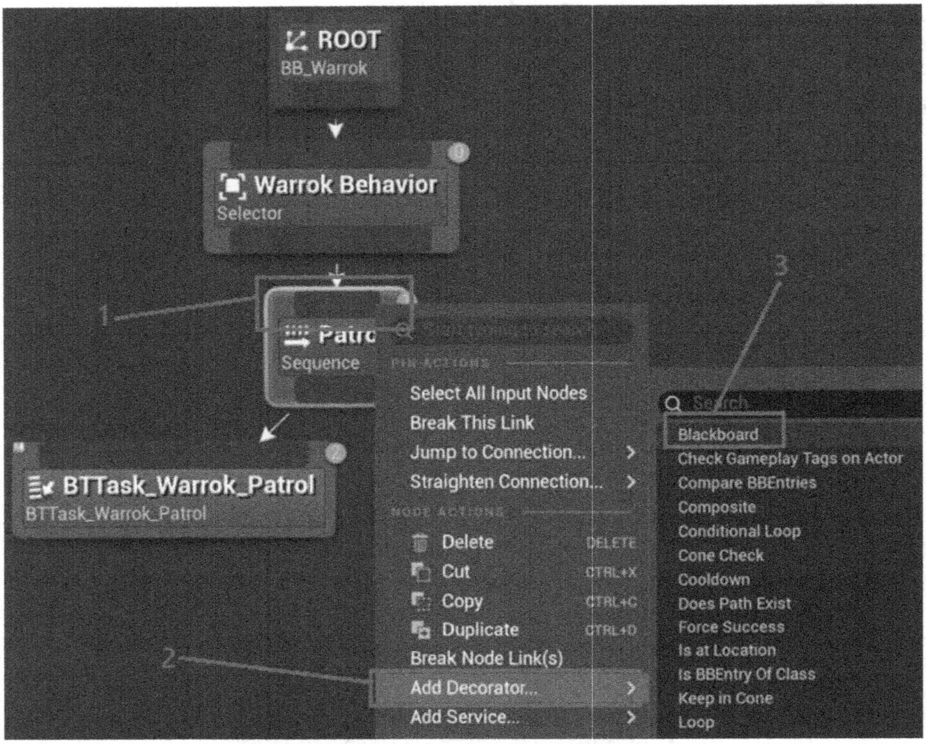

Figure 6.39 - Add a new decorator to Patrol

Select the new **Blackboard Decorator** and in the **Details** panel, set **Blackboard** properties as shown in *Figure 6.40*:

- **Key Query = Is Not Set**
- **Blackboard Key = PlayerTarget**

Add this **Decorator** to the **Patrol** Sequence node, not directly to `BTTask_Warrok_Patrol` or the **Wait** node. Placing the **Decorator** on the **Sequence** makes the condition apply to the entire patrol branch, as shown in *Figure 6.40*:

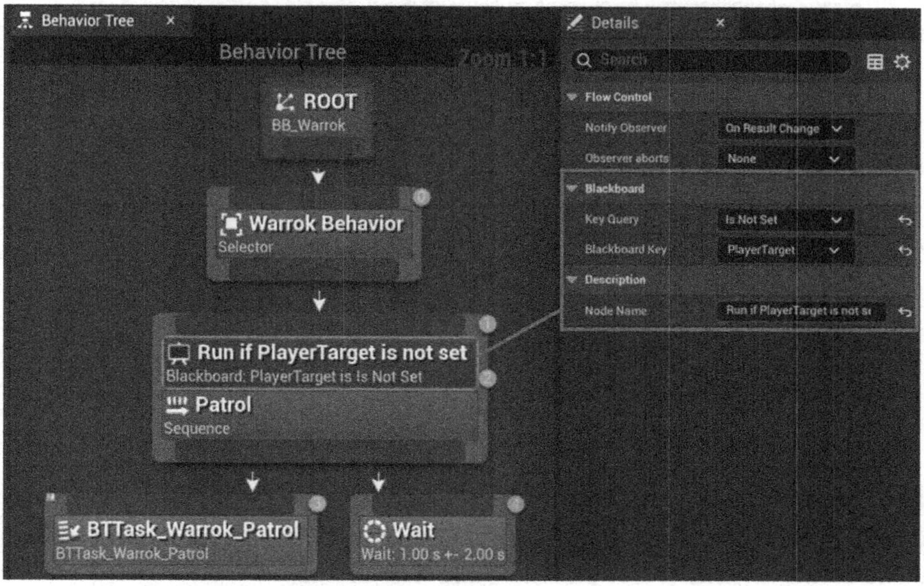

Figure 6.40 - Adding decorator to Blackboard

This allows the **Patrol** branch to run only while Warrok has not detected the player. Once AI Perception stores the player in `PlayerTarget`, this condition becomes False, and the **Selector** can move on to another branch, such as Chase behavior introduced in the next section.

This also means we can control Warrok's behavior by arranging the branches by priority. For example, if we have an attack branch for Warrok to attack the Hero character, this attack branch can be placed before the chase branch, so Warrok attacks first when the player is close enough. If the attack condition is not met, the **Selector** continues to the next branch and checks whether Warrok should chase or patrol.

Chasing and locking the player

Now that the patrol branch has a condition, we can create the chase branch. This branch will run when Warrok has detected the player and the `PlayerTarget` key has been set in the Blackboard.

Let's create a **Sequence** task and name it `Chase`. *Figure 6.41* shows how the `Chase` branch will look once the **Move To** node is added. We will add and configure this node shortly.

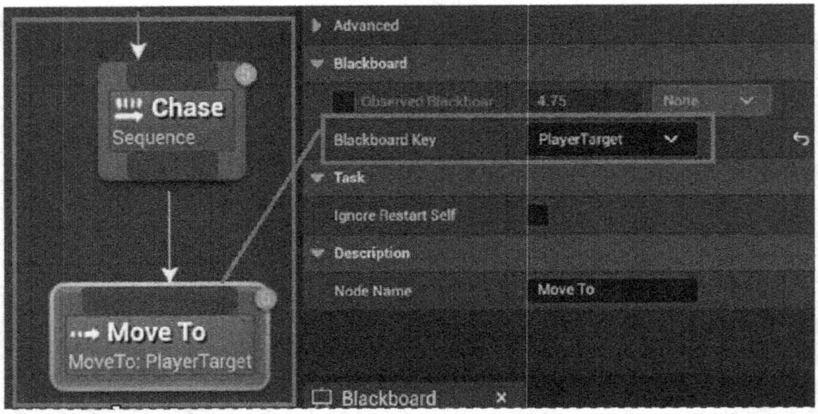

Figure 6.41 - Adding new Chase Sequence (left); and the detailed settings of Move To node (right)

The chase behavior needs a target Actor. The `PlayerTarget` key stores a reference to the player character. When Warrok detects the player, we will set this value. The Behavior Tree can then read it and decide whether to stop patrolling and start chasing.

It's time to explore how to use AI perception to change Warrok's behavior. This creates the first major behavior switch in Warrok's AI:

- Warrok patrols near `InitLocation`
- Warrok sees or hears `BP_Hero`
- `BP_Hero` is saved as `PlayerTarget`
- Behavior Tree stops patrol behavior
- Warrok starts chasing the player

This approach keeps the AI clean because the perception system does not directly perform every action. Instead, perception updates the Blackboard, and the Behavior Tree decides what to do with that information.

Note

It may be tempting to make Warrok chase the player directly from the perception event. For a very small prototype, that can work. However, for this chapter, we want to follow a cleaner AI structure:

- The perception event should answer this question: What did Warrok detect?
- The Behavior Tree should answer this question: What should Warrok do next?

> By separating these responsibilities, the AI becomes easier to expand.

Later, you can add more behaviors, such as searching, returning to patrol, calling nearby enemies for help, or choosing between multiple targets.

For now, perception's job is to detect the player and prepare the `PlayerTarget` value. With the target stored in the Blackboard, we can now create the actual chase branch that moves Warrok toward the player.

Creating the chase branch

Next, follow the steps to add the chase behavior to `BT_Warrok`:

1. Open `BT_Warrok`, create a new **Sequence** under **Warrok_Behavior** node, and rename the node to `Chase`.
2. Add a new **IsAtLocation** decorator to the **Chase** Sequence and name it **Is not within attack range**.
3. In the **Details** panel of the decorator, set **Acceptable Radius** to `200.0`, enable **Inverse Condition**, and set **Blackboard Key** to **PlayerTarget**, as shown in *Figure 6.42*. Enabling **Inverse Condition** makes the decorator succeed when Warrok is more than 200 Unreal units away from the Hero:

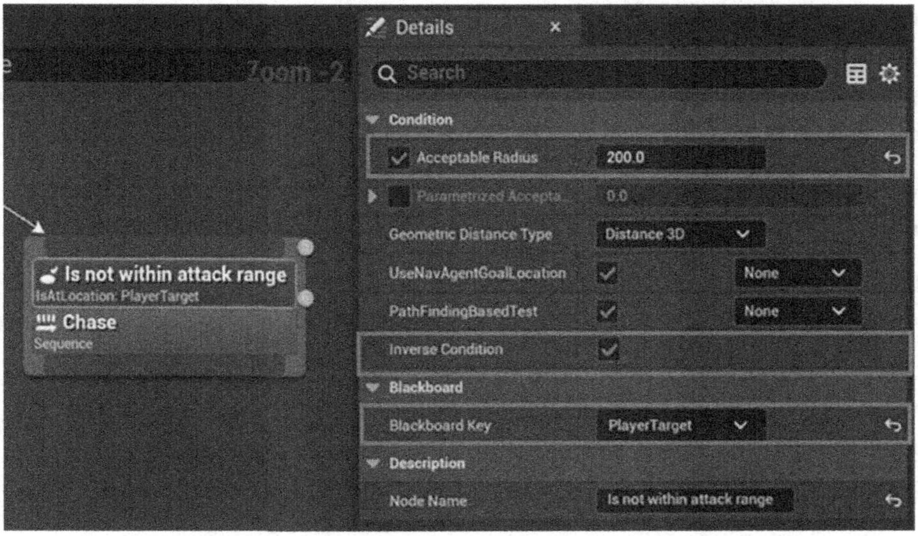

Figure 6.42 - Setting IsAtLocation decorator

4. Now, add a **Move To** Behavior Tree Task and configure it as shown in *Figure 6.43*:

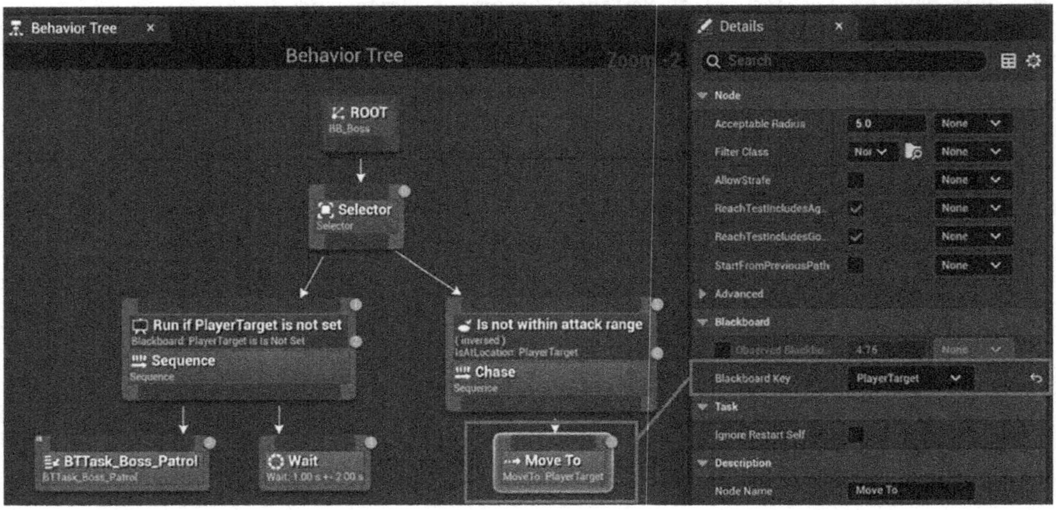

Figure 6.43 - Adding a Move To node to the Chase branch

The **Move To** node tells Warrok to move toward the actor stored in **PlayerTarget**.

Since **PlayerTarget** is an `Object` key that points to `BP_Hero`, Warrok will chase the player's current position.

The **Acceptable Radius** in the **Move To** node controls how close Warrok needs to get before the movement is considered successful. In practice, you may experiment with this value slightly depending on the size of Warrok's capsule and the desired attack distance. For now, we can keep the setup close to the planned value of `180`. This value controls how close Warrok needs to get to the Hero before the `Chase` task considers the movement successful.

However, Warrok's **Chase** node has a decorator **Is not within attack range**, and it also has an **Acceptable Radius** field, and the value is set to `200` Unreal units.

The chase stopping distance in the **Move To** node must be smaller than the distance in **Is Within Attack Range**; otherwise, Warrok could stop chasing before getting close enough to attack.

Warrok can now switch from patrolling to chasing when the player is detected. Next, we will extend this behavior into a full enemy combat loop by adding attack range checks and attack actions.

Developing an AI-controlled Enemy

Warrok can now patrol, detect the Hero, and chase the Hero when a target is available. It is time to make Warrok feel like a truly dangerous enemy warrior. The final step is to make Warrok behave like a complete AI enemy.

In this section, we will extend the **Behavior Tree** by adding a new `Attack` branch. The attack behavior will use a **Decorator** to check whether the player is within attack range, rotate Warrok to face the target, run a custom attack task, and wait briefly before attacking again. By the end of this section, Warrok's Behavior Tree will have three main branches:

- `Patrol`: Used when Warrok has no detected target.
- `Chase`: Used when the Hero has been detected but is not close enough to attack.
- `Attack`: Used when the Hero is close enough.

Because a **Selector** evaluates its child branches from left to right, with the leftmost branch having the highest priority, we will arrange the completed branches in this order: `Patrol` -> `Chase` -> `Attack`.

This means that Warrok patrols until it finds the Hero, chases the Hero until it is close enough to attack, and then executes the `Attack` action.

Handling animation states in AB_Warrok

Before the Behavior Tree can trigger Warrok's attack animation, `AB_Warrok` needs a variable that tells the Animation Blueprint which special animation should be played. Let's create it now:

1. Open `AB_Warrok`. In the **My Blueprint** panel, add a new variable named `AnimState`.
2. Set its type to **Integer**.
3. Compile the Blueprint and set its default value to `0`.

For this chapter, we will use the following `AnimState` values with Warrok's animations:

AnimState Value	State	Animation
0	Locomotion	BS_1D_Warrok
2	A_Warrok_Hit	A_Warrok_Hit
3	A_Warrok_Die	A_Warrok_Die
11	A_Warrok_Attack1	A_Warrok_Attack1
12	A_Warrok_Attack2	A_Warrok_Attack2

Table 6.3 - AnimState values and the animations they represent

This simple integer-based setup lets gameplay Blueprint logic request a special animation without building a more complex animation control system.

Adding the Attack states to AB_Warrok

Next, add the attack animation state to Warrok's Animation Blueprint.

Open the **AnimGraph** in `AB_Warrok`, then open the `Warrok State Machine`. This is the same **State Machine** that already contains the `Locomotion` state. Inside the **State Machine**:

1. Right-click in the **State Machine** graph and add a new state.
2. We have two different attack animations, so we need to create a state for each of them. Name them as `A_Warrok_Attack1` and `A_Warrok_Attack2`.
3. Connect the animation node to the state's final animation pose.
4. Return to the **State Machine** graph. Now we need to create transitions among Locomotion and the two attack states:
5. Create a transition from **Locomotion** to `A_Warrok_Attack1`.
6. Open the transition rule and add this condition: `AnimState == 11`. This means Warrok enters the `A_Warrok_Attack1` state when another Blueprint sets `AnimState` to 11.

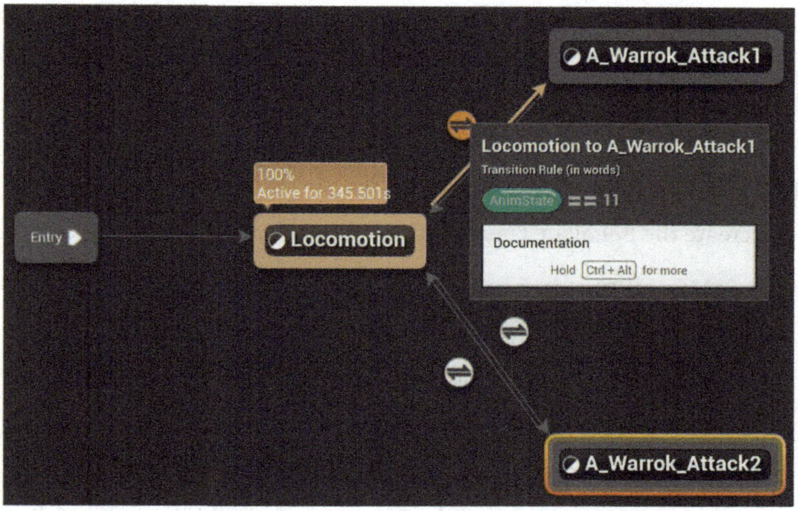

Figure 6.44 - Creating attack states and transitions

7. Next, create a transition from `A_Warrok_Attack1` back to the normal `Locomotion` state.
8. The attack animation should not stay active forever, so we need to reset **AnimState** to `0` after the attack animation finishes. Open Warrok's attack animation `A_Warrok_Attack1` and add an **Animation Notify** near the end of the animation. Name the notify: `EndOfAttack1`.
9. Return to Warrok's Animation Blueprint `AB_Warrok`. In the **Event Graph**, add the notify event: **AnimNotify_EndOfAttack1**.
10. From this event, set **AnimState** back to `0`, as shown in *Figure 6.45*.

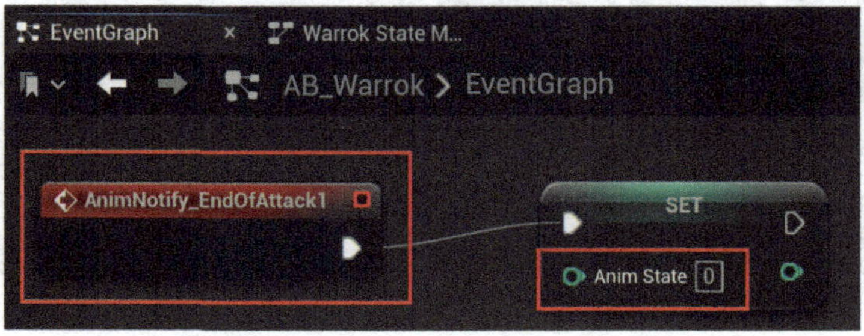

Figure 6.45 - Process AnimNotify_EndOfAttack1 to set AnimState to 0.

11. Repeat the same setup for `A_Warrok_Attack2` state. You need to create a new **Animation Notify** `EndOfAttack2` and add a new event **AnimNotify_EndOfAttack2** in the **Event Graph** of `AB_Warrok`.

With this setup, Warrok can enter the attack animations when **AnimState** becomes 11 or 12, then return to `Locomotion` when the corresponding `EndOfAttack1`/`EndOfAttack2` is triggered. We have made Warrok's animation state machine ready for attack. In the next section, we continue by creating the attack behavior task.

Creating Behavior Tree task BTTask_Warrok_Attack

It's time to create the Behavior Tree task that tells `AB_Warrok` to play the attack animation:

1. In the **Content Browser**, go to `Content/Pangaea/Characters/Warrok/AI/` and right-click in the folder, then select **Blueprint Class**.
2. In the parent class search window, search for: `BTTask_BlueprintBase`.
3. Select **BTTask_BlueprintBase** and create the Blueprint.
4. Name it `BTTask_Warrok_Attack`.

Now open `BTTask_Warrok_Attack`. In the **Event Graph**, build the task as follows:

1. Add or use the **Event Receive Execute AI** node.
2. From the **Controlled Pawn** pin, add **Cast To BP_Warrok** node.
3. From the successful cast output, get Warrok's **Mesh** component.
4. From the **Mesh**, add **Get Anim Instance**.
5. From the **Return Value** of **Get Anim Instance**, add **Cast To AB_Warrok**, as shown in *Figure 6.46*:

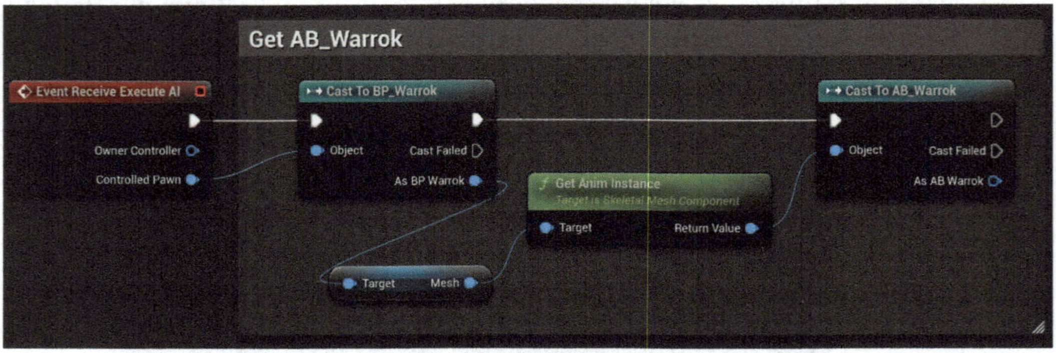

Figure 6.46 - Try to get AB_Warrok from BP_Warrok (Step 1 to 5)

6. From the successful cast output, add a comparison node to check if **AnimState** is set to `0` (Warrok in `Locomotion` state). This will return a Boolean value either **True** or **False**.
7. Add a **Branch** node from the execution pin of the **Cast to AB_Warrok** node.

8. Connect the Boolean result from *step 6* to the **Condition** input pin so that **Branch** can receive a Boolean result if Warrok is in `Locomotion` (standby or move) state. This is a green light to trigger a new attack.
9. If Warrok is currently busy with some other animations, there is no condition to launch an attack. In this case, create a **Finish Execute** node and return without **Success** checked (i.e. return **False**).
10. From the **True** output of the **Branch** node, create a **Switch on int** node.
11. Create a new **Random Integer** node, set the maximum value to 2 (change this number if you have several different attacks; currently our Warrok character has two attack animations mentioned before).
12. Connect the **Return Value** of **Random Integer** to the **Selection** input pin.
13. Add a **Set** node to assign **AnimState** to 11 from the output value **0** of the **Switch on Int** node.
14. Add a **Set** node to assign **AnimState** to 12 from the output value **Default** of the **Switch on Int** node.
15. Connect the **Target** pins of both **Set** nodes from **As AB Warrok** of **Cast To AB_Warrok** node as input.
16. Create a new **Finish Execute** node, connect the exec pin from both nodes.
17. Set the **Success** output of **Finish Execute** to True.

Figure 6.47 demonstrates *steps 6* to *17* as follows:

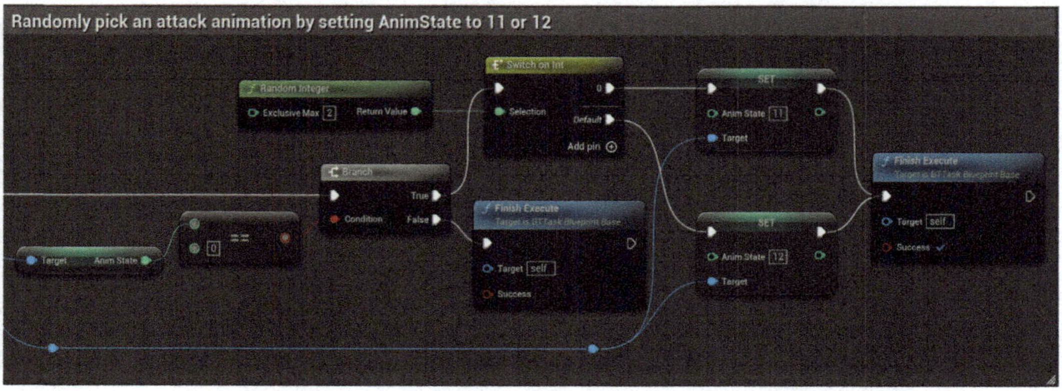

Figure 6.47 - Randomly select an attack and set AnimState (Step 6~16)

This part of the Blueprint handles the route of issuing an attack. We know Warrok has two different attack animations. In order to have Warrok randomly select one of the animations to attack, we use a **Random Integer** node to produce a random integer of either `0` or `1`. The

Switch on Int node then sets the **AnimState** variable to either of the attack animations (id 11 or 12), and returns **Success** checked in the final **Finish Execute** node.

The Behavior tree now has a way to check if this is the right moment to issue an attack. Let's continue the setup.

Look back in *Chapter 5* – we introduced Animation Notifies, which can be used to know when attack animations have finished. For now, we only need to trigger the attack animation from the Behavior Tree task. Near the end of the attack animation, it will fire an event to switch the animation back to idle.

For a beginner-friendly setup, the attack task does not need to apply damage immediately. Its first responsibility is to start the attack action. We will handle damage in a later section.

This task does not move Warrok directly. Its job is to request the attack animation by setting **AnimState** to 11/12 in `AB_Warrok`. The Animation Blueprint then handles the actual transition into the `A_Warrok_Attack1`/`A_Warrok_Attack2` state.

In the next section, we need to set up detailed attack parameters.

Rotating Warrok to face the player

Before playing an attack animation, Warrok should face the player. If Warrok attacks while facing the wrong direction, the result will look incorrect even if the logic works.

We can add a built-in **Rotate to Face BB Entry** node to the Attack branch. Set the **Blackboard Key** to **PlayerTarget** so it tells Warrok to rotate toward the player stored in the **PlayerTarget** key.

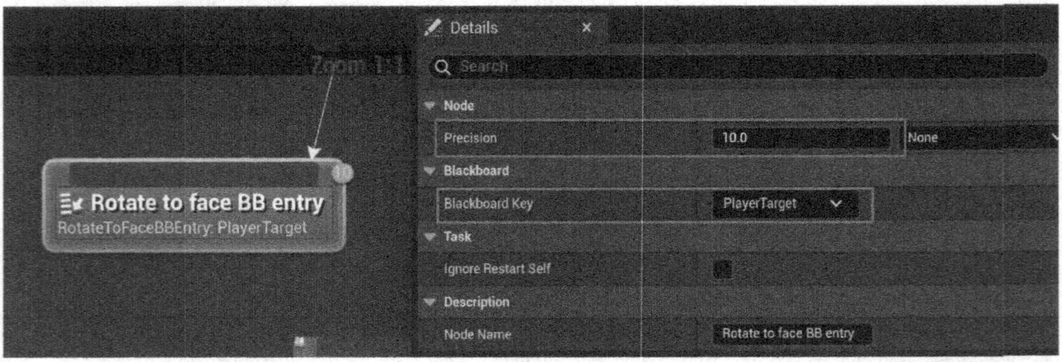

Figure 6.48 - Rotate to Face BB Entry node

The **Precision** value controls how closely Warrok needs to face the target before the node considers the rotation complete. A smaller value requires more accurate facing, while a larger value allows more tolerance. Setting **Precision** to `10` gives Warrok a small acceptable angle, so it does not need to be perfectly aligned before attacking, but it still turns close enough for the melee attack to look intentional.

This is especially important for melee attacks. The player needs to see that Warrok is intentionally attacking the target in front of it, not simply playing an animation in any direction.

Adding the attack branch to the Behavior Tree

Now we can add the `Attack` branch to the Behavior Tree.

Open `BT_Warrok`. At this point, your Behavior Tree should already have the `Chase` and `Patrol` logic. The final Behavior Tree should be organized under one main Selector.

The order under the Selector should be `Patrol` -> `Chase` -> `Attack`.

Add the `Attack` branch as follows:

1. Right-click under the `Warrok_Behavior` and add a **Sequence**. Rename the **Sequence** to `Attack`.
2. Move the **Attack** branch to the rightmost side of the **Selector** so that it has the lowest priority. Arrange the branches from left to right as `Patrol` -> `Chase` -> `Attack`.
3. Under the **Attack**, add the **Rotate to Face BB Entry** task.
4. Under the **Attack**, add the **BTTask_Warrok_Attack** task.
5. After **BTTask_Warrok_Attack**, add a **Wait** node.
6. Select the **Wait** node and set its wait time to match the attack rhythm. Here we set **Wait Time** to `0.5` and **Random Deviation** to `1.5`. This creates a 0~2 second cooldown between attacks. *Figure 6.49* shows the steps for adding the `Attack` branch.

   The **Wait** node prevents Warrok from restarting the attack task every frame. Without this pause, the Behavior Tree could repeatedly request the attack animation too quickly.

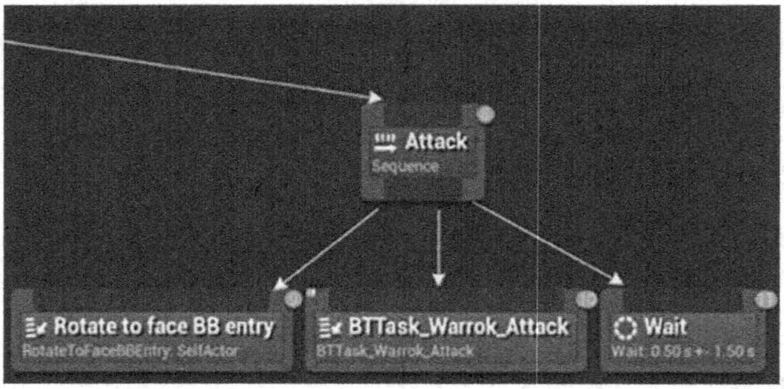

Figure 6.49 - Adding Attack branch

The final branch behavior is:

- The `Patrol` branch runs when `PlayerTarget` is not set.
- The `Chase` branch runs when `PlayerTarget` is set, but the Hero is not close enough to attack.
- The `Attack` branch runs when `PlayerTarget` is set, and the Hero is within attack range.

This creates the full decision loop: Warrok patrols until the Hero is detected, chases the Hero when the Hero is far away, and attacks when the Hero is close enough.

Testing the attack behavior

Press **Play** and move the Hero into Warrok's sight range. Warrok should now behave as follows:

1. If the Hero is not detected, Warrok patrols.
2. If the Hero is detected but far away, Warrok chases the Hero.
3. If the Hero is close enough, Warrok stops chasing and plays the attack animation.
4. After the attack animation reaches the `EndOfAttack` notify, Warrok returns to `Locomotion` and can attack again if the Hero is still in range.

If Warrok chases but never attacks, check the following:

- `PlayerTarget` must contain a valid reference to `BP_Hero` in the Blackboard.
- The `Attack` branch must be placed to the right of the `Chase` branch.
- The `Attack` branch's Blackboard decorator must check that `PlayerTarget` **Is Set**.
- The `Attack` branch's **Is within attack range** decorator must use **PlayerTarget**, an **Acceptable Radius** of `200.0`, and have **Inverse Condition** disabled.

- The Chase branch's **Is not within attack range** decorator must have **Inverse Condition** enabled.
- The **Move To** node's **Acceptable Radius** should be smaller than the 200-unit attack range.
- **Rotate to Face BB Entry** must use PlayerTarget as its **Blackboard Key**.
- BTTask_Warrok_Attack must set AnimState to 11 or 12.
- AB_Warrok must contain transitions into the A_Warrok_Attack1 and A_Warrok_Attack2 states using AnimState == 11 and AnimState == 12.
- Each attack animation must contain its corresponding EndOfAttack1 or EndOfAttack2 notify, which resets AnimState to 0.

With the Chase and Attack branches complete, Warrok can now behave like an active enemy. Next, we will make combat meaningful by allowing Warrok to receive damage, play hit reactions, and die when its health reaches zero.

Handling damage and death

Warrok can now patrol, detect the player, chase, and attack when close enough. However, an enemy character also needs to respond when it receives damage. Without health and death logic, Warrok can attack the player, but the player cannot properly defeat it.

In this section, we will add a simple health system to BP_Warrok, handle damage through Unreal Engine's **AnyDamage** event, and prepare the animation logic needed for hit and death behavior. We will also introduce an additional Behavior Tree task that helps the AI check whether Warrok is currently performing an action, such as attacking, being hit, or dying.

Adding hit and death states to AB_Warrok

Follow the steps to complete Warrok's animation states with additional hit and die states:

1. Open AB_Warrok and return to the **State Machine**.
2. Add a new state named: A_Warrok_Hit.
3. Open the Hit state and add Warrok's hit animation: A_Warrok_Hit.
4. Create a transition from the normal locomotion state to Hit with this condition: AnimState== 2.
5. Open the Hit animation and add an **Animation Notify** near the end of the animation. Name it EndOfHit.
6. In the **Event Graph** of AB_Warrok, add AnimNotify_EndOfHit and set AnimState back to 0.

7. Next, add a new state named A_Warrok_Die.
8. Open A_Warrok_Die, add the A_Warrok_Die animation asset, and connect it to **Output Animation Pose**.
9. Return to the **State Machine** graph and create a transition from **Locomotion** to A_Warrok_Die. Set its transition condition to AnimState == 3.
10. Create a transition from A_Warrok_Attack1 to A_Warrok_Die and set its condition to AnimState == 3.
11. Create a transition from A_Warrok_Attack2 to A_Warrok_Die and set its condition to AnimState == 3.
12. Create a transition from A_Warrok_Hit to A_Warrok_Die and set its condition to AnimState == 3.

Unlike the hit and attack animations, the death animation does not need to return to Locomotion. Once Warrok is dead, it should remain in the death state. Warrok's complete animation state machine is shown in *Figure 6.50*:

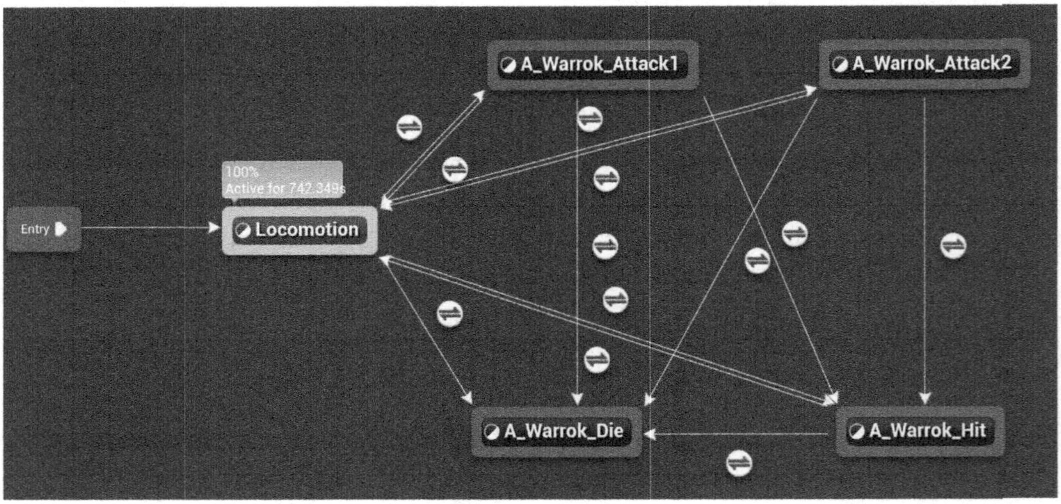

Figure 6.50 - Warrok's animation state machine

Adding health variables to BP_Warrok

We need to add two variables to represent Warrok's health:

1. Open BP_Warrok and create the following variables: **Health** and **MaxHealth**. Both are **Float** type variables.

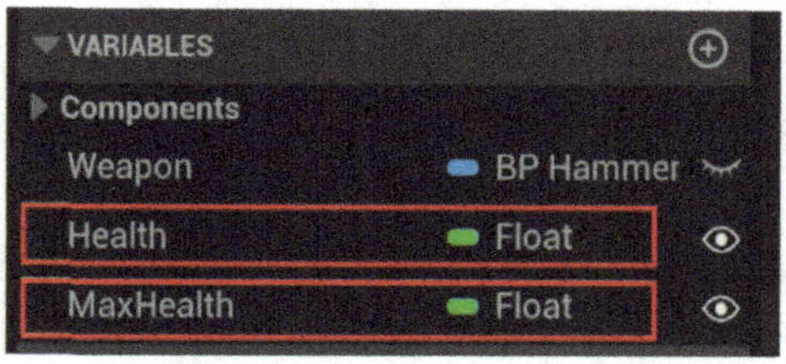

Figure 6.51 - Adding Health and MaxHealth variables

2. Make both variables public if you want to adjust them from the editor for testing. This allows you to tune different enemy instances without changing the Blueprint logic.
3. Compile and save, and then set the **MaxHealth** variable value to `300`.

The basic idea is simple:

1. **Health** starts at **MaxHealth**.
2. When Warrok takes damage, **Health** decreases.
3. When **Health** reaches 0, Warrok dies.

Initializing health in BeginPlay

After creating the variables, we should make sure Warrok starts with full health. This is done in the **BeginPlay** event. Let's set **Health** to **MaxHealth** after the **Attach Actor To Component** node.

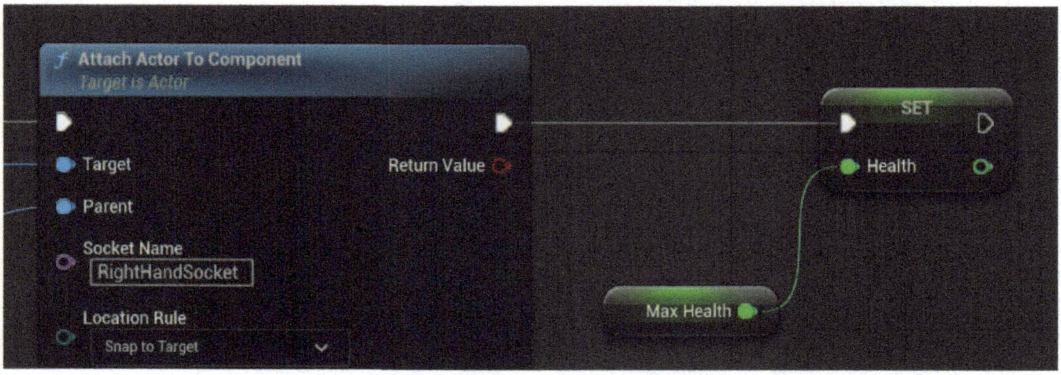

Figure 6.52 - Set health to MaxHealth in Blueprint

Even though both variables currently have the same default value, setting Health from `MaxHealth` during **BeginPlay** is a good habit. It allows `MaxHealth` to become the main tuning value, while Health represents the current runtime state.

Handling AnyDamage

Unreal Engine provides a built-in event called **AnyDamage**. This event is triggered when the actor receives damage through Unreal Engine's damage system.

In this project, Warrok cannot receive additional damage while the `A_Warrok_Hit` animation is playing. This is an *intentional gameplay design choice*. The brief damage immunity prevents several rapidly repeated damage events from reducing Warrok's health multiple times during a single hit reaction. It also allows the hit animation to finish without being repeatedly restarted or interrupted.

Therefore, the **AnyDamage** event processes damage only when Warrok is in `Locomotion` (`AnimState == 0`) or one of the two attack states (`AnimState == 11 or AnimState == 12`). When Warrok is already in the Hit state (`AnimState == 2`), the **Branch** condition is false, so the incoming damage is ignored. Once `AnimNotify_EndOfHit` resets `AnimState` to *0*, Warrok can receive damage again.

This short period is sometimes called an **invulnerability window** or **invulnerability frames**. You can include `AnimState == 2` in the allowed conditions if you want Warrok to remain vulnerable during its hit reaction instead.

For this beginner setup, we mainly need the `Damage` value. The basic logic is:

```
Event AnyDamage:
    → Health = Health - Damage
    → If Health <= 0
        → Die
      Else
        → Play hit reaction
```

This gives Warrok a simple damage response. If the player attacks Warrok, the damage reduces Warrok's health. If Warrok still has remaining health, it can play a hit reaction. If health reaches zero, Warrok should enter a death state.

Handling death and hit events

The Blueprint `BP_Warrok` handles the **AnyDamage** event. There are two major parts: calculating the current Health value and handling death:

1. Open `BP_Warrok`, create a new event node **Event AnyDamage**.
2. From the exec pin, create a **Cast To AB_Warrok** node.
3. Create a new **GetAnimInstance** function node, drag **Mesh** from the **Components** panel into the Blueprint, and connect it to the **Target** pin of the **GetAnimInstance** node.
4. Connect the **Return Value** pin of the **GetAnimInstance** to the **Object** pin of **Cast To AB_Warrok** node.
5. From the **As AB Warrok** output of **Cast To AB_Warrok**, get the **AnimState** variable.
6. Create three separate **Equal (Integer)** comparison nodes and connect **AnimState** to each one:
    - Compare `AnimState == 0` for the **Locomotion** state
    - Compare `AnimState == 11` for the `A_Warrok_Attack1` state
    - Compare `AnimState == 12` for the `A_Warrok_Attack2` state
7. Combine the three Boolean results using two **OR** Boolean nodes. Connect the results of `AnimState == 0` and `AnimState == 11` to the first **OR** node. Then connect the first **OR** node's result and the result of `AnimState == 12` to the second **OR** node. Connect the second **OR** node's output to the **Condition** pin of the **Branch** node.
   The resulting condition is:

   ```
   (AnimState == 0 OR AnimState == 11) OR AnimState == 12
   ```

   Therefore, the **Branch**'s **True** output continues the damage calculation only when Warrok is in **Locomotion**, `A_Warrok_Attack1`, or `A_Warrok_Attack2`.
8. Create a new **Set** node and read the health value directly from the `Health` variable.
9. Subtract the `Damage` value from the `Health` variable.

Figure 6.53 shows the setup for *steps 1–9*.

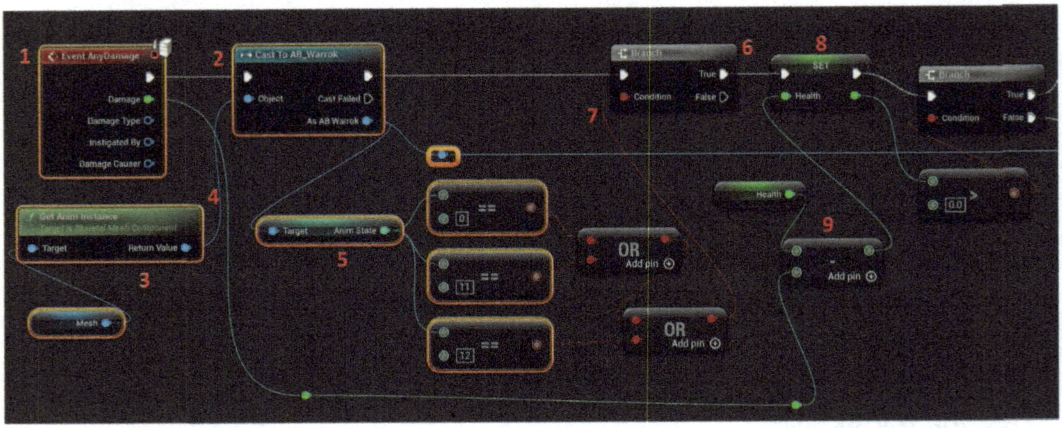

Figure 6.53 - Calculating the new Health value

> Note
>
> **Design note**
>
> `AnimState == 2` is intentionally excluded from the **Branch** condition. While the `A_Warrok_Hit` animation is playing, Warrok has a brief invulnerability window, so additional **AnyDamage** events do not reduce `Health`. Damage processing resumes when `AnimNotify_EndOfHit` resets `AnimState` to *0*.

To prevent Warrok from continuing to patrol, chase, or attack after death, we should track whether it is dead by checking if the `Health` value <= 0. This is handled in the **AnyDamage** event.

Figure 6.53 shows the damage-calculation portion of the **AnyDamage** execution flow. **Event AnyDamage** starts the logic and supplies the incoming **Damage** value. After obtaining `AB_Warrok` and confirming that the current `AnimState` allows damage processing, subtract `Damage` from `Health` and store the result back in the `Health` variable. The next **Branch** checks whether the updated Health is greater than 0. Its **True** output handles the hit reaction, while its **False** output handles **Warrok's** death.

Before setting the hit or die animation state, we must stop any movement Warrok is already performing. `BTTask_Warrok_CheckForAction`, which we will create in the next section, prevents the Behavior Tree from starting another action while Warrok is busy. However, it does not cancel a **Move To** request that has already started. Without explicitly stopping that request, Warrok may continue sliding while playing the Hit or Die animation.

Complete the two outputs of the `Health > 0` **Branch** as follows:

1. From the **True** output, add **Get AIController**, then call **Stop Movement** on the returned AI Controller.
2. After **Stop Movement**, set **AnimState** to 2 to enter the `A_Warrok_Hit` state.
3. From the **False** output, use **Get AIController** and call **Stop Movement** again.
4. After **Stop Movement**, set **AnimState** to 3 to enter the `A_Warrok_Die` state.
5. Add a five-second **Delay**, then destroy the hammer actor followed by `BP_Warrok`, as shown in *Figure 6.54*.

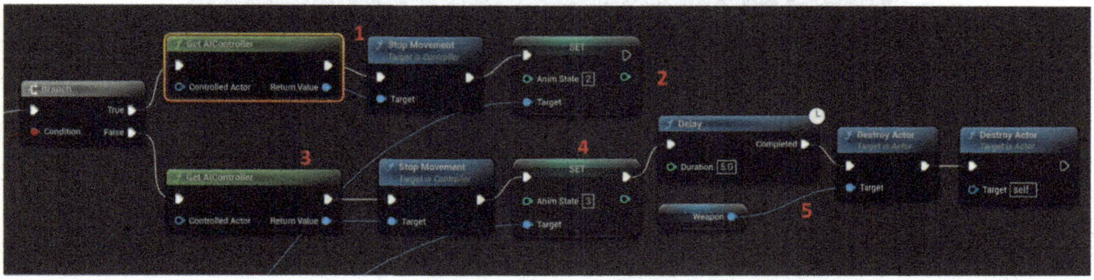

Figure 6.54 - Handling after death and hit status

Figure 6.54 shows the completed hit-and-death logic. If `Health > 0` is True, **Stop Movement** cancels the active navigation request before Warrok enters the `A_Warrok_Hit` state. When `AnimNotify_EndOfHit` later resets `AnimState` to 0, the Behavior Tree can resume patrol or chase behavior.

If `Health > 0` is False, Warrok is dead. In this case, we stop the active navigation request before setting `AnimState` to 3. Movement is not restored because Warrok must remain stationary after entering the `A_Warrok_Die` state.

The hammer must be destroyed separately because it was spawned as an independent actor and then attached to Warrok. Destroying `BP_Warrok` does not automatically destroy the spawned hammer actor, so explicitly removing it prevents an orphaned weapon actor from remaining in the level.

Using animation notifies for attack timing

In *Chapter 5*, we introduced how to use an **Animation Notify** to allow attack animation to send events back to the Blueprint at specific frames, so we can set the animation state back to 0 (`Idle`) after the attack.

We will apply the same mechanism to switching the animation states here too. Warrok has two attack animations, `A_Warrok_Attack1` and `A_Warrok_Attack2`. We need to add a notify near the end of each attack animation. Also, in `AB_Warrok`, we should handle these Animation Notify events to set the animation state back to `0`, as shown in *Figure 6.55*:

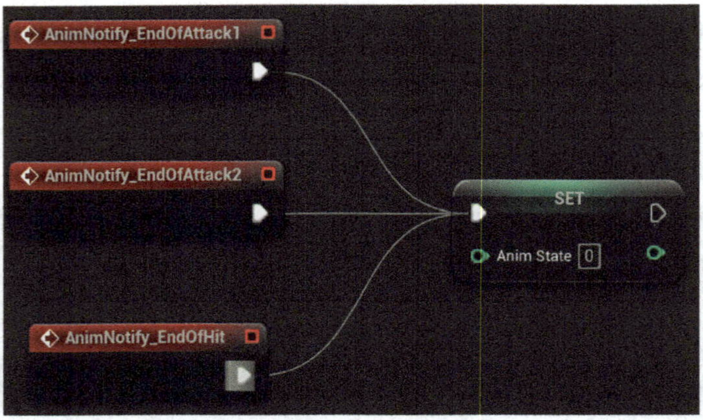

Figure 6.55 - Tracking end of attack animation in the Blueprint

Next, we want to prevent Warrok from starting another attack before the current attack animation is complete.

Preventing conflict of actions

At this point, Warrok has several possible next actions to perform: patrol, chase, attack, take a hit, and die.

Some of these actions should not happen at the same time. For example:

Conflict	Problem
Warrok attacks while dying.	Enemy behavior might look incorrect if Warrok continues attacking while dying.
Warrokmoves while playing hit animation	An active **Move To** request can continue moving Warrok even when the Behavior Tree is not starting a new action. The **AnyDamage** logic now calls **Stop Movement** before entering the `A_Warrok_Hit` state.
Warrok starts a new attack before the current attack finishes	The attack animation starts repeatedly

Conflict	Problem
Warrokcontinues to execute Behavior Tree after death	Warrok continues moving after dying.

Table 6.4 - Actions should not happen at the same time

We can create a separate task to check whether Warrok is currently busy with another action and put this as the highest priority branch, so it always gets executed first. Let's create a new Blueprint based on `BTTask_BlueprintBase` and name it `BTTask_Warrok_CheckForAction`.

This task can check the controlled Warrok pawn and determine whether it is allowed to continue normal AI behavior.

The logic can be described as:

```
Receive Execute AI
    → Get Controlled Pawn
    → Cast to BP_Warrok
    → Check IsDead, IsHit, or IsAttacking
    → Return success or failure based on the result
```

For example, if Warrok is dead, the task should prevent the AI from continuing normal behavior. If Warrok is currently attacking, the task can prevent another attack from starting too early.

A simple version of the task might ask: *is Warrok currently available for a new action?*

If yes, the Behavior Tree can continue. If not, it can wait or skip the current branch. The Blueprint is shown in *Figure 6.56*:

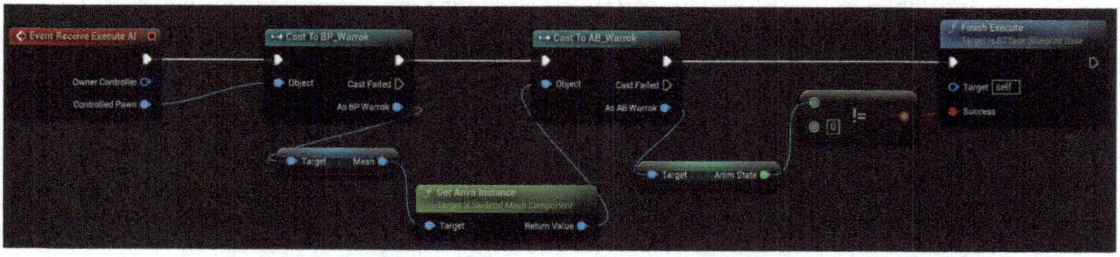

Figure 6.56 - The Blueprint of BTTask_Warrok_CheckForAction

`BTTask_Warrok_CheckForAction` checks whether Warrok is currently in the idle animation state by comparing `AnimState` with 0. If Warrok is not idle, it means another action, such as attacking, being hit, or dying, may still be in progress. In that case, the task prevents the Behavior Tree from starting a new action too early.

The exact structure depends on how you want to use the check task. The important idea is that the Behavior Tree should respect Warrok's current gameplay state. This makes enemy behavior more reliable and easier to debug.

After this check task is added to the Behavior Tree, Warrok has a safer action flow. The tree can avoid starting a new action while the current animation state is still busy.

Now we have a final version of the Behavior Tree, as shown in *Figure 6.57*:

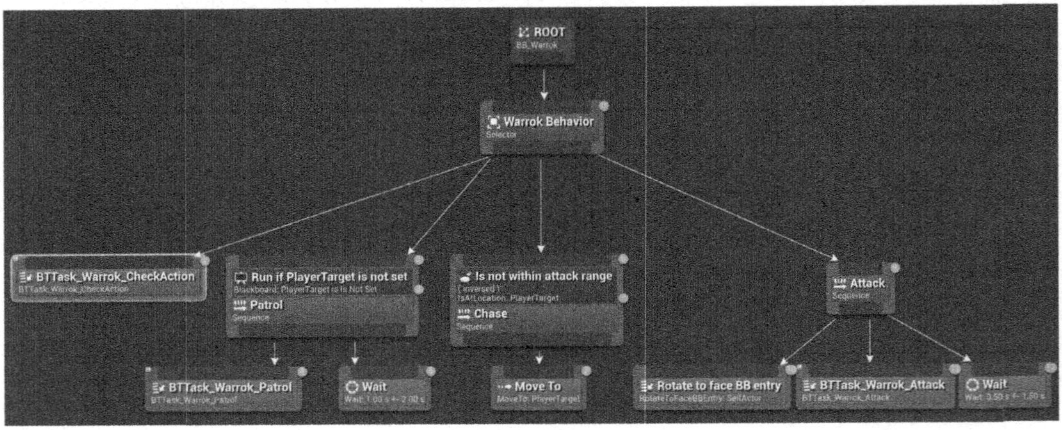

Figure 6.57 - The final Behavior Tree

After the final Behavior Tree is assembled, we need to test Warrok in the level.

Final testing

Start with the player outside Warrok's perception range. Warrok should patrol around its initial location. Then move the player into Warrok's sight range. Warrok should detect the player and chase. Once Warrok reaches attack range, it should stop moving, face the player, and attack.

Table 6.5 provides a quick checklist of expected behaviors for the main gameplay situations covered in this chapter:

Situation	Expected behaviors
Player is not detected	Warrok patrols around `InitLocation`
Player enters perception range	`PlayerTarget` is set

Situation	Expected behaviors
PlayerTarget is set	Warrokswitches from patrol to chase
Player is far away	Warrok moves toward the player
Player is within attack range	Warrok rotates and attacks
Warrok is attacking	It does not restart the attack every frame
Warrok takes damage	`Health` decreases
Warrok reaches zero health	Warrok stops normal AI behavior and dies

Table 6.5 - Quick Warrok checklist

If a branch of the Behavior Tree does not run as expected, check the Blackboard values first. Most Behavior Tree issues come from a key not being set, cleared, or checked correctly.

Once each item in *Table 6.5* works as expected, the Warrok enemy AI is complete and ready to be used as the main enemy behavior for this chapter.

Summary

In this chapter, we created a complete AI-controlled enemy character using Unreal Engine's AI framework. We began by setting up the Warrok enemy NPC with a Character Blueprint, Animation Blueprint, AI Controller, Behavior Tree, and Blackboard. These assets formed the foundation for controlling Warrok's behavior during gameplay.

We then enabled AI navigation by adding a Nav Mesh to the level, allowing Warrok to move through valid walkable areas. Using the `InitLocation` key, we created patrol behavior so Warrok could move around its starting position instead of remaining idle. We also improved the enemy's locomotion and turning so its movement looked more natural while navigating the level.

After movement was working, we added AI Perception so Warrok could detect the player through sight and hearing. By storing the detected player in the `PlayerTarget` Blackboard key, we connected perception to the Behavior Tree and allowed Warrok to switch from patrol behavior to chase behavior. We then extended the Behavior Tree with attack logic, allowing Warrok to stop chasing, face the player, and perform an attack when close enough.

Finally, we added health, damage, hit reaction, and death handling so Warrok could respond properly during combat. By combining Character Blueprints, AI Controllers, Behavior Trees, Blackboards, Nav Mesh navigation, AI Perception, and custom Behavior Tree tasks, we built a functional enemy NPC that can patrol, sense, chase, attack, and be defeated during gameplay. This completes the main Warrok enemy AI workflow.

You have now completed the basic combat gameplay for this chapter. In the next chapter, we will learn how to add UI elements to the game.

7

Game UI with Unreal Motion Graphics

In the modern gaming landscape, the User Interface (UI) serves as the vital bridge between the player and the virtual world. Whether it is a minimalist compass guiding a traveler through a dense forest or a complex command console in a flight simulator, the UI provides the essential data players need to make informed decisions. In Unreal Engine, this is handled through Unreal Motion Graphics (UMG).

UMG is a visual UI authoring tool that allows developers to create everything from basic menus and buttons to sophisticated, dynamic heads-up displays (HUDs). By utilizing a combination of the **Designer** tool and Blueprints, you can build interfaces that are both aesthetically pleasing and functionally robust.

This chapter introduces the core concepts and tools you need to create functional and interactive game user interfaces using UMG. You start by learning what UMG is and how the specialized UMG Editor provides a dedicated workspace for visual design and logic, distinct from the Level Editor you have used previously.

You will explore the interface panels unique to UMG, including the **Palette**, **Hierarchy**, **Designer Viewport**, **Animations**, and so on. This chapter also explains the dual nature of UMG assets with the drag-and-drop **Designer** tab for layout, and the **Graph** tab for visual scripting. This gives you a clear understanding of how visual elements translate into gameplay logic.

Following these foundational concepts, you will follow step-by-step instructions to create a functional Main Menu and a dynamic HUD. You will learn how to use Anchors to ensure your UI scales correctly across different screen resolutions and how to use **Bindings** to link player data, such as health and stamina, directly to the screen. Finally, you will integrate these UI elements into our *Pangaea* game project, allowing players to navigate between levels and view their progress in real-time.

In this chapter, we will cover the following main topics:

- What is Unreal Motion Graphics (UMG)?
- A brief introduction to the UMG Editor
- Creating the Main Menu
- Creating the HUD

By the end of this chapter, you will have a good understanding of Unreal Motion Graphics and its editor and will have worked through building a Main Menu system and HUD for the *Pangaea* game project. You'll have enough understanding to be capable of creating your own custom User Interfaces and combined logic, Main Menus, HUDs, and other real-time data visualization assets for your games in Unreal.

Technical requirements

The sample project for this chapter is available for download from the book's repository and branch:

- `Chapter07-Start` branch: The game project to begin learning this chapter.
- `Chapter07` branch: The completed game project for this chapter, featuring the main menu and in-game HUD.

You can download the example project and code files for this book by following the instructions in the *Download the example code/resource files* section in the *Preface* of this book.

This chapter's code/resource files are included in the downloadable code/resource bundle.

What is Unreal Motion Graphics (UMG)?

As described earlier, Unreal Motion Graphics (UMG) is a visual UI authoring toolset used to create interface elements such as menus, HUDs, and other overlays.

At its core, UMG is built upon Widget Blueprints. A Widget Blueprint is a specialized type of Blueprint that combines two distinct environments:

- A *visual layout designer* that forms a purely visual, drag-and-drop workspace (the canvas) where you act as an artist or graphic designer. Here, you assemble the look of your UI by placing and styling tangible elements like dragging a button onto the screen, choosing its color, and setting the **START GAME** text inside it

- A *standard Blueprint graph* for the logic-driven backend of the event graph, where you act as a programmer. Here, you use Unreal Engine's visual scripting nodes to dictate what those visual elements actually do during gameplay, such as catching the event of that specific button being clicked and triggering the command to load your game world.

UMG uses a system of **Widgets**, which are pre-made components, such as buttons, text blocks, images, and progress bars, that can be dragged, dropped, and styled. They allow you to create high-quality UIs that are capable of complex logic, such as reacting to player health changes or handling inventory management. Because they are Blueprints, they can easily communicate with other game systems (for example, Game Mode or the Player Character), allowing the interface to react instantly to in-game events and ensuring your UI is always in sync with the game state.

With an understanding of what Unreal Motion Graphics is, we will now examine the **UMG Editor**.

A brief introduction to the UMG Editor

Having previously spent time building the world of *Pangaea* in the **Level Editor**, you will now transition to a specialized toolset designed specifically for user interfaces. While the **Level Editor** is used to construct the 3D environments of *Pangaea*, the **UMG Editor** is a specialized workspace focused on the 2D and 3D user interface layer. Just as you used the **Level Editor** to manipulate Actors in world space, you will use the **UMG Editor** to manipulate Widgets in screen space.

To open the **UMG Editor**, you must first create or select a Widget Blueprint asset from the **Content Browser**. Once open, you will notice that the interface is specifically tailored for 2D layout and animation.

The **UMG Editor** includes a collection of tools that work in tandem to create a finished UI and comprises several panels, as highlighted in *Figure 7.1*:

Figure 7.1 - An overview of the UMG Editor interface layout

Each of these panels serves a distinct role in the UI development workflow, which we'll explore in the subsequent sections.

The main panels that you will use within this chapter are the Designer Viewport, the **Palette** panel, the **Hierarchy** panel, the **Details** panel, the **Animations** panel, and the **Graph** tab.

The Designer Viewport

The **Designer Viewport**, as shown in *Figure 7.2*, is the visual heart of the editor. It represents the player's screen and provides a canvas where you can drag, drop, and transform widgets to build the layout of your user interface.

Located in the center of the **UMG Editor**, it provides a *what-you-see-is-what-you-get* representation of how your UI will appear to the player. Unlike the 3D **Level Editor**, this Viewport is a 2D space where you manipulate Widgets to create the perfect layout for your game. It serves as the bridge between raw assets and a finished visual experience, allowing you to drag elements from the **Palette** panel and arrange them with pixel-perfect precision.

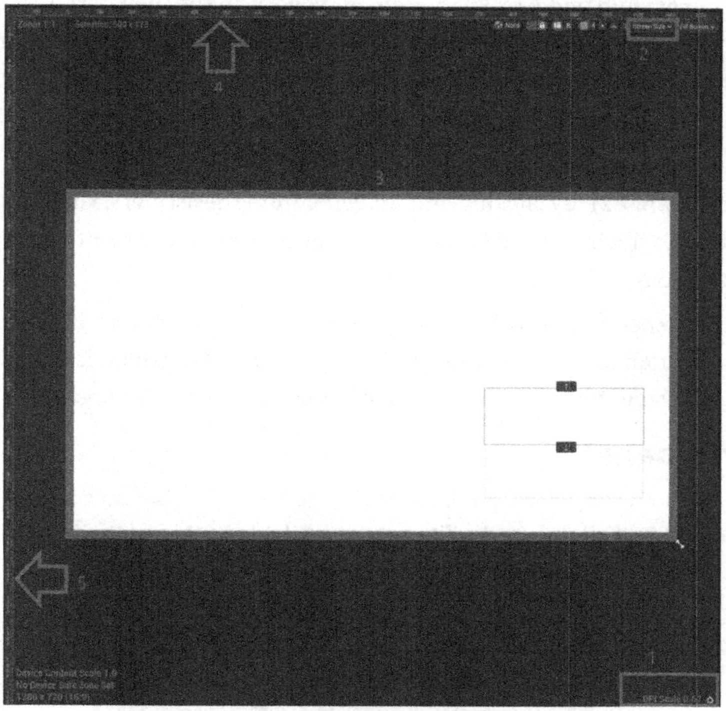

Figure 7.2 - UMG Designer Viewport

Understanding the layout and specific tools within the **Designer** Viewport is essential for creating a responsive UI:

- **Screen Size and Aspect Ratio**: Located at the top bar of the Viewport, this dropdown menu (**2** in *Figure 7.2*) allows you to switch between different device profiles, such as a 1080p monitor, a mobile phone, or a tablet. This is a critical area for beginners, as it helps you visualize how your UI will scale across various resolutions.
- **DPI Scaling**: In the bottom right of the Viewport, the current dots per inch (DPI) scaling is displayed (**1** in *Figure 7.2*). This informs you how Unreal is automatically resizing your UI to ensure it remains legible and correctly proportioned, and that widgets remain proportionally positioned regardless of the device's resolution.
- **Zoom and Pan**: You can navigate the Viewport using the mouse wheel to zoom in for detailed work or the right mouse button to pan across the layout. At the top-right of the Viewport, there is also a **Zoom percentage** indicator and a **Fill** button, which snaps the canvas back to fit the available screen space.
- **Canvas Panel**: By default, every new Widget Blueprint contains a **Canvas Panel** (**3** in *Figure 7.2*). This is the root container that allows for coordinate-based positioning and

anchoring of child widgets. Every element you see in the Viewport is a child of the root widget. By default, this is a **Canvas Panel**, and its boundaries are indicated by a dashed line. This line represents the safe zone where your UI elements live; anything placed outside this boundary will not be rendered on the player's screen.

- **Visual Guides and Rulers**: The Viewport features rulers along the top and left edges (**4** and **5** in *Figure 7.2*). By clicking and dragging from these rulers, you can pull out **Guidelines**, which are vital for aligning multiple buttons or health bars along a consistent axis.

By mastering these specific areas of the **Designer** Viewport, you gain total control over the player's visual experience, ensuring that every menu and HUD element is perfectly positioned and scales elegantly regardless of the hardware being used to play your game.

The Palette panel

Located in the top-left, the Palette panel, as shown in *Figure 7.3*, is your toolbox. It contains an expandable hierarchy of all the pre-built widgets available in Unreal Engine.

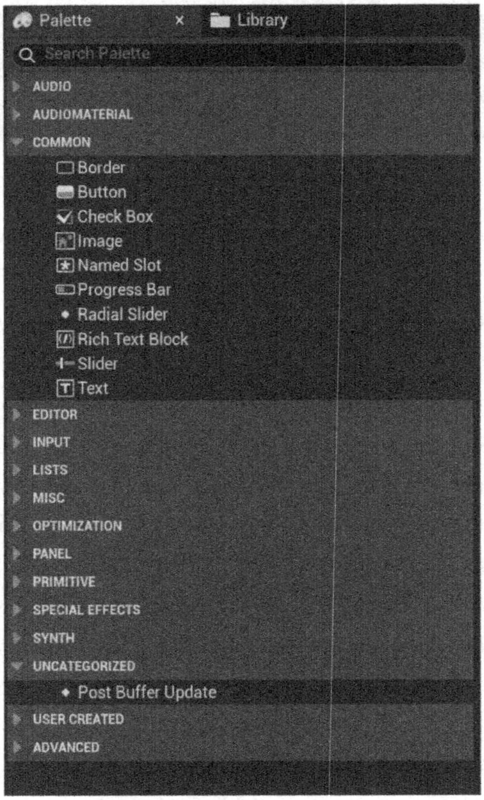

Figure 7.3 - UMG Palette panel

Some common widgets and their functionality are detailed below, but you should experiment with some of these widget groups to discover what functionality they bring:

- **Audio**: These include specialized controls for interacting with Audio and managing its playback and volume properties, such as **Audio** Sliders, **Audio Meters**, and **Audio Oscilloscope**.
- **Common**: These include essential elements like Buttons, Images, and Text.
- **Input**: These include interactive components, such as **ComboBoxes**, **Editable Text** (Single and Multi-Line), and **Spin Boxes**, which allow users to enter data or adjust game settings through direct manipulation.
- **Panel**: These are "containers" used for layout organization, such as **Horizontal Boxes**, **Vertical Boxes**, and **Grid Panels**.
- **Search functionality**: You can use the search bar at the top of the Palette to quickly find specific widgets without navigating through the categories.

The main widgets that you will use in this chapter are the Panel Widgets and the Button Widgets.

The Hierarchy panel

The Hierarchy panel, as shown in *Figure 7.4*, is situated below the **Palette** and displays a hierarchical tree structure of the widgets in your UI. Each widget item in the hierarchy is selectable, with selection causing that widget's properties to be editable in the **Details** panel.

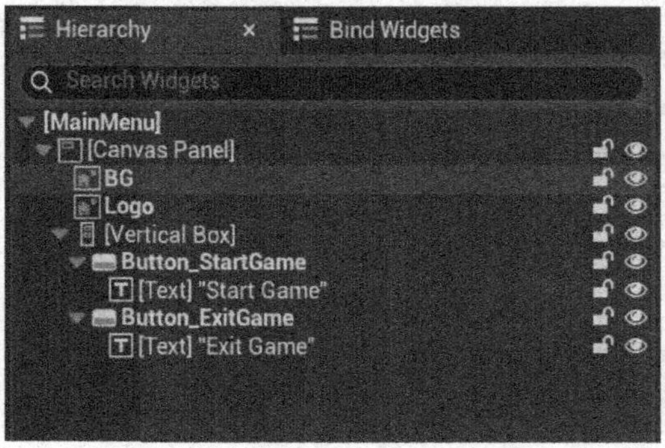

Figure 7.4 - UMG Hierarchy panel

Because UMG is based on a parent-child relationship, this panel is important for understanding your layout's logic and editing your UI. Some of its key features and functions are outlined as follows:

- **Parenting**: Dragging a Text block onto a Button in the **Hierarchy** makes the Text a *child* of the Button.

- **Slot properties**: When a widget is a child of a specific container (like a **Canvas Panel**), it gains **Slot** properties in the **Details** panel, which determine its anchoring and alignment within that parent.
- **Lock icon**: When a widget has its **Lock** icon clicked, it locks the widget and all its children to prevent them from being selected in the **Designer** Viewport.
- **Visibility (Eye) icon**: When a widget has its **Visibility** icon clicked, it toggles that widget's visibility in the **Designer** Viewport.
- **Search functionality**: You can use the search bar at the top of the Hierarchy to quickly locate and isolate specific widgets and their parents without navigating through the hierarchical tree, simplifying the view to the branch containing the widget you wish to focus on.

The Details panel

The Details panel, as shown in *Figure 7.5*, displays a hierarchical grouping of the settings and properties for the currently selected widget. It is the *command center* for fine-tuning the visual and functional properties of your selected widgets.

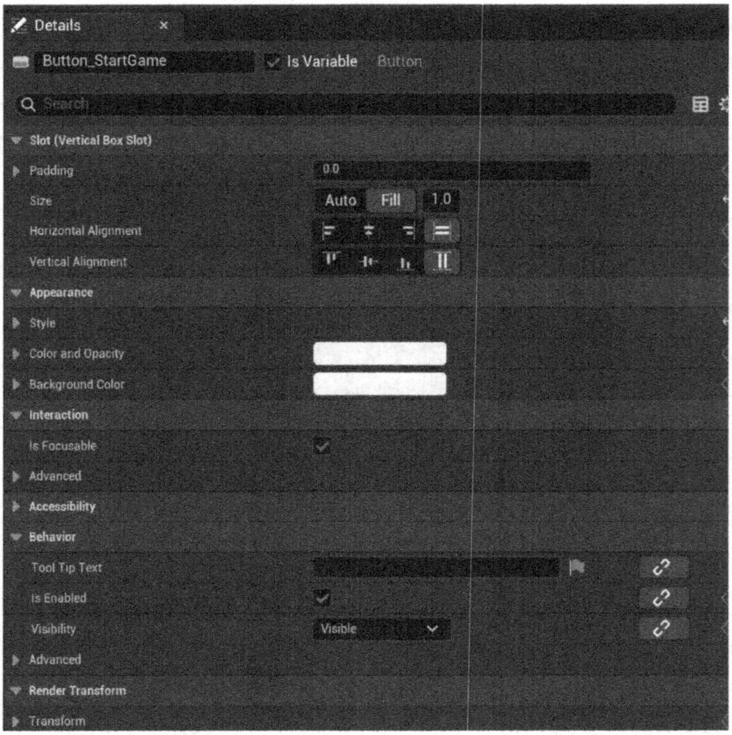

Figure 7.5 - UMG Details panel

Much like the **Details** panel in the **Level Editor**, it displays a comprehensive list of settings categorized into groups which generally include:

- **Is Variable**: At the top of the **Details** panel, checking this box is essential if you want to access that specific widget as a variable within the **Graph** tab to change its properties via Blueprints during gameplay.
- **Slot**: This category appears when a widget is a child of a **Canvas Panel** and contains critical layout properties such as **Anchors**, **Position**, **Size**, and **Alignment**. In *Figure 7.5*, the button is aligned to fill its parent container, which is the **Vertical Box**.
- **Appearance**: This is where you adjust the look of your widget, including the **Brush** (for images), **Tint** (for color overlays), and **Font** settings (for text blocks).
- **Behavior**: This section controls how the widget interacts with the game, including its **Visibility** state (**Visible**, **Hidden**, or **Collapsed**) and whether it is enabled for user interaction.

The Animations panel

The Animations panel, as shown in *Figure 7.6*, is the primary tool for breathing life into your static UI designs, allowing you to create dynamic transitions, button effects, and informative visual cues.

Located by default at the bottom-left of the **UMG Editor**, this panel operates on a timeline-based system similar to traditional video editing or motion graphics software. By creating an animation asset within this panel, you can *record* changes to a widget's properties, such as its opacity, position, or scale, over a set duration. This is essential for professional touches like a main menu fading in smoothly or a health bar pulsing red when the player's life reaches a critical threshold.

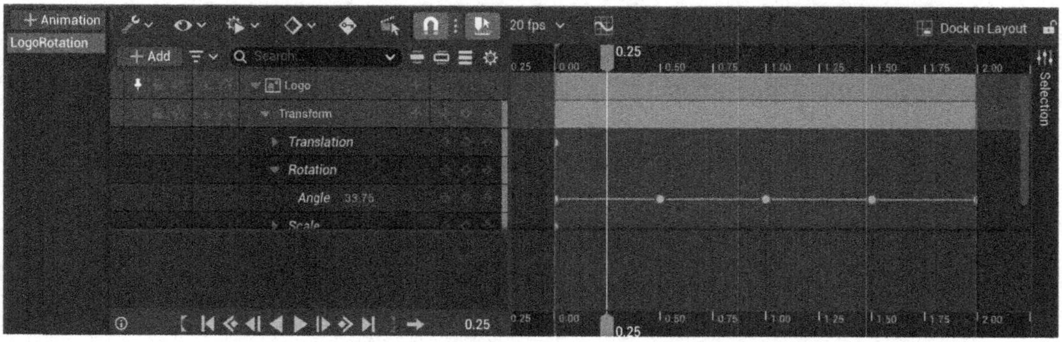

Figure 7.6 - UMG Animations panel

To effectively use the **Animations** panel, you must familiarize yourself with several key interface elements:

- **+ Animation button**: This is your starting point; clicking this allows you to create and name a new animation sequence, which then appears in the animation list.
- **Keyframes**: These are the essential *markers* on your timeline that store the specific value of a property, such as its position or color, at a particular moment. By setting two different keyframes (for example, a widget at 0% opacity and then at 100% opacity a second later or an Actor whose scale grows over the lifetime of an animation), Unreal Engine automatically calculates the transition between them, creating smooth, fluid transitions over time.
- **Timeline display**: Once an animation is selected, the right-hand side of the panel expands into a timeline where you can drag a timeline marker to a specific second or frame to set keyframes and their properties.
- **Keyframe icon (diamond)**: Found next to properties in the **Details** panel or on the timeline itself, clicking this icon locks in the current value of a property at that specific point in time.
- **Playback controls**: Standard buttons for **Play**, **Stop**, and **Loop** are located at the top of the timeline, allowing you to preview your UI motion directly within the **Designer** Viewport before ever running the game.

By gaining proficiency in using these controls, you can transition your interface from a series of static images into a polished, reactive experience that feels integrated into your game.

The Graph tab

The Graph tab, as shown in *Figure 7.7*, is the engine room of your Widget Blueprint, where you transition from visual design to functional logic. While the **Designer** tab defines how your UI looks, the **Graph** tab defines how it behaves. This environment uses the same Blueprint visual scripting system you used for characters and levels, as introduced in *Chapter 3*, but it is specialized for UI events. It is here that you bridge the gap between a button sitting on the screen and the action of the game starting, or between a player taking damage and the health bar visually depleting.

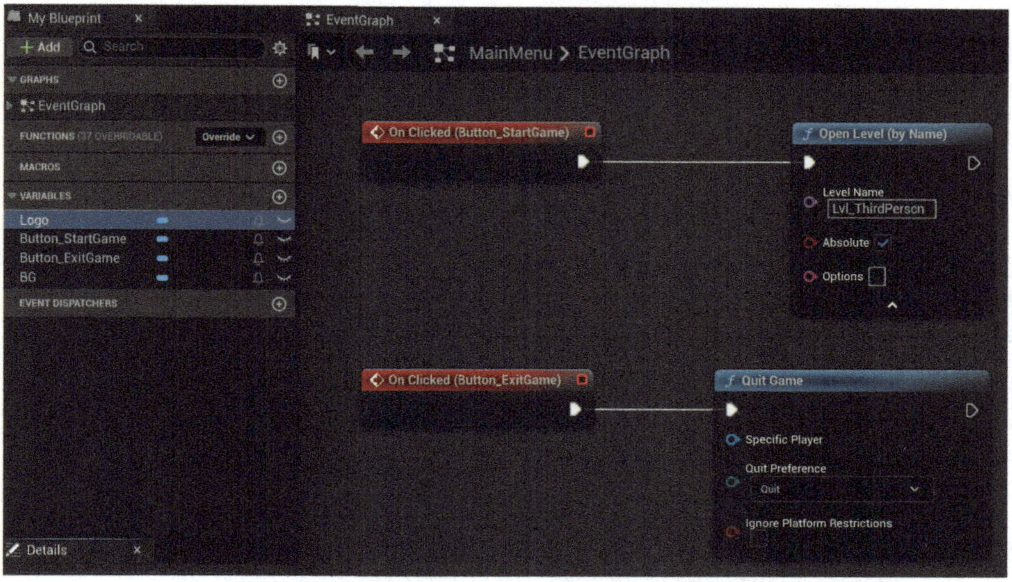

Figure 7.7 – The UMG Graph tab

Navigating the **Graph** tab requires an understanding of several distinct areas and functional nodes that are unique to the UMG workflow:

- **Toolbar**: At the top of the **Graph** tab, the **Toolbar** contains the **Compile** and **Save** buttons. It is vital to remember that any logic changes you make in the Graph will not take effect in the game until you hit **Compile**; a **yellow question mark** on the icon indicates that your latest changes haven't been *baked* into the widget yet.
- **My Blueprint panel**: Located on the left, this panel lists all the **Is Variable** widgets you marked in the **Designer** tab. It also displays any custom variables, functions, and macros you create. For a beginner, this is the go-to spot for dragging your buttons or progress bars into the graph to change their properties.
- **Palette (Graph Version)**: When in the **Graph** tab, the **Palette** changes to show a library of Blueprint nodes. You can find specialized UI functions here, such as **Play Animation**, **Set Visibility**, or nodes to get and set specific widget values.
- **Event Graph**: This is the large grid-based workspace where you arrange your nodes to script the logic for your widgets. In UMG, this area typically starts with a few default events like **Pre Construct** (which runs in the editor and at the start of the game), **Construct** (the UI version of **Begin Play**), and **Tick** (which runs every frame).

- **Variables**: Any widget marked as **Is Variable** in the **Designer** will appear here, allowing you to change its text, color, or progress percentage dynamically.
- **Variables and Bindings**: In the **Graph**, you can create variables to store data, such as a "Current Player Score." You can then use the **Variables** section to create getters and setters, allowing you to update the UI text blocks or images based on the data flowing through your game logic.

By utilizing the **Graph** tab, you transform your static UI into a responsive, "living" system that provides essential feedback to the player, making your game worlds feel interactive and reactive to their every move.

Having explored the various panels of the **UMG Editor**, you are now ready to begin constructing the visual elements of the *Pangaea* interface. In the next section, you will use these tools to build a functional Main Menu.

> **Note**
>
> If you would like more detailed information about building **user interfaces** in Unreal Engine, please refer to the official Unreal Engine documentation at `https://dev.epicgames.com/documentation/unreal-engine/building-your-ui-in-unreal-engine?application_version=5.6`.
>
> If you would like more detailed information about the **UMG Editor**, please refer to the official Unreal Engine documentation at `https://dev.epicgames.com/documentation/unreal-engine/umg-editor-reference-for-unreal-engine?application_version=5.6`.

Creating the Main Menu

Now that you have had an introduction to the **UMG Editor**, you will have the opportunity to get hands-on with the tools and create the Main Menu of the starting level for the *Pangaea* project.

Figure 7.8 - The completed Main Menu Level with working Main Menu UI

The Main Menu is very simple, as shown in *Figure 7.8*, and consists of the following elements:

- A background image
- A game logo image
- Two buttons: one to **Start** the game and the other to **Exit** the game

Through the following steps, you will learn how to structure the UI hierarchy and script the logic required to both launch your game and exit your game.

Creating the Main Menu Level

The following steps will guide you through creating the new Main Menu Level:

1. Open the `Pangaea` project that you have been using in the previous chapters.
2. In the **Content Browser**, navigate to **All** | **Content**| **Pangaea** folder.
3. Click on the **Add** button and select **New Folder**.
4. Name the new folder `Levels` and press *Enter*.
5. Right-click in the new `Levels` folder and select **Level** from the drop-down menu (see *Figure 7.9*) and name the level `MainMenu`.

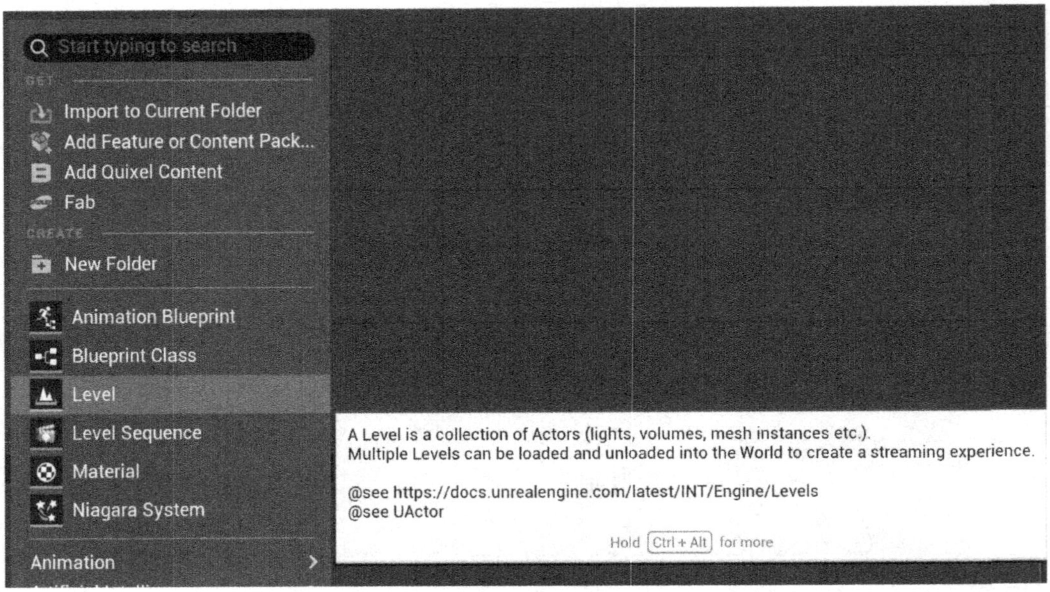

Figure 7.9 - Creating the Main Menu Level

6. Double-click on the **Main Menu Level** icon in the `Levels` folder to open the level.

Now that the **Main Menu** Level has been created and saved, the next step is to import the Main Menu background and game logo image resources to be used in the Main Menu.

Importing the Main Menu Resources

The following steps will guide you through importing the two image resources that are to be used within the Main Menu. You will first create a `UI` folder for holding the UI artifacts in the project.

Creating a dedicated `UI` folder is a development and project management best practice because it establishes a clean asset hierarchy, ensuring that all UI related artifacts are consolidated in one predictable location rather than cluttering core gameplay folders.

This disciplined organization drastically reduces development friction, allowing team members – or your future self – to instantly locate, update, and maintain interface assets as the project grows in scale.

Now, follow these steps:

1. In the **Content Browser**, navigate to **All** | **Content** | **Pangaea** folder.
2. Click on the **Add** button and select **New Folder**.
3. Name the new folder `UI` and press *Enter*.
4. Right-click in the new `UI` folder and select **Import to Current Folder**, and a File Browser should pop up, as shown in *Figure 7.10*:

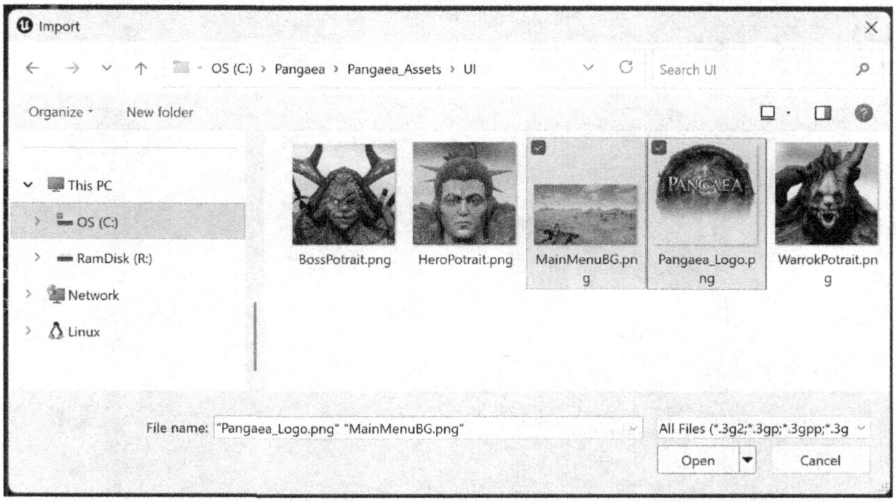

Figure 7.10 - Importing the Main Menu image resources

5. In the **File Browser**, navigate to the `Pangaea_Assets/UI` folder.
6. Hold *Shift* and select the `MainMenuBG.png` and the `Pangaea_Logo.png` files and click **Open**. These image files will then be imported into the project in the **All** | **Content** | **Pangaea** | **UI** folder.

With the **Main Menu** image resources imported, you will create the Main Menu Widget Blueprint next, which will be used to provide logic to the **Main Menu**.

Creating the Main Menu Widget Blueprint

The following steps will guide you through the creation of the Main Menu Widget Blueprint:

1. Right-click in the **All** | **Content** | **Pangaea** | **UI** folder and, from the drop-down menu, select **User Interface** | **Widget Blueprint**, as shown in *Figure 7.11*:

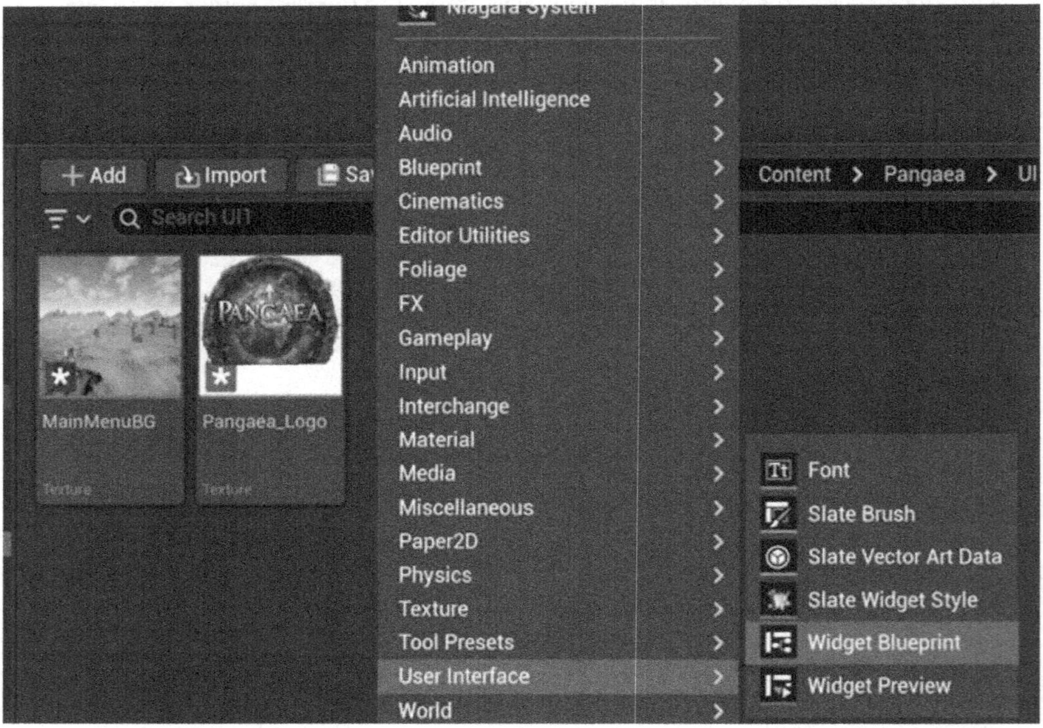

Figure 7.11 - Create the Main Menu Widget Blueprint

2. In the pop-up window that opens, choose **UserWidget** as the parent class for the new Widget Blueprint (see *Figure 7.12*), name it `MainMenu`, and press the **Select** button.

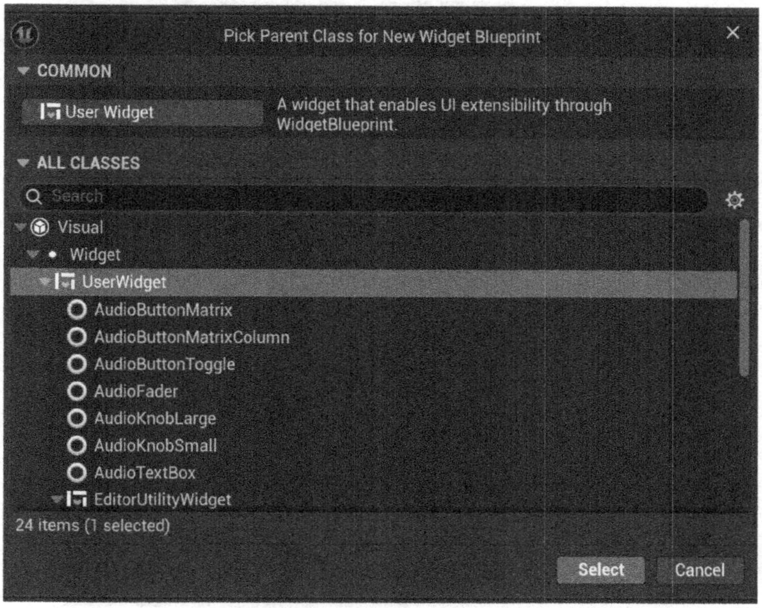

Figure 7.12 - Select UserWidget from the new Widget Parent Class pop-up

Now that you have created the Main Menu Widget Blueprint, you will begin creating the UI for the *Pangaea* game, starting with a **Canvas Panel**.

Adding the Canvas Panel

The Canvas Panel is a foundational layout widget that serves as the primary root container for most UI designs in UMG. Its main functionality is to provide a coordinate-based workspace where you can place child widgets at specific X and Y positions, allowing for precise, pixel-perfect arrangement.

Unlike Auto-Layout widgets (such as Horizontal or Vertical Boxes) that automatically stack their children, the **Canvas Panel** grants you total freedom over where an element sits on the screen. Most importantly, it introduces the concept of Anchors, which allow you to *pin* a widget to a specific part of the screen (such as a corner or the center), ensuring that your UI elements maintain their relative positions and scale correctly across various monitor resolutions and aspect ratios.

Use the following steps to guide you through adding a **Canvas Panel** to the game UI:

1. Double-click on the newly created `MainMenu` to open it in the UMG Editor.
2. Upon opening the UMG Editor, locate the **Canvas Panel** in the **Palette** panel under the Panel heading (**1** in *Figure 7.13*), and drag it into the **Hierarchy** panel to add it to the UI (**2** in *Figure 7.13*).

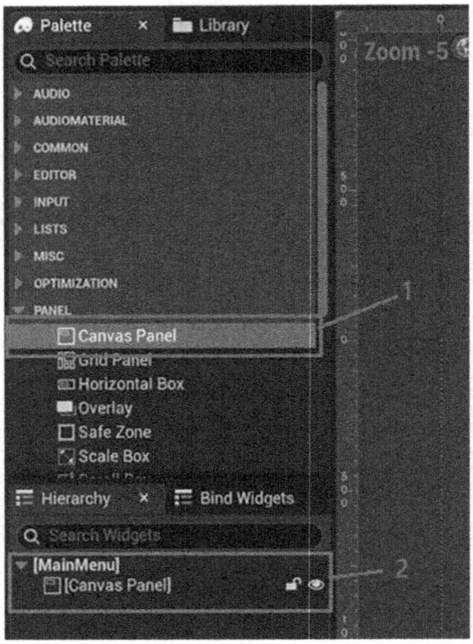

Figure 7.13 - Adding a Canvas Panel to the Main Menu hierarchy

With the **Canvas Panel** created as the root element for the game UI, the next step is to add a background and a logo to the *Pangaea* game's UI.

Adding the background and logo images

The Image component is a versatile visual widget used to display textures, materials, or solid colors within your UI. It is the primary tool for creating backgrounds, icons, health bar frames, and character portraits, providing the aesthetic *skin* for your interface elements.

Now, follow these steps to add two Image components to the UI hierarchy. One of these components will display the background image, and the other will display the logo image in the game UI:

1. Locate the **Image** component in the **Palette** panel under the **Common** heading (**1** in *Figure 7.14*) and drag it into the **Hierarchy** panel underneath the **Canvas Panel** to add it to the UI (**2** in *Figure 7.14*).
2. Right-click on the newly created Image component in the **Hierarchy** panel, select **Rename** in the pop-up menu, and name the component `IMG_Background`.

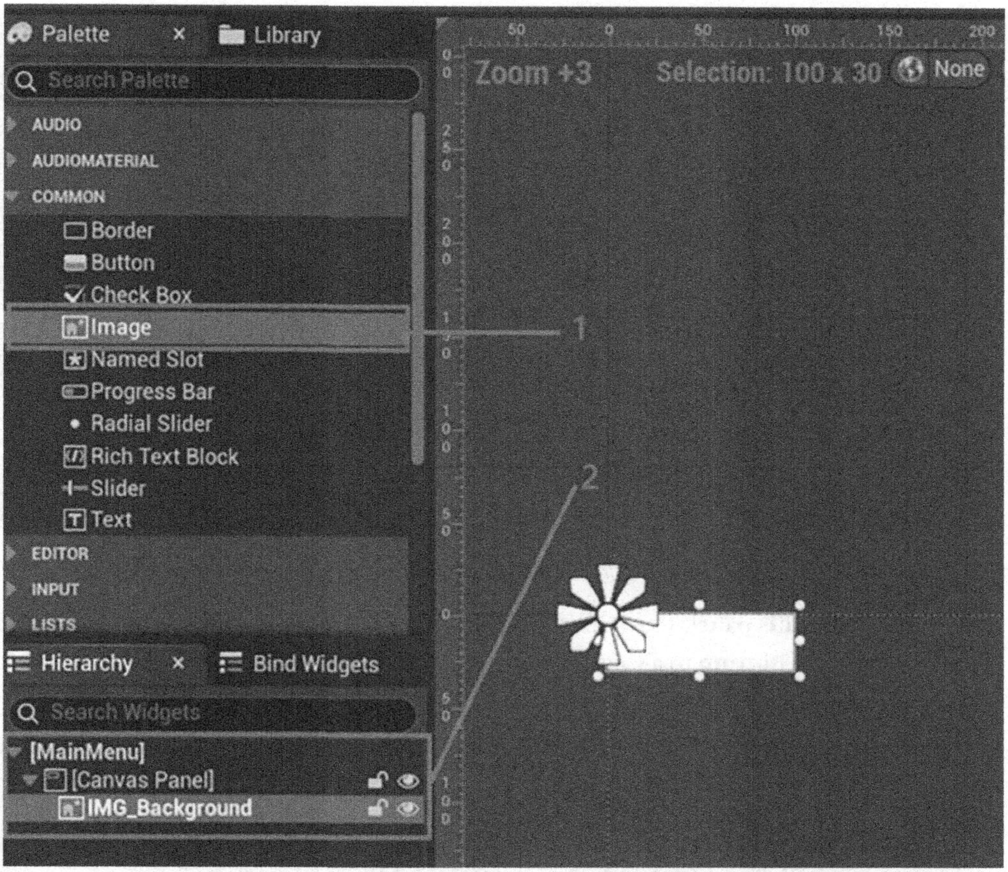

Figure 7.14 - Adding an Image component to the Main Menu hierarchy

3. To ensure that our background image will fill the entire screen, with the newly created `IMG_Background` component selected in the **Hierarchy** panel (**1** in *Figure 7.15*), click the **Anchors** drop-down in the **Details** panel (**2** in *Figure 7.15*). Here, select the bottom-right **Fill** preset, which is the **square** icon (**3** in *Figure 7.15*).

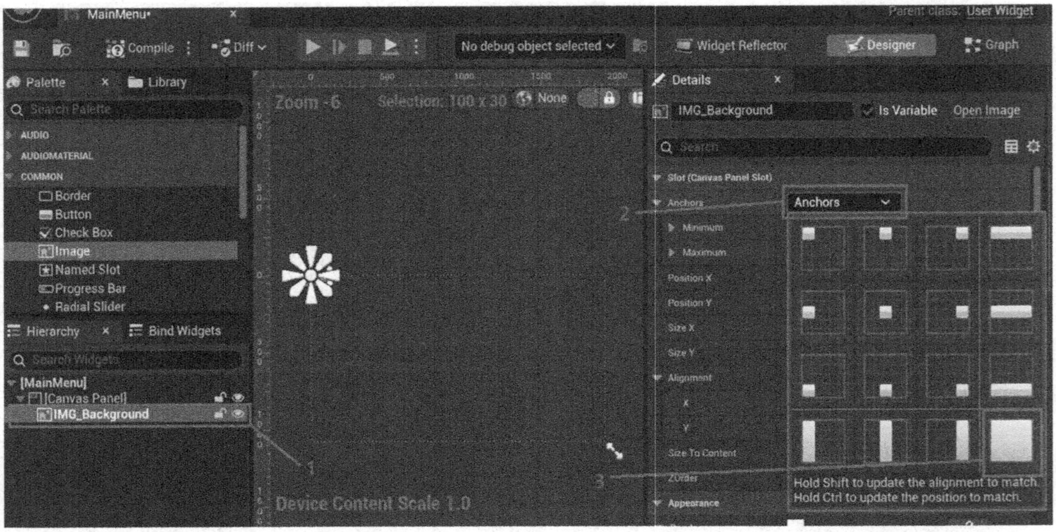

Figure 7.15 - Scaling the IMG_Background component in the Main Menu UI

4. In the **Details** panel, set all the Offset values for **Offset Left**, **Offset Top**, **Offset Right**, and **Offset Bottom** to a value of `0` (see *Figure 7.16*) to ensure that the background image stretches to fit any monitor.

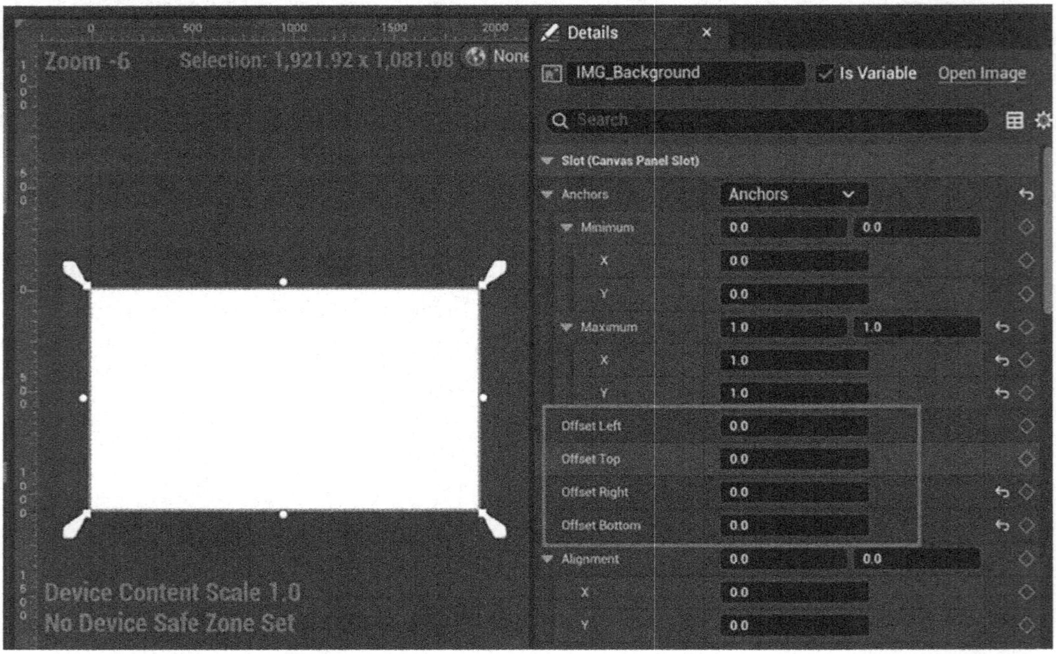

Figure 7.16 - Stretching the IMG_Background component to fill the Main Menu UI for any monitor

5. In the **Details** panel, navigate to the **Appearance** | **Brush** (**1** in *Figure 7.17*) headers. Here, click the **Image** drop-down, and use the *Search* text field to locate and select the `MainMenuBG.png` texture, which you imported earlier to set the UI background to that texture.
6. Now click the **Compile** button (**2** in *Figure 7.17*), and then the **Save** button (**3** in *Figure 7.17*) to save the UI at this step.

Figure 7.17 - Setting the Image background to the imported MainMenuBG texture

7. Repeat *steps 1 to 3* for a second **Image** component to hold the game logo. Then configure it as follows (see *Figure 7.18*):
    1. Drag the **Image** component onto the **Canvas Panel** in the **Hierarchy** panel – this should place it with the **Canvas Panel** as its parent but listed underneath the `IMG_Background` in the **Hierarchy**.
    2. Rename the Image component to `IMG_Logo`.
    3. In the **Details** panel, set its **Anchor** to the **Top-Center** preset. This preset pins the image's origin point directly to the top-middle edge of the player's screen (or parent container).
    4. In the **Details** panel, set the **Position X** value to `0` and the **Position Y** value to `50`. The new **Position** settings will adjust the image's position 50 units downward from the **Top-Center** anchor position.

5. In the **Details** panel, set the **Size X** value to `500` and the **Size Y** value to `420`.
6. In the **Details** panel, set the left **Alignment X** value to `0.5`. The new **Alignment X** setting will move the horizontal internal pivot point of the image to the exact midpoint of the image's width.
7. In the **Details** panel, navigate to the **Appearance | Brush** headers, click the **Image** drop-down. Here, use the Search text field to locate and select the `Pangaea_Logo.png` texture, which you imported earlier, to set the UI `IMG_Logo` image to that texture.
8. Now, click the **Compile** button, and then the **Save** button to save the UI and complete this step.

Figure 7.18 - Setting the logo Image to the imported Pangaea_Logo texture

When working with Image components, you will frequently manage the following properties in the **Details** panel:

- The **Brush | Image** dropdown is the core property of the **Image** widget and allows the user to select the specific Texture or Material you want to display. You can also adjust the **Image Size** to match the dimensions of your source asset.
- The **Brush | Draw As** setting determines how the image is rendered. You can choose **Image** for standard display, **Border** for elements that need to scale while maintaining edge proportions (9-slicing), or **Box** for simple tiled backgrounds.

- **Appearance | Color and Opacity** setting allows you to apply a color overlay to your texture. It is a powerful tool for UI designers, as it allows you to use a single white icon and change its color dynamically via Blueprints to represent different states (for example, turning an icon red when a skill is on cooldown).
- The **Appearance | Mirroring** property provides simple checkboxes to flip your image horizontally or vertically, which is useful for reusing symmetrical UI assets like corner flourishes.
- The **Advanced | Tiling** setting can be used if your image is intended to be a repeating pattern. You can set the tiling behavior to **Horizontal**, **Vertical**, or **Both**, allowing a small texture to fill a large area without stretching.

With the background and logo images both added to the *Pangaea* game UI, the next step is to add two buttons: one to start the game and the other to exit the game.

Adding the buttons

The Button component is the primary interactive element in UMG, designed to execute logic when clicked, hovered, or pressed by the user. It acts as a *wrapper* component, meaning it typically contains a child widget – most commonly a **Text** block – to provide a label for the action it performs.

The following steps will add two Button components (one for starting the game and the other for exiting the game) to the UI hierarchy and place them appropriately within the UI layout (a later step will add the functionality to allow them to start and exit the game). A visual of how the final UI hierarchy will look is shown in *Figure 7.19*.

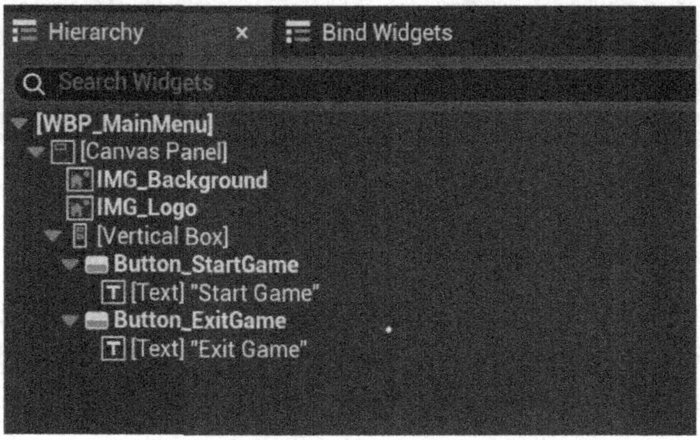

Figure 7.19 - Final Main Menu UI Hierarchy

First, we'll add the Vertical Box (see *Figure 7.20*) by following these steps:

1. Locate the **Vertical Box** component in the **Palette** panel under the **Panel** heading and drag it onto the **Canvas Panel** in the **Hierarchy** panel. This should place it with the **Canvas Panel** as its parent but listed underneath the `IMG_Logo` in the hierarchy.
2. In the **Details** panel, set its **Anchor** to the **Bottom-Right** preset.
3. In the **Details** panel, set the **Position X** value to `-350` and the **Position Y** value to `-300`.
4. In the **Details** panel, set the **Size X** value to `500` and the **Size Y** value to `300`.
5. In the **Details** panel, set the left **Alignment X** value to `0.5`, and right **Alignment Y** to also be `0.5`.

Figure 7.20 - Adding a Vertical Box to the UI

Next, add the buttons hierarchy (see *Figure 7.21*) by following these steps:

1. Locate the **Button** component in the **Palette** panel under the **Common** heading and drag two **Button** components onto the **Vertical Box** in the **Hierarchy** panel. This should place them with the **Vertical Box** as their parent in the hierarchy.
2. Rename the first (topmost) button in the hierarchy to `Button_StartGame` and rename the second (bottom) button in the hierarchy to `Button_ExitGame`.
3. In the **Details** panel under the **Slot** header, set the **Size** property for each button component to **Fill.** The **Horizontal Alignment** and **Vertical Alignment** settings

should be set to **Fill Horizontally** and **Fill Vertically**, respectively, for each button. This will align both buttons to expand but share the **Vertical Box** space equally.

4. In the **Details** panel under the **Appearance | Background Color** header, set the property **A** (the alpha channel) to **0**. This will ensure that the buttons will be displayed with a transparent background.

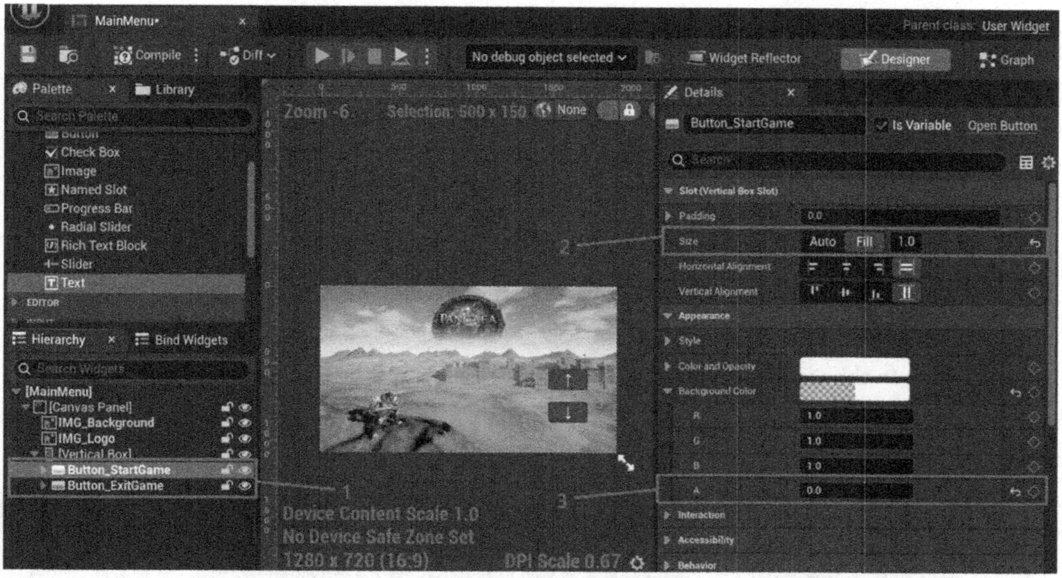

Figure 7.21 - Adding the two Button components to the UI

Let's also have a look at some of the properties in the **Details** panel that you will frequently manage while working with Button components:

- The **Style** property is where you define the button's visual response. It contains sub-menus for **Normal**, **Hovered**, and **Pressed** states. By setting different textures or tints for each, you provide the "affordance" that tells a player an element is interactive.
- The **Color and Opacity** setting affects the button and all of its children (for example, the text inside it).
- The **Interaction** header contains an **Is Focusable** toggle property, which allows a button to only be keyboard-focusable when it is checked.
- Located at the very bottom of the **Details** panel, the **Events** section provides the green + (**plus**) buttons for connecting events, such as **On Clicked**, **On Pressed**, and **On Released**. Clicking these + buttons will automatically create the corresponding event nodes in the **Graph** tab.

Now, we'll add the button texts (see *Figure 7.22*) by following these steps:

1. Locate the **Text** component in the **Palette** panel under the **Common** heading and drag a **Text** component onto each of the two buttons in the hierarchy. This should place them with each respective Button as their parent in the hierarchy.
2. For the **Text** component that is parented to `Button_StartGame` in the hierarchy (**1** in *Figure 7.22*):
    1. In the **Details** panel under the **Content** header, set the **Text** property value to **Start Game** (**2** in *Figure 7.22*).
    2. In the **Details** panel under the **Font** header, set the **Size** property value to `48` (**3** in *Figure 7.22*).
3. For the **Text** component that is parented to `Button_ExitGame` in the hierarchy:
    1. In the **Details** panel under the **Content** header, set the **Text** property value to **Exit Game**.
    2. In the **Details** panel under the **Font** header, set the **Size** property value to `48`.
4. Click the **Compile** button, and then the **Save** button to save the UI and complete this step.

Figure 7.22 - Adding labels to the Button components in the UI

To customize how text appears in your interface, you will commonly work with the following properties in the **Details** panel:

- The **Content** heading contains the **Text** property that holds the actual string of characters that will appear on the screen. It is also the area where you can click **Bind** to link the text to a dynamic variable, such as a player's score or current health.
- The properties under the **Appearance** | **Font** header enable the customization of the text appearance and allow you to change the **Font Family**, the **Typeface** (such as, **Regular**, **Bold**, or **Italic**), and the **Font Size** of the text that appears in your UI.
- The **Wrapping** | **Auto Wrap Text** property's checkbox can be enabled to ensure that long-running text automatically breaks into new lines once it reaches the edge of its container, rather than bleeding off the screen.

With the buttons and their labels added to the UI, the next step is to add functionality to the buttons using the UMG **Graph** view.

Connecting the buttons to Blueprints

The following steps will hook up the *Exit Game* and *Start Game* functionality in the **Graph** tab to the respective **Button** components in the UI hierarchy. Clicking these buttons in the UI will trigger the *Exit Game* and *Start Game* functionality.

1. With the `Button_ExitGame` in the **Hierarchy**, scroll down to the bottom of the **Details** panel and under the **Events** header, click the **+ (plus)** button that is next to the **On Clicked** event, as shown in *Figure 7.23*. This will switch to the **Graph** tab and create an **OnClicked** node in the graph.

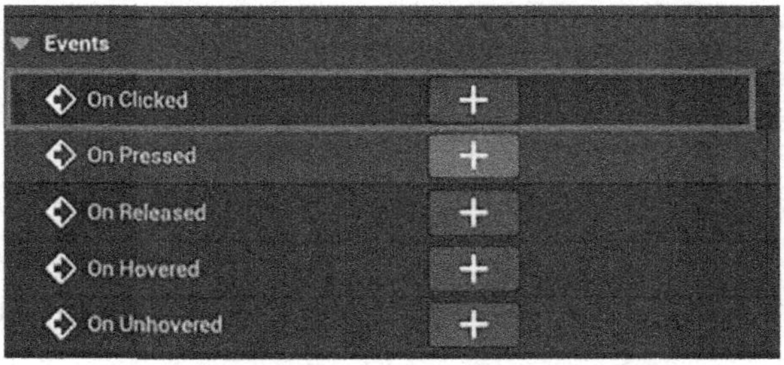

Figure 7.23 - Adding an On Clicked event to the Exit Game Button in the UI

2. In the **Graph** tab, drag the *white* node pin from the **OnClicked** node and drop it in the graph window, then search for the `Quit Game` node and hit *Enter* to select it. The **Quit Game** node immediately terminates the running gameplay session, safely closes the game application window, and returns the player to their desktop or console dashboard.

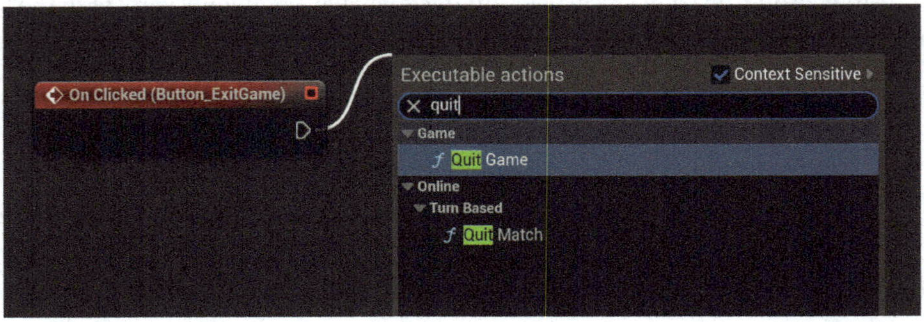

Figure 7.24 - Searching for the Quit Game node from the On Clicked event

3. This will add a **Quit Game** node into the graph and connect it to the **On Clicked** node with a *white* wire, as shown in *Figure 7.25*. Now click the **Compile** button, and then the **Save** button to save the UI and the Blueprint.

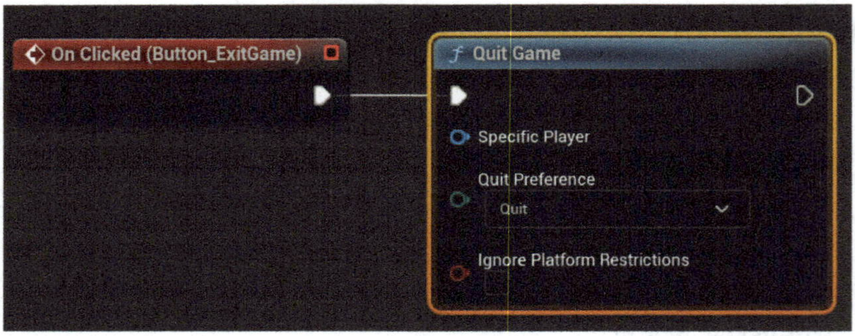

Figure 7.25 - Blueprint with the Quit Game node added and connected to the On Clicked node in the Graph tab

Now, go back into the **Designer** tab and repeat *steps 1 to 3* for the `Button_StartGame` in the hierarchy. For this button, however, you will use the **Open Level (By Name)** node to load the game level. Follow these steps:

1. In *step 2*, search for `Open Level (By Name)` and hit *Enter* to select it.
2. In the **Open Level (By Name)** node that is created, populate its **Level Name** property with the value `Lvl_ThirdPerson`. This will configure the button to start the game by loading the `Lvl_ThirdPerson` level. This level is located in the **Content Browser** under the **All** | **Content**| **ThirdPerson** folder.

When the button is clicked, the **Open Level (By Name)** node shuts down the current active scene and unloads its assets from memory while simultaneously loading and launching the specific level file matching the text name you provided – in our case, the `Lvl_ThirdPerson` level.

3. Now click the **Compile** button, and then the **Save** button to save the UI and the Blueprint, and then close the `MainMenu` Blueprint to complete this step. *Figure 7.26* shows the completed and configured **Graph** tab view for the `Button_StartGame` button:

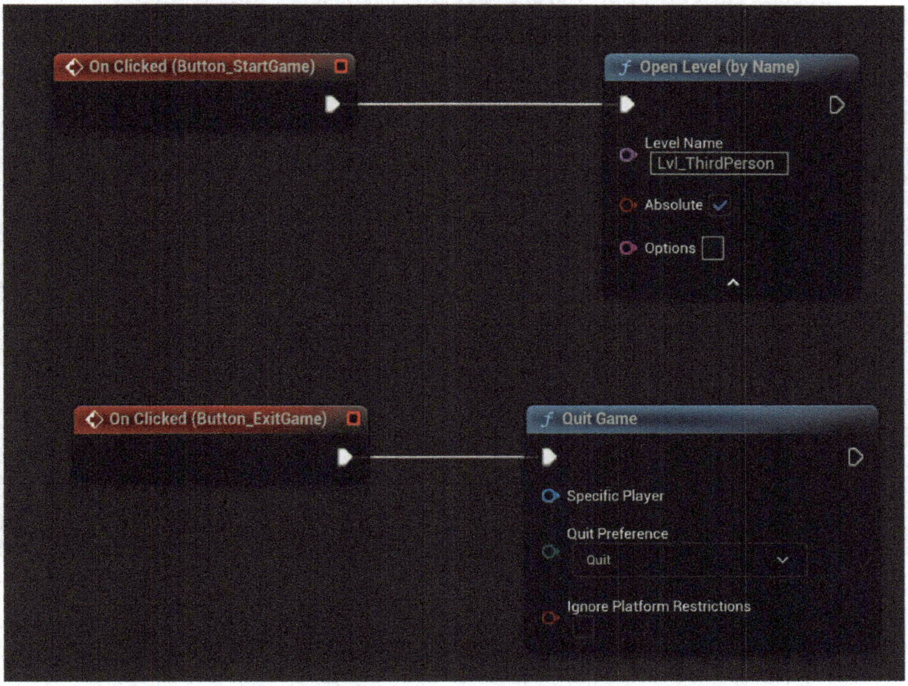

Figure 7.26 - MainMenu graph Blueprint with the Open Level (By Name) node added, configured to the Lvl_ThirdPerson level, and connected to the On Clicked node

With the UI buttons now configured with their functionality, the next step is to link the **Main Menu Widget Blueprint** to the **Main Menu** Level so that the main menu can be used in the *Pangaea* game.

Connecting the Main Menu Level to the Main Menu Blueprint

The following steps will create a **Level Blueprint** that will hook up the **Main Menu Widget Blueprint** to work in the **Main Menu** Level:

1. In the **Content Browser**, navigate to the **All** | **Content**| **Pangaea** | **Levels** folder and open the **Main Menu** Level.
2. Click the **List of World Blueprints...** button (**1** in *Figure 7.27*), and in the pop-up that appears, click on **Open Level Blueprint** (**2** in *Figure 7.27*) to open the **Level Blueprint** that is associated with the **Main Menu** Level.

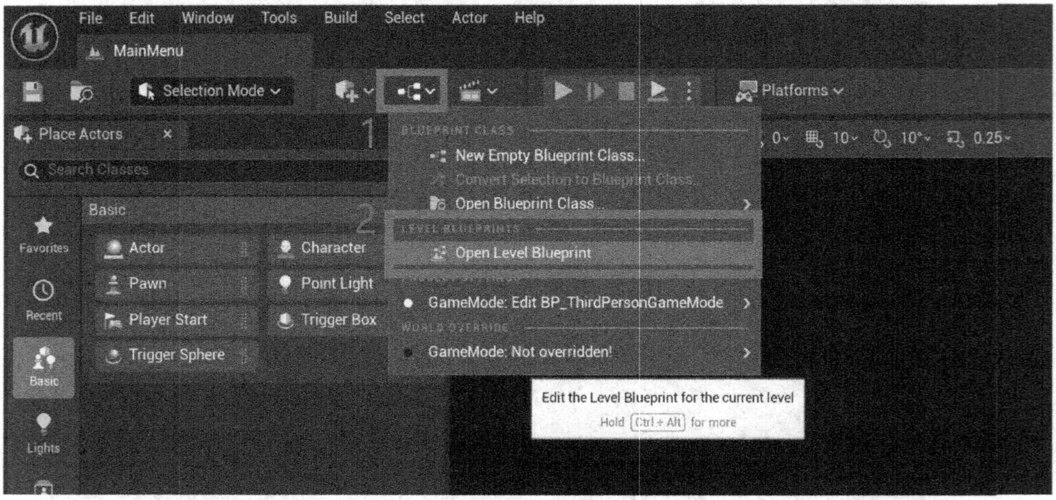

Figure 7.27 - Opening the Level Blueprint for the Main Menu level

3. In the opened Level Blueprint, drag the *white* node pin from the **Event BeginPlay** node and drop it in the graph window, then search for the `Create Widget` node and then hit *Enter* to select it. The **Create Widget** node spawned in this step is the critical component that actually generates the live, runtime instance of your UI asset in the game's memory.

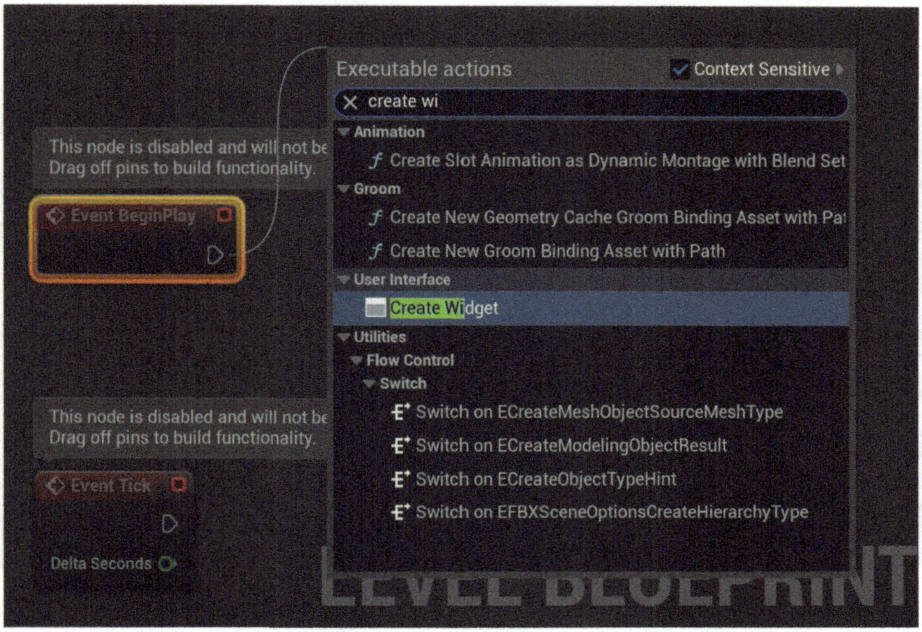

Figure 7.28 - Connecting the BeginPlay event to the Create Widget node in the Main Menu Level Blueprint

4. In the newly created node, populate its **Class** property with the value **MainMenu** (shown in *Figure 7.29*). This will configure the creation of an instance of the `MainMenu` Blueprint within the **Main Menu** Level.

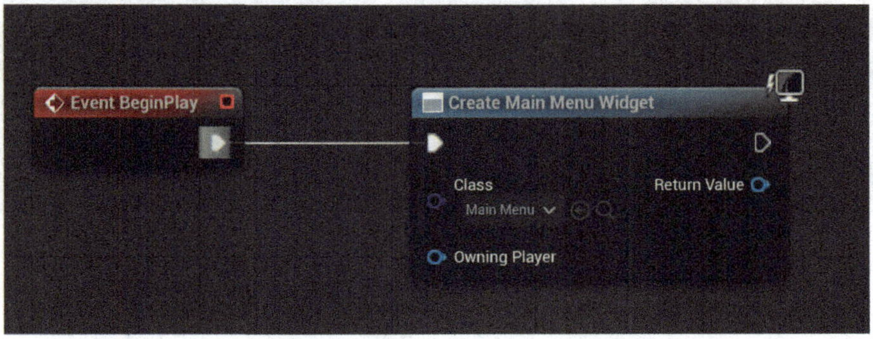

Figure 7.29 - Event BeginPlay connected to the Create Main Menu Widget node

5. In the Level Blueprint, drag the blue **Return Value** node pin from the newly created **Create Main Menu Widget** node and search for and add the **Add to Viewport** node (see *Figure 7.30*). Then, connect the execution output pin of the **Create Main Menu Widget** node to the execution input pin of the **Add to Viewport** node. The `MainMenu`

Blueprint will now be added to the Viewport of the **Main Menu** Level, allowing it to be used as the UI for that level and making it visible on the screen.

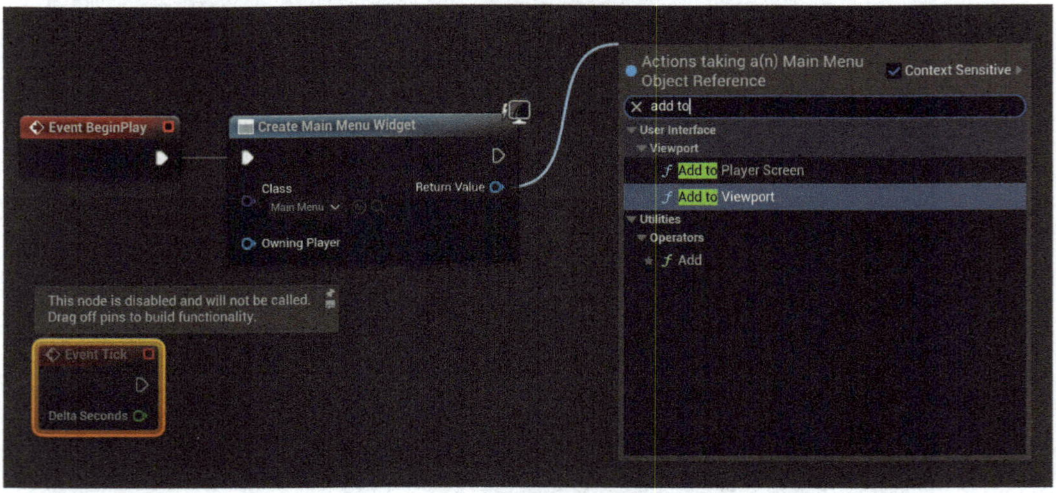

Figure 7.30 - Connecting the Create Main Menu Widget node to the Add to Viewport node in the Main Menu Level Blueprint

6. Now click the **Compile** button, and then the **Save** button to save the Level Blueprint. *Figure 7.31* shows the completed and configured Level Blueprint for the **Main Menu** Level.

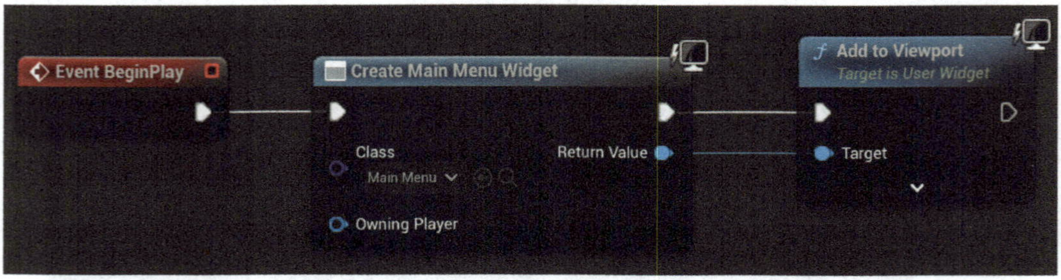

Figure 7.31 - Main Menu Level Blueprint with the Create Main Menu Widget node added, with the Return Value connected to the Add to Viewport node

The **Main Menu** is now complete (see *Figure 7.8*), and you can test the functionality of the **Main Menu** Level by pressing the **Play** button and interacting with the buttons in the UI. The **Start Game** button should load the `Lvl_ThirdPerson`, while the **Exit Game** button should exit the **Main Menu** Level.

Having created our first UI for the *Pangaea* main menu, in the next section, you will take this further and use these tools to build a functional HUD for the *Pangaea* game.

Unreal Engine has a lot of different UI components available within the **Palette** panel, and there are far too many to cover in this book, so we only introduced the ones used to build the *Pangaea* game. If you would like more detailed information about the UI components available in the **Palette** panel, refer to the official Unreal Engine documentation at `https://dev.epicgames.com/documentation/unreal-engine/umg-editor-reference-for-unreal-engine?application_version=5.6`.

Creating the HUD

With the Main Menu UI now in place, you will build out the *Pangaea* game UI further and create the game's heads-up display (HUD). The **HUD**, as shown in *Figure 7.32*, provides the player with constant visual feedback. In *Pangaea*, it is used to communicate the player and enemy health, as well as the current game state.

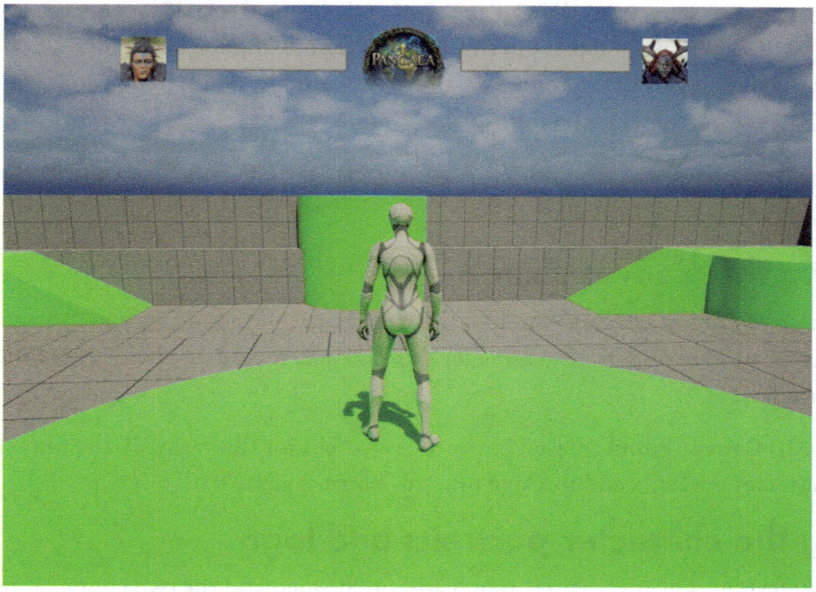

Figure 7.32 - Completed HUD UI displayed in the Third Person Level

Through the step-by-step guides in the subsequent sections, you will learn how to create the HUD UI and how to bind gameplay data to the components in the HUD UI.

Importing HUD resources

The following steps will guide you through importing the additional image resources that are to be used within the HUD:

1. In the **Content Browser**, navigate to **All** | **Content** | **Pangaea** | **UI** folder.

2. Right-click in the new `UI` folder and select **Import to Current Folder**, and a File Browser should pop up.
3. In the **File Browser**, navigate to the parent folder of the **Content** folder and from there navigate to the `Pangaea_Contents` folder.
4. Hold *Shift* and select the `HeroPortrait.png`, `WarrokPortrait.png`, and `BossPortrait.png` files and click **Open**. These image files will then be imported into the project in the **All** | **Content** | **Pangaea** | **UI** folder.

With the HUD image resources imported, you will now create the HUD Widget Blueprint, which will be used to provide logic to the HUD.

Creating the HUD Widget Blueprint

The HUD requires an underlying Widget Blueprint, similar to the Main Menu Blueprint UI. You can follow the same steps from the earlier *Creating the Main Menu Widget Blueprint* section to create a new HUD Widget Blueprint in the **All** | **Content** | **Pangaea** | **UI** folder. Choose **User Widget** as the parent class, but this time name it `HUD`. Finally, double-click on the newly created `HUD` to open it in the **UMG Editor**.

With the Widget Blueprint created for the game HUD, the next step is to add a root **Canvas Panel** into the *Pangaea* game's UI.

Creating the Canvas Panel

The HUD also requires a **Canvas Panel** for the UI to be displayed on. So, you can again follow the same steps used earlier in the *Adding the Canvas Panel* section to create the **Main Menu Canvas Panel**.

With the HUD **Canvas Panel** created as the root element for the game UI, the next step is to add the character portraits and the logo into the *Pangaea* game's UI.

Adding the character portraits and logo

The following steps will guide you through adding the logo and the two character portraits (one for the *player* and the other for the *enemy*), which appear at the top of the HUD:

1. Drag three **Image** components from the **Palette** panel into the **Hierarchy** panel, placing them underneath the **Canvas Panel**.
2. For the topmost **Image** component in the hierarchy:
   1. Rename the **Image** component to `IMG_Logo` (see *Figure 7.33*).
   2. In the **Details** panel, set the **Anchor** setting to **Top Middle**.
   3. In the **Details** panel, set the **Position X** value to `0` and the **Position Y** value to `40`.

4. In the **Details** panel, set the **Size X** value to `150` and the **Size Y** value to `150`.
5. In the **Details** panel, set the left **Alignment X** value to `0.5` and the right **Alignment Y** value to `0`.
6. In the **Details** panel, navigate to the **Appearance** | **Brush** headers, click the **Image** drop-down, and use the search text field to locate and select the `Pangaea_Logo.png` texture to set the UI `IMG_Logo` image to that texture.

3. For the second **Image** component in the hierarchy:
   1. Rename the **Image** component to `IMG_HeroPortrait`.
   2. In the **Details** panel, set the **Anchor** setting to **Top Middle**.
   3. In the **Details** panel, set the **Position X** value to `-420` and the **Position Y** value to `60`.
   4. In the **Details** panel, set the **Size X** value to `80` and the **Size Y** value to `80`.
   5. In the **Details** panel, set the **Alignment X** value to `1.0`, and the **Alignment Y** value to `0`.
   6. In the **Details** panel, navigate to the **Appearance** | **Brush** headers, click the **Image** dropdown, and use the search text field to locate and select the `HeroPortrait.png` texture to set the UI `IMG_HeroPortrait` image to that texture.
4. For the third **Image** component in the hierarchy:
   1. Rename the **Image** component to `IMG_EnemyPortrait`.
   2. In the **Details** panel, set the **Anchor** setting to **Top Middle**.
   3. In the **Details** panel, set the **Position X** value to `420` and the **Position Y** value to `60`.
   4. In the **Details** panel, set the **Size X** value to `80` and the **Size Y** value to `80`.
   5. In the **Details** panel, set the left **Alignment X** value to `0`, and the right **Alignment Y** value to `0`.
   6. In the **Details** panel, navigate to the **Appearance** | **Brush** headers, click the **Image** drop-down, and use the search text field to locate and select the `BossPortrait.png` texture to set the UI `IMG_EnemyPortrait` image to that texture.
5. Now click the **Compile** button, and then the **Save** button to save the UI and complete this step. The UI hierarchy and **Canvas** should look similar to that shown in *Figure 7.33*:

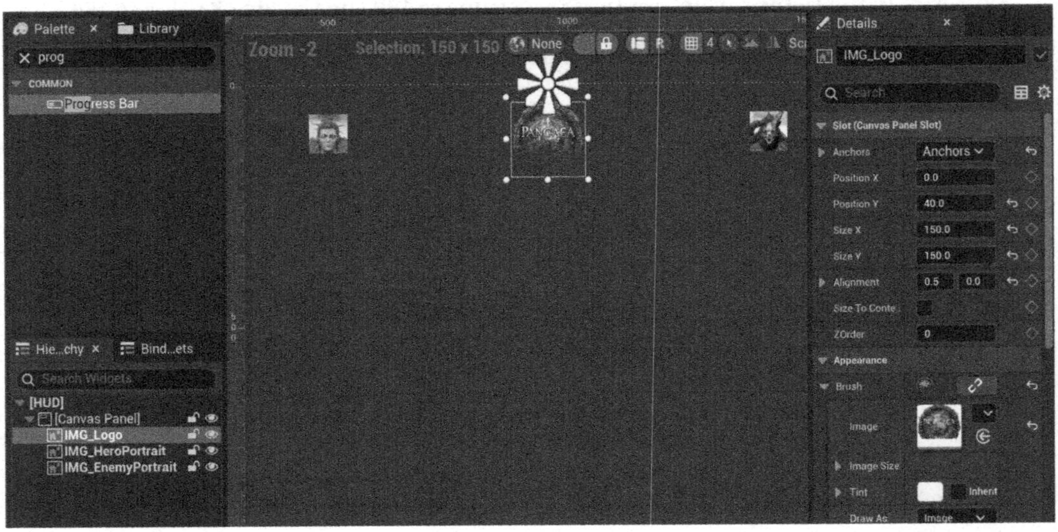

Figure 7.33 - HUD UI with Hero, Enemy, and Pangaea Logo

Having added the character portraits and the logo into the *Pangaea* game's HUD, the next step is to add the Hero and Enemy Health Bars into the HUD UI.

Adding the health bars

The following steps will guide you through adding the Health Bars, which appear at the top of the HUD, on either side of the character portraits:

1. Drag two **Progress Bar** components from the **Palette** panel into the **Hierarchy** panel, placing them underneath the **Canvas Panel**.
2. For the first **Progress Bar** in the hierarchy, follow these steps:
    1. Rename the **Progress Bar** component to `PB_HeroHealth` (see *Figure 7.34*).
    2. In the **Details** panel, set the **Anchor** setting to **Top Middle**.
    3. In the **Details** panel, set the **Position X** value to `-100` and the **Position Y** value to `80`.
    4. In the **Details** panel, set the **Size X** value to `300` and the **Size Y** value to `40`.
    5. In the **Details** panel, set the left **Alignment X** value to `1.0`, and the right **Alignment Y** value to `0`.
    6. In the **Details** panel, navigate to the **Progress** header, click the **Bar Fill Type** dropdown, and set its value to **Left to Right**.

3. For the bottommost progress bar in the hierarchy:
    1. Rename the **Progress Bar** component to `PB_EnemyHealth`.
    2. In the Details panel, set the **Anchor** setting to **Top Middle**.
    3. In the **Details** panel, set the **Position X** value to `100` and the **Position Y** value to `80`.
    4. In the **Details** panel, set the **Size X** value to `300` and the **Size Y** value to `40`.
    5. In the **Details** panel, set the left **Alignment X** value to `0`, and the right **Alignment Y** value to `0`.
    6. In the **Details** panel, navigate to the **Progress** header, click the **Bar Fill Type** dropdown, and set its value to **Right to Left**.
4. Now click the **Compile** button, and then the **Save** button to save the UI and complete this step. The UI hierarchy and canvas should look similar to that shown in *Figure 7.34*.

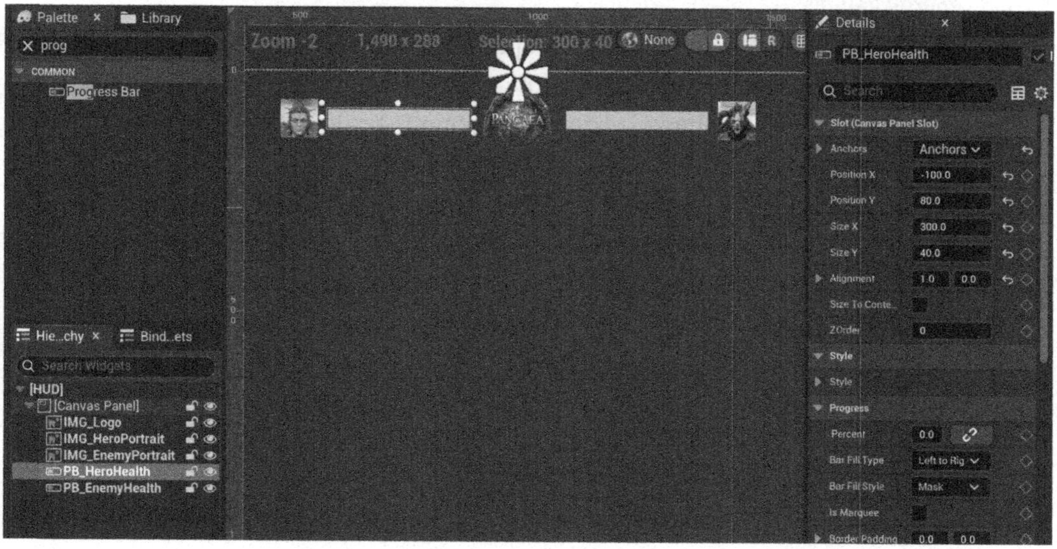

Figure 7.34 - HUD UI with the Hero and Enemy health bars added

Understanding the Progress Bar

The **Progress Bar** is a vital visual feedback component in UMG used to represent numerical values, such as health, stamina, or loading progress, as a percentage of a total. By translating raw data into a visual "fill," you provide players with an intuitive way to process information much faster than reading static numbers alone.

When setting up a Progress Bar, you will primarily interact with these key settings in the Details panel:

- The **Progress | Percent** setting is the core property that determines how much of the bar is filled. It operates on a **float scale** from **0.0** (completely empty) to **1.0** (completely full). If your character has a **CurrentHealth** variable of `50` and a **MaxHealth** of `100`, you would divide the **CurrentHealth** by the **MaxHealth** to get the `0.5` decimal required to fill the bar halfway.
- The **Appearance | Fill Color and Opacity** setting defines the specific color of the bar as it fills. You can use this to visually distinguish different resources, such as using vibrant *red* for health or *yellow* for stamina.
- The dropdown menu **Progress | Bar Fill Type** controls the direction of the filling animation. While **Left to Right** is the standard for most health bars, you can also select **Right to Left**, **Top to Bottom**, or even fill from the **Center** for more stylized meters or energy gauges.
- The **Style | Background/Fill Image** properties enable you to assign custom textures or materials to the **Background Image** (the empty part of the bar) and the **Fill Image** (the active part). This allows you to create a unique aesthetic that matches the specific art style of your game.
- The **Is Variable** check box at the top of the **Details** panel is mandatory if you intend to update the bar's progress dynamically via the **Graph** tab. Enabling this allows your character's logic to "talk" to the UI whenever they take damage or gain experience.
- The **Bind** button found next to the **Progress | Percent** bar in the **Details** panel allows you to create and bind a small piece of logic that performs a simple mathematical calculation to determine the fill amount of the data displayed by the Progress Bar. This ensures that the bar updates its fill level automatically whenever the underlying game data changes.

With the progress bars created to visualize the Hero and Enemy health in the game UI, the next step is to add the Game Over display functionality to the *Pangaea* game's UI.

Adding game over display

The following steps will guide you through adding the **Game Over** display to the HUD, which appears directly in the center of the HUD:

1. Drag a **Text** component from the **Palette** panel into the **Hierarchy** panel, placing it underneath the **Canvas Panel**. Then make the following adjustments:
    1. Rename the **Text** component to `TXT_GameOverDisplay`.
    2. In the **Details** panel, set the **Anchor** setting to **Center Middle.**
    3. In the **Details** panel, set the **Position X** value to `0` and the **Position Y** value to `0`.
    4. In the **Details** panel, set the **Size X** value to `500` and the **Size Y** value to `100`.
    5. In the **Details** panel, set the left **Alignment X** value to `0.5`, and the right **Alignment Y** value to `0.5`.
    6. In the **Details** panel, under the **Content** header, set the **Text** property value to **Game Over!**.
    7. In the **Details** panel, under the **Font** header, set the **Size** property value to `54.0`.
    8. In the **Details** panel, under the **Appearance** header, set the **Justification** property value to **Align Text Center** by pressing that property's middle button.
2. Now click the **Compile** button, and then the **Save** button to save the UI and complete this step.

Figure 7.35 - Completed HUD Widget Blueprint Design Layout

With the Game Over display added, the design part of the HUD Widget Blueprint is complete. The next step is to bind the Health Bars to the variables that store the Hero's and Enemy's health values in the *Pangaea* game.

Creating the Widget Blueprint UI variables

Creating and exposing widget variables makes them accessible to the **Graph** tab and external Blueprints and allows your game logic to dynamically pass real-time data, such as updated health values or player names, directly into the UI components for display.

The steps in this section will guide you through creating and adding three variables to the **Graph** tab of the HUD Widget Blueprint:

- One that will store the hero's health.
- Another that will store the enemy's health.
- Yet another that will store the text that is displayed at the end of the game.

Now, for the steps:

1. In the HUD Widget Blueprint, click the **Graph** tab button (highlighted in *Figure 7.36*) to switch over to the **Graph** tab in the **UMG Editor**.

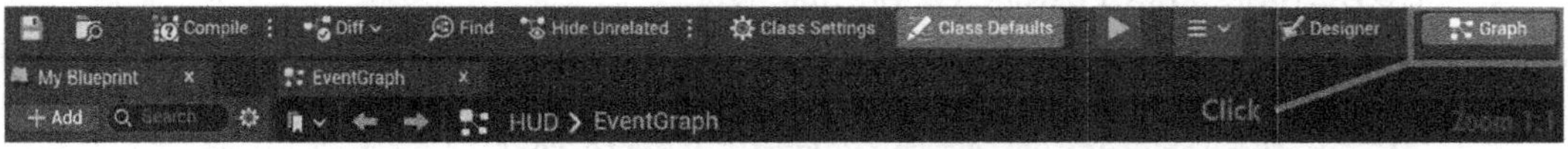

Figure 7.36 - The Graph tab button in the HUD widget Blueprint Design Layout

2. In the **Graph** tab, under the **VARIABLES** header (**1** in *Figure 7.37*), click on the **+** button (**2** in *Figure 7.37*) three times to create three new variables.

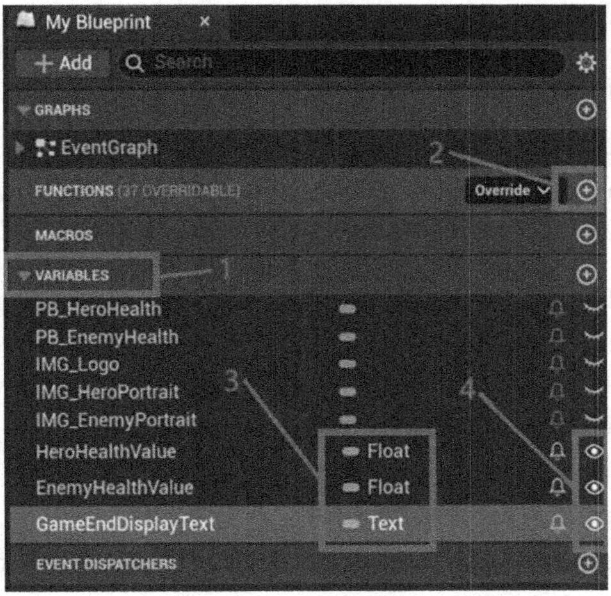

Figure 7.37 - Variable settings in the HUD widget Blueprint Graph Layout

3. For the topmost variable in the hierarchy:
    1. Rename the variable to `HeroHealthValue`.
    2. In the **Variables** list, set the **Variable Type** (**3** in *Figure 7.37*) to **Float**.
    3. In the **Variables** list, set the variable to be a *Public* variable (to make it accessible outside of the Blueprint) by clicking on the **Eye** icon and setting it to **Open** (**4** in *Figure 7.37*).
4. For the middle variable in the hierarchy:
    1. Rename the variable to `EnemyHealthValue`.
    2. In the **Variables** list, set the **Variable Type** to **Float**.
    3. In the **Variables** list, set the variable to be a *Public* variable by clicking on the **Eye** icon and setting it to **Open**.

5. For the bottommost variable in the hierarchy:
    1. Rename the variable to `GameEndDisplayText`.
    2. In the **Variables** list, set the **Variable Type** to **Text**.
    3. In the **Variables** list, set the variable to be a *Public* variable by clicking on the **Eye** icon and setting it to **Open**.
6. Now, click the **Compile** button, and then the **Save** button to save the UI and complete this step.

With the three Widget Blueprint UI Variables created, the next step is to bind these variables for display in the HUD of the *Pangaea* game.

Using Bindings and updating the display

In UMG, **Property Binding** is a mechanism that establishes a direct, live link between a visual widget property (such as a progress bar's fill percentage or a text block's content) and a specific data variable. Instead of forcing you to write complex code that constantly pushes updates to the screen, binding instructs the UI component to actively *watch* the assigned variable and automatically update its visual display the exact moment the underlying game data changes.

The following steps will guide you through the process of hooking the Widget Blueprint UI variables to their respective components in the HUD UI hierarchy.

1. In the HUD Widget Blueprint, click the **Designer** tab button to switch over to the **Designer** tab in the **UMG Editor**.
2. In the **Hierarchy** panel, select the `PB_HeroHealth` **Progress Bar**.
3. In the **Details** panel, navigate to the **Progress** | **Percent** property and click the **Binding** button to the right of the text box (**1** in *Figure 7.38*).
4. In the pop-up window that appears, select the `HeroHealthValue` variable (a normalized value that ranges from 0 to 1) from the list displayed at the bottom of the window (**2** in *Figure 7.38*).

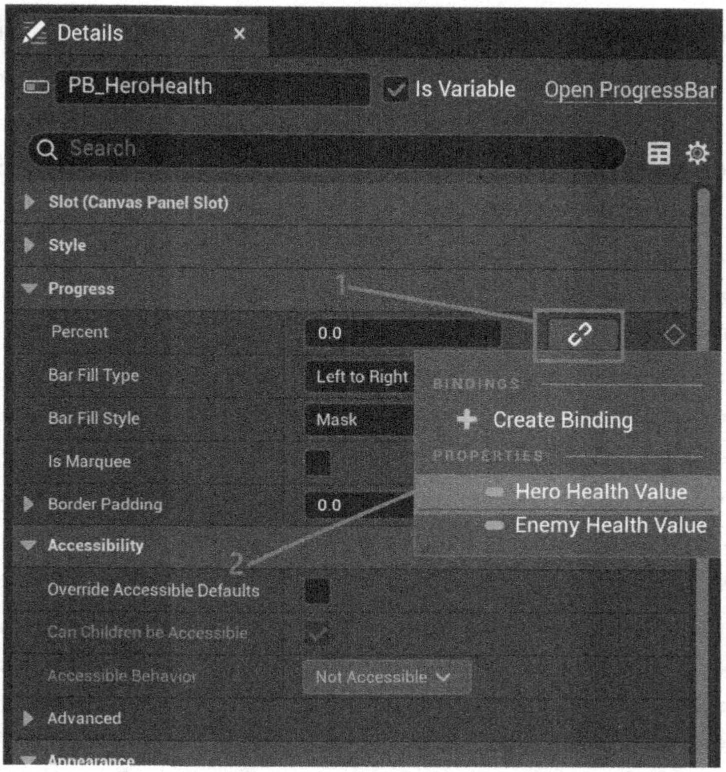

Figure 7.38 - Binding the PB_HeroHealth progress bar to the HeroHealthValue variable in the HUD

5. Repeat *steps 2* to *4* for the `PB_EnemyHealth` **Progress Bar**, but this time set the **Binding** for the **Progress** | **Percent** property to the **Enemy Health Value** variable that appears in the popup window. Additionally, set the **Bar Fill Type** to `Right to Left`.
6. Repeat *step 2* to *4* for the `TXT_GameOverDisplay` **Text** component, and this time set the **Binding** for the **Content** | **Text** property to the `GameEndDisplayText` variable that appears in the popup window.
7. Now click the **Compile** button, and then the **Save** button to save the UI and complete this step.

With the HUD Progress Bars and Game Over Text components now configured with their functionality, the next step is to link the HUD Widget Blueprint to the **ThirdPerson Level** so that the HUD UI can be used in the *Pangaea* game.

Connecting the Third Person Level to the HUD Blueprint

The following steps will create a **Level Blueprint** that will hook up the **HUD Widget Blueprint** to work in the **Third Person Level**:

1. In the **Content Browser**, navigate to the **All | Content| ThirdPerson** folder and open the **Lvl_ThirdPerson** level.
2. Click the **List of World Blueprints...** button, and in the pop-up that appears, click on **Open Level Blueprint** to open the Level Blueprint that is associated with the Third Person Level.
3. In the opened Level Blueprint, drag the white node pin from the **Event BeginPlay** node and drop it in the graph window, then search for the `Create Widget` node and hit *Enter* to select it.
4. In the newly created node, populate its **Class** property with the value `HUD`. This will configure the creation of an instance of the `HUD` Blueprint within the **Third Person** Level.
5. In the Level Blueprint, drag the blue **Return Value** node pin from the newly created **Create HUD Widget** node and drop it in the graph window, then search for the **Add to Viewport** node and hit *Enter* to select it. Then, connect the execution output pin of the **Create HUD Widget** node to the execution input pin of the **Add to Viewport** node. This adds the `HUD` Blueprint to the Viewport of the Third Person level, allowing it to be used as the UI for that level.
6. Now click the **Compile** button, and then the **Save** button to save the Level Blueprint. *Figure 7.39* shows the completed and configured Level Blueprint for the Third Person Level.

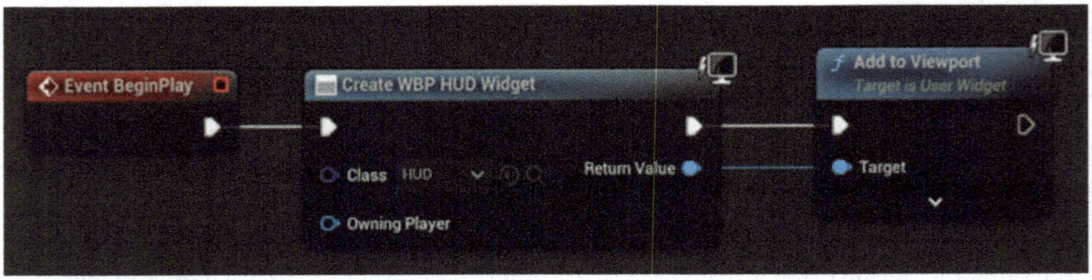

Figure 7.39 - Third Person Level Blueprint with the Create HUD Widget node added, with the Return Value connected to the Add to Viewport node

The HUD is now complete and hooked up to the Third Person Level, and you can verify that the HUD is being displayed by pressing the **Play** button with the Third Person Level open (see *Figure 7.32*).

This chapter provided you with an understanding of creating user interfaces through the **UMG Editor** in Unreal and gave you the opportunity to use this tool to create a Main Menu system and a HUD for the *Pangaea* game. With this knowledge, you will now be capable of creating your own custom User Interfaces and combined logic for your use in your own games.

Summary

In this chapter, you built a solid foundation for designing and implementing interactive user interfaces using **Unreal Motion Graphics (UMG)**. You explored the specialized **UMG Editor**, gaining familiarity with its common panels such as the **Designer** Viewport, **Palette**, **Hierarchy**, and the **Details** panel. Building on this, you learned how Widget Blueprints operate by balancing visual layout in the Designer tab with logic-driven scripting in the **Graph** tab. You examined core UI components, including **Canvas Panels**, **Vertical Boxes**, **Buttons**, and **Progress Bars**, and learned how to utilize **Anchors** and **DPI scaling** to ensure your interface remains responsive across various screen resolutions.

Through step-by-step hands-on examples, you walked through the creation of a Main Menu system and a dynamic Heads-Up Display (HUD) for the Pangaea project. You implemented level-loading and game exit functionality and gained experience in the process of data binding. By following guided exercises, you built functional health bars and character portraits that provide real-time feedback during gameplay.

With these skills, you now understand how to construct both the visual appearance and the underlying logic of a game's interface and are well-prepared to build your own custom UI systems through Unreal Engine's **UMG Editor**.

In the next chapter, we explore implementing gameplay, expanding on the Castle prototype, creating spawners, and building out a mission and objectives.

Part 3

Finishing Touches and Completing the Game

This part brings everything you have learned together to turn the project into a complete playable game. You will design the `Desert Castle` level and implement its gameplay flow, including objectives, enemy encounters, damage, progression, and win and lose conditions. You will then use **Sequencer** to create an introductory cut-scene with character animation and cinematic camera movement. Finally, you will polish the game by replacing prototype assets, refining gameplay, and adding audio and visual effects before configuring the project and packaging it as a standalone Windows game.

With this part, you will bring these systems together into a complete playable game that you can polish and package for others to play.

This part of the book includes the following chapters:

- *Chapter 8, Designing and Implementing Gameplay Mechanics*
- *Chapter 9, Creating Cinematics and Cut-Scenes*
- *Chapter 10, Polishing and Packaging Your Game*

8

Designing and Implementing Gameplay Mechanics

In this chapter, we move from learning individual tools to building a complete, playable game level. We will take the Desert Castle concept – a battle where the player fights through two guards (the `BP_Warrok` created in *Chapter 6*) and a Boss (another character, `BP_Boss`, created using the same workflow as `BP_Warrok` and provided in the project under the `Chapter08-Start` branch) to claim the castle – and turn it into a working gameplay experience that defines the gameplay goals, how the game responds to player actions, and what happens when the player wins or fails.

You will apply the knowledge gained from previous chapters, including Blueprint scripting, level editing, collision detection, and the characters, to create a structured mission with clear objectives. This establishes the essential building blocks of the game's gameplay: mechanics and progression systems. These define what players can do, why they do those things, and what they are working toward. These systems motivate players to overcome challenges, earn rewards, and stay engaged.

Understanding how to design and implement these systems is one of the most important skills a game developer can learn, and this chapter will give you hands-on experience building them.

This chapter covers the following topics:

- Designing the Desert Castle level
- Placing or spawning game Actors
- Using events to drive game progress
- Opening the gate

- Connecting the HUD to gameplay
- Applying and taking damage

By the end of this chapter, you will have a functional game level where players can fight enemies, track their progress, open gates, and win or lose based on their actions. This is the heart of game development: turning ideas into interactive systems that players can truly experience.

Technical requirements

The sample project for this chapter is available for download from the book's GitHub repository and branch:

- `Chapter08-Start` **branch**: This branch holds the game project with everything you need to start learning this chapter.
- `Chapter08` **branch**: This branch holds the completed game project for this chapter, including a mock-up prototype level for testing layout and mechanics, as well as a gameplay flow set up entirely in Blueprints that defines how missions and objectives function throughout the game.

You can download the example project and code files for this book by following the instructions in the *Download the example code/resource files* section in the *Preface* of this book.

This chapter's code/resource files are included in the downloadable code/resource bundle.

Designing the Desert Castle level

In previous chapters, we primarily worked within the `Lvl_ThirdPerson` level: a simple environment for creating and testing. While that level served its purpose for learning the basics, it isn't suitable for the *Pangaea* game you're building. Now it's time to shift focus from practice to production. In this chapter, you'll design a new game level called `Desert Castle`, which will serve as the main battlefield for *Pangaea*. This is where your gameplay systems will come to life, and where players will face their first real challenges.

A **game level** is more than just a space; it's the battlefield where players face challenges, test their skills, and experience the core of the game. The goal of level design is simple: make it fun. But achieving that goal requires thoughtful planning. In this section, we'll apply some important factors based on foundational level design theories to build the battle level for *Pangaea*. Complete game design theory is a deep and complex subject, and full exploration is beyond the scope of this book.

For the *Pangaea* game, we'll design a single battlefield level called `Desert Castle`. The concept is straightforward: the player fights through enemy guards, confronts the Boss, and ultimately claims victory by becoming the owner of the castle. While this premise is simple, the execution must be engaging.

We can reuse the existing assets, including the `Hero` and `Warrok` characters along with their Blueprint controllers, so that we can assemble the game level with minimum effort.

To make the game fun, we need to consider several key design factors, from how enemies are placed to how the player progresses through the space. Let's explore what makes a level a functional and enjoyable game.

Key design factors for the Desert Castle level

Before placing Actors in the editor, let's take a moment to think about what makes a game level work. A game level is basically built around a few fundamental design factors:

- Where the player begins
- How the game ends
- What the player is trying to achieve
- What obstacles stand in the way
- What happens upon success or failure

These factors form the backbone of the player's experience. In this section, we'll explore each factor in general terms, then apply it specifically to the `Desert Castle` level for *Pangaea*.

Game start

A gameplay scenario usually needs a defined starting point. The game start establishes where the player enters the level, what they first see, and how they are oriented to the challenges ahead. A well-designed **game start** does more than just place the player in the world; it sets expectations, hints at the goal, and provides immediate context for what the player is supposed to do.

Game end

A gameplay scenario must have a defined ending. The **game end** determines when the level is complete and what conditions trigger that completion. Typically, there are two possible outcomes: success and failure. Success occurs when the player achieves the primary goal, while failure occurs when the player's character is defeated before reaching that goal. Defining these conditions is essential to ensure the player has a clear sense of accomplishment or consequence.

Goal

A game level needs a clear goal. The **goal** is what the player is trying to accomplish – the reason they are playing the level in the first place. A well-defined goal provides direction, motivation, and a sense of purpose. At a high level, the goal is often expressed as a mission or story objective. Beneath that, specific, actionable objectives break the larger goal into manageable objectives that the player can track and complete one by one.

Challenges

Challenges are the obstacles that stand between the player and their goal. Challenges bring tension, risk, and satisfaction to the gameplay. Challenges are designed to test the player's skills, require strategy or quick reflexes, and make success feel earned. They also provide variety and pacing, breaking the gameplay into memorable encounters rather than a monotonous sequence of actions.

Outcomes

A gameplay scenario must end with a clear result. **Outcomes** provide closure, reinforce the stakes of the player's actions, and determine what happens next. Without a defined outcome, success and failure feel indistinguishable, and the player's efforts lack meaning. A proper outcome acknowledges what the player has accomplished, or where they fell short, and delivers a moment of emotional resolution, whether satisfaction or disappointment.

With the key design factors established, we need to translate them into a concrete playable space. In the next section, we'll create a rough map layout for `Desert Castle` that brings these factors to life.

Sketching the map for the Desert Castle level

With the key design factors defined, it's time to sketch the map of the level (see *Figure 8.1*). This sketch doesn't need to be a work of art. A simple diagram on paper or a mockup with simple shapes will do.

For the `Desert Castle` level, the layout is sketched using primitive shapes to match the final castle model that will replace it later. This approach demonstrates a common workflow: *designers can build and test gameplay using simple geometries, then let artists create high-quality assets based on the approved design.*

The purpose is to visualize how the player will move through the level space, where challenges are positioned, and how each objective connects to the next. By sketching first, we avoid the common mistake of building blindly and ending up with an unbalanced level. To keep the learning focused and reduce test time, we will place enemy characters in front of and behind the gate rather than distributing them throughout the entire level. This simplifies the setup while still allowing us to build and test the core gameplay mechanics effectively.

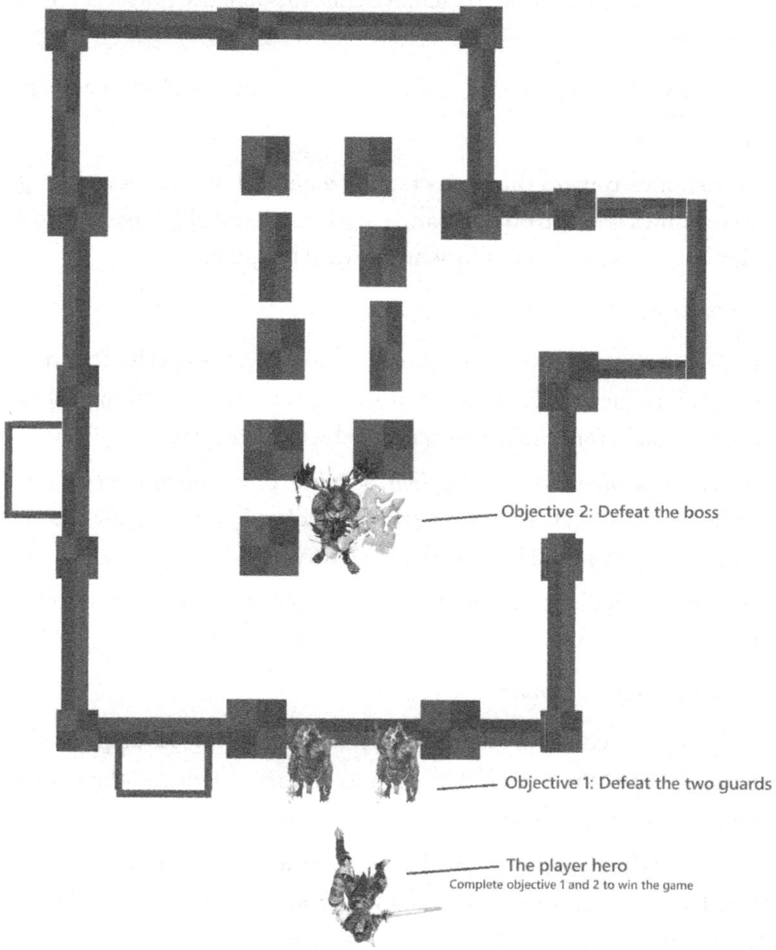

Figure 8.1 - Sketch the map for the Desert Castle level

The player's Hero character starts directly in front of the main entrance: the **Castle Gate**. This placement makes the objective instantly readable: the player must enter the castle. From this position, the player can see the gate ahead, establishing a clear direction to move. There is no confusion about where to go or what to do first. The game starts here, serving as a visual and spatial cue that guides the player naturally toward the first challenge.

The game's end is defined by two clear outcomes. The player succeeds by defeating the **Boss**. This marks the completion of the mission and triggers a victory state. The player fails if their own character is killed before defeating the Boss. In that case, the game ends in defeat, and the player must try again. These two outcomes bookend the experience, giving every encounter and every decision meaningful stakes.

The mission is to *occupy the castle*. To achieve this mission, the player must complete a series of objectives in order:

- Kill the two **Guards** (`Warrok 1` and `Warrok 2`) and reach the castle gate.
- Kill the **Boss**.

Each objective builds toward the next, creating a natural progression through the level. The player always knows what to do next, and each completed objective provides a small sense of accomplishment that drives them forward toward the goal.

The challenges come in two distinct forms:

- The *first challenge* is the *enemy guards*: smaller, less powerful foes positioned at the approach to the castle. These guards introduce the combat mechanics and build anticipation before the player reaches the main fortress.
- The *second challenge* is the *Boss fight*: a single, powerful enemy that waits inside the castle. The Boss tests everything the player has learned, demands careful execution, and serves as the final hurdle before victory.

Together, these two challenge types create a rising curve of difficulty that keeps the player engaged from start to finish.

There are two possible outcomes:

- If the player successfully defeats the Boss and completes all prior objectives, the game displays a **You Win** screen. This signals victory, celebrates the player's achievement, and provides a satisfying conclusion to the level.
- If the player's character is killed before defeating the Boss, the game displays a **You Failed** screen. This outcome is unambiguous, letting the player know they need to try again without hiding behind vague messaging.

These two simple, direct outcomes respect the player's time and make every encounter feel meaningful.

With your map sketch complete, it's time to bring that layout into Unreal Engine by building a prototype level using simple shapes.

Prototyping the level with Modeling Mode shapes

Now is the time to apply the level editing knowledge you learned in *Chapter 2*. We'll use those skills to create a prototype of the `Desert Castle` level in this section.

A **prototype level** serves three important purposes:

- First, it allows you to continue developing gameplay without being blocked. You can build and test missions, objectives, and enemy behavior using simple shapes before any final art is created.
- Second, it provides a testing platform to verify whether the gameplay is fun. If the prototype feels boring or frustrating, it's much easier to change simple shapes than to redo finished art.
- Third, the prototype acts as a reference for artists. They can see the exact size, scale, and layout of the level, then create final assets that fit perfectly into the space you've designed.

Before building the prototype level:

1. Navigate into the `Pangaea/Levels` folder structure in the **Content Browser**.
2. Right-click and choose Level to create a new game level, then rename the new level as `Desert_Castle.umap`.
3. Open the new level, create a folder named `Lighting`, and then add the lighting objects (see *Figure 8.2*) under the `Lighting` folder.

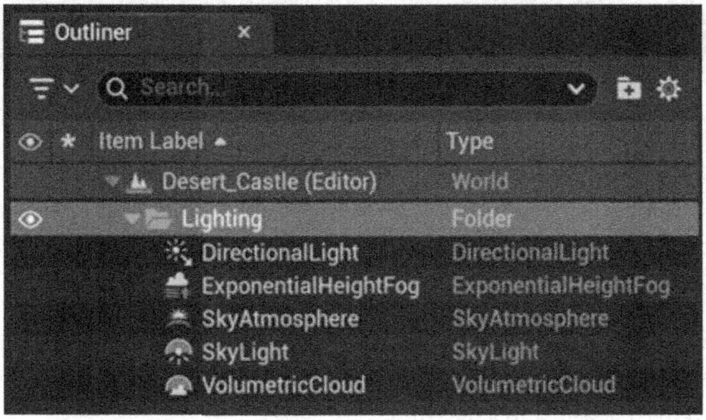

Figure 8.2 - Adding lighting objects to the Desert_Castle level

Now you are ready to build the prototype. Using the **Modeling Mode** tools introduced in the *Level prototyping and design* section in *Chapter 2*, create the basic shape of the castle with a simple plane and boxes, as shown in *Figure 8.3*. The goal is to capture the overall size, layout, and structure of the level so you can begin testing gameplay immediately.

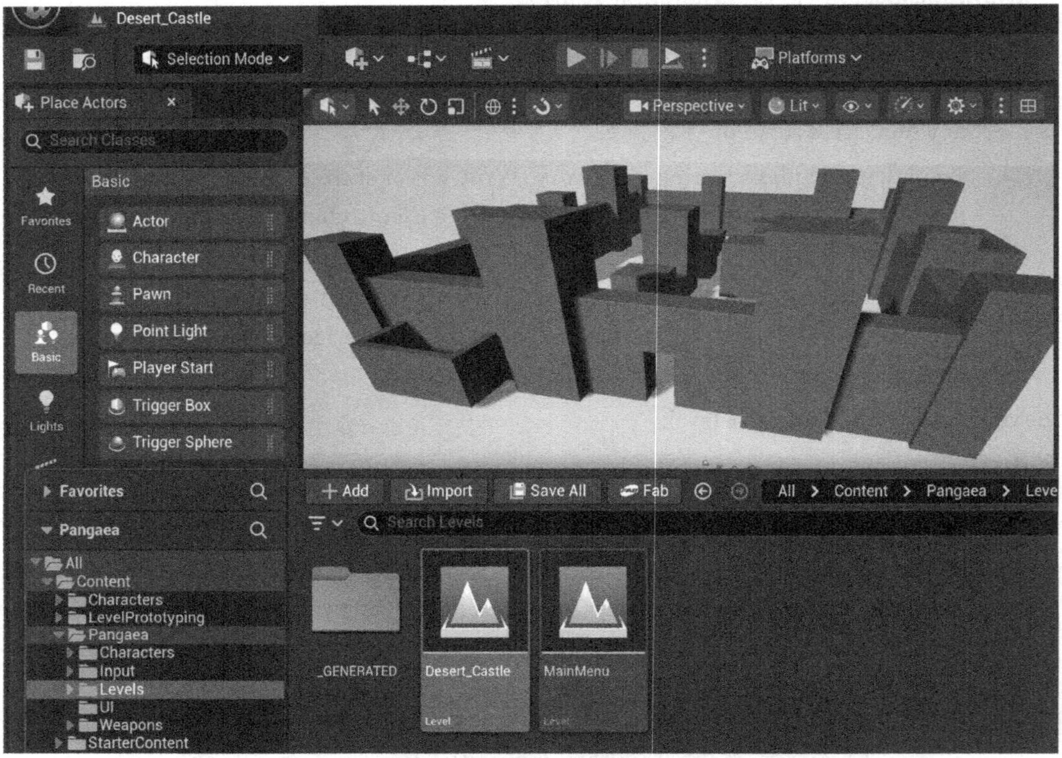

Figure 8.3 - Building the prototype of the Desert Castle level

With the layout sketched and the workflow in mind, it is time to build the prototype level using primitive shapes. Using the **Modeling Mode** tools, create a series of shapes (for example, boxes) to form the basic structure of the castle: ground platform, the towers, the walls, and so on.

If you sync the `Chapter08-Start` branch (see *Technical requirements* section; to access the GitHub repository, see the *Preface* for instructions), the castle primitives are already built for you, so you can skip that step and save time.

If you want to practice creating the castle prototype yourself, you can refer to *Tables 8.1*, *8.2*, and *8.3*, which provide the **Name**, **Scale**, and **Location** values needed to position each piece correctly. Name each box according to its entry on the table, then set its **Scale** and **Location** values exactly as listed.

Table 8.1 provides the scale and location values for the ground (a simple plane); the size (width, depth, height) values for the buildings; and the location values for both the ground and all buildings located inside the castle:

Group	Name	Shape	Scale (w,d,h)	Location
Ground	**Ground**	**Plane**	**1000,1000,1**	**0,0,0**
Group	**Name**	**Shape**	**Size (w,d,h)**	**Location**
Buildings	Building1	Box	800,800,1300	30,-8000,650
	Building2	Box	800,800,640	1320,-7950,320
	Building3	Box	820,640,680	-1320,100,340
	Building4	Box	440,1200,400	-2550,-8020,200
	Building5	Box	800,640,400	-3770,-7880,200
	Building6	Box	800,640,680	-3770,-9260, 340
	Building7	Box	800,640,680	-2570,-9460,340
	Building8	Box	440,1200,400	-1370,-9510,200
	Building9	Box	800,800,1000	10,-9480,500

Table 8.1 - Creating the ground and the buildings for the castle

Table 8.2 provides the size (width, depth, height) and location values for all wall towers surrounding the castle:

Group	Name	Shape	Size (w,d,h)	Location
Towers	Tower1	Box	560,560,1440	3810,-5380,640
	Tower2	Box	560,560,1440	1490,-5370,640
	Tower3	Box	560,560,1440	-810,-5370,640
	Tower4	Box	560,560,1440	-5560,-5200,640
	Tower5	Box	560,560,1440	-5590,-7500,640
	Tower6	Box	560,560,1440	-5640,-10760,640
	Tower7	Box	560,560,1440	-3220,-12030,640

Group	Name	Shape	Size (w,d,h)	Location
	Tower8	Box	560,560,1440	1480,-11880,640
	Tower9	Box	560,560,1440	3790,-11880,640
	Tower10	Box	800,800,1800	3770,-7790,760
	Tower11	Box	800,800,1800	3770,-10390,760
	Tower12	Box	800,800,1800	-910,-11960,760
	Tower13	Box	800,800,1800	-3200,-10640,760
	Tower14	Box	800,800,1800	-3210,-5360,760

Table 8.2 - Creating the towers for the castle

Table 8.3 includes the size (width, depth, height) and location values for the castle walls and the gate cutter. The **GateCutter** is a subtractive shape used to carve a hole in the castle wall where the gate will be placed. To create it, follow these steps:

1. Add a new **Box** shape in **Modeling Mode** and rename it to `GateCutter` in the **Details** panel.
2. Set its **Scale** and **Location** so that the cutter fully overlaps and penetrates through `WallEast1`.
3. Then, select the wall mesh first, hold *Ctrl* and select the **GateCutter**, open the **Boolean** tool, choose **Difference (A-B)**, and click **Accept**.

The cutter will be subtracted from the wall, leaving a clean gate-shaped opening. After the operation, the GateCutter is no longer needed and can be deleted or hidden from the level.

Group	Name	Shape	Size (w,d,h)	Location
Walls	WallEast1	Box	6400,360,1000	3810,-8640,520
	WallEast2	Box	1280,100,520	4640,-6550,320
	WallEast3	Box	100,600,520	4290,-5940,320
	WallEast4	Box	100,600,520	4290,-7150,320
	WallNorth1	Box	360,4800,1000	1270,-11880,520

Group	Name	Shape	Size (w,d,h)	Location
	WallNorth2	Box	360,2400,1000	-4530,-10770,520
	WallSouth1	Box	360,7200,1000	340,-5350,520
	WallSouth2	Box	360,2000,1000	-4450,-5200,520
	WallSouth3	Box	100,1300,520	320,-4450,320
	WallSouth4	Box	660,100,520	920,-4830,320
	WallSouth5	Box	660,100,520	-290,-4830,320
	WallWest1	Box	5200,360,1000	-5640,-8040,520
	WallWest2	Box	1200,360,1000	-3270,-11310,520
	WallWest3	Box	1200,260,760	-3240,-12930,370
	WallWest4	Box	1200,260,760	-1090,-12930,370
	WallWest5	Box	260,2400,760	-2160,-13670,370
	GateCutter Boolean (A-B)	Box	320,800,560	3789,-9080,300

Table 8.3 - Creating the walls for the castle

By following the values in the tables above, you should have a castle prototype that looks like the one shown in *Figure 8.3*. Now that the prototype is complete, let's discuss *concept art*, an essential step in commercial game development, in the next section.

Creating concept art for the game level

Concept art refers to early artwork that shows what a game's characters and environments should look like before they are built in the game. It helps the whole team agree on the game's visual style before spending time creating final assets.

In commercial game development, having one or more artists create concept art is an important step toward achieving higher visual quality. Concept art defines the game's visual style, color palette, lighting, mood, and overall artistic direction.

For the *Pangaea* game, you do not need to worry about creating any concept art. Simply learn the concept and be aware that this step exists in real game production. *Figure 8.4* provides an example of what the concept art for the `Desert Castle` level might look like:

Figure 8.4 - Concept art for the Desert Castle level

Now that you have enough knowledge to design the `Desert Castle` level, and the prototype level is ready, it's time to add Actors and gameplay logic to make the game come alive.

Placing or spawning game Actors

Placing a character means positioning it in the level manually during design time, while **spawning** a character means creating it dynamically during gameplay through Blueprint logic. Accordingly, game levels usually contain **static** and **dynamic Actors**.

Static Actors can be placed in the level during design time. The castle wall and the ground floor, for example, don't change position, so they can be static Actors. Static Actors require less computational effort to process, so marking non-moving actors can improve the overall performance of the game.

Dynamic Actors are moving Actors. The player character and enemies, for example, are marked as dynamic Actors. As a result, they need more CPU, GPU, and memory resources to process lighting effects, shadows, etc.

Actors can either be placed in a level in advance during design time or spawned dynamically during runtime. For example, if you know there will be exactly two guards in front of the gate, you can simply *place* them there.

However, if the number or type of guards is uncertain at design time and must be determined during gameplay, based on the player's actions or choices before reaching the gate, then you will need to *spawn* those guards dynamically.

Let's begin by placing the player character – our `Hero` – at the game's starting point in the prototype level.

Placing the Hero character

Unreal Engine provides a specific tool for setting the player's spawn location: the **Player Start** Actor. You can find it in the **Place Actors** panel under the **Basic** group. When the game begins, the designated player character will spawn at this exact location.

By default, the player character (in our case, `BP_Hero`) is defined in the **Project Settings** under the **Selected GameMode** settings. However, each game level can have its own settings that override the project's global settings. This is useful when different levels require different player characters.

For the `Desert Castle` level, we will practice overriding the global project settings by using the level's own **World Settings**.

Follow these steps to set up the level's overrides and place the player start location:

1. Open the `Desert_Castle` level and select the **World Settings** panel.

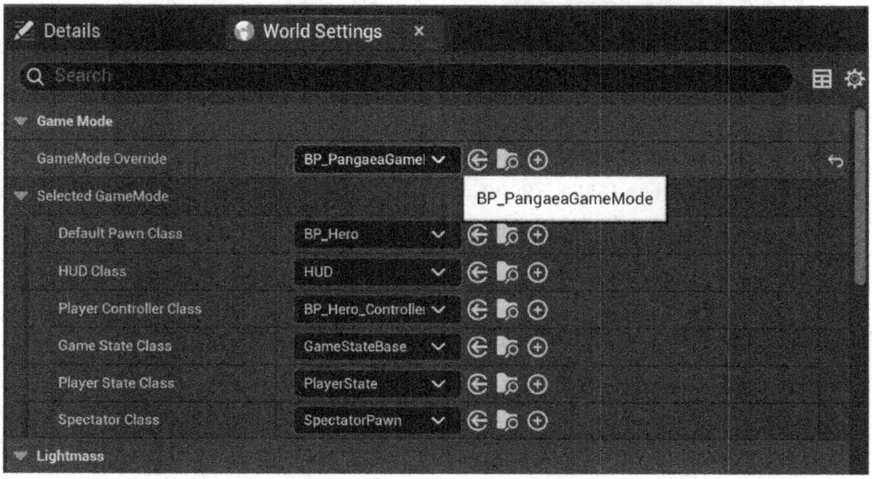

Figure 8.5 - Using World Settings to override the game's global project settings

2. Set **GameMode** Override to `BP_Pangaea_GameMode`.
3. Set the **Default Pawn Class** to `BP_Hero`. This tells the level which character the player will control.
4. Set **HUD Class** to `HUD`–the widget you created in *Chapter 7*. This ensures the correct interface displays during gameplay.
5. Open the **Place Actors** panel (via **Window** | **Place Actors** if it is not visible). Select the **Basic** group.
6. Drag and drop a **Player Start** Actor into the game level.

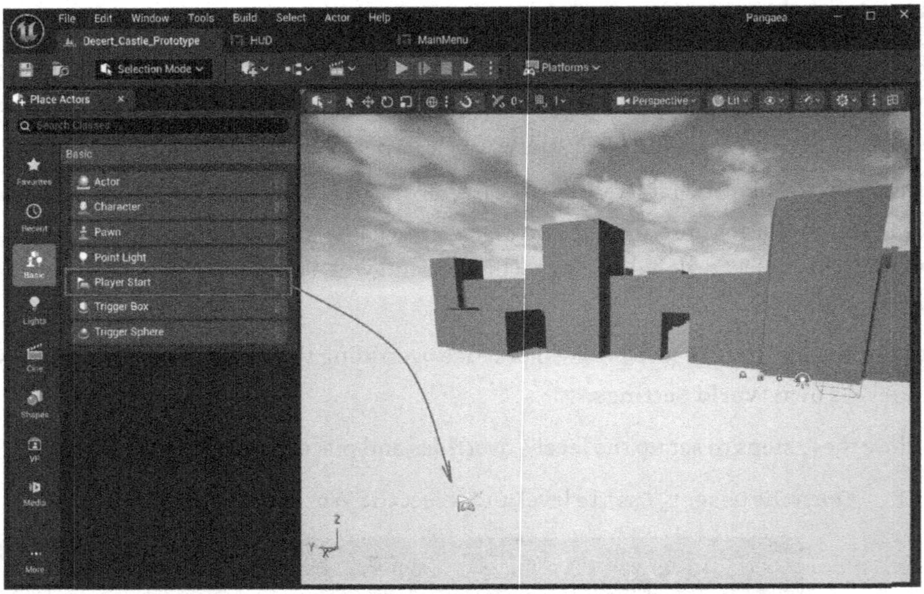

Figure 8.6 - Placing Player Start in the game level

7. Move the **Player Start** Actor to your preferred starting location. For example, you can set its **Location** to `(6851, -9000, 100)` and **Rotation** to `(0, 0, 180)` in the **Details** panel. This is where the player character will spawn when the game begins.

With the player set up, we now need to place two guards in front of the castle gate.

Placing the two guards in front of the gate

Follow these steps to place the two guards:

1. Open the **Content Drawer** and navigate to `Content/Pangaea/Characters/Warrok`.
2. Drag `BP_Warrok` from the **Content Drawer** and drop it into the game level.

3. Place the first `Warrok` character in front of the gate. In the **Details** panel, set its position to (4482, -8659, 92).
4. Repeat *steps 2* and *3* to add a second `Warrok` character and set its position to (4442, -9481, 92).

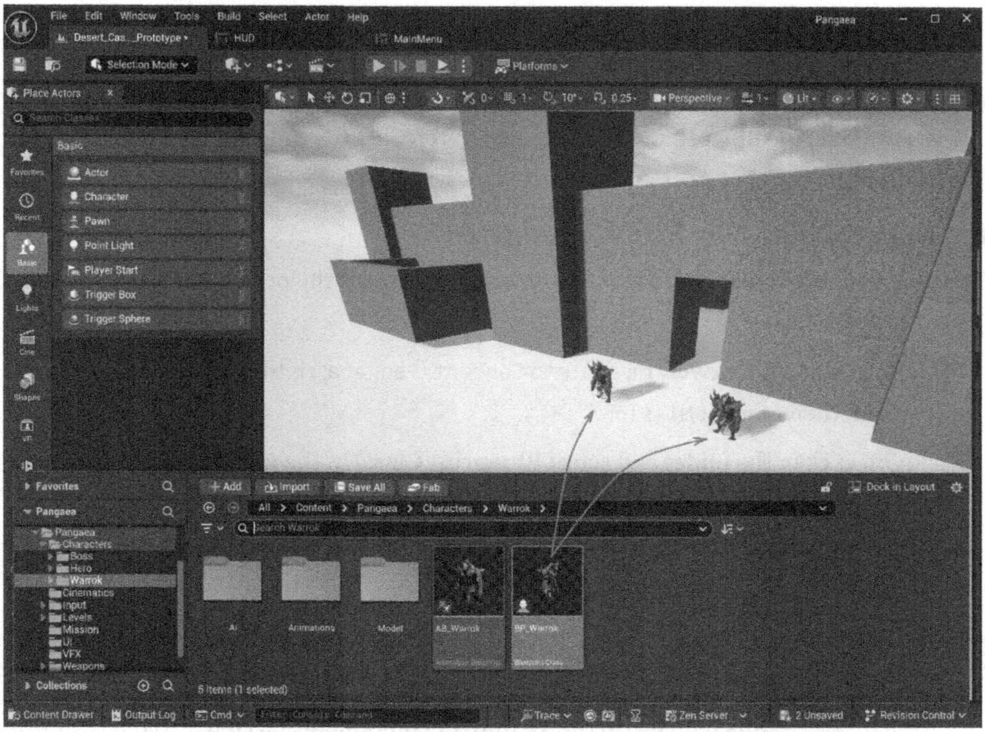

Figure 8.7 - Placing two guards in front of the gate

Both guards should now be positioned in front of the castle gate, ready to challenge the player. The two guards are placed manually at fixed positions. However, the Boss will behave differently; it will spawn inside the castle at a random position chosen from two possible locations.

Spawning the Boss at one of two random positions inside the castle

Before we make the Boss appear at a random location, we need to understand two important concepts: **Spawn Point** and **Spawner**.

Understanding Spawn Point and Spawner

Spawn Point is a simple marker placed in the level that defines a possible location where an Actor can appear. It does not create anything on its own but simply says *an Actor can spawn here*. In the *Pangaea* game, the Spawn Point is just a custom Blueprint that is named `BP_SpawnPoint`.

Spawner is a Blueprint responsible for creating (spawning) Actors at runtime. A spawner decides what, when, and where to spawn. It can choose from one or multiple spawn points. In the *Pangaea* game, the Blueprint `BP_BossSpawner` is created to randomly pick between two spawn points and spawn a Boss at the selected location.

Creating the Spawn Point Blueprint

Follow these steps to create `BP_SpawnPoint`, which will mark the possible locations where the Boss can appear:

1. In the **Content Drawer**, navigate to `Content/Pangaea`, right-click and select **New Folder**, then name it `Mission`.
2. Right-click in the folder and select **Blueprint Class**. In the **Pick Parent Class** window, search for and select `Actor`. Name the Blueprint `BP_SpawnPoint`.
3. Open `BP_SpawnPoint`. In the **Components** panel, click **Add** and select **Static Mesh**. Name this component `Visualizer`.
4. With the **Visualizer** component selected, go to the **Details** panel. Under **Static Mesh**, click the dropdown and search for `SM_Ball_01`. Select this mesh.
5. Still in the **Details** panel with the **Visualizer** component selected, expand the **Collision** section. Set **Collision Presets** to **NoCollision**.
6. Compile and save.

The `SM_Ball_01` mesh acts as a visual marker in the editor, helping you see where spawn points are placed. Since collision is disabled, it will not interfere with gameplay.

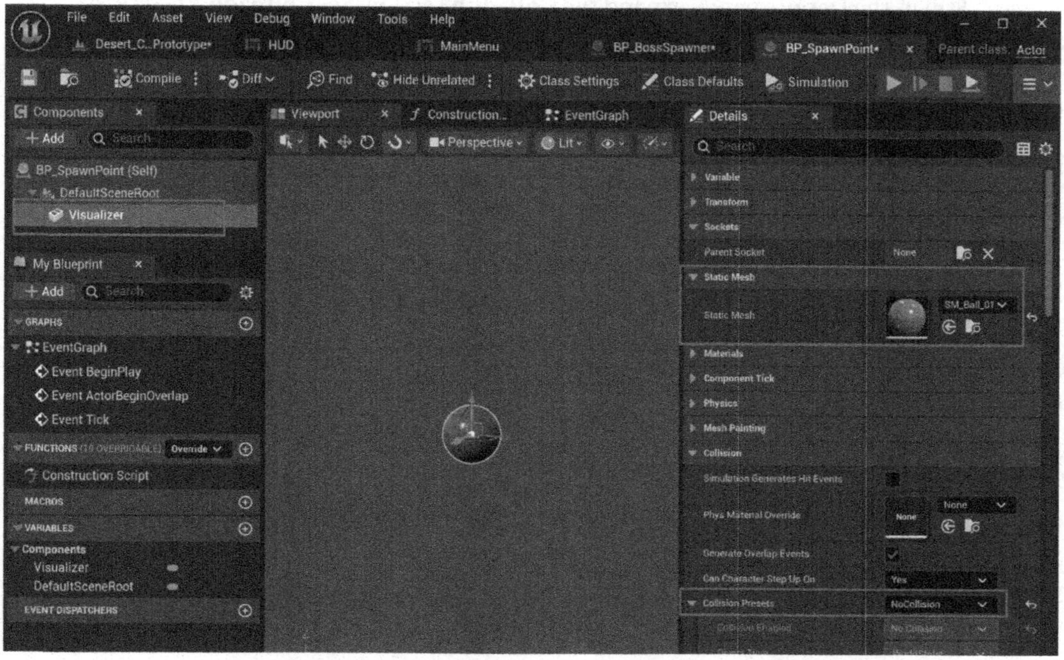

Figure 8.8 - Creating the BP_SpawnPoint Blueprint

With the spawn point Blueprint ready, we now need a spawner that will use those spawn points to create the Boss at a random location.

Creating the Boss Spawner Blueprint

Unlike the manually placed guards, the Boss will appear at runtime at one of two possible positions inside the castle, making each playthrough slightly different. This randomized spawning strategy adds variety to each playthrough, increases replayability, and keeps the experience unpredictable for the player.

Follow these steps to create the `BP_BossSpawner` Blueprint:

1. In the **Content Drawer**, navigate to `Content/Pangaea/Mission`. Right-click in the folder and select **Blueprint Class**. Select **Actor** as the parent class. Name the new Blueprint `BP_BossSpawner`.
2. Open `BP_BossSpawner`. In the **Components** panel, add a **Static Mesh** component and rename it `Visualizer`.
3. With the **Visualizer** component selected, go to the **Details** panel. Under **Static Mesh**, click the dropdown and search for `SM_Cylinder`. Select this mesh.

4. Still in the **Details** panel, expand the **Collision** section. Set **Collision Presets** to **NoCollision**.
5. Open the **Event Graph** of `BP_BossSpawner`. We will add logic to spawn the Boss. Add the following nodes:
    - **Get All Actors of Class**: Set the class to `BP_SpawnPoint`. This node finds every spawn point placed in the level.
    - **Random Integer**: Get a random integer value between 0 and the number of found spawn points minus 1 (the **ExclusiveMax** pin accepts the count of points and generates a random integer value between 0 and count - 1). Use this random index to pick one spawn point from the array.
    - **Get (or Array Get)**: Use the random index to retrieve the reference to a specific `BP_SpawnPoint` Actor from the array.
    - **SpawnActor**: Set **Class** to `BP_Boss` and set **Collision Handling Override** to `Always Spawn, Ignore Collisions`.

    Then, connect the execution flow, as shown in *Figure 8.9*. Trigger the spawning logic from **Event BeginPlay**. After retrieving the chosen spawn point, feed its transform (location and rotation) into the **SpawnActor** node.

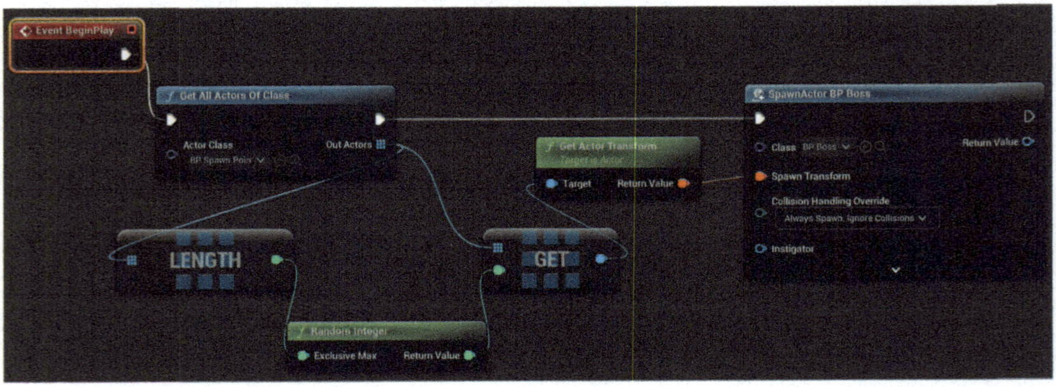

Figure 8.9 - Creating the BP_BossSpawner Blueprint

6. Compile and save.

With both Blueprints created, we now need to place them into the `Desert_Castle` level.

Placing two Spawn Points and the Boss Spawner

With the Desert_Castle level open, follow the steps below to place one Boss spawner and two spawn points in the game level:

1. In the **Content Drawer**, navigate to Content/Pangaea/Mission.
2. Drag BP_SpawnPoint and drop it into the level. Place it at the first desired Boss spawn location (for instance, (136, -6423, 100)) inside the castle.
3. Repeat the process to add a second BP_SpawnPoint at the second desired location (for example, (37, -10863, 100)).
4. Drag BP_BossSpawner from the **Content Drawer** and drop it into the level. The spawner can be placed anywhere. It does not need to be near the spawn points because it automatically finds them.

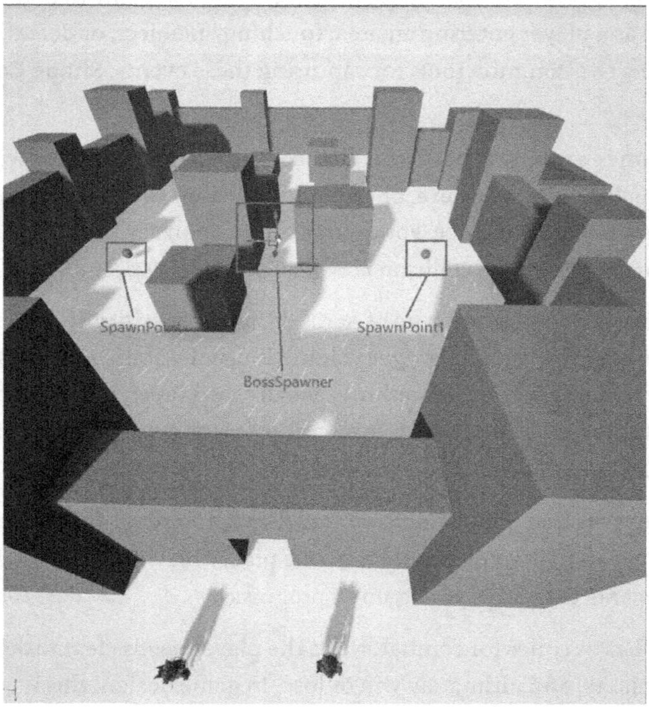

Figure 8.10 - Placing the two spawn points and the spawner in the game

When the game runs, the Boss spawner will locate both BP_SpawnPoint Actors, randomly select one, and spawn the Boss at that location.

With the spawn points and Boss spawner now placed in the level, the basic structure of `Desert Castle` is complete. However, a level with Actors placed and a Boss ready to spawn is still not a game. To make the game feel alive and responsive, we need *events*. In the next section, we will learn how to use events to drive game progress, from defeating the last guard to spawning the Boss and finally declaring victory.

Using events to drive game progress

Collisions and **triggers** are what make a game world feel responsive. They detect when the player enters an area, touches an object, or defeats an enemy, and fire events that drive game progress – such as opening a gate, spawning a Boss, or updating objectives. Without them, the game would have no way of knowing what the player is doing. **Events** are signals that tell the game when something has happened and what to do next.

To drive game progress with events, we need a way for the game to detect when something happens, such as a player entering an area, touching an object, or defeating an enemy. Unreal Engine provides two common tools for capturing these events: **Shape Collision** and **Trigger Volume**.

Shape Collision is a property built into almost every Actor. Any Actor with a collision component (such as a **Box**, **Sphere**, or **Capsule** collision) can detect when another Actor enters, overlaps, or exits its space. For example, a weapon can use shape collision to detect when it hits an enemy. Shape collision is typically tied to a specific Actor and moves with it.

Trigger Volume is a specialized type of Actor designed specifically for detecting overlap events. Unlike shape collision, a trigger volume is usually static and invisible during gameplay. It sits in the level and waits for something, usually the player, to walk into it. Trigger volumes are ideal for events like *"when the player reaches the castle gate, spawn the guards"* or *"when the player enters the throne room, start the Boss fight."*

The key difference is that Shape Collision travels with an Actor (like a weapon or moving character), while a Trigger Volume stays in one place and watches for Actors to enter its space. Both can fire events that drive your game's progress.

The level now has enemies for combat. Next, the player needs clear tasks: kill certain enemies, reach certain places, and ultimately win or lose. In game design, this is called a *mission* with its *objectives*. Let's define what that means for `Desert Castle`.

Mission and objectives

Now that we understand how to capture gameplay events using shape collision and trigger volumes, we can define what the player must do to succeed by creating the `BP_Mission` and `BP_Objective` Blueprints.

As explained earlier in the chapter, a **mission** represents the overall gameplay goal – what the player is trying to accomplish in the level. A mission contains **objectives**, which are the smaller sub-tasks that the player must complete to achieve the mission.

For the `Desert Castle` level, the mission is simple: **occupy the castle by defeating all enemies and confronting the Boss**.

To complete this mission and win the game, the player must fulfill specific objectives:

- Kill the two guards and move close to the gate to open it. The player cannot progress into the castle until both guards are defeated and the gate is triggered to open.
- Kill the Boss to win the game. Once inside the castle, the player must find and defeat the Boss. This is the final objective that leads to victory.

The player loses the game if the player's character is defeated at any point before completing all of the objectives; the game ends in failure.

With the mission and objectives defined, we can now create two Blueprints for them, respectively. We will use event tools to detect when the player reaches the gate and implement graph logic to detect when enemies are defeated and when the player wins the game.

Creating the BP_Objective Blueprint

Before we create the Blueprint, let's understand the variables that will be used.

- `Title`: A string that provides the title of the objective. This is a text description of the objective (for example, **"Kill the two guards and reach the gate"**) that can be displayed to the player as a task reminder.
- `IsActive`: A Boolean value that indicates whether this objective is active.
- `IsCompleted`: A Boolean value that indicates whether this objective has been finished. Once set to true, the objective will be inactive.
- `Actors`: A list of enemy Actors that must be destroyed (killed) before this objective can be completed. The objective will check each Actor in this array.

Now that we understand the variables, let's create the `BP_Objective` Blueprint by following these steps:

1. In the **Content Drawer**, navigate to `Content/Pangaea/Mission`. Right-click and select **Blueprint Class**. Choose **Actor** as the parent class. Name it `BP_Objective` (**1** in *Figure 8.11*).
2. Open `BP_Objective`. In the **Components** panel, click **+ Add** and select **Box Collision**. Name it `BoxTrigger` (**2** in *Figure 8.11*). This box will detect when the player enters the area.

3. In the **Variables** panel, click the + button to create four new variables (**3** in *Figure 8.11*). Make them all **public** by clicking on the **eye** icon so that they can be accessed by other Blueprints:
   - **Title**: Set its type to **String**
   - **IsActive**: Set its type to **Boolean**
   - **IsCompleted**: Set its type to **Boolean**
   - **Actors**: Set its type to an **Actor** Reference, and then change the **Variable Type** to `Array` on the **Details** panel (**4** in *Figure 8.11*).

> **Note**
>
> An **array** is a data structure that stores a collection of items of the same type, such as numbers, text, or Actor references, in a single variable. An array is used to group related items together and access them by their index position (starting from 0). For example, an *array of Actor references* in Unreal Engine can hold references to multiple Actor instances placed in the level – a list of enemy characters, for example.

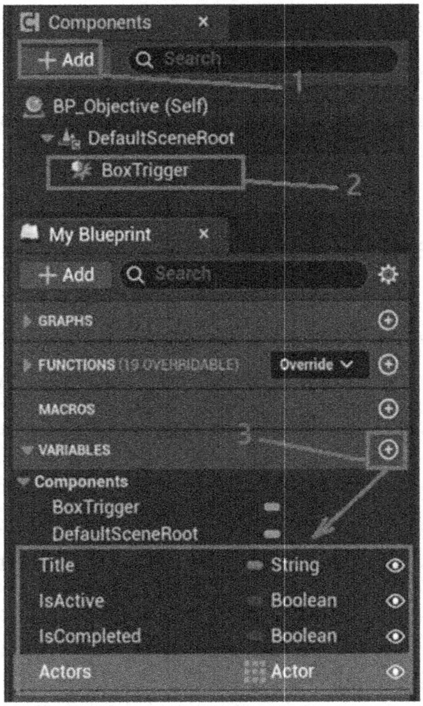

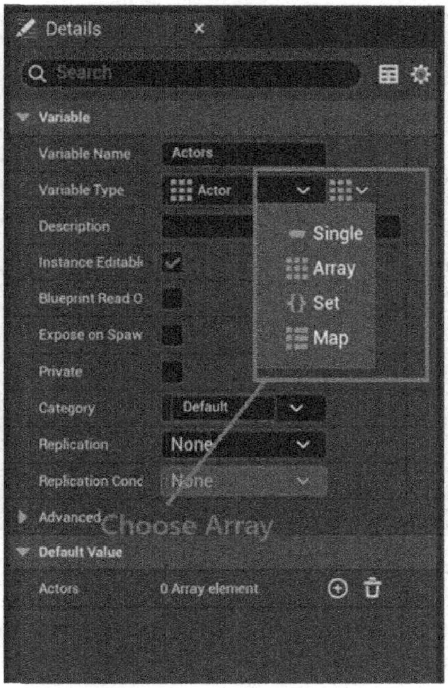

Figure 8.11 - Adding one Box Collision component and four variables to BP_Objective

4. Select `BoxTrigger` in the **Components** panel. In the **Details** panel, scroll to the **Events** section. Click the + button to add the **Event ActorBeginOverlap** (this node may already exist on the **Event Graph** and doesn't need you to add it manually).
5. In the **Event Graph**, locate **Event ActorBeginOverlap**. Add logic to check whether the overlapping Actor is the player (cast it to `BP_Hero`). If the cast succeeds, use a **Print String** node to display the objective's title on screen.

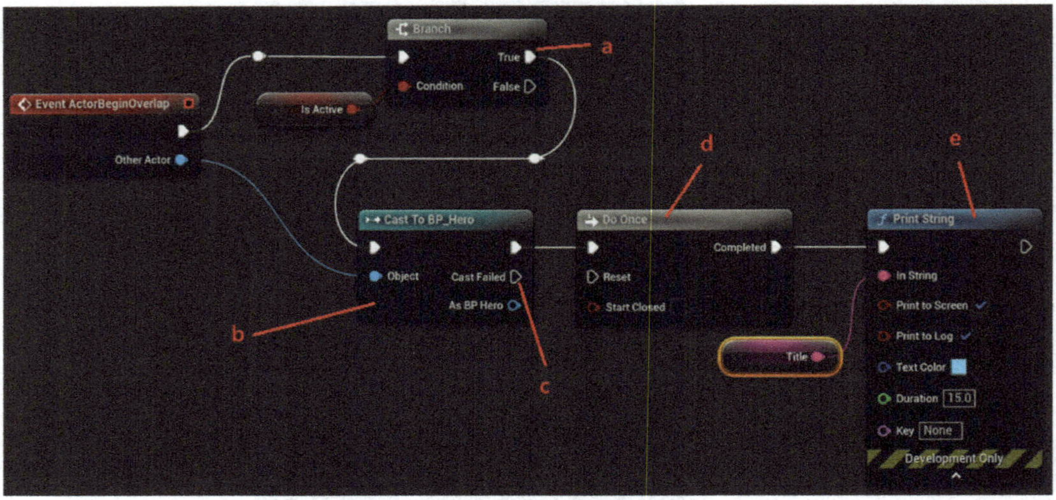

Figure 8.12 - Printing the objective title on screen when the player enters the BoxTrigger area

Figure 8.12 shows the Blueprint logic for the **Event ActorBeginOverlap** event. Here is how it works, step by step:

a. The first check is the **IsActive** flag. If **IsActive** is `False`, the execution stops. The objective only responds to overlaps when it is active.

b. If **IsActive** is `True`, the graph then attempts to cast the **Other Actor** (the Actor that entered the box) to `BP_Hero`. This determines whether the overlapping Actor is the player character.

c. If the cast fails (the overlapping Actor is not the player), the execution stops.

d. If the cast succeeds, the execution flows to a **Do Once** node. This node ensures that the objective's title is printed on screen only the first time the player enters the area.

e. Finally, a **Print String** node displays the objective's **Title** on the screen.

6. In the **Event Graph**, locate the **Event Tick** node and add logic to loop through the **Actors** array. For each Actor, check if it is still valid (not destroyed). If any Actor is still valid, the objective is not complete; otherwise, set **IsCompleted** to `True` and set **IsActive** to `False`.

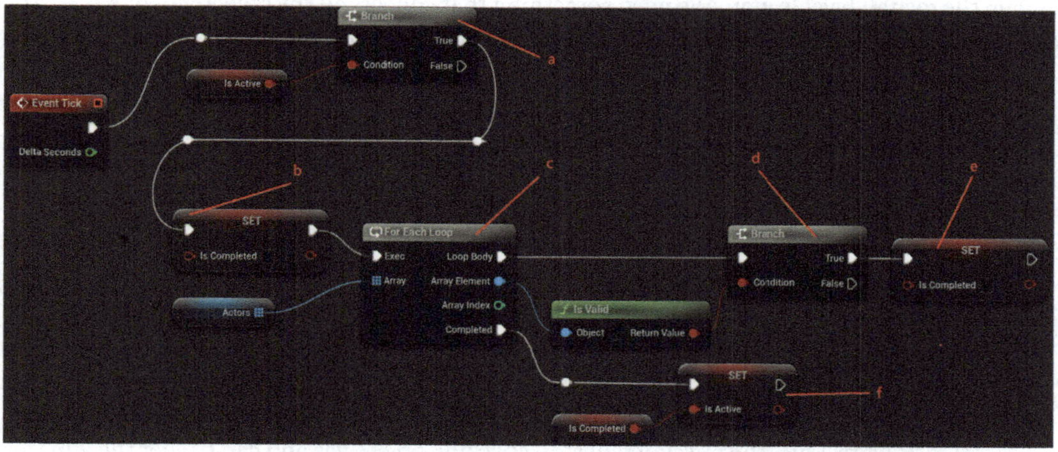

Figure 8.13 - Setting IsCompleted and IsActive flags by looping Actors

Figure 8.13 shows the Blueprint logic for checking whether an objective has been completed. The logic is designed to be clear and easy to follow, rather than optimized for performance, so that the underlying flow remains understandable. Here is how it works step by step:

a. The graph first checks the **IsActive** flag. If **IsActive** is `False`, the execution stops immediately.
b. If **IsActive** is `True`, the execution sets the **IsCompleted** flag to True. This operation assumes that this objective is completed before checking if all the actors have been destroyed.
c. The **For Each Loop** node iterates through the **Actors** array, checking if any Actor is valid or not.
d. Inside the loop body, an **Is Valid** node checks whether the current Actor is valid, which indicates whether the Actor is alive or not.
e. If the Actor is valid (still alive), the **IsCompleted** is set to `False`.
f. Once the loop completes, set the **IsActive** flag to the opposite of **IsCompleted** – meaning if **IsCompleted** is `True`, **IsActive** becomes `False`, which deactivates the objective.
g. Click **Compile**, then save.

With the `BP_Objective` Blueprint complete, we now have a way to track individual tasks, such as defeating the guards or entering the castle. However, an objective by itself does not know when the overall level is won. We need something that collects all the objectives and determines when every one of them is completed. This is where the mission comes in. Let's create `BP_Mission` to manage multiple objectives and trigger the game's win condition.

Creating the BP_Mission Blueprint

Before we create the Blueprint, let's understand the variables that will be used.

- `Goal`: This is a string value that describes the goal of this mission.
- `Objectives`: An array of `BP_Objective` references. This array holds all the objectives that belong to this mission. The mission will track each one to determine when the player has completed all the objectives.
- `IsCompleted`: A Boolean value that indicates whether the mission has been finished. Once set to True, the mission will stop checking objectives and can trigger the win condition.

Now that we understand the variables, let's follow these steps to create the `BP_Mission` Blueprint:

1. In the **Content Drawer**, navigate to `Content/Pangaea/Mission`. Right-click and select **Blueprint Class**. Choose **Actor** as the parent class. Name it `BP_Mission`.
2. Open `BP_Mission`. In the **Variables** panel, click the + button to create three *public* variables (with the open eyes).
   - **Goal**: Set its type to `String`
   - **IsCompleted**: Set its type to `Boolean`
   - **Objectives**: Set its type to **Array** of `BP_Objective` Reference

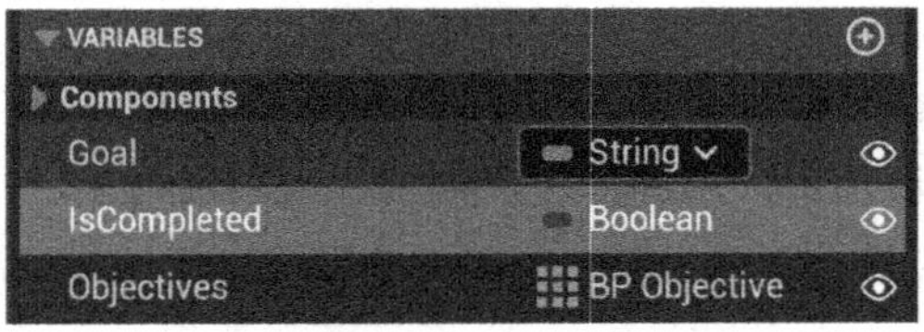

Figure 8.14 - Adding BP_Mission variables

3. In the **Event Graph**, locate the **Event BeginPlay** node. Add a **Print String** node to display the mission's goal on screen. The **Print String** node will display the string message in the top-left corner of the Viewport or the game window with the specified text color and duration.

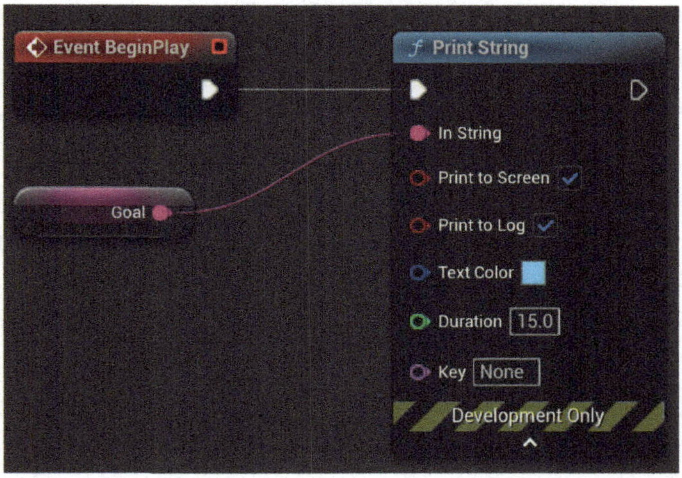

Figure 8.15 - Displaying the mission's goal on the game screen

4. In the **Event Graph**, locate the **Event Tick** node. Add logic to check whether all objectives are completed. Loop through the **Objectives** array. If any objective has **IsCompleted** set to `False`, the mission remains incomplete. Otherwise, if every objective is completed, trigger the player to win.

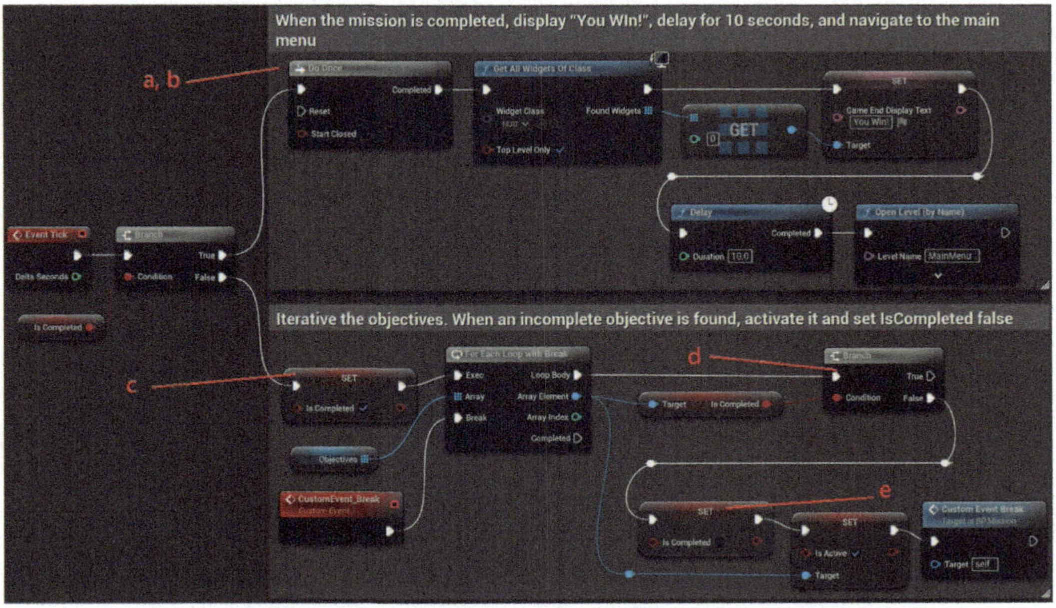

Figure 8.16 - Setting the mission's IsCompleted flag when all objectives are complete; otherwise, activating the first incomplete objective

Figure 8.16 shows the Blueprint logic for checking whether a mission has been completed. Here is how it works step by step:

a. First, check the **IsCompleted** flag. If it is already `False`, skip to *step c*.
b. If **IsCompleted** is `True`, display the game result on the HUD, wait for several seconds, and then navigate to the main menu.
c. Set the mission's **IsCompleted** flag to True before looping the **Objectives** array. All the objectives are supposed to be completed at this time.
d. Loop through the **Objectives** array using the **For Each Loop with Break** node. For each objective, check its **IsCompleted** flag.
e. If an incomplete objective is found, activate this objective, set the mission's **IsCompleted** flag to `False`, and then break the loop.

> **Note**
>
> To break a loop, right-click on an empty space in the graph and create a **Custom Event** node. Name it `CustomEvent_Break` and connect its execution pin to the **Break** pin of the **For Each Loop with Break** node. Whenever you want to exit the loop, simply call this custom event.

a. If the loop completes without finding any incomplete objectives (meaning all objectives are completed), let the mission's **IsCompleted** flag remain `True`.

5. Click **Compile**, then **Save**.

With the `BP_Objective` and `BP_Mission` Blueprints now created, let's put them to use by setting up the actual mission and objectives for the `Desert Castle` level.

Setting up the game mission and the objectives

Now, we need to place one `BP_Mission` and two `BP_Objective` actors into the `Desert_Castle` level and configure them to work with our specific gameplay goals.

Follow these steps to set up the mission and objectives:

1. Open the `Desert_Castle` level.
2. In the **Content Drawer**, navigate to `Content/Pangaea/Mission`. Drag `BP_Mission` into the level. Place it anywhere convenient; it works behind the scenes.
3. Drag the `BP_Objective` Blueprint into the `Desert_Castle` level twice to create the `BP_Objective` and `BP_Objective2` Actors.

4. Select each `BP_Objective` Actor in the level. In the **Details** panel, set up the two objectives according to the values in *Table 8.4* (see *Figure 8.17*).

Name	Title	Location	Scale	IsActive
`BP_Objective`	Kill the two guards	`4300, -9000, (0 )`	`30, 30, (20 )`	`True`
`BP_Objective2`	Kill the Boss	`2300, -9000, (0 )`	`30, 50, (20 )`	`False`

Table 8.4 - Setting up the two objectives for the Desert Castle level

5. In the **Outliner**, select the `BP_Objective` Actor. In the **Details** panel, under the **Default** section, add two Actor references to the **Actors** array: `BP_Warrok` and `BP_Warrok2`. We don't manually add the Boss Actor's reference for `BP_Objective2` because the Boss will be dynamically spawned at game start; therefore, we will let the `BP_BossSpawner` Actor handle adding the `BP_Boss` Actor reference to the **Actors** array for `BP_Objective2` in *step 7*.

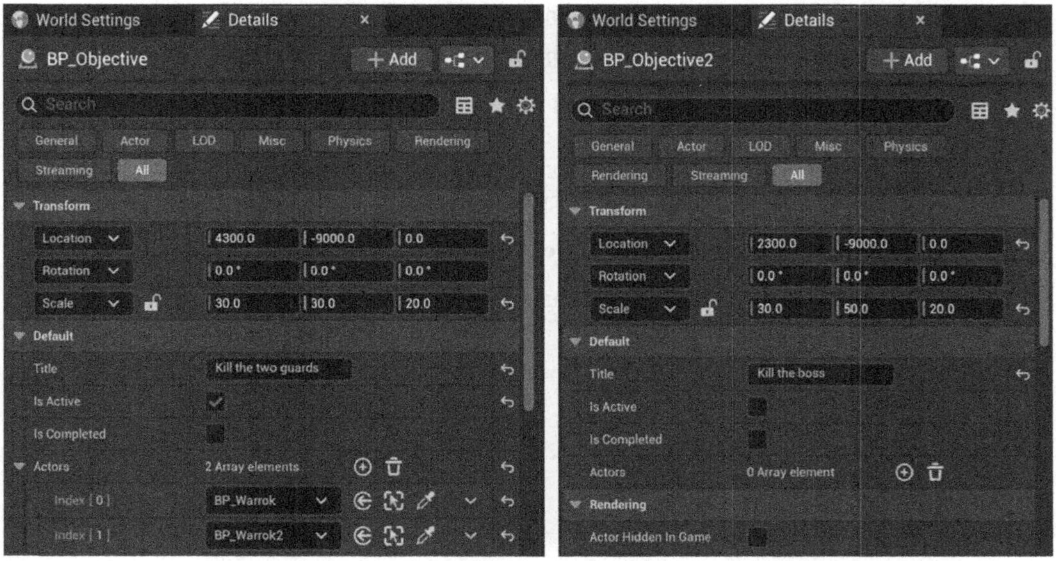

Figure 8.17 - Setting up BP_Objective and BP_Objective2

6. Select the BP_Mission Actor. In the **Details** panel, type `Capture the castle!` into the **Goal** field and add the BP_Objective and BP_Objective2 Actors to the **Objectives** array in the correct order.

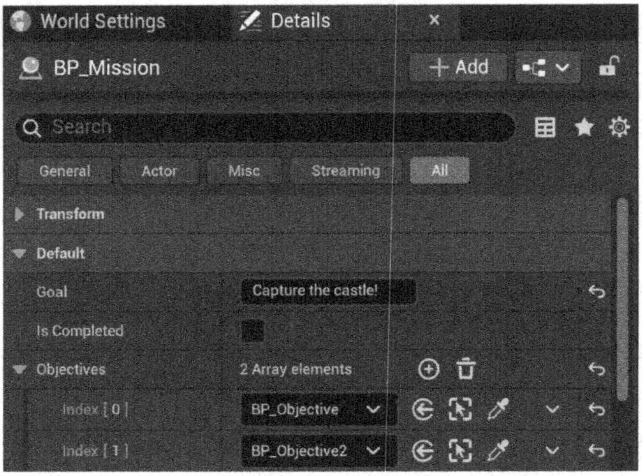

Figure 8.18 - Adding the two objectives to the mission's Objectives array

7. Add the BP_Boss Actor reference to the **Actors** array for BP_Objective2. This will require adding four nodes in the BP_BossSpawner's **Event Graph** after the BP_Boss Actor has been spawned (see *Figure 8.19*).
   a. Get all BP_Objective Actors.
   b. Retrieve the second (index = 1) Actor in the found BP_Objective Actors array, which is the BP_Objective2 Actor.
   c. Get the **Actors** array of BP_Objective2.
   d. Add BP_Boss onto the **Actors** array.

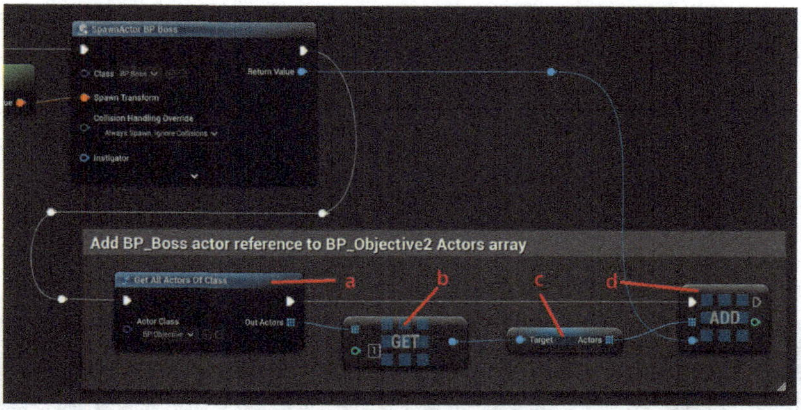

Figure 8.19 - Adding the BP_Boss Actor reference to the Actors array of BP_Objective2

Now that the mission and objectives are set up, it is time to test your current setup to ensure everything is working correctly.

1. Drag and drop a **Nav Mesh Bounds Volume** from the **Place Actors** panel to the game level, set the **Nav Mesh Bounds Volume** Actor's **Location** to (`-800, -9000, 600`), and **Scale** to (`80, 50, 20`).
2. Play through the level, defeat the two guards, and verify that the first objective is completed as expected.

Once the gameplay is confirmed, let's make the castle gate open when the first objective is completed.

Opening the gate

The gate should open once the first objective is completed. When the player defeats the two guards and approaches the castle gate, the gate opens. This creates a satisfying cause-and-effect sequence: defeat the guards, walk up to the gate, and watch it open as a reward for progress. This small moment reinforces that the player's actions have meaning in the game world.

Since the gate is at a fixed location, we will use a **Trigger Volume** to detect when the player approaches. Follow the steps below:

1. Add a **Trigger Volume** to the level. In the **Place Actors** panel, drag **Trigger Volume** under the **Volumes** group into the `Desert_Castle` level. Position and scale the volume so it covers the area of the castle gate:
   - **Location**: (`4000`, `-9000`, `100`)
   - **Scale**: (`5`, `5`, `5`)

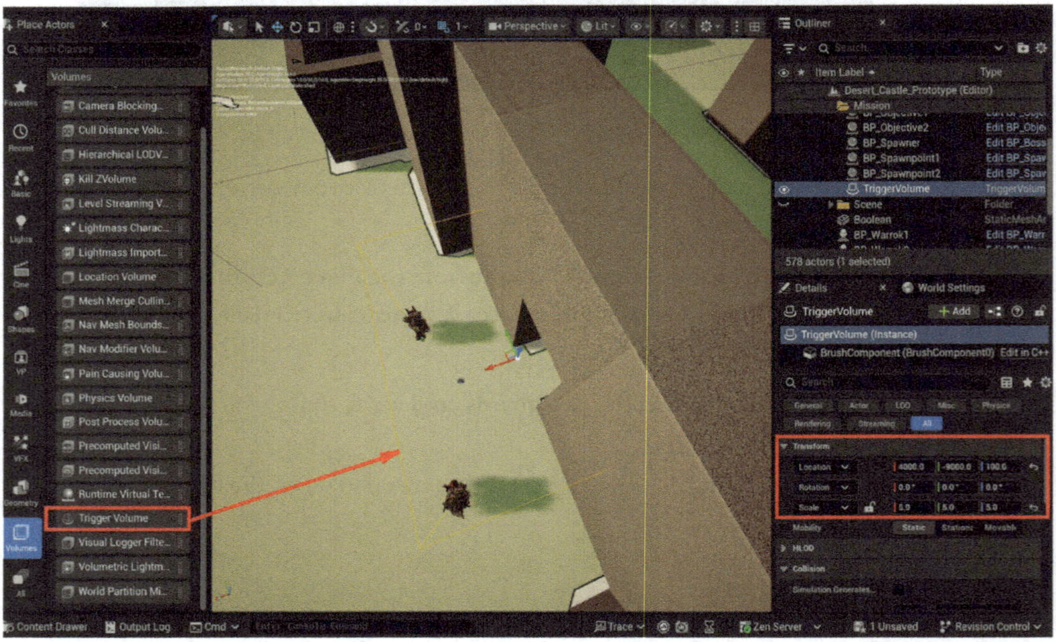

Figure 8.20 - Placing a Trigger Volume for opening the gate

2. Click **Open Level Blueprint** from the **List of World Blueprints** menu.
3. In the Level Blueprint, right-click and add an **On Actor Begin Overlap** event node for handling the corresponding event for the **Trigger Volume** you just placed.

4. Check if the overlapping Actor is the player's Hero character. From the **Other Actor** output of the overlap event, add a **Cast To BP_Hero** node. This ensures the gate only responds to the player, not to enemies or other objects.
5. Check if the first objective is completed. If the cast succeeds, you need to check whether the first objective (**Objective1**: kill the two guards and reach the gate) is completed. This can be done by:
    1. Using the **Get All Actors of Class** node to get the objectives array in the level
    2. Accessing the first objective (index 0) on the array to check its **IsCompleted** flag

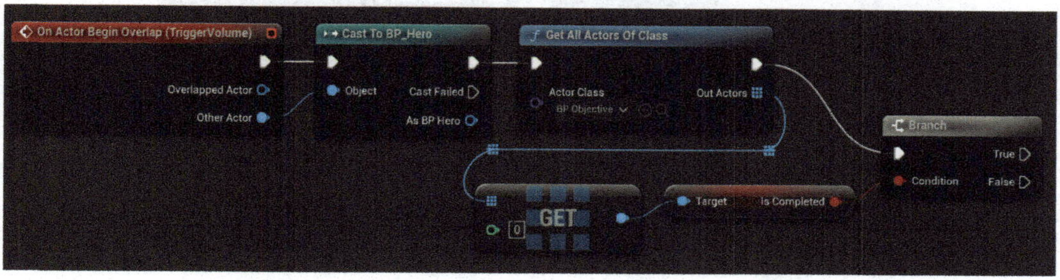

Figure 8.21 - Handling the On Actor Begin Overlap event in the Level Blueprint

6. If the first objective is completed, open the gate with the **Timeline** node:

> **Note**
>
> The **Timeline** node outputs interpolated values (e.g., between 0 and 1) over a set period of time. It is commonly used to create smooth animations, such as opening/closing a gate, fading the screen, or moving an object from one position to another.

    1. Add a **Timeline** node onto the Level Blueprint.

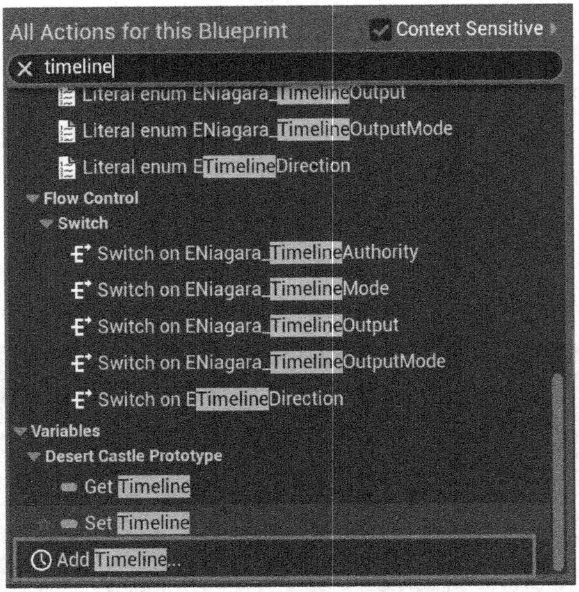

Figure 8.22 - Adding a Timeline node to the Level Blueprint

2. Double-click the new **Timeline** node to open the **Timeline Editor**.
3. Press the **+ Track** button to add a **Float Track**.

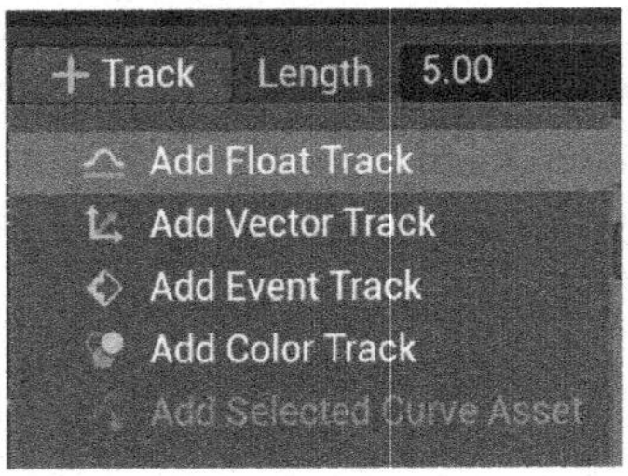

Figure 8.23 - Adding a Float Track

4. Edit the track by setting its **Length** to **3.00** seconds, renaming the track, and adding two keys on the timeline. When the node begins, it outputs **0** at the start and then linearly interpolates from **0** to **1** over the full **3** seconds.

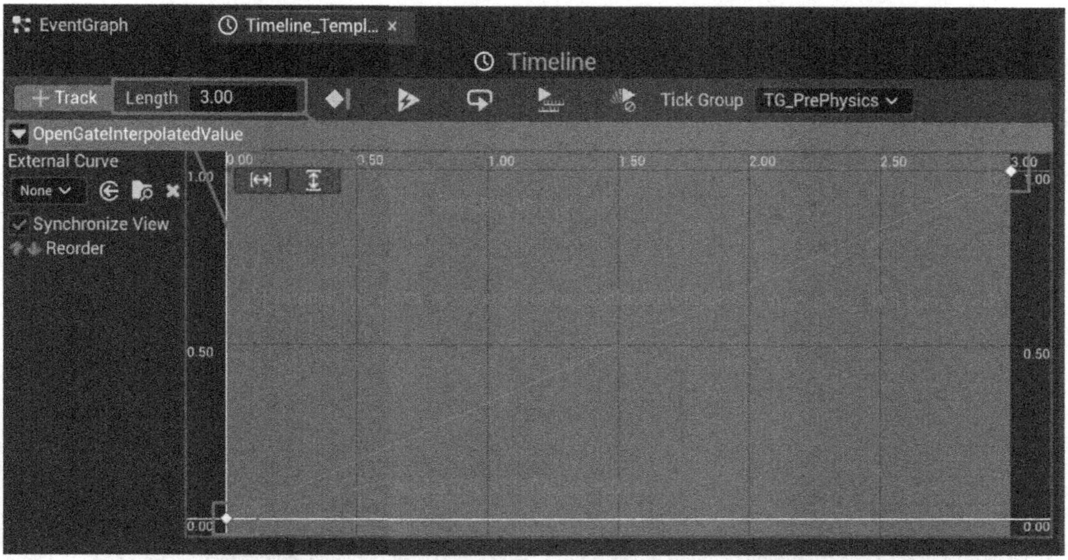

Figure 8.24 - Adding a Float track and configuring for opening the gate

5. Close the **Timeline Editor** and go back to edit the Level Blueprint.

7. Once the first objective is verified as complete, use a **Do Once** node first, then trigger the **Timeline** node. Over 3 seconds, the **Timeline** node outputs an interpolated value to the **Alpha** pins of the two **Lerp (Rotator)** nodes. The first **Lerp (Rotator)** rotates the left door's *Z* axis from 0 to 80 degrees, and the second rotates the right door's *Z* axis from 0 to -80 degrees. The results are fed into the **Set Actor Relative Rotation** nodes to smoothly animate the opening of the left and right gate doors.

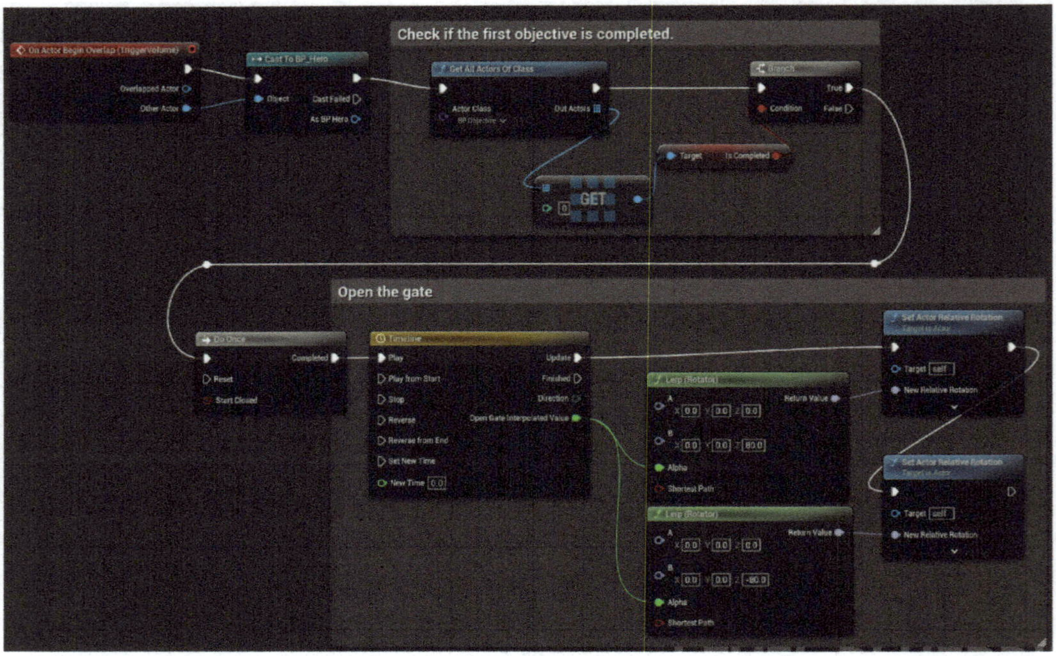

Figure 8.25 - Graph handling the On Actor Begin Overlap (Trigger Volume) event

Currently, we leave the **Target** input of the **Set Actor Relative Rotation** nodes set to **self**, so you won't see any gate movement when testing the game. This is because the gate meshes have not yet been added. We will connect the actual left and right gate door actors to these two nodes in *Chapter 10* when we polish the game.

Now, we have built the level layout, placed enemies, created spawn points, set up the mission and objectives, and implemented gate logic. The final piece is to hook up the HUD to display some gameplay information on screen. Let's take care of that now.

Connecting the HUD to gameplay

Based on the gameplay systems now in place, we need to display information to the player so that they understand what is happening. In this section, we will connect the HUD to show the following:

- **Hero health bar**: A progress bar representing, in percentage, how much health remains for the `Hero`.
- **Enemy portrait and health bar**: A visual image and a progress bar for the enemy under attack, indicating its identity and remaining health.

- **Lose and Win messages:** A text UI element that appears when the mission is failed or completed.
- **Mission and objectives information:** A text element that shows the mission goal and the objective title.

Before implementing the functions to display these elements, we need to perform some setup and ensure that the required screen visual elements and data bindings are configured properly. Open the HUD widget Blueprint under `Content/Pangaea/UI`, edit and verify the setup according to *Table 8.5*.

Component name	Component type	Value type	Value binding variable
PB_HeroHealth	Progress Bar	float	`HeroHealthValue`
PB_EnemyHealth	Progress Bar	float	`EnemyHealthValue`
IMG_EnemyPortrait	Image	Texture2D	`EnemyPortraitImage`
TXT_GameOverDisplay	Text	Text	`GameEndDisplayText`

Table 8.5 - HUD component and binding settings for gameplay displays

To enable changing the enemy portrait, the **IMG_EnemyPortrait** image widget needs to be bound to a `Texture2D` variable. This allows the portrait to update and display the correct image for the enemy currently under attack. Since the `EnemyPortraitImage` variable hasn't been added to the **HUD** graph yet, you should create it now and bind `IMG_EnemyPortrait` to it.

Figure 8.26 below illustrates the UI component and the corresponding bindings:

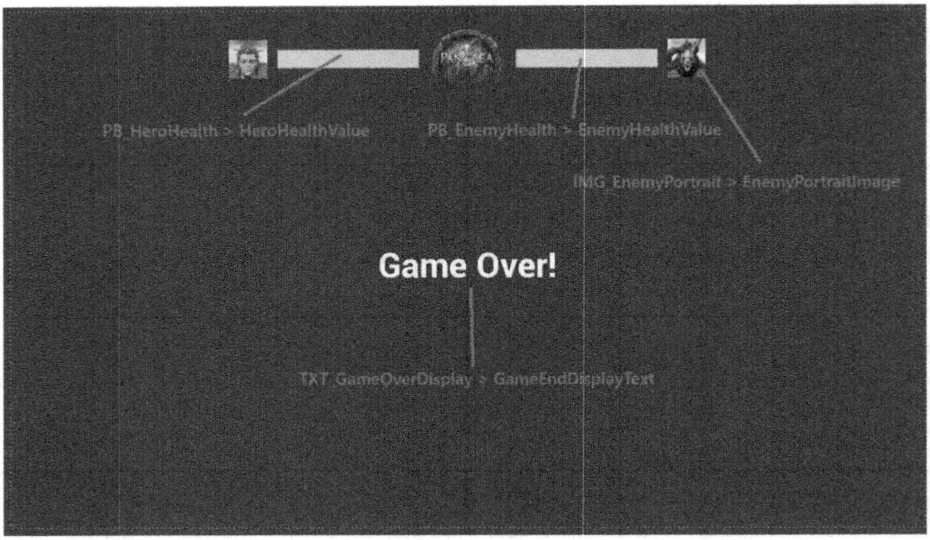

Figure 8.26 - Setting up the UI bindings

We can now start implementing the functions, `UpdateHero`, `UpdateEnemy`, and `ShowWinLose`, for updating the HUD widget. These functions will display the Hero's health, enemy portrait, enemy health, and the game's win/lose result.

Displaying Hero health

Follow the steps below to create the `UpdateHero` function in the HUD widget Blueprint:

1. Navigate to `Content/Pangaea/Characters/Hero` and open the `BP_Hero` Blueprint. Add two new variables of type **Float** – name them `Health` and `MaxHealth`. To make these variables accessible outside the Blueprint, set them to public by clicking the **eye** icon so it appears open.
2. Compile and save the `BP_Hero` Blueprint.
3. Set the `MaxHealth` value to `1000` on the **Details** panel.
4. Add the **Set Health** node to initialize the value for `Health` and connect it as the last execution task to the existing **Event BeginPlay** event execution sequence.

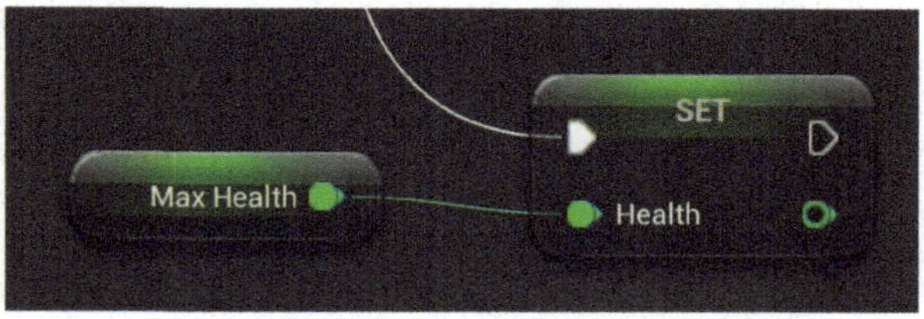

Figure 8.27 - Initializing the Health value from the pre-set MaxHealth value

5. With the HUD widget Blueprint open, select the **EventGraph** tab.
6. In the **Event Graph**, click the + button next to **Functions** in the **My Blueprint** panel. Name the new function `UpdateHero`.
7. With the function selected, go to the **Details** panel. Under **Inputs**, click the + button to add a new parameter. Name it `Hero`, set its type to `BP_Hero Reference`.
8. Inside the **UpdateHero** function graph, add nodes to retrieve the **Health** and **Max Health** values from the **Hero** input, divide **Health** by **Max Health** to calculate the percentage (a value between 0 and 1), and then assign that result to the **Hero Health Value** binding variable for display.

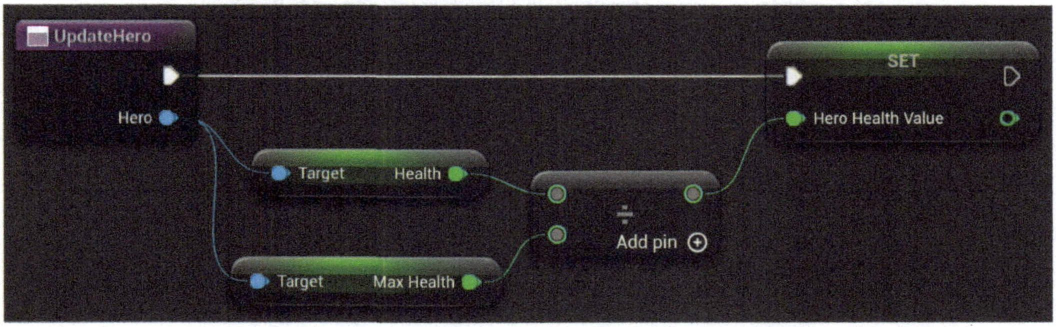

Figure 8.28 - Implementing the UpdateHero function graph

Displaying the enemy portrait and health

Follow the steps below to create the `UpdateEnemy` function in the HUD widget Blueprint:

1. Navigate to `Content/Pangaea/Characters/Warrok` and open the `BP_Warrok` Blueprint, set the MaxHealth to `300`, and then initialize the `Health` from the `MaxHealth` when the **Event BeginPlay** is called.
2. Navigate to `Content/Pangaea/Characters/Boss` and open the `BP_Boss` Blueprint, set the `MaxHealth` to `300`, and then initialize the `Health` from `MaxHealth` when the **Event BeginPlay** is called. Similar to displaying health for the Hero, the **Set Health** node

should be connected as the last execution task to the existing **Event BeginPlay** event execution sequence.

3. In the **My Blueprint** panel, click the + button next to **Functions** and name it `UpdateEnemy`.
4. Add an input parameter named `Enemy` with the type set to **Actor Reference** (since the enemy could be either a guard or a Boss).
5. Inside the `UpdateEnemy` function graph, add the following logic:
   a. First, attempt to cast the **Enemy** input to `BP_Warrok`.
   b. If the cast succeeds, retrieve the **Health** and **Max Health** values from the `BP_Warrok` reference.
   c. Divide **Health** by **Max Health** to calculate the percentage (value between 0 and 1) and assign the result to the **Enemy Health Value** binding variable for the health bar display.
   d. Set the **Enemy Portrait Image** binding variable using the appropriate texture for the guard.
   e. If the cast fails, attempt to cast the **Enemy** input to `BP_Boss`.
   f. If the cast to `BP_Boss` succeeds, retrieve the **Health** and **Max Health** values from the `BP_Boss` reference.
   g. Divide **Health** by **Max Health** to calculate the percentage (value between 0 and 1) and assign the result to the **Enemy Health Value** binding variable for the health bar display
   h. Set the **Enemy Portrait Image** using the appropriate texture for the Boss. Since we already bind the `IMG_EnemyPortrait` display to the `EnemyPortraitImage` variable when we created the HUD in *Chapter 7*, we can simply set the texture and change the portrait display on the game screen.

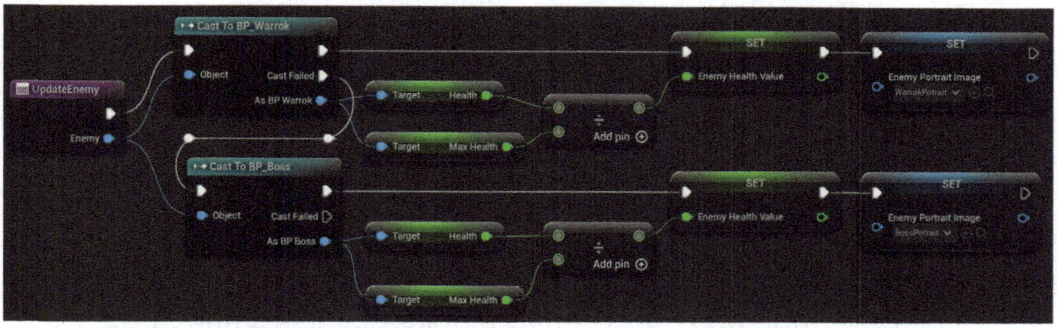

Figure 8.29 - Implementing the UpdateEnemy function graph

Showing Win and Lose messages

Follow the steps below to create the `ShowWinLose` function in the HUD widget Blueprint:

1. In the **My Blueprint** panel, click the **+** button next to **Functions** and name it `ShowWinLose`.
2. Add an input parameter named `WinOrLose` with the type set to **Boolean**.
3. Inside the **ShowWinLose** function graph, use a **Branch** node to check the **Win or Lose** input.
4. If **Win or Lose** is **True**, set the **Game End Display Text** binding variable to the string `You Win!`
5. If **Win or Lose** is **False**, set the **Game End Display Text** binding variable to the string `Game Over!`

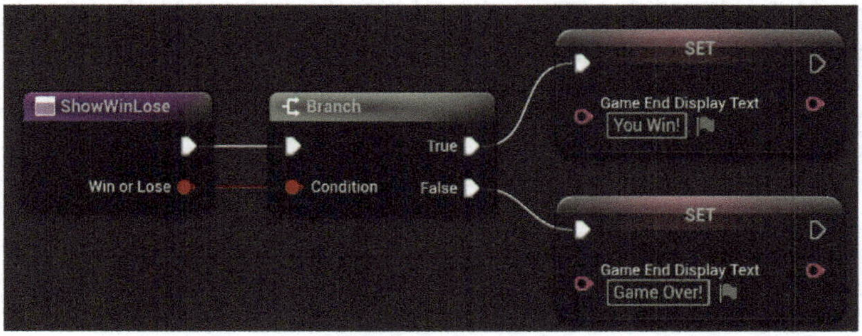

Figure 8.30 - Implementing the ShowWinLose function graph

Connecting HUD displays

To update the Hero's health bar, we can hook it into BP_Hero's **Event AnyDamage.** Follow these steps:

1. Open the BP_Hero Blueprint and navigate to the **Event Graph.**
2. In the **Event Graph**, add the **Get All Widgets of Class** node. Set its **Widget Class** to the HUD widget class. This node returns an array of all HUD instances in the level.
3. Since only one HUD instance exists for the game level, the array should contain only one element. Use a **Get (a copy)** node (index = 0) to retrieve that HUD reference.
4. Call the HUD's **Update Hero** function. Pass **Self** (the BP_Hero instance) as the **Hero** input parameter.

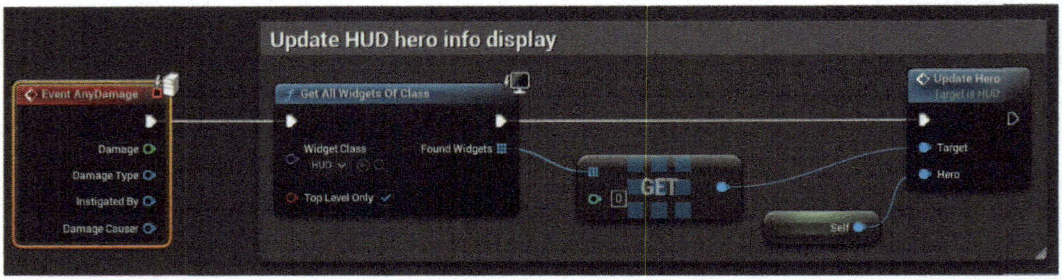

Figure 8.31 - Updating the player's Hero health bar display

Now, the Hero's health bar will update to reflect the current health percentage when the Hero is damaged.

To call the remaining display functions, follow the same process to get the HUD reference, then call the appropriate functions at the designated moments:

- UpdateEnemy: Call the UpdateEnemy function in BP_Warrok and BP_Boss when the **Event AnyDamage** is fired.

- `ShowWinLose`: Call the `ShowWinLose` function in `BP_Hero` when the **Event AnyDamage** event is fired, and `Health` reaches zero.

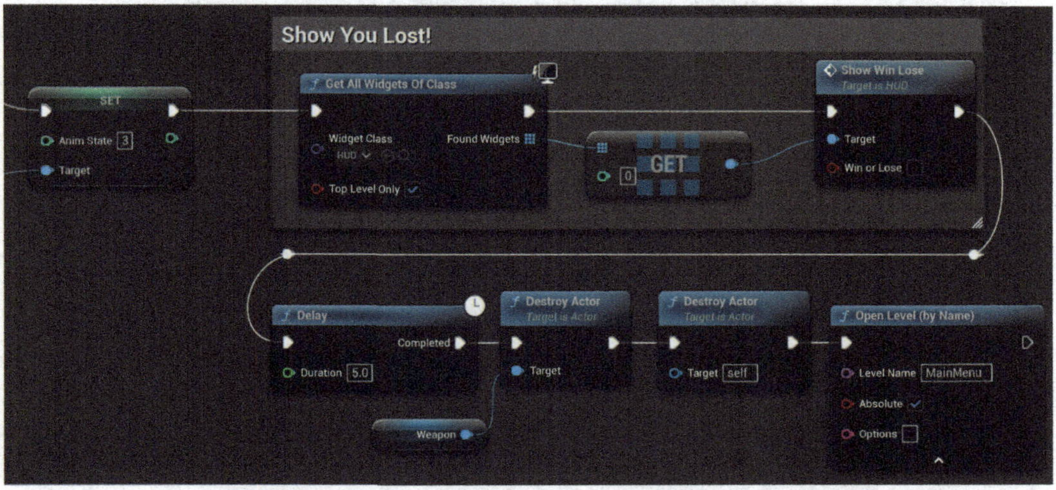

Figure 8.32 - Showing Win/Lose message and ending the game when the Hero is defeated

- `ShowWinLose`: In `BP_Mission`, call it when the mission is completed (either Win or Lose the game) to display the game result message.

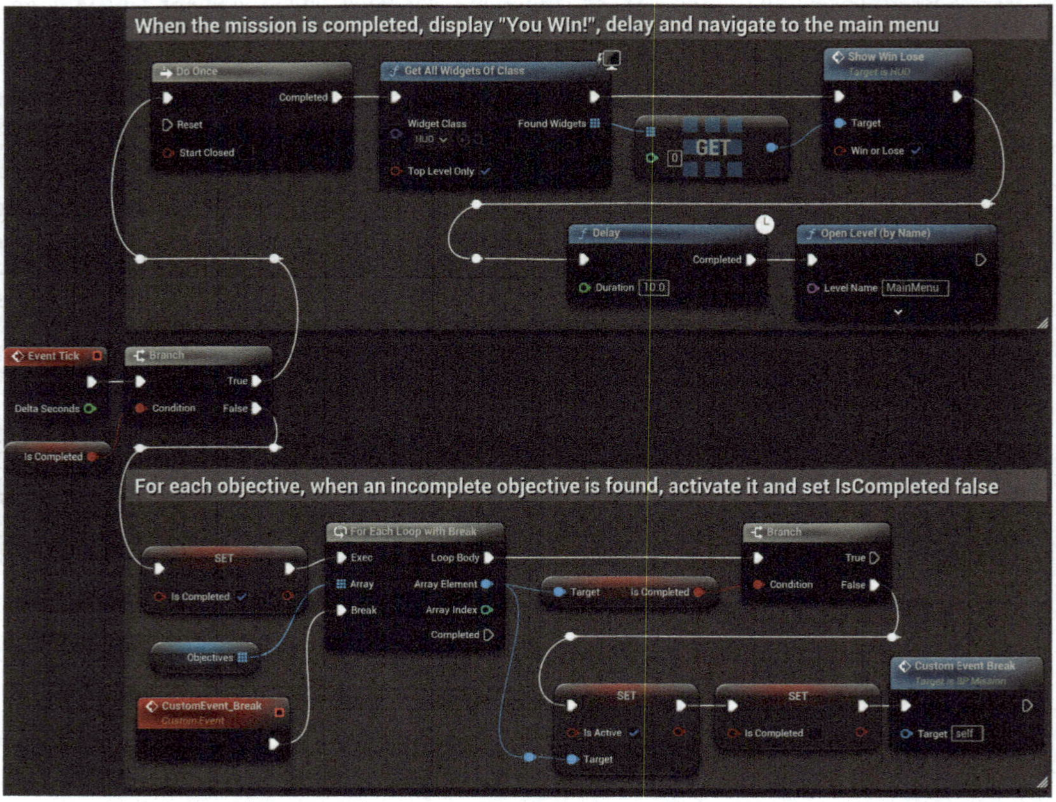

Figure 8.33 - Showing Win/Lose message and ending the game when the mission is completed

Now that the HUD can display the game information, the last thing we need to complete the game fight is to implement interactions between the game characters, including applying damage to opponents and taking damage.

Applying and taking damage

The attack and damage-taking mechanisms can be built based on several steps. First, we need to set up the weapon's collision so it can detect when it hits a target. Next, we implement the logic that applies damage when the weapon's overlap event is fired. Finally, we handle the target character's response by using the **AnyDamage** event, which triggers whenever damage is received and allows us to process health reduction, play hit reactions, and check for defeat.

Setting up weapon collision

Let's set up the sword's collision by opening the `BP_Sword` Blueprint. Select the **SwordMesh** component and configure its **Collision** settings as shown in *Figure 8.34*. This ensures that the weapon only overlaps with pawns and properly generates overlap events. Follow the annotations in *Figure 8.34* to complete the settings:

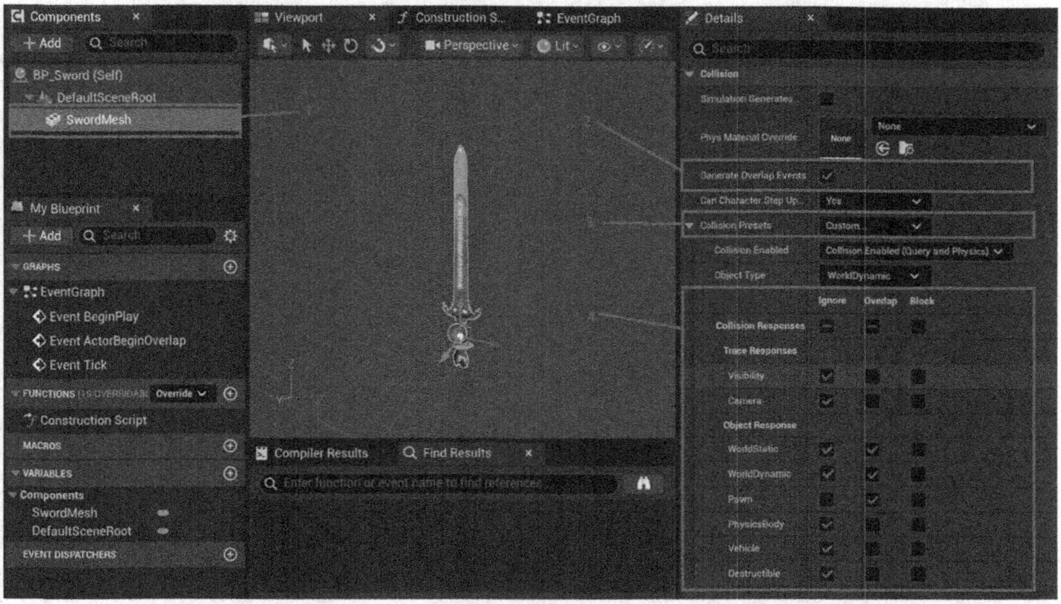

Figure 8.34 - Setting up the collision for BP_Sword

Remember to apply the same collision setup for the `BP_Hammer` and `BP_Hatchet` weapons.

Applying damage to the hit target

Now that the sword's collision is properly set up to detect overlaps with pawns, we need to implement the logic that actually applies damage to the hit target. When the sword's **Event ActorBeginOverlap** is triggered, we must first verify that the overlapping actor is not the Hero itself – this prevents the player from damaging themselves.

Next, we check whether the Hero is currently in the `Attack` state (`AnimState` = 1), ensuring that damage is only dealt during the active swing of the weapon. If both conditions are met, we retrieve the target actor and call the **Apply Damage** node, passing in the **Base Damage** value (e.g., `100`). This triggers the target's **AnyDamage** event, which will handle health reduction and any other reactions.

Figure 8.35 shows the Blueprint logic for applying damage when the weapon overlaps with a valid target:

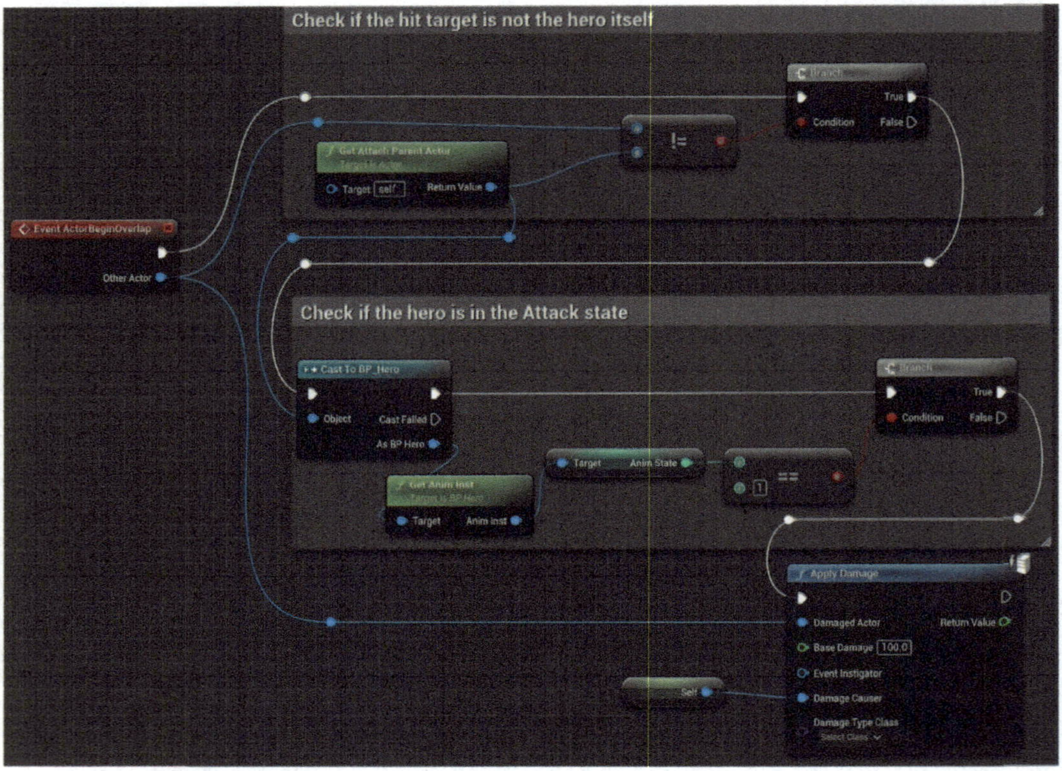

Figure 8.35 - BP_Sword handles the ActorBeginOverlap event to apply damage to the target

The same damage application logic should be applied to the `BP_Hammer` and `BP_Hatchet` weapons, with a few slight differences. For these weapons, the overlapping Actor remains the damage target, while the weapon's holder is cast to either `BP_Warrok` or `BP_Boss`, rather than `BP_Hero`. We then check the holder's animation state, ensuring it is either 11 or 12, which corresponds to the two attack animations. Once validated, the damage is applied to the target in the same way as the sword.

Taking damage

The Hero handles hit damage when the **AnyDamage** event is triggered. When the Hero takes damage, the **AnyDamage** event fires. Before applying the damage, we first verify that the Hero is in a state where damage can be received – specifically, when the animation state is either `Locomotion` (`AnimState = 0`) or `Attack` (`AnimState = 1`). This prevents the Hero from taking damage during invulnerable states such as the `Hit` (`AnimState = 2`) or `Die` (`AnimState = 3`) states.

To perform this check, we cast to `AB_Hero` to access the current animation state, then compare it to the valid states using an **OR** node (see *Figure 8.36*). If the condition passes, we subtract the damage value from the Hero's current health and update the `Health` variable accordingly.

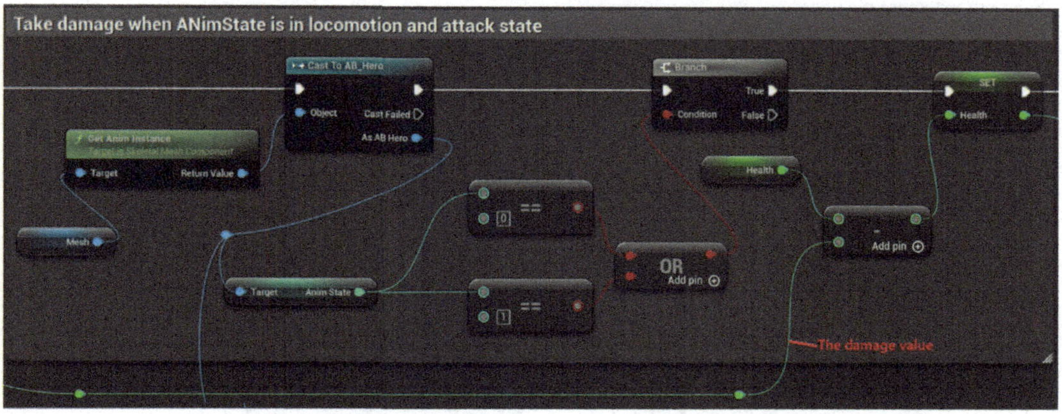

Figure 8.36 - BP_Hero handling the AnyDamage event to decrease the Hero's health

Once the damage is applied and the Hero's health is updated, the next step is to determine which animation to play. If the Hero is still alive (`Health` greater than zero), we set the animation state to 2, which triggers the `Hit` reaction animation. However, if the `Health` drops to zero or below, we set the animation state to 3, which plays the `Die` animation.

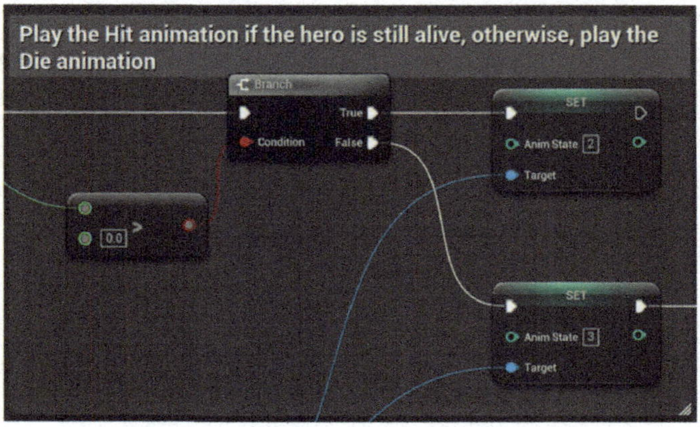

Figure 8.37 - BP_Hero handles the AnyDamage event to play the Hit or Die animation

The same damage handling logic should be applied to both `BP_Warrok` and `BP_Boss` characters. If you encounter any difficulties while implementing this, the `Chapter08` demo project in the GitHub repository (see the *Technical requirements* section; to access the GitHub repository, see the *Preface* for access instructions) provides a complete reference implementation that you can use to review and compare with your own work. The demo project provides a complete reference implementation that you can compare with your own work.

Summary

In this chapter, we moved from the simple testing environment to building a complete gameplay level for the *Pangaea* game. We designed the `Desert Castle` level by first establishing key design factors such as Game Start, Game End, Goal, Challenges, and Outcomes, then sketching a map layout and prototyping the level using **Modeling Mode** shapes.

We implemented several core gameplay systems. We manually placed two guards in front of the castle gate and created a dynamic Boss spawning system using spawn points and a spawner to randomly position the Boss inside the castle. We built `BP_Objective` and `BP_Mission` Blueprints to track player progress and determine win and loss conditions. We added gate logic using a **Trigger Volume** and a **Timeline** node to open the castle gate when the first objective was complete. Finally, we integrated the HUD by creating the display functions, `UpdateHero`, `UpdateEnemy`, and `ShowWinLose`, and hooked them up to the gameplay systems.

We also implemented a damage system that allows the Hero and enemies to apply and take damage during combat. This included handling hit reactions and death when an Actor's health reaches zero.

Now, by the end of this chapter, you have a functional game level where the player can fight enemies, complete objectives, open the gate, defeat the Boss, and see appropriate win or lose messages.

In the next chapter, we will shift from gameplay programming to cinematic storytelling by creating an intro cutscene using video editing techniques.

9

Creating Cinematics and Cut-Scenes

In the modern gaming landscape, cinematic storytelling and dynamic animations are essential for immersing players in a virtual world. Whether it is a dramatic opening cut-scene that sets the narrative stakes or a subtle camera fly-through that reveals a hidden temple, these sequences provide the visual polish and emotional weight that players expect. In Unreal Engine, this choreography is handled through the *Sequencer*.

This chapter introduces the core concepts and tools you need to create cinematic sequences using Unreal Engine's powerful animation framework. You start by learning what a **Sequencer** is and how the specialized **Sequencer Editor** provides a dedicated workspace for temporal design, distinct from the **Level Editor** you have used previously.

You will explore the unique **Sequencer Editor** interface, including the **Track List**, the **Timeline**, and the **Playback Controls**. This chapter also explains the modular nature of Level Sequence assets, which combine actors with specific property tracks, such as **Transform**, **Animation**, and **Camera Cuts**. This gives you a clear understanding of how linear time translates into dynamic in-game events.

Following these foundational concepts, you will follow step-by-step instructions to create an introductory cut-scene featuring character movement and animation, a camera fly-through, and a camera transition, and then integrate the cinematic sequence into our *Pangaea* game project, allowing players to automatically experience the cut-scene before starting gameplay.

In this chapter, we will cover the following

- Understanding the Sequencer
- Using the Sequencer

- Exploring keyframe animation
- Understanding Level Sequence Assets
- Understanding Level Sequence Actors
- Creating the cut-scene

By the end of this chapter, you will have a good understanding of the Unreal Engine **Sequencer Editor** and will have worked through creating an introductory cut-scene for the *Pangaea* game project. You'll have enough understanding to be proficient at creating your own custom cinematic sequences for your games in Unreal.

Technical requirements

The sample project for this chapter is available for download from the book's GitHub repository and branch:

- `Chapter09-Start` branch: This branch holds the game project with everything you need to start learning this chapter.
- `Chapter09` branch: This branch contains the completed game project for this chapter, which includes the introductory cut-scene for the Desert Castle level.

You can download the example project and code files for this book by following the instructions in the *Download the example code/resource files* section in the *Preface* of this book.

This chapter's code/resource files are included in the downloadable code/resource bundle.

Understanding the Sequencer

Sequencer is a multi-track nonlinear editor used to create in-game cinematics, cut-scenes, and complex animations within Unreal Engine. It serves as the primary tool for developers to choreograph actors, cameras, and events in a 3D space over a linear timeline.

At its core, **Sequencer** is built upon Level Sequence assets. A **Level Sequence** is a specialized asset that combines two distinct functional areas: a **Track List** for managing actors, such as characters, lights, and audio, and a **Timeline** for defining the specific values and properties of those actors at any given frame.

Sequencer uses a system of *tracks* and *sections*, which are modular components, such as **Transform** tracks, **Animation** tracks, and **Camera Cut** tracks, that can be added, edited, and layered. While these sequences are part of the broader **cinematics framework** (an expansive ecosystem that includes physical camera simulation, motion capture recording, and production management and rendering pipelines), **Sequencer** provides a user-friendly interface that allows designers to build cinematic-quality storytelling without the need for deep C++ knowledge or complex manual scripting.

This architecture allows you to create high-fidelity cinematics that are not only visually impressive but also deeply integrated with the game logic. Because Level Sequences are assets, they can interact with other game systems, such as the Level Blueprint or the player character, allowing the cinematic to trigger gameplay events or react to the current state of the world, ensuring a seamless transition between cut-scenes and play.

With an understanding of what **Sequencer** is, we will now examine the **Sequencer Editor**.

Using the Sequencer

While the **Level Editor** allows you to place Actors in 3D space, the **Sequencer Editor** allows you to manipulate those Actors and their properties along a temporal timeline. Whether you are moving a camera for a cut-scene or changing the intensity of a light during a gameplay trigger, **Sequencer** is the tool that orchestrates these changes.

To view the **Sequencer Editor**, you must first create a **Level Sequence** asset in the **Content Browser** (click the **Cinematics Clapperboard** button in the **Level Editor**'s main top toolbar, select **Add Level Sequence** from the dropdown, and save the asset in your project). When you open this asset, the **Sequencer** typically appears at the bottom of the screen, providing a dedicated interface for linear animation, as shown in *Figure 9.1*:

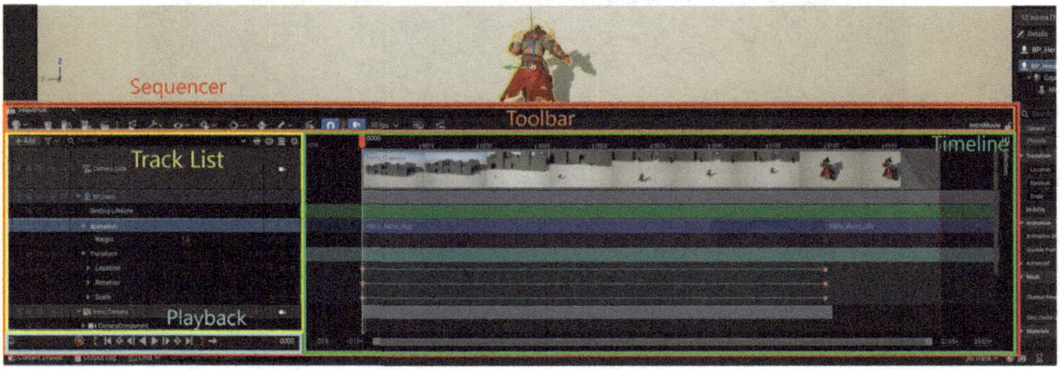

Figure 9.1 - Sequencer Editor Interface Layout

> **Note**
>
> Unlike the **Level Editor**, the **Sequencer** is *non-destructive* to your world state. You can move an Actor to the other side of the map in a sequence, and when the sequence ends or is closed, the Actor can snap back to its original position.

The **Sequencer** interface is designed to provide a clear relationship between the objects in your world and their movement over time. By breaking the interface down into two halves, the **Track List** on the left and the **Timeline** on the right, Unreal Engine allows you to manage "who" is moving and "when" that movement occurs with precision.

Track List (left column)

Think of the **Track List** (see *Figure 9.2*) as the *table of contents* for your cinematic. It identifies every Actor, component, and property that you have given the **Sequencer** permission to control:

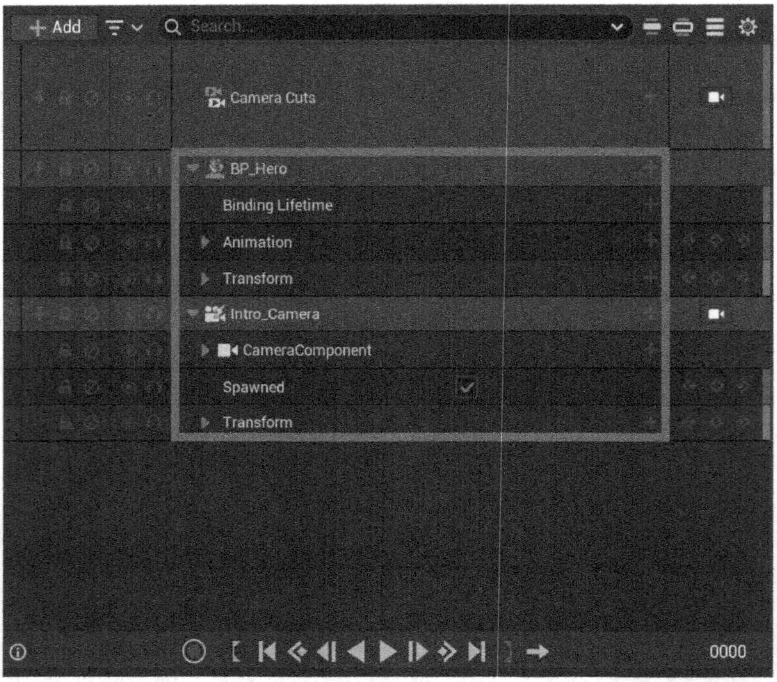

Figure 9.2 - Sequencer Track List Overview

Let's have a look at the important features of the Track List:

- **Hierarchy**: Objects are listed vertically. Click the *small arrow* next to **BP_Hero** at the top level; the list expands to show its sub-properties (see *Figure 9.2*), such as its **Transform** (controlling the Actor's location, rotation and scale) or its **Animation** (including animation speed, start/end offset, looping and event firing) property tracks.
- **Adding tracks and Actors**: Clicking the **+ Add** button at the top of the **Sequencer** (see *Figure 9.2*) adds a global (or master) track to the Track List, which is generally not

scoped to a specific object in the scene, although it is possible to use this to add an Actor from the Level into your Sequence.

You can bring new Actors into the **Sequencer** as either **Possessables** (existing Level objects such as your player or the scene environment) or **Spawnables** (objects that only exist for the duration of the clip such as a cinematic camera, a cinematic visual effect or a cut-scene prop). The main purpose of the **+ Add** button is to add master tracks that control the scene's overall sequence, such as camera cuts, events, or audio.

- **Adding sub-tracks and properties**: Clicking the + button that is located to the right of a specific Actor in the Track List (see *Figure 9.2*) adds component-specific **Sub-Tracks** or **Properties** that are available for that Actor. The options provided here are filtered based on what that specific Actor can do, and only the properties available in the **Track List** column can be animated. A practical example of animating a cube to move and rotate in the level would be achieved by adding the target cube Actor into the **Sequencer** Track List and adjusting the values of its **Location** (move) and **Rotation** (rotate) properties in the Timeline through **Keyframes** (explained in detail later in this chapter).

Timeline and Track lanes (right column)

To the right of the Track List is the **Timeline** (highlighted red in *Figure 9.3*), which is represented as a grid. This is where you visualize the passage of time, measured in either frames or seconds.

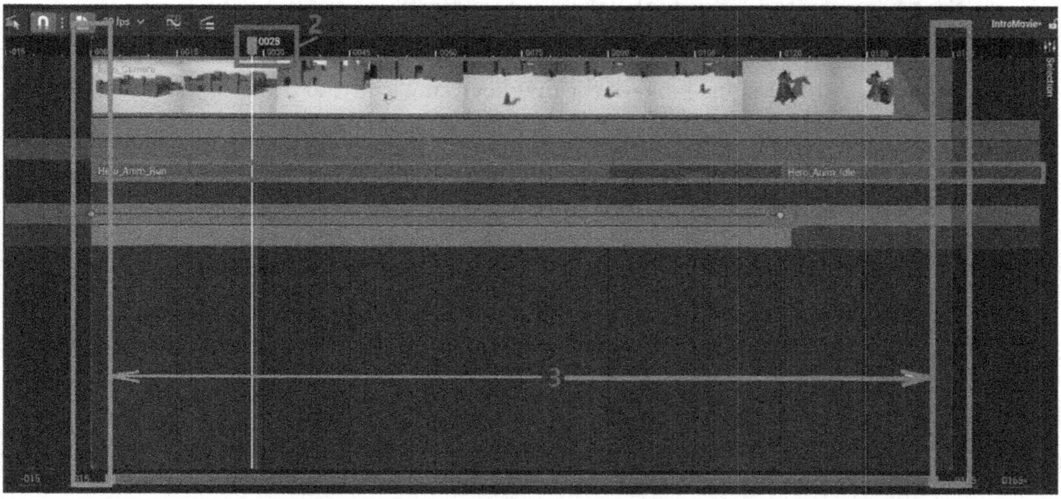

Figure 9.3 - Sequencer Timeline Overview

Here is a breakdown of the important features of the Timeline:

1. **Track lanes**: Each item in the Track List has its own dedicated horizontal row, known as a **track lane** (**1** in *Figure 9.3*). This ensures that the keyframes for your camera movement never get mixed up with the keyframes for your character's animation.
2. **The Playhead**: The *red* pointer with a vertical *white* line spanning across the Timeline is the **Playhead** (**2** in *Figure 9.3*). This represents the "current time". When you drag the Playhead back and forth (a process known as **scrubbing**), you will see the Actors in your **Level Editor** move and change according to your animation.
3. **The working range**: You will notice vertical markers on the timeline (**3** in *Figure 9.3*). These define the start (*green*) and end (*purple*) points of your sequence. Anything outside these bounds will not play when the sequence is triggered in-game.

Keyframes: connecting the two

Keyframes are the bridge between your list of properties and the timeline. They appear as small **red circular** icons within the track lanes (**4** in *Figure 9.3*). The following concepts explain how keyframes define and control changes over time in a sequence:

- **Defining a state**: When you place a keyframe, you are recording the exact value of a property at the Playhead's current position.
- **Visual alignment**: To read the **Sequencer**, you simply look at the intersection: find the property in the **Track List** (horizontal), follow its track lane to the right, and see where the keyframe sits relative to the playhead (vertical).
- **Interpolation**: The empty space between two keyframes in a lane is where the magic happens. Unreal Engine looks at the first keyframe icon and the second keyframe icon, then automatically calculates all the in-between values so the object moves smoothly from point A to point B. This is explained in more detail in the *Understanding interpolation* section later in the chapter.

Playback and toolbar

At the bottom or top of the interface (depending on your layout), you have the **Playback Controls** (**1** in *Figure 9.4*), which function like a standard video player (**Play, Pause, Skip to End**):

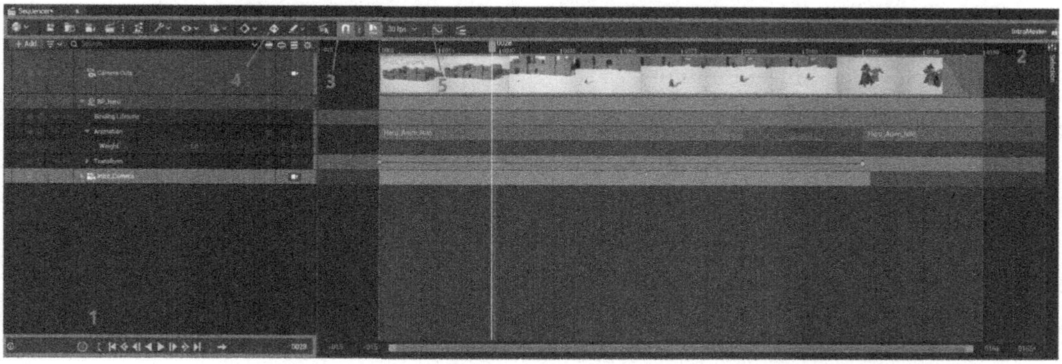

Figure 9.4 - Sequencer Playback and toolbar overview

The **toolbar** (**2** in *Figure 9.4*) provides essential utility tools, such as:

- **Snapping**: A **magnet** icon (**3** in *Figure 9.4*) that helps you align keyframes perfectly to the grid lines (frames).
- **Auto-Key**: A toggle (**4** in *Figure 9.4*) that automatically creates a keyframe whenever you move an Actor in the Viewport while the **Sequencer** is open.
- **Curve Editor Toggle**: A button (**5** in *Figure 9.4*) that transforms the Timeline from a series of lanes into a functional graph for fine-tuning the "feel" of your motion.

Understanding common track types

As you build cinematic sequences, you will work with different track types depending on what you want to animate or control:

- **Transform Track**: Controls the location, rotation, and scale of an Actor.
- **Audio Track**: Triggers sound effects or music at specific timestamps.
- **Event Track**: Allows you to fire off specific Blueprint logic at a precise moment in the timeline.
- **Cinematic Shot Track**: Used to organize different camera angles into a single cohesive movie.
- **Animation Track**: Specifically for Skeletal Meshes, this track allows you to trigger, loop, and blend skeletal animations. You can stack multiple clips and use **weighting** (a value between 0 and 1.0 that controls the influence a specific clip has over the character's body) to smoothly transition between them.

> **Tip**
>
> **Pro-tip for blending animations**
>
> One of the most powerful features of the **Animation Track** is the ability to overlap two animation clips. When you drag one clip over the end of another, **Sequencer** automatically creates a crossfade. This is an incredibly efficient way to transition a character from a *"Run"* animation into an *"Idle"* or *"Jump"* animation without needing to set up complex state machines in a separate Animation Blueprint.

Having explored the various sections of the **Sequencer Editor**, the next section will outline the importance of Keyframe Animation in the Unreal Engine **Sequencer**.

Exploring keyframe animation

As you learned in the previous section, animation in **Sequencer** is driven by keyframes. A keyframe is a data point that records the value of a property (like **Location**, **Rotation**, or **Light Color**) at a specific point in time.

To understand **keyframe animation** in **Sequencer**, think of it as the process of defining **milestones** for an Actor's properties. Instead of manually moving an object for every single frame of a 30-second clip, you define the "story beats" of its movement (*keyframes*), and Unreal Engine fills in the gaps (*interpolation*).

Understanding interpolation

The magic of animation happens between the keys. This is called **interpolation**. Unreal Engine looks at the value of keyframe A and keyframe B and calculates the mathematical path between them.

The *"feel"* of your animation depends entirely on the interpolation mode you choose (these can be changed by right-clicking a keyframe in the **Sequencer**).

The following interpolation modes are among the most commonly used in **Sequencer**:

- **Linear**: Moves at a constant, robotic speed from A to B. Best used for mechanical parts, elevators, or simple UI slides.
- **Constant**: No movement at all until the playhead hits the next key, then it "snaps" instantly. Best used for flickering lights, visibility toggles, or stop-motion effects.
- **Cubic (Auto)**: Adds a smooth Ease-In and Ease-Out curve (meaning the object gradually accelerates at the start and decelerates to a gentle stop, mimicking real-world

weight and momentum). Best used for organic movement, characters, and cinematic cameras.

By mastering these different interpolation modes, you can completely alter the emotional mood and professional quality of your scene, turning a rigid, robotic camera movement into a suspenseful cinematic sweep, or a jarring asset swap into a fluid, organic narrative transition. With an understanding of interpolation, you will now examine the keyframing workflow.

The keyframing workflow

At its heart, a keyframe is a snapshot of a specific property's state.

When you *key* a property, you are telling Unreal: *at exactly frame 60, this Actor must be at these X, Y, and Z coordinates.* The keyframing workflow can be broken down into four simple steps:

1. **Selection**: You first add an Actor to the **Sequencer** that you plan to manipulate or interact with during your cut-scene.
2. **Tracking**: You add a specific track for the property you want to change (e.g., **Transform**, **Intensity**, or **Color**) in the Track List section of the **Sequencer** (see *Figure 9.5*).

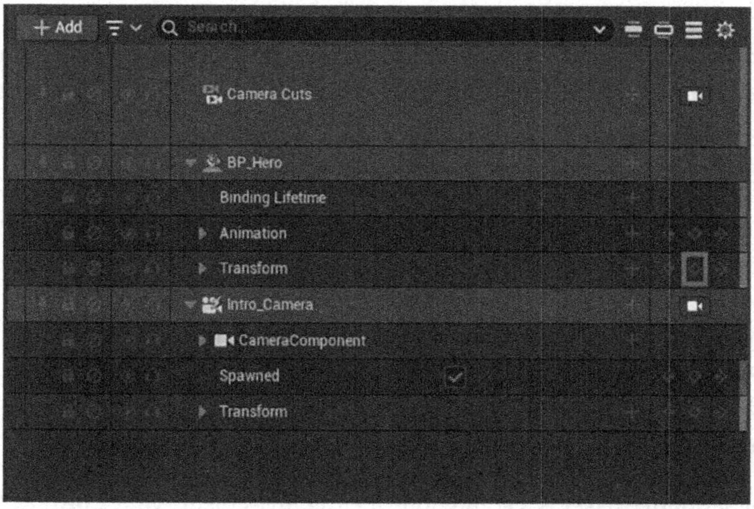

Figure 9.5 - Sequencer Track List

3. **Placement**: You move the Playhead (the red vertical pointer highlighted in *Figure 9.6*) to the desired time in the **Timeline** section of the **Sequencer**.
4. **Setting the Key**: You change the property in the **Details** panel or **Level Editor** and click the **Key Diamond** icon (highlighted in *Figure 9.5*).

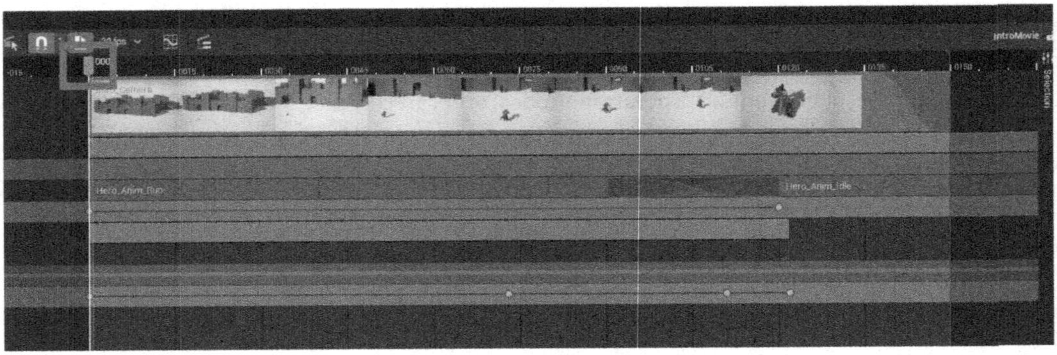

Figure 9.6 - Sequencer Timeline and Playhead

Keyframes aren't just for moving objects. In Unreal, almost any property with a **diamond** icon next to it in the **Details** panel can be keyed:

- **Post-Process Effects**: Keying **Vignette Intensity** or **Bloom** to create a dazed effect after an explosion.
- **Visibility**: Keying the **Actor Hidden in Game** checkbox to make items appear or disappear.
- **Material Parameters:** If you have a **Dissolve** parameter in your character's material, you can key that value in **Sequencer** to make them evaporate into dust.

You will have the opportunity to get hands-on with this workflow and explore it more deeply later in the chapter, when you will use it to create a custom cut-scene for the *Pangaea* game.

With an understanding of the basics of keyframe animation and its workflow in Unreal Engine, in the next sections, we will break down the two primary components that make the **Sequencer** system work: the data itself (the *Level Sequence Asset*) and the way it is brought into your game world (the *Level Sequence Actor*). Understanding the distinction between these two is vital, as it is a common point of confusion for those new to Unreal Engine.

Understanding Level Sequence Assets

The **Level Sequence asset** is a standalone file that lives inside your **Content Browser**, appearing as a **Clapperboard** icon as shown in *Figure 9.7*. This means it exists independently of any single level and contains the **Sequencer**'s data.

You can think of the Level Sequence asset as the *film reel* or the *master script* for your cinematic. The Level Sequence asset is assigned to a Level Sequence Actor to bind its data to a Level.

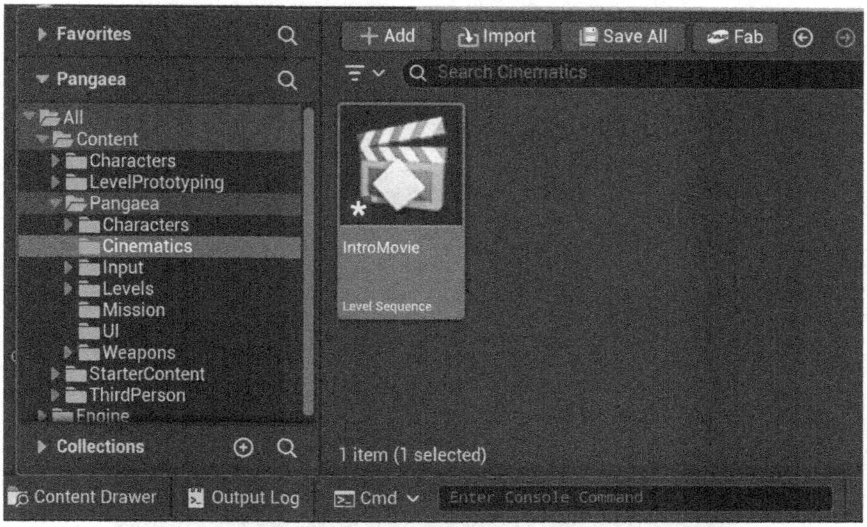

Figure 9.7 - Level Sequence asset in the Content Browser

The Level Sequence asset does all the heavy lifting of your cinematic, including:

- **Track Information**: The list of every **Actor**, **Light**, or **Camera** that has been *added* to the timeline.
- **Keyframes**: Every recorded data point for movement, color changes, or visibility.
- **Animations**: The specific clips of character movement that you have arranged on the timeline.
- **Audio and Events**: Triggers for sound effects or Blueprint logic that fire off at specific moments.

Because it is an asset in the **Content Browser**, it is *reusable*. You could, for instance, create a `Camera Shake` sequence and reuse that same asset across ten different levels. However, on its own, the asset is just *data on a shelf*, and it needs a way to be "read" by the level you are currently building. This is where the **Level Sequence Actor** comes in, which we'll explore in the next section.

Understanding Level Sequence Actors

The **Level Sequence Actor** is located within the Level and is the container for the Level Sequence asset. You can select it from the **Outliner** (shown in *Figure 9.8*) to expose its properties in the **Details** panel, which control how that cinematic behaves during live gameplay:

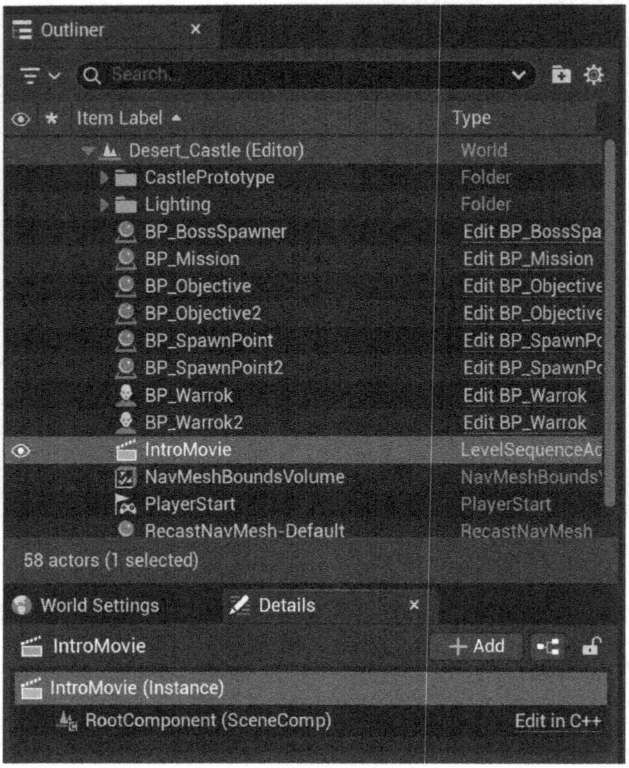

Figure 9.8 – Level Sequence Actor displayed in the Outliner (top) and Details (bottom) panels

The most critical properties are under the **Playback** group on the **Details** panel, which include:

- **Auto Play**: Determines if it should start playing the cut-scene automatically when the level loads.
- **Loop**: Determines if it should repeat playing the sequence.
- **Play Rate**: Controls the speed to play the sequence.

The Level Sequence Actor is the bridge between your data and your game world. While the Level Sequence Asset is the *film reel*, the Actor is the *projector* that actually plays that film within your scene.

How it works

One easy way to create a Level Sequence Actor is to drag the Level Sequence asset from your **Content Browser** into the Viewport. You can see this new item appear in your **Outliner**, as shown in *Figure 9.8*. Once created, the Level Sequence Actor is responsible for the following tasks:

- **Binding Data**: The primary job of this Actor is to bind the instructions in your Sequence Asset to the specific objects in your Level. For example, if your Level Sequence Asset says "Move the Chair", the Sequence Actor identifies which specific chair in your current room should move.
- **Controlling Sequence Behavior**: By selecting the Level Sequence Actor in your Level, you gain access to its settings in the **Details** panel. This is where you control how the sequence behaves during gameplay:
    - **Auto Play**: If checked, the sequence begins the moment the level starts.
    - **Loop**: It decides if the sequence plays once or repeats indefinitely.
    - **Play Rate**: This allows you to speed up or slow down the entire animation, such as for a slow-motion effect.

Think of the Level Sequence Actor as the physical representative of your cinematic within the 3D space. If you delete the Level Sequence Actor from your Level, your cinematic won't play in that Level anymore, but your hard work remains perfectly safe inside the Level Sequence asset back in the **Content Browser**.

Following an introduction to the **Sequencer Editor** and with a good understanding of the two underlying components that make the **Sequencer** system work (the Level Sequence Asset and the Level Sequence Actor), you are now ready to begin using these tools to create a custom cut-scene.

Creating the cut-scene

Now that you have had an introduction to the **Sequencer**, you will have the opportunity to get hands-on and create an "intro movie" for the *Pangaea* project, featuring a character running toward a desert castle and a smooth transition into active gameplay.

Through the following steps, you will learn how to create different tracks in the **Sequencer** to control the movement and animation of the player and the cinematic camera, how to choreograph these tracks in the Timeline so they work together, how to blend the cinematic camera back into the gameplay camera, and how to implement the logic required to start the cinematic cut-scene whenever you begin your game.

Creating the Intro Movie Sequence

The following steps will guide you through setting up your first cinematic sequence in the `Desert_Castle` level:

1. In the **Content Browser**, navigate to **All** | **Content** | **Pangaea** | **Levels** folder and open the `Desert_Castle` level from your **Levels** folder.
2. Navigate to **All** | **Content** | **Pangaea** | **Characters** | **Hero** folder, locate the `BP_Hero` Blueprint in the **Content Browser**, drag it into the **Viewport**, and in the **Details** panel set the following values:
    - Set the **Location** coordinates to (`7372`, `-9047`, `88`)
    - Set the **Rotation** values to (`0`, `0`, `180`)
3. Navigate to **All** | **Content** | **Pangaea** folder, and create a new folder called `Cinematics`.
4. In the top toolbar, click the **Cinematics** button (the **clapperboard** icon) and select **Add Level Sequence** to create a Level Sequence in the Level.
5. In the pop-up window that appears, navigate to **All** | **Content** | **Pangaea** | **Cinematics** folder, name the asset `IntroMovie`, and click **Save**. Once saved, the **Sequencer** will now open at the bottom of the Unreal Editor, as shown in *Figure 9.9*:

Figure 9.9 - Sequencer open in the Unreal Editor

Having now created a Level Sequence for the *Pangaea* cut-scene movie sequence and saved it within our project, you will move on to animating our Hero within the Level Sequence.

Animating the Hero

To make our Hero move, we need to add them to the **Sequencer** and define their movement using keyframes:

1. In the **Sequencer**, click the **+ Add** button (**1** in *Figure 9.10*) to add a track to the **Sequencer**. Then select **Actor Track**, and in the pop-up window that appears, search for and select **BP_Hero**. This **BP_Hero** is the reference to the `BP_Hero` we added into the level previously.

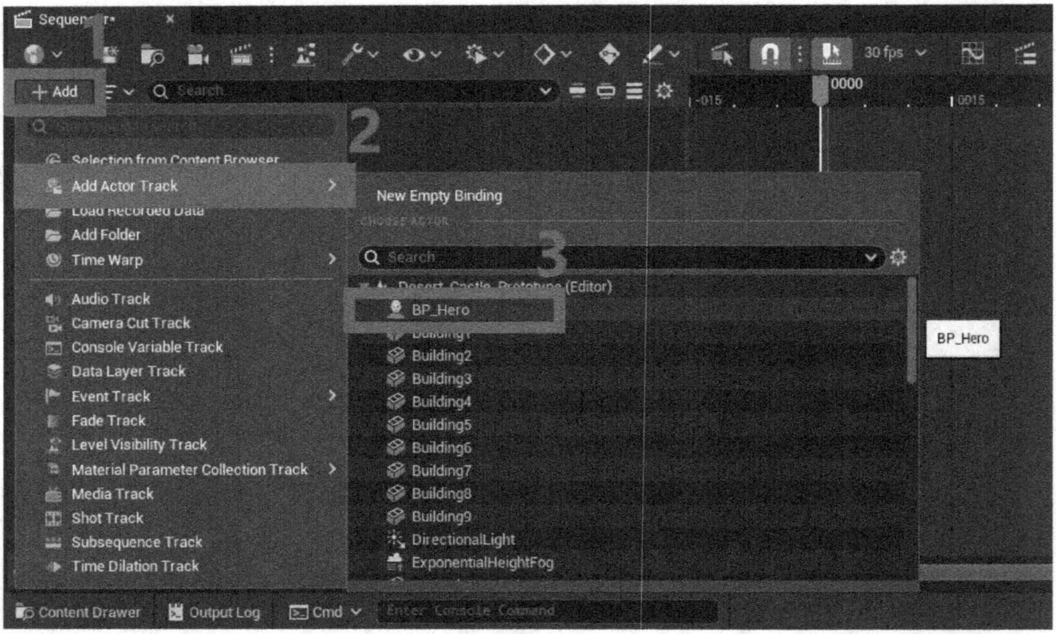

Figure 9.10 - Adding the BP_Hero to the Sequencer

2. In the Track List section of the **Sequencer**, click the + button next to **BP_Hero** (**1** in *Figure 9.11*) and select **Transform** from the pop-up list that appears.

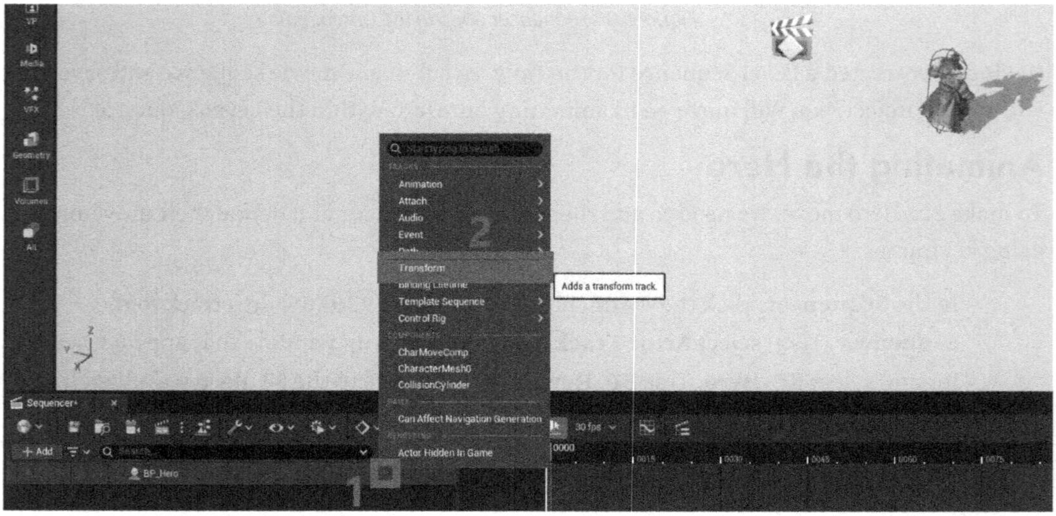

Figure 9.11 - Adding the BP_Hero Transform property to the Sequencer

3. With the **Transform** track selected in the Track List section of the **Sequencer**, ensure that the red **Playhead** pointer (**1** in *Figure 9.12*) in the **Timeline** section of the **Sequencer** is set at frame **0000**. Then, click the **Add Keyframe** button (**2** in *Figure 9. 12*) to create a keyframe that locks the initial starting position for the Hero.

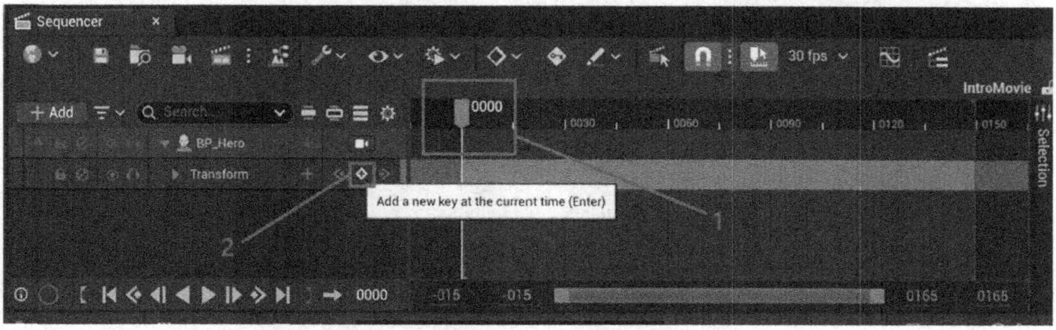

Figure 9.12 - Adding the initial BP_Hero Transform keyframe to the Sequencer

4. In the **Timeline** section of the **Sequencer**, move the red **Playhead** pointer to frame **0120**. In the **Viewport**, move the **BP_Hero** closer to the castle gate by setting his **Location** coordinates to (`5719`, `-9047`, `88`), and click the **Add Keyframe** button again to create a second keyframe that stores the second position of the **BP_Hero** in the cinematic sequence, as shown in *Figure 9.13*.

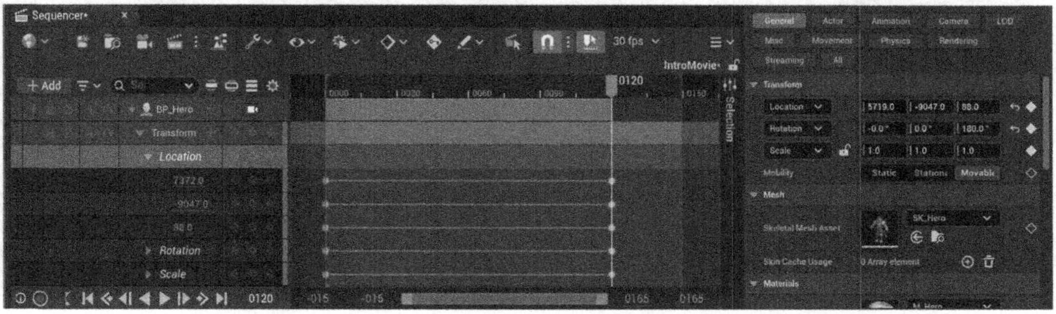

Figure 9.13 - Adding the second BP_Hero Transform keyframe to the Sequencer

5. In the **Timeline** section of the **Sequencer**, move the red **Playhead** pointer back to the starting frame of **0000**.
6. In the Track List section of the **Sequencer**, click the **+** button next to **BP_Hero** (**1** in *Figure 9.14*) and select **Animation** in the pop-up list that appears, then search for and select the `A_Hero_Run` animation in the search window to the right of the list.

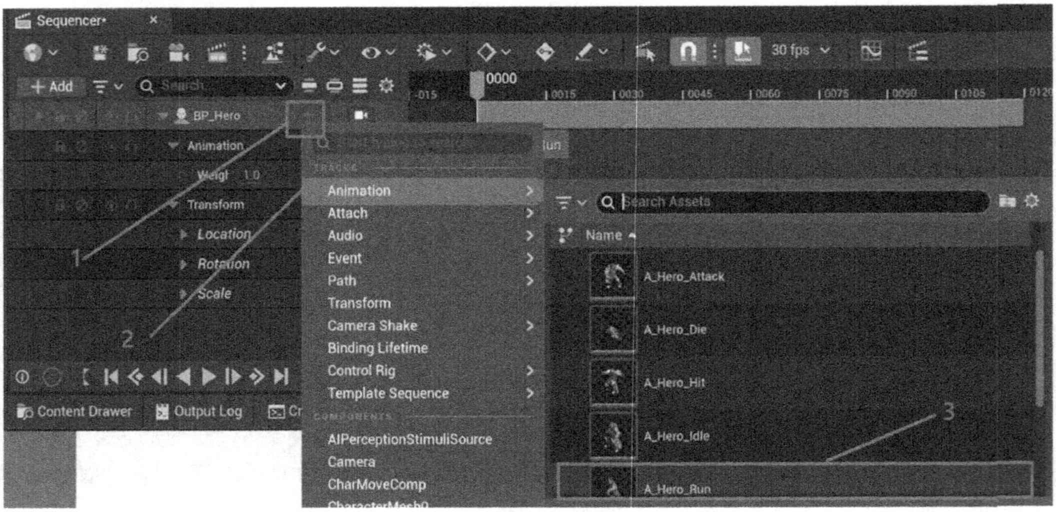

Figure 9.14 - Adding the A_Hero_Run animation to the Sequencer

7. In the **Timeline** section of the **Sequencer**, hover over the right-hand end of the newly created purple **A_Hero_Run** bar (highlighted in *Figure 9.15*) and drag the end so that the bar stretches to the right and extends to frame **0120**.

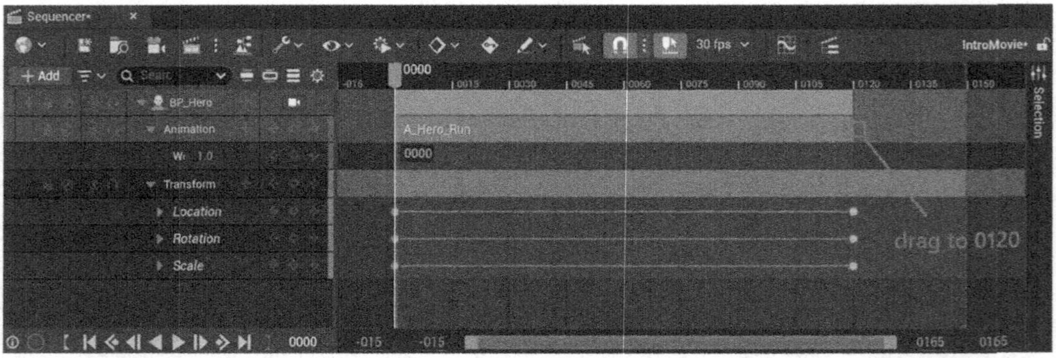

Figure 9.15 - Adjusting the length of the A_Hero_Run animation

8. In the Timeline section of the **Sequencer**, move the red **Playhead** pointer to the end of the **Animation** track by setting it to `0120`.

9. Move the red **Playhead** to frame **0090** and press the + button beside the **Animation** to add a new `A_Hero_Idle` animation (see *Figure 9.16*).

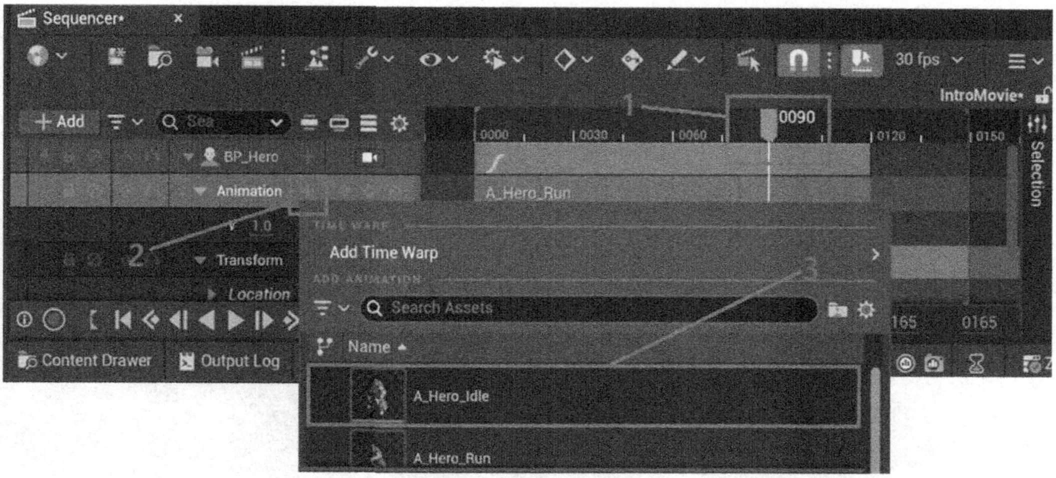

Figure 9.16 - Adding the A_Hero_Idle animation to the Sequencer

10. In the Timeline section of the **Sequencer**, drag the newly created `A_Hero_Idle` bar to the left, making sure to stay on the same **Animation** track, so that it overlaps the existing `A_Hero_Run` bar and starts at frame **0090** with the two animations merging into each other (see *Figure 9.17*). This overlapping area illustrates that the system will blend the two animations and generate a smooth transition from the running animation to the idling animation.

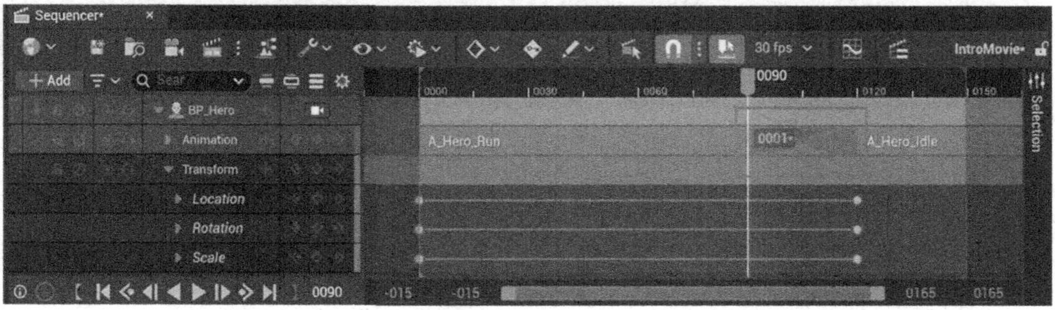

Figure 9.17 - Merging the transition between the A_Hero_Run and A_Hero_Idle animations

11. In the Timeline section of the **Sequencer**, right-click the `A_Hero_Run` animation bar, select **Properties** in the pop-up list that appears (**1** in *Figure 9.18*). Then, in the window to the right of the list, open the **Playback** dropdown and ensure that the **Force Custom Mode** property is checked. This allows the **Sequencer** to override the character's standard Animation Blueprint, which has control over the animation by default.

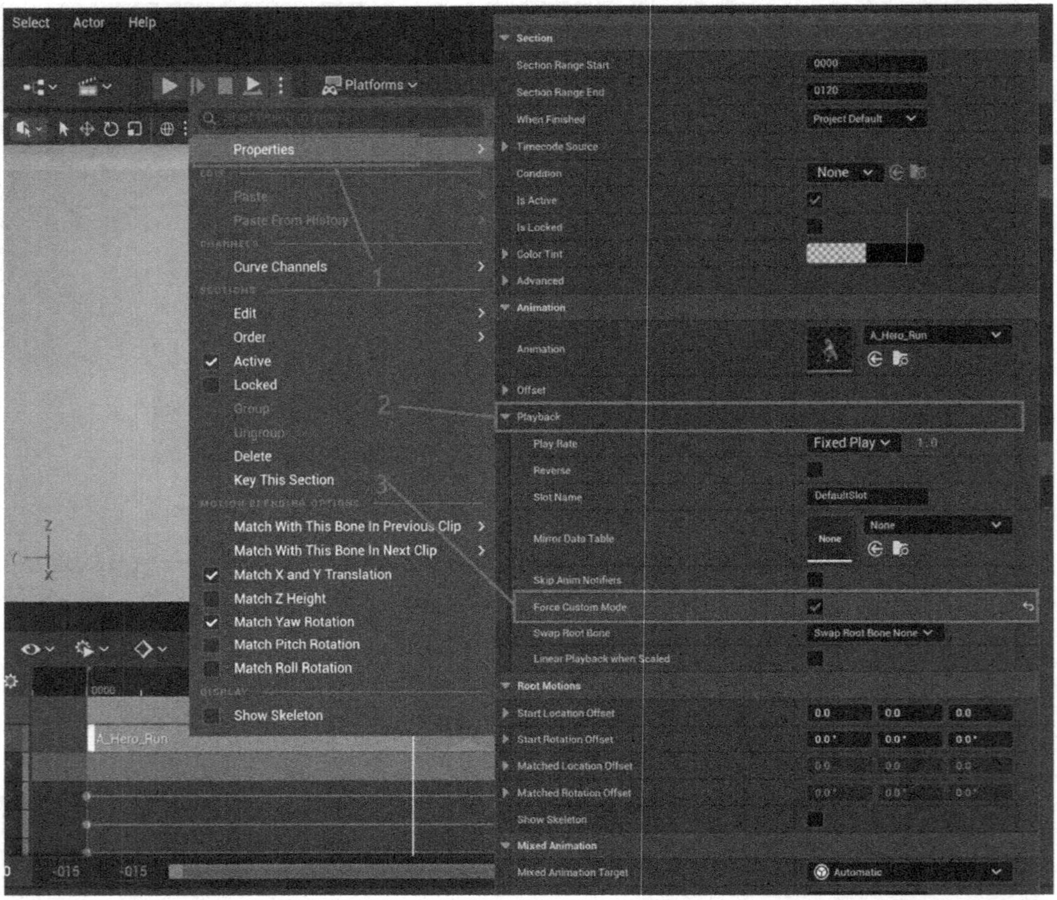

Figure 9.18 - Setting the Force Custom Mode property on the A_Hero_Run animation

12. Repeat *step 11* for the `A_Hero_Idle` animation bar, to allow the **Sequencer** to also override control of that animation.

With the Hero animation now added to the Level Sequence, you will move on to setting up the cinematic camera that will be used to display the *Pangaea* cut-scene movie sequence.

> **Note**
>
> **Cinematic versus Gameplay Cameras**
>
> In Unreal Engine, the fundamental difference between a **Cine Camera (CineCameraActor)** and a standard **Gameplay Camera** comes down to cinematic realism versus player function.

A **Gameplay Camera** is built for performance and responsive control; it features a basic digital lens designed to follow a character seamlessly through the world while giving the player a wide, clear view of the action.

In contrast, a **Cine Camera** is designed to mimic real-world Hollywood movie equipment. It introduces sophisticated physical camera attributes (such as customizable sensor sizes, focal lengths, lens presets, and an advanced tracking system) that allow you to pull focus dynamically, creating a shallow depth-of-field where the background is beautifully blurred to pull the audience's eyes to a specific narrative detail.

While you can animate a basic gameplay camera in **Sequencer**, using a **Cine Camera Actor** is the standard for cut-scenes because it instantly elevates the artistic mood and overall production value of your cinematic storytelling.

Setting up the cinematic camera

A great cut-scene needs a dynamic camera. Follow these steps to create a Cine Camera Actor and animate the camera's movement in the scene:

1. In the **Sequencer**'s toolbar, click the **Create a new camera** icon (highlighted red in *Figure 9.19*). This will automatically create a **CineCameraActor** camera in the level, and a related **Camera Cuts** track in the **Sequencer**'s Track List.

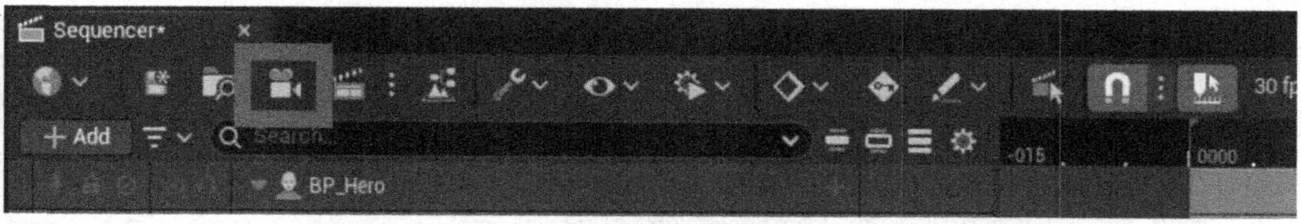

Figure 9.19 - Adding the Cinematic Camera to the Sequencer

2. In the **Outliner**, rename the **CineCameraActor** camera to `IntroCamera`.
3. In the Timeline section of the **Sequencer**, move the red **Playhead** pointer back to the starting frame of **0000**.
4. In the **Outliner**, select the `IntroCamera` camera, and in the **Details** panel, set the following values:
   - Set the **Location** coordinates to (`16662`, `-15238`, `2691`)
   - Set the **Rotation** values to (`0`, `-7.4`, `158`)

5. In the Track List section of the **Sequencer**, select the `IntroCamera` track (**1** in *Figure 9.20*), and make sure that the camera's **lock toggle** icon (**2** in *Figure 9.20*) is unlocked so that you can change the camera's **Transform** properties and reposition the camera.

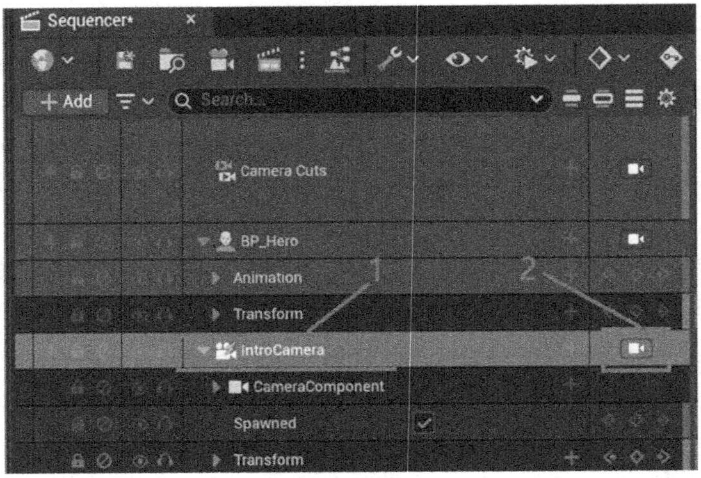

Figure 9.20 - Unlock the IntroCamera track in the Sequencer

6. In the Track List section of the **Sequencer**, select the **Transform** track that is located under the **IntroCamera** track and click the **Add Keyframe** button to create a keyframe that stores the initial **Location**, **Rotation**, and **Scale** of the **IntroCamera** in the cinematic sequence.

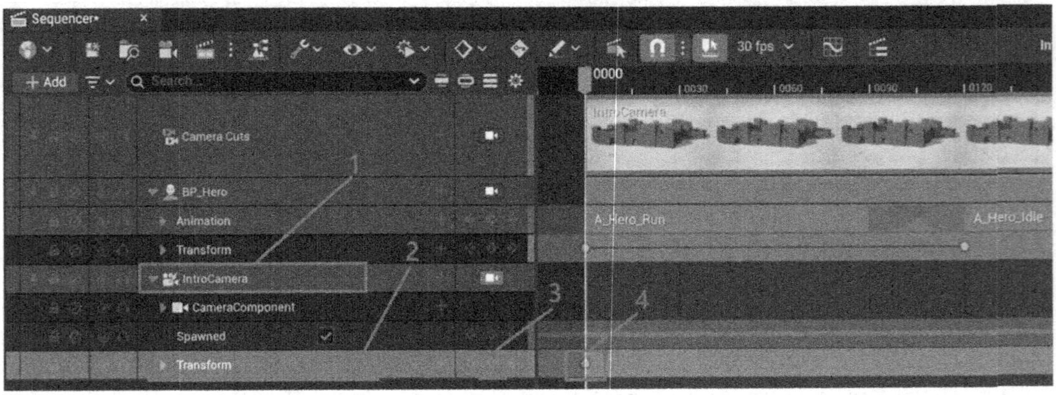

Figure 9.21 - Adding the initial IntroCamera Transform keyframe to the Sequencer

7. Click the **Save Sequencer** button (highlighted in *Figure 9.22*) at the top of the **Sequencer** toolbar to save the **Sequencer** in its current state.

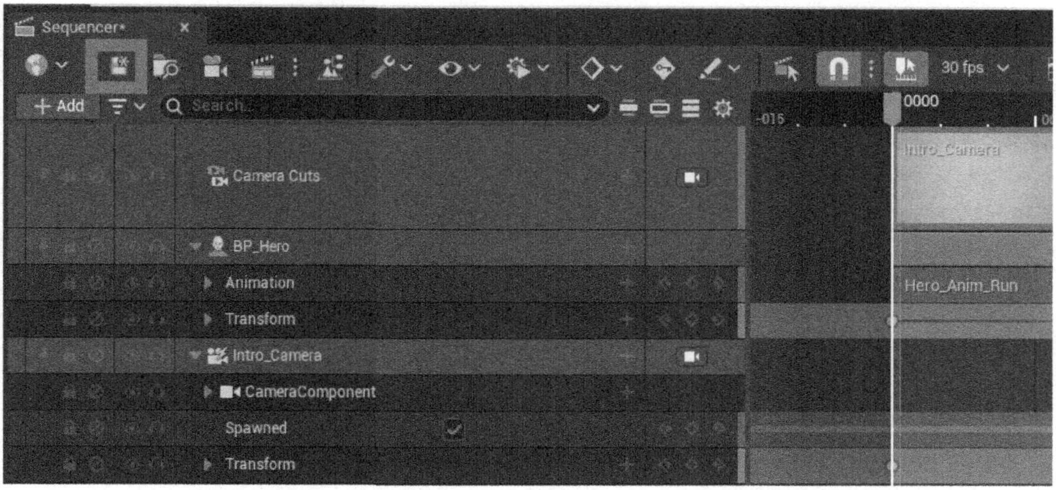

Figure 9.22 - Save Sequencer button

With your first **IntroCamera Transform** keyframes created (4 in *Figure 9.21*) and the **Location** and **Rotation** values set in the **Details** panel, you have now configured the starting position for the cut-scene camera within the animation sequence. You will now move on to create a further two positions that the camera will move through as it progresses through the cut-scene.

1. In the Timeline section of the **Sequencer**, move the red **Playhead** pointer to frame **0073**.
2. In the **Outliner**, select the **IntroCamera** camera, and in the **Details** panel, set the following values:
    - Set the **Location** coordinates to (`7758, -9647, 600`)
    - Set the **Rotation** values to (`0, -14, 168`)
3. In the Track List section of the **Sequencer**, select the **Transform** track that is located under the **IntroCamera** track, and click the **Add Keyframe** button to create a second keyframe that will store the second position of the **IntroCamera** in the cinematic sequence (highlighted in *Figure 9.23*).

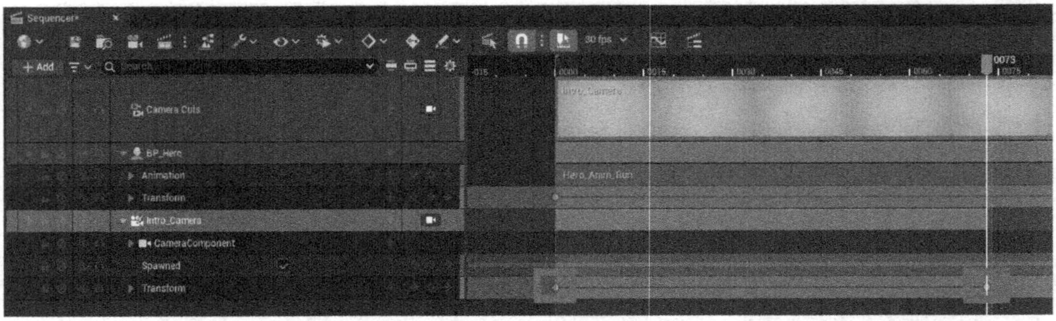

Figure 9.23 - Adding the second IntroCamera Transform keyframe to the Sequencer

4. Click the **Save Sequencer** button (highlighted in *Figure 9.22*) at the top of the **Sequencer** toolbar to save the **Sequencer** in its current state.
5. In the Timeline section of the **Sequencer**, move the red **Playhead** pointer to frame **0120**.
6. In the **Outliner**, select the **IntroCamera** camera, and in the **Details** panel**,** set the following values:
   - Set the **Location** coordinates to (`7360`, `-9094`, `860`)
   - Set the **Rotation** values to (`0`, `-19`, `177`)
7. In the Track List section of the **Sequencer**, select the Transform track under the **IntroCamera** track, and click the **Add Keyframe** button to create the third keyframe.
8. Click the **Save Sequencer** button to save the **Sequencer** in its current state.
   You should now have created the **IntroCamera** movement animation, with three keyframes defining the camera's location and rotation over time, as shown in *Figure 9.24*:

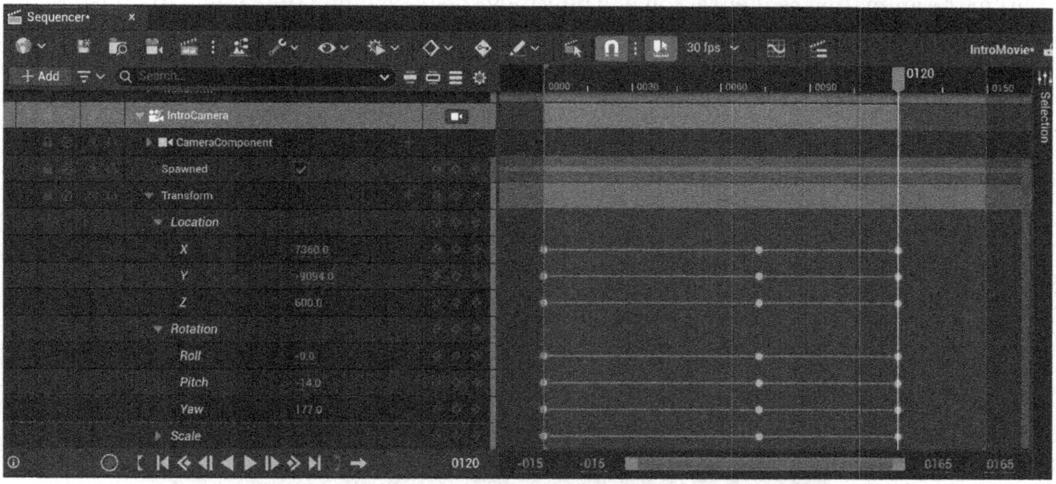

Figure 9.24 - The IntroCamera with three keyframes

9. In the **Outliner**, select the **IntroCamera** camera, and in the **Details** panel, under the **Camera Options** header, uncheck the **Constrain Aspect Ratio** checkbox to ensure the cinematic fills the entire player's screen.

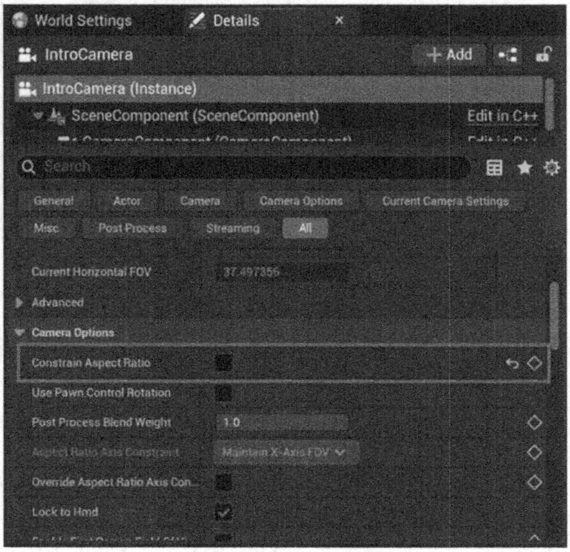

Figure 9.25 - Disabling the Constrain Aspect Ratio property on the IntroCamera

10. Click the **Save Sequencer** button to save the **Sequencer** in its current state.

With three sets of `IntroCamera` **Transform** keyframes created and the **Location** and **Rotation** values set in the **Details** panel, you have now configured all positions for the cut-scene camera within the animation sequence. You will now move on to enabling the camera to transition to gameplay as the cut-scene ends.

Transitioning to Gameplay

The goal of an intro cinematic is to hand control over to the player seamlessly, which will be achieved in the following steps:

1. In the Track List section of the **Sequencer**, select the **Transform** track that is located under the **BP_Hero** track.
2. In the Timeline section of the **Sequencer**, right-click the **Transform** bar, select **Properties** in the pop-up list that appears (see *Figure 9.26*), then set **When Finished** to **Keep State** in the dropdown list for that property. This prevents the Hero from snapping back to their original position when the movie ends.

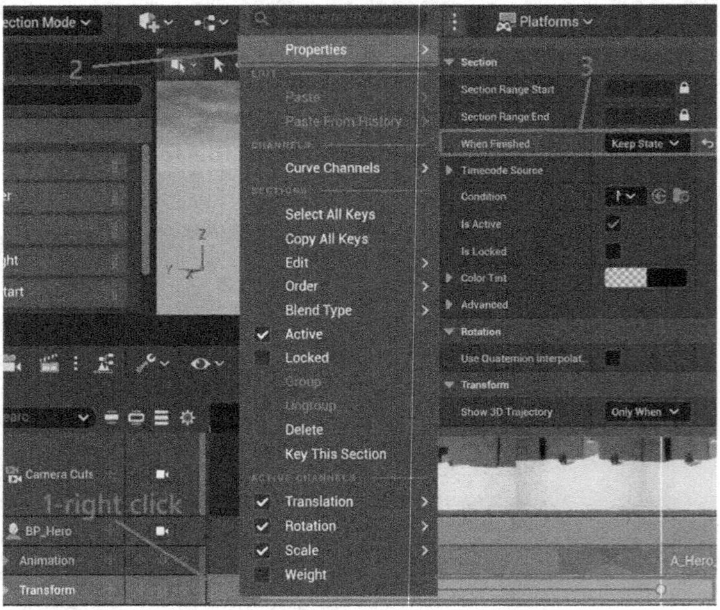

Figure 9.26 - Setting the When Finished property of the BP_Hero to Keep State

3. In the Track List section of the **Sequencer**, right-click on the **Camera Cuts** track (see *Figure 9.27*) and check the **Can Blend** checkbox to enable **Camera Blending**. This property allows you to create smooth visual transitions directly between different cameras in your timeline. We will use this technique in the next step to transition from our cinematic cut-scene camera back to the player's follow camera.

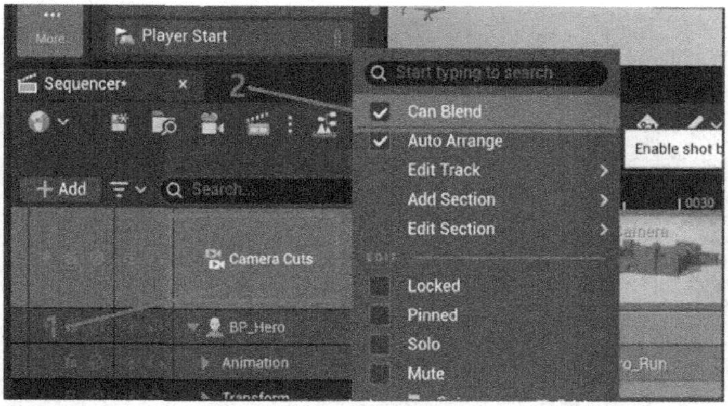

Figure 9.27 - Enabling the Can Blend property of the Camera Cuts track

4. In the Timeline section of the **Sequencer**, ensure the **Camera Cuts** section extends to at least frame **0135** first, and the **Camera Cuts' Can Blend flag** is set to `true`. Select the **Camera Cuts** bar and then drag the *yellow* triangle at the end of the **Camera Cuts** bar inwards to frame **0135**. This will create a "fade" or "blend" camera transition to smoothly interpolate from the cinematic camera back to the player's follow camera.

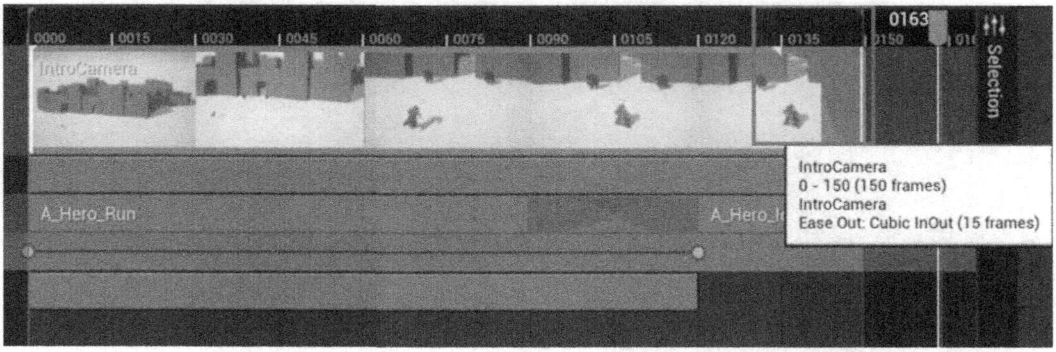

Figure 9.28 - Creating a fade transition to the Gameplay Camera from the Camera Cuts track

5. In the Timeline section of the **Sequencer**, right-click the **BP_Hero** track, select **Convert Selected Binding(s) To** in the pop-up list that appears, and then select **Spawnable Actor**.

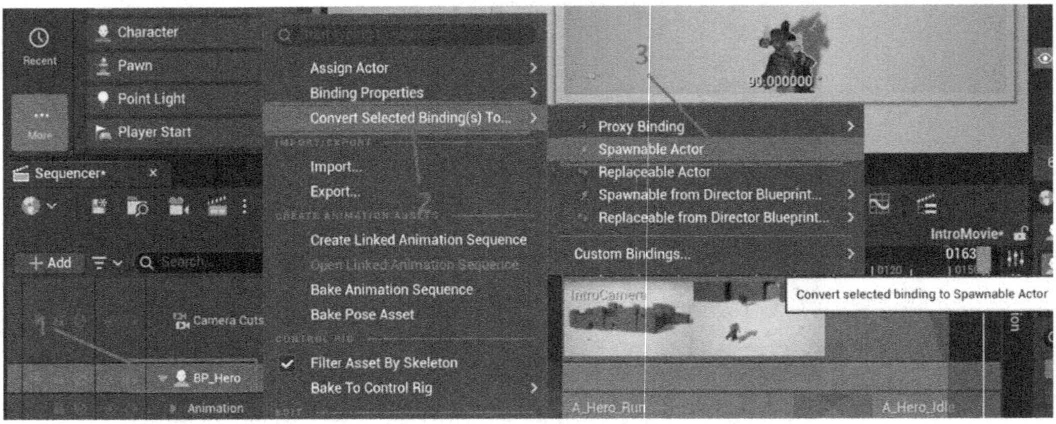

Figure 9.29 - Converting the BP_Hero binding to Spawnable Actor

6. In the Timeline section of the **Sequencer**, right-click the **BP_Hero** track, select **Convert Selected Binding(s) To** in the pop-up list that appears, then select **Replaceable from Director Blueprint**, then **Quick Bind**, and finally **Resolve to Player Pawn**. This tells Unreal to use the actual player pawn instead of a cinematic duplicate.

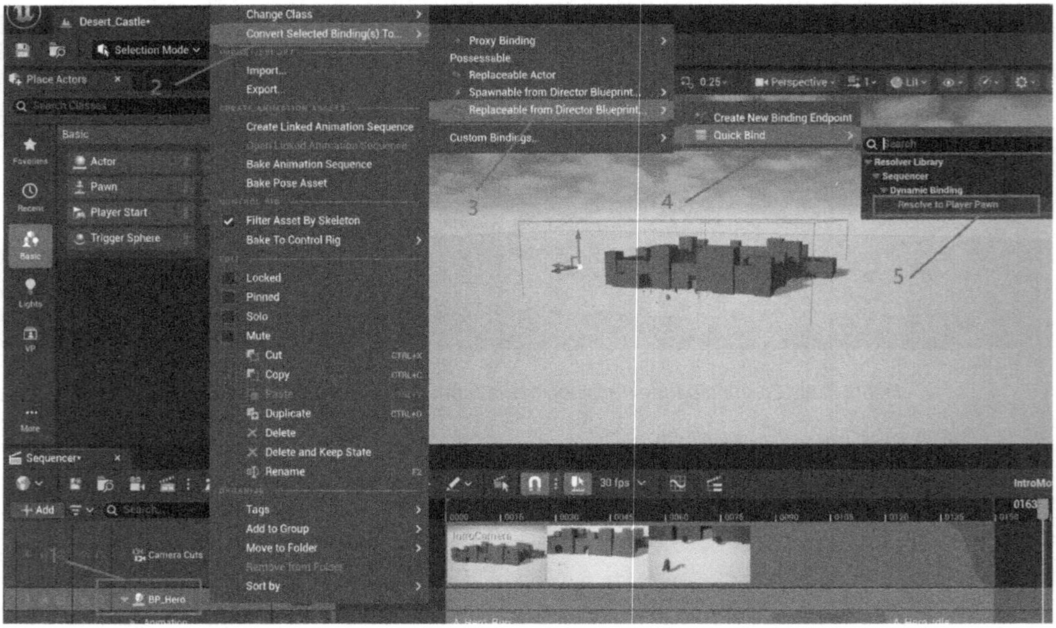

Figure 9.30 - Converting the BP_Hero binding to Resolve to Player Pawn

7. After completing the previous step, a Blueprint titled `IntroMovie_DirectorBP` will have been generated and will open in a new **Blueprint Editor** window (see *Figure 9.31*).

Make no changes to the Blueprint and simply save it and close the **Blueprint Editor** window.

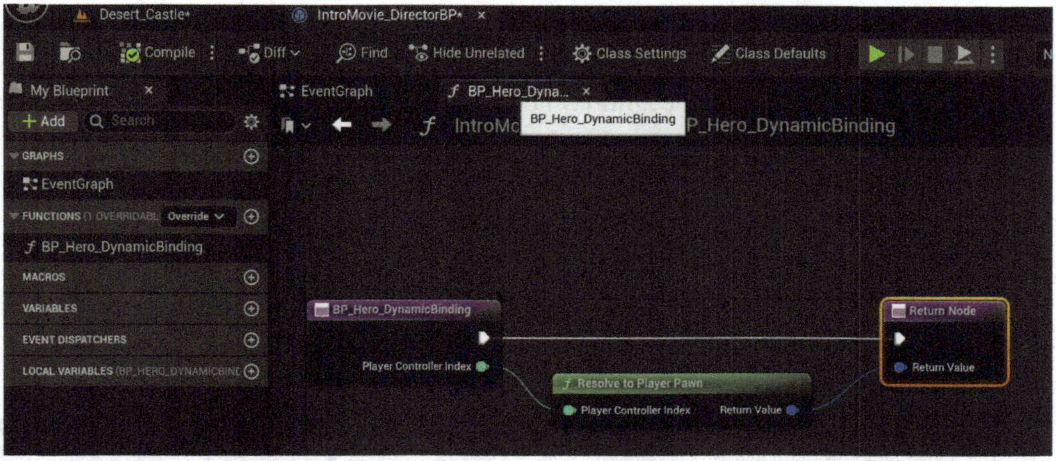

Figure 9.31 - The Generated IntroMovie_DirectorBP Blueprint

8. Click the **Save Sequencer** button to save the **Sequencer** in its current state.

Triggering the Sequence via Blueprints

Finally, we must tell the level to play this sequence as soon as the game starts. It is crucial to understand that a **Level Sequence asset** is completely passive by default and that simply creating an intro movie inside the Sequencer Editor does not mean Unreal Engine knows when, or even if, it should play during live gameplay.

When a player launches your game level, the engine executes the default gameplay startup logic – it immediately spawns the playable character at the Player Start location, initializes the user interface, and hands instant movement control over to the player's controller.

If we left things this way, the game would start playing normally in third-person mode while your cinematic intro sat completely ignored in your project files.

To prevent this, we must use the **Level Blueprint** to orchestrate a handoff. Think of the Level Blueprint as the director's cue. By intercepting the engine's standard startup event (**Event BeginPlay**), we can use code to instruct Unreal Engine to temporarily hold back normal player control, generate a Level Sequence Player in the game's memory to run our `IntroMovie` asset, and safely transition the camera and character states only after the cinematic story has been told.

The following node setup establishes this vital link, commanding your passive cinematic timeline to take center stage the exact millisecond the level loads.

1. Open the Level Blueprint that is associated with the `Desert_Castle` level.
2. In the **Level Blueprint Editor**, some HUD-related nodes will always be present that are triggered from the **Event BeginPlay** node. The playing of the sequence will be triggered after the HUD nodes have completed, so drag the *white* execution pin from the output of the **Add to Viewport** node and drop it in the graph window.
3. Search for the **Create Level Sequence Player** node and select it. This will create a **Create Level Sequence Player** node and connect it to the **Add to Viewport** node with a *white* wire (see *Figure 9.32*).
4. Inside the **Create Level Sequence Player** node, set the value of the **Level Sequence** dropdown to **IntroMovie**, as shown in *Figure 9.32*.

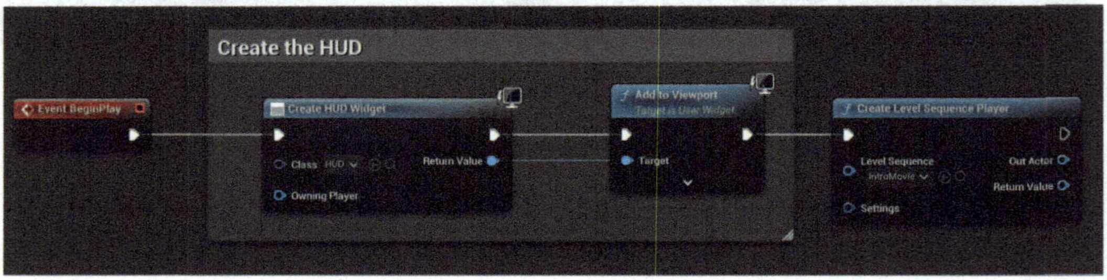

Figure 9.32 - Creating the IntroMovie sequence player

5. Drag the *white* execution pin from the output of the **Create Level Sequence Player** node and drop it in the graph window.
6. Search for the `Play` node and select it. This will create a **Play** node and connect it to the **Create Level Sequence Player** node with a *white* wire (see *Figure 9.33*).
7. Drag the blue **Return Value** pin from the output of the **Create Level Sequence Player** node and connect it to the **Target** input of the **Play** node to connect it with a blue wire.

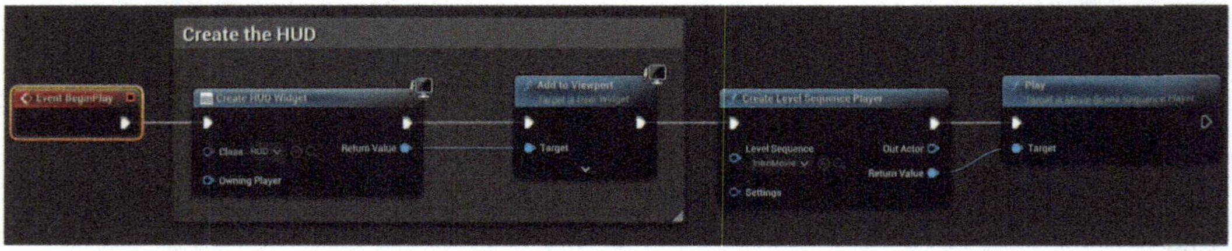

Figure 9.33 - Playing IntroMovie sequence

8. Click the **Compile** button and the **Save** button and then close the **Blueprint Editor**.
9. Finally, click the **Play** button, and you should see your cinematic intro play through, with the Hero running toward the castle, and the camera gliding into position.

This chapter provided you with an understanding of how to create in-game cinematic cut-scenes using the **Sequencer**, with a hands-on tutorial that enabled you to create an introductory cut-scene for the *Pangaea* game. With this knowledge, you will now be able to create your own simple custom cut-scenes for your projects.

Summary

In this chapter, you established a comprehensive understanding of cinematic storytelling and time-based animation using the Unreal Engine **Sequencer**. You explored the specialized **Sequencer Editor**, gaining familiarity with its core interface components, including the Track List for managing Actor properties and the Timeline for orchestrating events.

Building on these fundamentals, you mastered the mechanics of keyframe animation, learning how different interpolation modes (such as Linear, Constant, and Cubic) control the "feel" and flow of movement. You examined the essential relationship between the Level Sequence asset, which stores your cinematic data, and the Level Sequence Actor, which serves as the "projector" within your level.

Through a step-by-step hands-on example, you explored the process of creating an introductory cut-scene for your game, implementing character movement with animation and a fly-through camera, configuring this to automatically play at the start of your game and transitioning smoothly over to the gameplay camera.

With the skills learned here, you have the capability to create simple cinematic sequences in Unreal Engine. Gaining expertise in **Sequencer** is essential for high-quality game development, and you are encouraged to research and experiment with this tool further in your own games and projects.

In the next chapter, we explore polishing and packaging your game, replacing prototype elements with the final assets, fixing gameplay issues, adding polish through audio and visual effects, and finally turning the game project into a standalone build that can be run outside of the editor.

Further reading

Please refer to the following to get more information:

- If you would like more detailed information about the **Sequencer Editor**, please refer to the official Unreal Engine documentation at `https://dev.epicgames.com/`

documentation/unreal-engine/sequencer-cinematic-editor-unreal-engine?application_version=5.6.

- If you would like more detailed information about building **cinematics** in Unreal Engine, please refer to the official Unreal Engine documentation at https://dev.epicgames.com/documentation/unreal-engine/cinematics-and-movie-making-in-unreal-engine?application_version=5.6.

10

Polishing and Packaging Your Game

In the previous chapters, we have built the main parts of the *Pangaea* game step by step. You started by installing Unreal Engine and creating your first project. At this point, the project is no longer just a collection of separate Unreal Engine features. It has become a playable game experience. The player can control the Hero character, fight enemies, follow mission objectives, interact with the level, view gameplay information through the HUD, and experience a cinematic introduction before gameplay begins. However, a playable prototype is not the same as a finished game. Before a project is ready to share with others, it usually needs a final pass of polish, cleanup, testing, and packaging.

It's about time to focus on the final stage of the development process. We will continue improving the *Pangaea* project by replacing prototype elements with higher-quality assets, connecting the final gate-opening event, fixing noticeable gameplay issues, and adding basic audio and visual effects. These improvements may not completely change the game's core mechanics, but they make the game feel clearer, more responsive, more engaging, and complete to the player.

After polishing the game, you will learn how to prepare the project for packaging. **Packaging** is the process of turning your Unreal Engine project into a standalone build that can run outside the editor. You will configure important project settings, choose the correct maps, understand the difference between build configurations, and create a Windows build that you can test as a separate executable.

This chapter covers the following topics:

- Polishing the game

- Packaging the game
- Looking ahead

By the end of this chapter, you will have completed a final polish pass on the *Pangaea* project and prepared it as a standalone packaged game. You will also understand the basic steps required to continue improving the project after this book, whether you want to add more levels, expand the combat system, improve the AI, build more advanced UI, or prepare your own Unreal Engine game for release.

Technical requirements

The sample project for this chapter is available for download from the book's GitHub repository and branch:

- `Chapter10-Start` **branch**: This branch holds the game project with everything you need to start learning in this chapter.
- `Chapter10-Start-Castle` **branch**: This branch builds on the `Chapter10-Start` branch and already includes the `Desert Castle` assets imported into the project. This saves you time if you are unable to access the Epic Games Fab store to download and install the package yourself. You can simply start from this branch.
- `Chapter10` **branch**: This branch contains the completed game project for this chapter, which includes the introductory cut-scene for the `Desert Castle` level.

You can download the example project and code files for this book by following the instructions in the *Download the example code/resource files* section in the *Preface* of this book.

This chapter's code/resource files are included in the downloadable code/resource bundle.

Polishing the game

In the previous chapters, we focused on building the core systems of the *Pangaea* project. We created a playable Hero character, added player input, built enemy AI, designed the game UI, implemented gameplay objectives, and added an introductory cut-scene. These systems gave the project its main gameplay structure. The player can now enter the `Desert Castle` level, fight enemies, follow objectives, and complete the mission.

However, when developing a game, getting the core systems working is only one part of the process. Once the game is playable, the next step is to make it feel more complete, more readable, and more satisfying to play. This is where polishing becomes important. **Polishing** means improving the player's experience by refining what is already there. It may involve replacing temporary assets, connecting unfinished gameplay events, fixing noticeable problems, improving feedback, or adding small presentation details that make the game feel more responsive.

In this section, we will polish the *Pangaea* project on various features. We will start to improve the visual quality of the `Desert Castle` level by importing higher-quality environment assets. Then, we will connect the final gate-opening event so that the gate properly responds to the gameplay objective logic created earlier. After that, we will fix a few noticeable gameplay issues, including camera problems and animation state problems that can appear during combat.

Once the main issues are resolved, we will add basic audio effects to make the game feel more alive. Background music can help set the atmosphere of the level, while sound effects such as footsteps and attack sounds can give the player clearer feedback during gameplay.

Finally, we will add a simple visual effect to the Hero's sword attack by creating a Niagara-based sword trail. This will make the attack animation easier to read and more visually satisfying.

Polishing usually happens after the main gameplay systems have stabilized. If you polish too early, you may spend time improving assets, effects, camera behavior, or presentation details that later need to change when the gameplay structure changes.

In *Pangaea*, the core systems are now already connected: the Hero can move and attack, enemies can patrol and fight, objectives can update, the HUD can display gameplay information, and the level can reach a win or lose condition. Because the main flow is working, this is the right time to refine the player experience without constantly rebuilding the underlying gameplay logic.

Importing high-quality Desert Castle level assets

In *Chapter 2*, we used simple blockout geometry to prototype a basic level. Blockout geometry is useful during early development because it lets you quickly test the size, layout, and gameplay flow of a level without spending too much time on visual details. Later, in *Chapter 8*, we turned the Desert Castle concept into a playable gameplay level with enemies, objectives, the castle gate, and win or lose conditions.

Now that the gameplay structure is working, we can start improving how the level looks. Instead of using only simple placeholder shapes, we will import a higher-quality Desert Castle environment asset and use it to make the level feel closer to a finished game. This process is used to simulate importing artist-created assets in the common workflow in game development: first build and test the level with simple shapes, then replace or enhance those shapes with final art assets after the gameplay direction is clear.

For this chapter, we will use a `Desert Castle` asset from Fab, Epic Games' marketplace for digital content, including Unreal Engine assets. You can search for the asset from the Epic Games Launcher or the **Fab** page, then add it to the *Pangaea* project, as shown in *Figure 10.1* and described in the following steps:

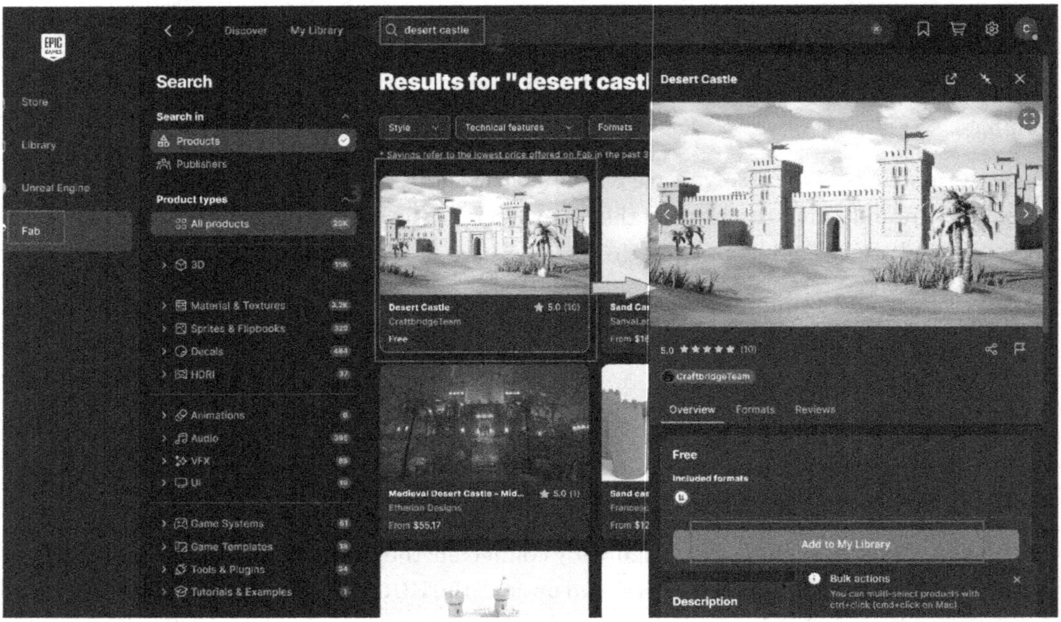

Figure 10.1 - Finding and adding the Desert Castle asset from Fab

1. Open the **Epic Games Launcher**. Select **Fab** from the left-side menu.
2. Search for `desert castle`.
3. Select the `Desert Castle` asset you want to use for this chapter.
4. Add the asset to the `Pangaea` project.
5. Wait for Unreal Engine to download and import the asset files.
6. After the import is complete, open the `Pangaea` project and check the **Content Drawer** for the newly added asset folder.

After the asset is imported into your project, you will see that Fab asset packs usually include multiple meshes, materials, textures, and sometimes example maps. After the asset is added to your project, you can use its meshes to improve the visual quality of the `Desert Castle` level.

If the imported asset pack creates its own folder, you do not need to move every file immediately. However, you should still understand where the meshes, materials, textures, and example levels are stored. Fab assets can contain many files, and each asset pack may organize its content differently.

After the asset is imported, it is useful to briefly inspect the folder structure before placing meshes into the level. This helps you understand which files are environmental meshes, which files are materials or textures, and whether the asset pack includes an example map that can be used as a reference. Use the following steps to understand the folder structure and find the pieces you need:

1. Open the **Content Drawer**.
2. Locate the imported `Desert Castle` asset folder.
3. Open the folder and identify common subfolders such as `Meshes`, `Materials`, `Textures`, `Maps`, or `Demo`, as shown in *Figure 10.2*.
4. Open the example map `Content/Desert_Castle/Maps/Desert_Castle.umap` only as a reference.
5. Return to the *Pangaea* `Desert Castle` level before placing assets.

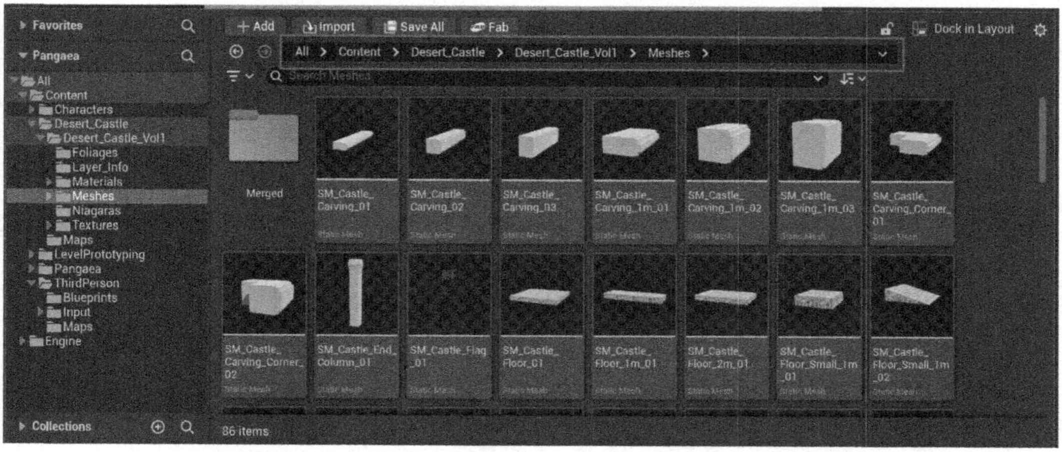

Figure 10.2 - Exploring the folder of Desert Castle level

As you begin replacing the blockout geometry with the imported assets, remember that you do not need to rebuild the entire level from scratch or copy the asset pack's example map. The example map is only a reference that helps you understand how the asset creator organized and used the environment pieces. Your actual work should continue in the *Pangaea* `Desert Castle` level, where you can improve the existing environment while preserving the gameplay flow you have already created. The intro cut-scene, the player's starting position, enemy placement, mission objectives, gate logic, Boss encounter, HUD updates, and win or lose conditions should remain connected to the gameplay flow from *Chapter 9*.

One option to bring in the castle meshes is to open the `Desert_Castle/Maps/Desert_Castle` level, select all the mesh actors, and press *Ctrl* + *C* to copy them. Then, open the `Pangaea/Levels/Desert_Castle` level and press *Ctrl* + *V* to paste the mesh actors.

Another way is to work in small sections one by one manually. Replace one wall, floor, tower, or gate piece, test the result, and then move on to the next piece. This makes it easier to find and fix problems if a new mesh blocks the player, changes the camera behavior, or interrupts the AI navigation.

After placing the real castle walls or gate mesh actors, check the following:

- The player can still move from the starting area toward the castle gate.
- The enemies still have enough space to patrol, chase, and attack.
- The Nav Mesh still covers the areas where AI characters need to move.
- The gate area still lines up with the gameplay objective.
- The camera does not become blocked too often by the new environment geometry.
- The player can still reach the Boss encounter after the gate opens.

Replacing prototype geometry with final assets can sometimes create new gameplay problems. A wall may block the player's path, a decorative object may interfere with AI movement, or a mesh may have a collision that prevents the player from entering an area. These issues are normal during a polish pass. The important habit is to *test the level after each major change instead of replacing everything at once and only testing at the end.*

After importing the `Desert Castle` asset and placing the main environment pieces, save the level and playtest it in the editor. The level should now look more like a real desert fortress while still keeping the gameplay structure you created earlier.

Now you can hide all the prototype shapes during gameplay. Select the shapes, and in the **Details** panel, set **Actor Hidden in Game** to `true`.

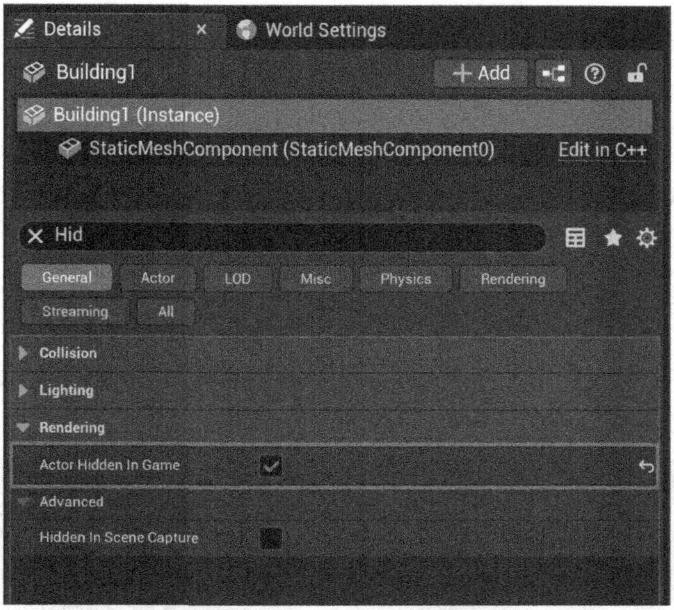

Figure 10.3 - Hiding the prototype shapes in game

In the next section, we will continue this polish pass by connecting the final gate mesh to the gate-opening event from the gameplay objective system.

Hooking up the gate opening event

In *Chapter 8*, we created the gameplay flow for the `Desert Castle` level. The player had to defeat the enemy guards, progress through the mission objectives, and eventually reach the castle entrance. We also prepared the logic for opening the gate, but at that point, the level was still using prototype geometry and temporary objects. Now that we have imported and placed higher-quality `Desert Castle` assets, we can connect the final gate mesh to the gameplay event.

This is an important part of the polishing process. The gameplay logic may already exist, but it needs to be connected to the correct final objects in the level. If the gate-opening event still points to a temporary actor, or if the gate mesh is not assigned correctly, the mission may progress internally, but the player will not see the gate open. In that case, the game logic is working, but the player experience is broken.

Follow the steps below to set up the gates:

1. Select the gate actors: `SM_Great_Wood_Door_Left` and `SM_Great_Wood_Door_Right` in the `Desert Castle` level in the **Outliner**.

2. In the **Details** panel, check the **Transform** section and make sure the **Mobility** setting for both actors is set to `Movable`.

> **Note**
>
> **Static objects** are intended to stay fixed in the level. If you try to move or rotate a static mesh during gameplay, Unreal Engine may ignore the movement or show warnings. Since our gate should open when the player reaches the correct stage of the mission, the gate actor must support runtime movement.

3. Also in the **Details** panel, in the **Transform** section, set the **Rotation** to be (`0`, `0`, `0`) for the two doors, so that the gates are closed by default.

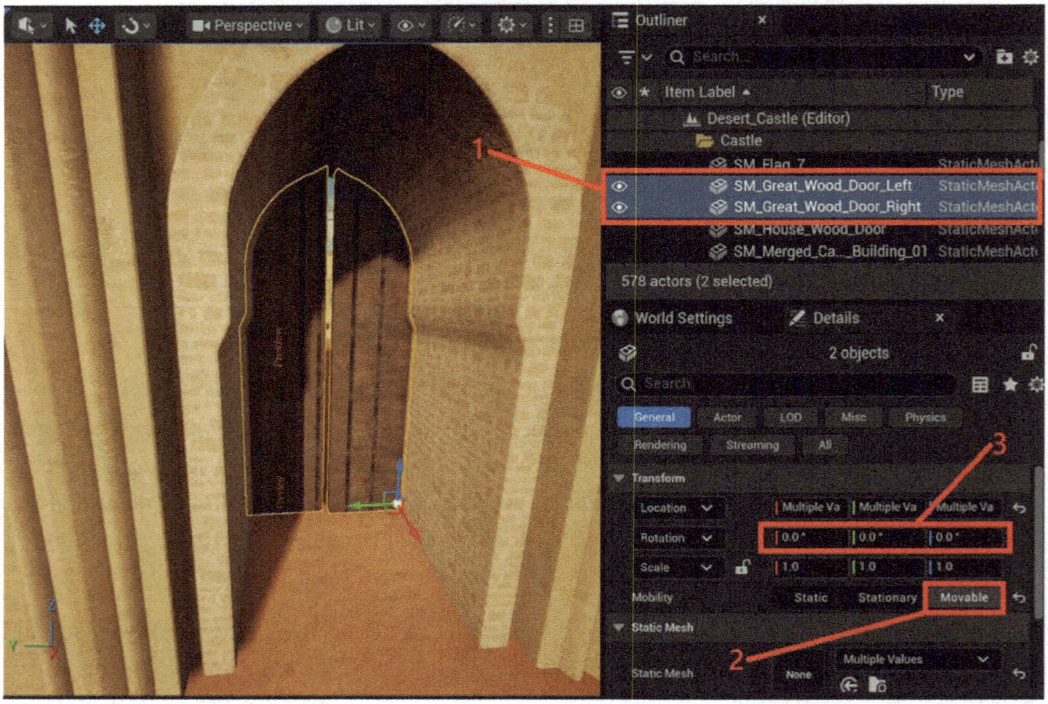

Figure 10.4 - Setting up the gate doors

4. Next, open the Level Blueprint, drag and drop the `SM_Great_Wood_Door_Left` and `SM_Great_Wood_Door_Right` actors from the **Outliner** onto the Level Blueprint's **Event Graph**. Then connect them to the **Target** pins of the **Set Actor Relative Rotation** nodes.

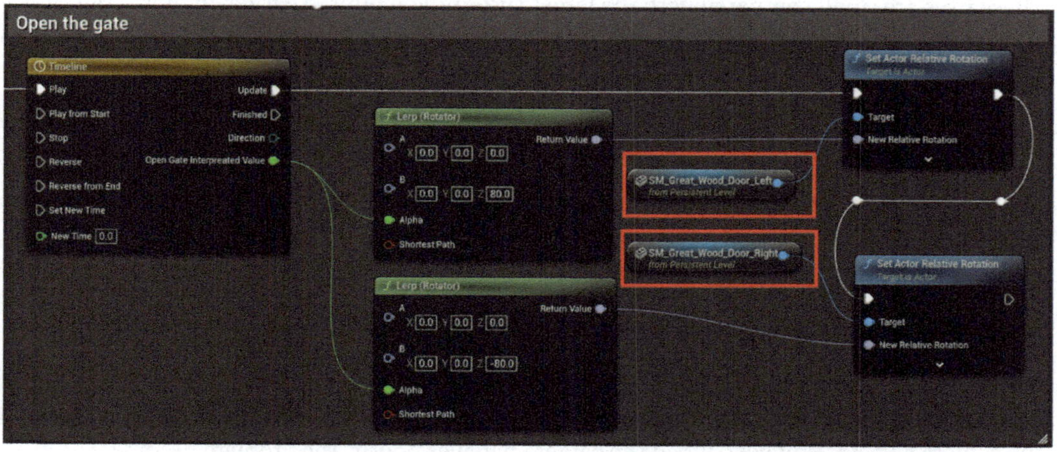

Figure 10.5 - Hooking up the gate doors with the rotation interpolation Blueprint

After replacing prototype assets and connecting the final gate-opening event, the `Desert Castle` level should look and feel closer to a complete game. However, as the project becomes more polished visually, small gameplay issues can become easier to notice. Problems that were acceptable during the prototype stage may now feel distracting because the rest of the game looks more complete. Next, we will try to fix some noticeable glitches.

Fixing noticeable glitches

This is a normal part of game development. When you improve one part of a game, it often reveals issues in another part. For example, after adding more detailed castle walls, towers, and props, the camera may collide with the environment more often. After improving the combat experience, repeated attack input may reveal animation state problems that were not obvious before. These kinds of issues are not always caused by new systems. They often appear because the game is now being tested more like a real game instead of a simple tutorial prototype.

In this section, we will fix two noticeable types of glitches in the *Pangaea* project:

- First, we will adjust the camera behavior so that the camera is less likely to cut through characters or create uncomfortable viewing angles during gameplay. A camera problem can quickly make a third-person game feel difficult to control, especially when the player is fighting enemies near walls or in tight spaces.
- Next, we will fix an animation problem related to the attack action. If the player triggers another attack while the previous attack animation is still transitioning back to the normal movement state, the character can become stuck or behave incorrectly. To solve this, we will add a simple action state check, so the character knows when it is currently attacking and when it is allowed to accept another attack command.

These fixes are small compared with the larger systems you built in earlier chapters, but they are important because they improve the stability and feel of the game. A polished game is not only about better assets, audio, and visual effects. It also needs to handle common player behavior reliably, especially when the player moves quickly, presses buttons repeatedly, or fights enemies in different parts of the level.

By the end of this section, the camera and attack animation behavior will feel more stable, and the *Pangaea* project will be better prepared for the final audio, visual effect, and packaging steps.

Fixing the camera problem

A third-person game depends heavily on a stable and readable camera. When the camera works well, the player can focus on movement, combat, and objectives without thinking about the camera system. However, when the camera behaves poorly, the problem becomes noticeable very quickly. The player may lose sight of the Hero character, see through walls, look inside a character mesh, or rotate the camera at an angle that makes combat difficult to read.

After replacing the prototype Desert Castle geometry with higher-quality environment assets, camera issues may become easier to notice. The new castle walls, towers, gates, stairs, and props can create tighter spaces than the simple blockout geometry. As a result, the camera may collide with the environment more often or move too close to the player character during gameplay. In this subsection, we will address two common third-person camera problems: camera clipping and camera rotation range.

Fixing camera clipping

Camera clipping happens when the camera cuts through another object. This may be a wall, a pillar, a gate, an enemy character, or even the Hero character's own body. When this happens, the player may see the inside of a mesh or temporarily lose a clear view of the action. This is especially distracting during combat because the player needs to clearly see the Hero, the enemy, and the surrounding environment.

As discussed in *Chapter 5* when we created the Hero character, Unreal Engine's third-person character setup usually attaches the camera to a **Spring Arm** component. The Spring Arm works like a camera boom that keeps the camera at a fixed distance behind the character. Instead of placing the camera directly on the character, the **Spring Arm** creates space between the character and the camera.

More importantly, it can also perform collision tests. If an obstacle is detected between the character and the camera, the Spring Arm can shorten itself automatically, so the camera moves closer to the character instead of passing through the obstacle.

To adjust the camera collision behavior, follow these steps (see *Figure 10.6*):

1. Open `BP_Hero`.
2. In the **Components** panel, select the camera boom or **Spring Arm** component.
3. In the **Details** panel, find the **Camera Collision** section.
4. Make sure **Do Collision Test** is enabled.
5. Check the **Probe Channel** setting and make sure it uses the **Camera** collision channel that can detect the environment objects in the level.
6. Adjust the **Probe Size** value if the camera still cuts through nearby objects (the variation in the **Probe Size** value is explained in the subsequent paragraphs).

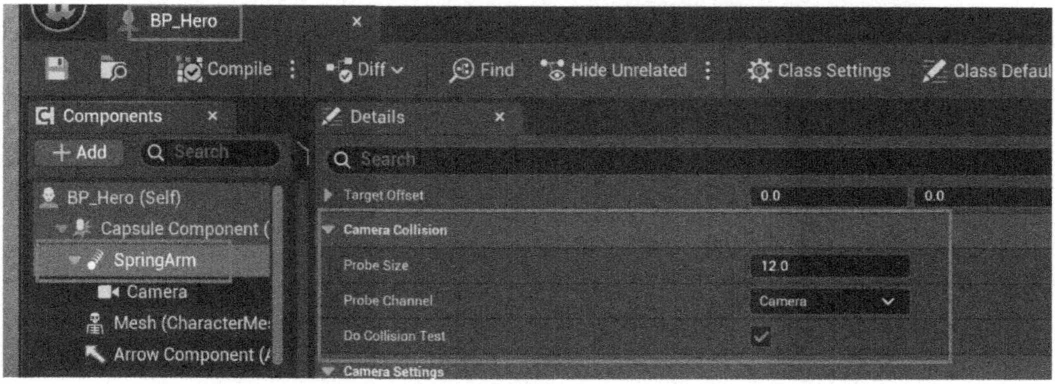

Figure 10.6 - Making sure collision test is on

7. Compile and save the Blueprint.
8. Play the level and move the Hero near walls, towers, the castle gate, and other large objects to test the camera.

When the **Do Collision Test** is enabled, Unreal Engine checks whether the normal camera position is blocked. If the camera is placed inside or behind an obstacle, the **Spring Arm** shortens temporarily and moves the camera closer to the Hero. This prevents the camera from passing through many common objects in the environment, such as walls, towers, pillars, and props.

The **Probe Size** value controls the size of the collision test used by the **Spring Arm**. If the value is too small, the camera may still get very close to walls before reacting. If the value is too large, the camera may pull in too aggressively and feel unstable. There is no single perfect value for every game, so you should test this setting in different areas of the `Desert Castle` level.

For *Pangaea*, test the camera in the following places:

- Near the castle gate
- Along narrow paths or corridors
- Close to large walls and towers
- Around decorative props
- During combat with Warrok enemies
- Near the Boss encounter area

Another camera problem can happen when the camera moves too close to the Hero character. Even if the **Spring Arm** prevents the camera from passing through walls, the camera may still move close enough that the player sees part of the Hero's body or weapon from the inside. For a beginner project, the simplest solution is usually to adjust the camera collision behavior by tuning the **Spring Arm** length, camera offset, and collision settings just introduced. You should also avoid placing important combat encounters in spaces that are too narrow for the third-person camera to work comfortably.

In some cases, the issue may not be caused only by the camera. A wall, pillar, or prop may be placed too close to the main gameplay path. If the camera repeatedly becomes blocked in the same location, consider slightly moving the environment object or widening the playable space. Camera polish often requires small adjustments to both the character camera settings and the level layout.

Restricting the camera rotation range

In addition to camera clipping, another common third-person camera issue is allowing the player to rotate the camera too far upward or downward. If the vertical rotation range is too wide, the player may accidentally look almost straight up into the sky or too far downward into the Hero's body or the ground. These extreme angles can make movement and combat harder to read, especially in tight areas near castle walls or during close-range fights.

To improve the gameplay experience, we can restrict the camera's vertical rotation range. This does not remove camera control from the player. Instead, it prevents the camera from reaching angles that are uncomfortable or unhelpful during gameplay.

Camera rotation is usually made up of three axes:

- **Yaw**: Rotating left and right
- **Pitch**: Rotating up and down
- **Roll**: Tilting sideways

For this fix, we are mainly concerned with pitch, because pitch controls how far the camera can look up or down. In most third-person action games, yaw should remain free so the player can look around the character, but pitch should be limited to a comfortable range.

Figure 10.7 shows the Blueprint version of this setup. Notice how the look input is read from **HeroLook**, the current **Spring Arm** rotation is separated with **Break Rotator**, the pitch value is limited with **Clamp (Float)**, and the final rotation is applied back to the **Spring Arm** with **Set Relative Rotation**.

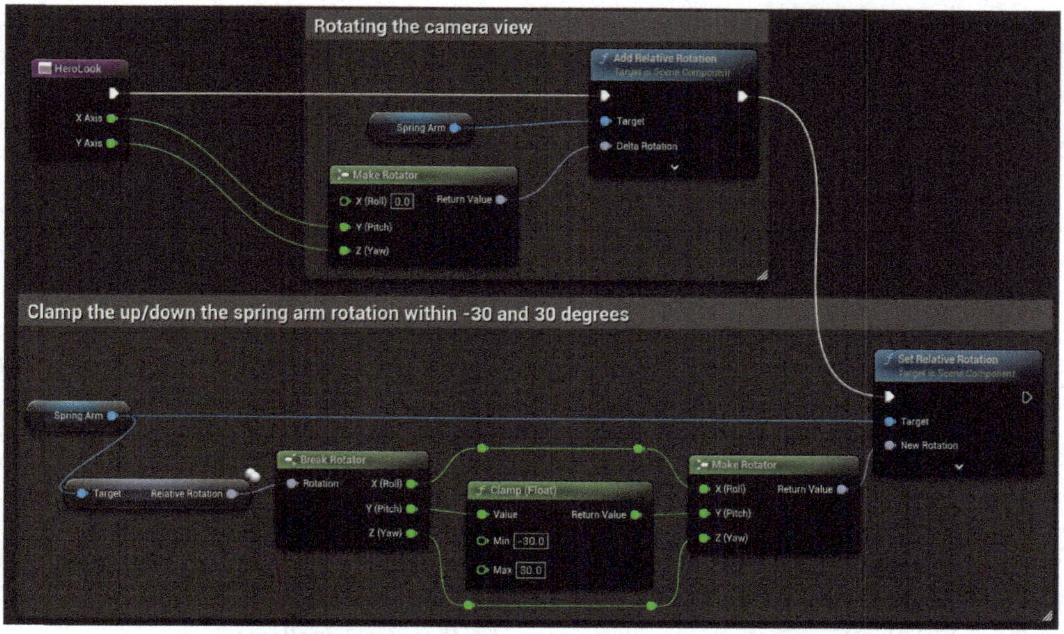

Figure 10.7 - Limiting the camera pitch rotation in BP_Hero

The important part of this setup is the **Clamp (Float)** node. It limits the pitch value before the Blueprint applies the new rotation to the Spring Arm. This prevents the camera from rotating too far upward or downward while still allowing the player to control the camera normally.

The exact minimum and maximum values depend on the game. A larger range gives the player more freedom, while a smaller range keeps the camera more controlled. For *Pangaea*, the goal is to allow the player to look up and down enough to understand the environment, but not so far that the camera becomes difficult to use during combat.

After applying the pitch clamp, test the camera in normal gameplay situations. Try rotating the camera upward and downward while moving and attacking. The camera should now stop at a comfortable upper and lower limit instead of rotating into extreme angles.

When testing camera fixes, do not only test in an open area. A third-person camera may feel fine in a wide space but become difficult to use near walls, props, enemies, or narrow paths. Remember to *always test the camera along the actual gameplay route the player will follow.*

After these changes, the *Pangaea* camera should behave more reliably around walls, gates, enemies, and tight spaces. The **Spring Arm** collision settings help prevent the camera from cutting through the environment, while the pitch restriction prevents uncomfortable vertical viewing angles. Together, these adjustments make exploration and combat easier to read.

In the next subsection, we will fix another noticeable gameplay issue: the Hero's attack animation can become stuck when repeated attack input happens at the wrong time.

Fixing the character animation freezing problem

The character animation may freeze if the Hero starts an attack or gets hit while the animation state is transitioning to the Locomotion state (`AnimState = 0`) from the previous Attack state (`AnimState = 1`) or Hit state (`AnimState = 2`).

An example to trigger this problem is when the Hero begins an attack, then the player quickly presses the attack button again before the animation has fully returned to the Locomotion state. If the Blueprint allows every attack input to start a new attack immediately, the character can become stuck in an incorrect animation state. This kind of bug often appears only after players begin testing the game more aggressively, because real players may press buttons faster or more often than expected.

To fix this issue, we need to add an extra animation state. The idea is straightforward: while the Hero is already attacking, it should not be allowed to start another attack. When the attack animation reaches the correct ending point, and the transition back to the Locomotion state has finished, the Hero can return to a state where another attack is allowed.

In our project, we already use the `AnimState` value to control whether the Hero is idle, attacking, or in another animation state. The attack input should only be accepted when `AnimState` is 0, which represents the idle or ready state. If `AnimState` is not 0, the Hero is already busy with another action, so the Blueprint should not start a new attack.

To update the attack state logic, follow these steps:

1. Open the **BP_Hero** Blueprint.
2. Navigate to the `Attack` function.
3. Find the condition that checks whether the Hero is allowed to attack.
4. Make sure the attack can only start when `AnimState` is equal to `0`.

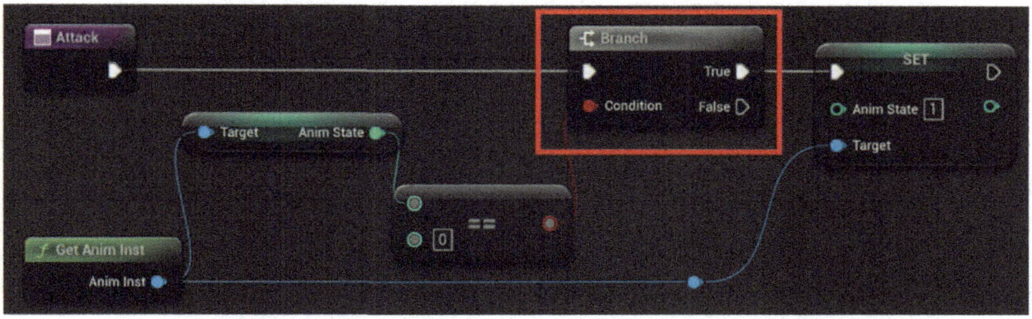

Figure 10.8 - Prevent Hero from performing the attack when AnimState is not 0

This prevents a new attack from starting while the Hero is already in the attack state. However, we also need to control what happens when the attack animation finishes.

Currently, the Blueprint may have set `AnimState` directly back to `0` when the attack finished. That can cause a problem because the attack animation may still be transitioning to the locomotion state. If the player presses the attack button during this short transition, the animation system may receive a new attack command before the previous animation has fully returned to a safe state. The solution to this problem is to set `AnimState` to `10` instead of `0` when the `EndofAttack1` Animation Notify is received. This value represents a short transition state after the attack. Since `AnimState` is no longer `0`, the player cannot issue a new attack during this transition period.

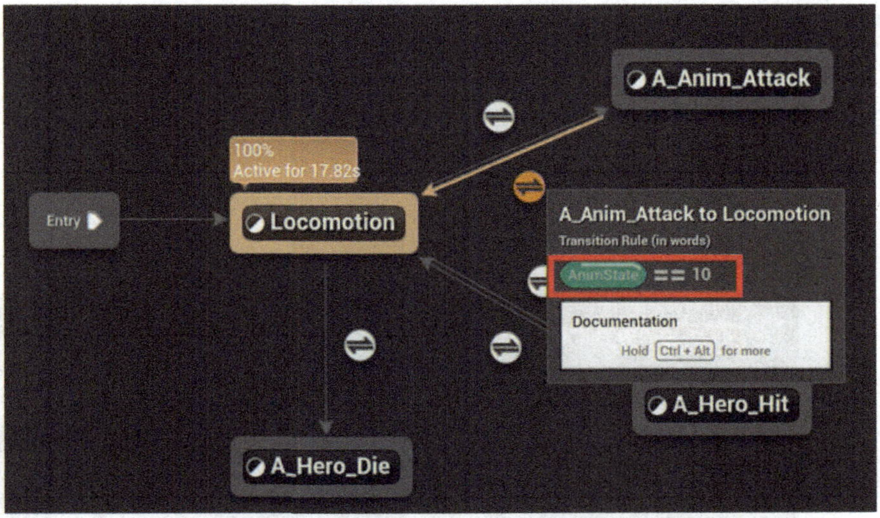

Figure 10.9 - Transitioning from the Attack state to the Locomotion state when AnimState is set to 10

To add this transition state, follow these steps:

1. Open the Animation Blueprint `AB_Hero` that responds to the end of the attack animation.
2. Find the place where `AnimState` is currently set back to `0`.
3. Change that value from `0` to `10`.
4. Compile and save the Blueprint.

Now the Hero has three important attack-related states:

- `AnimState` = `0`: The Hero is idle or ready and can accept a new attack input.
- `AnimState` = `1`: The Hero is currently attacking.
- `AnimState` = `10`: The Hero has finished the main attack motion but is still transitioning back to idle.

Next, we need to decide when `AnimState` should finally return to `0`. We will only set it back to 0 after the transition from the attack animation back to the idle animation has fully completed. This prevents the player from triggering another attack too early and helps avoid the animation becoming stuck.

To update `AnimState` at the correct times, we will use the existing Animation Notify events together with custom **End Transition** Events. The `EndOfAttack1` and `EndOfHit` Animation Notify events set `AnimState` to 10 when their animations reach the appropriate points. The **End Transition** Events then set `AnimState` back to 0 only after the transitions to Locomotion have fully completed.

To configure this timing, follow these steps:

1. Open the `AB_Hero` Animation Blueprint.
2. Set `AnimState` to `10` instead of `0` when the `EndOfAttack1` and `EndOfHit` notifications are received.

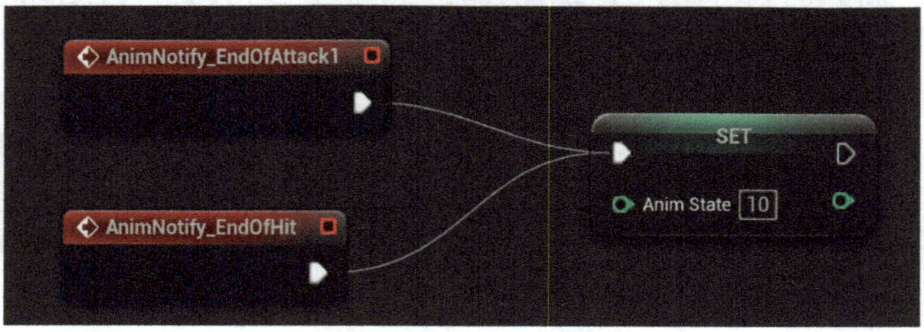

Figure 10.10 - Setting AnimState to 10 after the attack animation finishes

3. In the **Hero State Machine** window, select the transition which connects the `A_Anim_Attack` state to the `Locomotion` state.
4. Enter `EndOfTransitionFromAttack` into the **Custom Blueprint Event** field for the **End Transition Event.**

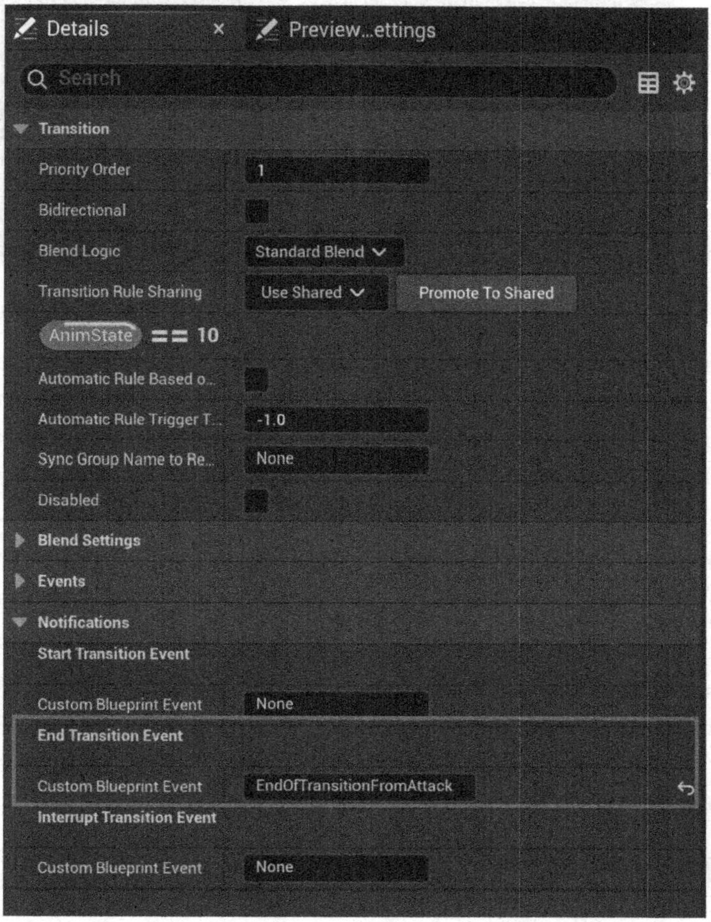

Figure 10.11 - Entering the custom event name for the End Transition Event

5. Compile and save. This step makes sure you can find the **AnimNotify_EndOfTransitionFromAttack** event node in the next step.
6. Go to the **Event Graph** of `AB_Hero`. Right-click in an empty area and search for `EndOfTransitionFromAttack`.

7. Select and add the **AnimNotify_EndOfTransitionFromAttack** node and connect its execution pin to a **Set AnimState** node, which will set **AnimState** to `0`.
8. Repeat *steps 3* to *7* to handle the `EndOfTransitionFromHit` event.

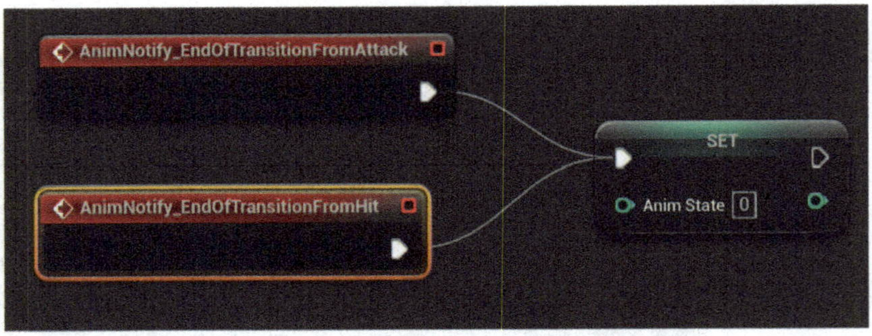

Figure 10.12 - Handling the transition end events and setting AnimState to 0

This fix is small, but it introduces an important gameplay programming idea: player actions often need state control. Without state control, repeated input can cause animations and gameplay logic to overlap in ways that were not intended. By tracking the Hero's current animation state more carefully, we make the combat behavior more stable and easier to maintain.

Please refer to the sample project and apply the same animation transition mechanism changes to the `BP_Warrok` and `BP_Boss` enemy characters (see the *Technical requirements* section for details; to access the GitHub repository, see the *Preface* for access instructions).

With the camera and animation issues fixed, the *Pangaea* project should feel more reliable during movement and combat. Next, we will continue polishing the game by adding sound effects, so the player receives clearer feedback from actions such as movement, attacks, and the overall atmosphere of the `Desert Castle` level.

Adding sound effects

So far, most of the *Pangaea* project has focused on visual and gameplay systems. The player can move through the `Desert Castle` level, fight enemies, follow objectives, see the HUD, and experience the intro cut-scene. However, a game does not feel complete through visuals alone. Audio plays an important role in how players understand, feel, and respond to what happens on screen.

Sound effects give feedback to the player. For example, when the Hero swings a sword, a sound effect helps the attack feel stronger. When footsteps are timed with the walking or running animation, the character feels more grounded in the world. Even simple audio additions can make the game feel much more polished because they help the player connect what they see with what they hear.

In this section, we will add basic sound effects to the *Pangaea* project by attaching sounds to animation clips. This is a practical, beginner-friendly approach because the Hero's movement and attacks are already driven by animations. By placing sound notifies directly on the animation timeline, we can make sounds play at the correct moment, such as when the Hero's foot touches the ground or when the sword swing reaches its strongest motion.

The goal of this section is not to build a complete professional audio system. A larger game may need sound classes, sound mixes, volume settings, surface-based footsteps, randomized sound variations, music transitions, and more advanced audio control. For this beginner project, we will focus on a simple implementation that improves the feel of the existing game without making the system too complex.

Before adding music to the level, let's begin with audio feedback that is directly tied to character actions. In *Pangaea*, the Hero's movement and attacks are driven by animation clips, so the best way to play sounds at the correct moment is to attach sound effects directly to those animations. This allows a footstep sound to play when the foot touches the ground, or an attack sound to play when the sword swing reaches its strongest motion.

Unreal Engine allows us to do this with an **Animation Notify**. When the animation reaches the **Animation Notify** marker during gameplay, Unreal Engine triggers the notify. Previously, we used this idea to control gameplay timing during attacks. In this section, we will use the same feature for audio timing, so a sound plays at the exact moment the animation reaches a footstep or sword swing.

For example, a running animation should not play a footstep sound randomly. The sound should happen when the character's foot contacts the ground. Similarly, a sword attack sound should play during the swing, not before the weapon starts moving or after the attack has already ended. By placing sound notifies directly on the animation timeline, we can match the sound timing to the motion of the character.

To add a sound effect to an animation clip, follow these steps:

1. In the **Content Drawer**, locate the animation clip you want to edit – the Hero attack animation, for example.
2. Double-click the animation asset to open it in the **Animation Editor**.
3. At the bottom of the editor, find the animation timeline.
4. Move the timeline marker to the frame where the sound should happen.
5. Right-click the **Notify** track, then select **Add Notify | Play Sound**, as shown in *Figure 10.13*:

Figure 10.13 - Adding a Play Sound notify at the correct animation timing

6. Select the `Drop_Item_From_ContentBrowser` in the **Sound** selection drop-down list in the **Details** panel.

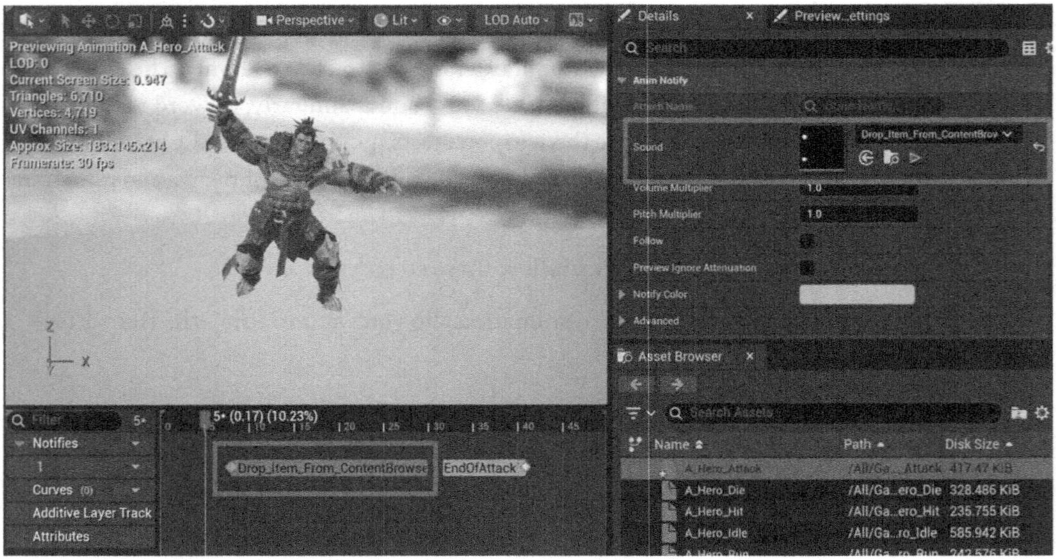

Figure 10.14 - Selecting an audio source for playing the attack sound effect

7. Adjust the notify position on the timeline until the sound matches the animation timing.
8. Save the animation asset.

The **Play Sound** notify should be placed at the exact moment when the sound should happen. For example, place a footstep sound when the Hero's foot touches the ground, or place an attack sound when the sword swing reaches the strongest part of the motion.

For a footstep sound, place the notify at the moment when the Hero's foot touches the ground. If the animation loop contains both left and right footsteps, add one notify for each foot contact. This will make the movement feel more natural because the sound rhythm follows the animation.

Repeat the same workflow for the Hero's attack animation but place the **Play Sound** notify near the main sword swing. The sound should happen when the attack motion becomes visible and forceful. If the sound plays too early, the attack may feel disconnected from the animation. If it plays too late, the player may feel that the input response is delayed. You can adjust the notify position by dragging it along the timeline and testing the result in gameplay.

After adding the notify, play the level, and test the animation during real gameplay. Walk, run, and attack several times to confirm that the sounds trigger correctly. Make sure the sound does not play repeatedly at the wrong time and that it does not feel delayed compared with the character's movement.

At this stage, we are only adding simple sound playback directly from animation clips. This is enough for the beginner version of *Pangaea* because it gives clear feedback for movement and combat without requiring a complex audio system. In larger projects, you may expand this with different footstep sounds for different surfaces, randomized sound variations, volume control, or audio mixing.

With the character action sounds in place, the Hero should feel more responsive and connected to the world. In the next section, we will continue improving the game's presentation by adding visual effects to the Hero's sword attack.

Adding visual effects

After adding audio effects, the *Pangaea* project should feel more responsive. The player can now hear feedback when the Hero moves or attacks. The next step is to improve the visual feedback of the game by adding a simple visual effect.

Visual effects, often called **VFX**, are used in games to make actions easier to read and more satisfying to watch. For example, a sword swing may have a trail effect, a spell may create glowing particles, an explosion may produce smoke and sparks, and a hit reaction may show a small impact effect. These effects do not always change the gameplay logic directly, but they help the player understand what is happening and make the action feel more complete.

In Unreal Engine, many modern visual effects are created with Niagara. **Niagara** is Unreal Engine's visual effects system for creating particle effects, trails, beams, smoke, sparks, magic effects, and many other dynamic visuals. It is a powerful system, and a full study of Niagara could fill an entire book by itself. In this beginner chapter, we will only use a very small part of Niagara to create a simple sword trail effect for the Hero's attack animation.

The purpose of this section is not to teach every part of Niagara. Instead, we will focus on a practical example that improves the *Pangaea* combat experience. You will create a Niagara System, configure a basic ribbon-style trail, attach it to the Hero's sword animation, and adjust its timing so the effect appears only during the attack swing.

This type of visual effect is a good example of game polish. The Hero already has an attack animation and attack logic, but the sword trail makes the action clearer and more visually satisfying. When the player attacks, the trail helps emphasize the motion of the weapon and makes the combat feel stronger.

By the end of this section, the Hero's sword attack will have a simple Niagara-based trail effect. This will give the combat a more polished appearance and introduce you to the basic workflow of adding visual effects to animation-driven gameplay.

Adding an attack trail to the Hero's sword

In the previous chapters, we created the Hero character, attached a sword, and added attack input so the player can perform an attack during gameplay. The attack already works as a gameplay action, but it can still look plain if the sword only plays the animation without any visual effect. To make the attack easier to read and more satisfying, we will add a simple trail effect that appears during the sword swing.

Creating a trail with Unreal Engine's Niagara effect system

A **sword trail** is a visual effect that follows the motion of a weapon. It helps emphasize the path of the attack and makes the animation feel faster and stronger. In this section, we will create the trail with Niagara, Unreal Engine's visual effects system. We will then attach the effect to the Hero's attack animation, so it appears only during the active part of the sword swing.

Before creating the effect, it is useful to understand the basic idea behind it. Niagara effects are stored as Niagara System assets. A **Niagara System** can contain one or more emitters. An **emitter** defines how particles are created, updated, and rendered. For a sword trail, instead of rendering individual sprite particles, we will use a **Ribbon Renderer**. A ribbon connects particles over time, creating a continuous strip-like trail. This makes it suitable for effects such as sword arcs, magic trails, and fast-moving energy streaks.

To create the sword trail Niagara System, follow these steps:

1. In the **Content Drawer**, navigate to the `Content/Pangaea` folder. If a `VFX` folder does not already exist, right-click an empty area, select **New Folder**, and name it `VFX`. Open the new `Content/Pangaea/VFX` folder. We will use this folder to store the sword-trail effect asset.
2. Right-click in the **Content Drawer**.
3. From the context menu, select **FX | Niagara System**.
4. In the Niagara System creation window, choose **Create Empty Niagara System**, as shown in *Figure 10.15*. This option gives us a blank Niagara System so we can build a simple sword trail from a minimal starting point.

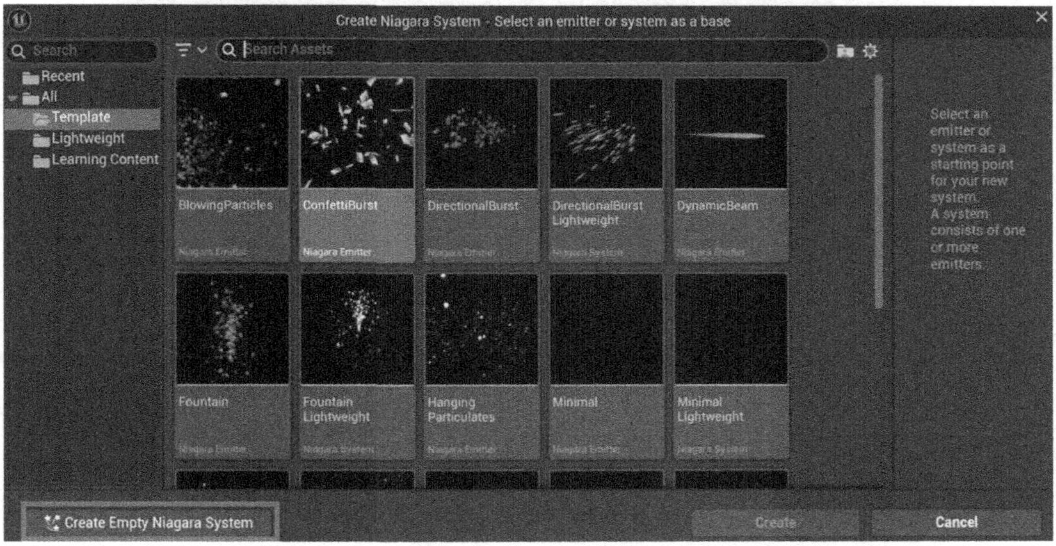

Figure 10.15 - Choosing Create Empty Niagara System in the Niagara System creation window

5. Click **Finish** or **Create**, depending on the editor window.
6. Rename the new Niagara System asset to `HeroSwordTrail`.
7. Double-click `HeroSwordTrail` to open it in the Niagara Editor.

First, the Niagara System is empty, so we need to add an emitter. The emitter controls how the effect generates, updates, and renders particles. For this beginner effect, we will start with a **Minimal** emitter. Let's continue:

1. Double-click the `HeroSwordTrail` asset to open the **Niagara Editor**. In the editor, right-click in the empty area.
2. Select **Add minimal emitter**.

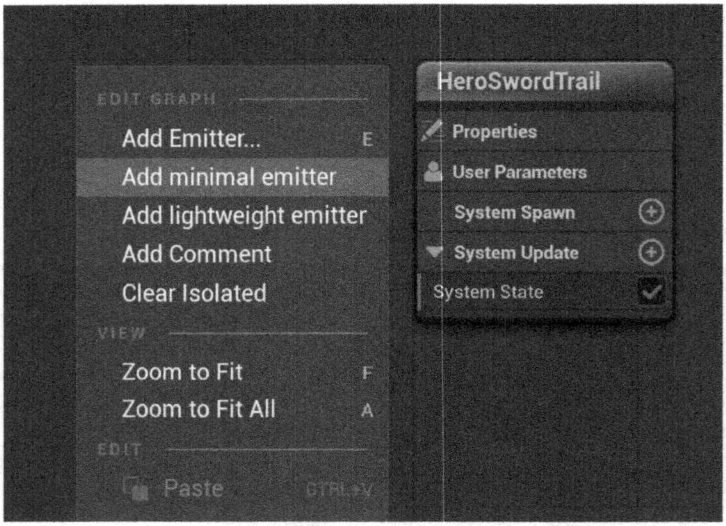

Figure 10.16 - Adding a new minimal emitter

3. Now you should see the **Minimal** emitter node on the **System Overview** window.

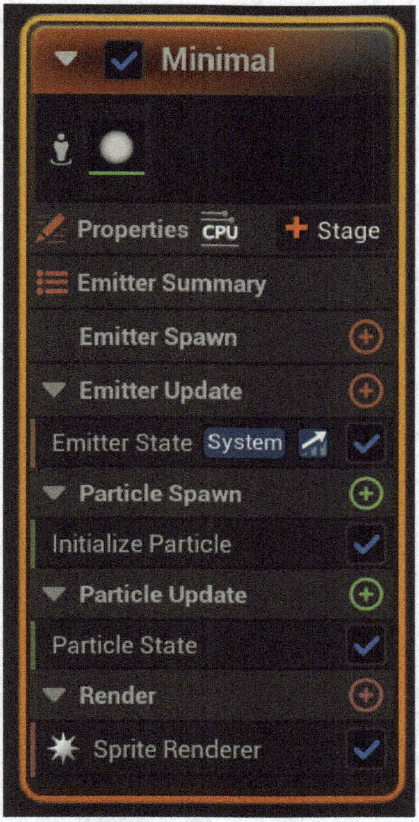

Figure 10.17 - The Minimal emitter is added to the Niagara System

The **Minimal** emitter gives us a simple starting point. Since we only need a basic sword trail, this emitter is enough for our first Niagara effect. Next, we need to configure the emitter so it creates a ribbon trail instead of regular sprite particles. Follow these steps:

1. In the **Minimal** emitter stack, locate the **Particle Spawn** section.
2. Click the **+** icon in the **Particle Spawn** section, then type `Add Velocity` in the search bar and select the **Add Velocity** module (see *Figure 10.18*). Then, set **Velocity** to (`0, 0, 100`) in the **Details** panel.

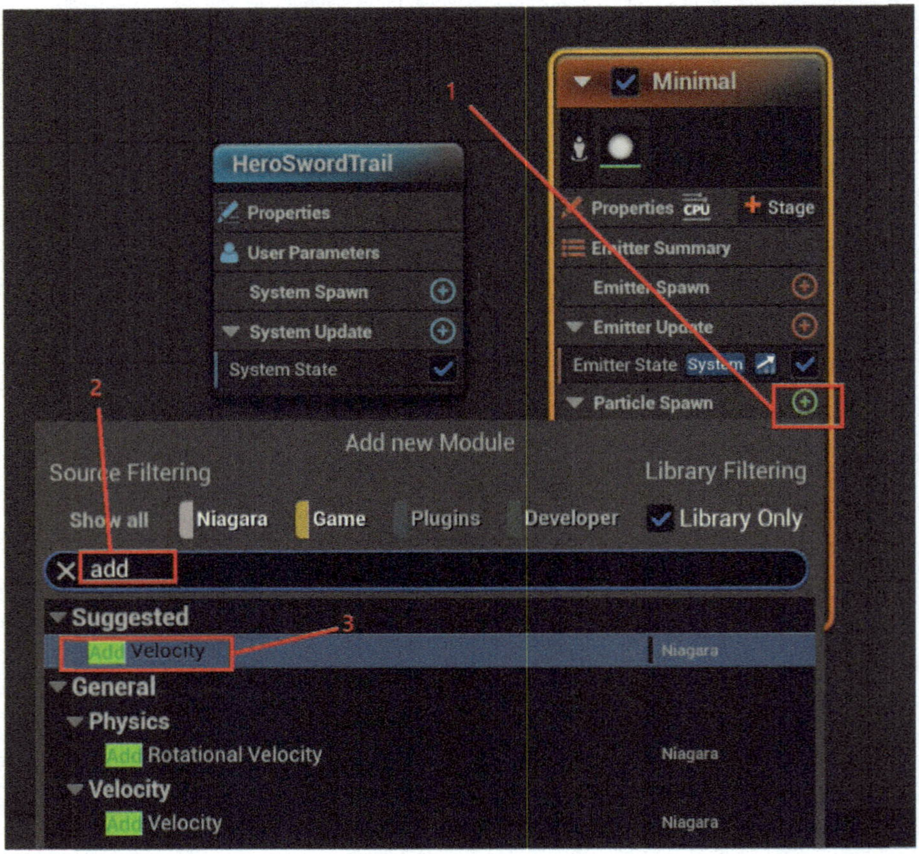

*Figure 10.18 - Adding the **Add Velocity** module to the Particle Spawn section*

3. Locate the **Render** section in the **Minimal** emitter.
4. Add a **Ribbon Renderer**.
5. Disable or remove the default **Sprite Renderer**, as shown in *Figure 10.19*. The sword trail should render as a connected ribbon, not as separate sprite particles.

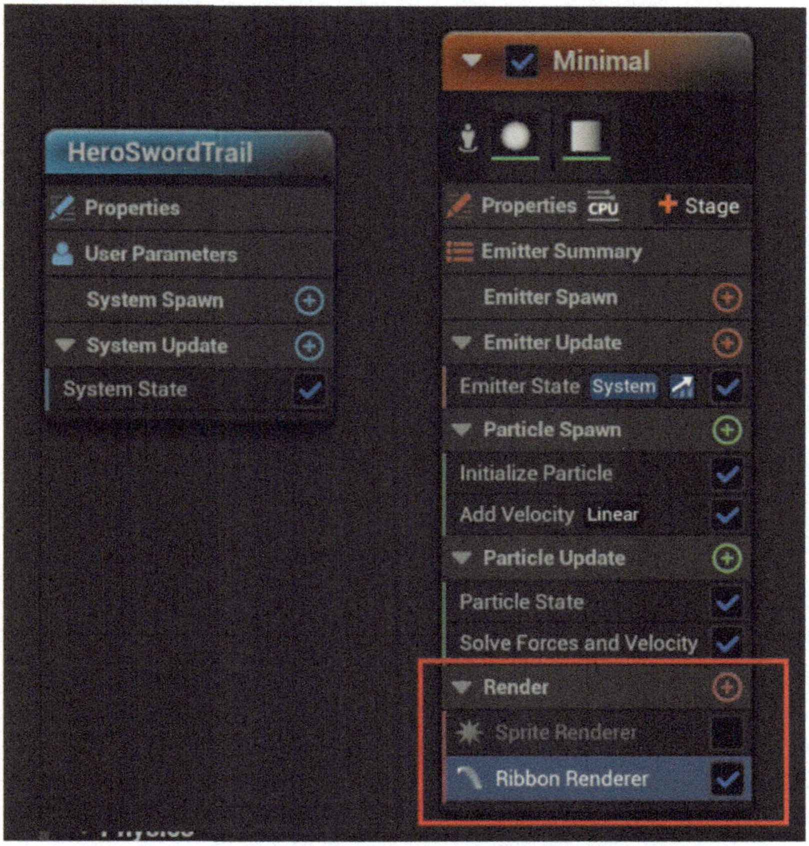

Figure 10.19 - Adding a Ribbon Renderer for the sword trail

6. In the **Emitter Update** section, add a **Spawn Rate** module if it is not already present (see *Figure 10.20*). Set the **Spawn Rate** to `50`.

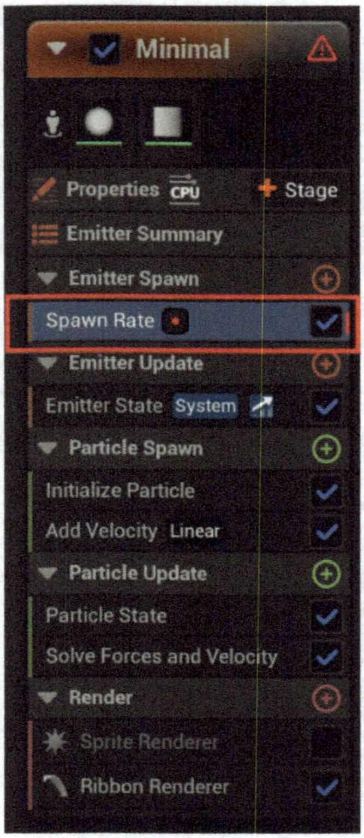

Figure 10.20 - Adding a Spawn Rate module to control how many particles are created

Spawn Rate controls how many particles the emitter creates over time. For a ribbon trail, this affects how continuous or sparse the trail appears during the sword swing.

7. Now adjust the rest of the settings for the effect. These values create a short, narrow trail that works well as a starting point for the Hero's sword attack:

    1. In the **Initialize Particle** module, change the following:

        - Set **Lifetime** to `0.1`
        - Under **Ribbon Attributes**, set **Ribbon Width Mode** to **Direct Set**
        - Set **Ribbon Width** to `5`

    2. In the **Ribbon Renderer** settings, under the **Rendering** group, change the following:

        - Disable **Cast Shadows**
        - Disable **Include in Hit Proxy**

> **Note**
>
> Select `hand_r_Trail_Socket` (which you will create in the next subsection) and position it near the tip of the sword. As a starting point, set **Relative Location** to `(-80, -24, 95)` and **Relative Rotation** to `(-38, 15, -50)`. Adjust these values if necessary so the trail follows the sword correctly.

The short **Lifetime** keeps the trail from staying on screen too long. The **Ribbon Width** controls how thick the trail appears. If the trail looks too thin, too thick, too short, or too long, you can return to these settings later and adjust them.

After changing the settings, save the Niagara System. You can preview the effect in the Niagara Editor, but the trail will be easier to judge after it is attached to the sword animation. A sword trail depends on motion, so it should be tested during the actual attack animation rather than only in the effect editor.

At this point, we have created the visual effect asset. However, it is not yet connected to the Hero character. In the next subsection, we will add a socket to the Hero's skeleton so Unreal Engine knows where the sword trail should appear during the attack.

Attaching the attack trail effect to the Hero's sword

Now that the `HeroSwordTrail` Niagara System has been created, we need to tell Unreal Engine where the effect should appear on the Hero character. Since the trail should follow the sword during the attack animation, we will attach it to the `hand_r_Trail_Socket` on the Hero's skeleton. Follow the steps below to add the sword trail effect to the Attack animation:

1. Locate and open `SK_Hero` under `Content/Pangaea/Characters/Hero/Models`. In the Skeleton Tree, find and right-click the `hand_r` bone, then select **Add Socket**.
2. Rename the new socket `hand_r_Trail_Socket`. Do not modify the existing `hand_rSocket` used to attach the sword, because changing its transform would also change the sword's position and orientation.
3. Position it close to the tip of the sword. For example, set **Relative Location** to `(-80, -24, 95)` and **Relative Rotation** to `(-38, 15, -50)`.

Figure 10.21 - Adding a new hand_r_Trail_Socket to the Hero's skeleton

4. In the **Content Drawer**, open the `Attack` animation in the **Animation Editor**.
5. In the animation timeline, find the part of the animation where the sword swing begins.
6. Right-click the Notify track and select **Add Notify State | Timed Niagara Effect**.
7. Select the new **Timed Niagara Effect** notify on the timeline.

> **Note**
>
> The sword attachment socket and trail-effect socket serve different purposes. Keep the existing `hand_rSocket` unchanged, and apply the trail transform values only to the new `hand_r_Trail_Socket`.

Figure 10.22 - Adding a Timed Niagara Effect notify state

8. In the **Details** panel, set the Niagara System to `HeroSwordTrail`.
9. Set the **Socket Name** to `hand_r_Trail_Socket`.

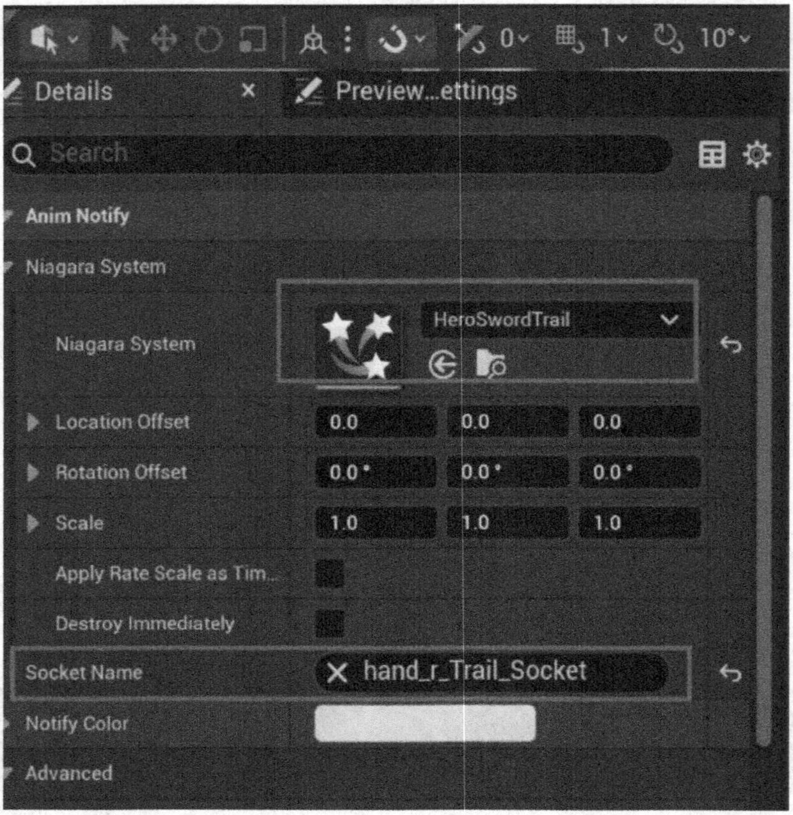

Figure 10.23 - Assigning the Niagara System and socket name

10. Drag the start and end points of the notify so the effect only appears during the sword swing.

Figure 10.24 - Adjusting the start and end timing of the sword trail effect

11. Save the animation asset.

The timing of the trail is *important*. If the effect starts too early, the trail may appear before the sword actually moves. If it ends too late, the trail may remain visible after the attack has already finished. A good starting point is to begin the effect shortly before the fastest part of the swing and end it shortly after the swing completes.

After setting up the notify, test the result in gameplay. Play the `Desert Castle` level and trigger the Hero's attack several times. Watch the sword carefully and check whether the trail follows the attack motion. If the trail appears in the wrong place, return to the skeleton and adjust the socket position. If the trail appears at the wrong time, return to the attack animation and adjust the **Timed Niagara Effect** notify.

You may also want to adjust the Niagara settings after seeing the effect in motion. For example:

- If the trail disappears too quickly, increase the particle **Lifetime** slightly
- If the trail looks too wide, reduce the **Ribbon Width**
- If the trail looks too sparse, increase the **Spawn Rate**

Small adjustments can make the effect feel better without changing the underlying combat logic.

The sword trail does not change the Hero's attack damage, collision, or enemy hit detection. It is purely a visual effect. However, it improves how the attack feels to the player because it makes the sword motion clearer and more satisfying. This is one of the key ideas behind game polish: *improving the player's experience by enhancing feedback around mechanics that already work.*

At this point, the *Pangaea* project has received several important polish improvements. The `Desert Castle` level has higher-quality environment assets, the gate-opening event is connected to the final gate mesh, noticeable camera issues have been addressed, audio feedback has been added, and the Hero's sword attack now has a visual trail effect. These changes help the project feel more complete inside the editor.

The final step is to prepare the game so it can run outside the editor. In the next section, we will package the *Pangaea* project into a standalone build.

Packaging the game

After polishing the *Pangaea* project inside the editor, the next step is to create a standalone build. Up to this point, most of our testing has happened through Unreal Editor by pressing the **Play** button. This is useful during development because it lets us quickly test gameplay, adjust Blueprints, modify levels, and fix problems. However, playing inside the editor is not the same as running the game as an independent application.

Packaging is the process of preparing an Unreal Engine project so it can run outside the editor. During packaging, Unreal Engine gathers the required game content, processes assets into a runtime-ready format, applies project settings, includes the required maps, and creates the files needed to launch the game on a target platform. For a Windows build, this means creating a standalone executable that can be opened without launching Unreal Editor.

In this section, we will prepare the *Pangaea* project for a standalone desktop build. We will first review the important project settings that affect packaging, such as the default game map and which levels need to be included in the packaged build. Then, we will look at a few simple runtime display options, such as windowed and full-screen modes. After that, we will discuss common build configurations, including **Debug Game**, **Development**, and **Shipping**, so you understand which type of build is appropriate for testing and which is more suitable for a final release.

Although Unreal Engine supports many target platforms, including Windows, macOS, Linux, Android, and iOS, this section is not intended to be a complete guide to mobile publishing. Packaging for Android or iOS requires additional platform-specific setup, such as SDKs, signing certificates, provisioning profiles, store requirements, device testing, and mobile performance considerations. Those topics are important, but they are beyond the beginner's scope of this chapter.

Instead, our focus will be on the **core packaging workflow** using a standalone desktop build. Once you understand this process, the same general idea applies to other platforms: configure the project, choose the target platform, package the game, test the build, and fix any issues that appear outside the editor. By learning the desktop packaging workflow first, you will build a foundation that can help you explore platform-specific deployment later.

Configuring the Project Settings

Before packaging the game, we should check the project settings that control how the game starts and which content is included in the build. In the editor, it is easy to open any level manually from the **Content Drawer**. In a packaged game, however, the player will not see the editor. The game needs to know which map to load first, which **Game Mode** to use, and which levels must be available at runtime.

To open the project settings, go to the main menu and select **Edit | Project Settings**. The **Project Settings** window contains many categories, but for this beginner packaging workflow, we will focus on the settings most directly related to launching and packaging the *Pangaea* project.

First, check the project's default maps. In the **Project Settings** window, select **Project | Maps & Modes**. This section controls which maps Unreal Engine uses when the project starts.

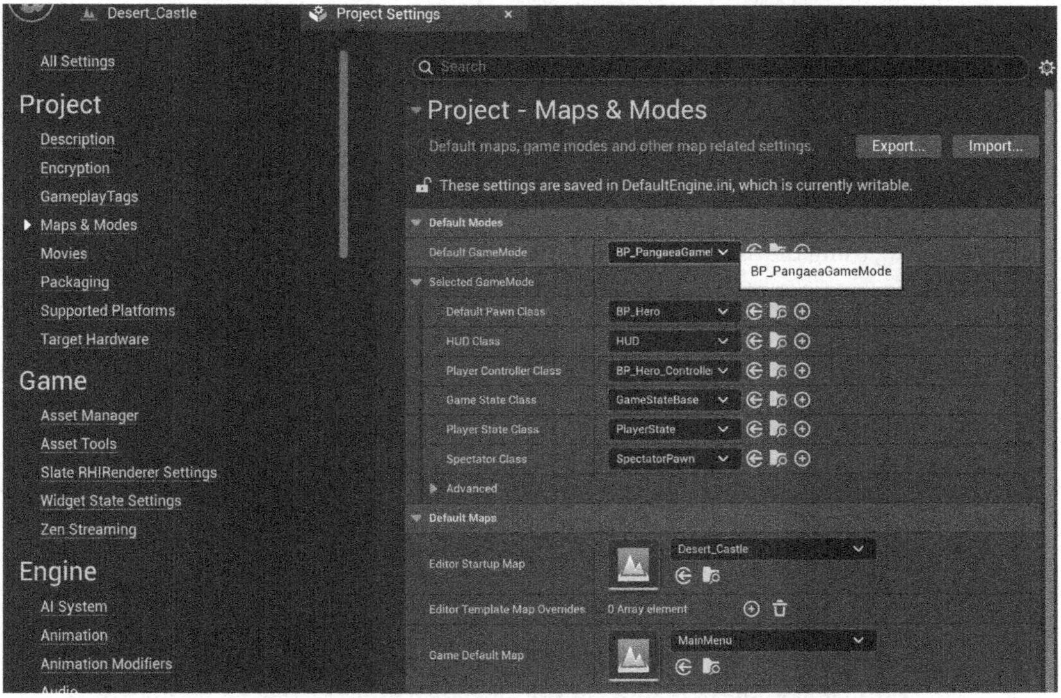

Figure 10.25 - Setting up map and modes for standalone build

Figure 10.25 shows the **Maps & Modes** settings that control which maps and gameplay classes Unreal Engine uses when the project starts. For this beginner packaging workflow, pay attention to the following settings:

- **Editor Startup Map**: This is the level that opens automatically when the project is opened in Unreal Editor.
- **Game Default Map**: It's the level that opens first when the game runs normally.
- **Game Instance Class**: This is the `Game Instance` class used for shared runtime data. This setting is available only if your project uses a Game Instance class.
- **Default GameMode**: It's the `Game Mode` used when a level does not override it.

For the packaged version of *Pangaea*, the most important setting is **Game Default Map**. This setting is more important than the others in this workflow because it controls which level opens first when the game runs as a standalone application.

In the editor, you can manually open any level from the **Content Drawer** before pressing **Play**. In a packaged build, the player does not have the editor, so Unreal Engine needs a clear starting map. If **Game Default Map** is not set correctly, the packaged game may start from the wrong level, skip the `Main Menu`, or fail to follow the intended game flow.

This should point to the first level you want the player to see when the standalone game starts. If your game starts with the Main Menu created in *Chapter 7*, set the **Game Default Map** to the `MainMenu` level. If you want the game to start directly in the Desert Castle gameplay level, set it to the `Desert_Castle` level instead.

For this project, using the `Main Menu` level as the **Game Default Map** is usually the better choice because it gives the packaged game a more complete flow. The player launches the game, sees the `Main Menu`, starts the game, watches or enters the introductory sequence, and then continues into the `Desert_Castle` level.

After setting the default map, make sure the required gameplay levels are included in the packaged build. This is important because a level that works in the editor may fail to load in the packaged game if it is not included correctly.

To check the map packaging settings, follow these steps and refer to *Figure 10.26*:

1. Open **Edit | Project Settings**.
2. In the left panel, select **Project | Packaging**.
3. Find the **List of maps to include in the packaged build** section under the **Advanced** group.
4. Add the required `MainMenu` and `Desert_Castle` maps to the list.

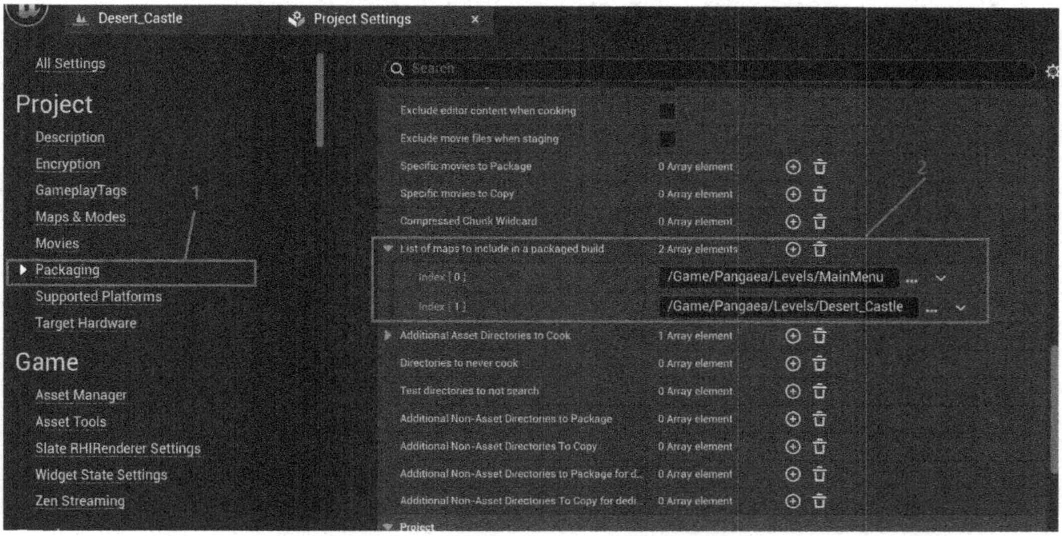

Figure 10.26 - Adding needed levels to the packaged build

Including the correct maps is one of the most common packaging requirements. If the packaged game opens to the wrong level, check the **Game Default Map**. If pressing a **Start** button or using an **Open Level** node fails in the packaged build, check whether the destination level has been included in the packaging settings.

You should also make sure that all recent changes have been saved before packaging. Save the current level, save modified Blueprints, save animation assets, and save any new audio or Niagara assets. Unsaved changes may still appear to work in the editor, but they may not be included correctly when the project is packaged.

Before moving on, make a final check:

- The correct **Game Default Map** is selected.
- The correct **Game Mode** is assigned.
- The `Main Menu` level is included if the game starts from a menu.
- The `Desert Castle` level is included.
- Any cut-scene-related level is included if needed.
- All modified assets and levels are saved.

Once these settings are configured, the project is ready for the next packaging preparation step. In the next subsection, we will look at how to control whether the packaged game runs in windowed mode or full-screen mode.

Making a windowed or full-screen build

After setting the correct default maps and packaging settings, the next thing to consider is how the game appears when it runs outside the editor. When testing inside Unreal Editor, the game usually runs in a **Play In Editor** (PIE) window or inside the editor Viewport. In a packaged build, however, the game opens as a standalone application. This means we should think about whether the game should start in windowed mode, full-screen mode, or allow the player to switch between the two.

For a beginner project like *Pangaea*, it is useful to understand the basic difference between these display modes:

- In **windowed mode**, the game runs inside a normal desktop window. This is convenient during testing because you can easily move between the game, the file explorer, and other applications.
- In **full-screen mode**, the game fills the display, which usually feels more like a final player-facing experience.

Unreal Engine allows you to control display behavior through project settings, console commands, and Blueprint logic. For this chapter, we will use simple Blueprint-based control because it is easy to understand and can be connected to UI buttons if needed.

One common approach is to use Unreal Engine's **Execute Console Command** node. This node allows a Blueprint to run a console command during gameplay. For example, the `r.setres` command can change the game resolution and display mode.

Here are two simple examples:

```
r.setres 1280x720w
r.setres 1920x1080f
```

In these commands, the resolution is written as width by height. The letter at the end controls the display mode:

- `w` means windowed mode
- `f` means full-screen mode

For example, `r.setres 1280x720w` sets the game to 1280 by 720 in windowed mode, while `r.setres 1920x1080f` sets the game to 1920 by 1080 in full-screen mode.

To test this in Blueprint, follow these steps:

1. Open the Blueprint where you want to control the display mode. For example, you can use the `Main Menu Widget` Blueprint created in *Chapter 7*.

2. Add a button for windowed mode, or use an existing menu button if you already have one.
3. In the button's **OnClicked** event, add an **Execute Console Command** node.
4. Set the command to:

```
r.setres 1280x720w
```

5. Add another button for full-screen mode.
6. In that button's **OnClicked** event, add another **Execute Console Command** node.
7. Set the command to:

```
r.setres 1920x1080f
```

8. Compile and save the Widget Blueprint.
9. Play the game and test both buttons.

This gives the player a simple way to switch between display modes. It is not a complete graphics settings menu, but it is enough to demonstrate how display behavior can be controlled in a packaged game.

You should also consider mouse cursor visibility. In a game with a `Main Menu`, the cursor should usually be visible so the player can click buttons. During gameplay, especially in a third-person action game, the cursor is usually hidden so mouse movement controls the camera instead of behaving like a desktop pointer.

To handle this, update the **Player Controller** settings when switching between the menu and gameplay:

1. In the main menu, set **Show Mouse Cursor** to true.
2. Use an appropriate UI input mode, such as **Set Input Mode UI Only** or **Set Input Mode Game and UI**.
3. During gameplay, set **Show Mouse Cursor** to false.
4. Use **Set Input Mode Game Only** so the player can control the character and camera normally.

If the cursor remains visible during gameplay, it can make the packaged game feel unfinished. If the cursor is hidden in the menu, the player may not be able to click the **Start** button. Therefore, cursor visibility should match the current state of the game.

After setting up windowed mode, full-screen mode, and cursor visibility, test the project in standalone mode or after packaging. Some display and input behavior can feel slightly different outside the editor, so it is important to test these features in the same way the player will experience them.

At this stage, the packaged game should have the correct startup level and more predictable display behavior. In the next subsection, we will look at the different build configurations Unreal Engine provides and decide which one is appropriate for testing and final packaging.

Choosing a package configuration

Before creating a packaged build, you need to choose a build configuration. A **build configuration** tells Unreal Engine what kind of executable it should create and how much debugging or development information should be included. Different configurations are useful at different stages of development.

When you are still testing your game, you usually want a build that is easy to debug and verify. When you are preparing a version for players, you usually want a cleaner build with fewer development features. Understanding the difference between these configurations helps you choose the correct option for the current stage of your project.

Unreal Engine provides several build configurations, but for this beginner workflow, we will focus on three common options, as shown in *Figure 10.27*:

- **Debug Game**
- **Development**
- **Shipping**

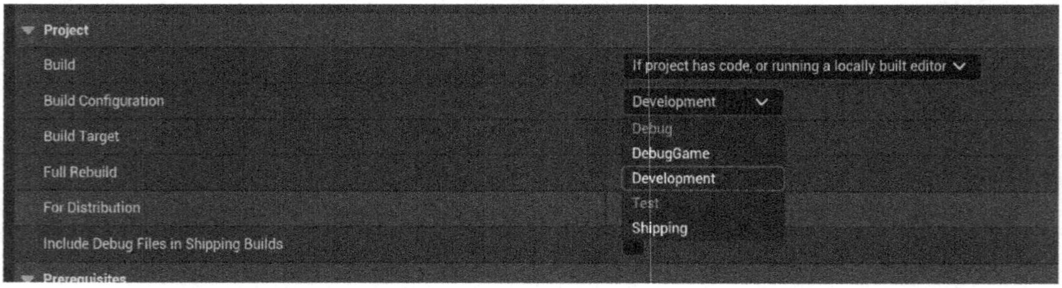

Figure 10.27 - Choosing different build configurations

Debug Game is mainly used when we need more debugging support. It is useful for programmers who need to inspect gameplay code and diagnose problems. However, it is not usually the best choice for a simple player-facing build because it includes extra debugging information and is not intended for final distribution.

Development is a good choice for testing packaged builds during development. It still keeps useful development information and makes it easier to identify problems if something behaves differently outside the editor. For the first packaged version of *Pangaea*, Development is usually the safest choice because it lets us test the standalone build before preparing a final version.

Shipping is intended for final player-facing builds. It removes many development and debugging features and is closer to what we would distribute to players. Once we have tested the game in a Development build and confirmed that the main menu, gameplay level, cut-scene, HUD, audio, visual effects, and win or lose conditions all work correctly, we can create a **Shipping** build.

For this chapter, we recommend creating a **Development** build first. This lets you check whether the game works correctly outside Unreal Editor while still keeping the build suitable for testing. After the **Development** build works as expected, you can repeat the packaging process with the **Shipping** configuration if you want a more final version.

To select the build configuration, follow these steps:

1. In Unreal Editor, open the **Platforms** menu from the main toolbar.
2. Select your target platform, such as **Windows**.
3. Find the build configuration option.
4. Choose **Development** for the first packaged test build.
5. Later, after testing is complete, choose **Shipping** if you want to create a final build.

The configuration you choose does not replace the need for testing. A **Shipping** build may behave differently from the editor, and even a **Development** build can reveal issues that were not obvious during **Play In Editor** testing. Always run the packaged game and test the full gameplay flow.

After choosing a build configuration, the next decision is the target platform. In the next subsection, we will briefly discuss platform selection and then focus on packaging a standalone Windows build for this beginner project.

Selecting the target platform

After choosing the build configuration, the next step is to select the target platform. The **target platform** tells Unreal Engine what kind of device or operating system the packaged game should run on. Unreal Engine supports many platforms, including Windows, macOS, Linux, Android, iOS, and game consoles. However, each platform has its own requirements, tools, and testing process.

For this beginner project, we will focus on creating a standalone Windows build. This means the game will be packaged as a desktop application that can run outside Unreal Editor. This is the most straightforward target for our current workflow because the book has been using a desktop Unreal Engine development environment, and Windows packaging does not require the same mobile-specific setup as Android or iOS.

You may notice that Unreal Engine also allows you to package for mobile platforms, such as Android and iOS. While the general packaging idea is similar, mobile deployment requires additional preparation. Android builds may require Android SDK, NDK (Native Development Kit), JDK (Java Development Kit), signing configuration, device permissions, and mobile performance testing. iOS builds require Apple developer tools, signing certificates, provisioning profiles, and usually a macOS-based build environment. These are important topics, but they are beyond the scope of this beginner closing chapter.

In this section, we will use **Windows** as the target platform so we can focus on the core packaging workflow: preparing the project, selecting the platform, creating the build, and testing the packaged game. Once you understand this process, you will have a foundation for learning platform-specific packaging later.

To select Windows as the target platform, follow these steps:

1. Save all open levels and modified assets.
2. Open the **Platforms** menu from the main toolbar.
3. Locate the **Windows** platform option.
4. Make sure the build configuration is set to **Development** for the first test build.
5. Select the option to **Package Project** for Windows.
6. Choose a folder where Unreal Engine should create the packaged build.
7. Wait for the packaging process to finish.

Depending on your computer and the size of the project, packaging may take some time. Unreal Engine needs to process the required assets, cook content, build the executable, and place the output files into the folder you selected. During this process, the **Output Log** may show warnings or errors. Some warnings may not stop the build, but errors usually need to be fixed before packaging can complete.

After the packaging process is complete, open the output folder. You should see a packaged Windows build folder that contains the executable file and the supporting files required to run the game. Double-click the executable to launch the standalone version of *Pangaea*.

When testing the packaged build, do not only check whether the game opens. Play through the main gameplay flow:

- Confirm that the correct startup level appears.
- Check that the Main Menu buttons work.
- Confirm that the player can enter the `Desert Castle` level.

- Test the intro cut-scene if it is included in the flow.
- Move the Hero character and test camera control.
- Fight the Warrok enemies.
- Confirm that the HUD updates correctly.
- Complete the required objectives.
- Check that the gate opens.
- Fight the Boss and test the win or lose condition.
- Listen for animation sound effects.
- Check that the sword trail visual effect appears during the attack.

Testing the packaged build is important because some issues only appear outside the editor. A level may open correctly in **Play In Editor** but fail in the packaged game if it was not included in the packaging settings. A UI button may work in the editor but fail if the map name is incorrect. A sound, material, or visual effect may be missing if the asset was not saved or referenced correctly.

If the packaged build works correctly, you have created a standalone version of the *Pangaea* project. This is an important milestone because the game is no longer limited to running inside Unreal Editor.

After testing the packaged Windows build, you have completed the final practical step of this beginner project. The *Pangaea* game can now run outside Unreal Editor as a standalone application. Throughout this chapter, you improved the game's presentation, fixed noticeable issues, added audio and visual feedback, configured the project for packaging, and created a build that can be tested like a real game.

This is an important milestone because it brings together everything you have learned across the book into one complete workflow: build, polish, package, and test. In the final section, we will look back at what you have learned and discuss how you can continue developing your Unreal Engine skills beyond this project.

Looking ahead

Congratulations! You have finished this book and followed the steps to complete the *Pangaea* game, building a playable third-person game from start to finish.

Throughout this book, we followed a focused learning strategy: learn what you need, when you need it (see *Preface*). Because game development covers an enormous range of topics, some concepts were introduced only to the level needed to complete the project, while other minor or redundant configurations were left out. Our goal was to give you a clear, focused path through the essential aspects of game development in Unreal Engine.

You now have an overall view of how these different parts come together, from level design, Blueprints, character setup, and player input to AI, UI, gameplay systems, cinematics, visual effects, and packaging. More importantly, you have built a foundation that you can use to explore each of these areas in greater depth.

Before we finish, let's look back at what you have learned and where you can go next:

1. In *Chapter 1*, you installed Unreal Engine, learned how to use the **Epic Games Launcher**, created your first project, and became familiar with the basic structure of an Unreal Engine project. You also learned how project settings, templates, and engine versions affect your development workflow.
    - You can continue learning how Unreal projects are structured on disk, how plugins extend the engine, how source control is used in real production, and how teams manage different engine versions across a project.
2. In *Chapter 2*, you learned how to build a game world in the Level Editor. You studied world and local coordinate systems, navigated the Viewport, placed Actors, transformed objects, used snapping, and created a `Castle` prototype level with blockout geometry. This gave you the foundation for thinking about level layout before final art is added.
    - Next, you can explore deeper level-design topics such as player guidance, encounter pacing, modular environment construction, lighting composition, environmental storytelling, and world partition for larger game worlds.
3. In *Chapter 3*, you learned the basics of Blueprints. You created Blueprint logic with nodes, graphs, variables, events, branches, loops, and simple flow control. This introduced you to visual scripting as a way to build gameplay without writing C++ code.
    - Beyond this book, you can continue learning Blueprint communication, Blueprint Interfaces, **Event Dispatchers**, **Blueprint Function Libraries**, data-driven design, debugging tools, and how to decide when a system should remain in Blueprint and when it should move into C++.
4. In *Chapter 4*, you created the player character. You imported character assets, organized meshes, textures, skeletons, and animations, created the Hero Character Blueprint, set up the Animation Blueprint, used **Blend Space** for movement animation, and attached a sword to the character.
    - You can explore more advanced character topics such as animation montages, layered animation, inverse kinematics, **Control Rig**, retargeting animations from other skeletons, motion matching, and more complex equipment systems.

5. In *Chapter 5*, you learned how to handle player input. You used Unreal Engine's **Enhanced Input** system to define Input Actions and **Input Mapping Contexts**, then routed player input into the Hero character so the player could move, look, and attack. You also learned how **Game Mode** helps connect the level to the correct player character and controller.
   - You can study input rebinding, multiple control schemes, gamepad support, local multiplayer input, touch input, accessibility settings, and more advanced Player Controller responsibilities.
6. In *Chapter 6*, you created an AI enemy character. You built Warrok as an AI-controlled NPC, added an AI Controller, used navigation so the enemy could move through the level, added perception so the enemy could detect the player, and used a Behavior Tree and **Blackboard** to organize patrol, chase, and attack behavior.
   - Next, you can continue learning advanced AI topics such as EQS, patrol path systems, squad behavior, ranged attacks, difficulty scaling, AI debugging tools, cover systems, and more complex decision-making patterns.
7. In *Chapter 7*, you created a game UI with Unreal Motion Graphics. You learned how Widget Blueprints work, how the **UMG Designer** and **Graph** tabs support both layout and logic, and how to create a main menu and HUD for the *Pangaea* project.
   - You can explore pause menus, settings screens, inventory UI, dialogue UI, animated UI transitions, UI sound effects, controller navigation, UI accessibility, and data-binding patterns that keep the interface synchronized with gameplay systems.
8. In *Chapter 8*, you designed and implemented gameplay mechanics for the `Desert Castle` level. You moved from isolated systems into a complete gameplay scenario with objectives, enemies, gates, mission progress, HUD updates, and win or lose conditions. This chapter showed how individual systems become a playable level when they are connected through gameplay logic.
   - You can study mission systems, save and load systems, checkpoints, damage types, combat balancing, level progression, Boss mechanics, quest tracking, and reusable gameplay frameworks.

9. In *Chapter 9*, you used **Sequencer** to create an introductory cut-scene. You learned how Level Sequence assets, tracks, keyframes, cameras, animation tracks, and **Camera Cuts** can be used to create cinematic storytelling inside Unreal Engine.
   - You can continue learning camera blocking, cinematic lighting, dialogue scenes, event tracks, gameplay-to-cinematic transitions, camera shake, facial animation, and how to trigger different sequences based on player progress.
10. In *Chapter 10*, you polished and packaged the game. You replaced prototype assets with higher-quality `Desert Castle` assets, connected the final gate-opening event, fixed noticeable camera issues, added audio feedback, created a Niagara sword trail visual effect, configured project settings, selected a build configuration, and packaged the game as a standalone desktop build.
    - You can learn more about optimization, profiling, platform-specific packaging, Android and iOS deployment, store submission requirements, automated build pipelines, quality assurance testing, and post-release updates.

The completed sample project included with this book also serves as a useful reference as you continue learning. If you encounter difficulties while experimenting with *Pangaea* or developing your own projects, you can compare your work with the completed implementation and revisit the techniques introduced in the book.

Moving forward, we will continue providing additional learning resources, such as tips, tutorials, documentation, and videos, to supplement the material covered here and support your ongoing development journey. Whether you want to improve your skills in Blueprint scripting, character animation, AI behavior, or visual effects, you can use these resources alongside other material and continue learning with greater confidence.

Summary

In this chapter, you learned how to take a playable game through a final polish and packaging pass. You improved the `Desert Castle` level with higher-quality environment assets, connected the final gate-opening event, and addressed camera and animation issues that affected gameplay. You also added audio feedback and created a Niagara-based sword trail to make character actions feel more responsive and visually polished.

Finally, you prepared the project for packaging by configuring the required maps and project settings, exploring display modes and build configurations, and creating and testing a standalone Windows build. These steps showed how testing and refinement continue beyond the Unreal Editor to ensure that the packaged game works as intended.

Looking back, the most important lesson is that game development is not a single feature or tool. It is a process of connecting many systems. A character needs input, animation, camera behavior, audio feedback, visual effects, UI support, and gameplay rules. A level needs layout, objectives, enemies, navigation, events, polish, and testing. A finished build needs correct project settings, included maps, saved assets, and careful verification outside the editor.

The *Pangaea* project you created in this book is intentionally small, but it follows the same general workflow used in much larger projects. This complete path is more important than any single feature because it shows how a game moves from an idea to something the player can actually run and experience.

From here, you can continue improving *Pangaea* or start a new Unreal Engine project of your own. You might add more levels, create new enemy types, improve combat, build a save system, add a settings menu, improve the Boss fight, replace more placeholder assets, or prepare the project for another platform. Each improvement will teach you more about how Unreal Engine systems work together.

Finishing this book does not mean you have learned everything about Unreal Engine. Instead, it means you now have a *foundation*. Every project you complete will bring you one step closer to becoming an experienced game developer. Keep building, keep learning, and most importantly, keep making games!

11

Unlock the Code/Resource Bundle and the PDF Version

Your copy of this book includes the following exclusive benefits:

Complete Code Bundle

Download the full source code for this book's examples and projects.

DRM-Free PDF Version

Download DRM-free PDF and ePub copies of this book.

7-Day Packt Library Access

Get 7-day unlimited access to 8,000+ books and videos. No credit card required.

Available for first-time Packt+ trial users only.

Next-Gen Reader Access

Read this book on Packt Reader with progress sync, dark mode and note-taking.

Follow this guide to unlock them. The process takes only a few minutes and only needs to be completed once.

Unlock this book's free benefits in three easy steps

Step 1

Have your purchase invoice ready for *step 3*. If you have a physical copy, scan it using your phone and save it as a PDF, JPG, or PNG.

For more help on finding your invoice, visit `https://www.packtpub.com/unlock-benefits/help`.

> Note
>
> **Note**: If you bought this book directly from the Packt website, no invoice is required. After *step 2*, you can access your exclusive content right away.

Step 2

Scan the QR code or go to `packtpub.com/unlock`.

On the page that opens (similar to *Figure 11.1* on desktop), search for this book by name and select the correct edition.

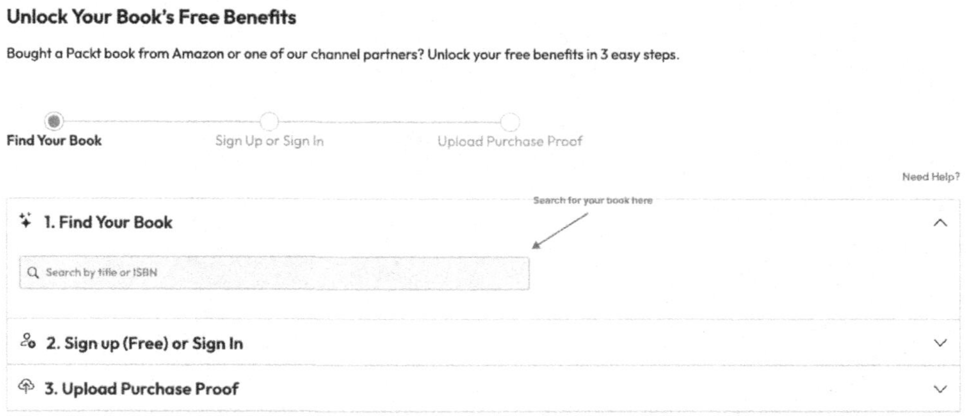

Figure 11.1: Packt unlock landing page on desktop

Step 3

After selecting the book, sign in to your Packt account or create one for free. Then, upload your invoice (PDF, PNG, or JPG, up to 10 MB). Follow the on-screen instructions to finish the process.

Need help?

If you get stuck and need help, visit `https://www.packtpub.com/unlock-benefits/help` for a detailed FAQ on how to find your invoice and more. This QR code will take you to the help page.

> Note
>
> **Note**: If you are still facing issues, reach out to `customercare@packt.com`.

Other Books You May Enjoy

If you enjoyed this book, you may be interested in these other books by Packt:

Unreal Engine 5 Best Practices

Tyson Butler-Boschma

ISBN: 978-1-83620-564-7

- Explore advanced lighting techniques to create dynamic, realistic lighting using Lumen
- Build and edit assets directly inside Unreal with its built-in modeling tools
- Craft compelling cinematic sequences with cameras and storytelling
- Design stunning, immersive worlds through layout and composition design
- Add destruction and realism with Chaos integration
- Profile and boost efficiency across your projects
- Solve real-world development challenges with tested UE5 strategies

Mastering Unreal Engine 5 Game Development with C++ Scripting

Marco Secchi

ISBN: 978-1-80666-592-1

- Write clean, optimized C++ code for Unreal Engine 5
- Work with Unreal Engine architecture for scalable systems
- Use pointers efficiently to improve runtime performance
- Apply event-driven programming with C++ and Blueprints
- Use Unreal Engine macros to extend gameplay systems
- Build Blueprint-accessible, optimized C++ components
- Implement data-driven gameplay systems in real projects

Packt is searching for authors like you

If you're interested in becoming an author for Packt, please visit `authors.packt.com` and apply today. We have worked with thousands of developers and tech professionals, just like you, to help them share their insight with the global tech community. You can make a general application, apply for a specific hot topic that we are recruiting an author for, or submit your own idea.

Share your thoughts

Now that you've finished *Unreal Engine 5 for Beginners*, we'd love to hear your thoughts! Scan the QR code below to go straight to the Amazon review page for this book and share your feedback or leave a review on the site that you purchased it from.

https://packt.link/r/1806105918

Your review is important to us and the tech community and will help us make sure we're delivering excellent quality content.

Index

Y

Made in United States
Orlando, FL
31 October 2026

89979537R00293